THE
INTELLECTUAL
MIGRATION

THE
INTELLECTUAL
MIGRATION

EUROPE AND AMERICA, 1930-1960

EDITED BY

DONALD FLEMING
AND
BERNARD BAILYN

The Belknap Press of
HARVARD UNIVERSITY PRESS
CAMBRIDGE · MASSACHUSETTS

1969

Contents

III

Illustrations

THE
INTELLECTUAL
MIGRATION

INTRODUCTION

O U R purpose in publishing this collection of memoirs and essays on the migration from Hitler's Europe to the United States should be clearly stated at the start. For like each of the many other waves of immigration that have peopled the United States, this movement affected both the migrants and the host country in uncountable ways. We did not intend to cover all its aspects, and chose instead to concentrate on what seemed to us to be its unique characteristics.

This migration was not a mass movement. Of the millions of Europeans uprooted by the fascist regimes, only a small proportion was able to reach safe refuges abroad, and of those only a trickle managed to settle in the United States.[1] In this relatively small group the level of education and the quality of professional skills were remarkable. This was the result partly of the connection that always exists between economic status (hence mobility) and professional occupations; partly it was a consequence of the international contacts that existed before the migration within the professions and among intellectuals; partly it reflects the special efforts that were made by professional groups abroad to rescue at least some of their colleagues from the general destruction; and partly it is the result of the fact that trained intelligence proved effective in managing escapes under difficult circumstances. ("You don't have to be much cleverer than other people," Leo Szilard writes of his departure from Germany, "just . . . one day earlier.")

The intellectual and creative power of the émigrés who settled in the United States has been generally recognized, but we were struck by the

1. For the numbers involved, and for a charming and valuable personal portrayal of leading intellectuals among the refugees, see Laura Fermi, *Illustrious Immigrants: The Intellectual Migration from Europe, 1930/41* (Chicago, 1968). We wish to thank Mrs. Fermi for her kindness in allowing us to see a portion of her book in manuscript, and for discussing the movement as a whole with us.

3

absence in the literature of recent American history of any effort to isolate the impact of this group on American intellectual life—to give an account of the influence of its leading figures on the substance of the various disciplines. We wanted to know the difference that was made in the major fields of the natural sciences, the social sciences, and the humanities by this exodus from Hitler's Europe, and if possible to assess this influence at a technical level. We knew before we started that we could never cover all areas equally or in just proportion to their historical importance, but we preferred an incomplete or unbalanced account to none at all, and felt that the effort to penetrate into the substance of the areas affected needed no apology.

We were struck too with the utility of our present vantage point in considering these questions. We are far enough away from the immediate impact of the migration of the 1930's and forties to be able to view it in at least rough historical perspective, yet we are close enough to hope for personal interpretations by some of the leading figures among the émigrés themselves. Our aim was to blend historical accounts of the effects of the migration written by experts in the various fields with memoirs written by participants, and in this way to add immediacy to the overall picture and to contribute to the historical documentation by eliciting personal commentaries that would not otherwise have existed.

Seeking then to stress what seemed to us to be the unique quality of this latest migration from Europe to America—its impact on intellectual life in the broadest sense and at the highest level—and to elicit interpretations of the movement by certain of the leading participants, we quickly faced the necessity of limiting and defining the scope of the project. Which of the refugees did we mean to include? Our decision was to limit the group to those who received their university training or equivalent in Europe. Thus three of our contributors, Peter Gay, Colin Eisler, and George Mandler, born in Europe and directly involved in the migration, appear here not as participants but as historians since all three received their higher education in this country.

We decided, second, to attempt to isolate influences that could be demonstrably associated with the physical movements of people. The professional world we are mainly concerned with is an international community: books and papers written abroad would have been read here in any case and would have had their effect. It was the consequence of the physical presence of the émigrés in this country, the immediate effect of their personalities, that we wanted to convey. We wished to trace the communication of ideas and attitudes through direct personal contacts—the personal contacts that exist between teachers and students; between lecturers and audiences; between artists, architects, and writers and their visible publics; and among members of research teams attempting to solve specific problems cooperatively. The consequence of this decision in some areas surprised us. In these terms we could not see what difference the actual presence of Thomas Mann in this country had made in the development of American literature—which is in no way to slight his importance as a writer or the broad and deep reception of his writing in this country but only to say that his personal presence here, as distinct from his publications, did not shape the course of literary history. We found in fact that the area of literature as a whole was surprisingly uninvolved in the story we were attempting to sketch, and not only for reasons intrinsic to literature or that result from language differences. The one conspicuous exception was the impact of the refugee literary critics and historians, notably Erich Auerbach, Leo Spitzer, and René Wellek; Harry Levin's essay is addressed to their influence. But in creative literature as such, there were no coteries of leading figures—as there were of physicists, psychologists, architects, and historians—that regrouped in this country and by their presence altered the development of the next American generation. Conversely, we found that there were certain areas where the impact of the émigrés was so pervasive as to defy specific analysis. Thus one field we considered—the advertising industry, where many of the creative minds are known to have been drawn from the migration—had to be ruled out. There was simply no way that we could see of isolating the émigré influence from the other factors that shaped the growth of the industry. We felt that the same general considerations applied to the great virtuosi and symphony conductors, with the further complication that they would almost certainly have been in and out of the United States even if Hitler had never existed.

Finally, we decided to limit the group to the German-speaking émigrés, including in this definition refugees not only from Germany and Austria but also from elsewhere in Central Europe—Hungary in particular—where German was the usual language of high culture. Though this decision was partly a matter of bringing our theme within manageable limits, we felt that it had some intellectual justification as well. Thus a very high proportion of the notable French refugees evidently thought of themselves as waiting out the war, and on its conclusion promptly returned to France. Though the impact of their actual presence in America was far from negligible, they represented by comparison with the refugees from Central Europe a deliberately transitory element in American life, a self-contained group that did not attempt to diffuse their influence through American culture at large. In this respect, the Spanish refugees fell somewhere between the French and the Central Europeans. *Their* war never did end, and for the most part they have remained in the United States. But though they have permanently altered the nature and raised the level of university instruction in Spanish literature and culture in this country, they have maintained a lively sense of constituting a community in exile, strongly though not exclusively oriented toward the ultimate fate of Spain.[2] By contrast with the French and Spanish refugees, the remarkable group of Italian émigrés became as unreservedly a part of American culture as the Central Europeans. We can only express our regret that a brilliant galaxy comprehending Toscanini, Fermi, and Poggioli is represented in the present volume by Salvador Luria alone.

We note still other gaps in the coverage of the present volume, and can only hope that these omissions will be repaired by others while memories are still fresh. We regret the absence of an account of the personal impact of Paul Tillich, a figure comparable in theology to John von Neumann in mathematics or Kurt Lewin in psychology. We are similarly disappointed in not being able to present an account of the émigrés' impact in the area of political thought, where the writings and personalities of Leo Strauss, Hannah Arendt, Hans Morgenthau, and Herbert Marcuse have been deeply influential. Four composers of world

2. The reverberations upon the whole Spanish tradition of this enforced scrutiny of Spain from abroad have been ably described by Juan Marichal in his article "Some Intellectual Consequences of the Spanish Civil War" in *The Texas Quarterly* for Spring 1961 and his book *El Nuevo Pensamiento Politico Español* (Mexico, D. F., 1966).

stature, Béla Bartók, Darius Milhaud, Arnold Schoenberg, and Igor Stravinsky, settled in America; and an account of Milhaud's and Schoenberg's activity as teachers of composition would certainly have been desirable. We recognize also that attention should have been given to the influence of émigrés upon economics and linguistics. Finally, on the institutional side, we believe that the New School for Social Research deserves a study in itself as a major organ for effecting the relocation of some of the most influential refugees.

Our contributors have, however, been able to cover a wide range of fields—biology, physics, mathematics, psychology, sociology, history, architecture, art history, literary criticism, and philosophy—not comprehensively (that was never our aim) but selectively, emphasizing central developments, unique influences, and characteristic experiences.

The essays that follow were undertaken separately and with only the most general suggestions by the editors. Yet the common themes that run through them are striking. The first and most important is introduced by Peter Gay in his essay on the Weimar background of the migration. The intellectuals, the scholars and scientists, who would emerge as leaders in the history of the diaspora were already alienated from the main currents of their native culture before they felt the necessity to emigrate. The great Budapest galaxy had already migrated to Germany before they scattered again to England and the United States. Though many of the alienated intellectuals eventually secured themselves in the establishments of their professions, they began as marginal men even before their societies were formally closed to them. The consequences of this fact are important not only for the individual careers involved but for the character of subsequent developments in the United States. In sociology its results are traced by Paul Lazarsfeld, in part impersonally, in his description of the merging of traditions that resulted in the creation of the Bureau of Applied Social Research at Columbia University, the parent organization of a numerous brood that has profoundly influenced the study of society in America; in part personally, in his "structural biography" of a marginal man,

who is part of two different cultures. He lives under cross pressures that move him in a number of directions. According to his gifts and external circumstances he may become a revolutionary, a surrealist, a criminal. In some cases his marginality may become the driving force for institutional efforts; the institution he creates shelters him and at the same time helps him crystallize his own identity.

Almost every one of these essays and memoirs turns at some point on the creative force of an interstitial situation on highly developed intellects. It was physicists moving from outside into the central problems of biology who supplied the "fostering environment" for the great breakthrough in genetics. It was the tension between Marxism and democratic liberalism that lay at the source of Franz Neumann's influence. It was the adjustment of the Bauhaus ideas to the peculiarities of American building needs and possibilities that defined the influence of Gropius, Mies, and Breuer. It was his extraordinary ability to live in the boundary areas of the traditional fields of mathematics and the sciences that allowed John von Neumann to launch a series of revolutionary developments. And it was Szilard's unconventional soarings into the region where science and politics meet that made nuclear fission a reality.

These developments are related to a second theme that runs through the essays: the high degree of readiness, the pregnancy, of the pre-existing situation in America. The German-born and -educated art historians would in any case have had a decisive influence in this country, but the way had been prepared for them by the work of a generation of native Americans who had made the United States, well before the refugees arrived, what Erwin Panofsky judged to be "a major power in the history of art"; the task of the German and Austrian scholars, John Coolidge writes, was "to establish [art history in this country] as a unified discipline and to bring it abreast of continental practice." The complex preparedness of American psychology for the reception of the ideas of the refugee Freudians is the central theme of Marie Jahoda's essay. The Bauhaus architects, Jordy writes, "found a receptive climate for their points of view"; there had been an "increasing understanding and, among liberal-minded students, increasing impatience as well for the kind of instruction that Gropius, Mies, and Breuer eventually offered." And American physics had vastly improved in the course of the 1920's as a result of the efforts that had been made by leaders in the field and by the foundations. As Weiner explains, leading European physicists, years before they became refugees, had participated as visitors in such successful American enterprises as the carefully unplanned summer sessions on theoretical physics at the University of Michigan. The one contrasting note is T. W. Adorno's account of his experiences in American social science projects in New York and California during the late thirties and through the forties. "I represent," he writes, "an extreme case, which, because it is extreme, sheds a little light on something seldom expounded." His paper is in fact a uniquely valuable testimony to a range of European attitudes and intellectual approaches that were *not* easily transferred to the United States and for which there was little pre-existing sympathy. A sensitive student of philosophy, music, and interpretative sociology, he was offended by the empiricism and commercialism of American life, and though he was one of the moving spirits behind the compiling and writing of *The Authoritarian Personality*, a milestone in applied social research, he continued to insist on "the fundamental importance of the mind—'Geist,' " and to condemn "adjustment," in Hegelian terms as "an extinction of the spontaneity and autonomy of the individual." The explanation he offers of his discontent with American cultural life and the reasons for his return to Germany in 1953 throw a sharp contrasting light on the cultural conditions that eased the reception into American society of the majority of the refugee intellectuals.

One cannot read through these fourteen selections, finally, without pausing at some point to note the general background importance of the Depression. The resistance of the American academic establishment to penetration by these sophisticated newcomers was undoubtedly related to the economic constraint that only gradually loosened in the late thirties. Szilard occupied a major academic position only very late in his career; Lazarsfeld did so much earlier, but only by creating a new institution that was eventually incorporated into a traditional university. The experimental psychologists settled at Swarthmore, Smith, and other collegiate centers but, with rare exceptions, did not become members of leading graduate faculties. And the poignant failure of Karl Bühler, the leading figure in Austrian psychology in the 1920's, to reestablish himself at all in this country is touched on again and again in the essays that deal with the social sciences.

The dominant note throughout these papers, however, is positive: the success of a group of highly trained individuals, specialists in almost every area of the arts and sciences, in transplanting themselves in mid-life to a new environment, and finding in this move creative challenges and a release of constructive energies.

In planning this volume we have been obliged again and again to call upon others for advice, and it is a pleasure now to acknowledge this assistance. Almost all of the contributors helped us in the early discussions of the project and later answered specific questions. In addition, we wish to note with thanks the assistance of Frederick H. Abernathy, James S. Ackerman, Lotte Bailyn, Garrett Birkhoff, John Clive, Burton S. Dreben, Herta Herzog, Louise Holborn, Gerald Holton, Fritz Jahoda, Rosi Kuerti, and Hans Zeisel. We also owe a great deal to the sympathetic cooperation of Oscar Handlin, director of the Charles Warren Center.

D.F.
B.B.

WEIMAR CULTURE:
THE OUTSIDER AS INSIDER

by PETER GAY

Der Deutsche ist im fremden Land
Meist als ein Vieh-losoph bekannt
Otto Reutter, "Der gewissenhafte Maurer"

THE exile holds an honored place in the history of Western civilization. Dante and Grotius, Bayle and Rousseau, Heine and Marx did their greatest work in enforced residence on alien soil, looking back with loathing and longing to the country, their own, that had rejected them. The Greek scholars from Byzantium who flooded the Italian city-states early in the fifteenth century and the Huguenot bourgeois who streamed out of France across Western Europe late in the seventeenth century brought with them energy, learning, and scarce, welcome skills; New England was founded by refugees who transformed a savage wilderness into blooming civilization.[1] But these mi-

* This essay is a first attempt to organize my ideas on the culture of Weimar; I hope to devote some years to an extensive study of what I propose to call the Weimar Renaissance. In the course of writing this essay, I have talked to a number of students and survivors of Weimar, to whom I am grateful for their time and effort, and for their permission to print some of their comments here, especially since I know that we do not always agree on our interpretation of this great and terrible age. I particularly thank Felix Gilbert for an invaluable conversation and an equally invaluable reading of the manuscript, and Hannah Arendt, James Marston Fitch, George Kennan, Heinz Hartmann, Hajo Holborn, Paul Lazarsfeld, Rudolph M. Loewenstein, Adolf Placzek, Rudolf Wittkower. I remember, with gratitude, an interview with the late Erwin Panofsky. In addition, I thank Joseph P. Bauke, Istvan Deak, George L. Mosse, and Theodore Reff for their assistance. This essay was first delivered, in slightly different form, as a series of four lectures on Weimar culture, at the Institute of Philosophy and Politics of Education, Teachers College, Columbia University. I am deeply grateful to the chairman of those lectures, my friend Lawrence A. Cremin, for providing such a stimulating occasion for testing my ideas.

1. For a systematic survey of the exile in Western history (a typical instance of the kind of theoretical thinking that refugee scholars brought to American universities), see Franz L. Neumann, "The Social Sciences," in Neumann, *et al.*, *The Cultural Migration: The European Scholar in America* (Philadelphia, 1953), pp. 4–26, especially pp. 4–14.

grations, impressive as they are, cannot compare with the exodus set in
motion early in 1933, when the Nazis seized control of Germany; the
exiles Hitler made were the greatest collection of transplanted intellect,
talent, and scholarship the world has ever seen.

The dazzling array of these exiles—Albert Einstein, Thomas Mann,
Erwin Panofsky, Bertolt Brecht, Walter Gropius, Georg Grosz, Wassily
Kandinsky, Max Reinhardt, Bruno Walter, Werner Jaeger, Wolfgang
Köhler, Paul Tillich, Ernst Cassirer—tempts us to idealize Weimar as
unique, a culture without strains and without debts, a true golden age.[2]
But to construct this flawless ideal is to trivialize the achievement of the
Weimar Renaissance, and to slight the price it had to pay for its existence. The excitement that characterized Weimar culture stemmed in
part from exuberant creativity and experimentation; but much of it was
anxiety, fear, a rising sense of doom. With some justice, Karl Mannheim, one of its survivors, boasted not long before its demise that future
years would look back on Weimar as a new Periclean age.[3] But it was a
precarious glory, a dance on the edge of a volcano. Weimar culture
was the creation of outsiders, propelled by history into the inside, for a
short, dizzying, fragile moment.

I. The Trauma of Birth:
From Weimar to Weimar

(i)

THE Weimar Republic was an idea seeking to become reality. The
decision to hold the constituent assembly at Weimar rather than
Berlin was taken primarily for prudential reasons, but it came to symbolize a prediction, or at least a hope, for a new start; it was tacit acknowledgment of the charge, widely made in Allied countries during
the war and indignantly denied in Germany, that there were really two
Germanies: the Germany of military swagger, abject submission to

2. Theodor Heuss, among others, later deplored the rise of the legend "von den
'goldenen zwanziger Jahren.' " *Erinnerungen, 1905–1933* (Tübingen, 1963), p. 348.

3. In conversation with Hannah Arendt, reported to author by Hannah Arendt. Bruno
Walter attributes the same term to the powerful Berlin theater critic Alfred Kerr; Walter,
Theme and Variations: An Autobiography (tr. James A. Galston, New York, 1946), p. 268.

authority, aggressive foreign adventure, obsessive preoccupation with form, and the Germany of lyrical poetry, humanist philosophy, and pacific cosmopolitanism. Germany had tried the way of Bismarck and Schlieffen, now it was ready to try the way of Goethe and Humboldt.

It is easy, too easy, to ridicule this solemn search for a usable past.[4] The Weimar Republic was born in defeat, lived in turmoil, and died in disaster; and from the beginning there were those who saw its travail with superb indifference or open *Schadenfreude*. But the Republic had its moments of greatness; its end was implied in its beginning, but it was not inevitable, and it was not inevitable because there were republicans who took the symbol of Weimar seriously and who tried, deliberately and bravely, to give the ideal real content.[5]

When we think of Weimar, we think of modernity in art, literature, and thought; we think of "the dancing of Mary Wigman, *The Threepenny Opera* of Brecht and Weill, avant-garde cinema like *The Cabinet of Dr. Caligari* and *Metropolis*, the novels of Werfel and Mann, the great *siedlungen* of Frankfort and Berlin," and, above all, of "the Bauhaus," which became "the capital of this imaginary country";[6] we think of

4. "History enjoys discrediting arbitrarily chosen symbols. The Republic sought to banish Prussian militarism. When, however, the National Assembly met in Weimar at the beginning of February, the Republic had created a new form of militarism in the Free Corps. . . ." Arthur Rosenberg, *A History of the German Republic* (trs. Ian F. D. Morrow and L. Marie Sieveking, London, 1936), p. 101. There is, as I shall show, some justice in Rosenberg's criticism, but the symbol of Weimar was not arbitrary; it had significance and for a time, a real chance. For the decision to choose Weimar, see Philipp Scheidemann, *Memoiren eines Sozialdemokraten* (Dresden, 1928), II, 352, which mentions the practical reason—the Spartakist threat—alone. For the other—symbolic—reason, see Rosenberg, *German Republic*, and Erick Eyck, *Geschichte der Weimarer Republik* (Zurich, 1956), I, 91.

5. As Toni Stolper has observed, historians have all too often written off the Weimar Republic as doomed from the start, and as a time of sheer misery and fear. She rightly objects that, after all, Weimar was characterized by splendid creativity in the midst of suffering, hard work in the midst of disappointment, hope in the face of pitiless and powerful adversaries. See Stolper, *Ein Leben in Brennpunkten unserer Zeit: Gustav Stolper, 1888–1947* (Tübingen, 1960), pp. 211–213. The argument that the end was not inevitable has recently been persuasively restated in the writings of Karl Dietrich Bracher, notably in Bracher, Wolfgang Sauer, Gerhard Schulz, *Die nationalsozialistische Machtergreifung: Studien zur Errichtung des totalitären Herrschaftssystems in Deutschland, 1933–34* (Wiesbaden, 1960), pp. 17–18.

6. I have here offered the list of a well-informed outsider observer, the American architectural historian James Marston Fitch, as typical. See Fitch, "A Utopia Revisited," *The Columbia University Forum*, 9 (Fall, 1966), 35.

rebellion—of sons against fathers, Dadaists against art, libertines against old-fashioned moralists. But while this striking mixture of cynicism and faith, this search for novelty and for roots—this solemn irreverence— was a child of war, revolution, and democracy, the elements that made it up came from both the distant and the recent past, remembered and revived by a new generation. Goethe and Schopenhauer, Kleist and Büchner, were living realities for the new Weimar, while the immediate, still passionately debated ancestry of the Weimar style went back to the turn of the century and the nineties: Frank Wedekind completed his first and still most important play, *Frühlings Erwachen*, in 1891, a year after William II had dismissed Bismarck, and long before the Emperor had fully tested his peculiar talent for disaster.[7]

Imperial Germany was studiedly hostile to the modern movement. The Emperor and his empress, Auguste Victoria, set the tone, and their taste ran to gaudy parades, glittering medals, sentimental heroic portraits: the *Siegesallee* in Berlin, an ambitious double row of marble statues commemorating the unmemorable, was expression, and symptom, of Wilhelminian taste. The universities, in which Germans took such ostentatious pride, were nurseries of a woolly-minded militarist idealism and centers of resistance to the new in art or the social sciences; Jews, democrats, socialists, in a word, outsiders, were kept from the sacred precincts of higher learning. The Empress interfered with the staging of Strauss's *Salome* and kept Strauss's *Rosenkavalier* from opening in Berlin, taking charming and talented decadence for impermissible immorality; the government harassed Käthe Kollwitz for her proletarian posters, while in 1908 the Emperor dismissed Hugo von Tschudi, director of the National Gallery in Berlin, for his subversive tastes in art. Four years later, when Kandinsky and Marc published their collective volume of essays, pictures, and musical examples, *Der Blaue Reiter*, they fittingly dedicated it to Tschudi's memory.[8] The new art made the ruling circles

7. Harry Graf Kessler reports a conversation of informed amateurs in the midst of revolution, on January 4, 1919: these friends agreed that "in German art the transition from bourgeois to popular"—that is, from Impressionist to Expressionist art—"had long preceded the Revolution." *Tagebücher, 1918–1937* (Frankfurt, 1961), p. 91.

8. The Kaiser vetoed a gold medal that was to be awarded to Kollwitz; in 1908, the Empress ordered the suppression of one of her posters, *Die Heimarbeiterin*, and in 1912, the police prohibited a Kollwitz poster designed for a children's playground. For these and other details, see Bernard S. Myers, *The German Expressionists: A Generation in*

literally sick: In 1893, the Bavarian statesman Prince Chlodwig zu Hohenlohe-Schillingsfürst went to see Gerhart Hauptmann's *Hanneles Himmelfahrt*. "A monstrous wretched piece of work," he noted in his diary, "social-democratic-realistic, at the same time full of sickly, sentimental mysticism, nerve-wracking, in general abominable. Afterwards we went to Borchards, to get ourselves back into a human frame of mind with champagne and caviar."[9]

But Wilhelminian Germany, though philistine and oppressive, was not a dictatorship; and the modern movement fed on opposition. Expressionism, which dominated Weimar culture during its formative years, was fully matured in the Empire. Expressionist painters and poets made inflammatory statements, exhibited outrageous pictures, published *avant garde* little magazines, and gathered, for collaboration and comfort, in informal groups like *Die Brücke* and *Der blaue Reiter*. Their ranks were decimated before the Revolution: Franz Marc and August Macke, whose eccentric colors and exotic landscapes haunted the twenties, were killed in the war; others, like Emil Nolde and Ernst Ludwig Kirchner, who survived, had found their final manner—their aggressive color, primitive subject matter, their untamed, urgent subjectivity—in the first decade of the twentieth century. The precise date of Kandinsky's first wholly non-objective painting remains a matter for controversy, but it is certain that it must be placed before the war.[10] And it was in 1914 that Walter Hasenclever completed his first Expressionist play, *Der Sohn*, as prophetic of the Weimar style as Marc's blue horses. Everywhere young artists broke away from the pomposity of academic art

---

Revolt (New York, 1966), p. 24; for the fate of Tschudi, see Klaus Lankheit's new documentary edition of *Der blaue Reiter* (eds. Wassily Kandinsky and Franz Marc, Munich, 1965), pp. 22–24, 255, 261–262.

9. The prince's spleen is really untranslatable: "Heute abend in 'Hannele.' Ein grässliches Machwerk, sozialdemokratisch-realistisch, dabei von krankhafter, sentimentaler Mystik, nervenangreifend, überhaupt scheusslich. Wir gingen nachher zu Borchard, um uns durch Champagner und Kaviar wieder in eine menschliche Stimmung zu versetzen." Diary of December 14, 1893, quoted in Paul Kampffmeyer, *Fritz Ebert* (Berlin, 1923), p. 41.

10. Kandinsky painted what he considered to be abstractions as early as 1910, and it was in the same year that he wrote his revolutionary manifesto *Über das Geistige in der Kunst* (Munich, 1912). But in 1914, it is clear, some of Kandinsky's paintings had no objective correlative whatever. Other abstract artists, Delaunay and Mondrian, made similar experiments before the war broke out.

and sought to rise above the bombast of their surroundings to cultivate their inner life, articulate their religious yearning, satisfy their dim longing for human and cultural renewal. In comparison with the circulation figures of popular magazines, Herwarth Walden's *Sturm* and Franz Pfemfert's *Aktion* were negligible; in comparison with the big publishing houses, Ernst Rowohlt and Kurt Wolff were mere amateurs: the Expressionists were a band of outsiders. But they were determined and active. The Republic would add to their lives nothing but success.

What was true of painting, poetry, and experimental short prose was true in other areas of culture: Thomas Mann's *Buddenbrooks, Tonio Kröger*, and *Tod in Venedig*, all published by 1911, already embodied the playful, irresponsible love affair with death, the relentless symbolism, and the strenuous effort to make ideas dramatically respectable, that were to distinguish, and partly to mar, Mann's work of the twenties. The unrestrained political satire that entertained and frightened visitors to the *Kabarett der Komiker* and readers of the *Weltbühne* during the Republic traced back its manner and matter to Heinrich Mann's *Der Untertan*, to Walter Mehring's early political *chansons*, to Frank Wedekind's eccentric dramas—and Wedekind, after all, had died in 1918— and to Carl Sternheim's clipped, mannered dissections of what Sternheim icily called "*bürgerliches Heldenleben*," a life, as he saw it, of surpassing vulgarity, crass scramble for status, and suicidal rush into a great war: "After us, collapse!" exclaims one of Sternheim's characters in a play he wrote in the last year of peace: "We are ripe."[11]

In a less ominous sense, the modern movement was ripe as well. Psychoanalysis was introduced into Germany in 1910, with the founding of the Berlin branch of the International Psychoanalytical Association. Friedrich Meinecke and Otto Hintze, who drew the attention of the historical profession in other countries to Berlin in the 1920's, had done significant work before the war: Meinecke's *Weltbürgertum und Nationalstaat*, which some of his pupils would later fondly remember as his best book, was published in 1907.[12] Max Reinhardt, the magician of the Weimar theater, had practically filled his bag of tricks by 1914. Arnold

11. This speech, which has been much quoted, is in the play *1913*, act III, scene ii.

12. Felix Gilbert, in conversation with the author. As Gilbert has pointed out to me, Meinecke was made a professor in Berlin before the war, which, once again, "shows the ambiguous nature of the era."

Schönberg, who completed the twelve-tone system in 1924, had broken through to atonality before 1912. Even Walter Gropius, whose Bauhaus buildings in Dessau appear as the archetypical expression of the Weimar style, had achieved his characteristic idiom before the war, partly as the pupil of Peter Behrens, partly in association with Adolf Meyer, with whom he built the Fagus Shoe Last Factory in 1911 and, in 1914, the celebrated buildings for the Werkbund Exhibition in Cologne. There can be no doubt: the Weimar style was born before the Weimar Republic. The war gave it a political cast and a strident tone, and saddled it with a deadly quarrel; the Revolution gave it unprecedented opportunities. But the Republic created little; it liberated what was already there.[13]

Just as the Weimar style was older than the Weimar Republic, so was it larger than Germany. Both in the Empire and in the Republic, German painters, poets, playwrights, psychologists, philosophers, architects, even humorists, were engaged in an international commerce of ideas; they were part of a Western community on which they drew and which, in turn, they fed; chauvinism was not merely offensive to the Weimar style, it would have been fatal to it. Kandinsky embodies this cosmopolitanism in one person: he was born in Russia, learned much from the French Fauves, and found his own style in Munich.[14] Other "German" painters—Kirchner, Heckel, Nolde, Pechstein, Marc, and Klee—each in his own way, went to school to the Norwegian Munch,

13. As I discovered after I had written these lines, Gropius himself was fully aware of this: "After I had already found my own ground in architecture before the First World War, as is evidenced in the Fagus Building of 1911 and in the Cologne Werkbund Exhibition in 1914 (Germany), the full consciousness of my responsibility as an architect, based on my own reflections, came to me as a result of the First World War, during which my theoretical premises first took shape." *Scope of Total Architecture* (New York, 1962 ed.), p. 19. Late in 1918, Gropius told James Marston Fitch, he was furloughed to Germany after successfully completing a mission on the Italian front, and he decided to travel to Berlin. During his trip the Revolution broke out, and as Gropius witnessed the indignities visited on officers by strangers, he remembers being seized by a sudden thought: "This is more than just a lost war. A world has come to an end. We must seek a radical solution to our problems." (Fitch, in conversation with the author.) This progression of Gropius' intellectual career—ideas fully developed in the Empire, given political and social direction by the War, and realized under the Republic—is characteristic of other representatives of the Weimar spirit as well.

14. As Myers has well said: "Kandinsky belongs, in spite of his Russian background and subsequent French canonization, to the Munich school of the period before the First World War. As in the case of Paul Klee, it is futile to bicker over nationality as such. . . ." *German Expressionists*, p. 165.

the Frenchman Gauguin, and the Netherlander Van Gogh. Munich, the capital of painters in the Empire, mounted influential exhibitions of French Neo-Impressionists, while Marc and Klee went directly to Paris on visits they would later describe as decisive for their artistic development.[15] Dada, the artists' rebellion against art, was born during the war in Zurich, flourished after the war in Paris, and made Berlin its headquarters during the first years of Weimar.[16] The German Expressionist theater is unthinkable without the experiments of Strindberg, while German social realism depended on the realistic phase of Ibsen whose plays were naturalized in Germany well before the First World War. A catalogue of Brecht's foreign sources—though Brecht's poetic diction is purely, superbly German—would have to be long to be at all meaningful, and range from Villon and Rimbaud to such improbable influences as Kipling, and from Chinese lyrics to Augustan satire.[17] Spirits as diverse as Franz Werfel and Ernst Ludwig Kirchner acknowledged the inspiration of Walt Whitman;[18] the philosophical irrationalism of Bergson, and the brooding poetic irrationalism of Dostoyevsky, appealed to sensitive spirits from the extreme left to the extreme right who could no longer bear the shape of modernity and were sickened by Wilhelminian culture. In architecture the American Frank Lloyd Wright, the Spaniard Antonio Gaudí, and the Belgian Henry van de Velde supplied the German rebels with most of their ammunition.[19] And in all areas Austrians —poets, playwrights, psychologists, cultural critics—transmitted to their German audience their obsession with decadence and their attempts to come to terms with eros: Sigmund Freud, Hugo von Hofmannsthal,

15. See *ibid., passim,* especially pp. 83, 100–101, 120–121, 131, 140, 178, 182, 187.

16. Hans Richter, *Dada: Art and Anti-Art* (New York, 1965).

17. Martin Esslin, *Brecht: The Man and His Work* (Garden City, N.Y., 1961), pp. 108–109, 113.

18. Myers, *German Expressionists,* p. 102; Walter H. Sokel, *The Writer in Extremis: Expressionism in Twentieth-Century German Literature* (New York, ed. 1964), pp. 3, 19, 160.

19. The "spectrum of stylistic movements" like Secession, Jugendstil, and others, and "highly personal idioms" like Wright's, "were bound to be confusing to the younger generation; it is the more remarkable how little they confused Gropius, how completely he seems to have digested all these stimuli by the time he did his first building in 1911. (Digested is the proper word because—already well-educated, well-traveled, and widely read, he would have been thoroughly familiar with them all.)" James Marston Fitch, *Walter Gropius* (New York, 1960), p. 19.

Karl Kraus, and Arthur Schnitzler had as many readers in Berlin, Munich, and Frankfurt, as they had in Vienna—perhaps more.

For the outsiders of the Empire as, later, for the insiders of the Republic, the most insistent questions revolved around the need for man's renewal, questions made nearly insoluble by the disappearance of God, the threat of the machine, the incurable stupidity of the upper classes, and the helpless philistinism of the bourgeoisie. Seeking answers to their questions, the rebels turned to whatever help they could find, wherever they could find it. There was nothing unusual in this; man's articulate misery or articulate delight has never been a respecter of frontiers. But it was precisely this—the commonplace quality of the cosmopolitanism of the Empire—that later gave the Weimar style its toughness of fiber: in its unself-conscious internationalism it shared the vitality of other cultural movements in European history.

What the war did was to destroy the ties of German culture, both to the usable past and the congenial foreign environment, for all but the most determined cosmopolitans.[20] It was the cultural task of the Weimar Republic to restore these ties, and thus create an atmosphere in which the Weimar Renaissance might enjoy its brief splendor.

(ii)

It is the tragedy of the Weimar Republic that while it succeeded in its cultural task—the brilliance of the refugees from Hitler is a measure of that success—the trauma of its birth was so severe that it could never enlist the wholehearted loyalty of all, or even many, of its beneficiaries. The Revolution had widespread support at the outset. It awakened the unpolitical architect Gropius to his social responsibility, and to the need for a democratic reconstruction of Germany. It aroused the enthusiasm of Bertolt Brecht who, like many other young men, had been revolted

20. Thus the Fabian Socialist and psychologist Graham Wallas wrote to his German friend, the Revisionist Socialist Eduard Bernstein, in the midst of war, in 1915: "Nowadays one lives from day to day and scarcely dares to think about the future. But sometimes I hope that when peace comes you and I may meet and shake hands, and tell each other that we have never had one thought of each other that was not kind, and then sit down to consider whether we can help in any way to heal the wounds of civilization." Peter Gay, *The Dilemma of Democratic Socialism: Eduard Bernstein's Challenge to Marx* (New York, ed. 1967), p. 280.

by years of slaughter.[21] It gave hope to conservative ideologists delighted to see the collapse of a regime that had not been idealistic enough to embody true conservatism.[22] It enlisted the support of bourgeois intellectuals like Friedrich Meinecke, filled though they were with rage against the allied powers.[23] It delighted soldiers and their families, and democrats, socialists, pacifists, and Utopians.

But events in the winter of 1918–1919, followed by the turmoil of the founding years, dissipated the capital of good will that had accumulated in the days of collapse and hope. As the Revolution had pleased, so its course and consequences disappointed many for different reasons. The new conservatives came to hate precisely the innovations introduced in the Republic; the radicals, for their part, the survivals left from the Empire: the Weimar Republic, it seems, was too successful to satisfy its critics, not successful enough to satisfy its wellwishers. As early as December 1918, the progressive publisher Paul Cassirer characterized the Revolution as "nothing but a great swindle—*Schiebung*"; nothing essential had been changed, he told Count Kessler, "only a few cousins" had been shoved into positions of profit and power.[24] Many of the young enthusiasts, like Brecht, turned their back on politics as quickly as they had taken it up; writers and artists like Wieland Herzfelde and George Grosz quickly joined the Spartakist opposition.[25] Indeed, quite early, while the enemies of the young republic remained steadfast in their enmity, its enthusiasts wavered and withdrew their support. In February 1919, the journalist Simon Guttmann spoke for this group with the

21. See Esslin, *Brecht*, pp. 8–9.

22. See Klemens von Klemperer, *Germany's New Conservatism: Its History and Dilemma in the Twentieth Century* (Princeton, 1957), part II, chap. i, "The Revolution of 1918–1919 and Its Conservative Aspects."

23. Perhaps most revealing is Meinecke's letter of October 21, 1918, slightly anticipating the events of November, to L. Aschoff, in *Ausgewählter Briefwechsel* (eds. Ludwig Dehio and Peter Classen, Stuttgart, 1962), pp. 95–98.

24. Kessler, *Tagebücher*, p. 78. It is worth noting that while Kessler's diaries are magnificently articulate, vivid, and detailed, they must be used with some caution; there are occasions when the aesthete will report what sounds striking rather than what really happened. (Thus the economist Friedrich Glum rightly takes exception to Kessler's reporting of the decisive day, November 9, 1918, as being too melodramatic. See Glum, *Zwischen Wissenschaft, Wirtschaft und Politik: Erlebtes und Erdachtes in vier Reichen* [Bonn, 1964], p. 187.) The diaries remain an invaluable source, however, and I have used them freely.

25. Kessler, *Tagebücher*, p. 109; Esslin, *Brecht*, p. 9.

savage pessimism of the disappointed lover: at the moment, he told
Kessler, the intellectuals almost without exception opposed the government; it was impossible, he added, to exaggerate their bitterness against
the present regime, which shied away from responsibility, did nothing,
and was active only when it came to shooting down fellow citizens.
Nothing, he said sadly, had been changed by the Revolution: everything
went on as before, in the old way.[26] And on May 1, 1919, a national
holiday, Kessler noted that the festivities gave the impression of "national mourning for a revolution that misfired."[27] It soon became common practice to compress disdain into a single phrase: 1918 was the
"so-called Revolution."[28]

There are many obvious reasons for this widespread disenchantment.
The bloody civil war, the reemergence of the military as a factor in
politics, the failure to discredit the aristocratic-industrial complex that
had dominated the Empire, the frequency of political assassination and
the impunity of right-wing political assassins, the imposition of the
Versailles treaty (which nearly everyone, including most left-wing Socialists, was quick to brand as an intolerable *Diktat*), the French occupation, the inflation—all this, as it gave new hope to monarchists, to
fanatical militarists, to anti-Semites and xenophobes of all sorts, to industrialists first frightened by the specter of socialization and then contemptuous of socialists who would not socialize, served to make the
Republic appear a fraud, and Republican politics, with its succession of
cabinets and torrents of rhetoric, unreal and comical at best, at worst a
treason beneath contempt. "We young students did not read the newspapers in those years," Hannah Arendt has recalled. "George Grosz's
cartoons seemed to us not satires but realistic reportage: we knew those
types; they were all around us. Should we mount the barricades for
that?"[29] The very birth of the Republic had its farcical elements: it was
proclaimed in the early afternoon of November 9, 1918, by Philipp

26. Kessler, *Tagebücher*, p. 123.
27. *Ibid.*, p. 182. The term is *"verfehlte Revolution."*
28. For examples see Lion Feuchtwanger, writing in 1928 in the *Weltbühne* (quoted in
Esslin, *Brecht*, p. 10); and Franz Neumann, "Social Sciences," p. 14; or, Siegfried Jacobsohn, editor of the *Weltbühne*, writing in his own journal on March 27, 1919: "We need
a second revolution. No: we need a revolution." *Ausnahmezustand*, an anthology of
selections from *Weltbühne* and *Tagebuch* (ed. Wolfgang Weyrauch, Munich, 1966), p. 24.
29. In conversation with author.

Scheidemann, not from pure Republican enthusiasm, but from an anxious desire to forestall the proclamation of a Soviet Republic by Karl Liebknecht. And when Ebert learned of Scheidemann's action a few minutes after, he was furious with the irregularity of the proceedings.[30] No one could fail to notice that the Republic came into the world almost by accident, and covered with apologies.

Beyond this there was another, subtler inducement to cynicism and unpolitical detachment. In August 1914, the Western world had experienced a war psychosis: the war seemed a release from boredom, an invitation to heroism, a remedy for decadence. But it was in Germany that this psychosis reached heights of absurdity. The old, the young, the unfit, volunteered with pure joy, and went to death filled with their mission. The war offered "purification, liberation, and enormous hope"; it "set the hearts of poets aflame" with a sense of relief that "a peaceful world had collapsed," a world of which "one was so tired, so dreadfully tired." Only "victory at any price" could give life meaning: the Germans had at last united as a *Volk*, Germans alone were "truthful, authentic, manly, objective," a land of heroes facing opponents saddled with "cowardice, mendacity, and baseness"; grand old words like *Volk* and *Reich* and *Geist* were now given new meaning by this great crusade for *Kultur*.[31] But this elation led to depression, often to mental collapse; the orgy of self-indulgent, self-deceptive chauvinism was followed by guilt and shame and, in some cases, a hollow insistence that one had been right all along—a sequence of oscillations scarcely calculated to induce political realism. Many of the enthusiasts lost their enthusiasm, but not their Utopianism. Some—Thomas Mann among them—learned from war and revolution: it was one of their incidental benefits that they acted as political educators to the few willing to be educated.[32] But

30. The most reliable description of these events is still to be found in Scheidemann's own *Memoiren eines Sozialdemokraten*, II, 309–314.

31. These may sound like imaginary quotations, but they are not; I have drawn them from Thomas Mann's essay, "Gedanken im Krieg," written in September 1914 and published in 1915; and from postcards by Friedrich Gundolf to Stefan George, dating from August 14 and August 30, 1914 (*Stefan George-Friedrich Gundolf Briefwechsel* [ed. Robert Boehringer, Munich, 1962]), pp. 256–257, 258–259.

32. Arnold Brecht has developed the idea of war, revolution, and republic as political education in his autobiography, *Aus nächster Nähe: Lebenserinnerungen, 1884–1927* (Stuttgart, 1966).

there were many who remained political innocents, ready to despise what they could not understand, and open to vendors of nostrums even more nauseating than the war they had greeted with such joy.

All this was bad enough, but doubtless the most effective enemy of the Weimar Republic was the civil war fought within the Republican left, the struggle, as Eduard Bernstein said, of "socialists against socialists,"[33] which broke out as soon as the Republic was born: its very proclamation, after all, was an act directed not merely against the monarchy but against the Spartakists.

This struggle was inevitable. Socialist unity had been shattered during, and over the issue of, the war; the Russian Revolution, and the manner of the German collapse, which gave socialists a rather artificial and tenuous prominence, were not very likely to restore it. With the definitive eviction of the Empire in November 1918, the moment for the confrontation of two competing socialist groups had come; the stakes in the struggle for immediate power were high, for the holders of power would determine the future of Germany—the Spartakists wanted to turn Germany into a Soviet republic, the majority socialists, into a parliamentary democracy. It is one of the saddest ironies of German history that while in 1918 no other alternatives seemed possible, the internecine struggle for either of the available alternatives gave room for forces seeking yet another alternative—a military dictatorship. The confrontation of socialist with socialist was everywhere, having swept away old institutions, the Revolution offered new, and many, surfaces for friction. Spartakists and moderate socialists fought in Berlin and in the provinces, in politicians' meetings and in the streets, in workers' councils and at funerals for victims of armed clashes. There were many harsh words—words never forgotten or forgiven—and words were not all. Everyone was armed, everyone was irritable and unwilling to accept frustration, many had been trained and remained ready to kill, disorder encouraged irrational mass action and offered protective cover to political assassins. For almost two months the government had maintained a specious unity among socialist forces; but on December 27, the Independent Socialists walked out. And even before that, there had been violence and death, and after there was more: Karl Liebknecht and Rosa Luxemburg

33. Eduard Bernstein, *Die deutsche Revolution* (Berlin, 1921), chap. viii.

were murdered on January 15, 1919, Kurt Eisner, the Bavarian prime minister, was murdered by an aristocratic student on February 21, and the Bavarian Soviet Republic which came out of the assassination was cruelly put down by regular and Free Corps troops at the end of April and the beginning of May—all events producing vehement recriminations and lasting distrust among forces on the left. The Spartakists denounced the governing socialists as servile butchers; the government socialists denounced the Spartakists as sanguinary revolutionaries and Russian agents. The enemy on the right needed only to wait.

Historians have made much of the failures of the politicians who governed the young Republic. Had they failed utterly, it would have been understandable. Ebert and his associates faced problems that would have abashed the coolest, most experienced statesman. There was widespread disorder, there was hunger, there was an army to be brought home and demobilized, there was a constitution to be written and put into practice. More: there was a peace to be made with vindictive politicians who wanted not settlement but revenge; the conduct of allied statesmen proves that it is not defeat alone that produces traumas—victory, too, after years of bloodshed and endless suffering, seemed somehow unbearable. Yet, in the midst of defeat and misery, domestic treason and foreign stupidity, the Revolution accomplished a great deal. It ended the war. It swept away—forever—the Prussian ruling house and the other German monarchies, large and small. It educated at least some Germans in the ways of practical politics. It established a democratic state. It gave new opportunities to talent ineligible for preferment in the Empire, opening centers of prestige and power to progressive professors, modern playwrights and producers, democratic political thinkers. Hugo Preuss, the architect of the Weimar Constitution, was a symbol of the Revolution—as a Jew and a left-wing democrat, he had been kept out of the University establishment for all his merits, and now he, the outsider, gave shape to the new Republic, *his* Republic.[34]

Yet great mistakes were made, and recriminations over them poisoned the atmosphere early, preparing the way for further mistakes. As the

34. For Preuss, see Walter Simons, *Hugo Preuss* (in the Series, "Meister des Rechts," Berlin, 1930); and the essay by Carl Schmitt, "Hugo Preuss: Sein Staatsbegriff und seine Stellung in der deutschen Staatslehre," no. 72 in a collection of lectures and writings, *Recht und Staat in Geschichte und Gegenwart* (Tübingen, 1930).

brilliant political journalist Carl von Ossietzky put it as early as June 1919, "There were three areas in which we had a right to expect an absolute break with old methods, and reconstruction: in the purely political, the economic, and the spiritual-ethical area." But "what has the Revolution accomplished? The answer is sad indeed. In foreign and domestic politics celebrities swagger around who for several decades have of right belonged into a reliquary. Economic reconstruction is steadily being postponed, while anarchy, egotism, profiteering triumph. No resisting hand, only soft persuasion. Poverty of ideas, lack of courage, lack of faith."[35] It is a stern indictment, but not without justice. The Republicans' search for order, their fear of bolshevism, the timidity of leaders themselves the product of the old society and better equipped to oppose than to govern—and, it must be added, the confusion, irresponsibility, and dictatorial pretensions of the Spartakist left—forestalled decisive action in area after area. Preuss, gravely worried by the hegemony of Prussia, wanted to destroy the old federal collection of states, break up Prussia into several *Länder*, and gather a number of small states into larger units. His plan was not adopted, and among its most effective adversaries were Social Democrats unwilling to yield what they had just acquired, or—as with Eisner in Bavaria—suspicious of the central regime. A compromise kept the old states intact, preserved Prussian dominance, and left the troublesome relations between the *Reich* and the *Länder* unappeased. The affair was to provide a painful lesson to Socialists jealous of their office: a short-range private gain proved to be a long-range public disaster.[36]

The nationalization of major industries had the same history; ambitious schemes and good will were never translated into action. The economist Rudolph Wissell pointed out the road to socialism through

35. Quoted in Raimund Koplin, *Carl von Ossietzky als politischer Publizist* (Berlin, 1964), p. 28.

36. "It remains a historical sin of omission that in that time of stormy progressive development the leap into the unitary state was not taken. Despite all Platonic obeisances to the idea of national unity, some Social-Democratic holders of power defended particular interests with an eagerness no smaller than that shown earlier by the dynasts." Friedrich Stampfer, *Die vierzehn Jahre der ersten deutschen Republik* (3rd ed., Hamburg, 1953), p. 134. The Preuss plan is reproduced, with map, in Arnold Brecht, *Federalism and Regionalism in Germany: The Division of Prussia* (New York and London, 1945), pp. 94–95. For Bavarian resistance see Rosenberg, *History of the German Republic*, p. 51; see also Eyck, *Geschichte der Weimarer Republik*, I, 81–83, 102ff.

planning, and the road was clear enough. But it was never taken; cautious Socialists were too timid to venture onto it, while big industry proceeded to "nationalize" the economy in its own way: through cartelization.[37]

These were fateful strategic errors, but the men of Weimar made an even more fateful error when they failed to tame, or transform, the machinery of the old order—the military, the civil service, and the courts. The military caste had come out of the war demoralized, its prestige shattered, in panic, ready for any compromise. The generals had led Germany into disaster, lying to themselves as much as to the world, wasting uncounted lives. Friedrich Meinecke acknowledged late in 1918 that "the unmeasured claims of the pan-German-militarist-conservative combine" had utterly discredited them.[38] Yet within a few years, this combine had regained its charisma for wide circles of the public and saddled the Republic with the legend of an undefeated German army stabbed in the back at home by Jews and Communists.

This resurgence was largely the responsibility of the Weimar leaders who had made the old army indispensable. On November 10, the day after the proclamation of the Republic, Ebert had concluded a far-reaching agreement with General Groener, accepting the aid of the army in keeping order. Regular troops, aided by hastily formed *Freikorps*, shot down militant Spartakists by the score; the Social Democrat Noske, the "bloodhound" of the Republic, gave the right-wing troops wide latitude for action—that is to say, for organized assassination. There were excesses on all sides—"these were terrible months," Arnold Brecht, a sober observer, later remembered—and the good will of Ebert and Noske is beyond question. Their judgment is something else again.[39] On February 2, 1919, more than a month before Noske's notorious edict commanding his troops to shoot on sight anyone found with arms

37. Franz L. Neumann, *Behemoth: The Structure and Practice of National Socialism, 1933–1944* (2nd ed., Toronto and New York, 1944), pp. 14–16; Rosenberg, *History of the German Republic*, p. 109.

38. See the letter of Meinecke to Aschoff, cited above, note 23; *Briefwechsel*, p. 97.

39. Brecht, *Aus nächster Nähe*, p. 247. The controversy over Noske remains unresolved. I am inclined to agree with Brecht (*ibid.*, pp. 231–247) that Noske had courage and took the task of being "bloodhound" from a sense of responsibility (the epithet is, after all, his own), but that he lacked foresight. For a favorable view of Noske, see Eyck, *Weimarer Republik*, I, 212–217; for severe criticism, H. and E. Hannover, *Politische Justiz, 1918–1933* (Frankfurt, 1966), pp. 40–45; there is much useful material in Francis L. Carsten, *Reichswehr und Politik, 1918–1933* (Cologne, 1964).

in his hands, and three months before the white terror vented its fury on the conquered Soviet Republic of Bavaria, Count Kessler prophesied that the present regime could not last: "The paradox of a republican-social-democratic government allowing itself and the capitalists' safes to be defended by hired unemployed and by royalist officers is simply too insane."[40]

The same air of unreality hovered around the continued employment of Imperial officials. The German civil service was world-famous for its efficiency and for its neutrality, but during the Republic it used its highly trained capacities mainly for administrative sabotage; their pro-verbial loyalty to their superiors apparently did not extend to Social Democratic or liberal ministers.[41] But the most astounding instance of this sophistic appeal to independence and objectivity—a fertile breeding ground for cynicism among the beneficiaries on the right as much as the victims on the left—was the conduct of judges, prosecutors, and juries in the Republic. The surviving judges of the Empire were taken into service after the Revolution; they were irremovable and, as their be-havior was to show, immovable as well: almost all of them came from the privileged orders; with close connections among aristocrats, officers, and conservative politicians, they had little pity for accused Commu-nists but suave forbearance for ex-officers. The consequences are notori-ous, but they deserve emphasis: between 1918 and 1922, assassinations traced to left wing elements amounted to 22; of these, 17 were fully expiated—10 with the death penalty. Right-wing extremists, on the other hand, found the courts sympathetic; of the 354 murders com-mitted by them, only 1 was fully expiated, and not even that by the death penalty. The average prison sentences handed out to these politi-cal murderers reflect the same biãs: 15 years for the left, 4 months for the right.[42] Right-wing putschists like Kapp, who had tried to over-

40. Kessler, *Tagebücher*, p. 117.

41. Decisive on this point is Arnold Brecht, "Bureaucratic Sabotage," *Annals of the American Academy of Political Science*, 179 (January, 1937), 48–57.

42. These figures, which have been accepted as authoritative by all historians, were collected and documented by the late German statistician Emil Julius Gumbel; see his *Zwei Jahre Mord* (Berlin, 1921), *Vier Jahr Politischer Mord* (Berlin, 1922), *Verräter Verfallen der Feme* (Berlin, 1929), *Lasst Köpfe rollen* (Berlin, 1932). His figures have been utilized in Neumann, *Behemoth*, pp. 20–23, 478–479; Hannover and Hannover, *Politische Justiz*, *passim*, especially p. 18.

throw the Republic by force and violence—his associates committed several revolting murders—were acquitted, freed on a technicality, or allowed to escape abroad. After the Hitler-Ludendorff Putsch of November 1923 failed, the trial of the putschists was degraded into a political farce; the court permitted the accused and their lawyers to insult the government in the most offensive and incendiary language and finally convicted Hitler to five years of *Festungshaft*, a comfortable form of detention of which, in any event, he served less than a year. The *Feme* murders committed by members of illegal "defense organizations," para-military vigilante groups, belong to the most atrocious crimes in a century filled with atrocities: unemployed fanatics and unemployable ex-officers clubbed men to death and strangled women often on the mere suspicion of "unpatriotic activities." Few of the murderers were tried, few of those tried convicted, and none of those convicted long detained or in any way deterred from later criminal activity. Indeed, one of these *Feme* murderers, Edmund Heines, one of Röhm's friends, actually served around a year and a half in jail and was finally disposed of, in an act of poetic justice, in the Nazi purges of June 30, 1934.[43] The two murderers of Erzberger were allowed to escape, the whole network of conspirators against him, though commonly known, was largely unmolested, and the chief conspirator was acquitted. Whenever the judges found it possible to twist the law in behalf of reaction, they twisted it: Hitler, as an Austrian, should have been deported after his Putsch, but was allowed to stay in Germany because he *thought* himself a German. Against Spartakists, Communists, or candid journalists, on the other hand, the courts proceeded with utmost rigor. Whoever was found to have had the slightest connection with the Bavarian Soviet Republic was harshly punished; writers who "insulted" the Reichswehr were convicted even if their exposé was proved to be true. In 1934, in exile, the Social Democratic party ruefully acknowledged its tragic mistake: "That the German working class movement, disoriented during the war, should have taken over the old state apparatus practically unchanged, was the grave historical error it committed."[44] True enough. Not content with inviting the Trojan horse into the city, the men of Weimar watched its construction and solicitously sheltered its designers.

43. For Heines, see Hannover and Hannover, *Politische Justiz*, pp. 154–157.
44. Quoted, *ibid.*, p. 34.

ii. The Roles of Reason:
Conciliators and Critics

(i)

THERE were thousands in Weimar—professors, industrialists, politicians—who hated the Nazis but did not love the Republic. Well-educated, intelligent, reluctant to exchange the values of the Empire for the dubious dispensations of democracy, many of these men were paralyzed by their conflicts and pursued, through the years of Weimar, public careers of honorable impotence punctuated by fitful activity. They learned to live with the Republic, judged its advent a historical necessity, and respected some of its leaders, but they never learned to love it, and never believed in its future. They came to be called "*Vernunftrepublikaner*"—republicans from intellectual choice rather than passionate conviction. On May 7, 1933, after the Nazis had been in power a little more than three months, Friedrich Meinecke confided to a fellow historian, Walter Lenel: "The German people was simply not ripe for parliamentary democracy, especially under the pressure of the Versailles Pcacc. I said that to myself, under my breath, from the beginning."[1] Here is the authentic voice of the *Vernunftrepublikaner*.

Like other intellectual republicans, Meinecke had prepared for this position even before the Emperor had abdicated. In the fall of 1918, he became convinced that Germany's only chance for survival was to "become democratic," to "throw overboard" the "ballast of conservative ideas," to fight any attempt at restoration, and to resign oneself to progress through a rational, courageous decision. And early in 1919 he was certain: "In the conflict between statesmanlike reason and inherited ideals, which we are all compelled to experience at this moment, I believe I must follow, with firm step, the demands of reason."[2]

What reason demanded, it seemed, was a republic with a strong President, a cautiously experimental regime ready to preserve the valu-

---

1. *Briefwechsel*, p. 138.
2. Meinecke to his wife, October 5, 1918; and to Siegfried A. Kaehler, (end of) January 1919, *ibid.*, pp. 95, 335. For Meinecke as *Vernunftrepublikaner* see above all, Waldemar Besson, "Friedrich Meinecke und die Weimarer Republik," *Vierteljahrshefte für Zeitgeschichte*, 7 (1959), 113–129.

able remnants of a great past, a state, above all, that would reconcile all classes with one another. As these reasonable republicans reasoned it out: in the old days, Bismarck's virulent anti-Socialist policies had frustrated class reconciliation; now it was threatened by the radical rhetoric of the Social Democrats. The form of government was less important than was its effectiveness in producing class collaboration and preventing radical polarization in politics: on this point Meinecke, who had loved the monarchy, agreed with Robert Bosch, the liberal engineer and industrialist, who had been indifferent to it. "In itself," Bosch wrote in 1923, "the Republic is not the decisive thing."[3] Earlier, Bosch had confessed that he was "not convinced that a Republic is the best thing for us." But, he insisted, "I am of the opinion that we should stay with the republic, now that we've got one."[4] This mood lasted through the twenties: to the *Vernunftrepublikaner* the Republic was, in a sense, the punishment that the Germans, aristocrats and bourgeois, deserved; it was infinitely preferable to the barbarism of the right and the irresponsibility of the left; it should enlist cooperation, even if it could not command enthusiasm.

This cool rationalism had its own characteristic virtues and vices: it was better equipped to discover defects than excellences; it was more likely to elicit dispassionate analysis of past errors than passionate loyalty to new possibilities. It encouraged a curious, rather limited, Machiavellianism: the *Vernunftrepublikaner* found it conceivable to collaborate with the military—had it not produced cultivated and moderate generals like Groener?[5]—or to see some pedagogic value in the Nazi electoral victory of 1930—might it not compel the Social Democrats to be "statesmanlike" and work with Bruening?[6] The *Vernunftrepublikaner* were reasonable men who had been willing to learn the first lesson of modernity but not the second: they acknowledged that nostalgia for the Empire was ridiculous, but they could not see that the Republic

3. Quoted in Theodore Heuss, *Robert Bosch: Leben und Leistung* (Stuttgart, 1946), p. 371.
4. Undated letter, but approximate date suggests itself from the reference to the National Assembly. Heuss, *Robert Bosch*, p. 371.
5. "Groener, the most overrated man in the Weimar Republic" (Felix Gilbert, in conversation with the author). It is time that such an opinion be at last publicly recorded.
6. This rather fantastic estimation of politics in 1930 is expressed in a letter from Friedrich Meinecke to his daughter and son-in-law, Sabine and Carl Rabl, October 30, 1930, *Briefwechsel*, p. 128.

might deserve passionate support—or, rather, that it might become deserving enough if deserving persons supported it.

Their very intellectual style kept the *Vernunftrepublikaner* from forming a party or laying down a program; in fact, some of them markedly changed during the brief life of the Republic. And not all of them were ineffectual: Gustav Stresemann, the politician for whom the name *Vernunftrepublikaner* might have been coined, became an active conciliatory force in German politics.[7] Stresemann's development—from lobbyist to politician, from politician to statesman—was a steady growth, a history of ambitions directed and disciplined, of ideas broadening under the pressure of insistent reality. Stresemann began as a typical, he ended up as an extraordinary German, and it was his tragedy—most of it enacted posthumously—that he could not persuade his own kind to accompany him on his voyage of discovery.

Neither Stresemann's origins nor his early career suggested such potentialities. Born into the Berlin bourgeoisie, Stresemann long retained a vivid affection for his environment, where men of middling origins aspired to higher things by reading the German classics but directed their education to practical affairs. His doctoral dissertation of 1900 was an exercise in nostalgia: it was on the bottled beer industry—his father's trade—and described small business as a way of life threatened by giant combines. In his early ventures into politics, too, he followed his father: wholly accepting the Empire, enthusiastic about German militarism, touched with the peculiar liberalism—mildly constitutionalist, vehemently imperialist—that had marked the Revolutionaries of 1848. When the war came, Stresemann, then in the Reichstag, lent his considerable eloquence to the war aims of the government; he was an uncritical, unmitigated annexationist, demanding a vast colonial empire in Africa, most of Belgium, and an Eastern Europe detached from Russia and subjected to German influence. Count Kessler, who came to know him well, likened the Stresemann of those years to one of Sternheim's less attractive dramatic personages: conventional, politically ambitious, cor-

7. The name seems to have been coined by Professor Wilhelm Kahl, like Stresemann a member of the German People's Party. See Henry Ashby Turner, Jr., *Stresemann and the Politics of the Weimar Republic* (Princeton, 1963), p. 112. Turner is quoting Gustav Stresemann's *Vermächtnis. Der Nachlass in drei Bänden* (ed. Henry Bernhard, Berlin, 1932–1933), I, 327.

rupted by industry and Old German cant.[8] The German collapse and the German Revolution depressed and disconcerted him; when he helped to form his new party, the *Deutsche Volkspartei*, he and his associates made their continued loyalties plain: "I was a monarchist," Stresemann wrote on January 6, 1919, "am a monarchist, and shall remain a monarchist."[9] His political line—and it was nothing more than that—now became the need for cooperation with an undesirable regime that had come to power in an unfortunate revolution and accepted a shameful peace treaty; this cooperation would save the country from civil war and dismemberment, and keep the way open for a possible restoration. In the Kapp Putsch of 1920, and later, Stresemann apologized for right-wing subversion and kept close connections with politicians and officers working for some form of monarchy.

Then something happened to Stresemann: history. It was not a dramatic conversion; it was perhaps not even a conscious process, but rather a conscious policy of gradual political adjustments for the sake of his party which masked an unconscious fading of old loyalties and growth of new connections: as early as 1919 Kessler subtly saw Stresemann as a "problematic phenomenon."[10] Certainly to the day in August 1923 when he became chancellor of the Republic, and beyond, Stresemann intimated his persistent hope for a restoration. But, just as his earlier pronouncements in defense of Weimar had smacked of political insincerity, his royalist pronouncements of the later years had a perfunctory air about them: the viciousness of the extreme right had taught Stresemann the virtues of Weimar; the exigencies of foreign and domestic politics had made him into a responsible statesman.

In January 1923, Arnold Brecht talked to Stresemann, trying to win him over to his plan for a seventy-fifth anniversary celebration of the Revolution of 1848, the liberal Revolution of the *Paulskirche* in Frankfurt, which had fathered the flag that had become the flag of Weimar.

When he hesitated (for he immediately saw, of course, that such a celebration would bring the colors black, red, gold to center stage) we reminded him that once, as a student, he himself had carried the black-red-gold flag at a celebration for the victims

---

8. Kessler, *Tagebücher*, p. 396.
9. Quoted in Turner, *Stresemann*, p. 30.
10. Kessler, *Tagebücher*, p. 138.

of March. We showed him a newspaper clipping about it. He then consented laughing-
ly and heartily, obviously much taken with the plan and especially enthusiastic about
the historic support which, he was sure, it would lend his policy of active collaboration
with the Weimar coalition. There, and at that moment, Stresemann was won over
emotionally to the Weimar Republic. The previous two years, with the fall of Social
Democratic predominance on the one hand, and the assassination of ministers and the
lust for dictatorship on the other, had made him into a *Vernunftrepublikaner*. But now
he was touched at the heart. Now more than tactical opportunism, more than mere
reason, came into play. As we sat with him in conversation about the *Paulskirche*, he
suddenly looked once more like that young idealistic student who had carried the
black-red-gold flag in honor of those who had fallen in the March days. His secret
attachment to the democratic republic shone from his eyes. The Stresemann of the
Wilhelminian policy of expansion—Stresemann the First, one might say, who had
still supported the Kapp Putsch—had long been dying. Stresemann the Second was
born, no longer a mere *Vernunftrepublikaner*, but—even if he could not plainly tell this
to the members of his own party—in the game with all his heart.[11]

Brecht's version of the scene sounds a little sentimental, but then, with
these *Vernunftrepublikaner* one could never be quite sure: their republi-
canism had its reasons which their reason did not know.

(ii)

The *Vernunftrepublikaner* placed their reason in the service of reconciliation: they sought to reconcile classes with each other, parties with the
state, Germany with the rest of the world—and themselves to republi-
canism. But there were other men of reason in Weimar, not intellectual
republicans but republican intellectuals, who placed their reason in the

11. Arnold Brecht, *Aus nächster Nähe*, pp. 399–400. While the controversy over Stresemann's policies and motives continues, the sources from which I have drawn here agree
on the impressive quality of Stresemann's growth. See especially Theodor Eschenburg,
"Gustav Stresemann," in *Die improvisierte Demokratie: Gesammelte Aufsätze zur Weimarer
Republik* (Munich, 1964), pp. 143–226, which, though not uncritical, sees Stresemann as
a great man; Stampfer, *Vierzehn Jahre*, pp. 344–345, which makes much of his "openness
to new and newest ideas, compounded with the old subservient spirit in strange ways;"
Arthur Rosenberg, who reports that Stresemann's belief in Weimar was known by
August 1923, and who sympathetically stresses Stresemann's isolation (*German Republic*,
pp. 199–202). Even Anneliese Thimme, caustic and revisionist, anxious to dispel what she
calls the "legends" that have formed around the "good European," acknowledges Stresemann's capacity for growth; while she denies, I think rightly, that a real "conversion"
took place, she does see a drastic change toward a realistic appreciation of the Republic.
Gustav Stresemann: Eine politische Biographie zur Geschichte der Weimarer Republik (Hanover, 1957).

service of criticism: they sought to uncover the arcana of government, the secrets of the unconscious, the legends of history. Nothing, no one, not even Bismarck, was safe from them.

There was neither novelty nor courage in criticizing the regime of Emperor William II—in fact it had become fashionable to make the Emperor a scapegoat—but then, in the time of the Republic, Bismarck himself came under attack: between 1925 and 1930 Johannes Ziekursch, a university professor and neither a Jew nor a Socialist, published a political history of the Empire from 1871 to 1918 in which he attacked Bismarck's authoritarianism and charged him with responsibility for the disasters that overtook his creation.[12] After this—did not the Weimar Republic still live in Bismarck's shadow?[13]—everything was possible. In fact, it was 1930, the year of Ziekursch's third volume and of Brüning that Erich Fromm, then an orthodox Freudian, offered a psychoanalytical account of the rise of the Christ dogma and in passing took issue with Troeltsch's attempt to "explain away" the class basis of early Christianity.[14] And it was in 1930 that the brilliant young historian Eckart Kehr published his provocative doctoral thesis, *Schlachtflottenbau und Parteipolitik*, which laid bare, in relentless and unimpeachable detail, the domestic economic sources of Germany's naval policy during the critical years from 1894 to 1901.

Eckart Kehr's tragically short career—he died in 1933 at the age of thirty—illustrates the high price a heretic had to pay, even in the Republic. His family swarmed with powerful figures in the intellectual establishment of the late Empire, but, shaken by war and defeat, he rebelled against the Prussian conservatism of his immediate environ-

12. *Politische Geschichte des neuen deutschen Kaiserreiches* (3 vols., Frankfurt, 1925–1930). The literature around Bismarck is enormous; on his reputation, see especially Andreas Dorpalen, "The German Historians and Bismarck," *The Review of Politics*, 15 (January, 1953), 53–67; Hans Rothfels, "Problems of a Bismarck Biography," *ibid.*, 9 (July, 1947), 362–380; Otto Pflanze, "Bismarck and German Nationalism," *American Historical Review*, 60 (April, 1955), 548–566; and a very useful thesis by Ludwig Freisel, *Das Bismarckbild des Alldeutschen Verbandes von 1890 bis 1933; ein Beitrag zum Bismarckverständnis des deutschen Nationalismus* (Oldenburg, 1964).

13. This is well expressed by Karl Dietrich Bracher, "Enstehung der Weimarer Verfassung," in *Deutschland zwischen Demokratie und Diktatur: Beiträge zur neueren Politik und Geschichte* (Berlin, 1964), pp. 11–13.

14. Now readily available in Fromm, *The Dogma of Christ and Other Essays on Religion, Psychology, and Culture* (Anchor ed., New York, 1966), pp. 1–95.

ment: by heritage an insider, his experience made Kehr into an outsider determined to compel the university world to grant him recognition. His studies of the intimate relations of business leaders, industrialists, and foreign-policy makers in the Empire forced him to the conclusion that profit had been a far more significant incentive for German imperialism than grandiose thoughts about the German mission: writing the dissertation had had a "revolutionizing effect "on him; he had begun, after all, with "political history and philosophy," but he discovered that social structure and economic interests influenced political decisions in ways that pious historians had always denied, or, rather, never seen.[15] His articles, which appeared in rapid succession in the late 1920's, were as scandalous as his book; they dealt, in biting language but impeccable scholarship, with such touchy subjects as the rise of the Prussian bureaucracy, the class struggles in the early Empire, the social and financial foundations of foreign policy, the sociology of the Reichswehr.

Predictably, Kehr's fellow historians did not know what to do with him. His articles were noticed; his book had some respectful and respectable reviews, but for the most part, it was a handful of young students in Germany and American progressive historians like Charles Beard who appreciated Kehr's true value. For the rest, there was patriotic denunciation and worried headshaking: Hermann Oncken called Kehr the "enfant terrible" of the profession; even Friedrich Meinecke, one of Kehr's teachers and one of his warmest, most disinterested sup porters, called him, more in friendly warning than in disapproval, "a complete Nihilist" who believed that "to understand all is to criticize all."[16] And this, of course, was precisely the point.

15. See Hans-Ulrich Wehler's Introduction to his collection of Eckart Kehr's collected articles, *Der Primat der Innenpolitik: Gesammelte Aufsätze zur preussisch-deutschen Sozialgeschichte im 19. und 20. Jahrhundert* (Berlin, 1965), pp. 3–4.
16. *Ibid.* p. 4. The transmission of Kehr's work to America is a splendid example of the impact that European scholarship had on American intellectual life. Beard, as Wehler points out (p. 8), had his attention drawn to Kehr by his German son-in-law, Alfred Vagts; after the war, at Columbia University, it was Franz Neumann who advised his students to read Kehr, and reinforced his advice by referring to Kehr's articles appreciatively in his own *Behemoth*, which all of his students, and not his students alone, read with great care. *Behemoth* refers to Kehr as an "extremely gifted German historian," and to his dissertation as "indispensable to an understanding of German imperialism." (See *Behemoth*, pp. 203, 206, 477, 488–489.)

(iii)

Kehr was a lonely operator, the *Steppenwolf* of the German historical profession. In contrast, his fellow critics, committed like him to the proposition that to understand all is to criticize all, generally joined in schools or institutions, huddling together for warmth, mutual support, and informed self-criticism. Surely there is nothing especially German, or Weimar-Republican, about the founding of institutes. New disciplines, seeking to clarify their purpose, train their personnel in their own way and propagate their findings, have often created institutions separate from, or only loosely affiliated with, old centers of higher learning. What is special about the institutes of the Weimar Republic is above all the quality of the work that was done in them.

At first glance, except for housing a high proportion of Jews, these institutes seem to have had little in common: the Kulturhistorische Bibliothek Warburg in Hamburg did its work in peaceful obscurity: the Psychoanalytische Institut in Berlin, though as unpolitical as the Warburg Institute, aroused much opposition among the members of the psychological guild; the Deutsche Hochschule für Politik attempted to establish a consensus among men of good will in all parties, and explicitly excluded only Communists and Nazis; while the Institut für Sozialforschung in Frankfurt was a center for left Hegelians persuaded that Weimar was only a way station to socialism. But, for all their differences, they were members of a real community of reason devoted to radical inquiry, open to ideas impossible or scandalous to traditional practitioners, and committed, all of them, not so much to Weimar institutions, but, with their lack of piety, their ruthless modernity, their search for reality through science, to the Weimar spirit.

While in retrospect the Warburg Institute appears as one of the greatest glories and most characteristic expressions of the Weimar spirit, its founder was a loyal monarchist, and the institute itself the intensely personal creation of one man, the realization of an obsessive wish. Rich, scholarly, extraordinarily sensitive and intermittently psychotic, Aby Warburg was haunted by the survival of classical antiquity in the civilization of the West. The subject had long engaged the attention of scholars, but not with the urgency and refined discrimination that Warburg himself brought to it; the precise shape of classicism, its precise impact on the Renaissance, seemed to him not dry scholastic matters but matters almost of life and death. There was in him, Panofsky has written, "an enormous tension between the rational and the irrational" which induced in him "not a romantic split, but a fascinating combination of brilliant wit and dark melancholy, the keenest rational criticism and most empathetic readiness to help."[17] It was Warburg's special achievement to recognize—I am tempted to say, to reexperience—the full range of the classical heritage, which was, after all, more than serene temples and Latin poems; it was dark as it was light, and its legacy was superstitious beliefs and magical practices quite as much as sculpture and poetry. Warburg's models—Burckhardt, Nietzsche, and Usener—set his problem and suggested its solution: the study of the survival of the classical heritage demanded a broad view of cultural history, an appreciation of the Dionysian aspects of life, and close attention to man's religious experience.[18]

For thirty years Warburg traveled, wrote highly original essays on the art and thought of the Renaissance and the Reformation, and collected a library of impressive diversity. In 1918, with the defeat, he fell ill, and two years later he broke down and went to a Swiss sanatorium. But he left his library which, in the charge of Fritz Saxl, was affiliated with the new University of Hamburg. Saxl and Erwin Panofsky both held university posts, but they did most of their writing and teaching in the Warburg Library, which soon acquired a wide reputation through its monthly lectures—later printed for general distribution—and its ambitious publications.

Ernst Cassirer's association with the Institute shows the Warburg style at work. Cassirer, already a well-known philosopher, had been appointed to the chair of philosophy at Hamburg; he moved there in October 1919, and then, sometime in the following year, he went to see the Warburg Library. It was, in Hamburg as elsewhere, a bewildering time: "Although the war had been lost by Germany," Fritz Saxl recalled later, "the air was full of hope. The collapse of material power had

17. "A. Warburg," *Repertorium für Kunstwissenschaft,* 51 (1930), 3.
18. See Fritz Saxl, "Die Bibliothek Warburg und ihr Ziel," *Vorträge der Bibliothek Warburg, 1921–1922* (Leipzig, 1923), pp. 1–2.

produced a strong and favorable reaction in the intellectual field"; the founding of Hamburg University, and the appointment of Cassirer, were obviously part of the reaction: Cassirer "lent a peculiar dignity to the young arts faculty, and an ever-growing number of students came to his courses, eager for the truth and for learning, after the many deceptions of the war years." It was in this atmosphere that Cassirer visited the Warburg Bibliothek. "Being in charge of the library," Saxl recalls, "I showed Cassirer around. He was a gracious visitor, who listened attentively as I explained to him Warburg's intention in placing books on philosophy next to books on astrology, magic, and folklore, and in linking the sections on art with those on literature, religion, and philosophy. The study of philosophy was for Warburg inseparable from that of the so-called primitive mind: neither could be isolated from the study of imagery in religion, literature, and art. These ideas had found expression in the unorthodox arrangement of the books on the shelves.

"Cassirer understood at once. Yet, when he was ready to leave, he said, in the kind and clear manner so typical of him: 'This library is dangerous. I shall either have to avoid it altogether or imprison myself here for years. The philosophical problems involved are close to my own, but the concrete historical material which Warburg has collected is overwhelming.' "[19] But this rebuff was not a rejection of the Library. It was Cassirer's way of protecting his own work in progress from being swamped by the massive confirmation he knew was on its shelves; he was then working on the first volume of *Die Philosophie der symbolischen Formen*, conceived wholly independently from, yet wholly congruent with, Warburg's philosophical ideas.

Cassirer did not resist long; he returned to the Institute and remained its most prolific author. And, appropriately enough, the first book the Warburg Institute published was Cassirer's *Die Begriffsform im mythischen Denken*; indeed his best work of the twenties—the three volumes of the philosophy of symbolic forms, his essay on language and myth, and his great book on Renaissance philosophy, this last dedicated to Warburg—was done under its auspices. He did not work alone; he was

19. Fritz Saxl, "Ernst Cassirer," *The Philosophy of Ernst Cassirer* (ed. Paul Arthur Schilpp, New York, 1949), pp. 47–48. For confirmation of the story, see Toni Cassirer, *Aus meinem Leben mit Ernst Cassirer* (New York, 1950), p. 106ff.

surrounded by productive art historians, philosophers and philologists: Eduard Norden's *Die Geburt des Kindes*, Percy Schramm's *Kaiser, Rom und Renovatio*, Paul Lehmann's *Pseudo-antike Literatur des Mittelalters*, Erwin Panofsky's *Idea, Dürers 'Melancolia I,' Hercules am Scheidewege*— all now classics in their field—were all Warburg Studies.

The severe empiricism of the Warburg style, the very antithesis of the anti-intellectualism and uncritical mysticism that were threatening to barbarize German culture in the twenties, was Weimar at its best; Warburg's celebrated formula that Athens must be recovered, over and over again, from the hands of Alexandria,[20] was not merely an art historian's prescription for the understanding of the Renaissance, which had painfully struggled with alchemy and astrology, but an *Aufklärer's* prescription for life in a world threatened by unreason.[21] But the influence of the Warburg Institute, if profound, was narrow; all of its survivors testify to its serene isolation. German right wingers looking for *Kultur-Bolsheviken* found no material for suspicion in the Warburg Institute's publications on the world view of St. Augustine, the contents of medieval encyclopedias, or the iconography of a Dürer engraving.

It was different with those other students of myth, the psychoanalysts, for the myths they studied were the—often unacknowledged—possessions of everyone. The Psychoanalytical Institute in Berlin, which had begun as a branch of the International Association in 1910, became independent in 1920, complete with clinic and training facilities—a decisive step, as Freud recognized, toward creating a body of well-trained analysts.[22] And, to judge from the names of those who trained and were

20. Aby Warburg, "Heidnisch-antike Weissagung in Wort und Bild zu Luthers Zeiten" (1920), *Gesammelte Schriften* (Leipzig, 1932), II, 491–492, 534. See also Gertrud Bing, *Aby M. Warburg* (Hamburg, 1958), p. 29.

21. "Warburg believed in the power of reason; he was an *Aufklärer*, precisely because he knew the legacy of demonic antiquity so well. Lessing's *Laocoon* had been the great influence on his youth, and he felt a deep obligation to the German Enlightenment of the eighteenth century." Bing, *Warburg*, p. 29. Other valuable reminiscences of Warburg include Carl Georg Heise, *Persönliche Erinnerungen an Aby Warburg* (New York, 1947), and the collective volume of memorial speeches, *Worte zur Beisetzung von Professor Dr. Aby M. Warburg* (Darmstadt, 1929). See also Dieter Wuttke, "Aby Warburg und seine Bibliothek," *Arcadia*, 1 (1966), 319–333, with excellent bibliography.

22. Sigmund Freud, "The Resistances to Psycho-Analysis," (1925), *The Standard Edition of the Complete Psychological Works of S. Freud*, XIX (London, 1961), 213–224.

trained in Berlin—Sandor Rado, Franz Alexander, Karen Horney, Otto Fenichel, Melanie Klein, Wilhelm Reich—the Institute participated in that sense of excitement so characteristic of Weimar culture: Max Eitingon was its founder, Hanns Sachs its chief training analyst, Karl Abraham its imaginative, disciplined theoretician. It was a rigorous school, and stiff: Rudolph Loewenstein, who was analyzed in Berlin by Hanns Sachs, found it "cold, very German." But even Loewenstein, with all his reservations, thought Sachs splendid ("a true empiricist") and Rado brilliant ("a magnificent teacher" and an "extraordinary intelligent man").[23] And, in addition to the excitement generated by the local talent, there was one unforgettable incursion by the Founder himself; at the Berlin Congress of 1922, the last he ever attended, Freud read a paper, "Some remarks on the Unconscious,"[24] which those present never forgot. It was in this paper, Loewenstein recalls, that Freud "introduced a whole new approach, a revolution in analysis," the "structural theory" of "the superego, the ego, and the id." The lecture was, Loewenstein says, "one of the greatest esthetic, scientific-esthetic experiences I've ever had in my life."[25]

However magnificent, such experiences had a limited public; in Germany, as elsewhere and perhaps more than elsewhere, psychoanalysis was viewed with considerable suspicion. Ironically enough, it was the war that called psychoanalysis to the favorable attention of a hostile profession; psychiatrists approached German analysts to administer rapid cures to shell-shocked soldiers that they might be fitted for combat once again, an access of pragmatic interest Abraham found unwelcome: "I did not like the idea," he wrote Freud, "that psychoanalysis should suddenly become fashionable because of purely practical considerations. We would rapidly have acquired a number of colleagues who would merely have paid lip service and would afterwards have called them-

23. "The Reminiscences of Rudolph M. Loewenstein," Oral History Research Office (1965), pp. 19–25. See Jeanne Lampl-de Groot, "Die Entwicklung der Psychoanalyse in Deutschland bis 1933," Sigmund Freud-Institut, Frankfurt am Main, *Ansprachen und Vorträge zur Einweihung des Instituts-Neubaues am 14. Oktober 1964* (Frankfurt, n.d.) pp. 26–30.

24. See Ernest Jones, *The Life and Work of Sigmund Freud*, III, *The Last Phase, 1919–1939* (New York, 1957), p. 87.

25. "Reminiscences of Loewenstein," p. 22.

selves psychoanalysts. Our position as outsiders," he concluded, in obvious relief, "will continue for the time being."[26]

There were few signs of change, but Abraham greeted each of them optimistically: he was asked, on occasion, to address meetings of psychiatrists, and in 1920, he even wrote a long piece for *Die neue Rundschau*, the Fischer Verlag's highly esteemed monthly, expounding the general principles of psychoanalysis. "Berlin," Abraham told Freud in October 1919, "is clamoring for psychoanalysis."[27] But the clamor remained muted. For some time there were rumors that Abraham would be appointed *ausserordentlicher Professor* in psychoanalysis at the University of Berlin but, as Freud rightly foresaw, nothing came of it. "Intellectuals" and "liberal advanced people," Loewenstein reports, looked upon analysis "with some interest" if not with much favor, and the general attitude remained one of hostility: medical students or young physicians studying and undergoing psychoanalysis kept this to themselves for fear that they would not get, or would lose, desirable positions.[28] Many intellectuals, all across the political spectrum, continued distrustful: Ricarda Huch, historian, essayist, poet, a decent and intelligent conservative, was so hostile that even though she was present at the meeting at which Freud's name had been proposed for the Goethe Prize, she "totally forgot" this—an amusing instance of a Freudian mechanism used to repress Freud himself. When a psychiatrist sent her a book "on Freud and against Freud," she found it "very fine" but not sharp enough.[29] And from the left Eckart Kehr condemned psychoanalysis as a bourgeois ideology inducing conformity and inviting escape

26. Abraham to Freud, October 27, 1918, *A Psycho-Analytic Dialogue: The Letters o, Sigmund Freud and Karl Abraham, 1907–1926* (eds. Hilda C. Abraham and Ernst L. Freud, trs. Bernard Marsh and Hilda C. Abraham, New York, 1965), pp. 279–280.

27. Abraham to Freud, October 19, 1919, *ibid.*, p. 292. See also, *ibid.*, 299–300, 305. Abraham's article was "Die Psychoanalyse als Erkenntnisquelle für die Geisteswissenschaften," *Die Neue Rundschau*, 31, part 2 (1920), 1154–1174.

28. "Reminiscences of Loewenstein," p. 32. At least one witness to the Weimar scene, Felix Gilbert, remembers the matter a little differently. "*I* (and I think this was typical) read Freud and Jung as a student in the twenties," he has written to me; "Freud was our 'daily talk.' I admit that there might have been few practicing analysts in Germany at that time, but Freud as an intellectual event had certainly permeated the entire intellectual scene."

29. Marie Baum, *Leuchtende Spur: Das Leben Ricarda Huchs* (Tübingen, 1950), pp. 329–330, 335–336.

from real social problems.[30] In 1929, Paul Tillich affirmed that the "philosophy of the unconscious, initiated by Freud" was "daily" growing in influence,[31] but the growth was halting, marked by professional squabbles and by widespread public misunderstanding, even among—perhaps especially among—the educated, who found it hard to discriminate among Freud, Adler, and Jung, and who often preferred Jung, with his acceptance of spirituality, to Freud, with his rejection of religion —a legacy, as Ernst Robert Curtius put it, of Freud's naturalism which would be overcome only after this final version of Enlightenment thought had been overcome as well.[32] In depth psychology, the outsider remained the outsider.

(iv)

Unlike the art historians and the psychoanalysts, the republican intellectuals practicing political science were directly, deliberately—I am tempted to say, defiantly—involved in the political life of the Republic and sought to influence its course—or, rather, those who were setting its course.

Political science had been a victim of the German Empire. German *Staatswissenschaft* of the 1850's and 1860's had made pioneering investigations into comparative government and public administration. But with the advent of Bismarck's Second Reich, political scientists, like other liberals, came to concentrate on the relatively harmless branch of political science, public law, which trained officials to defend, but not intellectuals to criticize the state. The study of "social and political reality," Franz Neumann wrote later, from his American vantage point, "found virtually no place in German university life. Scholarship meant essentially two things: speculation and book learning. Thus what we call social and political science was largely carried on outside the universities." Of course, Neumann continues, there was one exception: Max Weber, who possessed "a unique combination of a theoretical frame" combined with "a mastery of a tremendous number of data, and

30. "Neuere deutsche Geschichtsschreibung" (lecture given in Chicago in 1932), in *Der Primat der Innenpolitik*, pp. 254–268.

31. "The Protestant Message and the Man of Today," in *The Protestant Era* (ed. and tr. James Luther Adams, London, 1951), p. 190.

32. See *Deutscher Geist in Gefahr* (1932), pp. 24–25.

a full awareness of the political responsibility of the scholar." Yet Weber had little influence at home. "It is characteristic of German social science that it virtually destroyed Weber by an almost exclusive concentration upon the discussion of his methodology. Neither his demand for empirical studies nor his insistence upon the responsibility of the scholar were heeded." It is "in the United States," Neumann significantly concludes, "that Weber really came to life."[33]

The impulse for reform emerged from desperate practical need. Even before 1914, but with greater urgency during the war, a few German publicists, historians, and public officials, appalled by the political ignorance of statesmen and public alike, turned their attention to the *Ecole libre des sciences politiques* in Paris, a school, they believed, that had been the center of "the intellectual and national reconstruction" of France after its debacle in 1871.[34] Friedrich Meinecke, Friedrich Naumann, Carl Becker, who was to become *Kultusminister* in the Republic, Richard von Kühlmann, a highly placed and cultivated official in the foreign office, and Ernst Jäckh, an energetic, persuasive journalist, joined to seek ways of educating the unpolitical German in political affairs. They won over Robert Bosch, who supported his progressive convictions with munificent philanthropies, and early in 1918 founded a *Staatsbürger-schule*, with Naumann as its president. Naumann provided the rhetoric: Germans needed "education to politics," a training that would be provided by men and women in public life, and offer, not indoctrination or slogans, but insight. "The people," he argued, "is thirsty for political and socio-political truth and clarity," and a free school—free from the pressure of the state or private donors—must satisfy that thirst.[35]

Naumann died in August 1919; Ernst Jäckh became his successor. But Jäckh, whose only son was killed at the end of hostilities, the only victim in his unit, on his only day at the front, had ambitious plans, and

33. Neumann, "Social Sciences," pp. 21–22.

34. For the history of the Deutsche Hochschule für Politik, see Ernst Jäckh, *Weltsaat: Erlebtes und Erstrebtes* (Stuttgart, 1960), pp. 79–93 (the quotation is on p. 82); Jäckh, ed., *Politik als Wissenschaft: Zehn Jahre deutsche Hochschule für Politik* (Berlin, 1930); *Berichte der deutschen Hochschule für Politik*, 8 (October, 1930), 113–129 (report on 10th anniversary celebration of the school); and Fritz Stern, *The Politics of Cultural Despair: A Study in the Rise of the Germanic Ideology* (Berkeley, 1961), p. 235.

35. Theodor Heuss, *Friedrich Naumann, Der Mann, das Werk, die Zeit* (Stuttgart, 1937), pp. 538–542; see also Heuss, *Robert Bosch*, pp. 607–620 passim.

he transformed Naumann's "political school" into the Deutsche Hochschule für Politik. It opened in October 1920, beginning modestly with 120 students; by 1932, the last year of the Republic, it had more than 2,000 students, of whom over 500 were regularly matriculated. The course of study developed gradually, through experience. There were outside lectures, seminars, and a regular program. The faculty, both full- and part-time, was enthusiastic and outstanding; it included the philosopher Max Scheler; Theodor Heuss was director of studies for the first five years of the Hochschule; Arnold Wolfers and Hans Simons taught political science, Albert Solomon sociology; Sigmund Neumann was in charge of the newspaper archives; Franz Neumann, then a young trade union lawyer in Berlin, was among its occasional lecturers. And from the beginning, the Hochschule cultivated its ties to scholars and foundations abroad; in the course of the twenties, Charles Beard, Nicholas Murray Butler, G. P. Gooch, André Siegfried came to perform; and in 1931, Hajo Holborn came to the Hochschule from Heidelberg, filling a chair for history and international relations given by the Carnegie Endowment.

The program concentrated on political science in its broadest sense: political history, political sociology, foreign and domestic policy, "cultural politics" which included courses on the press, and the theory of the legal and economic foundations of politics. In its time, and in its place, the Hochschule was a radical departure. It began as an evening school, and never ceased to attract men and women of a type that had never enjoyed higher education before: trade union officials, employees, journalists, as well as diplomats and foreign students from many countries. There were students—and this, too, was revolutionary—who had no *Abitur*: in 1930, about a third had graduated from Gymnasium, a third had left Gymnasium after six years (*Sekundareife*), while the last third had only attended the free secondary schools (*Volksschulen*) which traditionally closed all access to academic training. And the Hochschule was radical also in its independence; the board of trustees accepted from the German government no more than 20 per cent of its budget, from the Prussian government only its building. And when a group of industrialists under the leadership of Hugenberg offered to support the school generously on condition that they control its program and name as its director the Conservative Revolutionist historian Martin Spahn, the trustees refused. It should surprise no one that in 1933, Joseph Goebbels took the Hochschule under his personal supervision.[36]

With its deliberately cultivated ties to high government officials—ties which did not compromise its autonomy but marked its readiness to participate in the shaping of policy—and its attempt to float, as it were, above parties—among its regular professors was the "Young Conservative" Max Hildebert Boehm, whose specialty was *Deutschtumspolitik*, the study of Germans on and beyond the frontiers drawn at Versailles, in a word, *irredentism*—the Deutsche Hochschule für Politik stood on the ground of bourgeois liberalism. This was too radical for many Germans. It was not radical enough for the political scientists and political theorists in the Institut für Sozialforschung in Frankfurt, for that institute was securely in the hands of Marxists.

If we read the bland histories of the International Institute of Social Research—as it came to be called in exile—written in the mid-1930's for American consumption, histories where unpleasant words like "Marx," "dialectic," "class struggle," and even "bourgeois" do not appear, we are tempted to compare its professors to characters in Bertolt Brecht's prose writings—and indeed to Brecht himself: telling their audience what it wants to hear and what, in their judgment, it is fit to absorb. For there can be no doubt: the Frankfurt Institute was left-Hegelian to the core. Founded in 1923 with several private endowments, and affiliated with the University of Frankfurt, the Institute did not really begin to function until 1924, when the veteran Socialist Carl Grünberg took the directorship.[37] In his lecture at the festivities inaugurating the Institut für Sozialforschung, Grünberg energetically stressed its function as a research institute—a function which, in Grünberg's candid logic, was revolutionary: most institutes, he argued, train "mandarins," social functionaries. That is understandable and just: the state needs loyal servants.

36. See Jäckh, *Weltsaat*, p. 88; Hajo Holborn to author (in conversation).

37. See *International Institute of Social Research: A Short Description of Its History and Aims* (New York, 1935?); *International Institute of Social Research: A Report on Its History, Aims and Activities, 1933–1938* (New York, 1939?); both compiled by the Institute, both wary, requiring much reading between the lines. The softening down of the hard edges of its teachings invades even the translations of titles; in addition to the instance cited in the text, note that repeatedly articles on "bourgeois society" are rendered as articles on "modern society."

But the Frankfurt Institute, he insisted, would train not servants but students of the state; by stressing the role of research and minimizing the roles of teaching and technical training, it would seek not to dull the capacity of the students for criticism, but sharpen it; it would teach them to understand the world, and, through understanding, change it. There are pessimists in the world, Grünberg said, prating of the decline of the West; but there are many, and "their number and influence is steadily growing," who not merely "believe, wish, and hope" that a new social order will come, but who are "scientifically convinced" that this order will be "socialism," and that this is the time of "transition from capitalism to socialism." "I may assume that it is well known," Grünberg added, "that I too hold this view. I too belong among the adversaries of the historically outmoded economic, social, and legal order and among the partisans of Marxism." To be sure, Grünberg reassured his listeners, his Marxism was a commitment neither to a party line nor to dogmatism; the students would be free. But there could be no question: the solution to pressing social questions offered in the Institute would be Marxist.[38] Nothing could be plainer than that.

For all his avowed radicalism, Grünberg's reign was less effective than that of his successor, Max Horkheimer, who became director of the Institute in 1931, when Grünberg retired after a long illness. Even under Grünberg's directorship, two major volumes had been published under the auspices of the Institute: Henryk Grossman's *Das Akkumulations- und Zusammenbruchsgesetz des Kapitalistischen Systems*, in 1929—The Law of Accumulation and Collapse of the Capitalist System, which, in the American bibliography of the Institute, appears a little less provocatively as The Law of Accumulation *in* the Capitalist System—and Friedrich Pollock's *Die planwirtschaftlichen Versuche in der Soviet Union, 1917–1927*, in the same year. With Horkheimer, the pace increased. His inaugural lecture, though more Aesopian than that of his predecessor, gave adequate clues to the attentive listener: Grünberg, Horkheimer said, had mainly cultivated "the history of the labor movement" and assembled a splendid library; but there were new tasks ahead: social philosophy must move beyond mere intellectual dispute to real effectiveness. This could

38. Karl Grünberg, *Festrede, gehalten zur Einweihung des Instituts für Sozialforschung.* . . . *June 22, 1924, Frankfurter Universitätsreden*, XX (Frankfurt, 1924).

be achieved only through a turn to empirical investigation in which "philosophers, sociologists, economists, historians, and psychologists could join in permanent collaboration."[39] Horkheimer hinted that this would not be a passive empiricism, an acceptance of things as they were; his rejection of metaphysical dogmatism and philosophical apologies, coupled with his demand for an understanding of the relations among the economic life of society, the psychological development of the individual, and changes in cultural life, and his free references to Hegel, made it obvious enough that the Frankfurt Institute would not surrender the Marxism that Grünberg had proclaimed.

Whatever Horkheimer's precise meaning, his intentions were brilliantly realized in a magazine, the *Zeitschrift für Sozialforschung*, founded in 1931, which published in its brief German phase—abruptly terminated in the spring of 1933—some important articles: Horkheimer himself wrote on a variety of philosophical subjects; Erich Fromm sought to develop a social psychology on Freudian grounds; Henryk Grossman wrote on Marx, Leo Lowenthal on the sociology of literature, Theodor Adorno on the sociology of music; while others, like Herbert Marcuse, Walter Benjamin, Franz Neumann, Paul Lazarsfeld, Otto Kirchheimer, and Karl August Wittfogel—then in his Communist phase—lectured at the Institute, did reviews or research, and published in journals sympathetic to its philosophical style. It was, one might say, quite a group.

(v)

To an American audience, especially in an academic setting, the names I have been listing stand like a screen before a complex reality. For, while these men may have been the heart of the Weimar spirit, and in their own way, the best of Weimar, they were not at the heart of public affairs; they met, cultivated, sometimes influenced insiders without really becoming insiders themselves.

To recall us to the reality behind the screen, then, let me offer two vignettes from the academic life of the period. "When I came in the spring of 1918 to the University of Breslau," Franz Neumann reports,

39. Max Horkheimer, "Die Gegenwärtige Lage der Sozialphilosophie und die Aufgaben eines Instituts für Sozialforschung," ("Antrittsvorlesung"), *Frankfurter Universitätsreden*, 37 (1931).

its celebrated economist—in his very first lecture—denounced the Peace Resolution of 1917 (peace without annexation and indemnities) and demanded the incorporation of Longwy and Brie, the transformation of Belgium into a German protectorate, the German colonization of large stretches of Eastern Europe and overseas colonies. The still more celebrated professor of literature, after having paid homage to Kantian idealism, derived from that philosophy the categorical imperative of a German victory, a German monarchy, and substantially the same peace terms. When I came to Leipzig in the fall of 1918, the economics professor thought it necessary—in October 1918—to endorse the peace terms of the Pan German Union and of the General Staff, while the historian proved conclusively that democracy was an essentially non-German form of political organization, suitable for the materialistic Anglo-Saxons, but incompatible with the idealism of the Germanic race. When I transferred to Rostock in the summer of 1919 I had to organize students to combat anti-Semitism openly preached by university professors. When I finally landed in Frankfurt, the very first task with which I was faced was to help protect a newly appointed Socialist university professor from attack—political as well as physical—by students secretly supported by a considerable number of professors.[40]

Berlin was equally infected. On November 15, 1922, Count Kessler attended a celebration in honor of Gerhart Hauptmann's sixtieth birthday at the University of Berlin. "New auditorium (*Aula*)," he wrote in his diary,

solemn, somewhat michelangelesque hall with an ugly mural by Arthur Kampf. Hauptmann sat on the speaker's stand, between Ebert and Löbe. Some professor of literature, I think his name was Petersen, gave a colorless, tiresome address, followed by a few further professorial essays . . .

The only speakers who had anything to say were a student and Löbe. The student spoke with so much fire and youthful freshness that he overwhelmed the audience. Only one professor, standing next to me, with gilded spectacles and in general corresponding to the prototype of the *boche*, who could barely master his rage through the whole ceremony, gave evidence of his displeasure by mumbling something. Hauptmann read a speech, short, not very profound, but happily pronouncing decisively in behalf of humanity and reconciliation.

The most remarkable thing about the festivities was the grotesquely narrow-minded conduct of students and professors. The Berlin fraternity council solemnly resolved—I believe with a majority of two to one—not to participate in the Hauptmann celebration because Gerhart Hauptmann is no longer to be considered a reliable German, after professing himself a republican! And I hear from Sam Fischer that the abovementioned Petersen who gave the official address had been to see him two days before

40. Neumann, "Social Sciences," pp. 15–16.

to ask him to disinvite Ebert, since it would not be agreeable to the university to have the republican chief of state appearing before it. And when Fischer refused, Petersen asked him at least to disinvite Löbe, for, after all, two Social Democrats at once were a little too much!

At the end of the celebration d'Albert played the Appassionata—beautifully. Whereupon once again one of the professors sitting next to me distinguished himself by whispering to his neighbor discontentedly: "That was of course the pianist's own composition, wasn't it?" Beethoven seems to be at home in the University of Berlin as little as Ebert.[41]

Whatever most Germans hungered for, evidently the men of reason in the Republic, whether they were conciliators or critics, were not providing it.

III. The Hunger for Wholeness: Trials of Modernity

(i)

ON a hot spring noon of the year 1913, a young student was walking through the main street of the town of Heidelberg. He had just crossed the *Brunngässlein* and noticed how the customary stream of pedestrians who usually strolled to the University and back from the *Ludwigplatz*, in casual noisy conversation and irregular groups, on sidewalk and in the street, now were crawling lazily over the red-hot pavement, exhausted by the unaccustomed heat. As all at once these tired people seemed to pull themselves together: with elastic carriage, light step, a solitary man came walking along—all stepped aside that nothing might encumber his progress, and, as though floating, as though winged, he turned the corner, toward the *Wredeplatz*.

The spectator stood motionless, rooted to the spot. A breath from a higher world had brushed him. He no longer knew what had happened, hardly where he was. Was it a man who had stepped through the crowd? But he was distinguished from all the men through whom he had walked, by an unconscious loftiness and an easy power, so that beside him all pedestrians appeared like pale larvae, like soulless stick figures. Was it a God who had divided the bustling throng and hastened, with easy step, to other shores? But he had worn man's clothing, though of an unusual kind: a thin yellow silk jacket fluttered around his slender body; a large hat sat on his head, strangely light

41. Kessler, *Tagebücher*, pp. 347–348.

and alien, and thick brown hair welled up under it. And in his hand there twirled a small, thin cane—was it the staff of Mercury, was it a human switch? And the countenance? The spectator recalled single features only indistinctly; they were chiseled, and the pallor of the cheeks contributed to arousing the impression of strangeness, statuesqueness, divinity. And the eyes? Suddenly the spectator knew: it was the beam from these eyes that had enchanted him; quick as lightning a look had darted toward him, had penetrated his innermost being, and had strolled on with a slight, fleeting smile. And now the certainty arose: if it was a man, then—Stefan George.[1]

It was indeed Stefan George, poet and seer, leader of a tight, humorless, self-congratulatory coterie of young men, a modern Socrates who held his disciples with a fascination at once erotic and spiritual—though this Socrates, who picked his Alcibiades at least in part for their looks, was handsomer than his antique model. Stefan George was king of a secret Germany, a hero looking for heroes in an unheroic time. The impression he made on Edgar Salin in 1913—an impression the young man recorded on that day[2]—was not at all unusual: there was a certain type of German to whom George was simply irresistible.

Stefan George died in voluntary Swiss exile in 1933, unwilling to lend his prestige to the triumphant Nazis whom he despised as ghastly caricatures of his elusive ideal. Friedrich Gundolf, his best-known disciple, the handsomest of his young men and the most productive, had died before him, in 1931, but most of the others survived him, some as Nazis, some as martyrs, some in exile. Sorcerers' apprentices all, they could not exorcise the spirits they had helped call up.

Like most of the elements making up the Weimar spirit, the George Circle, too, antedated the Republic, and drew on sources both German and foreign. Born in 1868, George had turned in loathing from a culture he despised to Baudelaire, cursed poet cursing his time, to Mallarmé, experimenter, musician in words, and prophet, and to German outsiders—to Hölderlin, the tendentious classicist, and to Nietzsche, the strident advocate of a new pagan aristocracy. In his journal of poetry and polemics, the *Blätter für die Kunst*, founded in 1892, and in his carefully staged conversations with his young men, Stefan George devel-

---

1. Edgar Salin, *Um Stefan George: Erinnerung und Zeugnis* (2nd ed., Munich, 1954), pp. 11–12.
2. Salin explicitly insists that this portrait was not a late elaboration, but based on a letter written that very day. *Ibid.*, p. 303.

oped his program, and sought an audience for his delicately chiseled poetry. George was not a racist; Gundolf's anti-French wartime fervor left him cold, while the right-wing mobs of the twenties only revolted him.[3] His task, as he saw it, was to perpetuate cultural values—the George Circle expended much energy expounding Goethe and translating Shakespeare and Dante—and to renew the aristocratic sense of life. It was Nietzsche's task: to be the good European, presiding over a transvaluation of values. But unlike Nietzsche, George did not choose to be alone; it was the heart of his method to build a secret empire for the sake of the new *Reich* to come, to find strength and possible inspiration in warm friendships and among the choice spirits of the past.

The George Circle, then, in addition to doing translations, polishing verses, and cultivating eccentricity in dress and typography, combed history for worthy subjects. Gundolf celebrated Caesar, Goethe, and Shakespeare, Ernst Bertram discovered new meaning in Nietzsche. These biographers were performing rituals; they did not analyze, they proclaimed their subjects, treating them as founders, as leaders, as judges, as supermen shrouded in myth, who, through their lives, shamed twentieth-century Germany, that new iron age. In 1930, Eckart Kehr noted and deplored a "Plutarch-Renaissance," and cited Gundolf's frenetic biography of Caesar as a leading example of this "historical belles-lettrism." The popularity of Plutarch among the George Circle, and indeed among a wider public, seemed to him symptomatic of disorientation; Plutarch had written of gods and heroes, of gigantic individuals, often inaccurately, and now modern Plutarchs, with the same contempt for precision, were offering a hungry public new giants to worship. Emil Ludwig and other best-selling biographers of the Ullstein world fitted smoothly into this pattern; Ludwig calmly announced that he preferred

3. In his moving autobiography, *Die verlorene Bibliothek* (Hamburg, 1964), p. 151, Walter Mehring portrays George playing the harp on top of the Olympus of war poets, while his *"geliebten Siegfried-Lustknaben"* marched off, but in justice it must be said that George felt nothing but loathing for the war, precisely because it was killing off his young men. Many of these holy fools, gravediggers of the Republic, were intelligent about the stupidities of others; George, about the war, and Spengler, about George: "The fundamental weakness of George (quite apart from the fact that the 'circle' has turned him into a sacred fool) is his lack of intelligence"—thus Oswald Spengler to Hans Klöres, January 6, 1917, in Spengler, *Briefe, 1913–1936* (ed. Anton M. Koktanek, Munich, 1963), p. 63.

graceful, unreliable storytelling to the cold accuracy of the expert. The biographers in the George Circle were often themselves experts, but they did not choose experts as their subjects; they chose whole men.[4]

The most notable biography produced in the George Circle was Ernst Kantorowicz' book on the great thirteenth-century Hohenstaufen emperor Frederick, *Kaiser Friedrich der II*. The text volume appeared in 1927; the second volume, which detailed the sources and analyzed technical problems, in 1931. The biography aroused immediate controversy and found a remarkably wide audience—an audience it fully deserved: it was, as Felix Gilbert has written, "a breath of fresh air in the muffiness of medieval history"; the "young people of all political shades (even Kehr!)" greeted it as "a work of opposition against the medieval establishment." The well-known medievalist Karl Hampe, who profoundly disagreed with Kantorowicz, was yet moved to concede him "exemplary mastery" of the material, patience with detail, and the kind of insight granted only to the knowledgeable scholar.[5]

Kantorowicz, then, was no crude propagandist; he was in fact not a propagandist at all. But he poured into his biography all of his experience and all of his expectations. By origin a Jew, by vocation a Prussian officer, Kantorowicz had joined the Freikorps after the war and taken up arms against the Left; to him, the Republic was the triumph of mediocrity, a leaderless age. He was an accomplished scholar, but as a member of the George Circle he professed contempt for the cold positivism of modern scientific scholarship, and sought historical understanding of great men, and historic moments, not through analysis but through vivid intuitions. Emperor Frederick—a superman who had defied all authority, voraciously tasted all of life, and become a legend in his own time—was an obvious subject for such a historian.

In one respect, as even hostile reviewers conceded, Kantorowicz' *Weltanschauung* served him well: rationalist historians had slighted the myths surrounding Frederick II, and Kantorowicz was ideally equipped to recognize them, and to understand their role in thirteenth-century

4. "Der neue Plutarch: Die 'historische Belletristik,' die Universität und die Demokratie," *Die Gesellschaft*, 7, part 2 (Berlin, 1930), pp. 180–188; the quotations from Ludwig, which are chilling, are on pp. 185, 187 (this piece now in Kehr, *Der Primat der Innenpolitik*, pp. 269–278).

5. Felix Gilbert to author, June 21, 1967; Hampe: "Das neueste Lebensbild Kaiser Friedrichs II," *Historische Zeitschrift*, 146 (1932), 441–475.

politics. But he was not content with detecting and penetrating myths. In a day when there were no more emperors, Kantorowicz said in his curt prefatory note, a "secret Germany" yearned for "its emperors and heroes." And the body of his book offered that secret Germany much palatable nourishment: Kantorowicz' Frederick II is the father of the Renaissance, a ruler rivalling the stature of Alexander the Great. He revived the classics, attained dizzying heights of the human spirit, embodied primeval forces, was strong, alert, vigorous despite all his intellect, and in combination of qualities superior even to Caesar and Napoleon, German to his core. He was dead and yet alive, waiting to redeem a German people as yet incapable of grasping his true semi-divine greatness. Kantorowicz did more than report medieval legends; his language in its hyperbole, its shimmering vagueness, its ecstatic approval, conveys a highly tendentious—I am tempted to say, erotic—engagement with its subject, and implies belief in these legends as deep truths, relevant to a suffering Germany. Kantorowicz put much reliable history into his biography, but that made his myth all the more persuasive to the educated, all the more dangerous to the Republic.[6]

It is impossible to measure the following for such books, or of the George *Kreis* as a whole; George's disciples vastly exaggerated their influence.[7] But there were many who found it seductive; it was a fresh wind in the stuffy atmosphere of the universities, and an exciting alternative to the routine cant of the politicians. Theodor Heuss later recalled that "the great works of historical prose that came out of the Stefan George circle became very important to me." Heuss never felt any real enthusiasm for the master himself; all the esoteric mumbo-jumbo (*Drum und Dran*) of the circle, all the "self-conscious verbal constructions" of its poetry, disturbed him. But, he confessed, the "works of Friedrich Gundolf, from his magnificent Shakespeare book on," and

6. For an interesting controversy around mythmaking in this biography see Albert Brackmann, "Kaiser Friedrich II. in 'mythischer Schau,' " *Historische Zeitschrift*, 140 (1929), 534–549, a review that challenges the very method—the search for living reality, the need to sense, feel, relive historical moments—characteristic of the George Circle, and Kantorowicz' results. Kantorowicz' reply, " 'Mythenschau,' Eine Erwiderung," *ibid.*, 141 (1930), 457–471, takes back nothing; while Brackmann returns to the attack, "Nachwort," *ibid.*, pp. 472–478.

7. This point has recently been made, persuasively, by Christian Graf von Krockow, *Die Entscheidung: Eine Untersuchung über Ernst Jünger, Carl Schmitt, Martin Heidegger* (Stuttgart, 1958), p. 36.

the historical writings of Wolters, Kommerell, and the others, meant a great deal to him: "What was decisive in my estimate was not what one could learn from George, though that was not negligible, but the high standards his circle imposed."[8] If even Heuss was taken into camp—and the hysterical bombast of these biographies is nearly intolerable today— the hunger for wholeness must have been great indeed.

(ii)

With its cult of youth, the George Circle especially touched many of the young. But German youth, often restless, bewildered, and incurably alienated from the Republic, also found other, less strenuous guides; the youth movement, which had had its modest beginnings at the turn of the century and flourished through the twenties, collected among its ranks and preserved among its graduates many would-be thinkers hunting for an organic philosophy of life.

It would be impossible to draw an ideological profile of the *Wandervogel* and their many offshoots. The youth movements had no real philosophy. Many were anti-Semitic, some accepted Jews. Many tied their members together in strong if unacknowledged homoerotic friendships, some encouraged girls to join. Many expounded a pantheistic love of nature and mystical love of the fatherland, some were casual associations devoted to healthful walks. Many repudiated attempts to introduce politics, some, especially after 1918, allied themselves with Communist, Socialist, or Nazi groups. But all *Wandervogel* except the most casual attached an enormous importance to their movement, an importance dimly felt but fervently articulated: as solemn, rebellious bourgeois— and they were nearly all bourgeois—they saw their rambling, their singing, their huddling around the camp fire, their visits to venerable ruins, as a haven from a Germany they could not respect or even understand, as an experiment in restoring primitive bonds that overwhelming events and insidious forces had loosened or destroyed, in a word, as a critique of the adult world.[9]

8. Heuss, *Erinnerungen*, p. 354.

9. The interest in the German youth movement, both nostalgic and sociological, has never flagged, and the literature that has grown up about it is quite unmanageable. I have relied heavily on Walter Z. Laqueur, *Young Germany: A History of the German Youth Movement* (London, 1962), a sound analysis equipped with a good bibliography.

The rhetoric of the leading spokesmen for the youth movements betrays this high idealism, unremitting search, and incurable confusion. Many of the youth leaders hailed an idealized, romanticized medieval Germany as a refuge from commercialism and fragmentation. Hans Breuer, who compiled the song book of the youth movement—one of the biggest bestsellers of twentieth-century Germany—made it clear in his prefaces that he had gathered his folksongs for "disinherited" youth, a youth "sensing in its incompleteness (*Halbheit*) the goad and longing for a whole, harmonious humanity."[10] What, he asks, "What is the old, classical folksong? It is the song of the whole man, complete unto himself (*in sich geschlossen*)."[11] The youth, singing these songs, was a self-conscious rebel against his father; indeed, Hans Blüher, first historian of the *Wandervogel* and apologist for its adolescent eroticism, insisted that "the period that produced the *Wandervogel* is characterized by a struggle of youth against age." Alienated sons sought out other alienated sons and formed a great "confederation of friendship."[12] To judge by these writers, the *Wandervogel* sought warmth and comradeliness, an escape from the lies spawned by mass culture, a clean way of life unmarked by the use of alcohol and tobacco, and, above all, a community that could rise above self-interest and shabby party politics.

As the philosopher Paul Natorp, full of sympathy and concern, warned as early as 1920, these aspirations were of doubtful value. The facile irrationalism of the *Wandervogel*, he said, their search for the soul and distrust of the mind, was bound to produce false ideals and lead to anti-social behavior: "You fear the dismemberment of your being in all the piece-work of human wishing and knowing, and fail to notice that you cannot achieve wholeness if you reject such large and essential parts of that which has been allotted to all mankind. You seek the indivisibility of man's being, and yet assent to its being torn apart."[13]

Natorp's warning was in vain. The unbridled neo-romanticism and emotional thinking of the prewar years had not been cured by the ex-

---

10. "Vorwort" to the 10th edition of *Der Zupfgeigenhansl* (1913), in *Grundschriften der deutschen Jugendbewegung* (ed. Werner Kindt, Düsseldorf, 1963), p. 67.

11. *Ibid.*, p. 66.

12. "Geschichte des Wandervogels," from vol. I (1912), in *Grundschriften*, p. 47.

13. "Hoffnungen und Gefahren unserer Jugendbewegung," a lecture first given in 1913; the quotation comes from the 3rd edition of 1920, in *Grundschriften*, p. 145.

perience of the war and the peace that followed it—these events, on which youth leaders dwelled obsessively, only compounded the confusion. The result was a peculiarly undoctrinaire, unanalytical, in fact unpolitical socialism—it was "a self-evident proposition," one observer noted, for all people in the youth movement to be socialists.[14] Young men and women, seeking purity and renewal, were socialists by instinct; the *völkisch*, right-wing groups demanded the "reawakening of a genuine Germanness (*deutsches Volkstum*) in German lands," while the left-wing groups called for "the restoration of a *societas*, a communally constructed society."[15] Everywhere, amid endless splintering of groups and futile efforts at reunion, there was a certain fixation on the experience of youth itself; novels about schools and youth groups, and the concentration of psychologists on youth psychology, exemplified, and strengthened, this fixation.[16] Flight into the future through flight into the past; reformation through nostalgia—in the end, such thinking amounted to nothing more than the decision to make adolescence itself into an ideology.

(iii)

The leaders of the youth movement did not need to generate their own ideas; if anything, Weimar enjoyed too many ideas, variegated, mutually (and sometimes internally) contradictory, unanalyzed and often unanalyzable. It was swamped with polemics designed to expose the inferiority of Republican culture to the imaginary glories of the First and Second Empire, or the imagined glories of the Third Empire to come. And for those who did not read books, authors provided slogan-like titles. Werner Sombart's indictment of the commercial mentality, winningly entitled *Händler und Helden*, was a characteristic product of the war, but kept its public during the 1920's; even more strikingly, Ferdinand Tönnies' classic in sociology, *Gemeinschaft und Gesellschaft*, first published as long ago as 1887, made its fortune in the Weimar Republic, with its invidious contrast between the authentic, organic harmony of

14. Elisabeth Busse-Wilson, "Freideutsche Jugend 1920," in *Grundschriften*, p. 245.
15. See Ernst Buske, "Jugend und Volk," in *Grundschriften*, p. 198.
16. Paul Lazarsfeld has commented (in conversation with author) on the plethora of studies on adolescence and the extreme scarcity of work on child psychology in the Germany and Austria of the 1920's.

community and the materialistic fragmentation of business society.[17] Perhaps most effective was the pairing offered in the title of Ludwig Klages' three-volume *Der Geist als Widersacher der Seele*, which assailed the intellectualism of mind in the name of the irrationalism of the soul.

Books spawned movements, which generally paraded before the public covered in deliberately incongruous labels—Conservative Revolution, Young Conservatism, National Bolshevism, Prussian Socialism—testifying ostensibly to a responsible attempt to get away from traditional political terminology, but actually to a perverse pleasure in paradox and a deliberate assault on reason.[18] Certainly Meinecke was right when he observed in 1924 that "the deep yearning for the inner unity and harmony of all laws of life and events in life remained a powerful force in the German spirit."[19]

The spokesmen for this yearning were as varied, and as incongruous, as the ideas they proclaimed: Hugo von Hofmannsthal was an exquisitely cultivated *Literat*, who sought to hold high the flag of civilization in an age of decay; Ernst Jünger translated his experiences of adventure and war-service—the *Kriegserlebnis*—into a nihilistic celebration of action and death; Walther Rathenau turned on the industry on which his fortune rested by constructing elaborate and ambitious indictments of machine civilization; Oswald Spengler impressed the impressionable with his display of erudition, his unhesitating prophecies, and his coarse arrogance.

In 1927, Hofmannsthal gave an address at the University of Munich rather strangely entitled, "Das Schrifttum als geistiger Raum der Nation." Not unexpectedly, it was a highly civilized performance; its diction was elegant and its cultural purpose unimpeachable. But it was also a mystification, elusive, strenuously vague: Hofmannsthal speaks of seekers and prophets, and discerns in the Germany of his day a "conservative revolution" of a "magnitude hitherto unknown in European history." But he does not identify the seekers and prophets, and specifies

17. See Krockow, *Entscheidung*, p. 32, 32n.

18. See on this point, and on the literature in general, Klemens von Klemperer, *Germany's New Conservatism: Its History and Dilemma in the Twentieth Century* (Princeton, 1957). In the end, the political pundits who proclaimed that they had "outgrown" the labels "left" and "right" usually ended up on the right.

19. *Staatsräson* (Munich and Berlin, 1924), p. 490.

the aim of the Conservative Revolution only as "form, a new German reality, in which the whole nation can participate." This elusiveness was itself, though perhaps not intentionally, a political act, for if the Germany of 1927 needed anything, it needed clarity, concreteness, demystification.

Yet a careful reading of Hofmannsthal's address suggests, if not a program, at least a coherent attitude. Evidently, Hofmannsthal believed that Germany failed, but needed to be a cultural organism in which spirit and life, literature and politics, the educated and the uneducated, might join in common possession of cultural goods, in a living tradition that all could enjoy. We are "connected to a community," Hofmannsthal argued, not by physical coexistence or intimacy, but by some "spiritual adherence." Indeed, only where there is "believed wholeness of existence—*geglaubte Ganzheit des Daseins*," *there* is reality. And now, in the 1920's, there are some seekers and prophets in Germany who are groping for this reality, and in two ways. They "seek, not freedom, but connection," and they have achieved the insight "that it is impossible to live without believed wholeness," that "life becomes livable only through valid connections," that "scattered worthless individuals" must become "the core of the nation"—that, in a word, "all partitions into which mind has polarized life, must be overcome in the mind, and transformed into spiritual unity."[20] Hofmannsthal was fortunate; he died in 1929, before he saw the consequences to which fatigue with freedom and denigration of individuality would lead.

In contrast with Hofmannsthal's dim vistas, Spengler's *Preussentum und Sozialismus*, first published in 1920 and often reprinted, is clear at least in the target of its scorn. Spengler had leaped into immediate prominence with the first volume of his *Untergang des Abendlandes*, in 1918, and retained his position as a deep thinker with *Preussentum und Sozialismus*, the first of his political pamphlets. It is one long insult to the Weimar Republic—"the revolution of stupidity was followed by the revolution of vulgarity." But it is also more than that: *Preussentum und Sozialismus* appropriates the word "socialism" to special purposes. Spengler agrees with most prophets of his day: socialism is inevitable.

20. The address is conveniently reprinted in a posthumous collection of Hofmannsthal's prose writings, *Die Berührung der Sphären* (Berlin, 1931), pp. 422–442.

But there are two types of socialism—English and Prussian—and we must learn to discriminate between them, and choose. To Spengler, Karl Marx, "the step-father of socialism," was an English socialist—the materialist imbued with unrealistic, "literary ideals"; the cosmopolitan liberal in action. The task, clearly, is "to liberate German Socialism from Marx." With frightening shrewdness, Spengler recognized that the so-called Marxist Socialist party of Germany really contained powerful anti-Marxist and true Prussian elements: "The Bebel-party had something soldierly, which distinguished it from the socialism of all other countries: clanking step of the workers' batallions, calm decisiveness, discipline, courage to die for something higher (*Jenseitiges*)." Class struggle is nonsense; and the German Revolution, the product of theory, is nonsense too. The German instinct, which, rooted in the blood, is truthful, sees things differently: "Power belongs to the whole. The individual serves it. The whole is sovereign. The king is only the first servant of his state (Frederick the Great). Everyone is given his place. There are commands and obedience. This, since the eighteenth century, has been authoritarian (*autoritativer*) Socialism, in essence illiberal and antidemocratic—that is, if we think of English liberalism and French democracy." The true German must recognize the needs of the day and, yielding to them, transform the authoritarian socialism of the eighteenth into the authoritarian socialism of the twentieth century. "Together, Prussianism and socialism stand against the England within us, against the world view which has penetrated the whole existence of our people, paralyzed it, and robbed it of its soul." The one salvation is "Prussian Socialism." Here are Hofmannthal's search for community and leadership in the language of the officer's barracks.

(iv)

Quite naturally, almost inevitably, the searchers for a meaningful life in a meaningless Republic turned to German history, to find comfort or models there. They found what they sought; German historians were ready to join them, and German history turned out to be singularly rich in oversized heroes and memorable scenes, both of them invaluable to mythmakers. One famous scene, from which nationalist and *völkische* elements derived much inspiration, had taken place in October 1817, three hundred years after Martin Luther had nailed his theses to the church door at Wittenberg. German students, wearing old-fashioned costume, gathered at the Wartburg, a historic and romantic spot; they shouted *Heil*, sang patriotic songs, said fervent prayers, and burned some books. They were members of the new *Burschenschaften*, radical, nationalistic, anti-Semitic, anti-French student associations with names drawn from the legendary past: Germania, Arminia, Teutonia. They were at the Wartburg to celebrate the liberation of their country—or, rather, countries—from the alien yoke, and in their celebration they linked the reformer Luther with the general Blücher as twin liberators of the German spirit and the German land, determined to draw strength from ancient myths for the political and moral tasks before them.[21]

This spirit survived into the Weimar Republic, drawing on a widening repertory of heroes: on Bismarck, the man of blood and iron, the tough realist who had unified the German nation by the sheer force of his will; on Frederick II of Prussia, invariably called "the Great," who with a historic display of self-discipline had grown from an effete flute player into the *Alte Fritz*, tough, sly, hardworking, in a word magnificent, gaunt from a lifetime of exhausting labor as first servant of his state;[22] on Martin Luther, defiantly forging a new faith and a new language, doing what he must do; on Wagnerian Teutons, who had inspired eighteenth-century French lawyers as they had inspired ancient Roman historians with their purity, their valor, their political prowess. It was a heady and, to susceptible spirits, poisonous amalgam. "The younger generation," wrote Ernst-Walter Techow, one of Rathenau's assassins, in 1933, "was striving for something new, hardly dreamed of. They smelled the morning air. They gathered in themselves an energy charged with the myth of the Prussian-German past, the pressure of the present and the expectation of an unknown future."[23]

The wholehearted commitment to Weimar demanded the repudiation of all such mythology. By its very existence, the Republic was a calculated affront to the heroes and clichés that every German child

21. Franz Schnabel, *Deutsche Geschichte im Neunzehnten Jahrhundert*, vol. II, *Monarchie und Volkssouveränitat* (2nd ed., Freiburg, 1949), 245–253.

22. See below, p. 79.

23. *Gemeiner Mörder?! Das Rathenau-Attentat* (Leipzig, 1933), p. 20, quoted in James Joll, *Three Intellectuals in Politics* (New York, 1960), p. 128.

knew, many German politicians invoked, and, it turned out, most Germans cherished. In the battle of historical symbols the Republicans were at a disadvantage from the start: compared with Bismarck and other charismatic leaders, at once superhuman and picturesque, the models available to Weimar were pallid and uninspiring: Goethe, with his benign ineffectual cosmopolitanism, the man everyone quoted and no one followed;[24] and the Revolutionaries of 1848, with their black-red-gold flag, their well-meaning speeches, and their decisive failure. Significantly, Heinrich Heine, perhaps the least ambiguous, most vital ancestor of the Weimar spirit, had found no fitting memorial even by the end of the Weimar Republic; for seventy-five years, proposals to erect a statue to him had called forth unmeasured and successful protests.[25]

While Weimar's need for a transvaluation of historical values was urgent, the hopes for achieving it were small; indeed, the need was great and the hope small from the same cause: the German historical craft, far from subjecting legends to criticism or the acid of humor, had long rationalized and refined them. With rare exceptions, like Theodor Mommsen, German historians had fitted easily into the Imperial system; professionally committed to a conservative view of things, more inclined to treasure established values than to urge change, they were thoroughly at home in the German university system, rejecting new men as much, and with equal vehemence, as they rejected new ideas. In 1915, the journalist and historian Gustav Mayer, a Jew and an independent political radical, wanted to "habilitate" himself at the University of Berlin, and was advised to take the step by Erich Marcks and Friedrich Meinecke. Mayer, skeptical whether "the old prejudices against democrats, Jews, and outsiders" had "really lost their power over the university clique," decided to risk it; he subjected himself to humiliating examinations only to find his skepticism justified—he did not get the appointment he obviously deserved. It was not until the Weimar years that he was imposed on Berlin University, but the dominant university clique of historians changed little.[26]

24. "Official Germany celebrates Goethe," wrote Carl von Ossietzky in the *Weltbühne* in 1932, "not as poet and prophet, but above all as opium." *Ausnahmezustand*, p. 286.
25. For the tragicomedy of the Heine statue, see Ludwig Marcuse, "Die Geschichte des Heine-Denkmals," *Tagebuch* (1932), in *Ausnahmezustand*, pp. 227–236.
26. Gustav Mayer, *Erinnerungen: Vom Journalisten zum Historiker der deutschen Arbeiter-*

The ideology that continued to dominate the German historical profession through the twenties was tenacious in part because it had a long history of its own; it could invoke a figure as charismatic for German historians as the personages of the German past were for the German people: Leopold von Ranke. Beyond doubt, Ranke was a very great historian: it must be confessed that if German historians often took a high tone of self-congratulation they had much to congratulate themselves on. Ranke was a pioneer in the use of archives, a master of complex materials, a splendid dramatist, and the founder of a new style of historical thinking. Ranke's central doctrines—the autonomy of the historian and his duty to understand each segment of the past from within —were of enormous service to the profession. But in the hands of German historians in the late Empire and the young Republic, the autonomy of history turned into its isolation. The segregation of history from ethics drove most German historians into a passive acceptance of things as they were, and the segregation of history from other disciplines alienated most German historians from the social sciences. For all his acknowledged historical erudition, most historians dismissed Max Weber as an "outsider";[27] for all his extravagance, the medievalist Georg von Below spoke for his fellows when he insisted that historians could "do without a new science of 'sociology.' "[28]

As their work shows, they did without it, and badly. What they could have learned from sociology, and from political science, was critical distance from the social and political structure in which they so comfortably lived. But then, the whole energy of Ranke's historical thinking had been away from the criticism, and toward the sunny acceptance of power; his celebrated insistence on the primacy of foreign policy was only a corollary of his cheerful resignation to the realities of the modern imperialistic state.

---

bewegung (Zurich, 1949), pp. 282–286, 310ff; the quotation, with the crucial word "*outsider*" in English, is on p. 282.

27. Hans Mommsen, "Zum Verhältnis von politischer Wissenschaft und Geschichtswissenschaft in Deutschland," *Vierteljahrshefte für Zeitgeschichte*, 10 (1962), pp. 346–347; the whole article (pp. 341–372) is extremely instructive.

28. See Georg von Below, autobiographical sketch in *Die Geschichtswissenschaft der Gegenwart in Selbstdarstellungen*, I (ed. Sigfrid Steinberg, Leipzig, 1925), p. 45; Below is referring to an article he had written in 1919. Earlier, during the war, he had predicted

Ranke's triumph as a historian was as fateful as it had been glittering; his legacy was ambiguous. While many of his epigoni were competent men—and few escaped being Ranke's epigone—they turned Ranke's pride into conceit, his diligence into pedantry, his acceptance of power into a mixture of servility at home and bluster abroad. This was perhaps less their fault than the fault of history itself—Ranke's teachings were more appropriate and less harmful to the nineteenth century than to the twentieth—but whatever the cause, the effects of these shifts were disastrous. We tend to make much of historians' efforts to revise the work of their predecessors; we make too little of the continuity of historical schools. Ranke's declared disciples before the First World War—capable historians like Max Lenz, Otto Hintze, Erich Marcks, Hans Delbrück—took Ranke's mystical belief in the nation-state and its ceaseless struggle for power, and projected it onto the world as a whole: in the history of modern Europe, the great powers had, through war or diplomacy, prevented any single state from gaining hegemony. But now, they reasoned, in an age of imperialism, Germany was threatened by the hegemony of a single naval state, Great Britain. Germany, therefore, must arm and, if necessary, fight to secure its proper place among the great powers.

The consequences of such thinking were inescapable: unquestioning support for the political-military machine that was ruling the country, and an unpolitical evasion of domestic conflicts. The historians of the post-Rankean generations thus displayed a curious mixture of bloodless rationalism and half-concealed mysticism; they coolly shoved armies and frontiers across the chessboard of international politics, and, at the same time, reveled in the mysterious workings of history, which had assigned to Germany a sacred part to play, a sacred mission to perform. They subscribed to the dictum of the democratic imperialist Friedrich

---

that "the monster of a major science of sociology will never be born." *Die deutsche Geschichtsschreibung von den Befreiungskriegen bis zu unseren Tagen: Geschichte und Kulturgeschichte* (Leipzig, 1916), p. 102. Hans Delbrück, whose political orientation was certainly quite different from Below's nationalism, did hold the same view of sociology. See A. Oberschall, *Empirical Social Research in Germany, 1848–1914* (Paris, 1965), p. 145. Meinecke, whom no one could accuse of undue prejudice in behalf of social science, conceded in 1922 that his profession had neglected disciplines from which they had much to learn. "Drei Generationen deutscher Gelehrtenpolitik," *Historische Zeitschrift*, 125 (1922), pp. 248–283.

Naumann, who defined nationalism as the urge of the German people to spread its influence over the globe.[29] Thus, when the war came, they simultaneously defended the unrestrained use of naked power and Germany's special mission to preserve, and spread, *Kultur*, a product in which Germans apparently excelled, and which they thought they must defend against the barbarous mass society of Russia, the effete decadence of France, the mechanical nightmare of the United States, and the unheroic commercialism of England. Distinguished historians—Troeltsch, Meinecke, Hintze—lent themselves to collective volume after collective volume proclaiming to an incredulous world the superiority of German *Kultur* over the mere *civilization* of the Allied Powers.

This type of historical thinking did not survive the Revolution unchanged; even historians noticed that something had happened in 1918. But the myth-making mentality that had produced such thinking went underground and emerged in disguised form, more inaccessible than ever to unmasking or self-criticism. The traditional boasts about German *Kultur* and Germany's mission had embodied elaborate fantasies, wish-dreams sprung from deep needs, and historians in the Weimar Republic found it psychologically more economical to patch up their fantasies than to discard them. The Weimar spirit, I have said, was born before the Weimar Republic; so was its nemesis. As in the Empire, so now too there were exceptions and, thanks to Weimar, there were more exceptions than before, but the bulk of the historical profession trafficked in nostalgia, hero-worship, and the uncritical acceptance—indeed, open advocacy—of apologetic distortions and sheer lies, like the notorious stab-in-the-back legend, the *Dolchstosslegende*.[30] "The full devotion to

29. Quoted in Ludwig Dehio, "Gedanken über die deutsche Sendung, 1900–1918," *Historische Zeitschrift*, 174 (1952), pp. 479–502. This article, and a bold and brilliant analysis of Ranke's epigoni, "Ranke und der deutsche Imperialismus" (also originally in the *Historische Zeitschrift*), as well as other important essays bearing on Ranke and his influence on historians and history, are now conveniently available in English: *Germany and World Politics in the Twentieth Century* (tr. Dieter Pevsner, New York and London, 1959). It is symptomatic that Dehio should still have thought it necessary (in 1950!) to introduce his essay on Ranke's followers with a modest disclaimer of arrogance, and professions of respect for the "great men of earlier generations." For the Ranke school, see also the careful analysis by Hans-Heinz Krill, *Die Ranke Renaissance: Max Lenz und Erich Marcks* (Berlin, 1962).

30. As Hans Mommsen has charged, German historians failed to prevent "the spread of the stab-in-the-back legend . . . in which the political fantasies (*politische Wunsch-*

Bismarck, and to the house of Hohenzollern," the cultural historian Walter Goetz lamented in 1924, "produced that profound aversion to democracy which was characteristic of German educated strata of the period between 1871 and 1914," an aversion that survived into the Republic, and was unhappily supported by leading historians. Respect has its value, but now, in the 1920's, it has become a burden: "The task of the historian is not cultivation of piety for a misunderstood past, but the pitiless exploration of the truth." But this, Goetz argued, was precisely what the German historical profession seemed incapable of grasping. What Germany needed was "clarity about itself" but what it got from its historians was yearning for the good old days, and misreading of recent history; historians were investing the old military caste with false glamor and the Republic with imaginary crimes. "Preceptors of the nation! Do you really think you are fulfilling an educational task if you command history to stop in its course and return to an old condition?"[31]

The vehemence of Goetz's outburst betrays his despair; he must have known that those who would listen to him did not need his warning, and those who needed his warning would not listen to him. Patriotic, antidemocratic myth-making went on. "Above all," wrote the aged historian Karl Julius Beloch a year after Goetz's article, "I do not want to close my eyes forever before I have seen Germany rise again to its old glory. But if this should not be my lot, I shall take with me the conviction that my people will one day remember that God, who made iron grow, wanted no slaves."[32] Beloch's quotation of Ernst Moritz Arndt's patriotic *Vaterlandslied* only underlined the continuing vitality of the old Wartburg spirit. And indeed, some of Beloch's most respected colleagues did their bit to restore Germany's glory. Felix Rachfahl was only one among many in the twenties to defend Germany's invasion of Belgium in 1914 as historically perfectly justified;[33] while von Below, coyly refusing to comment freely on the Revolution and the Republic,

denken) of the Wilhelminian period lived on." "Zum Verhältnis von politischer Wissenschaft . . . ," p. 348.

31. "Die deutsche Geschichtsschreibung der Gegenwart," in *Die deutsche Nation*, November 1, 1924, reprinted in Goetz, *Historiker in meiner Zeit: Gesammelte Aufsätze* (Cologne, 1957), pp. 415–424.

32. See Beloch's autobiography in *Geschichtswissenschaft der Gegenwart*, II (1926), 27.

33. See Rachfahl's autobiography in *ibid.*, II, 215.

in ostensible fear of the libel laws, did feel free to denounce democracy as "the great danger of our time," a force that was devouring, and devastating, the German people.[34] These were the voices of grand old men among German historians. It is not surprising that in 1931, Hajo Holborn should note little progress toward scientific objectivity among his colleagues. "The profound transformations experienced in all areas of intellectual, political, and social life as a consequence of the world war," he wrote in the *Historische Zeitschrift*, had "scarcely touched the core of scientific historical studies." Old academic "traditions and institutions" have been powerful enough to make "criticism of customary procedures, directions and aims of historical research and writing" extremely rare; what was far more in evidence was "a certain pride" in the discovery "how little one had to give up of inherited ideals." All too many historians thought themselves heroes for "swimming against the stream of the times." But, Holborn warned, these "inclinations to a kind of 'Faith of the Nibelungs'" were nothing better than "self-satisfaction," mere symptoms of thoughtlessness and self-deception which were threatening to "become dangerous to our craft."[35]

In retrospect, Holborn's solemn strictures are even more poignant than they must have seemed in their day, for they apply to some degree to Holborn's revered teacher Friedrich Meinecke, the best-known, and doubtless the most distinguished historian in the Weimar Republic.

Friedrich Meinecke is the Thomas Mann of German historical writing, and his *Idee der Staatsräson* is his *Zauberberg*, published, like the *Zauberberg*, in 1924, and written, like the *Zauberberg*, to confront recent history, to grasp the dialectical struggle of light and darkness battling one another in unappeasable conflict yet yoked together in indissoluble brotherhood. Like Mann, Meinecke was a cultural aristocrat converted to the Republic; like Mann, Meinecke was master of ponderous irony, enjoyed the subtle interplay of motives, sought the good but found evil fascinating, and derived, from the pains of war and defeat, the single lesson that if man is ever to conquer the demon that is within him, he can conquer him only by looking at him unafraid, and taking his meas-

34. See Below's autobiography in *ibid.*, I, especially 44.
35. "Protestantismus und politische Ideengeschichte," *Historische Zeitschrift*, 144 (1931), 15.

ure. Thomas Mann leaves his simple hero, Hans Castorp, on the battle-
field, his chances of survival uncertain, but sustained by the hopeful
question, Will from this universal lustful feast of death love arise some
day? Meinecke, wrestling with *his* demon, *raison d'état*, ends on a similar
note: "Contemplation cannot tire of looking into its sphinx-like countenance, and will never manage to penetrate it fully. It can only appeal
to the active statesman to carry state and God in his heart together, that
he may prevent the demon, whom he can never wholly shake off, from
becoming too powerful."[36]

Die Idee der Staatsräson is literature, philosophy, and autobiography,
but it is, I hasten to add, scholarly history as well.[37] In more than five
hundred closely printed pages, Meinecke traces the conception of *raison
d'état* from the origin of modern political thought in Machiavelli, through
its great representatives like Frederick the Great, to the twentieth century. And, in tracing it, Meinecke demonstrates its importance and its
problematic quality: the state has its needs—maintenance and expansion
of its power in a system of competing states—and the statesman finds
himself compelled to act in ways that he, as a moral man or in private
life, would condemn. Power, it seems, is dominated by a tragic duality:
seeking its own good, it is committed to evil means—to cold calculation, to fraud and force.[38]

There is much penetrating analysis here, informed by deep moral
passion and great subtlety—though, strange to say, not enough subtlety.
Meinecke, the master of words, is also their victim, and a victim in a
way peculiarly representative of the *Vernunftrepublikaner*: for all his crit-

36. *Staatsräson*, p. 542.

37. To call the book autobiographical is not to read into it what is not there; Meinecke
explicitly confesses that while he wrote it to follow up some themes he had first stated
before the war, in *Weltbürgertum und Nationalstaat* (Munich and Berlin, 1908), the grave
events of the war brought new perspectives, while "the shock of the collapse" pushed the
central problem into the forefront, "in all its terror." *Staatsräson*, p. 27.

38. The tragic nature of power is an important, always implicit and sometimes explicit theme of the book. It is, I think, an unfortunate way of analyzing power: it gives a
practical question metaphysical dignity. Waldemar Besson has charged, severely but not
without justice, that to see power tragically was to display resignation, impotence before
powerful forces, and thus to make an unwitting contribution to the destruction of
Weimar. "Friedrich Meinecke und die Weimarer Republik," *Vierteljahrshefte für Zeitgeschichte*, 7 (1959), 113–129, especially 124–128. More favorable, though by no means
sentimental, is Felix Gilbert, in John Higham, with Leonard Krieger and Felix Gilbert,
History (Englewood Cliffs, N.J., 1965), pp. 363–367.

ical energy, Meinecke cuts short criticism by taking rhetoric for reality, and mundane psychological conflicts for metaphysical problems.[39] "Hatred and revenge," he cites Bismarck, "are bad counselors in politics," but he does not stop to ask if Bismarck followed his own counsel;[40] "at least in his own eyes," he quotes Frederick the Great, "the hero must be justified," but he fails to inquire whether the word "hero" does not prejudge the issue, or whether Frederick was indeed justified in his own eyes;[41] he quotes some isolated high-flown moral pronouncements of Treitschke's and, despite some rather severe criticisms of Treitschke's aggressiveness and crude social Darwinism, grants him "deep ethical seriousness and spiritual breadth."[42] Meinecke takes his ideal of the state —an organic unity in which rulers and ruled join—for the reality, thus assuming as demonstrated what needed to be—and could not be— proved. Caught in his presuppositions, Meinecke never saw that the tragic view of the state helped to excuse its crimes, that the poor had no stake in the state's growth in power or glory, that the state was not nature's final answer to the problem of human organization, and, quite simply, that the state did not always, not often, represent the public interest. If Kantorowicz regressed by turning scientific questions into myths, Meinecke regressed by turning them into philosophical problems.

(v)

The complex of feelings and responses I have called "the hunger for wholeness" turns out on examination to be a great regression born from a great fear: the fear of modernity. The abstractions that Tönnies and Hofmannsthal and the others manipulated—*Volk, Führer, Organismus, Reich, Entscheidung, Gemeinschaft*—reveal a desperate need for roots and

39. See Eckart Kehr's discriminating review of Meinecke's *Geschichte des deutsch-englischen Bündnisproblems, 1890–1901* (Munich and Berlin, 1927): "Das ganze Lebenswerk Meineckes ist durchzogen von einer bewussten und disciplinierten Einschränkung seiner Problemstellungen—Meinecke's whole life work is colored by a conscious, disciplined limitation of his way of posing problems." *Die Gesellschaft*, 5, part 2 (1928), 27.
40. *Staatsräson*, p. 8.
41. *Ibid.*, p. 492.
42. *Ibid.*, p. 506. While Meinecke, as I have said, is far from uncritical of Treitschke, he is at pains to separate him from such intolerable disciplines as Dietrich Schäfer; it is worth adding that he is silent on Treitschke's anti-Semitism.

for community, a vehement, often vicious repudiation of reason accompanied by the urge for direct action or for surrender to a charismatic leader. The hunger for wholeness was awash with hate; the political, and sometimes the private world of its chief spokesmen was a paranoid world, filled with enemies: the dehumanizing machine, capitalist materialism, godless rationalism, rootless society, cosmopolitan Jews, and that great all-devouring monster, the city.[43] Othmar Spann, the Austrian Catholic social philosopher, whose fantasies were enormously popular in right-wing circles, offered a list of villains the others could accept with ease: Locke, Hume, Voltaire, Rousseau, Ricardo, Marx, Darwin, filthy—*unflätig*—psychoanalysis, impressionism, Dadaism, cubism, and the film drama.[44] It was this conglomerate of hostile feelings masquerading as philosophy that prompted Troeltsch in 1922, not long before his death, to warn against what he regarded as the peculiarly German inclination to a "mixture of mysticism and brutality."[45]

(vi)

Yet the Weimar situation was nothing if not complicated. Not all who, in the twenties, hungered for connection and unity were victims of regression; a few, outnumbered and not destined to succeed, sought to satisfy their needs not through escape from but mastery of the world, not through denunciation but employment of the machine, not through irrationalism but reason, not through nihilism but construction—and this last quite literally, for this modern, rationalist, democratic, organic philosophy was formulated most lucidly by architects.

The most articulate, as well as the finest, among these architects was Walter Gropius. In early 1919, Gropius opened the Bauhaus in Weimar, merging in the new venture two older schools, an academy of art and a

---

43. For these abstractions, see Kurt Sontheimer, *Anti-Demokratisches Denken in der Weimarer Republik: Die politischen Ideen des deutschen Nationalismus zwischen 1918 und 1933* (Munich, 1962). The anti-modernity of the German movement, its philosophical and psychological vagaries, are best analyzed in Fritz Stern, *The Politics of Cultural Despair: A Study in the Rise of the Germanic Ideology* (Berkeley, 1961). For the idea of "The Paranoid Style" I have drawn on Richard Hofstadter's title essay, *The Paranoid Style in American Politics and Other Essays* (New York, 1965).

44. See the list compiled in Ernst von Aster, "Othmar Spann's 'Gesellschaftsphilosophie'," *Die Gesellschaft*, 7, part 2 (1930), 230–241, especially 231.

45. Quoted in Klemperer, *Germany's New Conservatism*, p. 113.

school of applied arts. Clarifying and boldly advancing beyond principles first enunciated in the German Werkbund before the War, Gropius from the beginning dedicated his school to creating a single artistic unity—the building. "Architects, painters, and sculptors," he wrote in his opening manifesto of April 1919, "must once again recognize and grasp the complex shape (*vielgliedrige Gestalt*) of the building in its totality and its parts." Only then will their work be filled by the "architectonic spirit" now lost in "salon art." Older schools of art "could not produce this unity," since they had separated art from craft. This must change: "Architects, sculptors, painters, we must all turn back to craft." There is no essential difference between craftsmanship and artist: "The artist is the craftsman in his highest form (*Steigerung des Handwerkers*)." Let all, forgetting snobbish distinctions, collaborate in "the new building of the future, which will be everything together, architecture and sculpture and painting, in a single shape, rising to heaven from the hands of millions of craftsmen as a crystal symbol of a new emerging faith." Lyonel Feininger illustrated this call to a new unity with a woodcut depicting a tall slender secular cathedral, lit by stars.[46]

The course of studies at the Bauhaus was designed to turn this rhetoric into reality. After passing the elementary course, each student was trained in the workshop by two masters, who imparted, it was hoped, a mastery of materials as well as aesthetics, of content and form together. "A dual education of this kind," Gropius later wrote, "would enable the coming generation to achieve the reunion of all forms of creative work and become the architects of a new civilization." In 1922, Klee drew a symbolic representation of this program: a seven-pointed star is inscribed in a circular band; this band represents the preliminary training that encloses the several materials (glass, stone, wood) and the several courses (construction, color, composition) and leads to the heart of the star, another circle, in which the double aim of Bauhaus is proudly displayed: *Bau und Bühne*—building and stage.[47] The atmosphere of the new Bauhaus was experimental, cheerful, splendidly vigorous: one need only think of some of the teachers to recreate it: Klee, Kandinsky,

46. The manifesto is reproduced in full in *Das Bauhaus, 1919–1933: Weimar, Dessau, Berlin* (ed. Hans M. Wingler, n.p., 1962), pp. 38–41.
47. *Ibid.*, p. 10.

Feininger, Schlemmer, Adolf Meyer. Inevitably, there was some tension within: Johannes Itten, a painter and educator whom Gropius had imported from Vienna to conduct the all-important elementary course, was passionately dedicated to aesthetics and more indifferent to practical results than Gropius thought right—or possible. In 1923, he resigned, and the preliminary course was taken over by Josef Albers and Laszlo Moholy-Nagy. But with the passing of time and with an atmosphere congenial to open debate, these tensions relaxed, and the Bauhaus even profited from a rather premature exhibition on which Gropius had insisted against the better judgment of some colleagues. The true enemy, in any event, was not internal dissension, but outside hostility—the political and aesthetic aversion of right-wing, tradition-bound craftsmen to the revolutionary implications of the Bauhaus' experiments and to the Bohemian conduct of its students. In 1925, the Bauhaus migrated from the uncongenial atmosphere of Weimar to Dessau; there Gropius built his celebrated buildings—perhaps the most photographed artifact of the Weimar period—Klee and Kandinsky continued to be productive, Breuer built his furniture, and the workshop designed its lamps and china and silverware, clean, sturdy, and beautiful, which made the Bauhaus as famous abroad as it was becoming notorious at home. Finally, in 1932, politics and depression drove it to Berlin for its final twilight existence.

In the writings of his later years, Gropius simply developed the lines he had laid down in his opening manifesto of 1919; the new architecture sought for wholeness by seeking to satisfy both economic and aesthetic needs. Mechanization must be made to serve; the Bauhaus in fact had been designed "to avert mankind's enslavement by the machine by giving its products a content of reality and significance, and so saving the home from mechanistic anarchy. . . . Our object was to eliminate every drawback of the machine without sacrificing any one of its real advantages." True, modern man had been torn apart; but to abandon the division of labor would be not merely impossible but also undesirable. The tragedy of fragmentation was not caused by the machine or the minute subdivision of tasks, but by "the predominantly materialistic mentality of our age and the defective and unreal articulation of the individual to the community." What was needed was a thoroughly modern philosophy, unafraid of mechanization or of the right kind of standardization. "What we preached in practice was the common citizenship of all forms of creative work, and their logical interdependence on one another in the modern world." The "guiding principle was that artistic design is neither an intellectual nor a material affair, but simply an integral part of the stuff of life." Reason and passion here must collaborate. "It is true that a work of art remains a technical product, but it has an intellectual purpose to fulfill as well which only passion and imagination can achieve." The Bauhaus, in sum, had been a true community which, "through the wholeness of its approach" had "helped to restore architecture and design of today as a social art"; it had developed "total architecture."[48]

The language of architects is notorious for its imprecision, pretentiousness, and addiction to cliché, and Gropius himself did not always escape the temptation of playing oracle. Yet his work—the houses he designed, the products he supervised, the pupils he trained, the public he educated—gives solid, concrete meaning to his most fanciful expressions. What Gropius taught, and what most Germans did not want to learn, was the lesson of Bacon and Descartes and the Enlightenment: that one must confront the world and dominate it, that the cure for the ills of modernity is more, and the right kind, of modernity. It should surprise no one that the Bauhaus survived the Weimar Republic by only half a year.

48. I have drawn these quotations freely from Walter Gropius, *The New Architecture and the Bauhaus* (tr. P. Morton Shand, London, 1965), and the collection of Gropius' essays, *Scope of Total Architecture*. Interestingly enough, the Expressionist architect Erich Mendelsohn voiced similar opinions. The "primary element," he wrote, is "function," but Mendelsohn insisted on what he called his "program of reconciliation," in which beauty and utility were joined; the "dualism" of "God and man" disappears in the "organism" of architecture. Mendelsohn, *Briefe eines Architekten* (ed. Oskar Beyer, Munich, 1961), pp. 57, 73. When Albert Einstein walked through Mendelsohn's "Einstein Tower" in Potsdam in 1920, he whispered: "organic." Arnold Whittick, *Erich Mendelsohn* (London, 1940), p. 64.

IV. The Revenge of the Father:
Rise and Fall of Objectivity

(i)

THE history of Weimar culture runs parallel to the history of the Weimar Republic; culture was in continuous, tense interaction with society, an expression and criticism of political realities. This mixture of intimacy and hostility between art and life is characteristic of all modern society; in Weimar, where old centers of power—the universities, the bureaucracy, the army—had resisted outsiders while the theater, publishing, journalism was largely in their hands, it was particularly marked. The three lives of the Bauhaus—venturesome trials at the beginning, a secure accomplishment in the middle years, and frantic pessimism at the end—are expressive of the three periods of the Republic itself.[1] The time from November 1918 to 1924, with its revolution, civil war, foreign occupation, political murder, and fantastic inflation, was a time of experimentation in the arts; Expressionism dominated politics as much as painting or the stage.[2] Between 1924 and 1930, when Germany enjoyed fiscal stabilization, relaxation in political violence, renewed prestige abroad, and widespread prosperity, the arts moved into the phase of *Neue Sachlichkeit*—of objectivity, matter-of-factness, sobriety.[3] And then, between 1930 and 1933, the years of government by decree, decay of middle-class parties, resumption of violence, and disastrous unemployment, culture became less the critic than the mirror of events; the newspaper and film industries ground out right-wing propaganda, the best among architects, novelists, or playwrights were subdued and unproductive, and the country was inundated by the rising tide of *Kitsch*, much of it politically inspired.

If, by the early thirties, culture came to serve the counter-revolution, only a dozen years before it had done its best, by its lights, to serve the revolution. But expressionism was revolutionary without being political, or, at least, without being programmatic; its rebellion against stable

1. This parallelism in periodization has been noted by others: see Garten, *Modern German Drama*, p. 171; Kracauer, *From Caligari to Hitler*, p. 165.

2. The phrase "political expressionism" is, I think, Hannah Arendt's.

3. "Sachlichkeit" is a notoriously difficult term to translate; for some versions, including "sobriety," see Sokel, *The Writer in Extremis*, pp. 158–159.

forms and common sense reflected the longing for renewal, the discontent with actuality, and the uncertainty about means, that marked Germany as a whole. When the Revolution came, Expressionists of all persuasions firmly supported it, and drew other artists into the revolutionary circle. The *Novembergruppe*, founded in December 1918, and its offshoot, provocatively called the *Arbeiterrat für Kunst*, both dedicated to disseminating art appropriate to the new age, enlisted Expressionists from all parts of the political spectrum and artists from all parts of the artistic spectrum: Emil Nolde, the mystical, racist Christian, as much as Ernst Toller, the uncomfortable Communist; Erich Mendelssohn, whose flamboyantly curved designs were in the Expressionist idiom, as much as Walter Gropius, whose severe geometry offered the way out from Expressionism.[4] All artists, or nearly all, were seized with the quasi-religious fervor to make all things new: Bertolt Brecht and Kurt Weill, Alban Berg and Paul Hindemith, all joined the *Novembergruppe*. "The future of art," they proclaimed in December 1918, "and the seriousness of this hour forces us revolutionaries of the spirit (Expressionists, Cubists, Futurists) toward unity and close cooperation."[5]

This unity, like the unity of the Weimar coalition, did not last; but the revolutionaries of the spirit continued to assault their world, sometimes with great artistry, often hysterically. Expressionist films used dim lighting, distorted sets, antinaturalistic acting and stories murky with significance; Expressionist painters used strong simple aggressive colors, deliberately primitive draftsmanship, and abrupt movement; the dance, the cartoon, sculpture, all went through Expressionist phases, and no matter how placid their subject matter might be—some of the finest Expressionist paintings, after all, were landscapes and still-lifes—their artistic intention was as subversive of established tradition as George Grosz's savage drawings of revolting plutocrats, coquettish prostitutes, and maimed veterans.

Probably the most inventive Expressionists in early Weimar were the playwrights. Prolific and hostile—to the rules, to the audience, often to clarity—Georg Kaiser, Ernst Toller, Fritz von Unruh, Walter Hasenclever poured out plays eccentric in plot, staging, speech, characters, acting, and direction. Sets were merely indicated; lighting left the spec-

4. See Myers, *The German Expressionists*, pp. 217–223.   5. *Ibid.*, p. 220.

tator much to do; speech rose to declamation and, often, sheer yelling, as far removed from ordinary manner as possible. Characters were endowed with universality by being deprived of names and individual characteristics, and called simply "the man," "the young girl," "the soldier," "the mother." These plays had much life, little wit, and absolutely no humor; they were a direct appeal, a cry for help, and an emphatic demand for reformation.

Fortunately for these playwrights, producers and directors in the Republic were on the whole sympathetic to them. The most powerful man in the Weimar theater was Leopold Jessner, who had been imposed on the *Staatliche Schauspielhaus* in Berlin as *Intendant*—a strategic post—in the summer of 1919. The Prussian *Kultusminister*, Konrad Hänisch, was a Social Democrat; so was Jessner. But this was not Jessner's sole distinction; he was an experienced director and producer, who had successfully directed Ibsen, Hauptmann, Wedekind, and Schnitzler in Hamburg and in Königsberg. In fact, the last two plays he staged at Königsberg in 1919, before his call to Berlin, had been Wedekind's *Büchse der Pandora* and Kaiser's *Gas*. In Berlin he was to use his unprecedented influence with a curious mixture of daring and discretion.

The very first of his Berlin productions was, doubtless deliberately, a classic German play: Schiller's *Wilhelm Tell*. Jessner gave it an Expressionist production, obviously intent on demonstrating the critical function of art in the new republic. He took care to make the evening—it was December 12, 1919—as provocative as possible. He had engaged the best actors he could find—Albert Bassermann played Tell, Fritz Kortner the tyrant Gessler. The stage was dominated by what was to become Jessner's characteristic device, the *Jessnertreppe*, a jagged arrangement of bare steps on which actors could sit, which they could climb for declamation, and from which they could roll after they had been killed. The *Jessnertreppe* was an Expressionist assault on naturalism, and an Expressionist demand that the audience participate in the drama by using its imagination. Beyond this, Jessner had muted the patriotic tones of Schiller's drama by cutting a famous line about the fatherland, and converted the play into a call for revolution against tyranny. Gessler was dressed in a glittering uniform, dripping with medals, the very type of the hateful German general; his cheeks had been rouged to a furious red, to caricature the bestial Junker. The most obtuse among the spectators could not fail to guess the political message of the play before him.

Kortner records the course of the evening in his autobiography. The men of the theater, he writes, were left-wing; they had been outraged by the murder of Liebknecht and Luxemburg, and Jessner's production was an expression of this outrage. The premiere was interrupted from the start by demonstrations in the hall. Right wing and left were fully represented, there was yelling, whistling, stamping of feet; critics of various political directions and literary tastes stood on their seats and waved their programs at each other. Finally, Jessner, personally timid for all his radicalism, rang down the curtain, but the actors insisted that the play go on. The trumpets sounded, imitating the cadence of the ex-Kaiser's automobile, and this set off another noisy demonstration in the hall. Then Kortner, looking, he says, like an anticipation of Göring, jumped on stage, and shouted the demonstrators down. For a while there was quiet, and Bassermann could shoot the apple off his son's head to enormous applause. The curtain went down at the end of the act, and the company congratulated one another. They had celebrated too soon; the demonstrations resumed, until the yelling became deafening. And now Albert Bassermann, the refined actor, with his hoarse voice, ran through the curtain onto the stage. His unexpected appearance brought silence, and then, with a voice ringing clear for once, Bassermann shouted, "*Schmeisst doch die bezahlten Lümmel hinaus!*"—"Throw out the bums; they've been bought!" There were a few shouted disclaimers (they wanted to prove, Kortner suggests, that they were uncorrupted swine), but the resistance was over, and the play went on to a triumphant conclusion.[6] It was an Expressionist evening worthy of the production that had called it forth.

A style as self-consciously spontaneous and strenuously individualistic as Expressionism was not calculated to develop a single theme or leading preoccupation, beyond the rebelliousness itself and the urgent yearning to communicate. Some Expressionist writers recorded their fear of sex-

6. See Fritz Kortner, *Aller Tage Abend* (Munich, 1959), pp. 350–362. On Jessner, see the dissertation by Horst Müllenmeister, *Leopold Jessner: Geschichte eines Regiestils* (Cologne, 1956). Rudolf Bernauer, the producer and director, who did not like Jessner's expressionism, or his supple changes of direction, has some corrective remarks on him, *Das Theater meines Lebens: Erinnerungen* (Berlin, 1955), pp. 367–369.

ual inadequacy or of nothingness; others, their conversions to Christ or to a religion of humanity. Some celebrated, others caricatured machine civilization. A few glorified war and destruction. Most execrated militarism and propagated their ecstatic vision of a regenerated peaceful humanity.[7] The Expressionists had many heroes; the stranger, the sufferer, the suicide, the prostitute. But there is one theme that pervades their work: the son's revolt against the father. And here art comments quite directly on life: it would be simplistic to interpret the November Revolution as just one thing, but it was also, and significantly, a rebellion against paternal authority.

The first successful play to embody this theme was Hasenclever's *Der Sohn*, prophetically written in 1914. It is a pathetic drama pitting a tyrannical father against a son yearning to be free. The father beats the twenty-year-old boy, continually humiliates him, and is in the end defeated by the strength of his son. But the strength is borrowed: the boy is helped to maturity by a motherly *Fräulein*, and, while in the last act he threatens to shoot his father, he need not take responsibility for his threat: his father dies at his feet, the victim of a stroke.

For all its pathos—and what can one say of a revolution in which the tyrant, as it were, anticipates the slave's bid for freedom?—Hasenclever's play set a pattern.[8] "In that time," Carl Zuckmayer recalled later, "the father-son conflict was demanded of every good young writer."[9] Many good and many mediocre young writers complied, and, not surprisingly, drew contradictory morals from this single theme.

The pendant to *Der Sohn* was *Vatermord*, by Arnolt Bronnen, who later, appropriately enough, became a Nazi.[10] At first glance his play of parricide resembles Hasenclever's: here too a young man is harassed, intimidated, and beaten by his father, but the feeling is very different—while the young man of *Der Sohn* explicitly fights for freedom from tyranny, the young man of *Vatermord* lives in an atmosphere drenched in moral corruption, and his rebellion has purely subjective, vitalist significance. *Vatermord* is an unappetizing play about an unappetizing

7. See Sokel, *Writer in Extremis, passim*; Jethro Bithell, *Modern German Literature, 1880–1938* (2nd ed., London, 1946) especially chaps. xv and xviii.

8. Garten, *Modern German Drama*, p. 119; Sokel, *Writer in Extremis*, pp. 39–40.

9. Zuckmayer, *Als wär's ein Stück von mir* (Frankfurt, 1966), p. 324.

10. As Bithell writes in obvious disgust: *Vatermord* is "the most *awful* son-father tragedy" (italics his). *Modern German Literature*, p. 449.

family. Young Walter Fessel—the name, *shackle*, is surely not accidental
—is timid and indecisive; he whines and begs like a child to be allowed
to go to an agricultural school, while his father, a Socialist, wants him
to study and fight for the rights of the workers; the boy is passive
enough to be almost seduced by a homosexual school friend, but his
real passion is for his mother, still young and beautiful, who hates her
husband and lusts for her eldest son. As the play progresses through
senseless beatings and endless disputes—all presented in a pseudo-poetic
undifferentiated speech, a semi-stuttering, highly repetitive prose, obviously designed to hypnotize the audience—the mother becomes sexually
aroused and, like a bitch in heat, seeks the male that will satisfy her, first
in her husband and finally, after the son has stabbed his father to death,
in her son. But Walter Fessel, who has killed not the tyrant but all rational order, rejects his naked mother with a final stammering speech:

> I have enough of you.
> I have enough of everything.
> Go bury your husband, you are old,
> I am young however,
> I know you not,
> I am free.
> No one before me, no one beside me, no one above me,
> father dead,
> Heaven, I jump onto you, I am flying,
> It urges, trembles, moans, laments, must rise, swells, quells,
> bursts, flies, must rise, must rise,
> I,
> I blossom—[11]

The strains of adolescence—the burden of schooling and the stirring
of sex—had long attracted German writers of the modern movement:
Wedekind's pioneering *Frühlings Erwachen* is, after all, crudely put, a
play about puberty. In the early days of the Republic, Hermann Hesse
gave these themes a psychoanalytical twist, while Franz Werfel encouraged the son's rebellion against the authoritarian father in both
poems and novellas: it was in 1920 that Werfel published his short novel
of successful filial rebellion, *Nicht der Mörder, der Ermordete ist schuldig*—
not the murderer, the victim is guilty—an unfortunate saying which the
Nazis were to use much later, in a rather different context, and with a

11. Bronnen, *Vatermord*, (Berlin, 1925), p. 96.

different meaning. And it was the year before, in 1919, that Franz Kafka wrote, though he did not mail, his celebrated letter, a wounded son's indictment, to his father.

For many, the conflict went deeper than mere personal antagonism; it came to symbolize the political situation, or even the world's destiny. "Father and son," exclaims a character in Kaiser's play *Koralle*, "strain away from one another. It is always a struggle of life and death."[12] And in the confusion of the Weimar scene, writers agreed neither on the meaning of the father-son conflict, nor on its proper outcome. Socialists and republicans favored the son's bid for rational freedom against irrational authority; but there were many, hostile to rebellion, who sided with the father.

For this second group, the history of young Frederick of Prussia was the perfect subject. The story was well-known and thoroughly attested; myth here obtains the support of history. Frederick, still crown prince, defies his uncultivated martinet of a royal father; he would rather play the flute and write French poems than drill troops. He concerts with his friend Katte to run away, but the pair are betrayed, and the king takes his revenge. For a long time the king is determined to execute his son along with his son's friend, but good sense and the pleading of his advisors induce him to change course slightly: Katte will be executed before the crown prince's eyes, and Frederick, after a long hard penance, will be restored to the royal grace.

In the versions by right-wing writers, the father holds all the good cards: King Frederick William I is coarse and cruel, his decision to have his son executed reveals a streak of obstinacy and vindictiveness that is hardly praiseworthy; but the king is, after all, the finest Prussian type: honest, frugal, upstanding, passionately devoted to the welfare of the country that God has entrusted to him. If he is harsh, he is at least manly; if he is narrow, he embodies qualities that matter—loyalty, public service, piety. The son is intellectually superior, but he has effeminate leanings, yet he—we know it from history—will grow into greatness. But who can say that he would have become Frederick the Great if he had not gone through this purgatory, if he had not learned to bow down before his father, and take the royal burden upon himself by becoming precisely like his father?

12. Quoted in Bithell, *Modern German Literature*, p. 444.

The work that represents this genre most nakedly is a play by Joachim von der Goltz, which places the meaning of young Frederick's drama, though in itself obvious enough, into its very title: it is called *Vater und Sohn*. It holds no surprises: the division into acts is traditional, as is the management of the action; speech is naturalistic, filled with soldierly humor; characters are straight from the fairytale storehouse of a military nation: at moments of extreme tension, generals weep, while other characters face the mighty king in virile confrontation. When the flight has been discovered, and Frederick William I raves that both young men must be beheaded, Buddenbrok, a general and the king's close companion, steps forward: "If His Majesty wants blood, let Him take mine. (*He tears open his military coat.*) That other [that is, young Frederick's] you won't have, as long as I may speak a word." The King: "Buddenbrok!!" Buddenbrok, "*calmly*": "My King and Lord . . ." and so forth. And in the final scene, the young prince humiliates himself, as he is ordered to do, before his father and his father's companions, dryly, merely following orders, when the king suddenly melts, and comments on the prince's pallor "*in a transformed soft voice.*" This is enough: young Frederick "*meets the king's look and suddenly, deeply moved, drops to his father's feet*": "Father, forgive!" And the father forgives.

This was the kind of drama that conservative and *völkische* circles could appreciate. Goltz's play was saluted for its "manliness"; it reminded some critics of Kleist—which was, in the inflamed political situation of Weimar, a tendentious compliment, since Kleist's plays were being widely read as supporting the cause of militant nationalism. Goltz himself was hailed as a writer whose roots were deep in the soil, a soil called "*Volk, Deutschtum.*"[13] The "Fridericus" films that UFA began to produce in 1922 and continued to produce right to the end— "Fridericus Rex," "The Mill of Sans Souci," "The Chorale of Leuthen" —were a usually trashy but always popular tribute to Goltz's work.[14]

The presidential campaign of 1925 reenacted the son-father conflict in reality, and on a larger stage. The election of Hindenburg was the con-

13. See excerpts from reviews reproduced at the back of *Vater und Sohn* (Munich, 1922). As Felix Gilbert has pointed out to me, the interest in Kleist during the twenties was not simply patriotic; a number of productions stressed the unconscious, sexual component of his plays, and gave them a Freudian interpretation.

14. Kracauer, *From Caligari to Hitler*, pp. 115–119, 265–269.

sequence of miscalculations and self-serving, sectarian political decisions —of Socialist timidity, Communist obstructionism, and the endless stupid cleverness of bourgeois politicians. But it was symbolic as well: there was a vast outpouring of votes for the aged "hero of Tannenberg" who smelled of the old order; Hindenburg had been sold to the public as a man above parties, as the mystical representative of the German soul, the very embodiment of traditional values, as a sturdy paternal figure. With his election, the revenge of the father had begun.

(ii)

The real threat of Hindenburg's presidency was veiled for years by German recovery; a few skeptics like Count Kessler warned that Hindenburg's election would bring "one of the darkest chapters of German history"; Meinecke feared for the Republic and placed his hope in hope itself.[15] But most Germans, living from day to day, enjoyed the new calm, prosperous atmosphere. In life as in art, the time for revolutionary experimentation appeared to be over. In 1924, Paul Kornfeld, himself a leading Expressionist, had already called for an end to Expressionism: "No more about war, revolution and the salvation of the world!" he wrote. "Let us be modest and turn our attention to other and smaller things." And shortly after, Rudolf Kayser, editor of the *Neue Rundschau*, announced that "now after the exorbitant, gushing (*verströmten*) ecstasies, the tendency toward a new reality and objectivity—*Sachlichkeit*— is becoming palpable in all areas of life."[16] Some writers, in fact, had buried Expressionism even earlier; in 1922, Carl Zuckmayer had voiced his distaste for a style he thought alien to life, artificial, hysterical, worn out, and greeted the fresh talent of Bertolt Brecht: "There is a poet! A new tone. A power of speech and form which sweeps all that stale Expressionism into the ashcan."[17] It was a severe, and not wholly just verdict—the early work of Brecht owed much to Expressionist impulses—but it shows that the time for a slower pace was at hand.

The years of *Neue Sachlichkeit* were good years for the arts, but the

15. Kessler, *Tagebücher*, p. 439; Meinecke, *Politische Schriften*, p. 384.

16. Garten, *Modern German Drama*, p. 173; Wolfgang Grothe, "*Die Neue Rundschau des Verlages S. Fischer*," *Börsenblatt für den deutschen Buch-Handel* (Frankfurter Ausgabe), 17 (December 14, 1961), 2236.

17. Zuckmayer, *Als wär's ein Stück von mir*, p. 365.

men who first used the name were aware of its ambiguity. Gustav Hartlaub, the director of the Mannheim Museum who is credited with inventing the term, related the new mood "to the general contemporary feeling in Germany of resignation and cynicism after a period of exuberant hopes (which had found an outlet in expressionism). Cynicism and resignation are the negative side of the *Neue Sachlichkeit*; the positive side expressed itself in the enthusiasm for the immediate reality as a result of the desire to take things entirely objectively on a material basis without immediately investing them with ideal implications."[18] Carl Sternheim's acidulous comedy of 1926, *Die Schule von Uznach*, which was subtitled *Die neue Sachlichkeit*, took exception to the new cynicism and caricatured the "realism" of progressive educators as an excuse for promoting sexual license, and the film critic Siegfried Kracauer deplored the political passivity of the new style. But there were others, like Hartlaub himself, who greeted the disillusionment inherent in the *Neue Sachlichkeit* as a long overdue corrective to the intoxication of Expressionism; he chose to call it "healthy."[19]

Whatever its ultimate meaning—and that meaning differed from artist to artist—in substance the *Neue Sachlichkeit* was a search for reality, for a place to stand in the actual world; it was the struggle for objectivity that has characterized German culture since Goethe.[20] It called for realism in setting, accurate reportage, return to naturalistic speech, and, if there had to be idealism, sober idealism. It was a movement toward simplicity and clarity in which many of the Expressionists could join, not merely because they were weary with old modes, venally adapted themselves to new fashions or experienced outright conversion: Expressionism itself had contained impulses toward objectivity, which now gained the upper hand.[21] Carl Zuckmayer had begun, like so many others, as an Expressionist: his first play, *Am Kreuzweg*, produced in 1920 by Jessner, was everything his later work was not: declamatory and difficult. Then Zuckmayer shifted: his broad comedy of 1925, *Der*

18. Quoted in Myers, *The German Expressionists*, p. 224.
19. *Ibid.*, p. 224.
20. Goethe's struggle against what he regarded as morbid subjectivity and toward healthy objectivity, which was to become a model for his many imitators, has been brilliantly analyzed in Barker Fairley, *A Study of Goethe* (Oxford, 1947). The tradition is noted in Sokel, *The Writer in Extremis*, pp. 220–221.
21. See Sokel, *Writer in Extremis*, pp. 158–160.

fröhliche Weinberg, made him rich, and his realistic satire of 1931, *Der Hauptmann von Köpenick*, secured him a place in the history of German literature.[22] And Franz Werfel, a pioneer among Expressionist poets, also moved toward objectivity from conviction; his call for humane pacific cosmopolitanism, for plain goodness, never wavered, but his techniques developed from exuberant playfulness to meticulous precision. Around 1924 Werfel's metamorphosis was practically complete; in that year he published a major novel, *Verdi*, which portrays Verdi in the midst of an unproductive period, deeply jealous of Wagner and depressed about his own talent. It is only when he is freed from his sick admiration for that overripe seducer that Verdi can go on to the masterpiece of his advanced years, *Otello*. In style as in message, Werfel's *Verdi* reads like an awakening from Expressionism and a return to reality.

1924 was also the year that Thomas Mann published his most famous novel. *Der Zauberberg* follows its own laws; it did not transcend Expressionism, but quite simply skipped it, moving from *fin de siècle* decadence, nineteenth-century philosophizing, and traditional symbolism to superb naturalism in dialogue and description, and thoroughly modern psychological analysis. And it was in 1924 that Bertolt Brecht, already halfway beyond his nihilist experiments and into a new, cool lyricism peculiarly his own, moved from Munich to Berlin.

Brecht's move symbolizes the growing power of Berlin in the golden mid-twenties. As Germany's largest city, as the capital of Prussia and the Empire, Berlin had been the inevitable choice for capital of the Republic. But Berlin came to engross not merely government offices and party headquarters, but the leaders of culture, at the expense of the provinces. Other cities, like Munich or Hamburg, struggled to keep excellence in their universities, high quality in their theaters, and liveliness in their Bohemian quarters, but Berlin was an irresistible magnet. To go to Berlin was the aspiration of the composer, the journalist, the actor: with its superb orchestras, its hundred and twenty newspapers, its forty theaters, Berlin was the place for the ambitious, the energetic, the talented. Wherever they started, it was in Berlin that they became, and Berlin that made them, famous: young Erich Kästner, who became

---

22. There are some interesting comments on Zuckmayer's development in Gerhard F. Hering's "Nachwort" to Zuckmayer, *Meisterdramen* (Frankfurt, 1966), pp. 583–590.

notorious with his impudent verse before he became famous for his children's books, was fired from his post on the staff of a Leipzig newspaper and so in 1927, he recalls, he "went off, penniless, to conquer Berlin."[23]

Kurt Tucholsky wrote his affectionate *chansons* and nostalgic sketches about Berlin from the haven of Paris, but he, the native Berliner celebrating his city from a distance, was untypical. His like were greatly outnumbered by the likes of Kästner, *Wahlberliner*, men born in Hamburg or Breslau or Vienna, or points east and south, who chose to live in Berlin, or rather, who found any other city inconceivable. Bruno Walter, born in Berlin, had achieved fame in concert halls and opera houses all over Germany and Austria—and his name was associated with Munich, Vienna, and Salzburg. But Berlin in the twenties aroused him to real enthusiasm: "In his memoirs," he writes, "the English ambassador to Berlin, Viscount d'Abernon, speaks of the time after 1925 as of an epoch of splendor in the Reich capital's cultural life." It was "as if all the eminent artistic forces were shining forth once more, imparting to the last festive symposium of the minds a many-hued brilliance before the night of barbarism closed in." The accomplishments of the Berlin theaters "could hardly be surpassed in talent, vitality, loftiness of intention, and variety." Walter lists "Deutsches Theater and the Kammerspiele, in which Reinhardt held sway," which imparted to "tragedies, plays, and comedies the character of festival plays—from Shakespeare to Hauptmann and Werfel, from Molière to Shaw and Galsworthy, from Schiller to Unruh and Hofmannsthal." Then there was "The Tribüne, under Eugen Robert," devoted to "the careful and vivacious rendition of French, English, and Hungarian comedies." And the State Theater, where "Leopold Jessner's dramatic experiments caused heated discussion." Karlheinz Martin "conducted the destinies of the Volksbühne with a genuine understanding of the artistic popularization of plays and the theater." And there were other stages, which also tried to "raise dramatic interpretive art to new levels. Actors and stage directors alike were able to display the full scope of their talents. Contemporary native and international creations as well as those of the past had their day on the boards." There were many experiments: "there

23. Erich Kästner, "Meine sonnige Jugend," in *Kästner für Erwachsene* (Frankfurt and Zurich, 1966), p. 528. Felix Gilbert has commented on the impoverishment of the provinces through Berlin (conversation with author).

were oddities, and occasionally even absurdities." But the "character-istic sign of those days was an unparalleled mental alertness. And the alertness of the giving corresponded to the alertness of the receiving. A passionate general concentration upon cultural life prevailed, eloquently expressed by the large space devoted to art by the daily newspapers in spite of the political excitement of the times." Music was just as lively. "The Philharmonic Concerts led by Wilhelm Furtwängler; the 'Bruno Walter Concerts' with the Philharmonic Orchestra; a wealth of choral concerts, chamber music recitals, and concerts by soloists; the State Opera, deserving of high praise because of premieres such as that of Alban Berg's *Wozzeck* and Leos Janacek's *Jenufa* under Erich Kleiber's baton; the newly flourishing Municipal Opera under my guidance; the Kroll Opera under Klemperer." And many other institutions "matched the achievements of the dramatic stage." Add to all this "the visible arts and the outstanding accomplishments of science" and clearly, it was a great epoch.[24]

Bruno Walter's compilation, though copious, is far from complete. Berlin was headquarters for the political cabaret, where Otto Reutter performed his own dry compositions, lampooning the Germans for their rigidity in conduct and instability in politics, where Paul Graetz and Trude Hesterberg sang Walter Mehring's satirical songs, and Claire Waldoff her proletarian ditties; Berlin the city of publishing empires like Mosse and Ullstein; Berlin the center of political journalism, the biting commentary of Carl von Ossietzky, Leopold Schwarzschild, and —usually sent in from abroad—Kurt Tucholsky; Berlin the stage for Erwin Piscator's experiment in the political theater; Berlin the scene of Alfred Döblin's most remarkable novel, *Berlin Alexanderplatz*; Berlin the best possible town for premieres of charming trifling films, senti-mental Lehar operettas, and the *Dreigroschenoper*; Berlin the city of Samuel Fischer, the great publisher, who had on his list Thomas Mann, Hermann Hesse, Gerhart Hauptmann, Stefan Zweig, Carl Zuckmayer, Alfred Döblin, Hugo von Hofmannsthal. And Berlin was eminently the city of outsiders: "The overflowing plenty of stimuli," Gottfried Benn writes about the Jews in his apologetic autobiography, his racism intact, "of artistic, scientific, commercial improvisations which placed

24. Bruno Walter, *Theme and Variations*, pp. 268–269.

the Berlin of 1918 to 1933 in the class of Paris, stemmed for the most part from the talents of this sector of the population, its international connections, its sensitive restlessness, and above all its absolute (*totsicher*) instinct for quality."[25] Berlin, wrote Carl Zuckmayer—and he meant the Berlin of republican days—"was worth more than a mass. This city gobbled up talents and human energies with unexampled appetite"; it "sucked up into itself" talents real and spurious "with tornado-like powers." In those days "one spoke of Berlin as one speaks of a highly desirable woman, whose coldness and coquettishness are widely known." She was called "arrogant, snobbish, parvenu, uncultivated, common" but she was the center of everyone's fantasies and the goal of everyone's desires: "Everyone wanted her, she enticed everyone." The "man who had Berlin, owned the world." It was a city that demanded, and gave, energies: "We needed little sleep and we were never tired." It was a city of crooks and cripples, a city of hit songs and endless talk; with a press that was "cruel, pitiless, aggressive, filled with bloody irony, yet not discouraging," and with criticism that was, in the same way, harsh, nonconformist, but fair, in search of quality, delighted with excellence: "Berlin tasted of the future, and that is why we gladly took the crap and the coldness."[26]

(iii)

If Berlin tasted of the future, the taste of Berlin was cruelly deceptive; there was little future left. Life would not leave art alone. Beginning in 1929, the Republic suffered a series of traumatic blows from which neither the Republic not its culture was ever to recover. Gustav Stresemann died on October 3, 1929; whatever his limitations, he had been, both for Republicans at home, and conciliatory minds abroad, an irreplaceable force for good. Count Kessler was in Paris at the time; on October 4, he wrote in his diary: "All Parisian morning papers are reporting the news of Stresemann's death in the largest possible type. It is almost as though the greatest French statesman had died. Mourning is general and genuine. One gets the feeling that we do now have a European fatherland." And he quotes the *Times* of London: "Strese-

25. *Doppelleben*, in *Gesammelte Werke* (ed. Dieter Wellershoff, Wiesbaden, 1958–1961), IV, 73. But then Benn makes clear that some of his best friends were Jews.
26. Zuckmayer, *Als wär's ein Stück von mir*, pp. 311–314.

mann did inestimable service to the German Republic; his work for Europe as a whole was almost as great."[27] Then came the Depression, unemployment, continual political crisis culminating in the elections of September 1930, which decimated the bourgeois parties, gave the Nazis six and a half million votes and 107 deputies in the Reichstag, and led to Brüning's semi-dictatorship, to government by emergency decree. Survivors like Hannah Arendt and Hajo Holborn have testified to their dismay, and their conviction that the end had come. "The German intellectual's state of mind," Franz Neumann recalled later, "was, long before 1933, one of skepticism and despair, bordering on cynicism."[28] If that was the mood of some before 1930, September 1930 saddled intellectuals with it beyond hope of recovery. When late in 1935, in English exile, Arthur Rosenberg wrote his *History of the German Republic*, he concluded it with 1930, and treated the three years until Hitler's ascent to power as an epilogue. It was a tendentious periodization of Weimar history, but it reveals more than the mood of the disillusioned and displaced historian—it points to unpleasant realities.

By 1930, political divisions had deepened, and debate had grown ugly, scurrilous, often issuing in real violence. The realization of Hitler's boast in September 1930 that, if he came to power, heads would roll, was accompanied by clashes in the streets. In December of 1930, at the movie premiere of Erich Maria Remarque's *Im Westen Nichts Neues*—which as a novel had already aroused the right with its enormous sales, and its demonstration that war was hell and that German soldiers, far from having been stabbed in the back at home, had lost the war at the front—the Nazis, under Goebbels' leadership, led riots against the film, invaded the theater, throwing stink bombs and letting loose mice, and finally succeeded in having the film banned. In fury and prophetic despair, Carl von Ossietzky attacked the republicans for their torpor and cowardice: craven republicans, he wrote, have constructed an "especially lovely formula"; with a regretful smile, they are saying to one another: "What is one to do? The film, after all, is so bad!" But, Ossietzky objected, "this affair is political and not touched by aesthetic categories. It is completely irrelevant whether the film, and the book on which it is

27. Kessler, *Tagebücher*, pp. 595–596.
28. Neumann, "Social Sciences," p. 14; also Hannah Arendt and Hajo Holborn in conversation with author.

based, are works of art. The sole question is whether a deliberately moderate pacific way of thinking . . . should continue to be permitted or not." First it "was openly terrorized" by a fanatical mob "under the leadership of a club-footed psychopath," then it was "quietly quashed in the obscure censorship office of some obscure official." The banality every German and every foreign statesman utters on every possible occasion—that peace is preferable to war—"has now in Germany attained the charm of the forbidden." Fascism had scored another victory, and liberal cowardice, which simply stays home in moments of trouble, is now bankrupt. "Fascism can be beaten only in the streets. Against the National Socialist rabble party we have only one logic: the heavy knout; to tame them, we have only one doctrine: *A un corsaire—corsaire et demi!*"[29]

It was a brave and futile cry. The Social Democrats clung to Republican legality; the supple Jewish publishing house of Ullstein sought to accommodate itself to threatening conditions by purging its house of Jews and radicals, and by adopting a patriotic, even chauvinist tone—which shocked its friends and did not appease its enemies.[30] Anti-Semitism, long endemic in the universities and a standard battle cry of right-wing parties, became more virulent than ever.[31] In impatience and sheer disgust, a number of promising or prominent intellectuals made common cause with the Communists, joining the party or submitting to its discipline, thus mirroring, and exacerbating, the polarization of political life. Arthur Koestler, who arrived from Paris in September 1930,

29. Carl von Ossietzky, "Remarque-Film," *Weltbühne*, 1930, in *Ausnahmezustand*, p. 218; Eyck, *Geschichte der Weimarer Republik*, II, 368–369.

30. The history of Ullstein needs to be written; the reminiscences of members of this house, and the commissioned histories, obscure more than they clarify. Arthur Köstler, *Arrow in the Blue: An Autobiography* (New York, 1952), p. 249ff. is very helpful; Peter de Mendelssohn, *Zeitungsstadt Berlin: Menschen und Mächte in der Geschichte der deutschen Presse* (Berlin, 1959), though full of detail, and Hermann Ullstein, *The Rise and Fall of the House of Ullstein* (New York, 1943), full of irrelevancies, are not.

31. "In the German Republic," wrote the philosopher Theodor Lessing in 1932, "a popular state (*Volksstaat*) which guarantees every citizen freedom of conscience and protection of his honor, a collective crime is being perpetrated the like of which has never happened before. For it has never been permitted that the majority in a state could deliver over the defenseless minority to the instinct of the masses, in word and print, as hateful and parasitical." *Der jüdische Selbsthass* (Berlin, c. 1930), p. 409, quoted by George L. Mosse, "Die deutsche Rechte und die Juden," in *Entscheidungsjahr 1932: Zur Judenfrage in der Endphase der Weimarer Republik* (Tübingen, 1965), p. 183.

on the day of the fateful Reichstag elections, to join the staff of the Ullstein firm in Berlin, thought Weimar doomed, liberals and Socialists contemptible, and Communism the only hope. And Bertolt Brecht, who had been studying Marxism sympathetically since he had come to Berlin, steadily moved left. In 1928, he put his distaste for the bourgeoisie, and his new-found materialist philosophy, into the *Dreigroschenoper*: Mackie Messer taunts his bourgeois audience for loving its own fat belly and the docility of the workers, and assured it that however it might try to twist the truth, this much was certain: feeding one's face came first, ethics came after that. They are imperishable lines:

> Ihr, die ihr euren Wanst und unsre Bravheit liebt
> Das eine wisset ein für allemal:
> Wie ihr es immer dreht und wie ihr's immer schiebt
> Erst kommt das Fressen, dann kommt die Moral.[32]

But when the party criticized his cynicism and remoteness from social realities he shifted to didactic plays, radicalized his *Dreigroschenoper* into a crudely anticapitalist movie script and novel, assailed entertainment as "culinary opera," called for a drama committed to progress, and came to advocate a philosophy of self-sacrifice unto death for the sake of the cause.[33]

This political line was not without its appeal, and the Communists, like the Social Democrats, held firm in the face of the Nazi onslaught. But neither Communists nor Socialists could ever capture a sector of the population that was growing strategically more significant week by week: the youth.

The political history of the youth in the Weimar Republic is, among its many ironies, the most poignant. As the father-son literature had shown from the beginning, there was confusion not merely over who ought to win the contest, but even over who was who. The politicized youth movement, and the student organizations, nearly all right-wing and increasingly infiltrated and then dominated by Nazis, claimed to be speaking for youth and youthfulness. As they saw it, the men who had made the Republic—the *Novemberverbrecher*—were middle-aged, not

32. Bertolt Brecht, *Stücke*, III (Berlin, 1964), 99.
33. For the complex story, the collection of documents, including the play, the novel, and details on the lawsuit over the film script, Bertolt Brecht's *Dreigroschenbuch* (Frankfurt, 1960), is invaluable.

only in years but in ways of thinking: the Republic, they insisted, had been born elderly. They were both right and wrong: the Nazis were not simply reactionaries; some of their notions, whether nihilist or totalitarian, were a repudiation as much of the traditional authoritarianism of the dead Empire as of the modern democratic rationalism of the dying Republic. Some of the leaders of right-wing youth were true revolutionaries, or fellow youths intoxicated with death. To that extent, the youth were young, if fatally so: rushing, with their eyes closed, into the abyss. But whether they were demanding a Führer who would organize their energies and compel them to the voluptuous passivity of total obedience, a restored and purified monarchy, or a Prussian-Socialist dictatorship, they were also betraying their youth and enslaving themselves, not merely to political adventurers and psychotic ideologues, but to the old industrial-military bureaucratic machine disguised in new forms.

The Nazis were not slow to recognize the importance of the youth. The young who had so far abstained from the polls, and the young who were getting ready to cast their first ballot, were two sources of enormous potential voting strength for them: both groups were hungry for action—any action, brutalized, often imbued with notions of racial purity and sheer hatred for the most conspicuous of outsiders—the Jew —and in despair over the future; after all, it had become a rueful, common joke among students to reply when they were asked what they wanted to be after they had completed their studies: "Unemployed."

There is good evidence that the young, especially the students, anticipated their elders in turning toward the right. In 1930, the Social Democratic party reported that less than 8 per cent of its membership was under twenty-five, and less than half of its membership under forty.[34] In the same year, General Groener declared that the "radicalization" of students—radicalization toward the right—was a serious danger to the country;[35] and in the same year, students at the university of Jena cheered a new professor, the virulent anti-Semite Hans F. K. Günther, who had been forced on the university as professor of a new chair of Rassenkunde.[36] By 1930—certainly by 1931—the students in universities

34. For the statistics see Franz Neumann, *Behemoth*, p. 18.
35. Mosse, "Die deutsche Rechte und die Juden," p. 197.
36. *Ibid.*, p. 199.

and Gymnasia, many of whom had long staged anti-Semitic riots against Jewish and radical professors, and kept Jewish students out of their associations, were largely National Socialist in sympathy; perhaps half of them were Nazis, many of them were wholly unpolitical, and only a few openly republican.[37]

Responsible Republican publicists were not blind to the danger; much has been written about those who were complacent about Hitler and the Nazification of the young, but too little about those who wrote and spoke against it until they were compelled into silence. Thomas Mann was only one among many urging students toward patience, and toward an appreciation of true freedom that comes with rationality and discipline. In 1928, the popular novelist Jakob Wassermann took up the father-son conflict in a long tendentious novel, *Der Fall Maurizius*, which portrays the struggle of a brave adolescent boy against his cold, cruel, powerful father: the father, a prosecuting attorney, had long ago perpetrated an act of judicial injustice; the son, after diligent research, uncovers his father's crime, repudiates him—"I do not want to be your son"[38]—and with this declaration of independence drives the father into insanity. And the boy's only close school friend attacks right-wing students for being mere puppets in the hands of unknown forces, for "allowing themselves to be shoved back and forth, like stuffed dolls, by people of whom they do not even know whether they are paid agents of reaction."[39]

To judge from the literature, by 1932 this concern had deepened into alarm. In the first six months of that year, to give only one instance, the monthly *Neue Rundschau* published no fewer than six long articles, all worried, all intelligent, all understanding of the youth's problems,

37. *Ibid.*, pp. 187, 195.

38. Jakob Wassermann, *Der Fall Maurizius* (Berlin, 1928), p. 586. It was not always the father who was the victim; there was a whole genre of *Schülerselbstmordromane*, novels retailing stories of the suicides of adolescent students. One of these, an obscure novel by Friedrich Torberg, *Der Schüler Gerber* (Berlin, 1930), written in early 1929, bears a prefatory note in which the author asserts that in the course of a single week—January 27 to February 3, 1929—he had read in the newspapers of ten such suicides. And Ernst Toller—himself to die by his own hand in 1939—dedicated his autobiography to "the memory of my nephew Harry, who, in 1928, at the age of eighteen, shot himself." The prefatory "Blick 1933" of that autobiography helplessly laments the youth "which went many ways, followed false gods and false leaders, but steadily tried to find clarity and the laws of the spirit." Ernst Toller, *Prosa, Briefe, Dramen, Gedichte* (Hamburg, 1961), pp. 26, 27.

39. Wassermann, *Der Fall Maurizius*, p. 19.

all exhorting to reason and patience. Jakob Wassermann showed deep sympathy for the "hopelessness of student youth." Behind the young man, he wrote, "the war, in front of him, social ruin, to his left he is being pulled by the Communist, to his right by the Nationalist, and all around him there is not a trace of honesty and rationality, and all his good instincts are being distorted into hatred." Yet, he pleaded, not all is feeling, not all action is good simply because it is action: "Not every forty-year-old is a criminal and an idiot for the simple reason that he is twenty years older than you are, not every fifty- or sixty-year-old a reactionary and enemy, not every father a fool and not every son a hero and martyr."[40] Elsewhere in the magazine Ernst Robert Curtius described the growing crisis of the university and called for a revival of humanist standards,[41] while the philosopher Ernst von Aster, in a perceptive piece, dissected what he called "the metaphysics of nationalism" in which he noted what others had noted before: that "strange connection" among the young of "revolutionary mutiny against authority and tradition" and "blind discipline toward the 'Führer.' "[42] And in two alarming essays, the publicist and publisher Peter Suhrkamp traced the outlines, and intimated the outcome, of the father's revenge. Youth, he wrote, looks back on the heroic days of its movement—before the First World War. "Their thoughts are disguised impulses; in their discussion private ideas parade as *Weltanschauung*." And they are continuing to cling to hero worship. "Without heroes they feel nothing. They resign. They take off. They have never grasped the difficulties, the dangers, and the harsh laws of reality." They are, in a word, not yet grown up. Now, in deep spiritual and economic need, they are turning anti-intellectual; they repudiate thinking as impotent, and so they are turning away from liberal parties and gathering under the umbrella of platitudes and dependence; they "love drill, and are ready for anyone who will command them." This may be natural of youth, but so far, youth has never started a revolution. Yet today, Suhrkamp concludes,

40. Jakob Wassermann, "Rede an die studentische Jugend über das Leben im Geiste; Zum Goethetag 1932," *Die neue Rundschau*, 43, part 1 (1932), 530–544.

41. Ernst Robert Curtius, "Die Universität als Idee und als Erfahrung," *ibid.*, pp. 145–167. This, and other essays printed in *Die Neue Rundschau*, were later that year gathered in Curtius' celebrated call to reason, *Deutscher Geist in Gefahr* (Stuttgart, 1932).

42. Ernst von Aster, "Metaphysik des Nationalismus," *Die Neue Rundschau*, 43, part 1 (1932), 52.

alienated, impoverished, ready for anything, filled with "anguish, hatred, rage, and noble indignation," youth may be ready for a real revolution. All they need is a "genuine revolutionary idea."[43]

This, then, was the Weimar Republic in 1932: clear vision and political impotence, fear, suspicion, and moments of irrational hope; among
the politicians of the middle, politics as usual, but with everyone else,
a sense of emergency. Koestler, who lived at the very heart of this climate, among Berlin journalists, recalls, in his autobiography, a joke
that circulated among the editorial employees of Ullstein which, better
than a lengthy analysis, conveys the temper of 1932. There was once, so
the story runs, an executioner named Wang Lun, who lived in the reign
of the second emperor of the Ming Dynasty. He was famous for his
skill and speed in beheading his victims, but he had, all his life, a secret
ambition which he found impossible to realize: to behead a person so
rapidly that the victim's head would remain poised on his neck. He
practiced and practiced, and finally, in his seventy-sixth year, he realized
his ambition. It was on a busy day of executions; and he dispatched
each man with graceful speed, head rolling in the dust. Then came the
twelfth man; he began to mount the scaffold, and Wang Lun whisked
his sword, beheading his victim so quickly that he continued to walk up
the steps. When he reached the top, he spoke angrily to the executioner:
"Why do you prolong my agony?" he asked. "You were mercifully
quick with the others!" It was a great moment in Wang Lun's life; he
had crowned his life's work. A serene smile spread over his face, he
turned to his victim, and said, "Just kindly nod, please."[44]

A few months later, Adolf Hitler was chancellor of Germany, and
the men of Weimar scattered, taking the spirit of Weimar with them, into the Aesopianism of internal migration, into death in the extermination
camps, into suicide—suicide in a Berlin apartment after a knock on the
door, on the Spanish frontier, in a Swedish village, in a Brazilian town,
in a New York hotel room. But others took the spirit of Weimar into
life, into great careers and lasting influence in laboratories, in hospitals,
in theaters, in universities, and gave that spirit its true home, in exile.

43. Peter Suhrkamp, "Die Sezession des Familiensohnes: Eine nachträgliche Betrach-
tung der Jugendbewegung," *ibid.*, pp. 95–96; "Söhne ohne Väter und Lehrer: Die
Situation der bürgerlichen Jugend," *ibid.*, p. 696.
44. Köstler, *Arrow in the Blue*, p. 254.

REMINISCENCES*

by LEO SZILARD

edited by Gertrud Weiss Szilard and Kathleen R. Winsor

[EDITORS' NOTE: Leo Szilard at various times considered writing his own biography, but he never did. He had a sense of history, however, and carefully preserved, in folders marked "History," all correspondence and other documents which he thought to be of historical significance. In 1951, when he seriously contemplated writing the history of the Manhattan Project, he organized the pertinent documents into ten folders, by different topics and time periods. The documents which are appended here come largely from this collection which Szilard selected himself. He also drafted an outline for his memoirs.

During a period of serious illness in 1960, which kept him in the hospital for a year, he used a tape recorder—which had been put into his sick room for the purpose of an oral history project—to dictate instead the first draft of *The Voice of the Dolphins and Other Stories* (New York, 1961), a whimsical history of the future twenty-five years, which seemed vastly more important to him than the history of the past quarter century.

However, at times he enjoyed giving interviews to interested visitors. On a few such occasions his wife switched on his tape recorder. What follows is an exact transcription of parts of these tapes, with editing limited to the minimum necessary to change spoken to written English.

These highly personal, pungent, and incisive comments by a leading participant in three great episodes in recent American history—the migration of intellectuals from Hitler's Europe to America; the development of a nuclear chain reaction; and the effort to prevent the use of atomic bombs and to establish civilian control of atomic energy—are published here by courtesy of Mrs. Szilard and with the cooperation of the M.I.T. Press, which will include them in a forthcoming edition of Szilard's scientific and other writings.

The selection and editing has been a collaborative effort of Gertrud Weiss Szilard and Kathleen R. Winsor, with the help of Ruth Grodzins for part of the manuscript. The annotations were prepared by Kathleen R. Winsor. Unpublished papers referred to in the notes are in the possession of Mrs. Szilard. Although many others helped and advised in the project, Mrs. Szilard wishes particularly to thank Mr. Melvin Voigt, University Librarian, and his staff, who made available space and other facilities of the Library of the University of California, San Diego, to gather, store, and process the Szilard papers.]

I REACHED the conclusion something would go wrong in Germany very early. I reached this conclusion in 1930, and the occasion was a meeting in Paris. It was a meeting of economists who were called together to decide whether Germany could pay reparations, and just how much she could pay. One of the participants of that meeting was Dr. Hjalmar Schacht, who was at that time, I think, president of the German Reichsbank. To the surprise of the world, including myself, he took the position that Germany could not pay any reparations unless she got back her former colonies. This was such a frightening statement to make that it caught my attention, and I concluded that if Hjalmar Schacht believed that he could get away with it, things must look rather bad. I was so impressed by this that I wrote a letter to my bank and transferred every single penny I had out of Germany into Switzerland. I was not the only one, as I later learned. Within a few months after this speech of Schacht's, a very large sum of money, mainly by depositors from abroad, was drawn out of Germany. Apparently there are many people who are sensitive to this kind of signal.

I visited America in 1931. I came here on Christmas Day 1931, on the *Leviathan*, and stayed here for about three months [until May 4, 1932]. In the course of 1932 I returned to Berlin where I was privat-dozent at the University. Hitler came into office in January '33, and I had no doubt what would happen. I lived in the faculty club of the Kaiser Wilhelm Institute in Berlin-Dahlem and I had my suitcases packed. By this I mean that I literally had two suitcases which were packed standing in my room; the key was in them, and all I had to do was turn the key and leave when things got too bad. I was there when the *Reichstagsbrand* occurred, and I remember how difficult it was for people there to understand what was going on. A friend of mine, Michael Polanyi, who was director of a division of the Kaiser Wilhelm Institute for Physical Chemistry, like many other people, took a very optimistic view of the situation. They all thought that civilized Germans would not stand for anything really rough happening. The reason that I took the opposite position was based on observations of rather small and insignificant things. I noticed that the Germans always took a utilitarian point of view. They asked, "Well, suppose I would oppose this, what good would I do? I wouldn't do very much good, I would just lose my influence. Then why should I oppose it?" You see, the moral point of view was completely absent, or very weak, and every consideration was simply, what would be the predictable consequence of my action. And on that basis did I reach the conclusion in 1931 that Hitler would get into power, not because the forces of the Nazi revolution were so strong, but rather because I thought that there would be no resistance whatsoever.

After the Reichstag fire [February 27, 1933], I went to see my friend Michael Polanyi and told him what had happened, and he looked at me and said, "Do you really mean to say that you think that the secretary of the interior had anything to do with this?" and I said, "Yes, that is precisely what I mean," and he just looked at me with incredulous eyes. At that time he had an offer to go to England and to accept a professorship in Manchester. I very strongly urged him to take this, but he said that if he now went to Manchester, he could not be productive for at least another year, because it takes that much time to install a laboratory, and I said to him, "Well, how long do you think you will remain productive if you *stay* in Berlin?" We couldn't get together on this so I finally told him that if he must refuse this offer he should do so on the ground that his wife was opposed to it, because his wife always could change her mind, so that if he wanted to have the thing reconsidered, he would have an out. Later on when I was in England, in the middle of '33, I was active in a committee, this one was a Jewish committee incidentally, where they were concerned about finding positions for refugees from Germany. Professor Namier[1] came from Manchester and reported that Polanyi was now again interested in accepting a professorship in Manchester. He said that previously he had refused the offer extended to him on the grounds that he was suffering from rheumatism, but it appears that Hitler cured his rheumatism.

I left Germany a few days after the Reichstag fire. How quickly things move you can see from this: I took a train from Berlin to Vienna on a certain date, close to the first of April, 1933. The train was empty. The same train, on the next day, was overcrowded, was stopped at the frontier, the people had to get out and everybody was interrogated by the Nazis. This just goes to show that if you want to suceed in this

1. Sir Lewis Bernstein Namier, professor of modern history at the University of Manchester from 1931 to 1953.

world you don't have to be much cleverer than other people, you just have to be one day earlier than most people. This is all that it takes.

While I was in Vienna the first people were dismissed from German universities, just two or three; it was however quite clear what would happen. I met, by pure chance, walking in the street a colleague of mine, Dr. Jacob Marschak, who was an economist at Heidelberg and who is now [1960] a professor at Yale. He also was rather sensitive; not being a German, but coming from Russia he had seen revolutions and upheavals, and he went to Vienna where he had relatives because he wanted to see what was going to happen in Germany. I told him that I thought since we were out here we may as well make up our minds what needed to be done and take up this lot of scholars and scientists who will have to leave Germany and the German universities. He said that he knew a rather wealthy economist in Vienna who might have some advice to give. His name was Schlesinger and he had a very beautiful apartment in the Liechtensteinpalais. We went to see him and he said, "Yes, it is quite possible that there will be wholesale dismissals from German universities; why don't we go and discuss this with Professor Jastrow." Professor Jastrow[2] was an economist mainly interested in the history of prices, and we went to see him—the three of us now—and Jastrow said, "Yes, yes, this is something one should seriously consider," and then he said, "You know, Sir William Beveridge is at present in Vienna. He came here to work with me on the history of prices, and perhaps we ought to talk to him." So I said, "Where is he staying?" and he said, "He's staying at the Hotel Regina." It so happened that I was staying at the Hotel Regina, so I volunteered to look up Sir William Beveridge and try to get him interested in this.

I saw Beveridge and he immediately said that at the London School of Economics he had already heard about dismissals, and he was already taking steps to take on one of those dismissed, that he was all in favor of doing something in England to receive those who have to leave German universities. So I phoned Schlesinger and suggested that he invite Beveridge to dinner. Schlesinger said no, he wouldn't invite him to dinner because Englishmen, if you invite them to dinner, get very con-

2. Ignaz Jastrow, German economist, historian and sociologist, professor of political science at the University of Berlin.

ceited. However, he would invite him to tea. So we had tea, and in this brief get-together, Schlesinger and Marschak and Beveridge, it was agreed that Beveridge, when he got back to England, and when he got the most important things he had on the docket out of the way, would try to form a committee which would set itself the task of finding places for those who have to leave German universities. He suggested that I come to London and that I occasionally prod him on this, and that if I were to prod him long enough and frequently enough, he thought he would do it. Soon thereafter he left, and soon after he left, I left and went to London.

When I came to London I phoned Beveridge. Beveridge said that his schedule had changed and that he found that he was free and that he could take up this job at once, and this is the history of the birth of the so-called Academic Assistance Council in England. The English adopted a policy of mainly helping the younger people, but did not demand that somebody should have an established name or position in order to find a position in England, quite in contrast to American organizations. In addition to the Academic Assistance Council, there was a Jewish committee functioning. They raised funds privately and they found positions for people and provided them with fellowships for one or two years. The two committees worked very closely together, and in a comparatively short time practically everybody who came to England had a position, except me.

When I was in England, and after I no longer had to function in connection with placing the scholars and scientists who left the German universities—when this was more or less organized and there was no need for me to do anything further about that—I was thinking about what I should do, and I was strongly tempted to go into biology. I went to see A. V. Hill and told him about this. Now A. V. Hill himself had been a physicist and became a very successful biologist, and he thought it was quite a good idea. He said, "Why don't we do it this way? I'll get you a position as a demonstrator in physiology, and then twenty-four hours before you demonstrate you read up these things, and then you should have no difficulty in demonstrating them the next day. In this way, by teaching physiology, you would learn physiology and it's a good place to begin."

Now I must tell you why I did not make this switch at the time. In fact, I made the switch to biology in 1946. In 1932 while I was still in Berlin, I read a book by H. G. Wells. It was called *The World Set Free*.[3] This book was written in 1913, one year before the World War, and in it H. G. Wells describes the discovery of artificial radioactivity and puts it in the year of 1933, the year in which it actually occurred. He then proceeds to describe the liberation of atomic energy on a large scale for industrial purposes, the development of atomic bombs, and a world war which was apparently fought by allies of England, France, and perhaps including America, against Germany and Austria, the powers located in the central part of Europe. He places this war in the year 1956, and in this war the major cities of the world are all destroyed by atomic bombs. Up to this point the book is exceedingly vivid and realistic. From then on the book gets to be a little, shall I say, utopian. With the world in shambles, a conference is called in Brissago in Italy, in which a world government is set up.

This book made a very great impression on me, but I didn't regard it as anything *but* fiction. It didn't start me thinking whether or not such things could in fact happen. I had not been working in nuclear physics up to that time.

Now, this really doesn't belong here, but I will nevertheless tell you of a curious conversation which I had, also in 1932, in Berlin. The conversation was with a very interesting man named Otto Mandl, who was an Austrian, and who became a wealthy timber merchant in England, and whose main claim to fame was that he had discovered H. G. Wells at a time when none of his works had been translated into German. He went to H. G. Wells and acquired the exclusive right to publish his works in German, and this is how H. G. Wells became known on the Continent. In 1932 something went wrong with his timber business in London, and he found himself again in Berlin. I had met him previously in London and I met him again in Berlin and there ensued a memorable conversation.[4] Otto Mandl said that he not only thought,

3. *The World Set Free: A Story of Mankind* (London, 1914).
4. Otto Mandl (d. 1956) was the husband of the pianist Lili Kraus, to whom he was married in 1930. In a recent conversation, Miss Kraus told me that she remembered discussions of this kind between Szilard and her husband very well. When I showed her this portion of the tape she said, "Every word is true." [G.W.S.]

he *knew* what it would take to save mankind from a series of ever-recurring wars that could destroy it. He said that man has a heroic streak in himself. Man is not satisfied with a happy idyllic life. He has a need to fight and to encounter danger. And he concluded that what mankind must do to save itself is to launch an enterprise aimed at leaving the earth. On this start he thought the energies of mankind could be concentrated and the need for heroism could be satisfied. I remember my own reaction very well. I told him that this was somewhat new to me, and that I really didn't know whether I would agree with him. The only thing I could say was this: that if I came to the conclusion that this was what mankind needed, and if I wanted to contribute something to save mankind, then I would probably go into nuclear physics, because only through the liberation of atomic energy could we obtain the means which would enable man not only to leave the earth but to leave the solar system.

I was not thinking any more about this conversation or about H. G. Wells's book either, until I found myself in London about the time of the British Association meeting in September 1933. I read in the newspapers a speech by Lord Rutherford, who was quoted as saying that he who talks about the liberation of atomic energy on an industrial scale is talking moonshine.[5] This set me pondering as I was walking the streets of London, and I remember that I stopped for a red light at the intersection of Southampton Row. As the light changed to green and I crossed the street, it suddenly occurred to me that if we could find an element which is split by neutrons and which would emit *two* neutrons when it absorbed *one* neutron, such an element, if assembled in sufficiently large mass, could sustain a nuclear chain reaction. I didn't see at

5. A summary of the speech by Rutherford, delivered at the meeting of the British Association for the Advancement of Science, Leicester, September 11, 1933, and published in *Nature*, 132 (September 16, 1933), 432–433, contains the sentence: "One timely word of warning was issued to those who look for sources of power in atomic transmutations—such expectations are the merest moonshine." See also, A. S. Eve, *Rutherford, Being the Life & Letters of the Rt. Hon. Lord Rutherford, O.M.* (Cambridge, 1939), p. 374: "These transformations of the atom are of extraordinary interest to scientists but we cannot control atomic energy to an extent which would be of any value commercially, and I believe we are not likely ever to be able to do so. A lot of nonsense has been talked about transmutation. Our interest in the matter is purely scientific, and the experiments which are being carried out will help us to a better understanding of the structure of matter."

the moment just how one would go about finding such an element, or what experiments would be needed, but the idea never left me. Soon thereafter, when the discovery of artificial radioactivity by Joliot and Mme. Joliot was announced, I suddenly saw that tools were at hand to explore the possibility of such a chain reaction. I talked to a number of people about this. I remember that I mentioned it to G. P. Thomson[6] and to Blackett,[7] but I couldn't evoke any enthusiasm.

I had one candidate for an element which might be instable in the sense of splitting off neutrons when it disintegrates, and that was beryllium. The reason I suspected beryllium of being a potential candidate for sustaining a chain reaction was that the mass of beryllium was such that it could disintegrate into two other particles and a neutron. It was not clear why it didn't disintegrate spontaneously, since the mass was large enough to do that; but it was conceivable that it had to be tickled by a neutron which would shake the beryllium nucleus in order to trigger such a disintegration. I remember I told Blackett that we really ought to get a large mass of beryllium, large enough to be able to notice whether it could sustain a chain reaction. Beryllium was very expensive at the time, almost unobtainable, and I remember Blackett's reaction was, "Look, you will have no luck with such fantastic ideas in England. Yes, perhaps in Russia. If a Russian physicist went to the government and said, 'We must make a chain reaction,' they would give him all the money and facilities which he would need. But you won't get it in England." As it turned out later beryllium cannot sustain a chain reaction and is, in fact, stable. What was wrong was that a published mass of helium was wrong. This was later discovered by Bethe, and it was a very important discovery for all of us, because we did not know where to begin to do nuclear physics if there were an element which could disintegrate but didn't.

When I gave up the beryllium I did not give up the thought that there might be another element which could sustain a chain reaction. And in the spring of 1934 I had applied for a patent which described the laws governing such a chain reaction. It was the first time, I think, that

6. George Paget Thomson (son of J. J. Thomson), in 1933, professor of physics at University of London.
7. P. M. S. Blackett; in 1933 professor of physics at University of London.

the concept of critical mass was developed and that a chain reaction was seriously discussed. Knowing what this would mean—and I knew it because I had read H. G. Wells—I did not want this patent to become public. The only way to keep it from becoming public was to assign it to the government. So I assigned this patent to the British Admiralty.[8]

At some point I decided that the reasonable thing to do was to investigate systematically all the elements. There were ninety-two of them. But of course this is a rather boring task, so I thought that I would get some money, have some apparatus built, and then hire somebody who would just sit down and go through one element after the other. The trouble was that none of the physicists had any enthusiasm for this idea of a chain reaction. I thought, there is after all something called "chain

8. Beginning March 12, 1934, Szilard filed several British patent applications, which led to two British patents:

1) *No. 440,023*: "Improvements in or relating to the Transmutation of Chemical Elements" issued on December 12, 1935, covers the generation of radioactive elements by neutrons and the chemical separation of radioactive elements from non-radioactive isotopes.

2) *No. 630,726*: "Improvements in or relating to the Transmutation of Chemical Elements" was assigned to the British Admiralty and sealed secret in 1936; it was not published until September 28, 1949. This patent has as its subject the idea of the nuclear chain reaction, in which more than one neutron is emitted per neutron absorbed.

In a reply, dated January 15, 1957, to an inquiry from Samuel Glasstone, Szilard said:
In the Spring of 1934 I applied for a provisional British application on a chain reacting system which was based on the concept that beryllium may give off two neutrons when it reacts with one slow neutron. The general concepts of a chain reaction including the critical size of the chain reacting system, were derived in this application. This application contained also the following passage:
(a) Pure neutron chains, in which the links of the chain are formed by neutrons of the mass number 1 alone. Such chains are only possible in the presence of a metastable element. A metastable element is an element the mass of which (packing fraction) is sufficiently high to allow its disintegration into parts under liberation of energy. Elements like uranium and thorium are such metastable elements; these two elements reveal their metastable nature by emitting alpha particles. Other elements may be metastable without revealing their nature in this way.
About one year later a patent application was filed by me in England based in part on this provisional application. This patent application was subsequently divided into two parts, one part was issued as a patent and the other part was assigned without financial compensation to the British Admiralty and was sealed secret. I assigned this patent to the British Admiralty because in England a patent could at that time be kept secret only if it was assigned to the Government. The reason for secrecy was my conviction that if a nuclear chain reaction can be made to work it can be used to set up violent explosions.

reaction" in chemistry. It doesn't resemble a nuclear chain reaction, but still it's a chain reaction. So I thought I would talk to a chemist, and I went to see Professor Chaim Weizmann, the Zionist leader, who was a renowned chemist. I had met him on one occasion or another. And Weizmann listened and Weizmann understood what I told him. He said, "How much money do you need?" I said that I thought £2,000 would be enough, which would have been at that time about $10,000. So Weizmann said that he would try to get this money. I didn't hear from him for several weeks, but then I ran into Michael Polanyi, who by that time had arrived in Manchester and was head of the chemistry department there.[9] Polanyi told me that Weizmann had talked to him about my ideas for the possibility of a chain reaction, and wanted Polanyi's advice about whether he should get me this money. And Polanyi thought that this experiment ought to be done, but then he didn't hear anything further. As a matter of fact, I did not see Weizmann again until the late fall of '45, after Hiroshima. I was at that time in Washington and I ran into him in the Wardman-Park Hotel. He seemed to be terribly happy to see me, and he said, "Do you remember when you came to see me in London?" I said, "Yes." He said, "And do you remember what you wanted me to do?" I said, "Yes." And he said, "Well, maybe you won't believe me, but I tried to get those £2,000 and found that I couldn't."

Because of these thoughts about the possibility of the chain reaction, and because of the discovery of artificial radioactivity, physics became too exciting for me to leave it. So I decided not to go into biology as yet, but to play around a little bit with physics, and I spent some months in the spring at the Strand Palace Hotel, doing nothing but dreaming about experiments which one could do, utilizing this marvelous tool of artificial radioactivity which Joliot had discovered. I didn't do anything; I just thought about these things. I remember that I went into my bath —I didn't have a private bath, but there was a bath in the corridor in the Strand Palace Hotel—around nine o'clock in the morning. There is no place as good to think as the bathtub. I would just soak there and think,

9. Michael Polanyi, the Hungarian-born physicist and chemist mentioned at the beginning of these Reminiscences, had become professor of physical chemistry at the University of Manchester.

and around twelve o'clock the maid would knock and say, "Are you all right, sir?" Then I usually got out and made a few notes, dictated a few memoranda; I played around this way, doing nothing, and the summer came around. At that time, I thought that one ought to try to learn something about beryllium; I thought that if beryllium is really so easy to split, the gamma rays of radium should split it and it should split off neutrons.

I had casually met the director of the physics department of St. Bartholomew's Hospital, so I dropped in for a visit and asked him whether in the summer, when everybody is away, I could use the radium, which was not much in use in summer, for experiments of this sort. And he said, yes, I could do this; but since I was not on the staff of the hospital, I should team up with somebody on his staff. There was a very nice young Englishman, Mr. Chalmers,[10] who was game, and so we teamed up and for the next two months we did experiments. It turned out that in fact beryllium splits off neutrons when exposed to the gamma rays of radium. This later on became really very important, because these neutrons are slow neutrons, and therefore if they disintegrate elements like uranium—of course we didn't know that until after Hahn's discovery— and if in that process fast neutrons come off,[11] you can distinguish them from neutrons of the source, which are slow.

We did essentially two experiments. We demonstrated that beryllium emits neutrons if exposed to the gamma rays of radium, and we demonstrated something else, which is called the Szilard-Chalmers effect. These experiments established me as a nuclear physicist, not in the eyes of Cambridge, but in the eyes of Oxford.[12]

There was an International Conference on Nuclear Physics in London in September, where these two discoveries were discussed by the par-

10. T. A. Chalmers, then a member of the physics department, Medical College, St. Bartholomew's Hospital, London.

11. O. Hahn and F. Strassman, "Über den Nachweis und das Verhalten der bei der Bestrahlung des Urans mittels Neutronen entstehenden Erdalkalimetalle," *Naturwissenschaften*, 27 (January 6, 1939), 11–15.

12. L. Szilard and T. A. Chalmers, "Detection of Neutrons Liberated from Beryllium by Gamma Rays: A New Technique for Inducing Radioactivity," *Nature*, 134 (September 29, 1934), 494–495; L. Szilard and T. A. Chalmers, "Chemical Separation of the Radioactive Element from its Bombarded Isotope in the Fermi Effect," *Nature*, 134 (September 22, 1934), 462–463.

ticipants[13] and so I got very favorable notice; and this led within six months to an offer of a fellowship at Oxford. However, I didn't get this offer until I had left England and come to America, where I didn't have a position but had some sort of fellowship. When I received the offer from Oxford, I had the choice of either keeping on this fellowship in America or returning to Oxford. I then wrote to Michael Polanyi, describing my choice between these two alternatives, and saying that I would accept the fellowship at Oxford and would stay in England until one year before the war, at which time I would shift my residence to New York City. That was very funny, because how can anyone say what he will do one year *before* the war? So the letter was passed around and a few people commented on it when I finally turned up in England.

And this is precisely what I did. In 1937 I decided that the time had come for me to change my full-time fellowship at Oxford to one which permitted me to spend six months out of the year in America. And on the basis of that arrangement (I had to take a cut of salary, of course; I had to go on half pay, so my total income amounted to $1,000 a year) I came over to America.

I came to America [on January 2, 1938] and did nothing but loaf. I didn't look for a position; I just thought I would wait and see. Then came the Munich crisis. I was at that time visiting Goldhaber[14] in Urbana, Illinois. I spent a week listening to the radio giving news about Munich, and when it was all over I wrote a letter to Lindemann, later Lord Cherwell, who was director of the Clarendon Laboratory [at Oxford] where I was employed. The letter said that I was now quite convinced that there would be war, and therefore there would be little point in my returning to England unless they would want to use me for war work. If, as a foreigner, I would not be used for war work, I would not want to return to England but rather stay in America. And so I resigned at Oxford and stayed here.

I was still intrigued with the possibility of a chain reaction, and for that reason I was interested in elements which became radioactive when

13. A discussion of these experiments at the conference is quoted on pages 88 and 89 of *International Conference on Physics, London, 1934, Papers and Discussions in Two Volumes* (Cambridge, 1935), I (Nuclear Physics).

14. Maurice Goldhaber, in 1938 assistant professor of physics, University of Illinois.

they were bombarded by neutrons and where there were more radio-active isotopes than there should have been. In particular, I was interested in indium. I went up to Rochester [New York] and stayed there for two weeks and did some experiments on indium, which finally cleared up this mystery. It turned out that indium is not instable and that the phenomenon observed could be explained without assuming that indium is split by neutrons.

At that point I abandoned the idea of a chain reaction and of looking for elements which could sustain a chain reaction, and I wrote a letter to the British Admiralty suggesting that the patent which has been applied for should be withdrawn because I couldn't make the process work.[15] Before that letter reached them, I learned of the discovery of fission. This was early in January when I visited Mr. [Eugene] Wigner in Princeton. Wigner told me of Hahn's discovery: Hahn found that uranium breaks into two parts when it absorbs the neutron and this is the process which we call fission. When I heard this I saw immediately that these fragments, being heavier than corresponds to their charge, must emit neutrons; and if enough neutrons are emitted in this fission process, then it should be, of course, possible to sustain a chain reaction; all the things which H. G. Wells had predicted appeared suddenly real to me.

At that time it was already clear, not only to me but to many other people, and certainly it was clear to Wigner, that we were at the threshold of another world war. And so it became, it seemed to us, urgent to set up experiments which would show whether, in fact, neutrons are emitted in the fission process of uranium. I thought that if neutrons are in fact emitted in fission, this should be kept secret from the Germans; so I was very eager to contact Joliot and Fermi, the two men who were most likely to think of this possibility. I was still in Princeton and staying at Wigner's apartment (Wigner was in the hospital with jaundice).

I got up in the morning and wanted to go out. It was raining cats and dogs, and I said, "My God, I am going to catch a cold!" because at that time, the first years I was in America, each time I got wet I invariably

15. Szilard's letter to the British Admiralty withdrawing the patent was dated December 21, 1938. On January 26, 1939, he sent a telegram, followed by a letter on February 2nd, cancelling the December letter and reinstating the patent, which later issued as British patent 630,726.

caught a bad cold. However, I had no rubbers with me, so I had no choice, I just had to go out. I got wet and came home with a very high fever, so I was not able to contact Fermi. As I got ready to go back to New York, I opened the drawer to take my things out and saw there were Wigner's rubbers standing. I could have taken Wigner's rubbers and avoided the cold. But as it was I was laid up with fever for about a week or ten days. In the meantime, Fermi had also thought of the possibility of a neutron emission and the possibility of a chain reaction and he went to a private meeting in Washington and talked about these things. Since it was a private meeting, the cat was not entirely out of the bag, but its tail was sticking out. When I recovered I went to see Rabi,[16] and Rabi told me that Fermi had similar ideas and that he had talked about them in Washington. Fermi was not in, so I told Rabi to please talk to Fermi and say that these things ought to be kept secret because it was very likely that neutrons are emitted, that this might lead to a chain reaction, and this might lead to the construction of bombs. So Rabi said he would, and I went back home to bed at the Kings Crown Hotel.

A few days later I got up to see Rabi and asked, "Did you talk to Fermi?" Rabi said, "Yes, I did." I said, "What did Fermi say?" and he said Fermi said, "Nuts!" So I said, "Why did he say, 'Nuts!'?" and Rabi said, "Well, I don't know, but he is in and we can ask him." So we went over to Fermi's office, and Rabi said to Fermi, "Look, Fermi, I told you what Szilard thought and you said, 'Nuts!' and Szilard wants to know why you said, 'Nuts!'" So Fermi said, "Well, there is the *remote* possibility that neutrons may be emitted in the fission of uranium and then of course that a chain reaction can be made." Rabi said, "What do you mean by 'remote possibility'?" and Fermi said, "Well, 10 per cent." And Rabi said, "Ten per cent is not a remote possibility if it means that we may die of it. If I have pneumonia and the doctor tells me that there is a remote possibility that I might die, and that it's 10 per cent, I get excited about it."

From the very beginning the line was drawn; the difference between Fermi's position throughout this and mine was marked on the first day we talked about it. We both wanted to be conservative, but Fermi thought that the conservative thing was to play down the possibility

16. Isidor Isaac Rabi, professor of physics, Columbia University.

that this might happen, and I thought the conservative thing was to assume that it would happen and take all the necessary precautions. I then wrote a letter to Joliot in which I told Joliot that we were discussing here the possibility of neutron emission of uranium in the fission process and the possibility of a chain reaction, and that I personally felt that these things should be discussed privately among the physicists of England, France, and America; and that there should be no publication on this topic if it should turn out that neutrons are, in fact, emitted, and that a chain reaction might be possible. This letter was dated February 2, 1939. I sent a telegram to England to Professor F. A. Lindemann, at Oxford, asking them to send a block of beryllium which I had had made in Europe with the kind of experiments in mind which I now was actually going to perform.

Such a block of beryllium can be used to produce slow neutrons because if you put radium in the middle of it, under the influence of the gamma rays of radium, the beryllium splits and gives off slow neutrons. If uranium, in the process of fission, which can be caused by slow neutrons, emits fast neutrons, these fast neutrons can be distinguished from the neutrons of the source by virtue of their higher energy.

There was at Columbia University some equipment which was very suitable for these experiments. This equipment was built by Dr. Walter Zinn who was doing experiments with it. And all we needed to do was to get a gram of radium, a block of beryllium, expose a piece of uranium to the neutrons which come from beryllium, and then see by means of the ionization chamber which Zinn had built whether fast neutrons are emitted in the process. Such an experiment need not take more than an hour or two to perform, once the equipment has been built and if you have the neutron source. But of course we had no radium.

So I first tried to talk to some of my wealthy friends; but they wanted to know just how sure I was that this would work, so finally I talked to one of my not-so-wealthy friends. He was an inventor and he had some income from royalties.[17] I told him what this was all about, and he said, "How much money do you need?" and I said, "Well, I'd like to borrow $2,000." He took out his checkbook, he wrote out a check, I cashed

17. While this friend's name is mentioned in the tape, he has since informed me that he wishes to remain anonymous. [G.W.S.]

the check, I rented the gram of radium, and in the meantime the beryllium block arrived from England. And with this radium and beryllium I turned up at Columbia and, having talked previously to Zinn, said to the head of the department, "I would like to have permission to do some experiments." I was given permission to do experiments for three months. I don't know what caused this caution, because they knew me quite well; but perhaps the idea was a little too fantastic to be entirely respectable. And once we had the radium and the beryllium it took us just one afternoon to see those neutrons. Mr. Zinn and I performed this experiment.[18]

In the meantime Fermi, who had independently thought of this possibility, had set up an experiment. His did not at first work so well, because he used a neutron source which emitted fast neutrons, but then he borrowed our neutron source and his experiment, which was of completely different design, also showed the neutrons.

And now there came the question: Shall we publish this? There were intensive discussions about this, and so Zinn and I, and Fermi and Anderson, each sent a paper to the *Physical Review*, a "Letter to the Editor."[19] But we requested that publication be delayed for a little while until we could decide whether we wanted to keep this thing secret or whether we would permit them to be published. Throughout this time I kept in close touch with Wigner and with Edward Teller, who was in Washington. At this time I went to Washington. Fermi also went to Washington on some other business, I forget what it was, and Teller and Fermi and I got together to discuss whether or not this thing should be published. Both Teller and I thought that it should not. Fermi thought that it should. But after a long discussion, Fermi took the position that after all this is a democracy; if the majority was against publication he would abide by the wish of the majority, and he said that he would go back to New York and advise the head of the department, Dean Pegram,[20] to ask that publication of these papers be indefinitely delayed.

18. The experiment with Zinn was performed on March 3, 1939.

19. Leo Szilard and Walter H. Zinn, "Instantaneous Emission of Fast Neutrons in the Interaction of Slow Neutrons with Uranium," *Physical Review*, 55 (April 15, 1939), 799–800; H. L. Anderson, E. Fermi, and H. B. Hanstein, "Production of Neutrons in Uranium Bombarded by Neutrons," *Physical Review*, 55 (April 15, 1939), 797–798.

20. George B. Pegram, chairman of the physics department and dean of the Graduate Faculties, Columbia University.

While we were still in Washington, we learned that Joliot and his co-workers had sent a note to *Nature*, reporting the discovery that neutrons are emitted in the fission of uranium, and indicating that this might lead to a chain reaction.[21] At this point Fermi said that in this case we would now publish everything. I was not willing to do that, and I said that even though Joliot had published this, this was just the first step, and that if we persisted in not publishing, Joliot would have to come around; otherwise, he would be at a disadvantage, because we would know his results and he would not know our results. But from that moment on, Fermi was adamant that withholding publication made no sense. I still did not want to yield and so we agreed to put this matter up for a decision by the head of the physics department, Professor Pegram. Pegram hesitated for a while to make this decision, but after a few weeks he finally said that he had decided that we should now publish everything. He later told me why he decided this, and so many decisions were based on the wrong premises: Rabi was concerned about my stand because he said that everybody else was opposed to withholding publication, and I alone in the Columbia group wanted it. This would make my position difficult, in the end impossible, and he thought that I ought to yield on this. According to Pegram, Rabi had visited Urbana and found that Maurice Goldhaber in Urbana knew of our research at Columbia; and from this Rabi concluded that these results were already known as far as Urbana, Illinois, and there was no point in keeping them secret. The fact was that I was in constant communication with Goldhaber; I wrote him of these results, and he was pledged to secrecy. He had talked to Rabi, because of course Rabi was part of the Columbia operation. So on this false premise, the decision was made that we should publish.

In the following months Fermi and I teamed up in order to explore whether a uranium-water system would be capable of sustaining a chain reaction. The experiment was actually done by Anderson, Fermi, and myself. We worked very hard at this experiment and saw that under the conditions of this experiment more neutrons are emitted by uranium than absorbed by uranium. We were therefore inclined to con-

21. H. von Halban, Jr., F. Joliot, and L. Kowarski, "Liberation of Neutrons in the Nuclear Explosion of Uranium," *Nature*, 143 (March 18, 1939), 470–472.

clude that this meant that the water-uranium system would sustain a chain reaction. Whether finally we should have said that in print I do not know. However, the fact is that we believed it until George Placzek dropped in for a visit.[22] Placzek said that our conclusion was wrong because in order to make a chain reaction go, we would have to reduce the absorption of water; that is, we would have to reduce the amount of water in the system, and if we reduced the water in the system we would increase the parasitic absorption of uranium, and he recommended that we abandon the water-uranium system and use helium for slowing down the neutrons. To Fermi this sounded impractical, and therefore funny, and Fermi referred to helium thereafter as Placzek's helium.

I took Placzek more seriously, and while I had, for purely practical reasons, no enthusiasm for helium, I dropped then and there my pursuit of the water-uranium system. Thus, while Fermi went on examining this system in detail and trying to see whether by changing the arrangements he could not improve it to the point where it would sustain a chain reaction, I started to think about the possibility of perhaps using graphite instead of water. This brought us to the end of June. We wrote up our paper,[23] Fermi left for the summer to go to Ann Arbor, and I was left alone in New York. I still had no position at Columbia; my three months [March 1–June 1, 1939] as a guest were up, but there were no experiments going on anyway and all I had to do was to think. Some very simple calculations which I made early in July showed that the graphite uranium system was indeed very promising, and when Wigner came to New York, I showed him what I had done. At this point, both Wigner and I began to worry about what would happen if the Germans got hold of some of the vast quantities of the uranium which the Belgians had in the Congo. So we began to think, through what channels we could approach the Belgian government and warn them against selling any uranium to Germany.

It occurred to me then that Einstein knew the Queen of the Belgians, and I suggested to Wigner that we visit Einstein, tell him about the situation, and ask him whether he might not write to the Queen. We

22. George Placzek, in 1939 a physicist at Cornell University.
23. H. L. Anderson, E. Fermi, and Leo Szilard, "Neutron Production and Absorption in Uranium," *Physica Review*, 56 (August 1, 1939), 284–286.

knew that Einstein was somewhere on Long Island but we didn't know precisely where, so I phoned his Princeton office and I was told he was staying at Dr. Moore's cabin at Peconic, Long Island. Wigner had a car and we drove out to Peconic and tried to find Dr. Moore's cabin. We drove around for about half an hour. We asked a number of people, but no one knew where Dr. Moore's cabin was. We were on the point of giving up and about to return to New York when I saw a boy of about seven or eight years of age standing at the curb. I leaned out of the window and I asked, "Say, do you by any chance know where Professor Einstein lives?" The boy knew and he offered to take us there, though he had never heard of Dr. Moore's cabin.

This was the first Einstein heard about the possibility of a chain reaction. He was very quick to see the implications and perfectly willing to do anything that needed to be done. He was reluctant to write to the Queen of the Belgians, but he thought he would write to one of the cabinet members of the Belgian government whom he knew. He was about to do just that when Wigner said that we should not approach a foreign government without giving the State Department an opportunity to object. So Wigner proposed that Einstein write the letter and send a copy to the State Department with a covering letter. Einstein would say in that covering letter that if we did not hear from the State Department within two weeks, he would send the letter to Belgium.

Having decided on this course, in principle, we returned to New York and Wigner left for California. (This goes to show how "green" we were. We did not know our way around in America, we did not know how to do business, and we certainly did not know how to deal with the government.) I had, however, an uneasy feeling about the approach we had decided upon and I felt that I would need to talk to somebody who knew a little bit better how things are done. I then thought of Gustav Stolper. He used to live in Berlin, where he had published a leading German economic journal and had been a member of the German parliament; now he was living as a refugee in New York. I went to see him and talked the situation over with him. He said that he thought that Dr. Alexander Sachs, who was economic adviser to the Lehman Corporation and who had previously worked for the New Deal, might be able to give us advice on how to approach the American government, and whether we should approach the State Department or some other agency of the government. He telephoned Dr. Sachs and I went to see him and I told him my story. Sachs said that if Einstein were to write a letter to President Roosevelt, he would personally deliver it to the President, and that there was no use going to any of the agencies or departments of the government; this issue should go to the White House. This sounded like good advice, and I decided to follow it.

In the meantime, Teller arrived in New York and I asked Teller whether he would drive me out to Peconic. Teller and I went to see Einstein and on this occasion we discussed with Einstein the possibility that he might write a letter to the President. Einstein was perfectly willing to do this. We discussed what should be in this letter and I said I would draft it. Subsequently, I sent Einstein two drafts to choose from, a longer one and a shorter one.

We did not know just how many words we could expect the President to read. How many words does the fission of uranium rate? So I sent Einstein a short version and the longer version; Einstein thought the longer one was better, and that was the version which he signed. The letter was dated August 2, 1939. I handed it to Dr. Sachs for delivery to the White House.[24]

I should perhaps say that this was not the first approach to the government. Soon after we had discovered the neutron emission of uranium, Wigner came to New York and we met—Fermi and I and Wigner —in the office of Dr. Pegram. Wigner said that this was such a serious business that we could not assume the responsibility for handling it, we must contact and inform the government. Wigner said that he would call Charles Edison, who was the new secretary of the navy.[25] He told Edison that Fermi would be in Washington the next day and would be glad to meet with a committee and explain certain matters which might be of interest to the Navy.

So Fermi went there. He was received by a committee. He told in his

24. Accompanying the Einstein letter of August 2nd was a letter of transmittal, Szilard to Sachs, dated August 15, 1939, and a four-page Memorandum for the President by Leo Szilard, also dated August 15th. Both of these documents are reprinted in their entirety below as Appendix I to these Reminiscences.

25. Charles Edison, son of Thomas Alva Edison, assistant secretary of the Navy 1937– 1939; secretary of the Navy 1939–1940.

cautious way the story of uranium and what possibilities were involved. But there the matter ended. Nothing came of this first approach. I got an echo of this through Merle Tuve.[26] Ross Gunn, who was an adviser to the Navy and who attended this conference, telephoned Tuve and asked him, "Who is this man Fermi? What kind of a man is he? Is he a Fascist or what? What is he?"

In July, after I took a rather optimistic view of the possibility of setting up a chain reaction in graphite and uranium, I approached Ross Gunn and told him that the situation did not look too bad; that the situation, as a matter of fact, looked so good that we ought to experiment at a faster rate than we had done before; that we had no money for this purpose, and I wondered if the Navy could make any funds available. Afterward I had a letter in reply, in which Ross Gunn explained that there was almost no way in which the Navy could support this type of research, but that if we got any results which might be of interest to the Navy, they would appreciate it if we would keep them informed. This was the second approach to the government.

Einstein's letter was dated August 2nd. August passed and nothing happened. September passed and nothing happened. Finally I got together with Teller and Wigner and we decided we'd give Sachs two more weeks, and if nothing happened we would use some other channel to the White House. However, suddenly Sachs began to bestir himself, and we received a phone call from him in October saying that he had seen the President and transmitted Einstein's letter to him, and that the President had appointed a committee under the chairmanship of Lyman J. Briggs, director of the National Bureau of Standards. Other members of the committee were Colonel Adamson of the Army[27] and Commander Hoover from the Navy.[28] The committee was to meet on October 21st, and Briggs wanted to know who else he should include. I told Sachs that, apart from Wigner and me, I thought that Edward Teller ought to be invited because he lived in Washington and he could act as liaison between us and the committee. This was done. In addition,

26. Merle A. Tuve, physicist at the Carnegie Institution of Washington, Department of Terrestrial Magnetism, which was working closely with the Navy.
27. Colonel K. R. Adamson, Army Ordnance Department.
28. Commander G. C. Hoover, Navy Bureau of Ordnance.

Briggs invited Dr. Tuve. Dr. Tuve had to go to New York and so he suggested that Dr. Roberts[29] sit in for him.

It was our general intention not to ask the government for money, but to ask only for the blessing of the government, so that then, with that blessing, we would go to foundations, raise the funds, and get some coordinated effort going.[30] However, these things never go the way you have planned them.

After I presented the case, and Wigner had spoken, Teller spoke; and Teller spoke in two capacities. In his own name he strongly supported what I had said and what Wigner had said. Then he said, having spoken for himself, he would speak for Dr. Tuve. Dr. Tuve could not attend the meeting, but he had visited New York and had had a discussion with Fermi; it was Dr. Tuve's opinion that at this time it would not be advisable—in fact, it would not be possible—to spend more money on this research than $15,000.

We had not intended to ask for any money from the government at this point, but since the issue of money was injected, the representative of the Army asked, "How much money do you need?" And I said that all we need money for at this time is to buy some graphite; and the amount of graphite which we would have to buy would cost about $2,000. Maybe a few experiments which would follow would raise the sum to $6,000—something in this order of magnitude.

At this point the representative of the Army started a rather long tirade. He told us that it was naïve to believe that we could make a significant contribution to defense by creating a new explosive. He said that if a new weapon was created, it usually took two wars before one knew whether the weapon was any good or not. And then he explained rather laboriously that in the end, it is not weapons which win the wars, but the morale of the troops. He went on in this vein for a long time, until suddenly Wigner, the most polite of us, interrupted him. He said in his high-pitched voice that it was very interesting to hear this. He had always thought that weapons were very important and that this was

---

29. Richard B. Roberts, Carnegie Institution.

30. Letter and seven-page memorandum, Szilard to Briggs, dated October 26, 1939, but probably prepared earlier, according to the *Smyth Report* (cited in note 41) were "more or less the basis of the discussion at this meeting"; letter, Szilard to Pegram, dated October 21, 1939, reports on the meeting.

what costs money, that this is why the Army needed such a large appropriation. But he was very interested to hear that he was wrong: it's not weapons but morale which wins the wars. If this was correct, perhaps one should take a second look at the budget of the Army, maybe the budget could be cut. Colonel Adamson wheeled around to look at Mr. Wigner and said, "Well, as far as those $2,000 are concerned, you can have it." This is how the first money promise was made by the government.

I should mention that, until the government showed interest (and the first interest it showed was the appointment of this committee) I was undecided whether this development ought to be carried on by industry, or whether it ought to be carried on by the government. And so, just a week or two before the meeting in Washington, I had met with the director of research of the Union Carbon and Carbide Company, W. F. Barrett.[31] The appointment was made by Strauss, and there was some mix-up about it, because they expected Fermi, but it was I who turned up.

There were five people sitting around the table, and I told them that the possibility of a chain reaction between uranium and graphite must be taken seriously; that at this point we could not say very much about this possibility; and that we could talk about it with much greater assurance if we first measured the absorption of neutrons in graphite. It was for this purpose that we would need about two thousand dollars' worth of graphite, and I wondered whether they might give us this amount of graphite on loan; the experiment would not damage the graphite and we could return it to them.

W. F. Barrett said, "You know, I'm a gambling man myself, but you are now asking me to gamble with the stockholders' money, and I'm not sure that I can do that. What would be the practical applications of such chain reaction?" And I said that I really could not say what the practical applications would be at this point, that there was very little doubt in my mind that such a revolution was phenomenal and would find its practical applications ultimately, but it was too early to say that. We

31. The meeting with Barrett's group took place on Monday, October 16, just five days before the Uranium Committee meeting in Washington, according to Szilard's letter to Barrett of October 18, 1939.

had first to see whether we could get it going, and under what conditions it could be set up.

After I left the meeting I had an uneasy feeling that I did not convince anybody there. After all, I was a foreigner and my name was not so well known. I was not well known as a physicist, certainly not to these people. So I wrote a letter to Mr. Barrett in which I invited him to lunch the following week at Columbia with Dr. Pegram, who was head of the physics department and dean of the graduate school, and Dr. Fermi, who after all was a Nobel Prize winner and quite well known.[32] He replied that he would not be in town that week; he did not suggest an alternate date, and he wrote that they had decided that they would not be in a position to let us have any graphite except on a straight purchase basis. I remember that I was quite depressed by that letter, and showed it to Pegram, who thought that I was too easily discouraged. And maybe I was.

The Washington meeting was followed by the most curious period in my life. We heard nothing from Washington at all. By the first of February [1940] there was still no word from Washington—at least none that reached me. I had assumed that once we had demonstrated that in the fission of uranium neutrons are emitted, there would be no difficulty in getting people interested, but I was wrong. Fermi didn't see any reason to do anything right away, since we had asked for money to buy graphite but hadn't yet gotten it; at that point he was interested in working on cosmic rays. I myself waited for developments in Washington, and amused myself by making some more detailed calculations on the chain reaction of the graphite-uranium system.

It is an incredible fact, in retrospect, that between the end of June 1939 and the spring of 1940, not a single experiment was under way in the United States which was aimed at exploring the possibilities of a chain reaction in natural uranium.

Late in January or early in February of 1940, I received a reprint of a paper by Joliot in which Joliot investigated the possibilities of a chain reaction in a uranium–water system.[33] In a sense this was a similar ex-

32. Letter, with memorandum, Szilard to Barrett, October 18, 1939.

33. H. von Halban, Jr., F. Joliot, L. Kowarski, and F. Perrin, "Mise en évidence d'une réaction nucléaire en chaine au sein d'une masse uranifère," *Journal de Physique et le Radium*, série VII, tome x, no. 10 (October, 1939), 428–429.

periment to the one which Anderson, Fermi, and I had carried out and published in June 1939. However, Joliot's experiment was done in a different set-up, and I was able to conclude from it what I was not able to conclude from our own experiment: namely, that the water–uranium system came very close to being chain-reacting, even though it did not quite reach this point. However, it seemed to come so close to being chain-reacting, that if we had improved the system somewhat by replacing water with graphite, in my opinion we should have gotten over the hump.

I read Joliot's paper very carefully and made a number of small computations on it, and then I went to see Fermi, with whom I was no longer in daily contact because my work at Columbia had ceased. We had lunch together and Fermi told me that he was on the point of going to California. I asked him, "Did you read Joliot's paper?" He said he had, and I then asked him, "What did you think of it?" and Fermi said, "Not much." At this point I saw no reason to continue the conversation and went home.

I then went to see Einstein again in Princeton, and told him that things were not moving at all. And I said to Einstein that I thought the best thing I could do was to go definitely on record that a graphite-uranium system would be chain-reacting by writing a paper on the subject and submitting it for publication to the *Physical Review*. I suggested that we reopen the matter with the government, and that we propose to take the position that I would publish my results unless the government asked me not to do so and unless the government were willing to take some action in this matter.

Accordingly, I wrote a paper for publication and sent it to *Physical Review* on February 16th [1940].[34] I brought the paper to Pegram, who was somewhat embarrassed because Fermi was out of town and Pegram did not know what action he should take. However, he said that he

34. "Divergent Chain Reactions in Systems Composed of Uranium and Carbon." This paper was sent to the *Physical Review* twice, first as a shorter Letter to the Editor on February 6th, then in full on February 14 (received February 16), 1940. With each version Szilard sent a covering letter to John Tate, editor, asking that publication be delayed; it was delayed indefinitely. The paper became Report A–55 of the Uranium Committee. After the war it was given the Manhattan District declassified report number MDDC–446.

must take some action, so he went to see Admiral Bowen[35] in Washington, who, Pegram thought, might take some interest because, after all, atomic energy might be used for driving submarines.

On the basis of the conversation I had with him, Einstein wrote to Alexander Sachs, and Sachs wrote again to the President,[36] and the President replied that he thought that the best way to continue research would be to have another meeting of the Uranium Committee. And now something most tragic and comic happened. Having received a letter from the White House, Sachs called up Lyman J. Briggs, chairman of the Uranium Committee, and suggested a meeting be called. And Briggs said he was on the point of calling a meeting and wanted to invite Sachs and Dr. Pegram to attend. Sachs said, "Well, what about Szilard and Fermi?" and Briggs said, "Well, you know, these matters are secret and we do not think that they should be included."

At this point, Sachs blew up. This was, after all, his meeting, and why should the people who were doing the job and who produced the figures not be included? This, however, was a misunderstanding: Briggs did not want to call the meeting because he had heard from the White House; he wanted to call the meeting at the initiative of Admiral Bowen, whom Pegram had contacted, so that Sachs and Briggs talked to each other at cross purposes. They were in effect talking about different meetings. However, somehow things got straightened out and the meeting was called which Fermi and I did in fact attend.[37]

I now have to go back to the summer of 1939, when in July I made the first steps in computing the uranium-graphite system. As soon as I saw that the uranium-graphite system might work, I wrote a number of letters to Fermi telling him that I felt this was a matter of some urgency,

35. Admiral Harold G. Bowen, director of the Naval Research Laboratory.

36. Letter, Sachs to Roosevelt, March 15, 1940, forwarded the letter from Einstein to Sachs, March 7, 1940, which contains the following paragraph: "Dr. Szilard has shown me the manuscript which he is sending to the *Physics Review* in which he describes in detail a method for setting up a chain reaction in uranium. The papers will appear in print unless they are held up, and the question arises whether something ought to be done to withhold publication." Otto Nathan and Heinz Norden, eds., *Einstein on Peace* (New York, 1960), p. 299.

37. The Advisory Committee on Uranium met at the National Bureau of Standards on Saturday, April 27th. Present were Chairman Briggs, Colonel Adamson, Commander Hoover, Admiral Bowen, Dean Pegram, Fermi, Szilard, Wigner, and Sachs.

and that we should not waste our time by making detailed physical measurements of the individual constants involved, but rather try to get a sufficient amount of graphite and uranium to approach the critical mass and build up a chain-reacting system.[38] Fermi's response to this crash program was very cool.[39] He said that he had thought of the possibilities of using carbon instead of water, that he had computed how a homogeneous mixture of carbon and uranium would behave, and that he had found that the absorption of carbon would have to be indeed exceedingly low in order to make such a system chain-reacting. I knew very well that Fermi must have been aware of the fact that a homogeneous mixture of uranium and carbon was not as good as a heterogeneous uranium-carbon system; he computed the homogeneous mixture only because it was the easiest to compute. And this showed me that Fermi did not take this matter really seriously. It was one of the factors which induced me to approach the government quite independently of Fermi or Columbia University.

In July 1939 when I had reported to Pegram my optimistic views about graphite, and told him why I thought the matter was urgent, he took the position that even though the matter appeared to be rather urgent, it being summer and Fermi away, there was really nothing that usefully could be done until fall—September, or perhaps October. This was the second factor which induced me to disregard everything else and go to the government directly.

Now, in the spring of 1940, we were advised that the money, the $6,000 which the committee had promised us, was available. We bought some graphite, and Fermi started an experiment to measure the absorption of that graphite. When he finished his measurement, the question of secrecy again came up. I went to his office and said, "Now that we have this value, perhaps the value ought not to be made public." At this point Fermi really lost his temper; he really thought that this was absurd. There was nothing much more I could say, but next time I dropped in at his office he told me that Pegram had come to see him, and Pegram thought that this value should not be published. From that point on, secrecy was on.

38. Letters, Szilard to Fermi, July 3, July 5, July 8, and July 11, 1939.
39. Letter, Fermi to Szilard, July 9, 1939; letter, Fermi to Pegram, July 11, 1939.

[EDITORS' NOTE: This portion of the taped interviews ends here. However, in the fragmentary outline of his memoirs mentioned in the headnote above, Szilard described some of the subsequent events in 1940 and 1941 as follows:]

In May 1940 I received a letter from Turner[40] in Princeton, who pointed out that in the chain reaction which I hoped to be able to set up there would be formed a new element which might be capable of undergoing fission. As we now know, this is in fact the case, and the element formed in the chain reaction is now called plutonium. Neither Fermi nor I had thought of this possibility, which was obviously of the utmost importance, and this realization increased my sense of urgency.

On Rabi's advice, I enlisted the help of H. C. Urey, who prevailed on the chairman of the Uranium Committee to appoint those of us who were actively interested in this problem to serve as a technical subcommittee of the Uranium Committee. We thought this would put us in a position to approach various laboratories in the U. S. and to enlist their cooperation in pursuing the various aspects of the problem, including the possibility raised by Turner's suggestion.

The Committee,[41] having been duly appointed, met in Washington, and when the meeting was opened by the chairman, he told us that the committee would be dissolved upon termination of the current meeting, because if the government were to spend a substantial amount of money—we were discussing sums of the order of a half million dollars —and subsequently it would turn out that it is not possible to set up a chain reaction based on uranium, there might be a congressional investigation. If this were the case, in such a situation it would be awkward if the government had made available funds on the recommendation of a committee whose membership comprised men other than American citizens of long standing. Fermi and I were not American citizens. Though Wigner was an American citizen, he was not one of long standing. Thus the work on uranium in the United States was brought to a

40. Louis A. Turner, in 1940 associate professor of physics at Princeton. His letter to Szilard is dated May 27, 1940.

41. A special advisory group called together by Briggs met at the National Bureau of Standards on June 15, 1940. Attending were Briggs, Urey, Tuve, Wigner, Breit, Fermi, Szilard, and Pegram. Henry De Wolf Smyth, *Atomic Energy for Peaceful Purposes . . .* (Princeton, 1946), p. 48. (Hereafter referred to as *Smyth Report*.)

standstill for the next six months. Mr. Wigner wrote a very polite letter to the chairman of the Uranium Committee saying that he would hold himself in readiness to work for the government on all matters related to defense, with the exception of uranium.

After reorganization in Washington, which put the Uranium Committee under Dr. Vannevar Bush's committee, Columbia University was given a contract in the amount of $40,000 to develop the Fermi-Szilard system. On November 1, 1940, I was put on the payroll of Columbia University under this contract. Since I was instrumental in inducing the government to assume expenditures for exploring the possibility of setting up a chain reaction, and with a view to the possibility that our efforts might come to nothing, it was deemed advisable to set my salary at a low figure, *i.e.*, $4,000 a year.

While up to this point we had suffered from the lack of official recognition, during this period we were suffering from having official recognition. H. C. Urey was under orders not to discuss with Fermi and myself the possibility of preparing substantial amounts of Uranium 235. Because of this compartmentalization, we failed to put two and two together, and at no time were we or any other physicist able to say to the American government that atomic bombs could be made with amounts of Uranium 235 which it was practicable to obtain. Thus our project and Urey's remained projects of low priority until the British colleagues, who were not so compartmentalized (hamstrung?), pointed out that making atomic bombs of Uranium 235 must be regarded as a practical proposition.

This led to a reorganization of the project and the group working at Columbia University was transferred to Chicago [in February 1942].

[EDITORS' NOTE: In these oral reminiscences Szilard does not cover his activities at the "Metallurgical Laboratory" in Chicago from February 1942 to the spring of 1945. During that time his title was Chief Physicist. The scientific aspects of this period, in the form of some thirty reports written by Szilard, will be included in the forthcoming collected works. Szilard picks up the story again in 1945.]

In the spring of '45 it was clear that the war against Germany would soon end, and so I began to ask myself, "What is the purpose of continuing the development of the bomb, and how would the bomb be used if the war with Japan has not ended by the time we have the first bomb?"

Initially we were strongly motivated to produce the bomb because we feared the Germans would get ahead of us, and the only way to prevent them from dropping bombs on us was to have bombs in readiness ourselves. But now, with the war won, it was not clear what we were working for.

I had many discussions with many people about this point in the Metallurgical Laboratory of the University of Chicago, which was the code name for the uranium project which produced the chain reaction. There was no indication that these problems were seriously discussed at a high government level. I had repeated conversations with Compton[42] about the future of the project, and he too was concerned about its future, but he had no word of what intentions there were, if there were any intentions at all.

There was no point in discussing these things with General Groves[43] or Dr. Conant[44] or Dr. Bush,[45] and because of secrecy there was no intermediate level in the government to which we could have gone for a careful consideration of these issues.[46] The only man with whom we were sure we were entitled to communicate was the President. In these circumstances I wrote a memorandum addressed to the President, and was looking around for some ways and means to communicate the memorandum to him. Since I didn't suppose that he would know who I was, I needed a letter of introduction.

I went to see Einstein and I asked him to write me such a letter of introduction, even though I could tell him only that there was trouble ahead, but I couldn't tell him what the nature of the trouble was. Einstein wrote a letter and I decided to transmit the memorandum and the letter to the President through Mrs. Roosevelt, who once before had

42. Arthur Holley Compton, then director of the "Metallurgical Laboratory" at the University of Chicago.

43. Major General Leslie R. Groves, Manhattan Engineer District, director of all army activities of the Project at that time.

44. James B. Conant, President of Harvard University and chairman of the National Defense Research Committee at that time.

45. Vannevar Bush, director of the Office of Scientific Research and Development at that time.

46. The "Metallurgical Laboratory" was transferred from the civilian OSRD to the War Department Manhattan District in April 1943.

channelled communications from the project to the President. I have forgotten now precisely what I wrote to Mrs. Roosevelt; I suppose that I sent her a copy of Einstein's letter—but not the memorandum. This I could not do. The memorandum I couldn't send her, because the memorandum would have been considered secret.[47]

Mrs. Roosevelt gave me an appointment for May 8th. When I had this appointment I called on Dr. Compton, who was in charge of the project, and told him that I intended to get a memorandum to the President, and I asked him to read the memorandum. I was fully prepared to be scolded by Compton, to be told that I should go through channels rather than go to the President directly. To my astonishment, this is not what happened.

Compton read the memorandum very carefully, and then he said, "I hope that you will get the President to read this." Elated by finding no resistance where I expected resistance, I went back to my office. I hadn't been in my office for five minutes when there was a knock on the door and Compton's assistant came in, telling me that he had just heard over the radio that President Roosevelt had died [April 12, 1945].

There I was now with my memorandum, and no way to get it anywhere. At this point I knew that I was in need of advice. I went to see the associate director of the project, Dr. [Walter] Bartky, and told him of my plight. He suggested that we go and see Dr. [Robert M.] Hutchins, president of the University of Chicago. This was the first time that

47. Letter, Einstein to Roosevelt, March 25, 1945, introducing Szilard. Einstein recalls his letter of 1939 on the importance of uranium and Szilard's work, says he has "much confidence in his judgment," and explains that secrecy prevents his knowing about Szilard's current work:

However, I understand that he now is greatly concerned about the lack of adequate contact between scientists who are doing this work and those members of your Cabinet who are responsible for formulating policy. In the circumstances I consider it my duty to give Dr. Szilard this introduction and I wish to express the hope that you will be able to give his presentation of the case your personal attention.

This letter has been published in *Einstein on Peace*, cited in note 36 above, pp. 304–305.

The memorandum by Szilard to the President, entitled "Enclosure to Mr. Albert Einstein's Letter of March 25, 1945 to the President of the United States," warns of precipitating an atomic arms race between the United States and Russia, suggests delay in our use of the atomic bomb, calls for setting up a system of international controls, and asks for formation of a cabinet-level committee through which scientists could express their views to the government. The document is printed in its entirety below as Appendix II to these Reminiscences.

I had met Hutchins. I told him briefly what the situation was, and this was the first time he knew that we were close to having an atomic bomb, even though the Metallurgical project had been on his campus for several years. Hutchins grasped the situation in an instant. He used to be an isolationist before the war, but he was a very peculiar isolationist, because where most isolationists held that the Americans should keep out of war because those foreigners do not deserve to have American blood shed for them, Hutchins' position was that the Americans should keep out of war because they would only mess it up. After he heard my story he asked me what this all would mean in the end, and I said that in the end this would mean that the world would have to live under one government. Then he said, "Yes, I believe you are right." I thought this was pretty good for an isolationist. As a matter of fact, a few days after the bomb was dropped on Hiroshima, Hutchins went on the radio; he gave a speech about the necessity of world government.

In spite of the good understanding which I had with Hutchins, he was not able to help with the task immediately at hand. "I do not know Mr. Truman," Hutchins said. I knew any number of people who could have reached Roosevelt, but I knew nobody offhand who could reach Truman. Truman just did not move in the same circles, so for a number of days I was at a complete loss as to what to do. Then I had an idea. Our project was very large by then, and there ought to be somebody from Kansas City. And three days later we had an appointment at the White House.

I asked the associate director of the project, Dr. Bartky, to come to Washington; and armed with Einstein's letter and my memorandum we went to the White House and were received by Matt Connelly, Truman's appointment secretary. I handed him Einstein's letter and the memorandum to read. He read the memorandum carefully from beginning to end, and then he said, "I see now this is a serious matter. At first I was a little suspicious, because this appointment came through Kansas City." Then he said, "The President thought that your concern would be about this matter, and he has asked me to make an appointment with you with James Byrnes, if you are willing to go down to see him in Spartanburg, South Carolina." We said that we would be happy to go anywhere that the President directed us, and he picked up the phone and made an appointment with Byrnes for us. I asked whether I might bring Dr. H. C. Urey[48] along, and Connelly said I could bring along anyone whom I wanted. So I phoned Chicago and asked Urey to join us in Washington, and together we went down the next day to Spartanburg, taking an overnight train from Washington.

We were concerned about two things: we were concerned first about the role which the bomb would play in the world after the war, and how America's position would be affected if the bomb were actually used in the war; we were also concerned about the future of atomic energy, and about the lack of planning as to how this research might be continued after the war. It was clear that the project set up during the war would not be continued but would have to be reorganized. But the valuable thing was not the big projects; the valuable things were the numerous teams, which somehow crystallized during the war, of men who had different abilities and who liked to work with each other. We thought that these teams ought to be preserved even though the projects might be dissolved.

We did not quite understand why we had been sent by the President to see James Byrnes. He had previously occupied a high position in the government, but was now out of the government and was living as a private citizen in Spartanburg. Clearly the President must have had in mind appointing him to a govermnent position, but what position? Was he to be the man in charge of the uranium work after the war, or what? We did not know.

Finally we arrived in Spartanburg, and I gave Byrnes Einstein's letter to read and the memorandum which I had written. Byrnes read the memorandum, and then we started to discuss the problem. When I spoke of my concern that Russia might become an atomic power—and might become an atomic power soon, if we were to demonstrate the power of the bomb and use it against Japan—his reply was, "General Groves tells me there is no uranium in Russia."

I told Byrnes that there was certainly a limited amount of rich uranium ore in Czechoslovakia to which Russia had access; but apart from this, it was very unlikely that in the vast territory of Russia there should be no low-grade uranium ores. High-grade uranium ore is, of course,

48. Harold C. Urey, then professor of chemistry at Columbia University.

another matter: high-grade deposits are rare, and it is not at all sure whether new high-grade deposits can be found. In the past, only the high-grade deposits were of interest because the main purpose of mining uranium ores was to produce radium, and the price of radium was such that working low-grade uranium ores would not have been profitable. But when you are dealing with atomic energy you are not limited to high-grade ores; you can use low-grade ones, and I doubted very much that anyone in America would be able to say, in a responsible way, that there were no major low-grade uranium deposits in Russia.

I thought it would be a mistake to disclose the existence of the bomb to the world before the government had made up its mind how to handle the situation after the war. Using the bomb certainly would disclose that the bomb exists. As a matter of fact, even testing the bomb would disclose that the bomb exists. Once the bomb has been tested and shown to go off, it would not be possible to keep it a secret.

Byrnes agreed that if we refrained from testing the bomb, people would conclude that its development did not succeed. However, he said that we had spent two billion dollars on developing the bomb, and Congress would want to know what we got for the money spent. "How would you get Congress to appropriate money for atomic energy research if you do not show results for the money which has been spent already?"

I saw his point at that time, and in retrospect I see even more clearly that it would not have served any useful purpose to keep the bomb secret, waiting for the government to understand the problem and to formulate a policy; for the government will not formulate a policy unless it is under pressure to do so, and if the bomb had been kept secret there would have been no pressure for the government to do anything in this direction.

Byrnes thought that the war would be over in about six months, and this proved to be a fairly accurate estimate. He was concerned about Russia's postwar behavior. Russian troops had moved into Hungary and Rumania; Byrnes thought it would be very difficult to persuade Russia to withdraw her troops from these countries, and that Russia might be more manageable if impressed by American military might. I shared Byrnes's concern about Russia's throwing around her weight in the postwar period, but I was completely flabbergasted by the assumption that rattling the bomb might make Russia more manageable.

I began to doubt that there was any way for me to communicate with Byrnes in this matter, and my doubt became certainty when he turned to me and said, "Well, you come from Hungary—you would not want Russia to stay in Hungary indefinitely." I certainly didn't want Russia to stay in Hungary indefinitely, but what Byrnes said offended my sense of proportion. I was concerned at this point that by demonstrating the bomb and using it in the war against Japan, we might start an atomic arms race between America and Russia which might end with the destruction of both countries. I was *not* disposed at this point to worry about what would happen to Hungary.

After all was said that could be said on this topic, the conversation turned to the future of the uranium project. To our astonishment, Byrnes showed complete indifference. This is easy to understand in retrospect because, contrary to what we had suspected, he was not slated to be director of the uranium project but he was slated to be secretary of state.

I was rarely as depressed as when we left Byrnes's house and walked toward the station. I thought to myself how much better off the world might be had I been born in America and become influential in American politics, and had Byrnes been born in Hungary and studied physics. In all probability there would have been no atomic bomb, and no danger of an arms race between America and Russia.

When I returned to Chicago, I found the project in an uproar. The Army had violently objected to our visit to the White House, and to Byrnes. Dr. Bartky was summoned to see General Groves; General Groves told him that I committed a grave breach of security by handing a secret document to Byrnes, who did not know how to handle secret documents. To calm the uproar, Dr. Compton, the leader of the project, decided to regularize the discussions by appointing a committee under the chairmanship of James Franck[49] to examine the issue of whether or not the bomb should be used, and if so, how.[50] The report

49. James Franck, physicist at the Chicago Laboratory. Other members of the Franck Committee were Hogness, Hughes, Nickson, Rabinowitch, Seaborg, Stearns, and Szilard.

50. Szilard wrote an unpublished article called "The Story of a Petition," dated July 28, 1946, which essentially covers the same ground as the oral tape. In this article, he says the Franck report,

of the committee has been published, and it was meant to be presented to the secretary of war, Mr. Stimson. Whether it ever reached his desk I do not know.

On my way from Spartanburg to Chicago I stopped in Washington to see Oppenheimer, who had arrived there to attend a meeting of the Interim Committee.[51] I told Oppenheimer that I thought it would be a very serious mistake to use the bomb against the cities of Japan. Oppenheimer didn't share my view. He surprised me by starting the conversation by saying that the atomic bomb is no good.[52] "What do you mean by that?" I asked him. He said, "Well, this is a weapon which has no military significance. It will make a big bang—a very big bang—but it is not a weapon which is useful in war." He thought it would be important, however, to inform the Russians that we had an atomic bomb and that we intended to use it against the cities of Japan, rather than taking them by surprise. This seemed reasonable to me, and I know that Stimson also shared this view. However, while this was necessary, it was certainly not sufficient. "Well," Oppenheimer said, "don't you think if we tell the Russians what we intend to do and then use the bomb in Japan, the Russians will understand it?" And I remember that I said, "They'll understand it only too well."

The time approached when the bomb would be tested. The date was never communicated to us in Chicago, nor did we ever receive any of-

---

was rushed to Stimson and advised against the outright military use of atomic bombs in the war against Japan. It took a stand in favor of demonstrating the power of the atomic bomb in a manner which will avoid mass slaughter but yet convince the Japanese of the destructive power of the bomb. By the beginning of July it became evident, at least to me, personally, that the use of the bomb will be examined by the Interim Committee purely on the basis of expediency, and that great weight will be given by them to the immediate effect, rather than to the long range effects.

51. The Interim Committee was organized in early May of 1945 by Secretary of War Henry L. Stimson to consider uses of the bomb and possible international control. He was chairman; members were Bush, Conant, Karl T. Compton, Under Secretary of the Navy Ralph Bard, Assistant Secretary of State William Clayton, and as the personal representative of President Truman, James Byrnes, who at that point held no official position. Robert Oppenheimer, director of the Los Alamos laboratory, was on the scientific advisory panel to the Interim Committee, whose other members were Arthur Compton, Fermi, and Lawrence. Richard G. Hewlett and Oscar E. Anderson, Jr., *The New World, 1939/1946: A History of the United States Atomic Energy Commission* (University Park, Pa., 1962–), I, 344–346.

52. A stronger word was used in the tape.

ficial indication of what was afoot. However, I concluded that the bomb was about to be tested when I was told that we were no longer permitted to call Los Alamos over the telephone. This could mean only one thing: Los Alamos must get ready to test the bomb, and the Army tried by this ingenious method to keep the news from the Chicago project.

I knew by this time that it would not be possible to dissuade the government from using the bomb against the cities of Japan. The cards in the Interim Committee were stacked against such an approach to the problem. Therefore all that remained was for the scientists to go unmistakably on record that they were opposed to such action. While the Franck Report argued the case on grounds of expediency, I thought the time had come for the scientists to go on record against the use of the bomb against the cities of Japan on moral grounds. Therefore I drafted a petition which was circulated in the project.[53]

This was again violently opposed by the Army. They accused me of having violated secrecy by disclosing in the petition that such a thing as a bomb existed. What the Army thought that we thought we were doing all this time, I cannot say. However, we did not yield to the Army's demand. The right to petition is anchored in the Constitution, and when you are a naturalized citizen you are supposed to learn the Constitution prior to obtaining your citizenship.

The first version of the petition which was circulated drew about fifty-three signatures in the Chicago project. What *is* significant is that these fifty-three people included *all* the leading physicists in the project and many of the leading biologists. The signatures of the chemists were conspicuously absent. This was so striking that I went over to the chemistry department to discover what the trouble was. What I discovered

53. In "The Story of a Petition" Szilard wrote, "A petition to the President was thus drafted in the first days of July and sent to every group leader in the 'Metallurgical Laboratory,' with the request to circulate it within his group." Szilard's covering letter to the group leaders is especially intense on the moral position, raising the analogy of individual Germans' guilt for Germany's acts. The text of this letter, dated July 4, 1945, appears below as Appendix III. The first version of the petition was dated July 3, 1945, and was signed by fifty-nine scientists. The final paragraph states: "In view of the foregoing, we, the undersigned, respectfully petition that you exercise your power as Commander-in-Chief to rule that the United States shall not, in the present phase of the war, resort to the use of atomic bombs." The text of the petition is printed in full below, as Appendix IV.

was rather disturbing: the chemists argued that what we must determine is solely whether more lives would be saved by using the bomb or by continuing the war without using the bomb. This is a utilitarian argument with which I was very familiar through my previous experiences in Germany. That some other issue may be involved in dropping the bomb on an inhabited city and killing men, women, and children did not occur to any of the chemists with whom I spoke.

Some of the members of the project said that they would sign the petition if it were worded somewhat more mildly, and I therefore drafted a second version of the petition which drew a somewhat larger number of signatures—but not a significantly larger number.[54] The second petition was dated one day before the bomb was actually tested at Alamogordo, New Mexico.[55]

After the petition had been circulated we were faced with the decision of what channels to use to communicate it to the White House. Several

---

54. The second version was dated July 17, 1945, and drew seventy signatures. The final three paragraphs, concluding in a significant modification of the final paragraph of the original petition, are as follows:

If after this war a situation is allowed to develop in the world which permits rival powers to be in uncontrolled possession of these new means of destruction, the cities of the United States as well as the cities of other nations will be in continuous danger of sudden annihilation. All the resources of the United States, moral and material, may have to be mobilized to prevent the advent of such a world situation. Its prevention is at present the solemn responsibility of the United States—singled out by virtue of her lead in the field of atomic power.

The added material strength which this lead gives to the United States brings with it the obligation of restraint and if we were to violate this obligation our moral position would be weakened in the eyes of the world and in our own eyes. It would then be more difficult for us to live up to our responsibility of bringing the unloosened forces of destruction under control.

In view of the foregoing, we, the undersigned, respectfully petition: first, that you exercise your power as Commander-in-Chief, to rule that the United States shall not resort to the use of atomic bombs in this war unless the terms which will be imposed upon Japan have been made public in detail and Japan knowing these terms has refused to surrender; second, that in such an event the question whether or not to use atomic bombs be decided by you in the light of the consideration presented in this petition as well as all the other moral responsibilities which are involved.

Both petitions were declassified finally on July 23, 1957.

55. While Szilard mentions that the petition was dated one day before the Alamogordo test, which was July 16, 1945, we have not found in the files any version dated July 15th. There is one dated the 16th, the day of the test, which is almost identical to the July 17th version, but without any signatures. All the copies with signatures are dated either the 3rd or the 17th.

people, and above all James Franck, took the position that they would sign the petition because they agreed with it, but they could do this only if the petition were to be forwarded to the President through the regular channels rather than outside of these channels. I did not like this idea because I was just not sure whether the regular channels would forward the petition or whether they would sabotage it by filing it until the war was over. However, to my regret, I finally yielded and handed the petition to Compton, who transmitted it to Colonel Nichols,[56] who promised that he would transmit it to General Groves for immediate transmittal to Potsdam. I have no evidence that this petition ever reached the President.[57]

56. Letter of transmittal, Szilard to A. H. Compton, July 19, 1945, requesting that he "forward this petition to the President via the War Department." The final paragraph of this letter, significant for its anticipation of an arms race with Russia, reads:

It would be appreciated if in transmitting these copies you would draw attention in your covering letter to the fact that the text of the petition deals with the moral aspect of the issue only. Some of those who signed the petition undoubtedly fear that the use of atomic bombs at this time would precipitate an armament race with Russia and believe that atomic bombs ought not to be demonstrated until the government had more time to reach a final decision as to which course it intends to follow in the years following the first demonstration of atomic bombs. Others are more inclined to think that if we withhold such a demonstration we will cause distrust on the part of other nations and are, therefore, in favor of an early demonstration. The text of the petition does not touch upon these and other important issues involved but deals with the moral issue only.

In his memorandum to Colonel K. D. Nichols, July 24, 1945, entitled "In re: Transmittal of Petitions addressed to the President," A. H. Compton urged speed in transmitting the documents, and enclosed the result of an opinion poll of 150 scientists, conducted by Farrington Daniels, director of the Chicago laboratory. Compton commented that "the strongly favored procedure . . . to give a military demonstration in Japan, to be followed by a renewed opportunity for surrender before full use of the weapons is employed . . . coincides with my own preference . . ." Fletcher Knebel and Charles W. Bailey, "The Fight over the A-Bomb; Secret Revealed after 18 Years," *Look*, 27 (August 13, 1963), 22–23.

57. The petition never reached the President, according to Knebel and Bailey. Nichols delivered the petition on July 25 to Groves, they write, who kept it until August 1, when it was delivered to Secretary of War Stimson's office by messenger. But President Truman was then at the Potsdam conference, about to embark for home aboard the *U.S.S. Augusta*. On August 6, the day of Hiroshima, Truman was still on the Atlantic. Knebel and Bailey quote a memorandum written almost a year later, May 24, 1946, by Army Lieutenant R. Gordon Arneson, secretary of the Interim Committee. ". . . since the question of the bomb's use 'had already been fully considered and settled by the proper authorities,' . . . it was decided that 'no useful purpose would be served by transmitting either the petition or any of the attached documents to the White House, particularly since the President was not then in the country.' " "The Fight over the A-Bomb," p. 23.

After the bomb was dropped on Hiroshima, I called the responsible officer of the Manhattan District in Chicago and told him that I was going to declassify the petition and asked him if there were any objection. There could not have been any objection, and there wasn't, and so I declassified the petition. A short time thereafter I sent a telegram to Matt Connelly, the President's secretary, to advise him that it was my intention to make the contents of the petition public, and that I wanted to advise him of this as a matter of courtesy.[58] When the telegram was not acknowledged I phoned the White House, upon which I received a telegram saying that the matter had been presented to the President for his decision, and that I would be advised accordingly.[59] Shortly thereafter I received a call from the Manhattan District saying that General Groves wanted the petition reclassified "Secret." I said that I would not do this on the basis of a telephone conversation, but that I wanted to have a letter explaining why the petition, which contained nothing secret, should be reclassified. Soon after, I received a three-page letter, stamped "Secret," in which I was advised that while the officer writing the letter could not possibly know what was in General Groves's mind when he asked that the petition be reclassified "Secret," he assumed that the reason for this request was that people reading the petition might conclude that there must have been some dissension in the project prior to the termination of the war; this might have slowed down the work of the project which was conducted under the Army.[60]

Immediately after Hiroshima, I went to see Hutchins and told him that something needed to be done to get thoughtful and influential people to think about what the bomb may mean to the world, and how the world and America can adjust to its existence. I proposed that the Uni-

58. We have so far not found this telegram to Connelly, but have found a corresponding letter, Szilard to Connelly, August 17, 1945.

59. Telegram, Connelly to Szilard, August 25, 1945.

60. This letter, which is in the Szilard files, is from Captain James S. Murray, Intelligence Officer, Manhattan Engineer District, dated August 27, 1945. Page three contains a paragraph giving exactly the explanation here summarized by Szilard. This letter was eventually declassified on May 13, 1960, and returned to Dr. Szilard. A few days after receiving it in 1945, Szilard commented in a letter to Robert M. Hutchins, dated August 29, 1945: "The Manhattan District's definition of 'Secret' includes 'information that might be injurious to the prestige of any governmental activity,' which is, of course, very different from the definition adopted by Congress in passing the Espionage Act."

versity of Chicago call a three-day meeting and assemble about twenty-five of the best men to discuss the subject. Hutchins immediately acted on this proposal and he invited a broad spectrum of Americans ranging from Henry Wallace to Charles Lindbergh. Lilienthal attended this meeting; so did Chester Barnard, Beardsley Ruml, Jake Weiner.[61]

This was one of the best meetings that I ever attended. In a short period of time we discussed a variety of subjects. We discussed the possibility of preventive war; we discussed the possibility of setting up international control of atomic energy, involving inspection. The wisest remarks that were made at this meeting were made by Jake Weiner, and what he said was this: "None of these things will happen. There will be no preventive war, and there'll be no international agreement involving inspection. America will be in sole possession for a number of years, and the bomb will exert a certain subtle influence; it will be present at every diplomatic conference, in the consciousness of the participants, and will exert its effect. Then, sooner or later, Russia also will have the bomb, and then a new equilibrium will establish itself." He had certainly more foresight than the rest of us, though it is not clear whether what we have now is an equilibrium or whether it is something else.

One of those who attended the Chicago meeting was Edward Condon. Henry Wallace was at that time looking around for a director for the Bureau of Standards, because Lyman J. Briggs had reached the retirement age. I asked that Condon be invited, with the possibility in mind that he might be a suitable candidate. Wallace liked him at first sight, and Condon was interested in the position. What I did not know when I thought of Condon as a suitable candidate was the fact that Condon had admired Henry Wallace for a number of years. After the conference I had a discussion with Hutchins and Condon, and I proposed that Condon and I go to Washington for a few days and try to find out what thinking in Washington about the bomb might be.

William Benton, vice president of the University of Chicago, had just accepted an appointment as assistant secretary of state under Byrnes.

61. Chester I. Barnard, Bell Telephone Company executive, foundation officer, author, and government consultant; Beardsley Ruml, treasurer of R. H. Macy and Son and chairman of the Federal Reserve Bank of New York; Joseph Lee Weiner, deputy director of the Division of Civilian Supply, Office of Production Management.

When he heard that we were going down to Washington he offered to invite the top desk men of the State Department to dinner, and he asked whether Condon and I might give a short discourse on the bomb for the benefit of the Department of State. This we actually did, and I think that this was the first intimation that these people in Washington had, that the advent of the atomic bomb did not necessarily mean that American military power would be enhanced for an indefinite period of time.

While we were in Washington, we somehow picked up a copy of a proposed bill on the control of atomic energy which the War Department had prepared, and which went under the name of the May-Johnson Bill. I took this bill back home to Chicago and gave it to Edward Levi of the Chicago Law School to read, who promptly informed me that this was a terrible bill and we had better do something to stop its passage.

While I was in Chicago I read in the newspapers that the House Military Affairs Committee had held a hearing on the bill which lasted for a day, and then they closed the hearing and prepared to report out the bill. At that one-day hearing the proponents of the bill testified for the bill, but no opponent of the bill was heard. This was disquieting news, but I doubt very much that I would have swung into action had it not been for a more or less accidental circumstance.

When the war ended, we were asked not to discuss the bomb publicly. We were under the impression that this request was made because there were some important international negotiations on the control of atomic energy under way, and any public discussion at this point could have disturbed these negotiations. We were not actually told this, but we were permitted to infer it, and having inferred it, we all decided to comply. Therefore all of us refused the numerous requests to speak over the radio or before groups, on what the atomic bomb was and what it might mean to the world. We kept silent. S. K. Allison[62] was the only one who gave a speech, and he said that he hoped very much that the secrecy which was imposed upon this type of work during the war

62. Samuel K. Allison, senior physicist from Los Alamos and newly appointed director of the Institute for Nuclear Studies. He gave "Sam's butterfly speech" at a luncheon at Chicago's Shoreland Hotel, September 1, 1945, at which the University of Chicago announced formation of its new research institute. Alice K. Smith, *A Peril and a Hope: The Scientists' Movement in America, 1945–1947* (Chicago, 1965), p. 88.

would be lifted after the war; otherwise, he said, he personally would cease to work on atomic energy and would start to work on the color of butterflies.

When his speech became known, Colonel Nichols flew from Oak Ridge to Chicago, and gathered a number of physicists and asked them just for a little while to be quiet and not to stir things up. "There is a bill being prepared," he said, "on the control of atomic energy, and when that bill is introduced in Congress that will be the right time to discuss these matters. Hearings will be held, and everyone will have an opportunity to appear as a witness and to have his say."

On the day when the one-day hearing was held before the House Military Affairs Committee and the hearings were closed, A. H. Compton arrived in Chicago and he met with the members of the project. He told us on that occasion that the War Department had prepared a bill for passage through Congress, and that the request which was addressed to us to refrain from publicly speaking on the subject of the atomic bomb was due to the War Department's desire to pass this law without unnecessary discussions in Congress. I remember that I got mad at this point, and got up and said that no bill on the control of atomic energy would be passed in Congress without discussion if I could possibly help it.

Through pure chance I received a telephone call the next morning from Hutchins, who had lunched the previous day with Marshall Field, asking whether I would be willing to talk to somebody from the *Chicago Sun*. I said that I was eager to talk to the *Sun*, but I would not want to talk to the *Sun* without also talking to the *Chicago Tribune*, and would Hutchins call up Colonel McCormick and have somebody from the *Chicago Tribune* come and see me?

In two separate interviews I told the reporters who came to see me that there was an attempt on the part of the Army to pass a bill through Congress without "unnecessary discussions," and the physicists would see to it that this would not happen. Because the information came from Compton and I regarded it as confidential, I did not feel free to identify either myself or Compton in this context; and the *Chicago Tribune* told me that under these circumstances they could not use the story. The *Chicago Sun*, being a less well-run newspaper, did not care, and printed the story on its front page. In retrospect, I know that I made a mistake, and should have permitted the papers to use my identity and have the story printed both in the *Tribune* and the *Chicago Sun*.

But in any case, the fight was on.

I went back to Hutchins and called up Condon, who was at that time associate director of research of Westinghouse, and Condon and I once more went down to Washington to see what we could do. We could probably have done very little, had it not been for the excellent advice which we received from Bob Lamb, who was at that time legislative advisor of the C.I.O.[63] He was recommended to us very highly by a number of people, and even though we did not like the idea of working with somebody who was legislative advisor of the C. I. O., because we did not want to involve the C.I.O., we decided to overlook this for the sake of getting really first-class advice.

I don't think that anyone knew the Congress as well at that time as did Bob Lamb. When he read the bill, he agreed with us that this bill must not pass. He arranged for us to see Chet Holifield and George Outland. Chet Holifield was on the House Military Affairs Committee, and was picked by Bob Lamb for this reason; George Outland was a friend of Chet Holifield, and a highly intelligent and competent Congressman. Both Condon and I went to see these two gentlemen and explained the situation to them. In the evening Bob Lamb reported to us that they were convinced that we had a good case, and that Chet Holifield would fight for us. Chet Holifield then arranged for Condon and me to see the chairman of the House Military Affairs Committee, May, and Sparkman. He himself joined us at this conversation, and we presented the case to them. May was not impressed, and he shortly thereafter made it public that he was not going to reopen the hearing even though Dr. Condon and Dr. Szilard had asked him to do so.

By this time, however, the scientists in the project got organized in Chicago, in Oak Ridge, and in Los Alamos. Both Chicago and Oak Ridge came to the conclusion that the May-Johnson bill was a bad bill which must not pass, and they were so vocal about it that a larger and

63. Robert K. Lamb counseled Szilard and Condon, also Lyle B. Borst and Harrison Davies, two younger scientists from Clinton Laboratories, helping in the campaign to defeat the May-Johnson bill.

larger portion of the press got interested in the fight. Los Alamos, under the influence of Oppenheimer, took the opposite position, and was in favor of the passage of the bill.

Condon and I found that everybody in Washington was greatly interested in the issue. We set ourselves a schedule: everybody wanted to see us, and we decided that we would keep Cabinet members waiting one day, Senators for two days, and Congressmen for three days before we'd give them an appointment.

Henry Wallace was very much interested, and he arranged for us to meet Senator Lister Hill.

We went to see Ickes and Ickes grumbled that he had not read this bill at all. The War Department brought it over, left it there for half a day, and then took it away again. "This is not the first time," he said, "that Royall[64] has been giving me the bum's rush."

We went to see Lewis Strauss who was at that time in the Department of the Navy, and discovered that the Navy did not have any particular views about this bill. The bill was prepared in the War Department, and even though the President made some friendly remarks about the bill, it was not really in any sense an Administration bill. It was a War Department bill.

We then went to see James Newman, in Snyder's office,[65] which was supposed to steer the bill through Congress. James Newman had read the bill, and he said to us, "I don't believe that you really understand this bill." "Well," we said, "we didn't really claim to understand it, but we just didn't think it was a good bill."

"Well, I don't think it is a good bill either," said Newman, "but I doubt that you understand what it says. Look," he said, "here the bill says: 'there will be a Managing Director and an Assistant Managing Director, and the Managing Director has to keep the Assistant Managing Director informed at all times.' Now," said Newman, "have you ever seen a provision of this type in a bill? What does this mean? Clearly,

64. Brigadier General Kenneth C. Royall, who was co-author with William L. Marbury of the May-Johnson bill, later became secretary of war.

65. James Newman, head of the science section of OWMR, became *de facto* science adviser to the President. John Snyder was director, Office of War Mobilization and Reconversion (OWMR). On October 18, President Truman authorized OWMR to take charge of atomic energy legislation.

it means that the managing director will be someone from the Army and the assistant managing director will be someone from the Navy, and since the Navy and the Army don't talk to each other, you have to write into the bill that they must talk to each other on this occasion." For all I know it may well be that he was right.

Under public pressure, May, the chairman of the House Military Affairs Committee, in the end was forced to reopen the hearings. He reopened the hearings just for one more day. Towards six one evening I received a telephone call from the office of the Military Affairs Committee, asking me whether I could testify before the committee the next morning. I said that I would testify. Who else could testify? There was no one in town whom I knew had anything to do with atomic energy except Herbert Anderson, who had worked on the project mainly as Fermi's assistant. He was a spirited young man at that time. He is now director of the Enrico Fermi Institute of Nuclear Studies at the University of Chicago. I asked Anderson whether he was willing to testify and he said he would, so I gave his name to the committee. The War Department asked Oppenheimer and A. H. Compton to testify *for* the bill, and so there were four witnesses.

I worked through the night and ended up with some sort of a prepared testimony, which I delivered, and I was then questioned by members of the committee.[66] Herbert Anderson testified after me and then came Compton and Oppenheimer. Neither Compton nor Oppenheimer were really, at heart, in favor of the bill. Oppenheimer managed to give the most brilliant performance on this occasion, for he gave members of the committee the impression that he was in favor of the bill, and the audience, mostly composed of physicists, his colleagues, the impression that he was against the bill. He did that by the simple expedient of answering a question put to him by a member of the committee. He was asked, "Dr. Oppenheimer, are you in favor of this bill?" And he answered, "Dr. Bush is in favor of this bill, and Dr. Conant is in favor of the bill, and I have a very high regard for both of these gentlemen." To the members of the committee this meant that he favored the

66. Szilard's testimony is recorded in "Hearings before the Committee on Military Affairs," *House Report*, 79 Cong., 1 Sess., no. 4280 (October 9 and 18, 1945), 71–96. See also the text of Szilard's speech in *Cong. Record*, 79 Cong., 1 Sess. (1945), A4877–A4878.

bill; to the audience composed of physicists this meant that he did not favor the bill.

H. C. Urey was ready to testify and this was communicated to the chairman, but he was not called. After my testimony, the chairman dryly remarked that I had consumed two and a half hours of the committee's time. It was obvious that the chairman played ball with the War Department and that the committee was stacked against us. There was no hope of inducing the committee into amending the bill; but even if there had been some hope, it is not possible to get a good bill by writing a bad bill and amending it. The only hope was to have the bill bottled up in the Rules Committee, and in this we succeeded. The bill never reached the floor of the House.

One of the men whom I saw rather late in the game was Judge Samuel Rosenman, in the White House. There was no need to convince Rosenman. "I told the President," Judge Rosenman told me, "that it looks as though the Army wants to pass this bill by number only."

The Senate set up a Committee on Atomic Energy under the chairmanship of McMahon, and this committee started hearings on atomic energy legislation early in 1946. They heard a number of witnesses, and when I testified before this committee, delivering a carefully prepared testimony, I found a much friendlier reception than I had found before the House Military Affairs Committee.[67]

In retrospect it seems to me that at this point I could have left Washington because there was not very much more that I needed to do. There were plenty of other people interested who were more influential than I was, yet I stayed throughout most of the hearings and listened to the testimony of several distinguished witnesses. One of the most impressive of these testimonies was that of Langmuir.[68]

One of the things which we tried to get across, and tried to get across very hard, was the notion that it would not take Russia more than five years to develop an atomic bomb also. Even though all younger men and everybody who had a creative part in the development of atomic energy were of that opinion, this is a case of "youth did not prevail."

67. See U. S. Senate, *Hearings before the Special Committee on Atomic Energy*, 79 Cong., 1 Sess. (1945), 267–300.
68. Irving Langmuir, physicist at the General Electric laboratories.

In his book, *Speaking Frankly*, James Byrnes relates that when he became secretary of state he tried to find out how long it would take Russia to develop a bomb. He needed this information in order to evaluate
proposals for the control of atomic energy. He reports in his book that,
from the best information which he could gather, he concluded that it
would take Russia seven to fifteen years to make the bomb. He adds that
this estimate was based on the assumption that postwar recovery would
be faster than it actually was, and therefore he thinks that this estimate
ought to be revised upward rather than downward. Dr. Conant, Dr.
Bush, and Dr. Compton all estimated that it would take Russia perhaps
fifteen years to make the bomb. Why this should be so is not clear,
though it is of course possible to contrive a psychological explanation
for these overestimates. If you are an expert, you believe that you are in
possession of the truth, and since you know so much, you are unwilling
to make allowances for unforeseen developments. This is, I think, what
happened in this case.

APPENDIX I

A. LETTER OF TRANSMITTAL, SZILARD TO DR. ALEXANDER SACHS,
AUGUST 15, 1939

Dear Dr. Sachs:

Enclosed I am sending you a letter from Prof. Albert Einstein, which is addressed to President Roosevelt and which he sent to me with the request of forwarding it through such channels as might appear appropriate. If you see your way to bring this letter to the attention of the President, I am certain Prof. Einstein would appreciate your doing so; otherwise would you be good enough to return the letter to me?

If a man, having courage and imagination, could be found and if such a man were put—in accordance with Dr. Einstein's suggestion—in the position to act with some measure of authority in this matter, this would certainly be an important step forward. In order that you may be able to see of what assistance such a man could be in our work, allow me please to give you a short account of the past history of the case.

In January this year, when I realized that there was a remote possibility of setting up a chain reaction in a large mass of uranium, I communicated with Prof. E. P. Wigner of Princeton University and Prof. E. Teller of George Washington University, Washington, D.C., and the three of us remained in constant consultation ever since. First of all it appeared necessary to perform certain fundamental experiments for which the use of about one gram of radium was required. Since at that time we had no certainty and had to act on a remote possibility, we could hardly hope to succeed in persuading a university laboratory to take charge of these experiments, or even to acquire the radium needed. Attempts to obtain the necessary funds from other sources appeared to be equally hopeless. In these circumstances a few of us physicists formed an association, called "Association for Scientific Collaboration," collected some funds among ourselves, rented about one gram of radium, and I arranged with the Physics Department of Columbia University for their permission to carry out the proposed experiments at Columbia. These experiments led early in March to rather striking results.

At about the same time Prof. E. Fermi, also at Columbia, made experiments of his own, independently of ours, and came to identical conclusions.

A close collaboration arose out of this coincidence, and recently Dr. Fermi and I jointly performed experiments which make it appear probable that a chain reaction in uranium can be achieved in the immediate future.

The path along which we have to move is now clearly defined, but it takes some courage to embark on the journey. The experiments will be costly

since we will now have to work with tons of material rather than—as hitherto
—with kilograms. Two or possibly three different alternatives will have to be
tried; failures, set-backs and some unavoidable danger to human life will have
to be faced. We have so far made use of the Association for Scientific Collaboration to overcome the difficulty of persuading other organisations to take
financial risks, and also to overcome the general reluctance to take action on
the basis of probabilities in the absence of certainty. Now, in the face of
greater certainty, but also greater risks, it will become necessary either to
strengthen this association both morally and financially, or to find new ways
which would serve the same purpose. We have to approach as quickly as
possible public-spirited private persons and try to enlist their financial cooperation, or, failing in this, we would have to try to enlist the collaboration
of the leading firms of the electrical or chemical industry.

Other aspects of the situation have to be kept in mind. Dr. Wigner is taking the stand that it is our duty to enlist the co-operation of the Administration. A few weeks ago he came to New York in order to discuss this point
with Dr. Teller and me, and on his initiative conversations took place between Dr. Einstein and the three of us. This led to Dr. Einstein's decision to
write to the President.

I am enclosing memorandum which will give you some of the views and
opinions which were expressed in these conversations.

I wish to make it clear that, in approaching you, I am acting in the capacity
of a trustee of the Association for Scientific Collaboration, and that I have no
authority to speak in the name of the Physics Department of Columbia University, of which I am a guest.

Yours sincerely,

B. MEMORANDUM, SZILARD TO THE PRESIDENT,
AUGUST 15, 1939

Much experimentation on atomic disintegration was done during the past
five years, but up to this year the problem of liberating nuclear energy could
not be attacked with any reasonable hope for success. Early this year it became known that the element uranium can be split by neutrons. It appeared
conceivable that in this nuclear process uranium itself may emit neutrons, and
a few of us envisaged the possibility of liberating nuclear energy by means of
a chain reaction of neutrons in uranium.

Experiments were thereupon performed, which led to striking results. One
has to conclude that a nuclear chain reaction could be maintained under certain well defined conditions in a large mass of uranium. It still remains to
prove this conclusion by actually setting up such a chain reaction in a large-
scale experiment.

This new development in physics means that a new source of power is now being created. Large amounts of energy would be liberated, and large quantities of new radioactive elements would be produced in such a chain reaction.

In medical applications of radium we have to deal with quantities of grams; the new radioactive elements could be produced in the chain reaction in quantities corresponding to tons of radium equivalents. While the practical application would include the medical field, it would not be limited to it.

A radioactive element gives a continuous release of energy for a certain period of time. The amount of energy which is released per unit weight of material may be very large, and therefore such elements might be used—if available in large quantities—as fuel for driving boats or airplanes. It should be pointed out, however, that the physiological action of the radiations emitted by these new radioactive elements makes it necessary to protect those who have to stay close to a large quantity of such an element, for instance the driver of the airplane. It may therefore be necessary to carry large quantities of lead, and this necessity might impede a development along this line, or at least limit the field of application.

Large quantities of energy would be liberated in a chain reaction, which might be utilized for purposes of power production in the form of a stationary power plant.

In view of this development it may be a question of national importance to secure an adequate supply of uranium. The United States has only very poor ores of uranium in moderate quantities; there is a good ore of uranium in Canada where the total deposit is estimated to be about 3000 tons; there may be about 1500 tons of uranium in Czechoslovakia, which is now controlled by Germany; there is an unknown amount of uranium in Russia, but the most important source of uranium, consisting of an unknown but probably very large amount of good ore, is Belgian Congo.

It is suggested therefore to explore the possibility of bringing over from Belgium or Belgian Congo a large stock of pitchblend, which is the ore of both radium and uranium, and to keep this stock here for possible future use. Perhaps a large quantity of this ore might be obtained as a token reparation payment from the Belgian Government. In taking action along this line it would not be necessary officially to disclose that the uranium content of the ore is the point of interest; action might be taken on the ground that it is of value to secure a stock of the ore on account of its radium content for possible future extraction of the radium for medical purposes.

Since it is unlikely that an earnest attempt to secure a supply of uranium will be made before the possibility of a chain reaction has been visibly demonstrated, it appears necessary to do this as quickly as possible by performing a large-scale experiment. The previous experiments have prepared the ground to the extent that it is now possible clearly to define the conditions under which such a large-scale experiment would have to be carried out. Still two or three different setups may have to be tried out, or alternatively preliminary experiments have to be carried out with several tons of material if we want to decide in advance in favor of one setup or another. These experiments cannot be carried out within the limited budget which was provided for laboratory experiments in the past, and it has now become necessary either to strengthen —financially and otherwise—the organizations which concerned themselves with this work up to now, or to create some new organization for the purpose. Public-spirited private persons who are likely to be interested in supporting this enterprise should be approached without delay, or alternatively the collaboration of the chemical or the electrical industry should be sought.

The investigations were hitherto limited to chain reactions based on the action of *slow* neutrons. The neutrons emitted from the splitting uranium are fast, but they are slowed down in a mixture of uranium and a light element. Fast neutrons lose their energy in colliding with atoms of a light element in much the same way as a billiard ball loses velocity in a collision with another ball. At present it is an open question whether such a chain reaction can also be made to work with *fast* neutrons which are not slowed down.

There is reason to believe that, if fast neutrons could be used, it would be easy to construct extremely dangerous bombs. The destructive power of these bombs can only be roughly estimated, but there is no doubt that it would go far beyond all military conceptions. It appears likely that such bombs would be too heavy to be transported by airplane, but still they could be transported by boat and exploded in port with disastrous results.

Although at present it is uncertain whether a fast neutron reaction can be made to work, from now on this possibility will have to be constantly kept in mind in view of its far-reaching military consequences. Experiments have been devised for settling this important point, and it is solely a question of organization to ensure that such experiments shall be actually carried out.

Should the experiments show that a chain reaction will work with *fast* neutrons, it would then be highly advisable to arrange among scientists for withholding publications on this subject. An attempt to arrange for withholding publications on this subject has already been made early in March but was abandoned in spite of favorable response in this country and in England on account of the negative attitude of certain French laboratories. The experience gained in March would make it possible to revive this attempt whenever it should be necessary.

APPENDIX II

ENCLOSURE TO MR. ALBERT EINSTEIN'S LETTER OF
MARCH 25, 1945, TO THE PRESIDENT OF THE UNITED STATES,
BY L. SZILARD

The work on uranium has now reached a stage which will make it possible for the Army to detonate atomic bombs in the immediate future. The "demonstration" of such bombs may be expected rather soon and naturally the War Department is considering the use of such bombs in the war against Japan.

From a purely military point of view this may be a favorable development. However, many of those scientists who are in a position to make allowances for the future development of this field believe that we are at present moving along a road leading to the destruction of the strong position that the United States hitherto occupied in the world. It appears probable that it will take just a few years before this will become manifest.

Perhaps the greatest immediate danger which faces us is the probability that our "demonstration" of atomic bombs will precipitate a race in the production of these devices between the United States and Russia and that if we continue to pursue the present course, our initial advantage may be lost very quickly in such a race.

If a nation were to start now to develop atomic bombs, so to speak from scratch, it could do so without reproducing many of the expensive installations which were built by the War Department during the War. *For over a year now we have known that we could develop methods by means of which atomic bombs can be produced from the main component of uranium which is more than one hundred times as abundant than the rare component* from which we are manufacturing atomic bombs at present. We must expect that a cost of about $500 million some nations may accumulate, within six years, a quantity of atomic bombs that will correspond to ten million tons of TNT. A single bomb of this type weighing about one ton and containing less than 200 pounds of active material may be expected to destroy an area of ten square miles. Under the conditions expected to prevail six years from now, most of our major cities might be completely destroyed in one single sudden attack and their populations might perish.

In the United States, thirty million people live in cities with a population of over 250,000 and a consideration of this and other factors involved indicates that the United States will be much more vulnerable than most other countries.

Thus the Government of the United States is at present faced with the necessity of arriving at decisions which will control the course that is to be followed from here on. These decisions ought to be based not on the *present* evidence relating to atomic bombs, but rather on the situation which can be expected to confront us in this respect a few years from now. This situation can be evaluated only by men who have first-hand knowledge of the facts involved, that is, by the small group of scientists who are actively engaged in this work. This group includes a number of eminent scientists who are willing to present their views; there is, however, no mechanism through which direct contact could be maintained between them and those men who are, by virtue of their position, responsible for formulating the policy which the United States might pursue.

The points on which decisions appear to be most urgently needed are as follows:

1. Shall we aim at trying to avoid a race in the production of atomic bombs between the United States and certain other nations?

2. Can a system of controls relating to this field be devised which is sufficiently tight to be relied on by the United States and which has some chance of being accepted under otherwise favorable conditions by Russia and Great Britain?

3. Can we materially improve our chances to obtain the cooperation of Russia in setting up such a system of controls by developing in the next two years modern methods of production which would give us an overwhelming superiority in this field at the time when Russia might be approached?

4. What framework could immediately be set up within which the scientific development of such "modern" methods could vigorously be pursued both under present and postwar conditions? Should, for instance, this framework be set up under the Secretary of Commerce or under the Secretary of the Interior, or should the scientific development be under a Government-owned corporation jointly controlled by the Secretary of Commerce, the Secretary of the Interior, and the Secretary of War?

5. Should the scientific development work be based on the assumption that a race in the production of atomic bombs is unavoidable and accordingly be aimed at maximum potential of war, say in six years from now, or should the scientific development be rather aimed at putting us into a favorable position with respect to negotiations with our Allies two or three years from now?

6. Should, in the light of the decisions concerning the above points, our "demonstration" of atomic bombs and their use against Japan be delayed until a certain further stage in the political and technical development has been reached so that the United States shall be in a more favorable position in negotiations aimed at setting up a system of controls?

Other decisions, which are needed but which are perhaps less urgent, would come within the competence of the Department of the Interior.

If there were in existence a small subcommittee of the Cabinet (having as its members, the Secretary of War, either the Secretary of Commerce or the Secretary of the Interior, a representative of the State Department, and a representative of the President, acting as the secretary of the Committee), the scientists could submit to such a committee their recommendations either by appearing from time to time before the committee or through the secretary of the committee.

The latter, if so authorized, by the President, could also act as a liaison to the scientists prior to the designation of such a subcommittee. At his disposal could then be placed a memorandum which has been prepared in an attempt to analyze the consequences of the scientific and technical development which we have to anticipate. The memorandum was prepared on the basis of consultations with ten scientists from six different institutions in the United States. These and other eminent scientists who were not consulted would undoubtedly avail themselves of the opportunity of presenting their views to a man authorized by the President, assuming that such a man would have the time at his disposal which a study of this kind would require.

APPENDIX III

SZILARD TO GROUP LEADERS OF "METALLURGICAL LABORATORY,"
JULY 4, 1945

Dear ——:

Inclosed is the text of a petition which will be submitted to the President of the United States. As you will see, this petition is based on purely moral considerations.

It may very well be that the decision of the President whether or not to use atomic bombs in the war against Japan will largely be based on considerations of expediency. On the basis of expediency, many arguments could be put forward both for and against our use of atomic bombs against Japan. Such arguments could be considered only within the framework of a thorough analysis of the situation which will face the United States after this war and it was felt that no useful purpose would be served by considering arguments of expediency in a short petition.

However small the chance might be that our petition may influence the course of events, I personally feel that it would be a matter of importance if a large number of scientists who have worked in this field went clearly and unmistakably on record as to their opposition on moral grounds to the use of these bombs in the present phase of the war.

Many of us are inclined to say that individual Germans share the guilt for the acts which Germany committed during this war because they did not raise their voices in protest against those acts. Their defense that their protest would have been of no avail hardly seems acceptable even though these Germans could not have protested without running risks to life and liberty. We are in a position to raise our voices without incurring any such risks even though we might incur the displeasure of some of those who are at present in charge of controlling the work on "atomic power."

The fact that the people of the United States are unaware of the choice which faces us increases our responsibility in this matter since those who have worked on "atomic power" represent a sample of the population and they alone are in a position to form an opinion and declare their stand.

Anyone who might wish to go on record by signing the petition ought to have an opportunity to do so and, therefore, it would be appreciated if you could give every member of your group an opportunity for signing.

APPENDIX IV

A PETITION TO THE PRESIDENT OF THE UNITED STATES, JULY 3, 1945

Discoveries of which the people of the United States are not aware may affect the welfare of this nation in the near future. The liberation of atomic power which has been achieved places atomic bombs in the hands of the Army. It places in your hands, as Commander-in-Chief, the fateful decision whether or not to sanction the use of such bombs in the present phase of the war against Japan.

We, the undersigned scientists, have been working in the field of atomic power for a number of years. Until recently we have had to reckon with the possibility that the United States might be attacked by atomic bombs during this war and that her only defense might lie in a counterattack by the same means. Today with this danger averted we feel impelled to say what follows:

The war has to be brought speedily to a successful conclusion and the destruction of Japanese cities by means of atomic bombs may very well be an effective method of warfare. We feel, however, that such an attack on Japan could not be justified in the present circumstances. We believe that the United States ought not to resort to the use of atomic bombs in the present phase of the war, at least not unless the terms which will be imposed upon Japan after the war are publicly announced and subsequently Japan is given an opportunity to surrender.

If such public announcement gave assurance to the Japanese that they could look forward to a life devoted to peaceful pursuits in their homeland and if Japan still refused to surrender, our nation would then be faced with a situation which might require a re-examination of her position with respect to the use of atomic bombs in the war.

Atomic bombs are primarily a means for the ruthless annihilation of cities. Once they were introduced as an instrument of war it would be difficult to resist for long the temptation of putting them to such use.

The last few years show a marked tendency toward increasing ruthlessness. At present our Air Forces, striking at the Japanese cities, are using the same methods of warfare which were condemned by American public opinion only a few years ago when applied by the Germans to the cities of England. Our use of atomic bombs in this war would carry the world a long way further on this path of ruthlessness.

Atomic power will provide the nations with new means of destruction. The atomic bombs at our disposal represent only the first step in this direction and there is almost no limit to the destructive power which will become available in the course of this development. Thus a nation which sets the precedent of using these newly liberated forces of nature for purposes of destruction may have to bear the responsibility of opening the door to an era of devastation on an unimaginable scale.

In view of the foregoing, we, the undersigned, respectfully petition that you exercise your power as Commander-in-Chief to rule that the United States shall not, in the present phase of the war, resort to the use of atomic bombs.

ÉMIGRÉ PHYSICISTS AND THE
BIOLOGICAL REVOLUTION

by DONALD FLEMING

ONE of the most remarkable by-products of the European diaspora of the 1930's was the profound stimulus given by refugee physicists to the revolution in biology symbolized by the
Watson-Crick model of DNA unveiled in 1953. As Watson has made
clear in *The Double Helix*, the discovery of this model was the fruit of a
highly calculated assault on what he and Crick flatly called in advance
"the secret of life."[1] In some ways, the most surprising aspect of the entire enterprise was the brazen candor with which Crick and Watson
equated their work with this virtually metaphysical quest, of a kind
that was already suspect in 1900 and thought to have been quietly
interred with Ernst Haeckel (d. 1919) and Jacques Loeb (d. 1924).[2]
Even when biologists were on to something really big, they were no
longer supposed to talk about solving the ultimate cosmic riddles. The
double question becomes why Crick and Watson blithely conceived of
their research in these provocatively unfashionable terms and what fed
their expectations of victory.

In science, one of the best reasons for expecting victory is to see what
it would consist in. By this standard, incomparably the most important
single development in paving the way for Crick and Watson was a piece
of research published by the Americans O. T. Avery, Colin MacLeod,
and Maclyn McCarty in 1944.[3] In retrospect, this is often thought of as
the first conclusive demonstration that DNA (deoxyribonucleic acid) is

1. James D. Watson, *The Double Helix* (New York, 1968), pp. 35, 197.
2. Donald Fleming, "Introduction" to Jacques Loeb, *The Mechanistic Conception of
Life*, 1st ed. 1912 (Cambridge, Mass., 1964), pp. vii–xli.
3. "Studies on the Chemical Nature of the Substance Inducing Transformation of
Pneumococcal Types. Induction of Transformation by a Desoxyribonucleic Acid Fraction Isolated from *Pneumococcus* Type III," *Journal of Experimental Medicine*, 79 (1944),
137–158. Now photographically reproduced in J. Herbert Taylor, ed., *Selected Papers on
Molecular Genetics* (New York, 1965), pp. 157–178.

the carrier of heredity. Avery's private correspondence shows that this was his own interpretation of the research, and discreet hints to this effect appear in the published paper.[4] Yet the authors hedged their bet by saying that it was "of course" possible that "the biological activity of the substance described is not an inherent property of the nucleic acid but is due to minute amounts of some other substance adsorbed to it or so intimately associated with it as to escape detection." Even if these qualifications were discounted, all the paper actually demonstrated was that DNA was the carrier of a particular hereditary trait in a single bacterium. As one of Avery's disciples later said, it was very hard to tell from such limited evidence what kind of "biological generalization" could be "responsibly" drawn.[5] "Were traits transferable in certain bacteria only, all bacteria, or potentially all organisms; most urgently, were other than antigenic traits transmissible, and if so, would DNA be the active agent for all?" Apart from the sheer difficulty of knowing how far to extrapolate from their evidence, Avery and his collaborators were almost neurotically reluctant to claim that DNA was genes and genes were simply DNA.

Here Avery was undoubtedly influenced by the satisfaction bordering on pride that was taken by many geneticists in the "formalism" of genetical science as it had developed up to 1940—the rigor with which the gene concept could be manipulated to account for hereditary traits without knowing or caring what genes were made of. They were of course known to be aligned upon the chromosomes. The doughty proponent of "the mechanistic conception of life," Jacques Loeb, had called as early as 1911 for a determination of "the chemical substances in the chromosomes which are responsible for the hereditary transmission of a quality" and "the mechanism by which these substances give rise to the hereditary characters."[6] But Loeb had the reputation of a doctrinaire mechanist, prematurely heralding the simplistic reduction of all biological phenomena to physico-chemical terms. In point of

4. O. T. Avery to Roy Avery, May 1943; reproduced in Rollin D. Hotchkiss, "Gene, Transforming Principle, and DNA," in John Cairns, Gunther S. Stent, James D. Watson, eds., *Phage and the Origins of Molecular Biology* (Cold Spring Harbor, N.Y., 1966), pp. 185–187.
5. Hotchkiss, "Gene, Transforming Principle, and DNA," p. 194.
6. *Mechanistic Conception*, p. 23.

fact, the great German biochemist Albrecht Kossel had already won a Nobel Prize in 1910 for fundamental research upon the nucleic acids (of which DNA is one) and had actually identified the four crucial components, cytosine, thymine, adenine, and guanine, now known to be the alphabet of genetics.[7] But Kossel in his study of nucleic acids was not addressing himself to the problems of heredity, let alone genetics, which was just getting started on both sides of the Atlantic. On the other hand, the science of genes that emerged between 1910 and 1940 had virtually no affiliations with biochemistry. Even when a union between the two began to be consummated from 1935 forward by George W. Beadle, Boris Ephrussi, and Edward L. Tatum, they were not dealing with the biochemistry of the genes themselves but with the metabolic sequences controlled by genes.[8] In any event, in the early 1940's Beadle and Tatum were still the Young Turks of genetics. Many geneticists rightly felt that one of the most secure intellectual structures in modern science had been reared upon the classical gene concept with its total lack of biochemical content. No wonder Avery and his associates hesitated to say bluntly that genes were nothing but DNA—that crude materialism had broken in upon the beautiful abstractions of classical genetics.

The upshot was that the retrospectively famous article of 1944 was muffled and circumspect. The authors expressly said that something more than DNA might *conceivably* be involved; they framed no hypotheses about other organisms or other hereditary traits; and they gingerly skirted the biochemistry of genes. In short, they did not make the loud emphatic claims or revolutionary clarifications appropriate to a major turning-point in biology. The results were predictable. Skeptics eagerly seized upon the *pro forma* acknowledgment that DNA might not be the actual agent of transformation. The Nobel Prize committee, though definitely alerted to something important, hung fire to see how it would all turn out and then rewarded the second wave of disclosures about DNA, by Watson, Crick, and Wilkins.[9]

7. Nobel Foundation, *Nobel Lectures: Physiology or Medicine 1901–1921* (Amsterdam, 1967), pp. 387–407.

8. George W. Beadle, "Genes and Chemical Reactions in Neurospora," in Nobel Foundation, *Nobel Lectures: Physiology or Medicine 1942–1962* (Amsterdam, 1964), pp. 587–599.

9. Göran Liljestrand in H. Schück *et al.*, *Nobel: The Man and His Prizes*, 2d ed. (Amsterdam, 1962), pp. 280–281.

In contrast to the enormous circumspection of Avery and his colleagues in 1944, Watson and Crick in 1953 drew supremely confident inferences about the bearing of their own work on genetics. They did not argue the point, they simply took it for granted. Further evidence of the role of DNA in heredity had indeed appeared—most notably, the demonstration by A. D. Hershey and Martha Chase in 1952 that a bacteriophage (*i.e.*, a virus attacking bacteria) could be regarded as a kind of syringe for injecting its own DNA into a host bacterium and that only the DNA was implicated in the subsequent proliferation of the phage in the host cell.[10] Yet the fact is that Watson and Crick were prepared to put the most sweeping imaginable construction upon Avery's work without waiting for any confirmation or elaboration whatever. Long before Hershey and Chase's evidence had come to hand, Watson and Crick had predicated their collaboration upon the all-sufficiency of DNA for explaining genetics.[11] They were absolutely certain that the structure of DNA was the structure of genes and the secret of heredity—in fact, the secret of life. What is more, they thought that they and a handful of rivals were in striking distance of the golden fleece. How had they come to form these superbly arrogant ambitions, unbuttressed by any truly compelling evidence and offering total defiance to contemporary standards of good taste in biological discourse? Watson and Crick were undoubtedly slashing and imperious, conquistadors of science by native temperament. But what is equally important, they had come under the influence of a number of men who had begun to entertain in the 1940's some of the same extravagant hopes and vaulting ambitions as Jacques Loeb a generation before. They too were candidly drawing a bead on the secret of life.

10. "Independent Functions of Viral Protein and Nucleic Acid in Growth of Bacteriophage," *Journal of General Physiology*, 36 (1952), 39–56; now reproduced in Taylor, ed., *Selected Papers*, pp. 212–229.

11. Watson, *Double Helix*, pp. 118–119.

II

THE men who supplied this indispensable fostering environment for Watson and Crick were four: Erwin Schrödinger (1887–1961), Leo Szilard (1898–1964), Max Delbrück (b. 1906), Salvador Luria (b. 1912)—an Austrian, a Hungarian Jew, a German, an Italian. They were all men who had been uprooted by fascism and spun out to the rim of the world that they had previously inhabited—Schrödinger to Dublin, Szilard, Delbrück, and Luria to the United States. Three of them were physicists, and quantum mechanics men at that—Schrödinger of course was one of the founders of quantum mechanics. Luria, the odd man out, was a biologist but highly congenial to physicists, with a remarkable aptitude for getting the hang of other people's science. By force of numbers and certain messianic qualities, the physicists in the group played the key role in the process by which unfashionable ambitions were stirred up again.

In a way, it was simply the human process so often enacted in those days of beginning a new life. Even among those who were able to escape, many intellectuals were broken by the experience. But some people, including these four men, experienced an intoxicating liberation from their former selves. By giving up the effort to hold stingily on to what they had been in a world that had vanished, and making themselves deliberately vulnerable to new experience, they were saved out of the wreckage of Europe. For the three physicists, the passage to a new life was undoubtedly facilitated by the sense that one of the great creative phases in the history of physics itself had come to an end at roughly the same moment as the old European world. And it was precisely the phase that they themselves had been active in, the creation of quantum mechanics. Max Delbrück would later express the view that had already become orthodox by 1930, that quantum mechanics was "the final word" on "the behavior of atoms"—one of the rarely perfect and complete intellectual constructions that had ever been achieved.[1] Paradoxi-

---

1. "A Physicist Looks at Biology," Connecticut Academy of Arts and Sciences, *Transactions*, 38 (December, 1949), pp. 173–190; now reproduced in John Cairns, Gunther S. Stent, James D. Watson, eds., *Phage and the Origins of Molecular Biology* (Cold Spring Harbor, N.Y., 1966), pp. 9–22 (citation, p. 19).

cally, Erwin Schrödinger who got a Nobel Prize for erecting it, always remained (with Albert Einstein) one of the very few skeptics about the finality of quantum mechanics as an expression of ultimate limitations upon the intelligibility of nature.[2] But he had no practical suggestions for transcending the quantum mechanical formulations and did not deny that quantum mechanics *per se* had been brought to a high degree of perfection by 1930. If, now, he and others who had been busy at this task turned to new interests, it would not be a gesture of despair. They had completed their mission.

For Leo Szilard, another kind of epoch in the history of physics was also drawing to a close with his own active cooperation—the epoch when nuclear physics had been the most rarefied form of intellectual exercise for its own sake. Szilard was one of the brilliant galaxy of Budapest Jews, including Eugene Wigner, Edward Teller, and John von Neumann, who erupted into mathematics and physics after 1920.[3] Szilard's own explanation for this Budapest syndrome was that "physics was not taught in Hungary."[4] By the end of the twenties Szilard had made a fundamental contribution to what later became known as information theory.[5] He had also found a spiritual mentor in H. G. Wells, whom he visited in London to obtain translation rights for Central Europe. Szilard was particularly attracted by Wells's prediction of an atomic bomb and his program for an "open conspiracy" to bring about a world state run on scientific lines.[6] The conspirators would be scientists and other professional people with an assured position for gradually subverting the status quo from within. For generations to come, they would probably meet with great resistance from governments and public opinion alike; but Wells did envision that the tempo of subversion might be enormously speeded up if the politicians and bureaucrats were obliged to entrust the conspirators with strategic responsibilities in wartime.

2. Cf. William T. Scott, *Erwin Schrödinger: An Introduction to His Writings* (Amherst, Mass., 1967), especially chaps. IV, V.

3. Cf. Laura Fermi, "The Mystery of Hungarian Talent," *Illustrious Immigrants: The Intellectual Migration from Europe, 1930–1941* (Chicago, 1968), pp. 53–59.

4. Edward Shils, "Leo Szilard," *Encounter*, 23, no. 6 (December, 1964), 38.

5. W. Ehrenberg, "Maxwell's Demon," *Scientific American*, 217, no. 5 (November, 1967), 103–110.

6. Shils, "Leo Szilard." Cf. W. Warren Wagar, *H. G. Wells and the World State* (New Haven, 1961), chap. IV, "The Open Conspiracy," pp. 164–205.

Szilard's own not-particularly-open conspiracy began in 1932 when he decided that Hitler was coming to power and cleared out for Vienna.[7] There he made the contact with Sir William Beveridge that led to the initial arrangements for receiving refugee scientists and scholars in England. On Beveridge's suggestion, Szilard followed him to London to nag him about this. In 1934 Szilard conceived the idea of a nuclear chain reaction producing a violent explosion and actually took out a patent on the process (partly secret and assigned to the British government). But he had not hit upon the right element for sustaining a reaction and by 1939 had put the problem aside. In January of that year he and everybody else learned of the discovery of nuclear fission in uranium. Szilard, who had settled in New York in 1937, now undertook a three-pronged campaign—to get English, French, and American scientists to clamp a tight lid of security on their researches in this field; to demonstrate that with uranium a chain reaction would really work; and above all to impress upon the American government the importance of getting an atomic bomb before Hitler. In this cause, he drafted and induced Albert Einstein to sign the famous letter of August 1939 warning Franklin D. Roosevelt of the possibility of such a bomb—the letter that triggered the (initially very modest) efforts of the United States in that direction.[8] Szilard himself eventually became a member of the team at the University of Chicago that built the atomic pile, the device for producing a controlled chain reaction that he had envisioned from the beginning.

In January 1944, Szilard was still urging the wartime chief of research Vannevar Bush to accelerate the work on the bomb to be sure it was used before the war was over.[9] Otherwise he feared that the peoples of the world would not be scared enough to make the necessary sacrifices of sovereignty to achieve international control. But by June of 1945, with Hitler already beaten, Szilard was beside himself at the thought of the evil genie that he had unloosed, for defensive purposes against Hitler, but now destined for offensive purposes against Japan. One of his

7. Shils, "Leo Szilard."
8. Donald Fleming, ed., "Albert Einstein, Letter to Franklin D. Roosevelt, 1939," in Daniel J. Boorstin, ed., *An American Primer* (Chicago, 1966), II, 857–862.
9. Shils, "Leo Szilard," p. 40.

colleagues has left a vivid account of a moment of truth in the streets of Chicago in that apocalyptic June.

It was unbearably hot in Chicago at that time. As I walked through the streets of the city, I was overcome by a vision of crashing skyscrapers under a flaming sky.

Szilard now joined in the increasingly frantic efforts to persuade the President and the secretary of war to do everything they could to avoid dropping atomic bombs on the Japanese. Hiroshima and Nagasaki, when they came, left Szilard with a legacy of guilt. He said of his compatriot Teller when the latter was agitating for hydrogen bombs, "Now Teller will know what it is to feel guilty."[10] But a more profound expression of Szilard's desperate craving to balance his accounts with humanity lay in prosecuting his open conspiracy to bring the menace of nuclear weapons under control by founding the Pugwash conferences and applying his pyrotechnical ingenuity to incessantly amended schemes for nuclear disarmament and world peace.[11]

Another aspect of Szilard's desire to redress the balance of his own impact upon the world was his decision in 1945 to switch from physics to biology. He had already thought of doing this when he moved to London in 1933, but the intriguing idea of a chain reaction had swung him back again to physics.[12] Yet it would be obtuse to regard his decision of 1945 as merely that of 1933 postdated. He was thirty-five in 1933; he was forty-seven, virtually antique by scientific standards, when he actually made the switch. In 1933 he was little known. In 1945 he was on his way to being legendarily famous—The Father of the Bomb —as the veil of secrecy about the Manhattan Project began to lift. He had to be a valiant and deeply concerned man to begin all over again in a new field. One dimension of his concern was the desire to be part of some great scientific breakthrough that was unmistakably life-enhancing rather than destructive. Szilard was in a unique position with respect to the bomb. Yet when younger and less important physicists also switched over to biology at the end of the war—Francis Crick and

10. *Ibid.*, p. 41.

11. J. Rotblat, *Pugwash—the First Ten Years* (London, 1967); Shils, "Leo Szilard," pp. 35–37.

12. Untitled interview with Szilard in *International Science and Technology*, 5 (May, 1962), 34.

Maurice Wilkins among them; Wilkins had worked on the Manhattan Project—they too were operating against a backdrop of widespread anxiety about the impact of physical science upon human life.

Important as this factor must have been in a rather covert way, some of the physicists who made the switch were at least as powerfully motivated by a feeling that physics was not as much fun as it used to be. The gigantic apparatus, gigantically funded and staffed, that had begun to come in with the cyclotron and then with a rush under the impetus of crash programs during the war, had taken over. Szilard, who had triggered the biggest crash program of all, waxed sarcastic on the consequences:

The interesting portions of physics have moved to higher energies where you have to have a Committee and Planning and getting the Machine and getting the Money for the Machine and the Committee deciding which Experiment should be done first.[13]

It was not, he said, "the kind of physics I enjoy." Three people he could work with, even five, but no more. As a much younger man put it, he was drawn to biology "because in physics nobody could test his own theories any more," and he thought it was "dull" to test other people's theories and exasperating to have to talk them into testing yours.[14] The inference is clear that the physicists who went over to biology were more likely to be loners or small-team men who lamented the passing of do-it-yourself physics.

III

THEY did not cease to be physicists rather than biologists in their general attitude toward nature. The distinction is classically illustrated in the response to Avery's research on DNA. He and his colleagues were biologists by first intention and accordingly steeped in reverence for the infinite particularity of living things, the joyful discrimination of types that generated the study of natural history in the first place. It was professionally alien to them to extrapolate incisively

13. *Ibid.*
14. Cyrus Levinthal to N. Visconti, c. 1953. Visconti, "Mating Theory," in Cairns *et al.*, eds., *Phage*, p. 149.

from the role of DNA in a single bacterium to the role of DNA in general. They might have their hunches, and would certainly yield to the accumulating evidence, but they would not anticipate it by a breathtaking generalization. Physicists have exactly the opposite instinct: to reduce rather than cherish the particularity of phenomena, and arrange them under a few principles of the broadest possible scope. The great emotional as well as intellectual satisfaction in physics is to achieve a starker simplicity than ever before. For a physicist, there are *fewer* things in heaven and earth than are dreamt of in a biologist's philosophy. The physicists-turned-biologists retained this highly receptive attitude toward the grand simplifications in nature. They instantly cleared the hurdle that Avery shied at, and found it easy and natural to make the most resounding assumptions about DNA in heredity.

Leo Szilard at any rate was well aware that what he had brought to biology was "not any skills acquired in physics, but rather an attitude: the conviction which few biologists had at the time, that mysteries can be solved."[1]

If secrets exist, they must be explainable. You see, this is something which modern biologists [*i.e.*, post-1940] brought into biology, something which the classical biologists did not have. They often were astonished, but they never felt it was their duty to explain. They lacked the faith that things are explainable—and it is this faith . . . which leads to major advances in biology. An example is the Watson-Crick model for DNA, a model which immediately explains how the DNA can duplicate. Everyone knew that DNA can duplicate, but nobody asked how it does.

"Explain" is one of the slipperiest words in the entire philosophy of science, and this has to be regarded as an orphic utterance requiring interpretation. Perhaps the best clue to what Szilard was getting at was his curious reference to classical biologists as "astonished" but declining to go beyond astonishment. This would imply a certain reverential pleasure on their part in contemplating the mystery of living things, and almost preferring the mysterious to remain mysterious. Szilard might well have had in mind the persistent undercurrent of anxiety among biologists about seeing their subject-matter "reduced" to mere physics and chemistry—wrested from their own distinctive control. More specifically, one might surmise from the context that he was re-

1. Untitled interview with Szilard in *International Science and Technology*, 5 (May, 1962), 36.

ferring to the characteristic formalism of classical genetics, which was certainly a kind of explanation, and a powerful kind at that, but negatively defined by an almost total lack of interest in the physico-chemical explanation of genes. To Szilard any such attitude of settling for less than might be known was not only misguided but incomprehensible—a failure of scientific nerve at the point where science began to be really interesting, on the trail of the ultimate secrets. Szilard was palpably mistaken when he said that conventional biologists were not interested in explanations. He was perfectly correct in sensing that they were seldom driven by the same passion as himself for ultimate explanations. It was this alien impulse that he and other physicists brought to the new "molecular" biology—to strike for the ultimate secrets of life, and nothing less.

To aim at the ultimate explanations in biology was one thing. To expect to find them in the immediate future was another. Yet this too was part of the physicists' contribution to the new biology. They kept the faith cherished by Szilard that "mysteries can be solved," and not in the vague sense that something would eventually turn up but that the most fundamental secrets would promptly yield to concerted pressure. After all, the history of physics between the wars had been marked by finite assaults upon colossally important problems, triumphantly executed before the enthusiasm of the participants could flag. The birth and consolidation of quantum mechanics had been substantially contained within the bounds of the 1920's. The thirties in turn had seen the literally explosive growth of nuclear physics to the point where it could utterly transform the world of practical men. Such examples would have been powerful enough simply as models for a more urgently prosecuted science of biology; but over and above this, Erwin Schrödinger, one of the heroes of the quantum mechanical revolution, and Leo Szilard, the man who launched the Bomb, actually turned to biological questions themselves. Not only the example but two of legendary exemplars had passed over from physics to biology. Men with the habit of speedy success in great scientific undertakings had set their seal of approval upon the immediate prospects of biology. It became correspondingly easier to believe that biology would be the next science to be revolutionized. Biology would be brought abreast of physics.

It was not simply that the physicists believed in themselves. They heartily disbelieved in the biologists. They thought that nobody had even been trying to make biology less trivial. One great advantage that they conceived of themselves as possessing was not only that they had been physicists but that they had not been biologists. Evidence of their contempt for conventional biologists is everywhere—in Szilard's kindly but devastating remarks; in Maurice Wilkins' lamenting to J. D. Watson that most biochemists "weren't like the high-powered types he had worked with on the bomb project"; and above all in the attitudes propagated by the quantum mechanics man turned virologist Max Delbrück.[2] One of his disciples reports that Delbrück consistently "deprecated" biochemistry and influenced some of them to avoid it.[3] When he sent a young colleague to visit laboratories that were working on animal viruses, he got the congenial verdict that this had been a "sad and discouraging" experience revealing "the lack of a proper quantitative approach" and the generally "unconvincing" character of "the approaches, methods and goals of animal virology" as conventionally and even mindlessly practiced.[4] Delbrück himself was prepared to say in print that biology as he had found it was a "depressing" subject to a physicist "because, insofar as physical explanations of seemingly physical phenomena go, like excitation, or chromosome movements, or replication, the analysis seems to have stalled around in a semidescriptive manner without noticeably progressing towards a radical physical explanation."[5]

Physicists, clearly, did not believe in stalling around. They had come into biology to put a stop to these ineffectual motions leading nowhere; and they certainly had a record of glittering successes to lend credibility

2. James D. Watson, *The Double Helix* (New York, 1968), p. 72. For Delbrück, see below, fn. 5.

3. Seymour Benzer, "Adventures in the rII Region," in John Cairns, Gunther S. Stent, James D. Watson, eds., *Phage and the Origins of Molecular Biology* (Cold Spring Harbor, N.Y., 1966), p. 158. Cf. N. Visconti, "Mating Theory," in Cairns *et al.*, eds., *Phage*, p. 148.

4. Renato Dulbecco, "The Plaque Technique and the Development of Quantitative Animal Virology," in Cairns *et al.*, eds., *Phage*, p. 288.

5. "A Physicist Looks at Biology," Connecticut Academy of Arts and Sciences, *Transactions*, 38 (December, 1949), now reproduced in Cairns *et al.*, eds., *Phage*, p. 22.

to their new ambitions. And yet—when Schrödinger, Szilard, and Delbrück turned to biological issues in the course of the 1940's they could not have failed to recognize, for all of their superb assurance, that they were embarking upon a bafflingly difficult conversion. For the number of scientists who had ever succeeded in jumping their traces in this fashion was almost vanishingly small. There were of course actual professions of biochemistry and biophysics, though Max Delbrück thought they had been infected by the mediocrity of biology itself; but in any event these were populated by people trained from an early age to straddle the line. The difficulty was to have become a mature scholar of some repute squarely in the middle of traditional physics or chemistry and *then* to pass over the great divide and achieve the same distinction in biology. Biology might (or might not) be a poor thing, but in 1940 virtually the only persuasive examples of negotiating the transition were Helmholtz and Pasteur. They had been a long time ago and very great geniuses into the bargain. Only Schrödinger would have been entitled to think of himself as belonging to the same class of intellects. The physicists' gamble ought to pay off, they evidently believed on balance that it would; but it remained a gamble, and a surprisingly big one.

IV

THE greatest single problem confronting the physicist-turned-biologist was how to estimate his advantages. Should he confine himself to the boldness of attack, the feeling for fundamental issues, the faith in the solubility of problems, that Szilard had spoken of, and for the rest, begin again? Or should he frankly embrace the reductionist position, expounded by Jacques Loeb, that true biology was nothing more than physics or chemistry anyhow, and a physicist was merely claiming his own? Did he already know more that was relevant to biology than the biologists, or did he merely know how to begin?

For physicists of the period between the wars, these issues had become inextricably involved with the famous "Copenhagen interpretation" of quantum mechanics propagated by Niels Bohr from 1927 forward—the doctrine epitomized by the magical word "complementarity."[1] Bohr's object was to clarify the limitations upon the description of nature that followed from the discovery by Max Planck in 1900 of the quantum of action. Bohr had particularly in mind the necessity for regarding light as comprised of waves in some contexts but of particles in others, with no possibility of eliminating either conception from a comprehensive account of the phenomena. But he also pointed to Werner Heisenberg's enunciation of the indeterminacy (or uncertainty) principle, that owing to the uncontrollable quantum interaction between the instrument of observation and its intended object, one could never simultaneously specify with any rigor both the position and the velocity of an electron (or other particle). The experimental setup for determining one would interfere destructively with the specification of the other. In Bohr's view, these mutually exclusive yet equally legitimate, indeed indispensable, options obliged physicists "to adopt a new mode of description designated as *complementary* in the sense that any given application of classical concepts precludes the simultaneous use of other classical concepts which in a different connection are equally necessary for the elucidation of the phenomena."[2] The basic idea was that of joyfully renouncing the effort to encompass nature in any single perspective, while retaining the physicist's commitment to the deepest possible insights. The object now became to discover the most fundamental, because mutually exclusive, alternatives for describing nature and then to integrate these within the paradox that each was required to eke out the deficiencies of the other. In these more general terms, Bohr came increasingly to think of complementarity as a universal principle for clarifying thought. He applied it, glancingly but by no means trivially, to psychology, gave an entire address on its implications for anthropology, and repeatedly dwelt from the very beginning upon its significance for biology.[3]

1. Niels Bohr, "The Quantum Postulate and the Recent Development of Atomic Theory," Como, 1927; in Bohr, *Atomic Theory and the Description of Nature* (Cambridge, Eng., 1934), pp. 52–91. Cf. Bohr, "Introductory Essay," 1929, *Ibid.*, pp. 9–15. For a general account of complementarity, cf. Max Jammer, *The Conceptual Development of Quantum Mechanics* (New York, 1966), chap. VII, "The Copenhagen Interpretation," pp. 323–361 (differentiation of concept in Bohr from that in Wolfgang Pauli, p. 355).

2. "Introductory Essay"; Bohr, *Atomic Theory*, p. 10.

3. Psychology: "The Quantum of Action and the Description of Nature," June, 1929;

The theme was congenial, for Bohr's beloved father had been a well-known professor of physiology.[4] Christian Bohr was basically anti-reductionist in orientation—no vitalist but definitely unsympathetic to doctrinaire mechanism in the vein of Jacques Loeb. This was essentially the position that Niels Bohr assumed in endeavoring to apply complementarity to biology. He first broached the topic in 1929 and then returned to it in a major address on "Light and Life" of 1932. He did not deny, he said in 1929, that biology was a "fruitful" field for the application of physics and chemistry.[5] "Just as we do not need to distinguish, in principle, between the current in a water pipe and the flow of blood in the vessels, no more should we expect, beforehand, any profound fundamental difference between the propagation of sense impressions in the nerves and the conduction of electricity in a metal wire." Yet he went on to say that "the more profound biological problems" concerning "the freedom and power of adaptation of the organism in its reaction to external stimuli" might well enforce a complementary approach. By 1932 he had sharpened his point by arguing that there was a basic complementarity between the analysis of atomic phenomena in organisms and the study of the organism as a living entity.

Thus, we should doubtless kill an animal if we tried to carry the investigation of its organs so far that we could tell the part played by the single atoms in vital functions. In every experiment on living organisms there must remain some uncertainty as regards the physical conditions to which they are subjected, and the idea suggests itself that the minimal freedom we must allow the organism will be just large enough to permit it, so to say, to hide its ultimate secrets from us. On this view, the very existence of life must in biology be considered as an elementary fact, just as in atomic physics the existence of the quantum of action has to be taken as a basic fact that cannot be derived

---

in Bohr, *Atomic Theory*, pp. 92–101. Anthropology: "Natural Philosophy and Human Cultures," August, 1938, printed in *Nature*, 143 (1939), 268, now reprinted in Bohr, *Atomic Physics and Human Knowledge* (New York, 1958), pp. 23–31. Biology: "The Atomic Theory and the Fundamental Principles underlying the Description of Nature," 1929, in Bohr, *Atomic Theory*, pp. 117–119. Cf. "Biology and Atomic Physics," Bologna, 1937; in Bohr, *Atomic Physics*, pp. 13–22.

4. Christian Bohr: David Jens Adler, "Childhood and Youth," and Léon Rosenfeld, "Niels Bohr in the Thirties," in Stefan Rozental, ed., *Niels Bohr: His Life and Work as Seen by His Friends and Colleagues*, 1st ed. Copenhagen, 1964 (English ed., Amsterdam, 1967), pp. 11–14 and 132. Long quotation from Christian Bohr: Niels Bohr, "Physical Science and the Problem of Life," Copenhagen, 1949, completed 1957, in Bohr, *Atomic Physics*, pp. 95–96.

5. "Atomic Theory and Fundamental Principles," *Atomic Theory*, p. 118.

from ordinary mechanical physics. Indeed, the essential non-analyzability of atomic stability in mechanical terms presents a close analogy to the impossibility of a physical or chemical explanation of the peculiar functions characteristic of life.[6]

The seductions of complementarity had brought at least one physicist to the point of forswearing the pursuit of "ultimate secrets" in biology, though only in the same sense that he had stopped looking for unambiguously total revelations in physics. Yet Bohr is avowing an ultimate quest of his own, for the discovery and elucidation of the complementarity relationship that would be most deeply revealing for biology— the ultimate paradox by which different themes of investigation could be securely allocated between radically alternative but equally essential methods of observation. For he made clear in the same address that he was not retreating from his previous conviction that physics and chemistry could be fruitfully brought to bear upon certain biological issues. He did, however, insist that other issues could only be studied within the constraints imposed by allowing the living organism to remain intact. In one sense, the task became to maximize the yield of fundamental insights into living things by ensuring that alternative strategies were pressed as far, and only as far, as they legitimately could be for the end in view. But the secret of this was to get the basic complementarity relationship exactly right.

In all this, there was no suggestion that the complementarity appropriate to biology would bear any substantive resemblance to that in quantum physics, or that biologists would have to know quantum mechanics. Bohr was invoking an analogy to the situation in physics, and nothing more. As he portrayed the matter, the sole advantage that a quantum physicist might bring to the study of biology would lie in a greater alertness to complementary relationships in general. But to define the content of any relevant complementarities would require a humble immersion in the actual materials of biology and a respectful recognition of what was distinctive about them. Anyone who supposed that he had merely embarked upon another branch of physics or chemistry would be missing the point entirely, and paradoxically disabling himself from the application of the complementarity principle that

6. "Light and Life," Copenhagen, August, 1932, published in *Nature*, 131 (1933), 421, reprinted in Bohr, *Atomic Physics*, p. 9.

constituted his only advantage. The anti-reductionist implications of the entire argument are unmistakable. In fact, the only kind of ultimate revelation that Bohr authorized a biologist to hope for was precisely the discovery of a systematic prohibition upon reducing the whole of biology to physics.

V

NO one could have predicted that a promising young quantum physicist, instead of being daunted by this prospect, would be galvanized into becoming a biologist. Max Delbrück, then twenty-six and a visiting member of Bohr's own institute in Copenhagen, had been out of town but returned just in time to hurry from the railroad station to hear Bohr deliver his "Light and Life" address of 1932.[1] The summons that Delbrück then heard for the first time, to discover a complementarity situation in biology, became his "prime motive" in embarking upon a new career.[2] But this factor was undoubtedly reenforced by the conviction, embodied in Bohr's original complementarity principle, that quantum mechanics had supplied the "final word" on the behavior of atoms; and by the impending breakup of the European world that sent Delbrück scurrying to the United States in 1937. Though the contemporary impact upon Delbrück of Bohr's "Light and Life" address is well authenticated, the best source for Delbrück's mature attitudes is his revealingly entitled paper "A Physicist Looks at Biology," published in 1949—halfway between Avery's breakthrough and the Watson-Crick model, at a time when Delbrück was already a well-known biologist but evidently still thought of himself as on permanent loan from physics.

Delbrück, like Bohr himself, repudiated the charge of being a vitalist and emphasized that physics and chemistry had a "firm hold" upon

1. Léon Rosenfeld, "Niels Bohr in the Thirties," in Stefan Rozental, ed., *Niels Bohr: His Life and Work as Seen by His Friends and Colleagues*, 1st ed. Copenhagen, 1964 (English ed., Amsterdam, 1967), p. 134.
2. Delbrück, "A Physicist Looks at Biology," Connecticut Academy of Arts and Sciences, *Transactions*, 38 (December, 1949), now reproduced in John Cairns, Gunther S. Stent, James D. Watson, eds., *Phage and the Origins of Molecular Biology* (Cold Spring Harbor, N.Y., 1966), p. 22.

biology. Animate and inanimate objects were made of the same elements and both were subject to the conservation of energy. But Delbrück reserved his real scorn for the reductionists, whom he defied by using the kind of language that they despised, about "the meanest living cell" as "a magic puzzle box" outstripping all the chemical laboratories of man.[3] Where Bohr had dwelt upon the intact living organism as an irreducible unit in biology, Delbrück tended to scale the argument down to the individual living cell. The control of heredity by genes aligned upon the chromosomes, he said, merely underscored the importance of the fact that genes had never been known to reproduce except in the "intact functional cell."[4] To make his target in these animadversions unmistakable, Delbrück expressly singled out the legendary reductionist Jacques Loeb as exemplifying a naïve conception of biology as devoid of its own laws and indistinguishable from the physical sciences.[5] He said that Loeb was representative in this respect of several generations of biochemists. The link that Delbrück thought he discerned between biochemistry and reductionism was undoubtedly a major source of the hostility toward the former that he communicated to some of his students. In the same context of paying his disrespects to reductionism, he pointed out with some complacency that most branches of biology got along very well without any physics or chemistry at all. He provocatively took as a prime example the aspect of classical genetics that scandalized Szilard—its capacity to function as an exact science "without ever having to refer to the processes" by which the logically deduced hereditary factors turned into observable traits.[6] He certainly did not imply that these processes could not or should not be investigated in their own right—he personally was much interested in them—but he clearly did not feel any compelling attraction toward a reductionist account of them.

The real question becomes why he found reductionism uncongenial. There was at least one prudential, but more than prudential, factor that must have entered in. Delbrück knew that by the 1930's the doctrinaire reductionism exemplified in Loeb had fallen into considerable disrepute as premature at best. The issue was particularly acute for physicists attempting to move into biology. They could not help being almost

3. *Ibid.*, p. 10.   4. *Ibid.*, p. 13.   5. *Ibid.*, pp. 16–17.   6. *Ibid.*, p. 17.

wincingly aware that classical biologists would be expecting them to fall promptly into the trap of a crude and implausible reductionism and thereby forfeit any claim to be taken seriously. A man like Delbrück might think that conventional biologists had been "stalling around," but in the end he would have to command some measure of respect from their side. Yet over and above this, and beyond all prudential considerations, Delbrück was aesthetically offended by the unengaging simplicity, the unsurprising and unparadoxical quality of the typical reductionist arguments. He would have found them dull even if they had been true. He retained in his new calling a physicist's characteristic zest for reducing the world to order but rang his own changes upon the general theme by demanding a paradoxical order, a complex simplification incorporating tensely poised alternatives.

The masterpiece in this style—a kind of scientific-baroque—was quantum mechanics. The man who sketched in the lineaments of other sciences in the same style was Niels Bohr. His complementarity approach to biology met all of Delbrück's demands, prudential and aesthetic alike. It forbade reductionism. It exulted and abounded in ultimate paradoxes. Delbrück rehearsed with rising excitement the rich possibilities of "a conflict between separate areas of experience, which gradually sharpens into a paradox"—

Instead of aiming from the molecular physics end at the whole of the phenomena exhibited by the living cell, we now expect to find natural limits to this approach, and thereby implicitly new virgin territories on which laws may hold which involve new concepts and which are only loosely related to those of physics, by virtue of the fact that they apply to phenomena whose appearance is conditioned on *not* making observations of the type needed for a consistent interpretation in terms of atomic physics.[7]

In one of the throwaway phrases that light up an entire philosophy in a flash, Delbrück regretfully conceded in 1949 that biologists had not yet achieved the desideratum of "clear paradoxes."[8] But he already suspected that the replication of cells (and therefore genes) was one of the best places to look for "a mutually exclusive relationship" between cellular biology and quantum mechanics.[9] The biologist, he said, should operate "without fear of contradicting molecular physics."[10]

7. *Ibid.*, pp. 18 and 21.   8. *Ibid.*, p. 22.   9. *Ibid.*, p. 19.   10. *Ibid.*, p. 22.

Historically, at any rate, a whole train of paradoxes had begun to pile up as soon as Delbrück turned his attention to biology in 1933. His first contribution to the new field, and in some ways the most influential that he ever made, lay precisely in the application of quantum mechanics to genetics. From 1932 forward, the German radiation biologist K. G. Zimmer had been collaborating in Berlin with the Russian geneticist N. W. Timoféeff-Ressovsky in researches upon a theme that the latter had already broached, the physical process involved in the mutation of genes.[11] The issue had sprung to life in the wake of Herman J. Muller's classic demonstration in 1927 of artificial mutation by X-rays. When Delbrück joined the others in 1934 for excited sessions of talk that could run on for ten hours or more at a time, they produced together a little pamphlet *Über die Natur der Genmutation und der Genstruktur*, derisively known on publication in 1935 as the *Dreimännerwerk* from the oddity of interdisciplinary teamwork in German science of that period.[12] In its original context, the *Dreimännerwerk* was an elaboration of the so-called "target theory" that undertook to correlate artificially induced increases in the rate of mutation with the ionization of "sensitive volumes" deduced to have been the targets in the chromosomes that had to be hit to force the genes to mutate.[13] It was plausible to suppose that the size of the targets was the upper limit of the size of genes themselves. By 1940, however, Muller himself, after flirting with the target theory, had given a magisterial analysis of the irremediable fallacies involved in any such calculations.[14] Despite efforts to refurbish the target theory in the mid-1940's, it now ranks among the exploded theories in genetics, a cautionary example of the pitfalls in a highly deductive argument.[15]

---

11. K. G. Zimmer, "The Target Theory," in Cairns *et al.*, eds., *Phage*, pp. 33–36.

12. *Nachrichten der Gesellschaft der Wissenschaften zu Göttingen*, VI, N.F. (1935), 1: 189 sqq.

13. Cf. Elof Axel Carlson, *The Gene: A Critical History* (Philadelphia, 1966), chap. XVIII, "The Target Theory: A Successful Failure," pp. 158–165.

14. Summarized by Carlson, *Gene*, p. 161.

15. The principal advocate of the theory was Douglas Lea, *Actions of Radiations on Living Cells* (Cambridge, Eng., 1946). The two editions of Peter Alexander, *Atomic Radiation and Life* (Harmondsworth, Eng., 1957 and 1965) are very instructive for the declining fortunes of the target theory.

VI

THE *Dreimännerwerk*, however, survived the wreck of the target theory to become the keystone of one of the most influential scientific books of the twentieth century—a book that was in league with the future but scientifically antiquated before it was written. The agent of this curious salvage operation was the founder of quantum mechanics, Erwin Schrödinger. Schrödinger was reared in the ample culture of the prosperous classes of Vienna in the generation before Sarajevo.[1] His career was oddly punctuated by the two great upheavals in Central Europe. He expected in 1918 to become professor of theoretical physics at Czernowitz, a university of the second or third rank, but to give much of his attention to the philosophical interests with which he was "deeply imbued."[2] But Czernowitz was handed over to Rumania at the end of the war. Schrödinger went on instead to the dazzling career in physics that eventually took him to Berlin as Max Planck's own successor. Schrödinger was a Catholic and an Aryan but he could not breathe the air of Hitler's Germany or Austria. By his own choice, he was deflected in middle age to the kind of backwater that Czernowitz might have been, but in 1939 it was Dublin.

In this doubly marginal situation, Schrödinger felt at liberty to recover the amplitude of interests that he had known in his youth; to indulge his long-suppressed speculative, philosophical, and synthesizing bent in public lectures that exceeded his own or anybody else's expertise. He proposed to gratify at his own peril "the keen longing for unified, all-embracing knowledge."[3] As if to rub in his total defiance of the fashionable diffidence in these matters, he unblushingly tackled one of the hackneyed cosmic riddles that had long induced shuffling embarrassment—*What Is Life?* His soberer and more informative subtitle to these lectures, delivered in Dublin in 1943 and published in 1944, was "The Physical Aspect of the Living Cell."

1. William T. Scott, *Erwin Schrödinger: An Introduction to His Writings* (Amherst, Mass., 1967), chap. 1, pp. 1–14.
2. Erwin Schrödinger, *My View of the World*, 1st ed. 1961, trans. Cecily Hastings (Cambridge, Eng., 1964), pp. vii–viii.
3. Erwin Schrödinger, *What is Life?* (Cambridge, Eng., 1944), now most readily available bound with his *Mind and Matter* (Cambridge, Eng., 1958, combined ed. 1967), p. 1.

In his view, the crucial aspect was the control of every living cell by a "code-script" somehow inscribed upon its chromosomes. The portions of the code-script known as genes, Schrödinger regarded as aperiodic crystals, physically equivalent to molecules and subject to ordinary molecular forces. The genes were relatively stable—he honored his old pieties by instancing the perpetuation of the Habsburg lip—but at the same time subject to both spontaneous and artificial mutation. The question became how the preponderating stability was combined with the observed rates of mutation. Schrödinger drew upon the *Dreimännerwerk* both to sharpen the issue and to supply a solution. He pointed out that according to calculations by Delbrück premised upon the target theory, the upper limit for the size of a gene had been greatly reduced over previous estimates.[4] A gene seemed to be of the fantastically small order of a thousand atoms, yet displayed "a most regular and lawful activity" bordering upon the miraculous, namely the Habsburg lip.[5] How could a structure composed of so few atoms withstand the disturbing influence of random heat motion to which all material substances are exposed? Here too Schrödinger cited Delbrück in the *Dreimännerwerk*—what he roundly called "Delbrück's model" for the application of quantum mechanics to genetics.[6] The Heitler-London forces that accounted for chemical bonding upon quantum mechanical principles demonstrated that very steep energy thresholds would have to be surmounted on passing from one stable configuration of a molecule to an isomeric configuration (with the same atoms stably rearranged). In a chromosomal molecule, the process of gene mutation entailed supplying the substantial energy lift required to clear the threshold between two stable configurations. Delbrück had shown in 1935, on the basis of earlier work by two members of the Budapest galaxy, Michael Polanyi and Eugene Wigner, that the requisite energy lifts would be of the same order of rarity as spontaneous mutations.[7] The argument would not, however, have been airtight if energy could somehow accumulate over a period of time to effect the quantum jump; but one of the premises of

4. *What Is Life?* pp. 30–31 (older estimates) and 47, 49 (new).
5. *Ibid.*, p. 49.
6. *Ibid.*, chap. v, "Delbrück's Model Discussed and Tested," pp. 60–71.
7. *Ibid.*, p. 54.

the target theory, as Schrödinger duly recorded, was precisely that mutation is a "single event" produced by hitting the target once and only once.[8]

Schrödinger had accounted to his own satisfaction for the otherwise miraculous stability of the small assemblages of atoms constituting genes. He acknowledged that another problem often felt in the same context of the minuteness even of the complete chromosomal strands was how a "code-script" adequate to the total development and great diversity of living organisms could possibly be crammed into such tiny specks of material. But this difficulty he dismissed as imaginary in the most original and seminal part of *What Is Life?*[9] The vital clue, he said, was the Morse code, which showed how as few as two signs arranged in groups of four could generate thirty different arrangements, and three signs in groups of ten, more than eighty-eight thousand. The numbers of atoms in the chromosomes need not be very large to produce "an almost unlimited number of possible arrangements." It was no longer "inconceivable," Schrödinger concluded, that "the miniature code should precisely correspond with a highly complicated and specified plan of development and should somehow contain the means to put it into operation." How it was actually done, Schrödinger did not profess to know. He thought of himself as demonstrating that there were no barriers in principle to incorporating sufficient stability and complexity within the genes. For this purpose, he said, there was no alternative to the molecular picture of the gene. If this had failed to account for the evidence, we would have had to "give up further attempts."[10] As it was, the way to the future was open. Investigators would not be wasting their time in trying to discover how the genetic code-script was transcribed into a complete organism and itself accurately replicated.

Schrödinger constantly referred to the molecular conception of the gene as "Delbrück's model" or "Delbrück's picture." Nothing in Delbrück's career was more paradoxical than this belated appropriation of his first and least characteristic contribution to biology by a man whose philosophical stance was almost diametrically opposed to his own. Where Delbrück had been entranced by Bohr's complementarity principle and eager to apply it to biology, Schrödinger never found the idea appealing

8. *Ibid.*, pp. 45–46.   9. *Ibid.*, pp. 65–66.   10. *Ibid.*, p. 61.

even as an explication of quantum mechanics, and still less as a kind of philosopher's stone for dissolving all riddles. He had been deeply influenced by Indian mysticism, partly via Schopenhauer, and cherished what he called "the Vedantic vision" of the oneness of nature.[11] He had a metaphysical panacea of his own, and one that accorded very ill with the sharp disjunction between the observer and the observed that constituted one of the principal arguments for complementarity. In fact, he never mentioned complementarity in *What Is Life?* Elsewhere, in responding to a hypothetical inquiry as to why he didn't talk about it, he said flatly that he did not think that it had as much connection as currently supposed with "a philosophical view of the world."[12] In *What Is Life?* he never implied the existence of mutually exclusive biological laws and physical laws, any paradoxical situation where a choice would have to be made between them for the purpose in view. Delbrück rightly sensed that this refusal of paradoxes was the general posture of biochemists, and accordingly held them in low esteem. Schrödinger in direct contrast, but equally in keeping with his own basic position, spoke of biochemists glowingly as exactly the people who would score the coup of explaining how genes replicate and function.[13]

Schrödinger, however, did not like to think of himself as a reductionist. Indeed, he said that his "only motive" for writing *What Is Life?* was to emphasize a feature of living things that a physicist would find surprising.[14] They had the capacity for producing "order from order," of perpetuating well-ordered assemblages of comparatively few atoms. In the world that modern physicists prided themselves upon having discovered, order was statistically educed from disorder in very large collections of atoms individually subject to random heat motions. The inference that Schrödinger drew was that living matter, while not escaping the established laws of physics, probably involved "other laws of physics, hitherto unknown," but once they were found out forming "just as integral a part of this science as the former."[15] At first glance, this might appear to be an utterance in the authentic Delbrückian style, an acceptable tribute to the man whom Schrödinger repeatedly cited;

11. *Ibid.*, pp. 93–94; more fully expounded in *My View of the World*.
12. *View of the World*, pp. vii–viii. For his general view of complementarity, cf. Scott, *Schrödinger*, chap. IV, "Schrödinger's Interpretation of Quantum Mechanics," pp. 68–102.
13. *What Is Life?*, p. 72.   14. *Ibid.*, pp. 72–73.   15. *Ibid.*, p. 73.

but not on closer inspection. One of the missing ingredients is, of course, complementarity. In the argument that Schrödinger went on to elaborate, he nowhere suggested that there was any biological unit, whether the organism as a whole or the individual cell, that constituted a barrier to the application of ordinary physical and chemical concepts. They might have to be supplemented by new concepts, but that was the appropriate word, rather than complemented, for he never thought in terms of the true complementarity situation, entailing a choice between alternative points of view that were mutually exclusive. Still less did he contemplate biological laws complementarily set over against physical in the manner envisioned by Bohr and Delbrück. The "other" laws would be laws of physics.

The difficulty becomes to discern what he thought the general purpose of the other laws might be. They cannot be laws explaining the replication and functioning of genes; for he expressly said that these would probably come from biochemistry rather than physics. But if he had anything else in mind, one is hard put within the terms of his own argument to see why additional laws of physics would be needed. The key to biology turns out to be the Heitler-London forces that apply equally to all solids, crystals, or molecules—including "the aperiodic crystal . . . largely withdrawn from the disorder of heat motion" in which the code of life is embodied.[16] Yet as Schrödinger constantly reiterated, these were implications of quantum mechanics as applied to genetics by Delbrück as early as 1935. What other laws of this scope could possibly be required? The suspicion arises that Schrödinger thought the Heitler-London forces *were* the other laws. For on close scrutiny, the general air of expectancy that every reader recalls as pervading the book, the sense of rising excitement at greater revelations to come, may well have attached for Schrödinger to the logical progression of his own argument. He may have supposed that he was actually answering the question that he asked in his title.

If so, Schrödinger was much closer to being a highly sophisticated reductionist than he liked to admit. In fact, the possibility must have passed through his own mind; for near the close of the book, after begging the reader not to accuse him of saying that chromosome fibers

16. *Ibid.*, p. 91.

are merely "cogs in the organic machine," he adds the curiously permissive proviso "at least not without a reference to the profound physical theories on which the simile is based."[17] He obviously remained fearful of the conventional reductionist arguments as impoverishing the complexity of living things as he understood them. But he did believe, with however many elaborate qualifications, that biology was a branch of physics. By so much, he defined a radical antithesis between himself and Max Delbrück—the man who had most profoundly influenced his own conception of life.

VII

DELBRÜCK had sharpened the antithesis from his side as well. Though Schrödinger seems never to have known what had become of him after 1935, Delbrück had taken his own interpretation of the complementarity between biology and physics seriously and begun to cultivate biology from within. It did not follow that he learned to respect most of the biologists whom he found in possession. His object was to beat them at their own game. After fleeing Germany to Caltech as a Rockefeller Fellow in 1937, he first tackled in the following year the theme that he and his disciples were to make their own, the growth of bacteriophage, *i.e.*, bactericidal viruses. Not surprisingly, the initial interest in these had turned chiefly upon their hoped-for value in medicine, which, however, turned out to be nil. The possibility that now began to dawn upon Delbrück was to give phage research an entirely different orientation, toward the really basic issues in biology. He evidently thought that it was typical of biologists to miss their best opportunities for attacking fundamental problems. In this frame of mind, he headed for one of the crucial encounters in the history of twentieth-century biology.

At a meeting, significantly enough, of the American Physical Society, he met the refugee Italian bacteriologist Salvador Luria on December 28, 1940, and found in him the rare kind of biologist that he could

17. *Ibid.*

respect, a man of extraordinary intellectual scope and flexibility.[1] While serving in the Italian army in 1936–1937 Luria had seized the chance to study calculus and while waiting for his American visa at Marseille in 1940 he read G. N. Lewis' *Physical Chemistry*. In Italy he had frequently hung around with physicists, including his fellow refugees in America, Enrico Fermi and Franco Rasetti.[2] If all this was not enough, he had even begun phage research in Italy on the same general lines as Delbrück. In December 1940 they immediately adjourned to Luria's laboratory at the College of Physicians and Surgeons in New York to do experiments together. But Delbrück's job was then at Vanderbilt University in Nashville and the only way that they could think of to get on with their budding collaboration was to spend the summer of 1941 at the Cold Spring Harbor Laboratory on Long Island Sound. The new departure that they stood for was the orientation of phage research toward genetical problems, initially the development of phage-resistant mutants in bacteria but eventually the nature and replication of the genes in phage itself.[3] In retrospect, Delbrück and Luria by their phage researches were giving a fundamentally new turn to genetics, comparable with the earlier impetus given by T. H. Morgan and his school in focusing attention upon *Drosophila*. But more than this, phage genetics became a springboard for molecular biology, and that proved to be the greatest point of forward thrust in biology as a whole. By 1950 the quantum mechanics expert Delbrück had succeeded, against the odds, in becoming one of the most distinguished biologists in the world.

In the process he had also become one of the fabulous personalities in American science, noted for wryly deflating remarks that kept people coming back, a trifle apprehensively, for more. A *Festschrift*, he said to a prospective contributor to his own, consists in honoring a man by printing his friends' unpublishable papers; and "they" would probably do that to him.[4] (They didn't dare.) You don't have the talent to be an

1. Salvador Luria, "Mutations of Bacteria and of Bacteriophage," in John Cairns, Gunther S. Stent, James D. Watson, eds., *Phage and the Origins of Molecular Biology* (Cold Spring Harbor, N.Y., 1966), pp. 173–179.

2. Laura Fermi, *Illustrious Immigrants: The Intellectual Migration from Europe, 1930–1941* (Chicago, 1968), p. 316.

3. For a general conspectus of the early accomplishments of the phage geneticists, see Gunther S. Stent, *Molecular Biology of Bacterial Viruses* (San Francisco, 1963).

4. Jean Weigle, "Story and Structure of the λ Transducing Phage," in Cairns *et al.*, eds., *Phage*, p. 233.

artist, he said to a young colleague who was thinking of abandoning
science, so what does that leave except to be a scientist?[5] There are worse
things than writing a dull thesis, he told a young man who had done
exactly that; at least nobody wants you to follow it up.[6] A brilliant
discovery by two of his own disciples he described as a great triumph
for the "Principle of Limited Sloppiness."[7] Whether consciously or not,
Delbrück used his personal magnetism to make a phage world populated with phage people—one of the little communities of intellectual
purpose and excitement that constitute the only genuine utopias of the
twentieth century.[8] People reminisced about their early days in the
"phage group" as if they had been at Eton together, or even on the
road to Damascus. Many had conversion experiences to relate from the
summer when they took their first "phage course" under Delbrück at
Cold Spring Harbor—his and Luria's improvisation of 1941 had turned
into an annual institution, a College of Propaganda for molecular biology. It was here that Leo Szilard was received into the faith at the venerable age of forty-seven, and found that Delbrück had the knack of making biology "comfortable" for physicists.[9]

When people talked about joining the "phage church," and even on
occasion about falling away from the true faith they were joking. But
jokes are embarrassed glimpses of the truth and Delbrück actually had
some of the mingled iron and guile of a great religious organizer. He
even kept his followers under a kind of church discipline. He literally
locked the younger ones up when he thought they were ready to write
up their results but inclined to procrastinate; papally dispensed them
from the ordinary rules of the calendar by decreeing Wednesday-Thurs-
day "weekends" for desert retreats; and negotiated in 1944 a famous
"phage treaty," for all the world like the creeds promulgated by the
early church councils, that henceforth the true phage believers would
work exclusively upon one small set of phages multiplying in a single
host.[10] Delbrück's great object in all this, not unworthy of being soberly

5. N. Visconti, "Mating Theory," *Ibid.*, p. 149.
6. J. D. Watson, "Growing Up in the Phage Group," *Ibid.*, p. 243.
7. *Ibid.*, p. 242.
8. The collective memory of the phage group is enshrined in Cairns *et al.*, eds., *Phage*.
9. Aaron Novick (Szilard's collaborator in biology), "Phenotypic Mixing," *Ibid.*, p. 134.
10. Seymour Benzer, "Adventures in the rII Region," *Ibid.*, p. 158. Phage treaty:
Thomas F. Anderson, "Electron Microscopy of Phages," *Ibid.*, p. 73.

characterized as religious from his concern with final things, was to keep
the phage group in undistracted motion toward a transcendent goal,
with no stragglers from the main purpose of achieving in the near future
a truly ultimate breakthrough in biology. For him personally the gleam
that travelled on before but had to be nailed down was the great paradox by which all would be made clear in biology as in physics. What
exactly he meant by this was one of the ineffable secrets that he never
quite succeeded in communicating to his followers. Yet their uneasy
awareness of it must have been a part of his hold upon them. What they
did clearly grasp was that they were supposed to be rapidly closing in
upon absolutely final and central truths in biology—as definitive as
quantum mechanics had proved to be in physics. Nothing peripheral,
tentative, or diffident would constitute a fulfillment of the goal that he
had set before them. By no accident, members of the phage group
would be talking unabashedly in the mid-1950's about "the central
dogma" in molecular biology. It was the kind of language that conventional biologists would not have wished upon their worst enemies,
jarringly offensive to their ideal of modest decorum in research and the
avoidance of religious enthusiasm about the results, but a perfect expression of the Delbrückian temper in biology.[11]

VIII

THE heart of "the central dogma" was the Watson-Crick model of
DNA. Watson-before-Crick became the unsuspected point of convergence by whom the physicists' dreams for biology came true. J. D.
Watson (b. 1928) read as an undergraduate at the University of Chicago
the book of which he later said that it instantly "polarized" him toward
"finding out the secret of the gene"—Schrödinger's *What Is Life?*[1] That
meant that he had to go to graduate school in genetics. He was turned

11. For a classic statement, as of August 1961, of disgust at this kind of talk (and
"molecular biology" in general), see Erwin Chargaff, "Amphisbaena," *Essays on Nucleic
Acids* (Amsterdam, 1963), pp. 174–199 (*re* "central dogma," p. 190).

1. Autobiographical material in Watson, "Growing Up in the Phage Group," in John
Cairns, Gunther S. Stent, James D. Watson, eds., *Phage and the Origins of Molecular
Biology* (Cold Spring Harbor, N.Y., 1966), pp. 239–245 (reading of Schrödinger, p. 239).

down by Harvard, which was no place to do genetics in 1947, and by Caltech, which was bad luck for Delbrück and Beadle were there; but he got into the only acceptable alternative, Indiana. The great magnet at Indiana was the newly enNobeled Muller. Watson promptly decided that Muller and *Drosophila* had seen their best days. He decided almost as promptly that the man who was on to something really interesting, namely phage genetics, was Salvador Luria, who had gone to Indiana in 1943. Watson took a phage doctorate with Luria in 1950, but his intermittent encounters with Max Delbrück were at least equally important. For anybody who had taken up genetics after reading Schrödinger, Delbrück was bound to be "legendary" from his role in *What Is Life?* Watson says, in fact, that he chose to work with Luria partly because the latter was known to be Delbrück's friend and collaborator. The abstract knowledge of this was one thing, but in the spring of 1948 the mythical figure actually materialized in Luria's apartment in Bloomington. However historic, he was still only forty-two, trim and youthful, and to Watson's delight very plain-spoken. Watson was hooked. In contrast, he and Leo Szilard, who first met in the fall of 1948, never took to each other.[2] Szilard was a learner too, with little to teach Watson; and he never achieved the same status in biology as Delbrück, or the same claim upon the deference of the younger men in the field. Yet it seems clear that Szilard did become a felt presence, a ponderable weight, in the phage world, as legendary as Delbrück in his own way and another portent of the wind that must be rising in biology if physicists of their stature could get excited about it. For Watson, Delbrück was more than a vague authenticating presence, he was an irresistible force to be sought out again and again—at Cold Spring Harbor in the summer of 1948, at brief phage meetings in the spring of 1949, at Pasadena in the summer of 1949 and then again for a month in the spring of 1950, topped off by another six weeks at Cold Spring Harbor in the summer of 1950. For Watson, as for many others, Delbrück had become the flint that he hoped to strike a spark of approval from, or at any rate a spark of interest.

Delbrück had his own terms for being impressed. He was not interested in raw data unless they were fitted into some kind of "pretty

2. *Ibid.*, p. 242.

hypothesis."[3] But what he was really after was pointers toward the one big hypothesis that would account decisively for the replication of genes. His disciples were expected to share his contempt for the ordinary geneticists who persisted in nibbling around the edges of heredity rather than trying for a bull's eye. Watson, whose organs of contempt were vigorous, found this a highly congenial demand. It was part of Delbrück's impatience with what he regarded as side issues that he had no truck with the theories, highly fashionable at the end of the 1940's and beginning of the fifties, of cytoplasmic heredity, controlled by factors outside the chromosomes.[4] Admittedly, genes did function in a cytoplasmic environment. Early in the fifties, some of Delbrück's disciples were canvassing the hypothesis that genetic control of protein synthesis in the cytoplasm might be the key not only to cellular metabolism but to the replication of genes themselves.[5] Delbrück imposed a severe restraint upon these speculations by his distaste for reductionism, his antipathy to biochemistry, and his complacency about the free-standing quality of genetics—its logical sufficiency unto itself and exemption from the trammels of chemistry. He evidently felt that elucidating the chemistry of genes would be a deplorably flat solution to his quest for the secret of heredity, unlikely in the extreme to yield the devastating paradox, the ineluctable complementarity, that Bohr had led him to expect. And besides, he was not a chemist. A geneticist he had actually become, and he opted for some kind of "pure" genetics as the best strategy for smoking out the process of gene replication.[6]

   J. D. Watson was fascinated by Delbrück but not hypnotized. His actual mentor Luria, though harboring mildly idolatrous feelings toward Delbrück, could not help thinking that if you wanted to know how genes behaved, it would be useful to know what they were made of.[7] Watson heartily agreed. It was not his only dissent from the *echt* Delbrückian gospel. When Delbrück actually turned up in Bloomington in 1948, he had a more than physical shock to administer to Watson. For the Delbrück that Watson was excited about meeting was the Del-

3. *Ibid.*, pp. 242–243.   4. *Ibid.*, p. 241.
5. N. Visconti, "Mating Theory," in Cairns *et al.*, eds., *Phage*, p. 147.
6. James D. Watson, *The Double Helix* (New York, 1968), p. 23.
7. *Ibid.*

brück that got refracted through Schrödinger's *What Is Life?* Schrödinger had said absolutely nothing about complementarity, on Delbrück's behalf or his own, and a reader was entitled to suppose that they
were thoroughly kindred spirits attacking the problem of the gene in
unison. No doubt that was Schrödinger's opinion also. Instead of which,
Delbrück in person promptly began to talk about Niels Bohr and the
need for a complementarity principle in biology as in quantum mechanics.[8] Luria was more skeptical about this, for he had been put on his
guard against complementarity in general by Enrico Fermi while they
were still in Italy; and on inspecting Bohr's writings for himself had
found his worst suspicions confirmed—they were definitely "tainted
with idealism."[9] But he too, according to Watson, seemed to feel "on
most days" that the gene would be hard to lick and that really high-
powered brains like Delbrück's or Szilard's would be required to discover "the new laws of physics," or maybe chemistry, accounting for
the replication of genes.[10]

At this point, an intricate comedy of errors began to emerge. Schrödinger had spoken in *What Is Life?* of "other" laws of physics, "hitherto
unknown," as required in understanding life. It is at least arguable that
the laws he had in mind were those of the Heitler–London forces and
that "hitherto" meant before the application of quantum mechanics to
biology by himself and the early Delbrück. Yet nothing was simpler
than to interpret Schrödinger as calling for "new" laws that were totally unknown in 1943 and still undiscovered in 1950. In any event, of
the four phage geneticists who are known to have been excited by reading *What Is Life?*—Seymour Benzer, Salvador Luria, J. D. Watson, and
Gunther Stent—all but one have testified that what they were interested
in was the talk about the code-script and the aperiodic crystal rather
than about the laws of physics.[11] The one exception, Gunther Stent,
was not only intrigued by Schrödinger on this topic, but apparently
never hesitated for a moment to interpret the passage unequivocally as a

8. Watson, "Growing Up in the Phage Group," p. 240.
9. Luria to Stent in Gunther S. Stent, "That Was the Molecular Biology that Was,"
Science, 160 (April 26, 1968), 390–395, p. 395, fn. 10.
10. Watson, "Growing Up in the Phage Group," p. 240.
11. Stent, "That Was the Molecular Biology," p. 395, fn. 10. Seymour Benzer, "Adventures in the rII Region," in Cairns *et al.*, eds., *Phage*, p. 157.

call for laws that were still unknown.[12] What is far more important, he conflated this passage with Delbrück's pursuit of a complementarity principle in biology. Whatever Schrödinger was looking for, it was certainly not complementarity. Yet the identification, once made, had a great deal of specious plausibility. If Schrödinger based his book on Delbrück, why shouldn't they be in fundamental agreement? Readers who had passed lightly over the part about "other laws of physics" could easily be persuaded in retrospect that this was mere shorthand for Delbrück's invocations of complementarity. The fact that Schrödinger was the founder of quantum mechanics, and complementarity an effort to interpret quantum mechanics, must have made the fit seem perfect. Nobody who was deeply versed in Schrödinger's philosophy of the world could have been taken in by this, but in 1950 he had not yet supplied some of the principal texts for reading his mind.[13] In *What Is Life?*—the only publication of his that most of the relevant people had ever seen— he did not endorse complementarity; but he did not condemn it either. He simply ignored it. No wonder it was easy to bracket him comprehensively with Delbrück. Yet the joke was on Delbrück too. For the non-physicists in the phage group could never get clearly in mind that in calling for a complementarity principle in biology, he was *not* proposing to subordinate biology to quantum mechanics but rather insisting upon the autonomy of biological research and biological laws. His commitment to complementarity was to an abstract metaphysical principle that he and Bohr thought of as transcending its origin in quantum mechanics. The upshot, however, of confusing complementarity in general with complementarity in physics, and the latter with Schrödinger's "other laws of physics," was to persuade some members of the phage group that the breakthrough in biology would probably be reserved for those who knew quantum mechanics, or at any rate mathematical physics. Even Luria, who never set any store by complementarity, was sufficiently intimidated to threaten Watson with Delbrück or Szilard. Watson says that when he listened to Luria in this vein and

12. Stent, "Introduction: Waiting for the Paradox," *Ibid.*, pp. 3–4; Stent, "That Was the Molecular Biology," pp. 393–394.

13. *Mind and Matter*, published 1958; *My View of the World*, 1st German ed. 1961, English trans. 1964.

then reflected on his own "inability to think mathematically," he some-times got discouraged.[14]

Yet the fact is that Watson resisted Delbrück's and Stent's indoctrina-tion in the ineffable mysteries of the gene, and Luria's intermittent fits of gloom on the same topic. It was the kind of talk that got Watson's back up and made him want to prove the opposite—that the secret of the gene was extremely simple and didn't require any mathematics, let alone quantum mechanics, to understand; and in defiance of Delbrück, probably did require some chemistry. But Delbrück left his mark on Watson in a more positive way. He aroused the ambitions that Watson declined to believe were above him. Delbrück confirmed the impression that Schrödinger had made upon Watson, that the greatest conceivable disclosures in biology were almost in reach and somebody now at work would win the prize—today, tomorrow, next year, but very soon. Watson testified that he would come away from Delbrück's presence expecting to participate in "some great revelation."[15] The stimulus was more precise than that. Delbrück and Schrödinger, beyond all the con-fusions, truly did converge upon a clear specification of the central prob-lem in biology. The secret of life was the mode of replication of genes.

IX

IN 1950, Luria thought the trail was getting hot. On the basis of Avery's rather slowly digested work and in the general atmosphere of rising enthusiasm about somebody's cracking the secret soon, DNA began to "smell" like the essential genetic material.[1] Avery's evidence was inconclusive, but Luria had to anticipate the measured verdict upon it if he or any of his students were to have a chance, after all, of being in on the kill. In this cause, Luria dispatched Watson to Copenhagen at summer's end in 1950 to study the chemistry of DNA with the bio-chemist Herman Kalckar.[2] The dose did not take, but in the spring of

14. Watson, "Growing Up in the Phage Group," p. 240.
15. *Ibid.*
1. James D. Watson, *The Double Helix* (New York, 1968), p. 23.
2. *Ibid.*, p. 22.

1951 Watson became acquainted with Maurice Wilkins' work at King's College, London, on X-ray diffraction pictures of DNA, and then moved on unwittingly toward his ultimate rendezvous with Francis Crick at the Cavendish Laboratory in Cambridge.[3] Among other bonds, Crick and Watson had an ancestor in common, for Crick's decision to abandon physics for biology at the end of the war had been profoundly influenced by reading Schrödinger's *What Is Life?*[4] But more than this, Crick and Wilkins as physicists-turned-biologists were a familiar and congenial type to anybody who had grown up in the "phage group." Both men, according to their very different temperaments, expressed the same impatience with conventional biologists that Watson had imbibed from Delbrück and Szilard. Watson for his part was happy to chime in unison on the ineffectual dithering of the botanists and zoologists and the singular incuriosity of the classical geneticists about the actual nature of the genes.[5] It would be almost a kindness to wrest biology from their feeble grasp and put it in more capable hands.

One of the participants has taken up his own story at roughly this point, and other stories are on the way.[6] Yet despite the widespread impression that there must be great controversies still to be ventilated by the key figures, the main ingredients in Watson and Crick's success are perfectly clear; and so are their respective sources.[7] The Watson–Crick model of DNA as revealed in 1953 consists of two helically wound strands, a kind of spiral staircase with steps consisting of paired bases (cytosine with guanine, adenine with thymine, the alphabet of genetics), so that the strands are complementary and can replicate each other by the pairing of bases with their complements, as of a key with its lock. The idea of the helix as a fundamental molecular configuration in biology came in with Linus Pauling's epoch-making discovery in 1950 of the alpha helix in polypeptides (*i.e.*, fibrous proteins). The possibility of a helical structure in DNA was broached in 1951 by Maurice Wilkins.[8]

3. First encounter with Wilkins, *Ibid.*, pp. 32–33; with Crick, p. 48.

4. *Ibid.*, p. 13.

5. *Ibid.*, pp. 72, 74.

6. Crick has placed his own archives at the disposal of Robert Olby of Oxford, according to the latter. Olby to editor, *The Listener* (June 6, 1968). His projected date of publication is 1970.

7. Well set forth in Watson, *Double Helix*.

8. Cf. L. D. Hamilton, "DNA: Models and Reality," *Nature*, 218 (May 18, 1968), 633–637.

The pairing of complementary bases was a logical, though by no means obvious, inference from the quantitative (rather than structural) studies of DNA from 1944 forward by the Austrian refugee biochemist Erwin Chargaff of the College of Physicians and Surgeons of Columbia University. The fact that the bases had to be "inside" the strands, rather than on the outside, was first insisted upon by Rosalind Franklin of King's College, London—the turbulent "Rosy" of Watson's book. The basic constraints within which the helical structure had to be fitted came from X-ray crystallography of DNA by Wilkins, Rosalind Franklin, and R. G. Gosling. The "verification" of the double helix within these constraints was accomplished by tinkering with an actual model in imitation of Linus Pauling. None of this detracts in the least from the achievement of Watson and Crick. Only they put all of the hints and strategies together to produce the greatest coup in twentieth-century biology. After all, Linus Pauling was running in the same race and stumbled.

There was one remarkable footnote to the story. The celebrated German pioneer of quantum mechanics Pascual Jordan in various publications from 1938 to 1940 had discussed the possibility of the replication of genes and other biological molecules by a kind of stabilizing attraction between identical molecules—a process of "autocatalytic reproduction."[9] He invoked for this purpose, though not without serious reservations, the well-known "resonance" phenomenon in quantum mechanics. Max Delbrück called these speculations to the attention of Linus Pauling, who was then in the process of publishing his great book *The Nature of the Chemical Bond*, incorporating a resonance theory of bonding.[10] Pauling was dismayed by Jordan's hypothesis, however diffidently proffered, and persuaded Delbrück to collaborate in a definitive refutation. In an article of July 26, 1940, they demonstrated that quantum mechanical considerations actually precluded a stabilizing resonance interaction between identical molecules.[11] As an alternative, they proposed "well understood" interactions (other than by resonance)

9. Citations in rejoinder by Pauling and Delbrück, fn. 11 below.
10. Delbrück's initiative: Watson, *Double Helix*, p. 127.
11. Linus Pauling and Max Delbrück, "The Nature of the Intermolecular Forces Operative in Biological Processes," *Science*, 92 (July 26, 1940), 77–79.

... such as to give stability to a system of two molecules with *complementary* structures in juxtaposition, rather than of two molecules with necessarily identical structures; we accordingly feel that complementariness should be given primary consideration in the discussion of the specific attraction between molecules and the enzymatic synthesis of molecules.[12]

They went on to delimit their argument severely by pointing out that identical molecules could experience (non-resonance) attraction between complementary *groups*, so that autocatalytic reproduction on these terms was not ruled out. In biology, they were inclined to postulate both possibilities—complementary attraction between non-identical molecules and between appropriate groups in identical molecules. This article was in the minds of Watson and Crick as they were trying to solve the structure of DNA; and in the end they came up with the pairing of complementary bases.[13] Yet Pauling and Delbrück's argument in no sense dictated such a solution. All that they contributed was the negative assurance that resonance interactions need not be considered and that complementary attraction between non-identical molecules was not precluded by quantum mechanics. But these propositions were a great comfort to a man like Watson who had no quantum mechanics at all and certainly could not have soared into the empyrean of resonance theories. In his Nobel oration of 1962, he was still expressing his pleasure at fortifying empirically the theoretical arguments of Pauling and Delbrück against Jordan's hypothesis of gene replication by "still undiscovered long-range forces arising from quantum mechanical resonance interactions."[14] Something more than his own convenience as an investigator was involved; for he clearly found such ideas philosophically distasteful and bracketed them ominously with "mysticism."

If, as one cannot help suspecting, Watson was here thinking, just a little, about all the portentous talk of a great Delbrückian complementarity principle in biology, he must have relished the ironies of the situation. He and Crick had indeed found complementary relations at the heart of biology, but it was a totally mundane complementarity, exem-

12. *Ibid.*, p. 78.
13. Watson, *Double Helix*, p. 127.
14. James D. Watson, "The Involvement of RNA in the Synthesis of Proteins," in Nobel Foundation, *Nobel Lectures: Physiology or Medicine 1942–1962* (Amsterdam, 1964), pp. 785–808 (relevant passage, p. 786).

plified in locks and keys, and sharing nothing but a verbal echo with the complementarity principle of Bohr and Delbrück. Presumably Pauling and Delbrück intended to signify as much in 1940 by using the awkward term "complementariness" rather than the more natural but preempted "complementarity." Bohrian complementarity as embraced by Delbrück revolved about the paradox of having to choose between different lines of attack in research that could not be prosecuted with equal precision at the same time—a principle of mutual exclusion. The pairing of bases in DNA not only permitted but required that the complementary elements be thought of in immediate juxtaposition. Complementarity lay between different foci in research; complementariness between interlocking objects in a single field of vision. The two concepts were not only distinct but virtually antithetical. Yet Delbrück himself had collaborated with Pauling in giving the go-ahead signal for discovering the lamentably unparadoxical complementariness that actually occurred in biology. By the highest Delbrückian standards, the secret of life that he flogged people on to discover turned out to be dull. On top of that, he had paved the way for his own disappointment.

When the Watson-Crick model seemed to be in hand, early in March 1953, the first people that Watson thought of writing to were Luria and Delbrück.[15] Phage alumni were always asking themselves, What will Max think of it? Watson had measured himself triumphantly, with rather scanty equipment, against the biggest challenge that Delbrück could devise, and it was only natural to apply for the reward that was coming to him. But there must have been a trace of *Schadenfreude* as well, in confronting Delbrück with a solution that epitomized the temperamental gulf between them. Watson was a reductionist who had sought and found a devastatingly simple explanation of the "secret of life." Delbrück was an anti-reductionist in unavailing pursuit of a paradoxical solution to the same problem. In contrast with Delbrück, Erwin Schrödinger belonged, when the chips were down, to the great simplifiers and reductionists. He, rather than Delbrück, was the doctrinal progenitor of Watson's share in the model. But both men helped to stir up the requisite excitement about an impending biological revolution.

15. Watson, *Double Helix*, p. 205; letter to Delbrück photographically on unnumbered pages at end of book.

A NEW SITE FOR THE SEMINAR:
THE REFUGEES AND AMERICAN
PHYSICS IN THE THIRTIES

by CHARLES WEINER

NOT long after the detonation of the first nuclear explosions it became evident that a rather extraordinary group of scientists was at work in the United States. Prominent in this group were scientists who had come to the United States before the war as refugees from Fascist-dominated countries. Between 1933 and 1941, more than one hundred of these men and women joined the ranks

* This essay, essentially a summary of work in progress, is focused at the expense of much rich and relevant detail. Little detail, for example, is offered regarding the migrations of physicists from countries other than Germany. It must not be imagined, however, that these scholars constituted an unimportant part of the refugee group, either numerically or in eminence or in impact on science in America; quite the contrary. (The term "refugee physicist" here applies to those who were either dismissed or resigned from their positions as a result of the Fascist policies, rather than those physicists who came as émigrés prior to 1933.) Further, it has not seemed necessary in many instances to describe the experiences and outstanding achievements of some of the best known refugee physicists. It is nevertheless worth bearing in mind that the Nobel Prize had been awarded to Peter Debye, Albert Einstein, Enrico Fermi, James Franck, and Victor F. Hess before they came to America, and that Hans A. Bethe, Felix Bloch, Emilio G. Segrè, and Otto Stern subsequently became Nobel Laureates, as did Eugene P. Wigner and Maria Mayer who came as émigrés in 1930. Still others have played leading roles within the scientific community and in the realm of science policy, higher education, and international relations. Again the experiences of only a few of them have been included here, to provide examples of the conditions that influenced the reception of the refugees within the American physics community in the 1930's. A more comprehensive study must take into account the experiences and influence of a much larger proportion of the refugee physicists, the differences between their reception in the United States and that in England and other countries, and the correlation of similar experiences in various fields of science.

I am grateful to Gerald Holton of Harvard University for many valuable suggestions and rewarding discussions during the course of the research for this essay, and for his detailed comments on the draft manuscript. I have also profited from the critical reading of the manuscript by Robert K. Merton of Columbia University.

of American physicists.[1] Many of the new arrivals had already achieved eminence in physics while others had been identified by their colleagues as likely to do so. But the rapid growth of physics in America in the 1930's was under way before the refugees arrived. During the same period nearly thirteen hundred other physicists, Ph.D. graduates of American universities, entered the profession.[2] Before 1930, American institutions of learning and research were already attracting more European postdoctoral physics fellows than institutions in any other country.[3] This background is not usually appreciated, however, and the visible achievements of the refugee physicists have invited the popular view that it was the refugees who "made" American physics. The story of the effect of the refugee physicists is clearly more complex than that and, to be understood, it must be related to the changing environment for physics in America when they arrived.

The response of the refugees to their new surroundings was described in 1966 by Robert Oppenheimer:

> They all did an enormous amount, and the fact that they were all very good and yet wonderfully adaptable—in the sense that they genuinely came to this country not as a temporary and resented alternative but as something that could be lived with and enjoyed—made a great difference to American physics. I don't think it would have been so successful had there not been, by that time, a rather sturdy indigenous effort in physics . . . They all, I think, were right to appreciate what was good in this country, coming from Europe in the thirties. They came with a good heart, very eager to do the physics they knew how to do, and very anxious to have companionship in that.[4]

1. This estimate is based on a list of about one hundred names of physicists, compiled from various sources, including biographical data in the collections of the American Institute of Physics' Center for History and Philosophy of Physics of which the author is Director; correspondence of scientists involved in efforts to assist their colleagues; lists of displaced scholars circulated in the 1930's; and card files recording biographical information on refugee scholars in all fields who came to America. (These card files were generously made available by Betty Drury of the Institute of International Education who was a key staff member of the Emergency Committee in Aid of Displaced Foreign Scholars from 1935 to 1945.) The list is not yet complete.

2. M. Lois Marckworth, comp., *Dissertations in Physics: An Indexed Bibliography of All Doctoral Theses Accepted by American Universities, 1861–1959* (Stanford, 1961), p. xi.

3. *Natural Science Fellowships of the Rockefeller Foundation* (New York, 1930), p. 170.

4. Filmed interview with Robert Oppenheimer, November 1, 1966, conducted by the author for the documentary film on Enrico Fermi, produced by Harvard Project Physics. All quotations from interviews referred to in this essay are used by permission.

Several major developments were involved in the interaction of the refugee physicists and their new American environment. These developments include the internationalization of physics in the 1920's, the self-improvement movement within the American physics community in the late 1920's and early 1930's, the dissolution of physics in Germany and the response to this by scientists in other countries, the refugees' experiences during their nomadic stage, and the reception of the newly-arrived physicists in America. These developments can now be studied in detail, thanks to the joint efforts of physicists and historians since 1961 to identify and preserve relevant documentary source materials on the history of twentieth-century physics and to record the recollections of the participants themselves. This essay is at the same time one of the early fruits of these efforts and one of the first glimpses of what is contained in some of the documentary source materials already collected.[5]

1. The Traveling Seminar

WHEN the exodus from Nazi-controlled universities began in the spring of 1933, members of the academic communities of many nations quickly came to the aid of their displaced colleagues. Lord Beveridge, the English economist who was a leader in the organized attempt to aid the refugee scholars, was deeply impressed by the scientists who joined the effort, and in describing their role he used a significant phrase: "They began by knowing all about the work and worth of their fellow scientists in all countries. They showed their study

5. Major resources for this study have been: a) the manuscript and oral history collections that have been developed since 1961 at the American Institute of Physics' Center for History and Philosophy of Physics in New York City, including materials developed by the Institute's joint project with the American Academy of Arts and Sciences on the history of the initiation and growth of nuclear physics and other research fields in physics that have developed especially rapidly in the United States since 1930; b) the interviews documenting the history of quantum physics deposited at the American Philosophical Society Library in Philadelphia as a result of the joint American Physical Society-American Philosophical Society project, "Sources for the History of Quantum Physics," initiated in 1961.

and themselves as *truly international.*"[6] The scientific internationalism of this group was neither accidental nor superficial. An understanding of how this internationalism developed and how it influenced American institutions of learning and research helps to clarify the effect of the refugees on American physics.

During the years immediately preceding the rise of the Third Reich, Europe was bubbling with intellectual activity in many fields of scholarship. Physics was exceptionally ebullient. The relatively small group of scientists in this field had a profound awareness of recent radical change in the concepts of physics and expectations of more to come. European physicists and their students were constantly in motion, traveling back and forth to exchange newly-born ideas. As today, travel and communication were essential aspects of the life of physicists, contrary to the folkloric image of the scientist locked up in his laboratory, uninterested in personal interactions. Major stops on their itineraries included universities and laboratories in Munich, Leipzig, Göttingen, Leyden, Zurich, Cambridge, Copenhagen, and Berlin. In the 1920's it was essential for physicists to have first-hand experience of the work being performed in the capitals of research. The new quantum theory of matter, after its emergence as a collective triumph of physicists between 1925 and 1927, was being extended rapidly, and in the scattered centers of research its analytical force was being tried on a wide variety of physical problems. The intellectually charged atmosphere of the 1920's has recently been described by the American theoretical physicist John C. Slater:

> [It was] the decade in which the quantum theory really grew up, probably the most fruitful decade which the science of physics has ever known . . . Those of us who started our careers at that particular time found ourselves probably in the most competitive situation that has ever been seen in physical science. Here was the decade in which the most momentous physics discoveries in a century were being made, and here were fifty or more ambitious young men, entering a field with a smaller number of older and very distinguished workers, all trying to be in on the exciting discoveries that all were convinced were going to be made. The inevitable result of this effort was a great deal of duplication; almost every idea occurred to several people simultaneously. No one had time to follow through a line of work without having someone break in on

---

6. Lord Beveridge, *A Defence of Free Learning* (London, 1959), p. 9. Beveridge was the major initiator of the Academic Assistance Council, organized in England in 1933.

his developments before they were finished. It is probable that any one of a dozen theoretical physicists . . . given the situation that faced physics in 1924 just before the development of quantum mechanics, would have worked out its principles eventually, had he been free to take his time about it. But as things were, no one had the time to do it all by himself, and wave mechanics is the composite of the work of many men. Certainly it attained a richness and variety of approach in this way that it never would have had if it had been the work of one or a few isolated scientists.[7]

European physicists were hardly isolated from each other in the 1920's. Their mobility was facilitated by fellowships which allowed them to travel from one center of research to another. In Europe these places were within easy geographical reach and one had merely to present oneself to listen to, participate in, or to observe any particular seminar or laboratory. Indeed, there developed what can be described as a traveling seminar as groups of distinguished physicists attended a series of international conferences and seminars during this period, at Brussels, Leipzig, Rome, Copenhagen, Lake Como, London, or elsewhere.

Young physicists traveled to learn new experimental techniques, to supplement their background by exposure to different ideas, styles, and traditions of research, and sometimes simply to meet their colleagues. Members of the group of physicists under the leadership of Enrico Fermi in Rome, for example, were regularly dispatched to different laboratories during the heat of each summer to take advantage of larger research facilities or to learn new techniques in the relative coolness of London, Copenhagen, Hamburg, New York, or Pasadena.

In the course of these migrations Emilio G. Segrè visited Otto Stern in Hamburg and Pieter Zeeman in Amsterdam, Franco Rasetti visited Lise Meitner in Berlin and Robert A. Millikan in Pasadena, Edoardo Amaldi visited Peter Debye in Leipzig, and Enrico Fermi crossed the Atlantic to lecture at the University of Michigan. Reciprocally, Rome was host to other physicists from all over the world.[8]

One visitor to Rome, in turn, was Hans A. Bethe, who spent five months there in 1931 and another four in 1932. Bethe, a student of Ar-

7. John C. Slater, "Quantum Physics in America Between the Wars," *Physics Today* (January 1968), 44–45.

8. Tape-recorded interview with Emilio Segrè, February 13, 1967, conducted by the author. Oral History Collection, Center for History and Philosophy of Physics, American Institute of Physics (AIP). [Hereafter cited as Oral History Collection, AIP.]

nold Sommerfeld, had been a graduate student in Munich in 1927 when the Americans I. I. Rabi, Edward U. Condon, and Howard P. Robertson attended Sommerfeld's renowned seminar on theoretical physics. Now he was traveling on a Rockefeller Foundation fellowship obtained for him by Sommerfeld. Bethe's first stop was the Cavendish Laboratory in Cambridge, where the work of Rutherford was the chief attraction. From there he went on to Rome, having been advised by Sommerfeld that the research of Enrico Fermi would be well worth knowing. Sommerfeld had also recommended that Bethe go to the Bell Telephone Laboratories in the United States to see Clinton J. Davisson and Lester H. Germer, but Bethe had already worked on their specialty (electron diffraction) and was more interested in work being pursued in Cambridge and Rome.[9]

Rutherford's preeminent position in early nuclear physics had made the Cavendish Laboratory a Mecca for physicists the world over. Sir John Cockcroft, then a young researcher at "the Cavendish," recalled the atmosphere of the laboratory about 1930:

There were a very large number of short-term visitors from the Continent, people like Heisenberg and Gamow and Schrödinger, Einstein, Bohr. A continual stream of visitors who would come for two or three days and give a talk, a colloquium; and then, of course, there were the overseas research people who would come for two or three years to take their Ph.D. degree, people like Oliphant. So roughly half the laboratory group were from overseas, I would say . . . there were quite a lot of Americans.[10]

American physicists were also participants in the traveling seminar. I. I. Rabi recalls that when he was in Europe between 1925 and 1927 he met many other young American scientists who were also on the move, including Edwin C. Kemble, Edward U. Condon, Howard P. Robertson, F. Wheeler Loomis, Robert Oppenheimer, William V. Houston, Linus C. Pauling, Julius Stratton, John C. Slater, and William W. Watson.[11]

9. Tape-recorded interview with Hans Bethe, November 17, 1967, conducted by the author. Oral History Collection, AIP.

10. Tape-recorded interview with Sir John Cockcroft, March 28, 1967, conducted by the author. Oral History Collection, AIP.

11. Tape-recorded interview with I. I. Rabi, December 8, 1963, conducted by Thomas S. Kuhn. Archive for History of Quantum Physics, American Philosophical Society Library.

11. Internationalization and American Self-Improvement

FELLOWSHIPS from the Rockefeller Foundation or from the Rockefeller-backed International Education Board, which granted funds to individuals for a year at a time, played an essential role in internationalizing science in the 1920's. In particular, they made visits to the United States attractive to young European physicists. From 1924 through 1930, the Rockefeller Foundation granted fellowships to 135 European physicists for postdoctoral study abroad. Most of the fellowships went to physicists in Germany (31), Russia (22), and England (18). More of the fellows were attracted to the United States than to any other country. One-third of the physicists from European institutions chose to use their fellowships for study at American institutions, including sixteen of the thirty-one German physics fellows. The European fellows clustered at thriving centers of research in the United States, especially where there were superior facilities for experimental research.[12]

The increasingly attractive research environment in American universities was a consequence of the deliberate attempts made in the 1920's by physicists and by private foundations to improve teaching and research in physics. These efforts had taken hold by the late 1920's. At the California Institute of Technology Robert A. Millikan began developing a first-rate physics faculty immediately after arriving from Chicago in 1921 to head the science-oriented Pasadena institution. Among the new additions to the faculty before the end of the decade were Robert Oppenheimer, Linus C. Pauling, and William V. Houston, all of whom had been visiting the European physics centers during this period; Paul Epstein, who came from Europe in 1921; and Fritz Zwicky, who had originally come from Zurich in 1925 on a Rockefeller fellowship. Millikan was sensitive to the geographical isolation of California Institute of Technology from the older centers of physics on the East Coast and in Europe and wanted to bring the world of physics to California. He invited the most distinguished European physicists to deliver a series

12. *Natural Science Fellowships of the Rockefeller Foundation*, p. 170. The four countries that attracted most of the physics fellows were: United States (44), Germany (26), England (25), and Denmark (16). The United States was also the most popular choice for chemists and for biologists.

of lectures or to stay on for an entire quarter. Max Born, Erwin Schrödinger, Albert Einstein, Arnold Sommerfeld, Niels Bohr, and Paul
Ehrenfest were among the great physicists who accepted.[13]

A similar program was under way at the University of California in
Berkeley. By the late 1920's, the department of physics included Leon-
ard B. Loeb, Raymond T. Birge, Robert Brode, Ernest O. Lawrence,
Samuel K. Allison, and Robert Oppenheimer (who held professorships
both there and at the California Institute of Technology). Gerhart
Dieke, who had been a student of Paul Ehrenfest at the University of
Leyden, had arrived at Berkeley in 1925 to complete his studies there.
In his letters to Samuel Goudsmit, another Ehrenfest student still in
Leyden, he stated that he felt his experiences were beneficial but he was
critical of the relative isolation of physicists at California institutions
from the newer work being developed in Europe. Like others, he felt
that even a short delay in learning of new work was a handicap when
ideas in physics were developing so rapidly. Here again, transatlantic
visitors helped speed up scientific communication, as implied by Dieke
in a letter to Goudsmit from Pasadena early in 1927: "All of you are
much better off in Europe because the new work appears there a few
weeks sooner. Next month Schrödinger will be coming here, and I
hope he will have something new to tell."[14]

Goudsmit himself, along with yet another Ehrenfest student, George
Uhlenbeck, soon joined the faculty at the University of Michigan in
Ann Arbor, where still another determined effort was being made to
raise the standards of research and teaching, and to provide professional
companionship. The chairman of the department of physics, Harrison
M. Randall, felt that he needed more young theoretical physicists. He
managed to reallocate his budget to provide supporting funds for addi-

13. This survey of some of the major American physics departments, based largely on
departmental histories and oral history interviews deposited at the AIP Center for History
and Philosophy of Physics, leaves out similar developments under way at other universities. Stanley Coben, in his study of the cultural changes in America in the 1920's, used
these and other materials to document the development of American physics during the
period in his paper "The 'New Men': Transmission of Quantum Physics to America,
1919–1932," read at the annual meeting of the American Historical Association, December 29, 1967.

14. Gerhard Dieke to Samuel Goudsmit, January 20, 1927. Manuscript Collection,
Center for History and Philosophy of Physics, AIP. [Hereafter cited as Manuscript Collection, AIP.]

tional faculty and dispatched Walter F. Colby to Europe as a talent scout. Having been a postdoctoral student in Europe, Colby knew the young European physicists of particular merit and was able to persuade both Goudsmit and Uhlenbeck to come to the University. It was no accident that there were two rather than one; Ehrenfest had suggested that the difficult period of adjustment could be better weathered by two of his students together than either alone.

In addition to Goudsmit and Uhlenbeck, between 1925 and 1927 Randall added two more young theoretical physicists, thus achieving a "critical mass": Otto Laporte, who came to America on a Rockefeller fellowship after completing his studies with Sommerfeld in Munich in 1924; and David Dennison who had studied with Bohr in Copenhagen after receiving his degree from Michigan. Bohr's assistant, Oskar Klein, had been on the Michigan staff during 1923–1925.[15]

Another of Randall's innovations was to establish a summer school for theoretical physics in 1927, staffed by his own faculty and supplemented by invited lecturers drawn from the ranks of the most distinguished physicists in Europe and America. The school was enthusiastically attended by physicists from all over the country and from Europe. Those who participated in the summer schools, which lasted throughout the 1930's, find it hard to pinpoint exactly what happened there except that they found the atmosphere stimulating.

Writing of that period, Goudsmit notes:

The important thing, however, was not the formal lectures but the informal atmosphere during these summer sessions. The lectures were held to a minimum, just one hour every morning. There were usually two distinguished lecturers present at each time. The afternoon was free for discussions, excursions, picnics, games, swimming. Thus both lecturers and visitors had a lot of leisure time which was used in a most productive way. It is no wonder, therefore, that such an arrangement attracted at one time or another all the active theoretical physicists and many experimenters, young and old, from all over the country . . .

The day usually started rather late with the morning lecture by the visiting scientist.

15. David M. Dennison, "Physics and the Department of Physics Since 1900," in *Research—Definitions and Reflections: Essays on the Occasion of the University of Michigan Sesquicentennial* (Ann Arbor, 1967), p. 130; and tape-recorded interview with Harrison Randall, February 19, 1964, conducted by D. M. Dennison and W. J. King, and Randall's manuscript autobiography, 1964, Manuscript Collection, AIP.

A large fraction of the listeners accompanied the lecturer to the Michigan League for lunch where we had either a separate room or a large table set aside for us. After lunch, some played tennis and later gathered in the physics building or on the lawn, to continue the scientific discussion which had been going on during lunch and even during the tennis game. Heisenberg, an accomplished pianist, would withdraw himself every day for at least an hour, to practice his music. Others would go swimming or canoeing . . .

During all these social activities the participants never lost sight of their physics problems, sometimes to the despair of their relatives who couldn't care less about the intricacies of quantum mechanics. Several of the visitors, often including the lecturers, were housed in the Delta Upsilon fraternity on Hill Street, which the Physics Department had taken over for the summer. This further promoted the interplay of ideas, and often discussions continued until late at night.[16]

The roster of lecturers at the summer sessions was very impressive. For the summer of 1929, the lecturers at Michigan were P. A. M. Dirac and E. A. Milne from England; Leon Brillouin from France; Karl F. Herzfeld, who had left Munich to join the Johns Hopkins faculty in 1926; and Edward U. Condon and David Dennison from the United States. In 1930 the lecturers included Ehrenfest and Fermi as well as Goudsmit and Uhlenbeck, and Philip Morse from Princeton. In 1931 the roster included Arnold Sommerfeld, Wolfgang Pauli, H. A. Kramers from Holland, Robert Oppenheimer, Otto Laporte, Colby, and Uhlenbeck. The average attendance at these summer sessions in the late twenties and thirties was about sixty graduate students and thirty faculty.

At the University of Illinois, even more isolated from other centers, similar efforts were under way. In 1929, F. Wheeler Loomis had come from New York University to head the department of physics. His first annual report summarizes the intentions and activities of the department:

The following steps have been taken with the intention of stimulating the interest of staff and students and directing it toward the more vital parts of modern physics: an informal seminar consisting of several members of the Departments of Physics, Chemistry, and Mathematics has met weekly for the study of topics in the wave mechanics . . . a number of outside lecturers have been brought to the campus and have spoken on various new problems and results in modern physics. Only one out of eleven lectures

16. Samuel A. Goudsmit, "The Michigan Symposium in Theoretical Physics," *Michigan Alumnus Quarterly Review* (May 1961), 179–181.

so given was in any sense popular. The rest were intended for our own graduate students and faculty and have, it is thought, contributed effectively to keeping us informed and interested in the progressive parts of physics . . . The list of speakers follows: L. Prandtl, University of Göttingen; Otto Oldenberg, University of Göttingen; Gregor Wentzel, University of Zurich; Otto Stern, University of Hamburg; and Edward Condon, University of Minnesota.[17]

At Princeton, H. P. Robertson and K. T. Compton developed programs to raise the level of teaching and research in physics. The Michigan pattern of importing European physicists two at a time, as suggested by Ehrenfest, was repeated at Princeton when John von Neumann and Eugene P. Wigner were added to the faculty in 1930. Both had come from Hungary by way of the lively Berlin circle of physicists and mathematicians. At Princeton there were strong ties between the mathematics department and the physics department, and Wigner and von Neumann helped to strengthen these connections. Like the California Institute of Technology, Princeton benefited from the largesse of the Rockefeller-supported General Education Board, which gave nineteen million dollars in the 1920's to help develop science departments in American universities.

The commitment to build better departments of physics at universities throughout the United States was made by many physicists like I. I. Rabi and Edward Condon who had traveled in Europe during the preceding years and had developed definite ideas about how to improve physics in the United States when they returned home. In the fall of 1928, when most physicists still relied on the German journals, John Tate, editor of the *Physical Review*, asked forty-five leading American physicists whether they thought a new type of journal, containing "reports and critical comments on the various branches of current thought and research," was needed in the United States. Edward Condon, who had returned from his postdoctoral tour of Europe a year earlier, was one of the many who gave strong support to the idea:

I have been thinking ever since I returned from Germany that the greatest handicap to physical research work here is the lack of an adequate literature in English . . . There is no question but what our laboratories are better now than those abroad, but we lack

17. Quoted in G. M. Almy, "Life with Wheeler [Loomis] in the Physics Department 1929–40," manuscript of talk presented May 24, 1957. Manuscript Collection, AIP.

the literature which brings the young men quickly into step with the research work in the various fields.[18]

The visiting Rockefeller fellows from Europe, the stream of distinguished European physicists who could be found at any time lecturing at one or another American university in the late twenties or early thirties, and the conscious effort to upgrade physics programs to develop a more productive atmosphere at a number of institutions—these elements added up to a unique and vigorous physics enterprise in the United States. It occurred precisely at the time when the new quantum mechanics was being applied successfully to one field after another. American institutions were thus in close touch with these developments and in the forefront of many fields, including the newly developing field of nuclear physics. Despite the Depression, more and more students were being attracted to physics, and research support and fellowships were available.[19]

By 1933 these developments were clearly evidenced during meetings of the American Association for the Advancement of Science which were held in Chicago over a two-week period in June to coincide with the Century of Progress Exposition. The meeting of the American Physical Society, the organization of American research physicists, was also held in June 1933 in connection with the Exposition. Among the forty foreign guests who participated in the Chicago meetings were the physicists Frederick Aston and John Cockcroft from the Cavendish Laboratory, Niels Bohr, and Enrico Fermi. John Slater recalled recently that the thing that impressed him most was "not so much the excellence of the invited speakers as the fact that the younger American workers on the program gave talks of such high quality on research of such importance that, for the first time, the European physicists present were here to learn as much as to instruct."[20]

18. Edward Condon to John Tate, October 2, 1928. Manuscript Collection, AIP.

19. In 1931 United States philanthropic foundations gave an estimated $10,000,000 for encouragement of research, exclusive of medicine and public health. Karl T. Compton, "The Government's Responsibilities in Science," *Science*, 81 (April 12, 1935), 349. See also the National Research Council's *Funds Available in the United States for the Support and Encouragement of Research in Science and Its Technologies* (Washington, 1928 and 1934).

20. Slater, "Quantum Physics," p. 43. In 1932, more than 10,000 foreign students were enrolled in American universities. See Clarence Shedd, "Higher Education in the United States," in Walter M. Kotschnig and E. Prys, eds., *The University in a Changing World* (London, 1932), p. 140.

In other words, the self-conscious attempts of American physicists to improve their own discipline were beginning to pay off. The American involvement in the mixing of people and ideas in the preceding decade had helped to reduce the geographic isolation of American research centers from the cluster of European centers. As a result, many American scientists knew their European colleagues and they also knew the needs of their own institutions.

iii. The Dissolution of German Physics

AT the same time that science in the United States was undergoing rapid quantitative and qualitative growth, the scientific atmosphere in Germany was also changing, but in a far different way. Even though university enrollments had greatly increased, the number of faculty positions remained relatively static.[21] As a result, many young Germans interested in science initially had doubts about entering the field because of the uncertainty of obtaining a suitable position when their education was completed.

By 1927, the deteriorating scientific situation in Germany had become noticeable. The American geneticist Leslie C. Dunn went to Europe to make a study for the General Education Board on the state of research in the field of genetics. Dunn found severe limitations on opportunities for research in all fields. In part, this resulted from students taking degrees in the sciences faster than the academic and technical market could absorb them. Young German graduates were inclined to go abroad, where greater opportunities for research and teaching positions existed. German scientists told him that conditions were steadily worsening and moreover that "they couldn't see any prospect for the kind of political stability that would be likely to support steady scientific progress."[22]

21. Edward Y. Hartshorne, Jr., *The German Universities and National Socialism* (London, 1937), pp. 74ff., discusses the problems of overcrowding. For a German view of the university situation in 1932, see Martin Doerne, "Problems of the German University," in Kotschnig and Prys, *The University in a Changing World*, p. 66.

22. Interview with Leslie C. Dunn, November 1967, conducted by the author.

Hans Bethe has recalled how he reacted to the general atmosphere in Germany during the 1920's:

Many of my colleagues and professors were terrible chauvinists, and talked of nothing else but restoring the glory of Germany and the unfair treatment that Germany had received at Versailles . . . so I found life in Germany in the 1920's unsatisfactory in every respect except work. I found that I could not talk politics to anybody, and that colored my outlook generally . . . People were grumbling all the time. They were dissatisfied. I had a very small circle of friends, two or three, with whom I got along very well, with whom I went on walks in the mountains near Munich . . . But apart from that, I just felt that I didn't fit into the surroundings.[23]

By 1933 many of the bright young men who had been educated in German universities during the 1920's and had taken part in the international round of scientific travels had assumed their first faculty positions in the German universities and were starting to train their own students. At that time Hans Bethe had completed the first two months of the winter semester in his new post at the University of Tübingen where he was a *"beauftragte Lehrkraft,"* charged with instruction in the field of theoretical physics. Recently he recalled: "I enjoyed it a lot because it was the first time that I really was responsible for the teaching of theoretical physics and arranged my own schedule of courses . . . As far as the work went, it was very satisfactory."[24]

But there was another side to life in Tübingen:

Personally it was most unsatisfactory because Tübingen was one of the most Nazi-infested towns of southern Germany, and I was quite lonely . . . I remember they had any number of victory celebrations after elections and after many events in the early days of the Nazi government. They came to power on the 30th of January in '33, and I kept myself very much out of the mainstream in the city . . .[25]

On the first of April they had the first boycott of Jewish stores and about the same time they published a law according to which anyone who had one Jewish grandmother could not hold an official appointment. Well, since I had a Jewish mother, not only a grandmother, it was clear that this meant me and that sooner or later I would have to leave. I didn't expect it to be quite so soon. I had a somewhat interesting experience one day in April when I got a letter from one of the two people who were taking their doctor's degree with me, saying that he had read in a small town paper in Wuert-

23. Tape-recorded interview with Hans Bethe, November 17, 1967, conducted by the author. Oral History Collection, AIP.

24. *Ibid.*   25. *Ibid.*

temberg that I had been dismissed—and what should *he* do? This was the first news I had.

Then I wrote a letter to the professor of experimental physics who had been very friendly to me and who had indicated that he liked my work and would like me to remain there. I got back a very stiff letter saying that presumably the lectures in theoretical physics would have to be arranged differently the next term. About a week after the first letter from the student, I finally got a letter from the minister of education of the state of Wuerttemberg, saying that I was dismissed according to the law effective the first of May but that the salary for May could still be paid to me, and that was that.

So I went back to Munich, to my old teacher Sommerfeld who without much difficulty got a fellowship for me [at Munich] for the next three or four months.[26]

The sudden disruption of university life caught different scientists at different stages in their careers. For example, the experimental physicist, Otto R. Frisch, who had been working with Otto Stern at the University of Hamburg, had been scheduled to spend time with Enrico Fermi in Rome in 1933 on a Rockefeller International Education Board fellowship. Under the new laws, however, Frisch was unable to take advantage of the fellowship because he would have no post to return to in Germany, and the existence of a permanent position was one of the requirements of the fellowship.[27]

The unprecedented situation vividly impressed scholars and others abroad on May 19, 1933, when the *Manchester Guardian* devoted a full page to a list of the professors who had been dismissed from their posts in German universities during the three-week period between April 13 and May 4. The list covered institutions from every part of Germany and read like a Who's Who of scholarship. Compiled for the most part from announcements in the German press, it included 196 entries and was by no means complete.[28]

By mid-June, things had become even worse. On-the-scene reports by visiting scientists from America described the despair of those affected and alerted their colleagues in the United States to the growing crisis. Selig Hecht, an American biologist on leave from Columbia Univer-

26. Tape-recorded interview with Hans Bethe, October 28, 1966, conducted by the author. Oral History Collection, AIP.

27. Tape-recorded interview with Otto R. Frisch, May 3, 1967, conducted by the author. Oral History Collection, AIP.

28. "Nazi 'Purge' of the Universities: A Long List of Dismissals," *The Manchester Guardian Weekly*, May 19, 1933, 399. The page is reproduced as an appendix to this essay, p. 234.

sity in 1933 to do research at Cambridge, visited Germany in June. In a letter to a colleague he wrote:

It is really a terrifying situation when viewed close to hand. Not merely the obvious agony which the dismissed Jewish professors and others are up against, but the extraordinary callousness of the rest of the population in the face of it. Most people don't give a darn; a large proportion is rather glad it all happened. Those extremely few who are upset by it are disinclined to do or say anything publicly or even privately. In Munich everyone says not to speak too loudly or one will land in Dachau (the nearest concentration camp).[29]

In another letter, written on the same day, Hecht reported:

With the exception of a few outstanding instances of men who have been untouched or who have been dismissed outright, Jewish professors have been placed on leave. That means that they must absent themselves from their institutes, they cannot give any lectures, and cannot have any contact with their assistants and graduate students ... The situation of the Privatdozenten is much simpler ... they are being rapidly dismissed since they have practically no tenure. The assistants are worst off. They have usually been given one or two months' notice and have been dismissed. People working on funds from the Notgemeinschaft are in the same situation. Many of the appropriations have already terminated and, like those which terminate July 31, are not renewable for Jewish applicants.[30]

Another visitor to Germany in June of 1933 was the mathematician John von Neumann whose appointment at Princeton permitted him to spend six months of each year in Europe. On June 19 von Neumann wrote to the Princeton mathematician Oswald Veblen from Budapest:

Germany, on the other hand, was very depressing. We have been three days in Göttingen and the rest in Berlin, and had time to see and appreciate the effects of the present German madness. It is simply horrible. In Göttingen, in the first place, it is quite obvious that if these boys continue for only two more years (which is unfortunately very probable), they will ruin German science for a generation—at least—.[31]

29. Selig Hecht to Leslie C. Dunn, June 20, 1933. L. C. Dunn Papers, American Philosophical Society Library. (Hereafted cited as L. C. Dunn Papers.)

30. Selig Hecht to Alfred Cohn, June 20, 1933. L. C. Dunn Papers.

31. John von Neumann to Oswald Veblen, June 19, 1933. Oswald Veblen Papers, Manuscripts Division, Library of Congress. (Hereafter cited as Oswald Veblen Papers.) Hitler apparently was aware of this possibility. An American sociologist who made a firsthand study of the Nazi impact on academic life has stated that Hitler was reported to have said: "Our national policies will not be revoked or modified, even for scientists. If the dismissal of Jewish scientists means the annihilation of contemporary German science, then we shall do without science for a few years." See Hartshorne, *The German Universities*, p. 112.

Von Neumann was particularly disturbed by the situation in Götting-
en: "I met Courant, too, who is perhaps the most unhappy of all, as
the Göttingen 'Mathematisches Institut,' an essential part of his lifework, will be lost to him if he loses his position—which is probable—."[32]
Von Neumann then provided Veblen with a list of mathematicians
whom he knew to be in danger of losing their positions. He also named
outstanding theoretical physicists who were similarly forced into
"Beurlaubungen": Max Born, Hans Bethe, Felix Bloch, Walter Heitler,
Lothar Nordheim, Fritz London, Edward Teller, and Victor Weisskopf. In addition, von Neumann, like Hecht, was especially concerned
about the fate of other scientists, younger men whose reputations had
not yet been established. He despaired that "there is a great number of
gifted students, immediately before or after the Ph.D., whose existence
in Germany will be rendered impossible."[33]

Von Neumann's predictions were of course perfectly correct. By
April 1936, more than sixteen hundred scholars, about one-third of them
in the sciences, had been dismissed from German universities and scientific institutions.[34] The student enrollment in the German universities
had plunged, and large numbers of those still enrolled joined the ranks
of the bookburners. Even before 1933, students had played an active
role in supporting the Nazis, often making it impossible to establish an
atmosphere conducive to creative learning and scholarship in the universities.

iv. The Response of the Scientific Community

THE mass dismissals of scientists unacceptable to the regime in Germany were accompanied by concerted government efforts to direct science into channels that were compatible with the Nazi programs.
The subsequent fate of the dismissed scientists was influenced by how
the scientific community itself reacted to these developments.

32. Von Neumann to Veblen, June 19, 1933. Oswald Veblen Papers.
33. *Ibid.*
34. Hartshorne, *The German Universities*, p. 99.

Most members of the German scientific societies apparently were unwilling to speak out or were unconcerned about the effects of the Nazi policies on their dismissed colleagues and on science itself. When Albert Einstein resigned from the Prussian Academy of Science and the Bavarian Academy of Science in the spring of 1933, he condemned these scientific organizations for their acquiescence to the Nazi policies:

> The primary object of an academy is to protect and enrich the scientific life of a country. Yet, to the best of my knowledge, the learned societies of Germany have stood by passively and silently while substantial numbers of scholars, students, and academically-trained professionals have been deprived of employment and livelihood. I do not want to belong to any society which behaves in such a manner, even if it does so under pressure.[35]

Einstein had accepted a position in 1932 as the first faculty member of the newly founded Institute for Advanced Study at Princeton where he intended to spend six months of every year, returning to Berlin for the summer semesters. Long an outspoken critic of German nationalism, when he condemned the Nazi attack on Jews Einstein was denounced by the Prussian Academy for "atrocity-mongering." Had he not resigned, he certainly would have been expelled.

Einstein was anathema to the Nazis, not only because he was a Jew, a pacifist, and boldly critical of the regime, but also because he was a world symbol of theoretical physics. A series of pamphlets and magazine articles was published in Germany, attacking all theoretical physicists as Jews or products of the "Jewish spirit." Leading the attack on this brand of physics was the experimental physicist Johannes Stark, who had won the Nobel Prize in 1919. His assault on Jewish scientists was based on his notion that they were "the chief exponents and propagandists of the dogmatic spirit" in contemporary theoretical physics which had a "crippling and damaging effect on the development of physical research" in Germany.[36] Rebuttals to such arguments were offered within

---

35. Otto Nathan and Heinz Norden, eds., *Einstein on Peace* (New York, 1960), p. 216; see also "Professor Einstein and the Prussian Academy," *Science*, 77 (April 7, 1933), 346.

36. J. Stark, "The Pragmatic and Dogmatic Spirit in Physics," *Nature*, 141 (April 30, 1938), 771. See also, "Letter from J. Stark on International Status and Obligations of Science," with reply from A. V. Hill, *Nature*, 133 (February 24, 1934), 290–291; "Letter from J. Stark on the Attitude of the German Government Towards Science," with reply from A. V. Hill, *Nature*, 133 (April 21, 1934), 615–616. For an account of similar pub-

Germany by the physicists Max Planck, Max von Laue, Erwin Schrö-dinger, and Werner Heisenberg, who extolled the merits of theoretical physics without dealing with the issue of anti-Semitism.

Despite many notable exceptions, most German scientists went along with the Nazi tide. Their dismissed colleagues looked to scientists in other lands for help.

Reactions abroad to the events taking place in Germany deplored the attacks on academic freedom, the sacrifice of true scientific research, and the subordination of scholarship to political and other irrelevant consid-erations. Initially, however, there was a deliberate attempt to avoid what was considered the politics of the situation and to emphasize the need to uphold the ideal of the international nature of scholarship. In the spring of 1933, for example, the American Association of University Professors issued a public resolution which was transmitted to the Com-mittee on Intellectual Cooperation of the League of Nations: "The council has no wish to express any opinion on the political life or ideals of any nation, but science and scholarship long since have become inter-national, and the conditions of intellectual life in every important country are a matter of legitimate concern to every other."[37] This state-ment was an expression of conviction and of sympathy for "members of the profession who have been subjected to intolerant treatment in these difficult times."[38] More than four years later, when the effects of the programs of the Nazi regime were clear for all to see, the American Asso-ciation for the Advancement of Science issued a statement on a similarly mild note, resolving that "science is wholly independent of national

---

lications, see Morris Goran, "Swastika Science," *The Nation*, 148 (June 3, 1939), 641–643. Einstein was subjected to similar attacks throughout the 1920's. See Philipp Frank, *Einstein: His Life and Times* (New York, 1947), pp. 158–166.

Another German Nobel Prize physicist, Philip Lenard, was also a prominent spokes-man for the Nazi view of science. His four-volume *Deutsche Physik* (Munich, 1936) was loaded with attacks on "the Jewish spirit" in physics. In the preface, written in August 1935, and in subsequent prefaces in 1937 and 1942, he emphatically denied that science is international and maintained that, as a human product, science was "racial and condi-tioned by blood." See volume I, pp. ix–xviii.

37. "The Academic Situation in Germany and the American Association of University Professors," *School and Society*, 37 (June 10, 1933), 742.

38. *Ibid.*

boundaries and races and creeds and can flourish only when there is peace and intellectual freedom."[39]

Some scientists, however, adopted a more militant stand: that "the freedom of science [in the fascist countries] has been threatened or entirely destroyed." In 1934 a group of fourteen distinguished European scholars from many fields issued "a call to scientists" in which they condemned the uses to which science was being limited in Germany:

> In that country the exact sciences have been openly degraded to jobbing for war industries. During the education of young physicists and chemists, much time is devoted to lectures and practical exercises in 'defensive science': gas protection, air protection, study of explosives, war intelligence service, which have no relation to the scientific significance of this field. Moreover, only such investigations are favored which are likely to bring about a direct technical advance . . .[40]

The call to scientists to protect "free international science" referred to a statement by Bernhard Rust, Nazi Reichsminister for Science, Education, and Popular Instruction, who had maintained that "National Socialism is not unscientific, but only hostile to theories." As a result, the signers of the call pointed out, "all branches of physics which cannot be made to serve political and economic imperialism are therefore hampered and restricted. Studies which have contributed essentially to the broadening of our concept of the physical universe are thrust aside openly as vain and fruitless intellectualism."[41] Similarly, this group of scholars denounced Nazi-style genetics, the pseudo-science created in the service of racist doctrine.

In December 1938, Franz Boas made public a manifesto, signed by 1,284 American scientists, commenting on an article by Stark in the British journal, *Nature*, which set forth the official Nazi position on science. The article, declared the signers of the manifesto, was "an attack on all theoretical physics, and by obvious implication, on scientific theory in general. It introduces the official racialism of the Nazis to divide physicists into good, that is, nontheoretical and Aryan, and bad,

39. "Science and the Dictator Nation," *School and Society*, 48 (December 17, 1938), 800–802. Quoted from the *New York Herald Tribune*.
40. "A Call to Scientists," *The New Republic*, 80 (August 29, 1934), 76–77. Among the signers were Harold Laski, J. B. S. Haldane, Julian Huxley, Ernest Rutherford, Paul Langevin, and Jean Perrin.
41. *Ibid.*

that is, theoretical and Jewish." American scientists were warned that "any attack upon freedom of thought in one sphere, even as non-political a sphere as theoretical physics, is in effect an attack upon democracy itself."[42] The indignation over the Nazi attack on science was matched by strenuous efforts to assist the scientists victimized by these policies.

v. Internationalism in Practice

THE plight of the scientists who had been displaced or soon would be was immediately evident, and the close international links in science led to action by their colleagues in other countries. As individuals and in groups they swiftly came to the aid of their fellows: finding out who was in need, raising funds to assist them, and finding positions where they could continue to be productive with their scientific work.

Niels Bohr was one of the first to see the implications of the events in Germany. Otto Frisch, whose career at the University of Hamburg came to an abrupt end in the spring of 1933, remembered Bohr's concern:

Niels Bohr came visiting because he was concerned with the fate of all the displaced persons likely to come out of Germany. So he had decided to go around and talk to his various colleagues to get an idea of the problems; if possible, to meet the people who were in danger.[43]

Frisch himself found a haven at Bohr's Institute for Theoretical Physics in Copenhagen a year later. Through the efforts of Otto Stern and the support of the newly-formed Academic Assistance Council, Frisch first journeyed to P. M. S. Blackett's physics laboratory at Birkbeck College in London.

The Academic Assistance Council was established in May 1933 in

42. "Intellectual Freedom," *School and Society*, 48 (December 17, 1938), 787. The argument that science needs a free, democratic atmosphere to survive, often articulated since the 1930's, needs examination in the light of post-World War II developments. Daniel Kevles, who is preparing a social history of physics in America, to be published by Knopf in 1969, maintains that the argument had its origins in the ferment of the 1930's.

43. Tape-recorded interview with Otto R. Frisch, May 3, 1967, conducted by the author. Oral History Collection, AIP.

England "to defend the principle of academic freedom and to help those scholars and scientists of any nationality who, on grounds of religion, race, or political opinion, are prevented from continuing their work in their own country."[44] Lord Rutherford, a dominant figure in English science, was its president. Sir William Beveridge played a major role in founding the Council. Its offices were in the rooms of the Royal Society. The Council soon took a major part in giving assistance to displaced scholars. It circulated lists of such scholars to individuals and institutions that might be able to find places for them and it provided funds for temporary assistance and research positions in England.

An initiator and active supporter of the Council was the physicist Leo Szilard who in the twenties and early thirties was part of the "Hungarian circle" of scientists in Berlin. His first thought had been to establish an international university in Switzerland where scholars could be free to pursue their work. In the spring of 1933, Szilard was introduced to Beveridge in Vienna, and expressed his conviction that it would be necessary to provide at least temporary refuge for scholars. Soon after, the Academic Assistance Council was founded in London and Szilard, through his wide circle of friends in Europe, publicized the Council's existence, urging scientists to take advantage of its resources. Unlike many scientists during the period, Szilard had no illusions that things would get better soon, and he urged his displaced colleagues to reestablish themselves permanently.[45]

In 1933 a meeting attended by ten thousand persons was held in London to raise funds for refugee assistance and to hear and honor Albert Einstein. By that time a number of German scientists had found positions in England at London, Cambridge, Oxford, Manchester, and other universities. Many English scholars were contributing regularly

44. Lord Rutherford of Nelson, "Exiles in British Sanctuary," *Science*, 79 (June 15, 1934), 533. The Council's history appears in Lord Beveridge's *A Defence of Free Learning*. In 1937, the Council became the Society for Protection of Science and Learning. The major organized efforts are described by Norman Bentwich, *The Rescue and Achievement of Refugee Scholars* (The Hague, 1953).

45. Interview with Esther Simpson in London, September 12, 1967, conducted by the author. It was through Szilard that Miss Simpson joined the staff of the new Council in 1933; Edward Shils has described Szilard's role in "Leo Szilard: A Memoir," *Encounter*, 23 (December 1964), 38–39.

a percentage of their salary to help create and support temporary positions for the new arrivals.

Other groups to aid refugee scholars were formed in Europe in 1933, including the *Notgemeinschaft Deutscher Wissenschaftler im Ausland* set up by refugee scholars themselves in Zurich in 1933, with financial help from British learned societies. The *Notgemeinschaft* succeeded in placing German scholars in a number of countries, and was especially successful in finding a temporary haven for many at the newly reorganized University of Istanbul in Turkey. It soon moved from Zurich to London.

Early American responses to the situation took the form of spontaneous and independent efforts to assist the refugees and to find places for them in the United States. Leslie Dunn at Columbia University had been in touch with his European colleagues in biology and in other scientific fields since the 1920's when he had reported on conditions there for the General Education Board. He recalls that when the *Manchester Guardian* list of 196 displaced scholars reached the United States near the end of May, he, Alvin Johnson of The New School for Social Research, and John Dewey, Franz Boas, and Wesley Mitchell of Columbia met for lunch at the Columbia Faculty Club to discuss the situation. By the end of the luncheon, they had planned a Faculty Fellowship Fund at Columbia designed to aid their displaced colleagues by providing an opportunity for some of them to work at Columbia and had discussed what other steps might be taken on a national basis.[46]

A letter was sent to all Columbia professors, signed by John Dewey as temporary chairman and by other members of the faculty. They suggested "that since the continuity and integrity of scholarly work is a matter which vitally concerns us all, we at Columbia might take a lead in initiating effective help to our German colleagues who have been dismissed."[47] The letter solicited opinion on establishment of temporary fellowships at Columbia for refugee scholars, asking whether the faculty were willing to contribute toward funds to be raised for this purpose. The response was immediate. By the end of November 1933, 125 Columbia faculty members had contributed nearly $4,000 in cash and

46. Interview with Leslie Dunn, November 1967, conducted by the author.
47. John Dewey, *et al.*, to Members of the Faculties of Columbia University [1933]. L. C. Dunn Papers.

pledges and additional funds were obtained from outside agencies. As a result, provision was made to add four displaced scholars as visiting professors without financial responsibility on the part of the university. This group included the anthropologist Julius Lips, the archeologist Margaret Bieber, the mathematician Stefan Warschawski, and the theologian Paul Tillich.[48]

The appropriate departments of the university would invite a displaced scholar as a "faculty guest," and the needed financial support would be provided by the Faculty Fellowship Fund. In that way individuals would be selected on the basis of scholarly ability, not only need.

The principle of selection by their academic peers was characteristically employed in all of the American efforts to place refugees in either temporary or permanent university positions in the United States. The major group concerned with aiding displaced scholars in the United States was the Emergency Committee in Aid of Displaced German Scholars which, like the Academic Assistance Council in England, had been organized in May 1933. The Committee later substituted the word "Foreign" for "German" in its name. The origins of the Emergency Committee can be traced to a number of discussions in the period, such as the one that had taken place at Columbia.[49] As the Committee was beginning to take shape, Oswald Veblen, head of the School of Mathematical Sciences at the Institute for Advanced Study at Princeton, discussed ways of providing aid in a letter to Simon Flexner on May 10, 1933:

The idea which seems to receive most favor is that of having a committee for the natural sciences, which should be composed in a large part of what the Germans would call aryan scientists, together with a few men of affairs who would know how to raise funds. The idea would be to distribute the German scientists . . . so as not to cause undue concentration anywhere but so as to allow them to continue their scientific work.

48. Interim Report of Faculty Fellowship Fund, November 27, 1933. L. C. Dunn Papers.

49. A history of the Emergency Committee has been written by its chairman and executive secretary, Stephen Duggan, and Betty Drury, *The Rescue of Science and Learning* (New York, 1948). Valuable information is included in an excellent study by Charles John Wetzel, "The American Rescue of Refugee Scholars and Scientists from Europe, 1933–1945" (unpub. Ph.D. diss., Univ. of Wisconsin, 1964), which provides a comprehensive account of the organization, financing, policies, and operation of the various formal committees established to aid refugee scholars.

The scientific membership of the committee could be selected in such a way that the committee would possess firsthand knowledge of the individuals who are to be helped.[50]

The Emergency Committee assisted scholars from all fields of learning. They received applications to assist in the appointment of displaced scholars only from universities and not from individual scholars. When the university wanted to add a displaced scholar to its faculty but lacked funds for the position, it could submit a request to the committee for a grant to support the specific individual proposed for the position. The committee restricted its assistance to "mature scholars of distinction who had already made their reputations." Younger foreign scholars, they felt, would be in direct competition with American scholars who had recently completed their graduate work and were most affected by Depression-forced cutbacks in university faculties.[51] Further, since the committee did not want to place heavy pension burdens on the already strained universities during the Depression period, they did not make grants to scholars more than fifty-eight years old. Thus their assistance was largely limited to scholars between the ages of thirty-five and fifty-eight years of age whose reputations had already been established well enough to warrant an invitation from an American university.

The harsh edges of the committee's policies were largely a result of the Depression. But the committee also wanted to head off possible native anti-Semitism, conflicts with the economic self-interest of American scholars, and professional jealousy. Moreover, throughout the 1930's the immigration laws of the United States demanded of a non-quota immigrant teacher that he should have taught in Europe and could provide evidence that a job awaited him in the United States. Refugee aid work was strictly a private enterprise and aid committees had to work out policies that would win the support of private foundations. A major supporter of the Emergency Committee was the Rockefeller Foundation whose grants in aid of refugee scholars continued its established tradition of supporting science and individual scholars at specific institutions.

50. Oswald Veblen to Simon Flexner, May 10, 1933. Oswald Veblen Papers.
51. For the effect of the Depression on younger scholars, see "Academic Unemployment," American Association of University Professors *Bulletin*, 19 (1933), 354–355; and F. K. Richtmyer and H. M. Willey, "The Young College Instructor and the Depression," American Association of University Professors *Bulletin*, 22 (December, 1936), 507–509.

There were, however, many ways around the committee's policy of accepting applications only from institutions that needed aid in order to consummate an appointment. Scientists working with the Emergency Committee and a network of colleagues in universities throughout the country let it be known that certain scientists were available and that, if they were offered a specific position at an institution, the institution could probably obtain a grant to sustain that position. To avoid the age limit, Harlow Shapley, who had attracted many of the European Rockefeller fellows to the Harvard Observatory in the 1920's, helped establish a group known as the National Research Associates which provided funds to maintain senior scholars at Harvard.

In physics, possibly to a greater degree than in other fields, there was a tendency to bypass the committees aiding refugee scholars and to make direct arrangements. Again, this was facilitated by the high degree of internationalization of the field and by the personal contacts that had been established so effectively during the 1920's and early thirties. Leslie Dunn, who served on the executive board of the Emergency Committee, recalls that physicists seemed to know when someone who was doing interesting work wanted to move or when it was time to urge him to move. There were, in consequence, fewer applications to the Columbia Faculty Fellowship Fund or the Emergency Committee for funds in aid of physicists than for scientists and scholars in other fields.[52]

Not only did physicists in America react individually to the needs of their colleagues, but they also made efforts to enlist support throughout the profession. In December 1933 Rudolf Ladenburg and Eugene Wigner circulated a letter, written in German, to twenty-seven other physicists at American institutions, asking for their support in aid of German physicists who had lost their posts and had not yet found other positions. The senders and all but two of the physicists who received the letter had emigrated from Europe and taken up positions in American universities, eighteen of them before 1933 and seven as refugees from the Nazis. A list of twenty-eight physicists in need of help was attached. Wigner had obtained many of the names when he visited Berlin in 1933 and wrote to his friends at various German universities, asking who was being dismissed. Most of the individuals on the list were from Berlin,

52. Interview with Leslie Dunn, November 1967, conducted by the author.

Göttingen, and Breslau, where Wigner and Ladenburg had many contacts. They asked their colleagues to set aside 2 to 4 per cent of their income for two years in order to provide stipends for physicists in need.[53]

Other lists of displaced scholars, classified according to their fields, were already circulating widely in the United States before the list was compiled by Wigner and Ladenburg. Most of these lists had been compiled by the Academic Assistance Council in London and sent to the Emergency Committee in the United States. One, dated September 5, 1933, listed sixty-seven displaced physicists who had not yet found permanent positions. In most cases the names were well known in physics, making biographical data and comments on the list unnecessary.[54]

The information on the mimeographed lists was updated regularly by personal communications from Europe to America between scholars in specific fields. For example, the American Mathematical Society appointed an informal committee to represent the mathematicians in co-operative efforts with other committees to aid ousted scholars. Oswald Veblen, chairman of the committee, relied heavily on Niels Bohr and his mathematician brother Harald for news about the availability and needs of European scholars. Harald Bohr scoured Europe, reporting to Veblen almost daily by cablegrams and letters. By 1934 Veblen and others felt they had reached the saturation point in placing mathematicians in the United States as they took note of the large number of unemployed native mathematicians as well as signs of growing anti-Semitism in America.[55]

The placement of refugee scientists in America can be compared to

53. R. Ladenburg and E. Wigner to "Sehr verehrter Herr Kollege!" December 14, 1933. William F. Meggers Papers, Manuscript Collection, Center for History and Philosophy of Physics, AIP; and interview with Eugene Wigner, November 16, 1967, by the author. A translation of the letter appears as an appendix to this essay, pp. 229–233.

54. On May 9, 1934, Edward R. Murrow, who was on the Emergency Committee staff until 1935, sent Oswald Veblen a list of available mathematicians and physicists compiled by the Academic Assistance Council. By that time eighty-one physicists were listed. E. R. Murrow to Oswald Veblen, May 9, 1934. Oswald Veblen Papers.

55. Harald Bohr to R. G. D. Richardson, May 30, 1933; Richardson to Harald Bohr, June 29, 1933; Richardson to H. F. Blichfeldt, H. L. Rietz, and O. Veblen, June 25, 1933. Oswald Veblen Papers.

American scholars and European visitors were aware of anti-Semitic attitudes and unwritten policies within the science departments of many American universities. They recalled that even under ordinary circumstances in the 1920's and early 1930's it was often especially difficult to find faculty positions for well qualified Jewish graduates.

the refereeing system used by the editors of scholarly journals and by foundation executives. Panels of experts examined the credentials of refugee scholars, commented on their qualifications, and evaluated their suitability for specific situations. The Emergency Committee and other refugee aid groups in specific disciplines maintained "refugee" files containing a *vita*, references, "referees' comments," and, in at least one field, specific ratings from A to D in three categories: Scholarship, Personality, Adaptability and Teaching Ability. Given a limited number of available positions, the aim was to place qualified people where they could be most effective.

Too often it was difficult to evaluate the credentials of younger scholars. Leslie Dunn recalls that judgment in the field of genetics was not very difficult but it meant that only people who had a reasonable amount of publications could be judged. The situation of the younger displaced scholar can be tragically characterized as "to have published or to have perished." Nevertheless, additional places were found through the continuing efforts within the American scientific community, backed by the financial support of individuals and foundations.

VI. On the Way to America

ABOUT one hundred refugee physicists came to the United States between 1933 and 1941. Most of them had come from Germany and Austria and had been trained in the centers of European physics research that had been so active in the 1920's. Most of the refugee physicists who took up positions in America were under forty and had received their doctorates since 1921 and thus were beginning or about to begin their careers at the time of great excitement and intellectual ferment in physics in the late 1920's. They found jobs in the United States at universities throughout the country, without clustering at any single institution but tending to go to the universities that had been developing strong physics departments in the late twenties and early thirties.[56]

56. This description is based on a preliminary analysis of available biographical information for most of the one hundred physicists listed thus far by the author. For a descrip-

Many had obtained temporary refuge en route to the United States, in France, Copenhagen, Istanbul, and especially England. The pattern was first to find a refuge in Europe and then, because of the increasing threat of war and because of the inability of these havens to provide permanent or at least long range positions, to move on. But in many cases the physicists became involved in research in these temporary homes, learning new techniques and observing new styles of research. In P. M. S. Blackett's laboratory at London, in the Cavendish Laboratory at Cambridge, with Niels Bohr in Copenhagen, and at other institutions, these young physicists became involved in research at a time when new concepts and techniques were being rapidly developed, especially in nuclear physics.

The experiences that German-trained physicists had in other countries before turning to the United States differed according to their own education and the new environments in which they found themselves. Bethe in Manchester and Bristol, Goldhaber at the Cavendish Laboratory, and Weisskopf in Zurich and Copenhagen were among those who worked at institutions outside of Germany for varying times before their ultimate arrival in the United States. Their experience in these "interim" positions was to have a significant influence not only on their professional skills but on their ability to adjust rapidly to their more permanent positions in the United States.

In England and throughout Europe it soon became clear that the refugees could not be permanently supported. In 1934 Ernest Rutherford made a public appeal for financial support of the work of the Academic Assistance Council, explaining that although the Council had been able to provide temporary positions for scholars in England, the problem of permanent positions had not been solved:

Temporary fellowships are useful in saving the scholars from scientific sterility, in giving them the opportunity of strengthening their qualifications by further publication and the acquisition of new languages, and in giving them the active cooperation of their colleagues in discovering permanent positions; but they are justified only insofar as they assist to self-supporting existence once more.[57]

---

tion of the entire group of professionals and scientists, see Maurice Davie, *Refugees in America* (New York, 1947), pp. 300–323.

57. Lord Rutherford of Nelson, "Exiles in British Sanctuary," *Science*, 79 (June 15, 1934), 534. Reprinted from the *London Times*.

There was little possibility of permanent positions in England. Sir John Cockcroft in 1967 reflected on the problems they faced:

Well, you see, there was a very limited number of jobs in the Cavendish. At that time the staff was limited. Whatever positions became vacant, there were a lot of young people about to be appointed. Local people like Oliphant, or myself, or Feather, or Dee were in the running for jobs as they came along, so you see there were certainly no spare jobs available. You couldn't go to any other source and get money for a new post. So it wasn't very easy to fit a large number of refugees into the Cavendish organization at that time.[58]

England had only a limited ability to absorb refugees because there was just not enough room or money or will. The Depression was taking its toll, and the universities had not yet experienced large increases in enrollment. Lack of flexibility in the English academic world and the limited opportunities for the new arrivals meant that many had to move on, although they would have liked to stay and would indeed have been welcomed by their English colleagues. Even so, by 1935 temporary appointments in England rose to 155, and fifty-seven scholars had been absorbed on a permanent basis.[59]

Once again Leo Szilard was in the forefront of those recognizing the difficult new situation. He was among the first to recognize the need for refugee scientists to move on. For example, Maurice Goldhaber, who had studied at the University of Berlin and who had gone to the Cavendish Laboratory in 1930 to obtain his Ph.D., had been maintained there on a fellowship for several years after he completed his degree. Especially after Rutherford's death in 1937, he knew that the situation was not a permanent one and was advised by Esther Simpson of the Academic Assistance Council to try to find a job in the United States, when she heard that he was going there in 1938 for a six-week visit "to have a look." At a meeting of physicists in Washington, D.C., he was invited to visit the University of Illinois which, as we have noted, since 1929 had been building a strong physics faculty under the leadership of F. Wheeler Loomis. Szilard, who had himself emigrated to America by this time, was at the Washington meeting and encouraged him to look

58. Tape-recorded interview with Sir John Cockcroft, March 28, 1967, conducted by the author. Oral History Collection, AIP.

59. Bentwich, *Refugee Scholars*, p. 13.

into the situation. When Goldhaber returned to Cambridge, he had the job at the University of Illinois which included a grant of $3,000 from the graduate school for research on nuclear physics. Like so many others who preceded him, he saw a better opportunity for research in the United States.[60]

VII. A New Site for the Seminar

THE transition to America was not an easy one. These were difficult times in the personal lives of the refugees. After having been suddenly uprooted, they had made hasty arrangements to find temporary refuge in new lands. It was sadly difficult to break ties with relatives and friends and with a familiar environment. Once away from Germany they were plagued with uncertainty about the future, and anticipated the need to move on again. For those with children, this nomadic period was even more trying. The prospect of taking up new positions in American institutions often involved feelings of both relief and apprehension. They felt that there were greater opportunities for scientific work in the United States than elsewhere and that, somehow, even if their new positions were not permanent, they could eventually find others that were suitable. Many of the physicists felt that America was the end of the trek, and that once there they could begin to seek a normal life once again. At the same time, crossing the Atlantic only symbolized the great cultural distance between the continents. They had known what to expect when they migrated to the geographically proximate and culturally familiar countries in Europe. But they were not so sure about what would await them when they completed the long journey to America.

Life in the American communities in which the new arrivals settled was filled with odd, inexplicable ways. There were the usual problems relating to food, shelter, and transportation. Enrico Fermi, who had stopped off at Stockholm to receive his Nobel Prize while en route from

60. Tape-recorded interview with Maurice Goldhaber, January 10, 1967, conducted by the author. Oral History Collection, AIP.

Rome to New York, first settled with his wife Laura and their two children in a Manhattan apartment amidst the enclave of Columbia University professors already there. Laura Fermi's experiences during those first months in 1939 must have been like those of other wives of newly arrived scholars. She remembered her encounters with the mysteries of automatic refrigerators, an endless variety of packaged and canned foods, translating unmetric measures in the course of shopping and cooking, and the problems of making herself understood in day-to-day conversations in the neighborhood.[61] The ease of personal adjustment varied with the size of the community, the age of the new arrivals and their previous experiences. But, in general, the American tradition of assimilating new immigrants helped to soften the transition.

In the physics departments and in the larger community of physicists in the United States, most of the new arrivals felt at home almost from the start. Language difficulties were limited for most of them, not only because of their previous experiences but also because of the ease of communications in physics at a stage in its development when there was agreement on the basic facts, concepts, and techniques which could often be described by internationally accepted terms and by mathematics. The international journal and monograph literature of physics was available at the universities, so that the loss of a personal library was less of a handicap to refugee physicists than to refugee scholars in the humanities.

The sociability within and between departments contrasted strongly with the rigidity of the German universities, and contributed to the rapid adjustment of the newcomers. Some of the physicists, however, encountered a certain degree of hostility stemming from resentment of their "intrusion" into the departments when faculty positions were limited because of the Depression. In some cases they encountered anti-Semitism. Moreover, many of the refugee physicists had no permanent position and found it difficult to obtain new posts when their temporary appointments expired. On the whole, however, the physicists rapidly

61. Laura Fermi, *Atoms in the Family* (Chicago, 1954), pp. 141–144. Mrs. Fermi has also written an account of the "European-born atomic scientists" and their role in the development of the atomic bomb and its political aftermath in her recent study of the entire intellectual migration to America, *Illustrious Immigrants: The Intellectual Migration from Europe 1930–1941* (Chicago, 1968), pp. 174–214.

found places and began to contribute within their new professional environment.

Victor Weisskopf arrived in 1937 after spending a productive period with Wolfgang Pauli in Zurich and with Niels Bohr's international assembly of physicists in Copenhagen. Weisskopf describes his first few years at the University of Rochester as "a period when you were asked if you were expecting children, and you said, 'No, first we expect parents.' It was literally so. Of what little money we had, we had to pay the way of my mother, my brother, and my sister coming over. They were facing death and they had to come over. It was a difficult time."[62] Nevertheless, the personal transition was eased for the Weisskopfs because they had many friends who were warm and helpful, and he was completely accepted at Rochester.

Shortly after Weisskopf arrived, he began visiting other physicists at other universities, starting with colleagues he had known in Europe who had preceded him to the United States. He visited Bethe at Cornell, Teller in Washington, and Wigner at Princeton. Within a short time he had been invited to lecture in the summer school at Stanford University by Felix Bloch who had found a position there when he was forced to leave Europe. These summer sessions had become a regular part of American academic life, patterned after the example of the Michigan summer school. On the way to Stanford, Weisskopf would stop at the Robert Oppenheimer ranch in New Mexico where he met the young theorists associated with Oppenheimer.

Weisskopf's characterization of his reactions to America typifies many of the special features of American scientific life in the 1930's that contributed to the rapid acclimatization of the newly arrived European physicists:

Within the shortest time one was in the midst of a society that was extremely appealing and interesting and active; and in fact we felt much more as refugees in Europe than here . . . You had easier access to everybody . . . It was an extremely productive period for me. I worked, as you know, in nuclear physics and in field theory. I learned a lot. I was very close to experimental physics. For the first time I had systematic teaching duties, which broadened my knowledge a lot. It was the first time I really had many graduate students to work with.[63]

62. Tape-recorded interview with Victor Weisskopf, September 22, 1966, conducted by the author. Oral History Collection, AIP.
63. *Ibid.*

The informality of teacher-student relations was similarly important to Eugene Wigner, who emigrated in 1930, and recalls that "the great experience for me in the United States, and the condition which made work here very attractive and very pleasant was the possibility of working with graduate students. It was a new and stimulating experience to work with someone who was deeply interested in the subject, who was interested in exactly the same thing as you were at that time."[64]

Hans Bethe was impressed with the liveliness of teaching at Cornell when he arrived there in 1935:

It was customary in Europe to let the professor address the class and talk and write formally on the blackboard and then leave. The students would listen and try to understand. Occasionally a few came forward at the end of the lecture to ask a question or two; whereas here, whenever a student feels like it, he asks a question. I think it's much better.[65]

Bethe had not been prepared for this, but when it happened, he approved.

The traveling seminar soon began again for the refugees, but now in a new environment and on an expanded scale. Within a week after Bethe's arrival at Cornell, he presented a paper at the American Physical Society meeting where he came in contact with many new people. He was soon in touch with both Europeans and Americans here, visiting Columbia frequently to see Rabi whom he had first met while still a graduate student in Munich. He visited Van Vleck at Harvard and also attended the theoretical physics meetings in Washington, taking time to look into the experimental nuclear physics work in Merle Tuve's laboratory at the Carnegie Institution's Department of Terrestrial Magnetism. Bethe recalls with enjoyment his visits to the annual meeting of the American Physical Society in Washington every spring: "I spent many hours on the lawn at the Bureau of Standards where the Washington meeting was held in the spring, discussing papers and nuclear physics with other physicists . . . I certainly got the feeling that it was

64. Tape-recorded interview with Eugene Wigner, November 30, 1966, conducted by the author. Oral History Collection, AIP. Wigner's graduate students in the early 1930's included Frederick Seitz, John Bardeen, and Conyers Herring, all of them now outstanding leaders in the field of solid state physics.

65. Tape-recorded interview with Hans Bethe, November 17, 1967, conducted by the author. Oral History Collection, AIP.

much easier to get to know the other physicists here, and to get to know them from all over the country. I just liked it . . . I felt very much accepted from the very beginning."[66]

Bethe's visits to other universities and to frequent meetings of physicists in the United States brought him into direct contact with experimentalists, and he eagerly became involved in their problems. At Cornell he worked closely with M. Stanley Livingston, who had taken his doctorate with Ernest O. Lawrence and who had played a major role in building the first cyclotron at Berkeley in the early 1930's. He encountered no artificial barriers separating theoreticians from experimentalists. In the United States there were no distinct boundaries between these two groups, and they were most often found together in a single department, giving rise to a close interplay between theory and experiment. One consequence of this interaction for Bethe was the project he launched with the assistance of Livingston and Robert F. Bacher, his colleagues in the physics department at Cornell, to write a comprehensive three-part series of review articles on nuclear physics, including both the theoretical and experimental aspects of the subject in an integrated form. In the course of this work many experiments were redone, results were recalculated, existing theoretical interpretations were evaluated, and new ones were proposed. This series of articles was a tremendous stimulus to the development of nuclear physics and it was at the time, and still is, affectionately known among physicists as the "Bethe bible." The review articles came at a time when the field of nuclear physics was at the center of interest and more than any other single publication it marked the coming of age of that field.[67]

During the mid-1930's, the United States provided a special opportunity for theoretical physicists with an interest in current experimental

---

66. *Ibid.*

67. The review article consisted of three parts: a) H. A. Bethe and R. F. Bacher, "Stationary States of Nuclei," *Reviews of Modern Physics*, 8 (1936), 83–229; b) H. A. Bethe, "Nuclear Dynamics, Theoretical," *Reviews of Modern Physics*, 9 (1937), 69–244; and c) M. S. Livingston and H. A. Bethe, "Nuclear Dynamics, Experimental," *Reviews of Modern Physics*, 9 (1937), 245–390.

Bethe has commented on the relation between theory and experiment in Germany and America in one of the interviews with refugee scholars conducted for Radio Bremen and subsequently published as *Auszug des Geistes* (Bremen, 1962), pp. 31–40.

work. Experimental nuclear physics was highly developed in the United States, and the experimental results were outrunning theory. For a theoretician like Bethe, who had always been interested in theory useful to experimenters, this situation was made to order. The opportunity for theoretical physicists in Germany to work closely with their experimental colleagues had varied in different institutions. Bethe had been at Munich and Tübingen where there was little collaboration between the two groups. At Göttingen, however, Max Born and James Franck had established close ties between theory and experiment.[68]

Work in theoretical physics had been increasing steadily in the United States since the late 1920's, during a period when the new and powerful quantum mechanics required a closer link between theory and experiment than had existed anywhere before. This change in physics occurred at the time when American institutions were growing and were fluid, so that native and refugee theoreticians were able to turn their attention to new problems and to develop styles of work appropriate to these problems.

Not all the refugee physicists who came to America were theoreticians; many were experimentalists. But whether theorists or experimentalists, they were invited to contribute and had the opportunity to do so. The characteristics of American physics during the period included a high level of technological awareness and capability. Many American experimentalists and theoreticians had tinkered with ham radios or Model T Fords in their youth and had entered college with engineering as their original career goal. The high technological level and consciousness of American society was especially significant in the field of nuclear physics, which depended so much on ingenious apparatus and engineering techniques and on ready access to cheap replacement parts. One refugee physicist recalls how much he was impressed

68. Pure and applied mathematics were also closely linked at Göttingen. However, when Richard Courant arrived in the United States in 1934 after his mathematical institute had been destroyed by the Nazis, he found that American mathematicians tended to be concerned with abstract problems and had little interest in the application of mathematics to physics and other fields. His new mathematical institute at New York University helped to develop close connections between pure and applied mathematics in the United States. See the interview of Courant by Irmgard Bach in *Auszug des Geistes*, pp. 199–201.

when he learned that a vacuum tube needed in his nuclear research could be purchased at the corner drugstore.[69]

Close ties existed between many academic physics departments and industry. As a consequence, physicists gained experience with large scale technical work. Awareness of the existing technological capabilities was an advantage for physicists who could turn this technology to the uses of basic research in science. There was a permissive atmosphere in American departments of physics, and both professors and students felt free to innovate. They could afford to make mistakes for the hardware was relatively cheap. Although funds were restricted, enough was available for some unfocused research, to satisfy the needs of experimental physicists who derived enjoyment just from working with the apparatus, whether or not the experiments were in step with the state of theory at the time.[70]

In the 1930's, when the refugees were absorbed into the physics community, the scientific enterprise in the United States was growing rapidly. The refugee physicists, who came from the centers of physics research in Europe, were able to move freely in their new environment, adding their knowledge and individual research styles to work under way at American institutions, or seeking out new fields for exploration. Their opportunity to contribute was enlarged because a large number of them had been carefully placed by their American colleagues at institutions where they were needed and could be most productive.[71]

69. Tape-recorded interview with Maurice Goldhaber, January 10, 1967, conducted by the author. Oral History Collection, AIP.

70. These characteristics of American physics in the 1930's have been identified by many of the American and European physicists who made major contributions to the development of nuclear physics in the United States during the period, in a series of oral history interviews done for the American Institute of Physics—American Academy of Arts and Sciences project on the history of nuclear physics, and at the project's first Exploratory Conference on the History of Nuclear Physics, at the Academy in Brookline, Mass., May 18 and 19, 1967.

71. The social environment for science and the organization of the scientific community in the United States in the 1930's suggest that the conditions for a "brain drain" already existed at that time, and that large numbers of European scientists would have emigrated to the United States even without the stimulus of the political upheavals of Nazism. Recent studies of the large-scale emigration of scientists from all over the world to the United States in the past two decades emphasize that they have come because of the greater opportunities for professional development and self-expression in their work, better pay, and the better facilities available. See James A. Wilson, "The Emigration of

"The outlook would seem to be that the Americans are to be brought into a central place in the republic of learning . . ."[72] Thorstein Veblen's forecast was made in 1918. In June 1941 it appeared on the cover of the annual report of the Emergency Committee in Aid of Displaced Foreign Scholars, the organization which had assisted hundreds of refugee scholars placed in American institutions of higher learning since 1933. The implication was clear. American scholarship had been enriched by the wave of new arrivals who pursued their work in this country after their exodus from the fascist-dominated countries where they were genealogically or politically *persona non grata*. The ability to absorb and utilize the talents of the refugee physicists demonstrates that Veblen's hopeful prophecy had already begun to be fulfilled in physics by the early 1930's.

The success of the refugee physicists in America has been linked here to developments dating from the 1920's when the vigorous international mixing of people and ideas in physics brought many Americans into close contact with their European colleagues at a time of great intellectual excitement in the field. During the late 1920's and early 1930's American physicists, aided by a sympathetic society, were self-consciously developing their own institutions into first-rate centers of graduate education and research. At the same time opportunities for scientific careers in Germany were limited, and with the coming of Hitler, the careers of large numbers of physicists abruptly came to a halt. The response of their colleagues in other countries enabled them to continue their work in temporary havens where many of them were exposed to new problems and different styles of research. American scientists who knew the needs of their own institutions and who knew the work of the refugees helped them find permanent positions that would meet

---

British Scientists," *Minerva*, 1 (Autumn, 1966), 20–29; Stevan Dedijer, "Why Did Daedalus Leave?" *Science*, 133 (June, 1961), 2047–2052; Thomas J. Mills, "Scientific Personnel and the Professions," *The Annals of the American Academy of Political and Social Science*, 367 (September, 1966), 33–42; H. G. Grubel and A. D. Scott, "The Immigration of Scientists and Engineers to the United States, 1949–61," *The Journal of Political Economy*, 74 (August, 1966), 368–378; and *Scientists and Engineers from Abroad: 1962–64* (National Science Foundation, Washington, D.C., NSF 67–3).

72. Thorstein Veblen, *The Higher Learning in America* (New York, 1918), p. 48, quoted in *The Emergency Committee in Aid of Displaced Foreign Scholars* report as of June 1, 1941 (New York).

their personal needs while enriching American science. The refugees came at a time of rapid growth in the ideas and techniques of new fields such as nuclear physics, and the social structure in American physics was uniquely suited to provide niches for newcomers and to absorb and assimilate new talents, ideas and styles.

By the end of the 1930's, just prior to America's involvement in the war, the refugee physicists were fully immersed in the scientific community and, in collaboration with their American colleagues, were making major contributions to their field. They had come as physicists and refugees, and even more strikingly than was so often true in earlier periods of American history, they were rapidly assimilated into and helped to transform the field of activity which opened itself to them in the United States.

Palmer Physical Laboratory
Princeton, New Jersey
December 14, 1933.

ehr verehrter Herr Kollege!

Wir erlauben uns, Ihnen beiliegend eine Liste derjenigen
ollegen unseres Fachgebietes zu schicken, die, soweit uns bekannt, ihre
tellungen in Deutschland verloren und noch keine andere Stellung gefunden
aben. Einige unter ihnen erhalten ihre normalen Bezüge noch eine Zeit lang,
ekommen aber dann entweder gar nichts, oder eine ausserordentlich kleine
ension. Ein Teil dieser Kollegen wird daher in naher Zukunft in schwere
etlage geraten.

Zweck dieses Schreibens ist, Sie anzufragen, ob Sie bereit wären,
ür zwei Jahre, angefangen am 1 Jan 1934, einen gewissen Prozentsatz Ihres
ehaltes (2 - 4%) zur Verfügung zu stellen, damit jenen, die in Not sind
eholfen werden kann. Dieser Brief geht an alle Kollegen, die durch
eziehungen zu deutschen Hochschulen besonderes Interesse an Ihren alten
ollegen haben dürften. Eine Liste liegt bei.

Es besteht die Möglichkeit, dass wir auch von Weiterstehenden
terstützt werden. Es ist aber wahrscheinlich, dass wir bei dritten
ersonen mehr erreichen können, wenn wir uns darauf berufen können, dass
r uns auch unsererseits zu schweren Opfern entschlossen haben. In diesem
sammenhang sei bemerkt, dass in England alle Professoren (also nicht nur
ne, die von früher her mit Deutschland stärker verbunden waren) an einer
rartigen Sammlung teilgenommen haben, und dass z;B. bei der Londoner School
 Economics 3% vom gesamten Gehalt erzielt werden konnte. Der mittlere
ozentsatz für ganz England ist noch nicht endgültig bekannt, dürfte aber
gefähr 1% betragen.

Wir bitten Sie, gleichzeitig mit Ihrem Antwort, uns mitzuteilen,
en Ihnen noch weitere Kollegen bekannt sind, die entlassen sind und noch
ine Stellung anderswo haben. Auch wenn Ihnen bekannt wäre, dass einige der

ven uns angeführten Herren in der Zwischenzeit eine Stellung gefunden haben, bitten wir Sie, dies uns mitzuteilen. Ausserdem, falls Ihnen noch jemand bekannt ist, der soviel Interesse an den deutschen Kollegen hat, dass er in die Reihe derer, die diesen Brief erhalten, einbezogen werden könnte.

Schliesslich bitten wir Sie, in Ihrem Schreiben zwei Kollegen zu nennen, denen Sie die Verteilung des gesammelten Geldes übergaben möchten. Diese hätten dann – im Einvernehmen mit uns allen – zu entscheiden, welchen Kollegen die Unterstützung in erster Reihe zufliessen soll und in welcher Form sie gewährt werde. Den meistversprechenden jüngeren Kollegen könnten etw Stipendien zugebilligt werden, so dass sie in einem Lande mit niedrigem Preisniveau wissenschaftlich tätig sein könnten. Wie den älteren geholfen werden kann, muesste noch entschieden werden. Z. B. koennten ausserdeutschen Universitaeten nach Anfrage Geldbetraege zur Einladung der betreffenden Kollegen für Gastvorlesungen zur Verfügung gestellt werden.

Als Vertrauenskollegen möchten wir, um auch in dieser Beziehung einen Anhaltspunkt zu geben, Herrn Professor K. F. Herzfeld und Frau Dr. Maria Mayer Göppert (beide in Baltimore) in Vorschlag bringen; sie haben prinzipiell ihre Bereitwilligkeit erklärt. Bis zur Wahl unserer Vertrauensmänner würden die unterzeichneten die Korrespondenz in Empfang nehmen.

Wir hoffen, dass auch Sie die Wichtigkeit einer solchen Hilfsaktic empfinden und Ihre Unterstützung und Mitwirkung nicht versagen werden.

Mit freundlichen Grüssen

R. Ladenburg   und E. Wigner

[Translation of letter written in German in 1933 by Rudolf Ladenburg and Eugene Wigner to twenty-seven physicists at American institutions asking for their support in aid of displaced German scientists who are listed by name, age, position, field, and institution. The original letter is in the Manuscript Collection of the Center for History and Philosophy of Physics at the American Institute of Physics in New York City.]

Palmer Physical Laboratory
Princeton, New Jersey
December 14, 1933

Dear Colleague:

We are taking the liberty of sending you the attached list of former colleagues in our field who, so far as we know, have lost their posts in Germany and have not yet found another position. Some of them will receive their normal salary a while longer, but after that, nothing at all, or an extraordinarily small pension. A number of these colleagues in the near future will be in real need.

The purpose of this letter is to ask you if you would be ready to set aside a specific percent of your income (2–4%) for two years, starting January 1, 1934, in order that we may be able to help those in need. This letter is going to all those colleagues who through their connections with German higher education, may have a particular interest in their former colleagues. . . .

There is also the possibility that we shall also receive some support from additional sources. However, it is probable that we can achieve more through such third parties if we could inform them that from our side we have decided to make a big sacrifice. In this connection, it may be noted that in England all the professors (not just those who had strong ties with Germany earlier) took part in a similar collection, and that, for example, at the London School of Economics, the result was 3% of the total income. The average percent for all of England is not yet known in its entirety, but should run about 1%.

We are requesting that, at the same time as you answer, you let us know if there are additional colleagues who have been dismissed and have not yet found a position elsewhere. Moreover, if you should know of any on the list who in the meantime have found a position, please let us know. In addition, [inform us] if you know of someone who has such an interest in our German colleagues that he might be included in the list of those to receive this letter.

In conclusion, in your letter please name two colleagues to whom you would entrust the distribution of the money collected. These then would have to decide, in agreement with all of us, which colleagues should receive support of the first order and in which form it should be given. The most promising of the younger colleagues could be given smaller stipends, so that they could be scientifically employed in a country with a lower price level. How we shall be able to help the older [ones] must still be decided. As an example, on request, sums of money could be made available to non-German universities for inviting the colleagues in question as guest lecturers.

In this connection, we should like to suggest Frau Dr. Maria Mayer Goeppert and Prof. K. F. Herzfeld (both in Baltimore) as trustee colleagues; they have expressed their willingness in principle. Until the selection of our trustees, the undersigned will accept correspondence.

We hope that you, too, feel the importance of such assistance and will not deny your support and cooperation.

With friendly greetings,
(s) R. Ladenburg and E. Wigner

[List of displaced scientists attached to Wigner and Ladenburg letters]

ABBREVIATIONS

PD	=	Privat Dozent	Ch.	= Chemistry
Pr.	=	Professor	Astr.	= Astronomy
A	=	Assistant	Coll.	= Colloidal
Exp.	=	Experimental	T.H.	= Techn. High School
Th.	=	Theoretical	K.W.I.	= Kaiser Wilhelm Institut
Ph.	=	Physics	Un.	= University

	Age			
BAERWALD, Hans	53	PD	Exp. Ph.	Darmstadt T.H.
BECK, Guido	30?	PD	Th. Ph.	Leipzig
BYK, Alfred	50?	PD	Ph. Ch.	Berlin T. H. Un.
DRUCKER, C.	50?	PD	Ph. Ch.	Leipzig
FROMMER, Leopold	39	A	Ph. Ch.	B /Dahlem, K.W.I.
GROSSMAN	27?	A	Exp. Ph.	Breslau T.H.
HERMANN, C.	?	PD	Ph.	Stuttgart T.H.
HERTZ, Paul	52	PD	Th. Ph.	Göttingen
JAFFE, Georg	53	Pr.	Th. Ph.	Giessen
KALLMANN, Hartmut	35?	PD	Exp. Ph.	B /Dahlem, K.W.I.
KOHN, Hedwig	45?	PD	Exp. Ph.	Breslau Un.
KORNFELD, Gertrud	42	PD	Th. Ch.	Berlin Un.
LEHMANN, Erich	55?	Pr.	Photo.Ch.	Berlin T.H.
LION, Kurt	29	A	Exp. Ph.	Darmstadt T.H.
LUDLOFF, H.	30?	PD	Th. Ph.	Breslau Un.
MARX, Erich	60	Pr.	Exp. Ph.	Leipzig
NORDHEIM, Lothar	34	Pr.	Th. Ph.	Göttingen
OROWAN, Egen	30	A	Ph.	Berlin T. H.
PESE, Herbert	32	A	Exp. Ph.	Breslau Un.
REICHE, Fritz	50	Pr.	Th. Ph.	Breslau Un.
REIS, Alfred	51	PD	Ph. Ch.	Berlin, K.W.I.
RONA, Peter	62	PD	Coll. Ch.	Berlin
ROSENTHAL	30?	A	Astr. Ph.	Frankfurt /M
SALINGER, Hans	42?	P	Tech. Ph.	Berlin T.H.
SCHARF, Karl	30	A	Exp. Ph.	Dresden T.H.
SZILARD, Leo	35?	PD	Ph.	Berlin Un.
WEISSENBERG, Karl	40	PD	Ph.	Berlin, K.W.I.
WOLFSOHN, G.	33?	A	Exp. Ph.	Berlin, K.W.I.

NAZI "PURGE" OF THE UNIVERSITIES

A Long List of Dismissals

We publish below a detailed list of the professors who have been dismissed from their posts in German universities between April 13 and May 4. There are also in the list a few assistants or lecturers who have been dismissed and several professors who have resigned their posts.

The list is for the most part compiled from announcements in the German press, and we have made it as complete and accurate as the sources permit. Many famous names are included in the list, and if many others are unknown to British readers we think that the list will be found impressive both in itself and in the comprehensiveness of the subjects covered. Most of the professors have been dismissed because of their Jewish origin, a few possibly because of their liberal sentiments.

DISMISSED ON APRIL 13

Frankfort-on-Main

Professor Heller, Public Law. Formerly of Berlin. (Acted for the Prussian Government before the Supreme Court in its appeal against the appointment of a Commissar.)
Professor Horkheimer, Philosophy. Head of the Institute of Sociology.
Professor Loewe, Economics. (Formerly of Kiel.)
Professor Mannheim, Sociology.
Professor Tillich, Philosophy and Sociology. (Well-known religious Socialist. Formerly editor of "New Pages for Socialism.")
Professor Sinzheimer, Sociology and Law. One of the creators of German labour legislation.

Berlin—Commercial Hochschule

Professor Bonn, Economics. Twice Rector of the Hochschule. A Liberal. Sometimes referred to as "the German Keynes."

Berlin

Professor Emil Lederer, Economics. (Formerly of Heidelberg. Editor of the "Archiv für Sozialwissenschaft und Sozialpolitik.")

Breslau

Professor Cohn.
Professor Marck, Philosophy of Law.

Halle

Professor Dehn, Practical Theology.

Konigsberg—Commercial Hochschule

Professor Feiler, Economics. A Liberal. Well known through his books on U.S.A. and Russia. Formerly financial editor of the "Frankfurter Zeitung."

Bonn

Professor Kantorowicz, Dentistry.
Professor Loewenstein, Psychiatry.

Ki

Professor Kantorowicz, Criminal Law.

Cologr

Professor Kelsen, Public Law. (Formerly of Vienna, where he collaborated in the drafting of the Austrian Constitution. One of Germany's greatest constitutional lawyers. A Liberal.)

Heidelberg

Professor Hans von Eckardt. Principal of the Institute of Journalism.

Dresden—Art Academy

Professor Otto Dix, Teacher. (Not under Civil Service law, but on the ground that some of his pictures offended against morality, others were calculated to lessen the German people's will to defend itself (Wehrwille). His famous picture "War," a huge oil-painting, represents the horrors of modern warfare.)

Gottingen

Resigned in protest on April 18.—Professor James Franck, Experimental Physics. Nobel Prizeman, 1925. (As a war veteran not affected by the Civil Service law.)

Heidelberg

Professor Gerhard Anschutz, Public Law (resigned on April 22). One of the greatest German authorities on international law.
Professor Alfred Weber, Sociology (resigned on April 22).

DISMISSED ON APRIL 22

Hanover—Technical Hochschule

Professor Lessing, Philosophy (from lecture courses).

Berlin—Technical Hochschule

Professor Chajes, Industrial Hygiene (from lecture courses).
Professor Holde, Chemistry (from lecture courses).
Professor Fritz Frank, Chemical Research.
Professor Igel, Railway Construction.

DISMISSED ON APRIL 26

Frankfort-on-Main

Professor Salomon, Sociology.
Professor Mennicke.
Professor M. Wertheimer, Psychology.
Professor Strupp, International Law, Well known through his book on the legal structure of the Locarno protocols.
Professor Weil, Oriental Languages.
Professor Pribram, Economics.
Professor Richard Koch, History of Medicine.
Dr. Glatzer, Jewish Religion.
Professor Plessner, Oriental Languages.
Professor Sommerfeld, German Philology.
Professor Walter Fränkel, Metallurgy.
Professor Fritz Mayer, Chemistry.
Professor Ernst Kahn, Commercial Journalism.
Professor Neumark, Economics.
Professor Ernst Cohn, Private and Commercial Law.
Professor Braun, Hygiene and Bacteriology.
Professor Ludwig Wertheimer, Banking Law.
Professor Altschul, Methods of Marketing Research.

Marburg

Professor Röpke, Political Science.
Professor Jacobsohn, Indogermanic Philology. On April 27 he threw himself in front of a train and was killed at once. He was 53 years old.

Gottingen

Professor Honig, Criminal Law.
Professor Courant, Mathematics.
Professor Born, Theoretical Physics.
Professor Emmy Noether.
Professor Bernstein, Statistics.
Professor Bondi.

Konigsberg

Professor Hensel, Public Law (may be reappointed).

Konigsberg—Commercial Hochschule

Professor Rogowsky, Practical Economics.
Professor Hänsler.
Professor Kürbs.

Kiel

Professor Colm, Economics.
Professor Neisser, Economics.
Professor Adolf Fränkel, Mathematics.
Professor Husserl, Roman Law.
Professor Stenzel, Philosophy.
Professor Liepe, Modern German Philology and Literature.
Professor Rauch.
Professor Schücking, International Law. The chief German exponent of the legal conceptions on which the League of Nations is based. Has represented Germany at the Hague Court.
Professor Opet, German Law.

Berlin-Schoneberg—State Art School

Professor Georg Tappert.
Professor Curt Lahs.
Lehrer Joseph Vinecky.

Berlin—Combined State Schools for Free and Applied Art

Professor Karl Hofer. One of the greatest of modern German painters.
Professor Edwin Scharff.

Dusseldorf Art Academy

Professor Paul Klee. One of the pioneers of "expressionism." Well known in Paris and London.
Professor Oskar Moll, Director.

DISMISSED ON APRIL 27

Berlin—Hochschule for Music

Professor Dr. Daniel.
Professor Kreutzer.
Professor Feuermann
Professor Hörth.
Professor Dr. Schünemann, Director.

Konigsberg

Professor Paneth, Chemistry.
Professor Reidemeister, Mathematics.

Elbing

Professor Dr. Otto Haase, Director.
Professor Dr. Karl Thieme.
Professor Hans Haffenrichter.
Professor Emil Gossow.
Professor Frau Helene Ziegert.
Dozent Johannes Kretschmann.

Halle

Professor Dr. Julius Frankenberger, Director.
Professor Frau Dr. Elisabeth Blochmann.
Professor Dr. Fritz Mascheck.
Professor Frau Anna Dernehl.
Professor Martin Rang.
Professor Herbert Kranz.
Professor Dr. Adolf Reichwein.
Professor Dr. Karl von Hollander.
Professor Fritz Kauffmann.
Professor Dr. Hans Hoffmann.

Kiel

Professor D. Emil Fuchs.
Professor Wilhelm Oppermann.
Dozent Dr. Friedrich Copei.

Dortmund

Professor Dr. Johannes Sippel.
Dozent Dr. Hans Pflug.
Dozent Dr. Conrad Ameln.

Frankfort-on-Main

Professor Martin Schmidt.
Professor Frau Dr. Marie Anne Kuntze.
Professor Frau Dr. Gerda Simons.
Professor Dr. Hermann Semiller.
Professor Dr. Friedrich Wilhelm Spemann.
Dozent Hans Thierbach.
Dozent Frau Berta Kieser.

Bonn

Professor Dr. Hans Rosenberg.

DISMISSED ON APRIL 28

Heidelberg

Professor Radbruch (former Reich Minister of Justice). Criminal Law. Well known as a champion of penal reform.

Berlin—German Hochschule fur Politik

A free institution founded in 1920. Transformed into a State institution (end of April) with resignation of the President and Directors—Professor Dr. Jäckh (a well-known writer on international affairs), Professor Dr. Simons, Professor Dr. Drewe.

Berlin—University Institute for Cancer Research

Director resigned on May 1.—Professor Dr. Ferdinand Blumenthal, a pioneer of cancer research. A special chair was established for him in this subject in 1929.

DISMISSED ON MAY 1

Halle

Professor Fränkl, History of Art.
Professor Kisch, History of German Law.
Professor Kitzinger, Criminal Law.
Professor Utitz, Philosophy.
Professor Hertz, Sociology (Viennese by birth, and now in Vienna. He wrote as a young man a well-known book, "Moderne Rassentheorien," opposing the theories of Stewart Houston Chamberlain).
Privat Dozent Dr. Baer, Pure Mathematics.

DISMISSED ON MAY 2

Berlin

Professor Dr. Peter Rona, Colloid Chemistr and Physiology.
Professor Dr. Friedrich Franz Friedmann, Tubercular Research.
Professor Dr. Hans Friedenthal, Physiology.
Professor Dr. Franz Blumenthal, Dermatology.
Professor Dr. Birnbaum, Psychiatry.
Professor Dr. Mittwoch, Semitic Philology.
Professor Dr. Julius Pokorny, Celtic Philology, author of studies of the culture and literature of Ireland.
Professor Dr. Issai Schur, Mathematics. One of the leading mathematicians in Germany.
Professor Dr. Manes, Insurance.
Professor Dr. Byk, Quantum Theory of Physics.
Professor Dr. Fischel, History of Art.
Professor Dr. Jollos, Zoology.
Professor Dr. Walter Norden, Municipal Administration.
Professor Dr. Richter, Medicine.
Professor Dr. Hans Pringsheim, Chemistry.
Professor Dr. Hermann Grossmann, Technology.
Dozent Dr. Otto Lipmann, Applied Psychology.
Dozent Dr. Konrad Cohn, Dentistry.

Deprived of their Lecture Courses

Dozent Dr. Fritz Baade, a Socialist. Authority on agrarian questions.
Dozent Dr. Balogh.
Dozent Dr. Kurt Haentzschel, Press Law.
Dozent Dr. Walter Lande.
Professor Dr. Wolff-Eisner, Medicine.

Cologne

Professor Schmalenbach, Economics.
Professor Schmittmann, Economics (arrested May 3 on charges of Separatist activity).
Professor Spitzer.
Professor Cohn-Vossen, Mathematics.
Professor Braunfels.
Professor Lips, Sociology.
Professor Esch, Communications.
Professor Beyer, Industrial and Technical Pedagogy.
Professor Honigsheim, Philosophy and Sociology.

Jena

Professor Emil Klein, Medicine.
Professor Theodor Meyer-Steinegg, History of Medicine.
Professor Hans Stimmel.
Professor Mathilde Vaerting, Theory of Education.
Professor Dr. Wilhelm Peters, Psychology (at own request).
Professor Schaxel, Zoology.
Professor Berthold Josephy, Economic and Social Sciences.
Privat Dozent Leo Brauner, Botany.

Aachen—Technical Hochschule

Professor Hopf, Higher Mathematics.
Professor Fuchs.
Professor Meusel, Economics.
Professor Mautner, Iron Construction.
Professor Levy, Organic Chemistry.
Privat Dozent. Strauss, Literature.
Privat Dozent Pick.

DISMISSED ON MAY 3

Berlin—Technical Hochschule

Professor Dr. Kurrein, Technical Research.
Professor Dr. Schlesinger, Industrial Machinery.
Professor Dr. Schwerin, Theory of Elasticity.
Professor Dr. Levy, Economics.
Professor Dr. Lehmann, Photographic Chemistry.
Professor Korn, Photo-telegraphy.
Professor Traube, Colloid Chemistry.
Professor Salinger, Low-tension Electricity Technique.
Privat Dozent Dr. Kelen, Hydraulic Structures.
Herr Grabowski, Lecturer.

Greifswald

Professor Klingmueller, Roman and Private Law.
Professor Ziegler, Classical Philology.

Munster

Professor Freud.
Professor Bruck, Economics.
Professor Heilbronn, Botany.

Berlin

Professor James Goldschmidt, Criminal Law (resigned).
Professor Fritz Haber, Physical Chemistry. Nobel Prizeman (resigned). (Inventor of the synthetic ammonia manufacturing process on which Germany depended during the world war. It has been said that but for him Germany would have had to capitulate early in the war.)
Professor Freundlich, Colloid Chemistry (resigned).
Professor Polanyi, Physical Chemistry (resigned).
Professor Spranger, Philosophy and Pedagogy (resigned).

Berlin—Agricultural Hochschule

Professor Dr. Karl Brandt, Agricultural Marketing Research.

DISMISSED ON MAY 4

Leipzig

Professor Witkowski, Literary History. (A noted student of Goethe.)
Professor Walther Goetz, History. (One of the foremost German historians. Editor of the Propyläen Weltgeschichte. Democratic member of the Reichstag 1920-1928.)
Professor Apelt, Public Law. (Formerly Saxon Minister of the Interior.)
Professor Everth, Journalism.
Professor Hellmann, Mediæval History.
Privat Dozent Dr. Becker.

Dresden—Technical Hochschule

Professor Dr. Holldack, Law.

Leipzig—Teachers' Training College

Professor Dr. Johannes Richter (Principal).

JAPAN AND THE LEAGUE

Lord Cecil's Call for Firm Policy

In the House of Lords last week Lord Cecil raised the question of the position in the Far East and at the Disarmament Conference and asked for a statement of the Government's policy. He said there had been a partial failure of the peace machinery so laboriously set up at the Paris Conference, but the position would have been much worse if the League of Nations had not existed.

The Foreign Secretary in the House of Commons had stated quite definitely that Japan had not acted in accordance with her treaty obligations. Japan, too, had almost insolently defied and ignored the recommendations of the League Committee which considered the whole position. "That," he declared, "seems to me to be a perfectly clear case of deliberate defiance of the whole process and machinery by which we hoped to have erected a barrier against hostilities in the future." The situation was one of extreme seriousness, and yet the attitude of the Government on the matter appeared to be lacking in firmness and consistency. They had taken part in a solemn condemnation of the actions of Japan, and they had agreed to the proposition that she had broken the Covenant of the League, and therefore he asked what was their policy in the present position. He agreed that this was a matter for international action, but there was something which could be done by this country.

Recently the Government took very strong action with reference to their grievances against the Russian Government when they placed an embargo on Russian imports.

"If that was right against Russia," he went on, "it is surely right in the case of Japan. Are we going to stand for the peaceful settlement of international disputes or not? That is the whole question, and the answer to that may well be the difference between peace and war.

We had reached a crisis in foreign affairs, said Lord Cecil, and it was of the utmost importance that we should have a vigorous, rigorous, and consistent policy, and should not allow ourselves to be deflected because of any difficulties or dangers.

Lord Hailsham (C.—Minister for War) said the Government's policy with regard to Manchuria remained as it had been throughout, to act as a loyal member of the League of Nations in the closest possible collaboration and consultation with the members of the League.

Replying to Lord Cecil's suggestion that we should place an embargo on Japanese imports as we had done in the case of Russia, Lord Hailsham said the two cases were not parallel. In the case of Russia notice had been given to terminate the trading agreement. We had a commercial treaty with Japan which could not be denounced in less than twelve months.

He did not dispute that Japan's attitude did throw a very grave slur upon the efficiency of the Covenant of the League and was a matter which must be of grave concern to all its members. The Government was considering the matter very anxiously, with a real desire to fulfil their obligations as a member of the League.

JOHN VON NEUMANN, 1903–1957*

by S. ULAM, H. W. KUHN, A. W. TUCKER, and CLAUDE E. SHANNON

I N John von Neumann's death on February 8, 1957, the world of mathematics lost a most original, penetrating, and versatile mind. Science suffered the loss of a universal intellect and a unique interpreter of mathematics, who could bring the latest (and develop latent) applications of its methods to bear on problems of physics, astronomy, biology, and the new technology. Many eminent voices have already described and praised his contributions. It is my aim to add here a brief account of his life and of his work from a background of personal acquaintance and friendship extending over a period of twenty-five years.

John von Neumann (Johnny, as he was universally known in this country), the eldest of three boys, was born on December 28, 1903, in Budapest, Hungary, at that time part of the Austro-Hungarian empire. His family was well-to-do; his father, Max von Neumann, was a banker. As a small child, he was educated privately. In 1914, at the outbreak of the First World War, he was ten years old and entered the gymnasium.

Budapest, in the period of the two decades around the First World War, proved to be an exceptionally fertile breeding ground for scientific talent. It will be left to historians of science to discover and explain the conditions which catalyzed the emergence of so many brilliant individuals (—their names abound in the annals of mathematics and physics of the present time). Johnny was probably the most brilliant star in this constellation of scientists. When asked about his own opinion on what contributed to this statistically unlikely phenomenon, he would say that it was a coincidence of some cultural factors which he could not make precise: an external pressure on the whole society of this part of Central Europe, a subconscious feeling of extreme insecurity in individuals, and the necessity of producing the unusual or facing extinction. The First World War had shattered the existing economic and social patterns. Budapest, formerly the second capital of the Austro-Hungarian empire, was now the principal town of a small country. It became obvious to many scientists that they would have to emigrate and find a living elsewhere in less restricted and provincial surroundings.

According to William Fellner,[1] who was a classmate of his, Johnny's unusual abilities came to the attention of an early teacher (Laslo Ratz). He expressed to Johnny's father the opinion that it would be nonsensical to teach Johnny school mathematics in the conventional way, and they agreed that he should be privately coached in mathematics. Thus, under the guidance of Professor Kürschak and the tutoring of Fekete, then an assistant at the University of Budapest, he learned about the problems of mathematics. When he passed his "*matura*" in 1921, he was already recognized a professional mathematician. His first paper, a note with Fekete, was composed while he was not yet eighteen. During the next four years, Johnny was registered at the University of Budapest as a student of mathematics, but he spent most of his time in Zurich at the Eidgenössische Technische Hochschule, where he obtained an undergraduate degree of "*Diplomingenieur in Chemie*," and in Berlin. He would appear at the end of each semester at the University of Budapest to pass his course examinations (without having attended the courses, which was somewhat irregular). He received his doctorate in mathematics in Budapest at about the same time as his chemistry degree in Zurich. While in Zurich, he spent much of his spare time working on mathematical problems, writing for publication, and corresponding with mathematicians. He had contacts with Weyl and Polya, both of whom were in Zurich. At one time, Weyl left Zurich for a short period, and Johnny took over his course for that period.

---

1. This information was communicated by Fellner in a letter to Ulam recalling von Neumann's early studies.

It should be noted that, on the whole, precocity in original mathematical work was not uncommon in Europe. Compared to the United States, there seems to be a difference of at least two or three years in specialized education, due perhaps to a more intensive schooling system during the gymnasium and college years. However, Johnny was exceptional even among the youthful prodigies. His original work began even in his student days, and in 1927, he became a Privat Dozent at the University of Berlin. He held this position for three years until 1929, and during that time, became well-known to the mathematicians of the world through his publications in set theory, algebra, and quantum theory. I remember that in 1927, when he came to Lwów (in Poland) to attend a congress of mathematicians, his work in foundations of mathematics and set theory was already famous. This was already mentioned to us, a group of students, as an example of the work of a youthful genius.

In 1929, he transferred to the University of Hamburg, also as a Privat Dozent, and in 1930, he came to this country for the first time as a visiting lecturer at Princeton University. I remember Johnny telling me that even though the number of existing and prospective vacancies in German universities was extremely small, most of the two or three score Dozents counted on a professorship in the near future. With his typically rational approach, Johnny computed that the expected number of professorial appointments within three years was three, the number of Dozents was forty! He also felt that the coming political events would make intellectual work very difficult.

He accepted a visiting professorship at Princeton in 1930, lecturing for part of the academic year and returning to Europe in the summers. He became a permanent professor at the University in 1931 and held this position until 1933 when he was invited to join the Institute for Advanced Study as a professor, the youngest member of its permanent faculty.

Johnny married Marietta Kovesi in 1930. His daughter, Marina, was born in Princeton in 1935. In the early years of the Institute, a visitor from Europe found a wonderfully informal and yet intense scientific atmosphere. The Institute professors had their offices at Fine Hall (part of Princeton University), and in the Institute and the University departments a galaxy of celebrities was included in what quite possibly constituted one of the greatest concentrations of brains in mathematics and physics at any time and place.

It was upon Johnny's invitation that I visited this country for the first time at the end of 1935. Professor Veblen and his wife were responsible for the pleasant social atmosphere, and I found that the von Neumann's (and Alexander's) houses were the scenes of almost constant gatherings. These were the years of the Depression, but the Institute managed to give to a considerable number of both native and visiting mathematicians a relatively carefree existence.

Johnny's first marriage terminated in divorce. In 1938, he remarried during a summer visit to Budapest and brought back to Princeton his second wife, Klara Dan. His home continued to be a gathering place for scientists. His friends will remember the inexhaustible hospitality and the atmosphere of intelligence and wit one found there. Klari von Neumann later became one of the first coders of mathematical problems for electronic computing machines, an art to which she brought some of its early skills.

With the beginning of the war in Europe, Johnny's activities outside the Institute started to multiply. He undertook an enormous amount of work for various scientific projects in and out of the government.

In October 1954, he was named by presidential appointment as a member of the United States Atomic Energy Commission. He left Princeton on a leave of absence and discontinued all commitments with the exception of the chairmanship of the ICBM Committee. Admiral Strauss, chairman of the Commission and a friend of Johnny's for many years, suggested this nomination as soon as a vacancy occurred. Of Johnny's brief period of active service on the Commission, he writes:

> During the period between the date of his confirmation and the late autumn, 1955, Johnny functioned magnificently. He had the invaluable faculty of being able to take the most difficult problem, separate it into its components, whereupon everything looked brilliantly simple, and all of us wondered why we had not been able to see through to the answer as clearly as it was possible for him to do. In this way, he enormously facilitated the work of the Atomic Energy Commission.

Johnny, whose health had always been excellent, began to look very fatigued in 1954. In the summer of 1955, the first symptoms of a fatal disease were discovered by x-ray examination. A prolonged and cruel illness gradually put an end to all his activities. He died at Walter Reed Hospital in Washington at the age of fifty-three.

Johnny's friends remember him in his characteristic poses: standing before a blackboard or discussing problems at home. Somehow, his gesture, smile, and the expression of the eyes always reflected the kind of thought or the nature of the problem under discussion. He was of middle size, quite slim as a very young man, then increasingly corpulent; moving about in small steps with considerable random acceleration, but never with great speed. A smile flashed on his face whenever a problem exhibited features of a logical or mathematical paradox. Quite independently of his liking for abstract wit, he had a strong appreciation (one might say almost a hunger) for the more earthy type of comedy and humor.

He seemed to combine in his mind several abilities which, if not contradictory, at least seem separately to require such powers of concentration and memory that one very rarely finds them together in one intellect. These are: a feeling for the set-theoretical, formally algebraic basis of mathematical thought, the knowledge and understanding of the substance of classical mathematics in analysis and geometry, and a very acute perception of the potentialities of modern mathematical methods for the formulation of existing and new problems of theoretical physics. All this is specifically demonstrated by his brilliant and original work which covers a very wide spectrum of contemporary scientific thought.

His conversations with friends on scientific subjects could last for hours. There never was a lack of subjects, even when one departed from mathematical topics.

Johnny had a vivid interest in people and delighted in gossip. One often had the feeling that in his memory he was making a collection of human peculiarities as if preparing a statistical study. He followed also the changes brought by the passage of time. When a young man, he mentioned to me several times his belief that the primary mathematical powers decline after the age of about twenty-six, but that a certain more prosaic shrewdness developed by experience manages to compensate for this gradual loss, at least for a time. Later, this limiting age was slowly raised.

He engaged occasionally in conversational evaluations of other scientists; he was, on the whole, quite generous in his opinions, but often able to damn faint praise. The expressed judgment was, in general, very cautious, and he was certainly unwilling to state any final opinions about others: "Let Rhadamantys and Minos . . . judge. . . ." Once when asked, he said that he would consider Erhard Schmidt and Hermann Weyl among the mathematicians who especially influenced him technically in his early life.

Johnny was regarded by many as an excellent chairman of committees (this peculiar contemporary activity). He would press strongly his technical views, but defer rather easily on personal or organizational matters.

In spite of his great powers and his full consciousness of them, he lacked a certain self-confidence, admiring greatly a few mathematicians and physicists who possessed qualities which he did not believe he himself had in the highest possible degree. The qualities which evoked this feeling on his part were, I felt, relatively simple-minded powers of intuition of new truths, or the gift for a seemingly irrational perception of proofs or formulation of new theorems.

Quite aware that the criteria of value in mathematical work are, to some extent, purely aesthetic, he once expressed an apprehension that the values put on abstract scientific achievement in our present civilization might diminish: "The interests of humanity may change, the present curiosities in science may cease, and entirely different things may occupy the human mind in the future." One conversation centered on the ever accelerating progress of technology and changes in the mode of human life, which gives the appearance of approaching some essential singularity in the history of the race beyond which human affairs, as we know them, could not continue.

His friends enjoyed his great sense of humor. Among fellow scientists, he could make illuminating, often ironical, comments on historical or social phenomena with a mathematician's formulation, exhibiting the humor inherent in some statement true only in the vacuous set. These often could be appreciated only by mathematicians. He certainly did not consider mathematics sacrosanct. I remember a discussion in Los Alamos, in connection with some physical problems where a mathematical argument used the existence of ergodic transformations and fixed points. He remarked with a sudden smile, "Modern mathematics can be applied after all! It isn't clear, a priori, is it, that it could be so . . ."

I would say that his main interest after science was in the study of history. His knowledge of ancient history was unbelievably detailed. He remembered, for instance, all the anecdotical material in Gibbon's *Decline and Fall* and liked to engage after dinner in historical discussions. On a trip south, to a meeting of the American Mathematical Society at Duke University, passing near the battlefields of the Civil War he amazed us by his familiarity with the minutest features of the battles. This encyclopedic knowledge molded his views on the course of future events by inducing a sort of analytic continuation. I can testify that in his forecasts of political events leading to the Second World War and of military events during the war, most of his guesses were amazingly correct. After the end of the Second World War, however, his apprehensions of an almost immediate subsequent calamity, which he considered as extremely likely, proved fortunately wrong. There was perhaps an inclination to take a too exclusively rational point of view about the cases of historical events. This tendency was possibly due to an over-formalized game theory approach.

Among other accomplishments, Johnny was an excellent linguist. He remembered his school Latin and Greek remarkably well. In addition to English, he spoke German and French fluently. His lectures in this country were well known for their literary quality (with very few characteristic mispronunciations which his friends anticipated joyfully, *e.g.*, "integhers"). During his frequent visits to Los Alamos and Santa Fe (New Mexico), he displayed a less perfect knowledge of Spanish, and on a trip to Mexico, he tried to make himself understood by using "neo-Castilian," a creation of his own—English words with an "el" prefix and appropriate Spanish endings.

Before the war, Johnny spent the summers in Europe on vacations and lecturing (in 1935 at Cambridge University, in 1936 at the Institut Henri Poincaré in Paris). Often he mentioned that personally he found doing scientific work there almost impossible because of the atmosphere of political tension. After the war he undertook trips abroad only unwillingly.

Ever since he came to the United States, he expressed his appreciation of the opportunities here and very high hopes for the future of scientific work in this country.

To follow chronologically von Neumann's interests and accomplishments is to review a large part of the whole scientific development of the last three decades. In his youthful work, he was concerned not only with mathematical logic and the axiomatics of set theory, but, simultaneously, with the substance of set theory itself, obtaining interesting results in measure theory and the theory of real variables. It was in this period also that he began his classical work on quantum theory, the mathematical foundation of the theory of measurement in quantum theory and the new statistical mechanics. His profound studies of operators in Hilbert spaces also date from this period. He pushed far beyond the immediate needs of physical theories, and initiated a detailed study of rings of operators, which has independent mathematical interest. The beginning of the work on continuous geometries belongs to this period as well.

Von Neumann's awareness of results obtained by other mathematicians and the inherent possibilities which they offer is astonishing. Early in his work, a paper by Borel on the minimax property led him to develop in the paper, "Zur Theorie der Gesellschaftsspiele,"[2] ideas which culminated later in one of his most original creations, the theory of games. An idea of Koopman on the possibilities of treating problems of classical mechanics by means of operators on a function space stimulated him to give the first mathematically rigorous proof of an ergodic theorem. Haar's construction of measure in groups provided the inspiration for his wonderful partial solution of Hilbert's fifth problem, in which he proved the possibility of introducing analytical parameters in compact groups.

In the middle thirties, Johnny was fascinated by the problem of hydrodynamical turbulence. It was then that he became aware of the mysteries underlying the subject of non-linear partial differential equations. His work, from the beginning of the Second World War, concerns a study of the equations of hydrodynamics and the theory of shocks. The phenomena described by these non-linear equations are baffling ana-

2. "Zur Theorie der Gesellschaftsspiele," *Mathematische Annalen*, 100 (1928), 295–320.

lytically and defy even qualitative insight by present methods. Numerical work seemed to him the most promising way to obtain a feeling for the behavior of such systems. This impelled him to study new possibilities of computation on electronic machines, ab initio. He began to work on the theory of computing and planned the work, to remain unfinished, on the theory of automata. It was at the outset of such studies that his interest in the working of the nervous system and the schematized properties of organisms claimed so much of his attention.

This journey through many fields of mathematical sciences was not a result of restlessness. Neither was it a search for novelty, nor a desire for applying a small set of general methods to many diverse special cases. Mathematics, in contrast to theoretical physics, is not confined to a few central problems. The search for unity, if pursued on a purely formal basis, von Neumann considered doomed to failure. This wide range of curiosity had its basis in some metamathematical motivations and was influenced strongly by the world of physical phenomena—these will probably defy formalization for a long time to come.

Mathematicians, at the outset of their creative work, are often confronted by two conflicting motivations: the first is to contribute to the edifice of existing work—it is there that one can be sure of gaining recognition quickly by solving outstanding problems—the second is the desire to blaze new trails and to create new syntheses. This latter course is a more risky undertaking, the final judgment of value or success appearing only in the future. In his early work, Johnny chose the first of these alternatives. It was toward the end of his life that he felt sure enough of himself to engage freely and yet painstakingly in the creation of a possible new mathematical discipline. This was to be a combinatorial theory of automata and organisms. His illness and premature death permitted him to make only a beginning.

In his constant search for applicability and in his general mathematical instinct for all exact sciences, he brought to mind Euler, Poincaré, or in more recent times, perhaps Hermann Weyl. One should remember that the diversity and complexity of contemporary problems surpass enormously the situation confronting the first two named. In one of his last articles, Johnny deplored the fact that it does not seem possible nowadays for any one brain to have more than a passing knowledge of more than one-third of the field of pure mathematics.

1. Game Theory

THE subject forms a new, rapidly developing chapter in present-day mathematical research; of the many areas of mathematics shaped by von Neumann's genius none shows his influence more clearly.

This modern approach to problems of competition and cooperation was given a broad foundation in his superlative paper of 1928.[3] In scope and youthful vigor this work can be compared only to his papers of the same period on the axioms of set theory and the mathematical foundations of quantum mechanics. A decade later, when the Austrian economist Oskar Morgenstern came to Princeton, von Neumann's interest in the theory was reawakened. The result of their active and intensive collaboration during the early years of World War II was the treatise *Theory of Games and Economic Behavior*,[4] in which the basic structure of the 1928 paper is elaborated and extended. Together, the paper and treatise contain a remarkably complete outline of the subject as we know it today, and every writer in the field draws in some measure upon concepts which were there united into a coherent theory.

The crucial innovation of von Neumann, which was to be both the keystone of his Theory of Games and the central theme of his later research in the area, was the assertion and proof of the Minimax Theorem. Ideas of pure and randomized strategies had been introduced earlier, especially by Émile Borel.[5] However, these efforts were restricted either to individual examples or, at best, to zero-sum two-person games with skew-symmetric payoff matrices. To paraphrase his own opinion expressed in *Econometrica*,[6] von Neumann did not view the mere desire to mathematize strategic concepts and the straight formal definition of a

3. *Ibid.*

4. John von Neumann and Oskar Morgenstern, *Theory of Games and Economic Behavior* (Princeton, 1944).

5. "La Théorie du jeu et les équations intégrales à noyau symétrique," *Comptes Rendus hebdomadaires des séances de l'Académie des Sciences*, 173 (1921), 1304–1308; "Sur les Jeux où interviennent l'hasard et l'habileté des joueurs," *Théorie des probabilités* (Paris, 1924), pp. 202–224; "Sur les Systèmes de formes linéaires à déterminant symétrique gauche et la théorie générale du jeu," *Comptes Rendus hebdomadaires des séances de l'Académie des Sciences*, 184 (1927), 52–54.

6. "Communication on the Borel Notes," *Econometrica*, 21 (1953), 124–125.

pure strategy as the main agenda of an "initiator" in the field, but felt that there was nothing worth publishing until the Minimax Theorem was proved.

As the *leitmotiv* of this article, the Minimax Theorem requires at least informal statement at the outset. For any finite zero-sum two-person game in a normalized form, it asserts the existence of a unique numerical value, representing a gain for one player and a loss for the other, such that each can achieve at least this favorable an expectation from his own point of view by using a randomized (or mixed) strategy of his own choosing. Such strategies for the two players are termed optimal strategies and the unique numerical value, the minimax value of the game. This is the starting point of the von Neumann-Morgenstern solution for cooperative games, where all possible partitions of the players into two coalitions are considered and the reasonable aspirations of the opposing coalitions in each partition measured by the minimax value of the strictly competitive two-party struggle between them. In the area of extensive games, the solution of games with perfect information by means of pure strategies assumes importance only by contrast to the necessity of randomizing in the general case. The Minimax Theorem reappears in a new guise, when von Neumann turned to analyze a linear model of production. Finally, in the hands of von Neumann, it was the source of a broad spectrum of technical results, ranging from his extensions of the Brouwer fixed point theorem, developed for its proof, to new and unexpected methods for combinatorial problems.

Throughout von Neumann's work there is evidence of a strong drive to supply rigorous axiomatic foundations for the subjects which he treated. For game theory, his contribution of this sort was a set-theoretical formulation of a very wide class of finite games. When presented in terms of this system, a game is said to be in *extensive form*. Although the extensive description of a game is stripped of all the technical apparatus peculiar to the particular game, it retains the full combinatorial complexity of play according to the original rules. As such, it is in contrast with the so-called *normalized form*, with but one choice per player, that results when the game is simplified through the introduction of pure strategies.

Von Neumann's achievements in this direction were many. First, and most important, he recognized the necessity of characterizing games of strategy in an unequivocal manner; otherwise the field would necessarily remain a mere collection of examples. This program he carried out in masterful style, so that the essential elements which he isolated, such as play, chance and personal moves, payoffs, and information partitions, are still the starting points of any description of a game. It is difficult to appreciate, in retrospect, the genius of von Neumann's abstraction of the essential elements of a general game of strategy into a mathematical system. For this area, perhaps more than any other he worked in, had little mathematical tradition. Yet the mathematical system he created has served as a rallying point for much mathematical research which otherwise would not have been possible.

He placed in bold relief the pioneering theorem that every game with perfect information has a minimax solution in pure strategies. This theorem, used implicitly by many writers, could have no general proof until the theory of extensive games was on sound footing. By repeated emphasis, he underlined the role of incomplete information as the source of many interesting game-theoretic results. The ability to describe rigorously the state of information at each move in a game, separating out "inferences" and "signals," and to construct strategies which take full account of this information had a decisive role in the development of a theory of extensive games.

The fundamental problem of the theory of games is to find the methods by which a player can obtain a "most favorable result." At first, von Neumann identified the "most favorable result" with the greatest expected (monetary) value,[7] remarking that this or some similar assumption was necessary in order to apply the methods of probability theory. While doing so, he was well aware of the objections to the principle of maximizing expected winnings as a prescription for behavior, but wished to concentrate on other problems.

Parallel to his interest in the mathematical treatment of competitive economic situations by means of games of strategy, von Neumann was concerned with the formulation of models of general economic equilibrium. In 1932, he presented an economic model of his own devising at a

---

7. "Zur Theorie der Gesellschaftsspiele," p. 298.

colloquium in Princeton. This paper,[8] together with work of Wald[9] marks a new era in mathematical economics in which rigorous arguments replace mere "equation counting" as a means of establishing the existence of economic equilibrium. It also shares with Wald's work the credit for recognizing explicitly that inequalities as well as equations are forced on the system by the economic context, and for utilizing this fact to advantage in the mathematical treatment. In its linear approach to production, with alternative processes and the possibility of intermediate goods, it is the direct ancestor of linear programming and activity analysis.

The impact of von Neumann's Theory of Games extends far beyond the boundaries of this subject. By his example and through his accomplishments, he opened a broad new channel of two-way communication between mathematics and the social sciences. These sciences were fortunate indeed that one of the most creative mathematicians of the twentieth century concerned himself with some of their fundamental problems and constructed strikingly imaginative and stimulating models with which to attack their problems quantitatively. At the same time, mathematics received a vital infusion of fresh ideas and methods that will continue to be highly productive for many years to come. Von Neumann's interest in "problems of organized complexity,"[10] so important in the social sciences, went hand in hand with his pioneering development of large-scale high-speed computers. There is a great challenge for other mathematicians to follow his lead in grappling with complex systems in many areas of the sciences where mathematics has not yet penetrated deeply.

8. "Über ein Ökonomisches Gleichungssystem und eine Verallgemeinerung des Brouwerschen Fixpunktsatzes," *Ergebnisse eines Mathematischen Kolloquiums*, 8 (1935–36), 73–83. The translation, "A Model of General Economic Equilibrium," appears in *Review of Economic Studies*, 13 (1945–46), 1–9.

9. "Über die Eindeutige Positive Lösbarkeit der Neuen Produktionsgleichungen," *Ergebnisse eines Mathematischen Kolloquiums*, 6 (1933–34), 12–20; "Über die Produktionsgleichungen der Ökonomischen Wertlehre," *Ergebnisse eines Mathematischen Kolloquiums*, 7 (1934–35), 1–6; "Über Einige Gleichungssysteme der Mathematischen Ökonomie," *Zeitschrift für Nationalökonomie*, 7 (1936), 637–670. The English translation appears in *Econometrica*, 10 (1951), 368–403.

10. An apt designation of Warren Weaver, "Science and Complexity," *American Scientist*, 36 (1948), 536–544.

It was von Neumann's philosophy[11] that the mathematician may choose to work in any of a wide variety of fields, and that the selection of working material and the resulting measure of success are largely influenced by aesthetic values. However, he warned that mathematics loses much of its creative drive when too far removed from empirical sources. This philosophy is exemplified in a most brilliant and enduring way by the Theory of Games. It is a tribute to his great genius that in his 1928 paper he built such a sound and comprehensive mathematical foundation for games of strategy, an area almost new to mathematics, that he was able to see it explode in his lifetime into a broad and influential field of research.

11. Dynamics and Meteorological Calculations

THE formidable mathematical problems presented by the hydrodynamical equations of the motions of the earth's atmosphere fascinated von Neumann for a considerable time. With the advent of computing machines, a detailed numerical study at least of simplified versions of the problems became possible, and a large program of such work was started by him. At the Institute in Princeton, a meteorological research group was established;[12] the plan was to attack the problem of numerical weather solution by a step-by-step investigation of models which were to approximate more and more closely the real properties of the atmosphere. A numerical investigation of truly 3-dimensional motions is at present impractical even on the most advanced electronic computing machines. (This may not be the case, say five years from now.)

The first highly schematized computations which von Neumann ini-

11. See von Neumann's essay "The Mathematician" in *The Works of the Mind* (Chicago, 1947), pp. 180–196; reprinted in *The World of Mathematics* (ed. J. R. Newman, New York, 1956), pp. 2053–2063.

12. J. Charney was working closely with him on problems of meteorology, *e.g.* von Neumann, Charney, and R. Fjortoft, "Numerical Integration of the Barotropic Vorticity Equation," *Tellus*, 2 (1950), 237–254.

tiated dealt with a 2-dimensional model and for the most part in the so-called geostrophic approximation. Later, what might be called "$2+\frac{1}{2}$" dimensional hydrodynamical computations were performed by assuming two or three 2-dimensional models corresponding to different altitudes or pressure levels interacting with each other. This problem was dear to his mind, both because of its intrinsic mathematical interest, and because of the enormous technological consequences which a successful solution could have. He believed that our knowledge of dynamics of controlling processes in the atmosphere, together with the development of computing machines, was approaching a level that would permit weather prediction. Beyond that, he believed that one could understand, calculate, and perhaps put into effect processes ultimately permitting control and change of the climate.

In one paper[13] he speculated on the approach of the time when one could produce, with the now available vast nuclear sources of energy, changes in the general circulation of the atmosphere of the same order of magnitude as "the great globe itself." In such problems where the physics of the phenomena are already understood, it might be that a future Mathematical Analysis will enable the human race to extend vastly its control over nature.

III. Theory and Practice of Computing on Electronic Machines; Monte Carlo Method

VON NEUMANN'S interest in numerical work had different sources. One stemmed from his original work on the role of formalism in mathematical logic and set theory, and his youthful work was concerned extensively with Hilbert's program of considering mathematics as a finite game. Another equally strong motivation came from his work in problems of mathematical physics including the purely theoretical work on ergodic theory in classical physics and his contributions to quantum theory. A growing exposure to the more practical

13. "Can We Survive Technology?" *Fortune*, June, 1955.

problems encountered in hydrodynamics and in the manifold problems of mechanics of continua arising in the technology of nuclear energy led directly to problems of computation.

I remember quite well how, very early in the Los Alamos Project, it became obvious that analytical work alone was often not sufficient to provide even qualitative answers. The numerical work by hand and even the use of desk computing machines would require a prohibitively long time for these problems. This situation seemed to provide the final spur for von Neumann to engage himself energetically in the work on methods of computation utilizing the electronic machines.

For several years von Neumann had felt that in many problems of hydrodynamics—in propagation and the behavior of shocks, and generally in cases where the non-linear partial differential equations describing the phenomena had to be applied in instances involving large displacements (that is to say, in cases where linearization would not adequately approximate the true description) numerical work was necessary to provide heuristic material for a future theory.

This final necessity compelled him to examine, *from its foundations*, the problem of computing on electronic machines and, during 1944 and 1945, he formulated the now fundamental methods of translating a set of mathematical procedures into a language of instructions for a computing machine. The electronic machines of that time (*e.g.*, the Eniac) lacked the flexibility and generality which they now possess in the handling of mathematical problems. Speaking broadly, each problem required a special and different system of wiring, in order to enable the machine to perform the prescribed operations in a given sequence. Von Neumann's great contribution was the idea of a fixed and rather universal set of connections or circuits in the machine, a "flow diagram," and a "code" so as to enable a fixed set of connections in the machine to have the means of solving a very great variety of problems. While, a priori at least, the possibility of such an arrangement might be obvious to mathematical logicians, the execution and practice of such a universal method was far from obvious with the then existing electronic technology.

It is easy to underestimate, even now, many years after the inception of such methods, the great possibilities opened through such theoretical experimentation in problems of mathematical physics. The field is still new and it seems risky to make prophesies, but the already accumulated mass of theoretical experiments in hydrodynamics, magneto-hydrodynamics, and quantum-theoretical calculations, etc., allow one to hope that good syntheses may arise from these computations.

The engineering of the computing machines owes a great deal to von Neumann. The logical schemata of the machines, the planning of the relative roles of their memory, their speed, the selection of fundamental "orders" and their circuits in the present machines bear heavily the imprint of his ideas. Von Neumann himself supervised the construction of a machine at the Institute for Advanced Study in Princeton, so as to have an acquaintance with the engineering problems involved and at the same time to have at hand this tool for novel experimentation. Even before the machine was finished, which took longer than anticipated, he was involved in setting up and executing enormous computations arising in certain problems at the Los Alamos Laboratory. One of these, the problem of following the course of a thermonuclear reaction, involved more than a billion of elementary arithmetical operations and elementary logical orders. The problem was to find a "yes" or "no" answer to the question of propagation of a reaction. One was not concerned with providing the final data with great accuracy but, in order to obtain an answer to the original question, all the intermediate and detailed computations seemed necessary. It is true that guessing the behavior of certain elements of the problem, together with hand calculations, could indeed throw considerable light on the final answer. In order to increase the degree of confidence in estimates thus obtained by intuition, an enormous amount of computational work had to be undertaken. This seems to be rather common in some new problems of mathematical physics and of modern technology. Astronomical accuracy is not required in the description of the phenomena; in some cases, one would be satisfied with predicting the behavior "up to 10 percent" and yet during the course of the calculations, the individual steps have to be kept as accurate as possible. The enormous number of elementary steps then poses the problem of estimating the reliability of final results and problems on the intrinsic stability of mathematical methods and their computational execution.

In receiving the Fermi prize of the Atomic Energy Commission, von

Neumann was cited especially for his contribution to the development of computing on the electronic machines, so useful in many aspects of nuclear science and technology.

The electronic computing machines with their speed of computation surpassing that of the hand calculations by a factor of many thousands invite the invention of entirely new methods not only in numerical analysis in the classical sense, but in the very foundations of procedures of mathematical analysis itself. Nobody was more aware of these implications than von Neumann. A small example of what we mean here can be illustrated by the so-called Monte Carlo Method. The methods of numerical analysis as developed in the past for hand work, or even for the relay machines, are not necessarily optimal for computations on the electronic machines. So, for example, it is obvious that instead of employing tables of elementary functions, it is more economical to compute the desired values directly. Next, it is clear that the procedures of integration of equations by reduction to quadratures, etc., can now be circumvented by schemes so complicated arithmetically that they could not even be considered for hand work, but which are very feasible on the new machines. Literally dozens of computational tricks, "subroutines," *e.g.*, for calculating elementary algebraical or transcendental functions, for solving of auxiliary equations, etc. were produced by von Neumann during the years following the World War. Some of this work, by the way, is not as yet generally available to the mathematical public, but is more widely known among the now numerous technological and scientific groups utilizing the computing machines in industrial or government projects. This work includes methods for finding eigen-values and inversion of matrices, methods for economical search for extrema of functions of several variables, production of random digits, etc. Much of this exhibits the typical combinatorial dexterity, in some cases, of virtuoso quality, of his early work in mathematical logic and algebraical studies in operator theory.

The simplicity of mathematical formulation of the principles of mathematical physics hoped for in the nineteenth century seems to be conspicuously absent in modern theories. A perplexing variety and wealth of structure found in what one considered as elementary particles, seem to postpone the hopes for an early mathematical synthesis. In applied physics and in technology one is forced to deal with situations which, mathematically, present mixtures of different systems: for example, in addition to a system of particles whose behavior is governed by equations of mechanics, there are interacting electrical fields, described by partial differential equations; or, in the study of behavior of neutron-producing assemblies, one has, in addition to a system of neutrons, the hydrodynamical and the thermodynamical properties of the whole system interacting with the discrete assembly of these particles.

From the point of view of combinatorics alone, not to mention the difficulties of analysis in the handling of several partial differential and integral equations, it is clear that at the present time, there is very little hope of finding solutions in a closed form. In order to find, *even only qualitatively*, the properties of such systems, one is forced to look for pragmatic methods.

We decided to look for ways to find, as it were, homomorphic images of the given physical problem in a mathematical schema which could be represented by a system of fictitious "particles" treated by an electronic computer. It is especially in problems involving functions of a considerable number of independent variables that such procedures would be applied. To give a very simple concrete example of such a Monte Carlo approach, let us consider the question of evaluating the volume of a subregion of a given *n*-dimensional "cube" described by a set of inequalities. Instead of the usual method of approximating the volume required by a systematic subdivision of the space into its lattice points one could select, *at random*, with uniform probability, a number of points in space and determine (on the machine) how many of these points belong to the given region. This proportion will give us, according to elementary facts of probability theory, an approximate value of the relative volumes, *with the probability as close to one* as we wish, by employing a sufficient number of sample points. As a somewhat more complicated example, consider the problem of diffusion in a region of space bounded by surfaces which partly reflect and partly absorb the diffusing particles. If the geometry of the region is complicated, it might be more economical to try to perform "physically" a large number of such random walks rather than to try to solve the integro-differential equations classically. These "walks" can be performed conveniently on machines and such a procedure in fact reverses the treatment which in probability theory reduces the study of random walks to the study of differential equations.

Another instance of such methodology is, given a set of functional equations, to attempt to transform it into an equivalent one which would admit of a probabilistic or game theory interpretation. This latter would allow one to play, on a machine, the games illustrating the random processes and the distributions obtained would give a fair idea of the solution of the original equations. Better still, the hope would be to obtain directly a "homomorphic image" of the behavior of the physical system in question. It has to be stated that in many physical problems presently considered, the differential equations originally obtained by certain idealizations, are not, so to say, very sacrosanct any more. A direct study of models of the system on computing machines may possess a heuristic value, at least. A great number of problems were treated in this fashion towards the end of the war and in following years by von Neumann and the writer [Ulam]. At first, the probabilistic interpretation was immediately suggested by the physical situation itself. Later, problems of the third class mentioned above were studied. A theory of such mathematical models is still very incomplete. In particular, estimates of fluctuations and accuracy are not as yet developed. Here again, von Neumann contributed a large number of ingenious ways, for example by playing suitable games, of producing sequences of numbers in the given probability distributions. He also devised probabilistic models for treatment of the Boltzmann equation and important stochastic models for some strictly deterministic problems in hydrodynamics. Much of this work is scattered throughout various laboratory reports or is still in manuscript. One certainly hopes that in the near future, an organized selection will be available to the mathematical public.

iv. Automata Theory

THE theory of automata is a relatively recent and by no means sharply defined area of research. It is an interdisciplinary science bordered mathematically by symbolic logic and Turing machine theory, bordered engineering-wise by the theory and the use, particularly for general non-numerical work, of large-scale computing machines, and bordered biologically by neurophysiology, the theory of nerve-nets and the like. Problems range from Gödel-type questions (relating to Turing machines and decision procedures), to questions of duplication, of various biological phenomena in a machine (*e.g.*, adaptation, self-reproduction and self-repair).

Von Neumann spent a considerable part of the last few years of his life working in this area. It represented for him a synthesis of his early interest in logic and proof theory and his later work, during World War II and after, on large-scale electronic computers. Involving a mixture of pure and applied mathematics as well as other sciences, automata theory was an ideal field for von Neumann's wide-ranging intellect. He brought to it many new insights and opened up at least two new directions of research. It is unfortunate that he was unable to complete the work he had in progress, some of which is in the form of rough notes or unedited lectures, and for some of which no record exists apart from his colleagues' memories of casual conversations.

We shall not here discuss his tremendously important contributions to computing machines and their use—his ideas on their logical organization,[14] the use of flow diagrams for programming,[15] methods of pro-

14. John von Neumann, A. W. Burks, and H. H. Goldstine, *Preliminary Discussion of the Logical Design of an Electronic Computing Instrument*, part I, vol. I (Report prepared for U. S. Army Ordnance Department under Contract W–36–034–ORD–7481 [June 28, 1946; 2nd ed. Sept. 2, 1947]); John von Neumann and H. H. Goldstine, *Planning and Coding of Problems for an Electronic Computing Instrument*, part II, vol. I (Report prepared for U. S. Army Ordnance Department under Contract W–36–034–ORD–7481 [1947]).

15. von Neumann and Goldstine, *Planning and Coding*; John von Neumann and H. H. Goldstine, *Planning and Coding of Problems for an Electronic Computing Instrument*, part II, vol. II (Report prepared for U. S. Army Ordnance Department under Contract W–36–034–ORD–7481 [1948]); John von Neumann and H. H. Goldstine, *Planning and Coding of Problems for an Electronic Computing Instrument*, part II, vol. III (Report prepared for U. S. Army Ordnance Department under Contract W–36–034–ORD–7481 [1948]).

gramming various problems such as the inversion of matrices,[16] the Monte Carlo method, and so on,—but restrict ourselves to the automata area proper.

One important part of von Neumann's work on automata relates to the problem of designing reliable machines using unreliable components.[17] Given a set of building blocks with some positive probability of malfunctioning, can one by suitable design construct arbitrarily large and complex automata for which the overall probability of incorrect output is kept under control? Is it possible to obtain a probability of error as small as desired, or at least a probability of error not exceeding some fixed value (independent of the particular automaton)?

We have, in human and animal brains, examples of very large and relatively reliable systems constructed from individual components, the neurons, which would appear to be anything but reliable, not only in individual operation but in fine details of interconnection. Furthermore, it is well known that under conditions of lesion, accident, disease and so on, the brain continues to function remarkably well even when large fractions of it are damaged.

These facts are in sharp contrast with the behavior and organization of present-day computing machines. The individual components of these must be engineered to extreme reliability, each wire must be properly connected, and each order in a program must be correct. A single error in components, wiring, or programming will typically lead to complete gibberish in the output. If we are to view the brain as a machine, it is evidently organized for protection against errors in a way quite different from computing machines.

The problem is analogous to that in communication theory where one wishes to construct codes for transmission of information for which the reliability of the entire code is high even though the reliability for the transmission of individual symbols is poor. In communication theory this can be done by properly introduced redundancy, and some similar device must be used in the case at hand. Merely performing the same

16. John von Neumann and H. H. Goldstine, "Numerical Inverting of Matrices of High Order," *Bulletin of the American Mathematical Society*, 53 (1947), 1021–1099.

17. "Probabilistic Logics and the Synthesis of Reliable Organisms from Unreliable Components," in *Automata Studies* (eds. C. E. Shannon and J. McCarthy, Princeton, 1956), pp. 43–98.

calculation many times and then taking a majority vote will not suffice. The majority vote would itself be taken by unreliable components and thus would have to be taken many times and majority votes taken of the majority votes. And so on. We are face to face with a "Who will watch the watchman?" type of situation.

To attack these problems, von Neumann first set up a formal structure for automata. The particular system he chooses is somewhat like the McCullough–Pitts model; networks made up of a number of inter-connected components, each component of a relatively simple type. The individual components receive binary inputs over a set of different input lines and produce a binary output on an output line. The output occurs a certain integer number of time units later. If the output were a function of the inputs, we would have a reliable component that might perform, for example, operations of "and," "not," "Sheffer stroke," etc. However, if the output is related only statistically to the input, if, for example, with probability $1-\epsilon$ it gives the Sheffer stroke function and with probability ϵ the negative of this, we have an unreliable component. Given an unlimited number of such unreliable elements, say of the Sheffer stroke type, can one construct a reliable version of any given automaton?

Von Neumann shows that this can be done, and in fact does this by two quite different schemes. The first of these is perhaps the more elegant mathematically, as it stays closely within the prescribed problem and comes face to face with the "watchman" problem. This solution involves the construction from three unreliable sub-networks, together with certain comparing devices, of a large and more reliable sub-network to perform the same function. By carrying this out systematically throughout some network for realizing an automaton with reliable elements, one obtains a network for the same behavior with unreliable elements.

The first solution, as he points out, suffers from two shortcomings. In the first place, the final reliability cannot be made arbitrarily good but only held at a certain level ϵ (the ϵ depending on the reliability of the individual components). If the individual components are quite poor the solution, then, can hardly be considered satisfactory. Secondly, and even more serious from the point of view of application, the redundancy requirements for this solution are fantastically high in typical cases. The number of components required increases exponentially with the number n of components in the automaton being copied. Since n is very large in cases of practical interest, this solution can be considered to be only of logical importance.

The second approach involves what von Neumann called the multiplex trick. This means representing a binary output in the machine not by one line but by a bundle of N lines, the binary variable being determined by whether nearly all or very few of the lines carry the binary value 1. An automaton design based on reliable components is, in this scheme, replaced by one where each line becomes a bundle of lines, and each component is replaced by a sub-network which operates in the corresponding fashion between bundles of input and output lines. Von Neumann shows how such sub-networks can be constructed. He also makes some estimates of the redundancy requirements for certain gains in reliability. For example, starting with an unreliable "majority" organ whose probability of error is $1/200$, by a redundancy of 60,000 to 1 a sub-network representing a majority organ for bundles can be constructed whose probability of error is 10^{-20}. Using reasonable figures this would lead to an automaton of the complexity and speed of the brain operating for a hundred years with expectation about one error. In other words, something akin to this scheme is at least possible as the basis of the brain's reliability.

Another branch of automata theory developed by von Neumann is the study of self-reproducing machines—is it possible to formulate a simple and abstract system of "machines" which are capable of constructing other identical machines, or even more strongly, capable of a kind of evolutionary process in which successive generations construct machines of increasing "complexity." A real difficulty here is that of striking the proper balance between formal simplicity and ease of manipulation, on the one hand, and approximation of the model to real physical machines on the other hand. If reality is copied too closely in the model we have to deal with all of the complexity of nature, much of which is not particularly relevant to the self-reproducing question. However, by simplifying too much, the structure becomes so abstract and simplified that the problem is almost trivial and the solution is unimpressive with regard to solving the philosophical point that is involved. In one place, after a lengthy discussion of the difficulties of formulating the problem satisfactorily, von Neumann remarks: "I do not want to be seriously bothered with the objection that (a) everybody knows that automata can reproduce themselves (b) everybody knows that they cannot."

Von Neumann spent a good deal of time on the self-reproduction problem, discussing it briefly in the Hixon Symposium paper[18] and later in more detail in uncompleted manuscripts.[19]

He actually considered two different formulations of the problem. In the Hixon Symposium paper and in earlier lectures on this subject, a model is discussed in which there are a small number of basic components from which machines are made. These might be, for example, girders, a sensing organ (for sensing the presence of other parts), a joining organ (for fastening other parts together), etc. Machines are made by combinations of these parts and exist in a geometrical environment with other similar parts freely available.

Certain machines, made from these parts, are capable of gathering and working with components from the environment. It is possible also to construct "programmed" machines which follow a long sequence of instructions much as a computer does. Here, however, the instructions relate to manipulating parts rather than carrying out long calculations. The situation is somewhat analogous to that of Turing machines and indeed there is a notion of a *universal constructing machine* which can, by proper programming, imitate any machine for construction purposes. Von Neumann indicates how such a universal machine, together with a program-duplicating part, can be made into a self-reproducing machine.

This model is a very interesting one but, involving as it does complex considerations of motion of parts in a real Euclidean space, it would be tremendously difficult to carry out in detail, even if one ignored problems of energy, noise in the environment, and the like. At any rate, von Neumann abandoned this model in his later work in favor of a simpler construction.

18. "The General and Logical Theory of Automata," *Cerebral Mechanisms in Behavior; The Hixon Symposium* (ed. Lloyd A. Jeffress, New York, 1951), pp. 1–31.

19. *Theory of Self-reproducing Automata* (ed. and completed by Arthur W. Burks, Urbana, 1966).

The second type of self-reproducing system is described in an unfinished book for the University of Illinois Press. This second model is perhaps a little more suggestive of biological reproduction in the small (say at the cellular or even molecular level) although it is not closely patterned after any real physical system. Consider an infinite array of squares in the Euclidean plane, each square or "cell" capable of being in any of a number of states. The model that von Neumann developed had cells with twenty-nine possible states. Time moves in discrete steps. The state of a cell at a given time is a function of its state at the preceding time and that of its four nearest neighbors at the preceding time. As time progresses, then, the states of all cells evolve and change according to these functional relations. A certain state of the cells is called "quiescent" and corresponds to an inactive part of the plane. By proper construction of the functional equations it is possible to have groups of neighboring "active" cells which act somewhat like a living entity, an entity capable of retaining its identity, moving about and even of reproduction in the sense of causing another group of cells to take on a similar active state.

In addition to the self-reproducing question, he considers to some extent the problem of "evolution" in automata—is it possible to design automata which will construct in successive generations automata in some sense more efficient in adapting to their environment. He points out the existence of a *critical size* of automaton built from a given type of component such that smaller automata can only construct automata smaller than themselves, while some automata of the critical size or larger are capable of self-reproduction or even evolution (given a suitable definition of efficiency).

A field of great interest to von Neumann was that of the relation between the central nervous system and modern large-scale computers. His Hixon Symposium paper relates to this theme as well as to the problem of self-reproducing machines. More particularly, the Silliman Memorial Lectures[20] (which he prepared but was unable to deliver) are largely concerned with this comparison.

While realizing the similarities between computers and nerve-nets, von Neumann was also clearly aware of and often emphasized the many

20. *The Computer and the Brain* (New Haven, 1958).

important differences. At the surface level there are obvious differences in order of magnitude of the number and size of components and of their speed of operation. The neurons of a brain are much slower than artificial counterparts—transistors or vacuum tubes, but on the other hand they are much smaller, dissipate less power and there are many orders of magnitude more of them than in the largest computers. At a deeper level of comparison von Neumann stresses the differences in logical organization that must exist in the two cases. In part, these differences are implied by the difference in the kind of problem involved, "the logical depth," or the number of elementary operations that must be done in sequence to arrive at a solution. With computers, this logical depth may reach numbers like 10^7 or more because of the somewhat artificial and serial method of solving certain problems. The brain presumably, with more and slower components, operates on a more parallel basis with less logical depth and further, the problems it confronts are much less of the sequential calculation variety.

In the Silliman lectures, von Neumann touches briefly on a curious and provocative idea with some relevance to the foundations of mathematics. Turing, in his well known paper on computability, pointed out how one computing machine could be made to imitate another. Orders for the second machine are translated by a "short code" into sequences of orders for the first machine which cause it to accomplish, in a generally roundabout way, what the first machine would do. With such a translating code the first machine can be made to look, for computing purposes, like the second machine, although it is actually working inside in a different language. This procedure has become a commonplace and very useful tool in the everyday use of computers.

If we think of the brain as some kind of computing machine it is perfectly possible that the external language we use in communicating with each other may be quite different from the internal language used for computation (which includes, of course, all the logical and information-processing phenomena as well as arithmetic computation). In fact von Neumann gives various persuasive arguments that we are still totally unaware of the nature of the primary language for mental calculation. He states "Thus logics and mathematics in the central nervous system, when viewed as languages, must be structurally essentially different from those languages to which our common experience refers.

"It also ought to be noted that the language here involved may well correspond to a short code in the sense described earlier, rather than to a complete code: when we talk mathematics, we may be discussing a *secondary* language, built on the *primary* language truly used by the central nervous system. Thus the outward forms of our mathematics are not absolutely relevant from the point of view of evaluating what the mathematical or logical language *truly* used by the central nervous system is. However, the above remarks about reliability and logical and arithmetic depth prove that whatever the system is, it cannot fail to differ considerably from what we consciously and explicitly consider as mathematics."

In summary, von Neumann's contributions to automata theory have been characterized, like his contributions to other branches of mathematics and science, by the discovery of entirely new fields of study and the penetrating application of modern mathematical techniques. The areas which he opened for exploration will not be mapped in detail for many years. It is unfortunate that several of his projects in the automata area were left unfinished.

v. Nuclear Energy; Work at Los Alamos

THE discovery of the phenomenon of fission in uranium caused by absorption of neutrons with a consequent release of more neutrons came just before the outbreak of the Second World War. A number of physicists realized at once the possibility of a vast release of energy in an exponential reaction in a mass of uranium, and discussions started on quantitative evaluation of arrangements which would lead to utilization of this new source of energy.

Theoretical physicists form a much smaller and more closely knit group than mathematicians and, in general, the interchange of results and ideas is more rapid among them. Von Neumann, whose work in foundations of quantum theory brought him early into contact with most of the leading physicists, was aware of the new experimental facts and participated, from the beginning, in their speculations on the enormous technological possibilities latent in the phenomena of fission. The outbreak of war found him already engaged in scientific work connected with problems of defense. It was not until late in 1943, however, that he was asked by Oppenheimer to visit the Los Alamos Laboratory as a consultant and began to participate in the work which was to culminate in the construction of the atomic bomb.

As is now well known, the first self-sustaining nuclear chain reaction was established by a group of physicists headed by Fermi in Chicago on December 2, 1942, through the construction of a pile, an arrangement of uranium and a moderating substance where the neutrons are slowed down in order to increase their probability of causing further fissions. A pile forms a very large object and the time for the e-folding of the number of neutrons is relatively long. The project established at Los Alamos had as its aim to produce a very fast reaction in a relatively small amount of the 235 isotope of uranium or plutonium, leading to an explosive release of a vast amount of energy. The scientific group began to assemble in late spring of 1943 and by fall of that year a great number of eminent theoretical and experimental physicists were settled there. When von Neumann arrived in Los Alamos, diverse methods of assembling a critical mass of fissionable material were being examined; no scheme was a priori certain of success, one of the problems being whether a sufficiently fast assembly is possible before the nuclear reaction would lead to a mild or mediocre explosion preventing the utilization of most of the material.

E. Teller remembers how Johnny arrived in Lamy (the railroad station nearest Los Alamos), was brought up to the "hill," surrounded at that time by great secrecy, in an official car:

When he arrived, the Coordinating Council was just in session. Our Director, Oppenheimer, was reporting on the Ottawa meeting in Canada. His speech contained lots of references to most important people and equally important decisions, one of which affected us closely: We could expect the arrival of the British contingent in the near future. After he finished his speech he asked whether there were any questions or comments. The audience was impressed and no questions were asked. Then Oppenheimer suggested that there might be questions on some other topics. After a second or two a deep voice (whose source has been lost to history) spoke, "When shall we have a shoemaker on the Hill?" Even though no scientific problem was discussed with Johnny at that time, he asserted that as of that moment he was fully familiar with the nature of Los Alamos.

The atmosphere of work was extremely intense at that time and more characteristic of university seminars than technological or engineering laboratories by its informality and the exploratory and, one might say, abstract character of scientific discussions. I remember rather vividly that it was with some astonishment that I found, upon arriving at Los Alamos, a milieu reminiscent of a group of mathematicians discussing their abstract speculations rather than of engineers working on a well defined practical project—discussions were going on informally often until late at night. Scientifically, a striking feature of the situation was the diversity of problems, each equally important for the success of the project. For example, there was the problem of the distribution, in space and time, of the neutrons whose number increases exponentially; equally important was the problem of following the increasing deposition of energy by fissions in the material of the bomb, the calculation of hydrodynamical motions in the explosion, the distribution of energy in the form of radiation, and finally, following the course of the motions of the material surrounding the bomb after it has lost its criticality. It was vital to understand all these questions which involved very different mathematical problems.

It is impossible to detail here the contributions of von Neumann; I shall try to indicate some of the more important ones. Early in 1944 a method of *implosion* was considered for the assembly of the fissionable material. This involves a spherical impulse given to the material, followed by the compression. Von Neumann, Bethe, and Teller were the first to recognize the advantages of this scheme. Teller told him about the experimental work of Neddermeyer and collaborated with von Neumann on working out the essential consequences of such spherical geometry. Von Neumann came to the conclusion that one could produce exceedingly great pressures by this method and it became clear in the discussion that great pressures would bring about considerable compressions as well. In order to start the implosion in a sufficiently symmetrical manner, the original push given by high explosives had to be delivered by simultaneously detonating it from many points. Tuck and von Neumann suggested that it be supplemented by the use of high explosive lenses.

We mentioned before von Neumann's ability, perhaps somewhat rare among mathematicians, to commune with the physicists, understand their language, and to transform it almost instantly into a mathematician's schemes and expressions. Then, after following the problems as such, he could translate them back into expressions in common use among physicists.

The first attempts to calculate the motions resulting from an implosion were extremely schematic. The equations of state of the materials involved were only imperfectly known, but even with crude mathematical approximations one was led to equations whose solution was beyond the scope of explicit analytical methods. It became obvious that extensive and tedious numerical work was necessary in order to obtain quantitatively correct results and it is in this connection that computing machines appeared as a necessary aid.

A still more complicated problem is that of the calculation of the characteristics of the nuclear explosion. The amount of energy liberated in it depends on the history of the outward motions which are, of course, governed by the rate of energy deposition and by the thermodynamic properties of the material and radiation at the very high temperatures which are generated. One had to be satisfied for the first experiment with approximate calculations; however, as mentioned before, even the order of magnitude is not easy to estimate without intricate computations. After the end of the war the desire to economize on the material and to maximize its utilization prompted the need for much more precise calculations. Here again von Neumann's contributions to the mathematical treatment of the resulting physical questions were considerable.

Already during the war, the possibilities of *thermonuclear* reactions were considered, at first only in discussions, then in preliminary calculations. Von Neumann participated actively as a member of an imaginative group which considered various schemes for making possible such reactions on a large scale. The problems involved in treating the conditions necessary for such a reaction and in following its course are even more complex mathematically than those attending a fission explosion (whose characteristics are indeed a prerequisite for following the larger problem). After one discussion in which we outlined the course of such a calculation, von Neumann turned to me and said, "Probably in its execution we shall have to perform more elementary arithmetical steps than the total in all the computations performed by the human race heretofore." We noticed, however, that the total number of multiplications made by the school children of the world in the course of a few years sensibly exceeded that of our problem!

Limitations of space make it impossible to give an account of the innumerable smaller technical contributions of von Neumann welcomed by physicists and engineers engaged in this project.

Von Neumann was very adept in performing dimensional estimates and algebraical and numerical computations in his head without using a pencil and paper. This ability, perhaps somewhat akin to the talent of playing chess blindfolded, often impressed physicists. My impression was that von Neumann did not visualize the physical objects under consideration but rather treated their properties as logical consequences of the fundamental physical assumptions; but he was able to play a deductive game with these astonishingly well!

One trait of his scientific personality, which made him very much liked and sought after by those engaged in applications of mathematical techniques, was a willingness to listen attentively even to questions sometimes without much scientific import, but presenting the combinatorial attractions of a puzzle. Many of his interlocutors were helped actively or else consoled by knowing that there is no magic in mathematics known to anyone containing easy answers to their problems. His unselfish willingness to be involved in perhaps too diverse and certainly too numerous activities where mathematical insight might be useful (they are so increasingly common in technology nowadays) put severe demands on his time. In the years following the end of the Second World War, he found himself torn between conflicting demands on his time almost every moment.

Von Neumann strongly believed that the technological revolution initiated by the release of nuclear energy would cause more profound changes in human society, in particular in the development of science, than any technological discovery made in the previous history of the race. In one of the very few instances of talking about his own lucky guesses, he told me that, as a very young man, he believed that nuclear energy would be made available and change the order of human activities during his lifetime!

He participated actively in the early speculations and deliberations on the possibility of *controlled* thermonuclear reactions. When in 1954 he became a member of the Atomic Energy Commission, he worked on the technical and economical problems relating to the building and operation of fission reactors. In this position he also spent a great deal of time in the organization of studies of mathematical computing machines and the means to make them available to universities and other research centers.

This fragmentary account of von Neumann's diverse achievements and this cursory peregrination through the mathematical disciplines in which he left so many permanent imprints, may raise the question whether there was a thread of continuity throughout his work.

As Poincaré has phrased it: "*Il y a des problèmes qu'on se pose et des problèmes qui se posent.*" Now, fifty years after the great French mathematician formulated this indefinite distinction, the state of mathematics presents this division in a more acute form. Many more of the objects considered by mathematicians are their own free creations, often, so to say, special generalizations of previous constructions. These are sometimes originally inspired by the schemata of physics, others evolve genetically from free mathematical creations—in some cases prophetically anticipating the actual patterns of physical relations. Von Neumann's thought was obviously influenced by both tendencies. It was his desire to preserve, so far as possible, the connection between the pyramiding mathematical constructions and the increasing combinatorial complexity presented by physics and the natural sciences in general, a connection which seems to be growing more and more elusive.

Some of the great mathematicians of the eighteenth century, in particular Euler, succeeded in incorporating into the domain of mathematical analysis descriptions of many natural phenomena. Von Neumann's work attempted to cast in a similar role the mathematics stemming from set theory and modern algebra. This is of course, nowadays, a vastly more difficult undertaking. The infinitesimal calculus and the subsequent growth of analysis through most of the nineteenth century led to hopes of not merely cataloguing, but of understanding the contents of the Pandora's box opened by the discoveries of physical sciences. Such hopes are now illusory, if only because the real number system of the Euclidean space can no longer claim, algebraically, or even only topologically, to be the unique or even the best mathematical substratum for physical theories. The physical ideas of the nineteenth century, dominated mathematically by differential and integral equations and the theory of analytic functions, have become inadequate. The new quantum theory requires on the analytic side a set-theoretically more general point of view, the primitive notions themselves involving probability distributions and infinite-dimensional function spaces. The algebraical counterpart to this involves a study of combinatorial and algebraic structures more general than those presented by real or complex numbers alone. Von Neumann's work came at a time when the whole complex of ideas stemming from Cantor's set theory and the algebraical work of Hilbert, Weyl, Noether, Artin, Brauer, and others could be exploited for this purpose.

Another major source from which general mathematical investigations are beginning to develop is a new kind of combinatorial analysis stimulated by the recent fundamental researches in the biological sciences. Here, the lack of general method at the present time is even more noticeable. The problems are essentially non-linear, and of an extremely complex combinatorial character; it seems that many years of experimentation and heuristic studies will be necessary before one can hope to achieve the insight required for decisive syntheses. An awareness of this is what prompted von Neumann to devote so much of his work of the last ten years to the study and the construction of computing machines and to formulate a preliminary outline for the study of automata.

Surveying von Neumann's work and seeing how ramified and extended it is, one could say with Hilbert: "One is led to ask oneself whether the science of mathematics will not end, as has been the case for a long time now for other sciences, in a subdivision of separate parts whose representatives will barely understand each other and whose connections will continue to diminish? I neither think so nor hope for this;

the science of mathematics is an indivisible whole, an organism whose vital force has as its premise the indissolubility of its parts. Whatever the diversity of subjects of our science in its details, we are nonetheless struck by the equivalence of the logical procedures, the relation of ideas in the whole of science and the numerous analogies in its different domains . . . ."[21] Von Neumann's work was a contribution to this ideal of the universality and organic unity of mathematics.

21. David Hilbert, "Problèmes futurs des mathématiques," *Compte Rendu du Deuxième Congrès International des Mathématiciens tenu à Paris du 6 au 12 août 1900* (Paris, 1902).

AN EPISODE IN THE HISTORY
OF SOCIAL RESEARCH:
A MEMOIR

by PAUL F. LAZARSFELD

Introduction

AUTOBIOGRAPHIES deserve to be written under any one of three conditions: if the author is a man of great achievement (Einstein, Churchill); if, due to his position, he has been in contact with many important people or important events (a foreign correspondent); or if by external circumstances he can be considered a "case" representing a situation or development of interest.

In this last sense biographies have long been a tool of social research. Critical situations, like extreme poverty, culture conflicts, and concentration camps, have been studied through the medium of personal documents. In general the source of the material and the analyst who tries to draw conclusions from them are separate: the witness and the expert play distinct roles. The present essay is an effort to combine their two functions. I define myself as an expert witness.

But witness of what? I suppose I am included in this volume because I have been involved in two developments: the expansion of social research institutes in American universities and the development of a research style which prevails in many of them. Both of these elements have their roots in my previous European experience. My task in this paper becomes therefore to analyze as clearly as possible the steps, the social and psychological mechanisms, by which the European part of my professional biography came into play after I moved to this country, thirty-six years ago.

The general theme of this essay is rather easily stated. When my academic career began, the social sciences in Europe were dominated by philosophical and speculative minds. But interest in more concrete work was visible—symbolized, for instance, by the fact that Ferdinand Tönnies, the permanent president of the German Sociological Society, instituted in that organization a section on sociography. Without any formal alignment my research interests developed in this empirical direction. At the same time in the United States behaviorism and operationalism dominated the intellectual climate; and yet here too a minority interest began to make itself felt, exemplified, for example, in the publication by the Social Science Research Council of a monograph on the use of personal documents, and the intense interest in intervening variables and attitudes.[1]

In this situation I became a connecting cog. A European "positivist" was a curiosity welcomed by men aware of the subtler trends in the American social sciences. While in Europe the development of social science was arrested with the coming of Hitler, in America the evolving trends broadened, became diversified and refined, and required new institutional forms. My experiences and interests permitted me to play a role in this development. Obviously most of the things I did would have come about anyhow. Still, intellectual transportation needs carriers, and it was my good luck that I was one of them.

The present essay tries to account for my experiences by a procedure applicable, I believe, to any descriptive material, personal or collective. If I were forced to devise an academic title for the pages that follow I would call them a contribution to the study of innovation in higher education. I have included documentary material to enable the reader to form his own judgment of certain questions and to illustrate the available historical sources. At the same time I have tried to organize such material around a number of general ideas—integrating constructs —which I hope will be of interest to students of innovation. This relieves me of the problem of assessing the merit of the innovation and puts the weight on the mode of analysis.

On a recent occasion I urged my colleagues to study the work of social scientists from the point of view of "the decisions lying behind the final product; there is no reason why some of this exegesis should not be written by the authors themselves. We shy away too much

---

1. Gordon Allport, *The Use of Personal Documents in Psychological Science* (New York, 1942); Louis Gottschalk, Clyde Kluckhohn, and Robert Angell, *The Use of Personal Documents in History, Anthropology and Sociology* (New York, 1945).

from intellectual autobiographies."[2] I am indebted to the editors for providing me with the opportunity for such an exercise.

1. Calendar of External Events

IN the general character of life in Vienna after the First World War, three elements proved to be decisive for the story that follows: the political climate, interest in what was then called "psychology," and concern with what today is described as efforts at "explication."

I was active in the Socialist Student Movement, which was increasingly on the defensive before the growing nationalistic wave. We were concerned with why our propaganda was unsuccessful, and wanted to conduct psychological studies to explain it. I remember a formula I created at the time: a fighting revolution requires economics (Marx); a victorious revolution requires engineers (Russia); a defeated revolution calls for psychology (Vienna).

No sociology was taught at the University except for some lectures by a social philosopher, Othmar Spann.[3] My social reference group was the movement around Alfred Adler whose opposition to Freud had a strong sociological tinge. He had a considerable following among teachers, and was influential in the educational reform movement sponsored by the socialist municipality of Vienna.

Education in a broad sense was of great concern. As a schoolboy— well before entering the university at the age of eighteen—I tried to combine the ideas of the German youth movement with socialist propaganda among my colleagues.[4] Once I became a student I adhered to the rules of the earlier years: now I was "too old" to be a *revolté* and so I

2. "Problems in Methodology," in Robert K. Merton, Leonard Broom, and Leonard S. Cottrell, eds., *Sociology Today* (New York, 1959), p. 78.

3. There was a Viennese branch of the German Sociological Society, but as far as I remember I had no contact with it. I later found some of their members mentioned as discussants in printed reports of the yearly German *Soziologentag*.

4. One of the rare reports in English on the interesting German youth movement of that period is Walter Laqueur's *Young Germany: A History of the German Youth Movement* (New York, 1962).

became an amateur "educator." I took jobs as counselor in socialist children's camps and as a tutor in high schools for working-class youngsters. All this was part of an effort to promote the spirit of socialism.[5]

Intellectually, the main influence was a group of writers famous in science and the philosophy of science: Ernst Mach, Henri Poincaré, and Einstein. I was impressed by the idea that mere "clarification" was a road to discovery. Euclid's theorem on parallels was not truth but an axiom; it made no sense to say that an event on the moon and another on earth occurred simultaneously. All the ideas which later became known as "explications" held a great fascination for me, and this interest often merged into the conviction that "knowing how things are done" was an educational goal of high priority. When, as a student, I worked in the field of labor education, I often lectured on "how to read a newspaper": what is a news service, how does one take into account the sources of news, what should one watch for in different countries? One of Alfred Adler's main collaborators edited a series of small pamphlets applying his ideas to various substantive areas; I wrote my contribution under the title "behind the schools' backdrops." The main idea was that much anxiety could be avoided if families understood how schools are organized, how report cards come about, how teachers differ from each other in their perceptions of their students, etc.[6] At that time I had virtually no contact with the "Wiener Kreis" although its main leaders had already settled in Vienna. The obvious similarity of what I have just described with their teachings is probably more due to a common background than to direct influence.

Attending the university was a matter of course in a middle-class family, even one of limited means. The natural field of study for someone actively participating in political events was a doctorate in *Staatswissenschaft*, a modified law degree with a strong admixture of eco-

---

5. My first publication, at the age of twenty-three, (*Gemeinschaftserziehung durch Erziehungsgemeinschaften* [Vienna, 1925]) was a report on a camp which, together with my late friend Ludwig Wagner, I organized for the development of a socialist spirit in young people.

6. Paul F. Lazarsfeld, "Hinter den Kulissen der Schule," in Sofie Lazarsfeld, ed., *Technik der Erziehung* (Leipzig, 1929). One who has read the introduction to Paul F. Lazarsfeld and Morris S. Rosenberg, eds., *The Language of Social Research* (New York, 1955), will see the extent to which such intellectual inclinations have endured over a period of forty years.

nomics and political theory. But for me mathematics was a second pole of attraction, and for several years I took courses in both fields. It was almost accidental that I ended with a doctorate in applied mathematics. Immediately after the degree, I began teaching mathematics and physics in a *Gymnasium*.

While I was still a student, my interest in social science took a new turn with the arrival of two famous psychologists at the University of Vienna. There had been no real psychology there until Charlotte and Karl Bühler were appointed in 1923 to build up a new department. Karl Bühler was a leading academic figure who, as a younger man, had contributed to a major revolution in experimental psychology through his work on the psychology of thinking. His wife, Charlotte, considerably younger than he, was made associate professor, and was, in fact, the administrator of the department. (I will hereafter use the correct European term, Institute.) I participated in their early seminars and, after a while, was asked to give a course in statistics.

Slowly, my work as assistant at the university expanded, and I also taught courses in social and applied psychology. I received a small remuneration, by no means sufficient to give up my position in the *Gymnasium*. Still, my desire to shift entirely to the Psychological Institute increased, and around 1927 I got the idea that I would create a division of social psychology at the Institute. This would permit work on paid contracts, and from such sources I would get a small but adequate salary, in keeping with the generally low standard of living. The idea was realized in the form of an independent Research Center (*Wirtschaftspsychologische Forschungsstelle*, a term connoting broadly the application of psychology to social and economic problems), of which Karl Bühler was the president. From then on, I directed the applied studies of this Center, and at the same time gave my courses at the University Institute and supervised dissertations. A number of students worked at the Research Center, and quite a few dissertations were based on data collected there.[7]

7. My position as assistant at the Psychological Institute was rather vague and insecure. As a safeguard against possible collapse, I maintained my position in the secondary school system by taking an extended leave of absence.

Among our clients was the Frankfurt Institut für Sozialforschung. Its director, Max Horkheimer, had conceived the series of inquiries which were reported finally in *Autorität*

Charlotte Bühler divided her work between child and adolescent psychology. My own activities were closely connected with hers in the latter field. She had organized a series of monographs on adolescent psychology, and I was commissioned to write one on youth and occupation. The volume, *Jugend und Beruf*, appeared in 1931. It contained a number of papers by other members of the Institute as well as some of my own. A large part of the book was devoted to a ninety-page monograph in which I summarized all the literature then available on occupational choices among young people. At the same time, I published papers on statistical topics, and—in various magazines of the Socialist Party—on topics in industrial and political sociology. My statistical lectures were published as a "Manual for Teachers and Psychologists." It was probably the first European textbook on educational statistics, and was used widely in various universities.[8]

Around 1930, I began to organize a study of Marienthal, a village south of Vienna whose population was almost entirely unemployed.[9] My two main collaborators were Hans Zeisel, now professor at the University of Chicago, and Marie Jahoda, now professor at Sussex University in England. (The latter subsequently did important reports on unemployed youth for the League of Nations and the International Labor Office.) The Marienthal study brought me to the attention of the Paris representative of the Rockefeller Foundation, and in 1932 I

---

und Familie. One of the studies by Erich Fromm required the filling in of questionnaires by young workers, and we were asked to organize the part of the field work done in Austria. I did not meet any of the Horkheimer group when I was in Europe but got well acquainted with them after they and I came to the United States. As a matter of fact in the United States in 1934 I worked with Fromm on the analysis of the questionnaire we had undertaken in Austria.

8. *Jugend und Beruf* (Jena, 1931); *Statistisches Praktikum für Psychologen und Lehrer* (Jena, 1929). Subsequently, in this country, I have worked and published in the field of mathematical sociology. But this has never been an integral part of what has been called the Vienna-Columbia research tradition. I shall therefore not deal with it in this essay.

9. Marie Jahoda, Paul F. Lazarsfeld, and Hans Zeisel, *Die Arbeitslosen von Marienthal* (Leipzig, 1932; 2nd ed., Frankfurt, 1961). As part of the activities of my new Research Center in Vienna, I wanted to do some kind of social survey to balance its market research activities. For reasons I cannot remember, I was interested in doing a leisure-time study, and I discussed it with a leader of the Socialist Party, Otto Bauer. He considered it silly to study leisure problems at a time of severe unemployment, and it was he who suggested the new topic, to which I shall return repeatedly in this essay.

obtained a traveling fellowship to the United States, where I arrived in September 1933.[10]

During the first year of my fellowship in America, I participated in various studies and visited the few university centers where social research was taught. In February 1934, the Conservative Party in Austria overthrew the constitution, outlawed the Socialist Party, and established an Italian-type fascism. My position in the secondary school system was cancelled and most members of my family in Vienna were imprisoned, but my vague position as assistant at the university was nominally unaffected. This gave the sympathetic officers of the Rockefeller Foundation the pretext for extending my fellowship another year, nominally obeying the rule that it was necessary for a Fellow to have an assured position to which he could return.

At the end of the fellowship, in the fall of 1935, I decided to stay in this country. With the help of Robert Lynd, Professor of Sociology at Columbia, I obtained a position in New Jersey as a supervisor of student relief work for the National Youth Administration, whose headquarters were at the University of Newark. In the fall of 1936, a Research Center was established at that university, with me as director. This Center was patterned along the lines of its Viennese predecessor, and will be discussed in connection with it.

In 1937, the Rockefeller Foundation established at Princeton University a major research project on the effect of radio on the American society. I was appointed director of this new "Office of Radio Research" which, in 1939, was transferred to Columbia University. For one year I was a lecturer there, and in 1940 I became a permanent member of the Department of Sociology, as associate professor. The Office of Radio Research, later transformed into the Bureau of Applied Social Research, had a tenuous existence in the beginning, but in 1945 it was incorporated into the university structure. I have remained at Columbia, working at the Bureau and in the Department of Sociology, ever since.

10. The way I received my fellowship has its own interest. The Rockefeller representative gave me an application form. Living in the pessimistic climate of Vienna at the time, I was sure I would not get the fellowship, and did not apply. In November 1932 I got a cable from the Paris Rockefeller office informing me that my application had been misfiled, and that they wanted another copy. They had obviously decided to grant me the fellowship on the recommendation of their representative and it had never occurred to them that I had not applied. I mailed a "duplicate," and the fellowship was granted.

II. A Research Style and Its Probable Roots

TO describe the origin of the new research style, I shall use two sources: publications which appeared in German while I was still in Austria, and papers I wrote immediately after coming to the United States in order to explain the Viennese work to a new audience. In a way, I am extending this latter effort here, adding interpretation. I am organizing my remarks around three factors which seem to me significant: an ideological component, an intellectual "press," and certain personal characteristics.

1. *The ideological component.* The political motivation is most noticeable in the emphasis on *social stratification*, which permeated the main Austrian publications. *Jugend und Beruf* stresses that the then flourishing literature on adolescent psychology really dealt only with middle-class adolescents; it urged separate attention to the problems of working-class youths, who at that time started work at the age of fourteen. The whole monograph was organized around a sharp distinction between the two groups.[11]

The discussion of a "proletarian youth" was tied up with a socio-psychological reinterpretation of the notion of "exploitation." The idea was that working-class youths, by going to work at the age of fourteen, were deprived of the energizing experience of middle-class adolescence. Because of this, the working-class man never fully developed an effective scope and could, therefore, be kept in an inferior position. This theme reappeared in the Marienthal study: the effect of unemployment was to reduce the "effective scope" of working-class men. The frequently cited paper by Genevieve Knupfer, "Portrait of the Underdog,"[12] comes from a Columbia doctoral dissertation of 1947, which was the first work to assemble stratification data taken from public opinion surveys. Here the emphasis was on the low level of aspiration and the narrow "life space" prevailing in low income groups.[13] The line of

11. A condensation of the book in English will soon be published by Random House; its political influence will be traced in a new Introduction. It is hard to realize today how neglected the notion of social stratification was at that time.

12. *Public Opinion Quarterly*, 11 (1947), 103–114.

13. The main conceptual idea was taken over from a psychoanalyst, Siegfried Bernfeld,

argument was practically identical to that which now forms the ideological basis of New York's "Mobilization for Youth." And one could make an interesting comparison between my early book and the contribution of Herbert Gans in the recent *Uses of Sociology* volume,[14] although I am sure that there is no direct continuity. An important difference is that Gans stresses community action, while in the original case emphasis was placed on a delay in the beginning of manual work and changes in the educational system.

This attention to stratification and the social significance of working-class adolescence had a visible Marxist tinge. One other trace of this influence is not as explicit, but is easily documented. In *Jugend und Beruf* there was special pride in showing the effect of objective factors upon individual reactions. Various tables indicate that the occupational structure of German cities, as well as fluctuations of the business cycle, are reflected in the occupational plans of young people of working-class background. I also reported findings to the effect that the religious background of the family is related to the occupational plans of middle-class youths.[15]

In this early work there was another emphasis which we would today attribute to Durkheim, although I am quite sure that at the time I did not know of his existence. In the introduction to *Marienthal* I stressed that we wanted to study "the unemployed *village* and not the unemployed men." In another sentence it was stated that, because of this, we did not introduce personality tests, with no further explanation of what was meant by the phrase. But the implication was clear that the social structure has dominance over individual variations.

------

who had characterized a creative value of middle-class adolescence under the term "extended puberty." American sociologists have recently taken up this notion under the term "deferred gratification." The relation between Bernfeld, Bühler, and myself is described in a monograph by Leopold Rosenmayr, the current professor of sociology at the University of Vienna, on early adolescent research in Austria: *Geschichte der Jugendforschung in Oesterreich, 1914–1931* (Vienna, [1962]).

14. Herbert Gans, "Urban Poverty and Social Planning," in Paul F. Lazarsfeld *et al.*, eds., *The Uses of Sociology* (New York, 1967).

15. A similar table was used at the same time by Robert Merton in his dissertation, *Science, Technology and Society in Seventeenth-Century England* (Bruges, Belgium, 1938). I suppose that both of us got the idea from Max Weber, although I do not remember having known at the time the table on religion and occupational choice that Weber includes in a footnote to the monograph on the Protestant Ethic.

Another trace of the political climate can be found in the emphasis on decision making. The Austro-Marxist position put all hope on the winning of elections rather than on the Communist belief in violence, and therefore there was great interest in how people voted. From this origin a rather curious and important functional displacement occurred. At that time, the University of Vienna was dogmatically conservative, and it would have been unwise for staff members to undertake the unbiased study of people's voting decisions. As a conscious substitute, I turned to the question of how young people develop their occupational plans. A series of detailed case studies was collected with the help of a group of students. But then I was faced with the well-known difficulty of analysis.

For many months, I did not know how to proceed, until finally, in a rather strange way, I found a solution. Among the students working with me was a young woman who came to the attention of one of the earliest American market research experts. He needed some interviews in Austria at the time, and because of the training of this student (she subsequently was my main collaborator in the field work for the Marienthal study), he asked her to do some of the interviews on why people bought various kinds of soaps. Market research was then completely unknown in Austria, and she told me about this commission as a kind of curiosity. I immediately linked it up with my problem of occupational choice. Obviously, my difficulty was that such choices extended over a long period of time, with many ramifications and feedbacks. If I wanted to combine statistical analysis with descriptions of entire choice processes, I had better, for the time being, concentrate on more manageable material. For the methodological goal I had in mind, consumer choices would be much more suitable.

Such is the origin of my Vienna market research studies: the result of the methodological equivalence of socialist voting and the buying of soap.[16]

Still, I had learned enough from the case studies on occupational

16. Just after I came to this country, I published a paper on the "Art of Asking Why" (*National Marketing Review*, 1 [1935], 32–43), which summarizes the resulting interviewing techniques. Though reprinted and widely quoted, I am not sure that it had any great influence on American research. See, however, the extensive entry on "Reason Analysis," written by my former student, Charles Kadushin, in the new *International Encyclopedia of the Social Sciences* (New York, 1968).

choice to make one more political point in *Jugend und Beruf*. The implications for a planned society were quite clear: most young people do not have decided occupational plans and therefore would not mind being guided—as a matter of fact might like to be guided—to an occupational choice; it should, consequently, be easy to fill the occupational quotas established through a central economic plan.

2. *The intellectual climate.* I have mentioned some of the episodes that directed me toward empirical studies. Given this inclination, it is relevant to clarify the specific shape it took in the European climate in which I did my early professional work, for it is this force which will help to explain the role I was destined to play in the United States.

The Bühlers, in the newly created Psychological Institute at the University of Vienna, had begun to concentrate on the integration of approaches, an effort best exemplified by the important book of Karl Bühler, *Die Krise der Psychologie.* He had become prominent as an introspectionist, and he was also well acquainted with the tradition of cultural philosophy, and especially the thought of Wilhelm Dilthey, as a result of his broad philosophical training; in addition, during a trip to the United States he had come into contact with American behaviorism. His book is an effort to analyze these three sources of psychological knowledge: introspection; interpretation of cultural products such as art, folklore, biographies, and diaries; and the observation of behavior. But the key to Bühler's thought throughout was the need to transcend any one approach or any one immediate body of information to reach a broad conceptual integration.

It is difficult for me to say now whether I was genuinely influenced by this ecumenical spirit, but I certainly never missed the chance to show that even "trivial" studies, if properly interpreted and integrated, could lead to *important* findings, "important" implying a higher level of generalization. Thus, I once summarized a number of our consumer studies by carving out the notion of the proletarian consumer. He is:

... less psychologically mobile, less active, more inhibited in his behavior. The radius of stores he considers for possible purchases is smaller. He buys more often at the same store. His food habits are more rigid and less subject to seasonal variations. As part of this reduction in effective scope the interest in other than the most essential details is lost; requirements in regard to quality, appearance and other features of merchandise are the less specific and frequent the more we deal with consumers from low social strata.

One of the studies that contributed to the notion of the proletarian consumer dealt with preferences for sweet and bitter chocolate; low-income people preferred the former (and quite generally prefer sweet smells, loud colors, and many other strong sense experiences). And yet this study also shows that one can quite easily miss an important point. The president of the sponsoring concern joined the Board of the Vienna Research Center and at the first meeting gave a fine testimonial of how this study had increased the sales of his chocolate division. In fact, however, the study had not yet been delivered, and all I could conclude was that he wanted to be helpful with this white lie. I know now what had really happened: I failed to discover the Hawthorne Effect; the chocolate division got so involved in our study that they simply became active and sold more.

Altogether, the consumer purchase became a special case of a problem which had great sanctity in the European humanistic tradition: *Handlung*,[17] action. Bühler himself had written a fundamental paper on language as a special form of action,[18] and it was in these terms that I reported on the nature of the Austrian market studies soon after I came to this country.[19] In "The Psychological Aspect of Market Research" (1934) I included in a half-dozen pages on "the structure of the act of purchasing" diagrams and new terms ("Accent on Motivation") intermingled with, if I may say so, interesting examples on the purchase of

17. I have traced the importance of the notion of action in a paper read at the Max Weber Centennial, organized by the American Sociological Association: Paul F. Lazarsfeld and A. R. Oberschall, "Max Weber and Empirical Social Research," *American Sociological Review*, 30 (1965), 185–192.

18. In France "structural linguistics" is today considered the great glory of modern social science. The Founding Father is Ferdinand de Saussure and the second generation is represented by the circle of Prague, with Troubetzkoy and Jakobson as the leaders. The latter corroborates my memory that he and his associates frequently traveled to Vienna to obtain Karl Bühler's wise counsel.

19. Published in the *Harvard Business Review* in October of that year. The Viennese university structure made me classify myself at the time as a "psychologist." The fact that six years later I became a member of the Columbia Department of Sociology did not change the character of my work. I am now Professor of Social Science, which resolved for me a terminological embarrassment. Incidentally, this paper cited above was rejected by two psychological journals, which considered the topic not appropriately psychological.

sweaters and soaps. The general idea was that "the action of a purchase is markedly articulated and that different phases and elements can be distinguished in it." The trend toward deducing a "theoretical outlook" from specific data may be exemplified by the following quotation:

The "time of deliberation," the "anticipated features of the purchase," "the relation to previous purchases" are only examples of what we could call the psychological "co-ordinates" of a purchase. It seems to us that one of the outstanding contributions of the psychologist to the problem of market survey is the careful, general study of the structure of the purchase, in order to prepare us to find in a special study what could possibly be characteristic for the investigated commodity.

It would have been unacceptable just to report that x per cent of people did or thought this or that about some topic. The task was to combine diverse findings into a small number of "integrating constructs." At the same time, it was imperative to explicate as clearly as possible the procedures by which such greater depth was achieved.[20] In a paper written in 1933 summarizing the Austrian experience, the following four rules were singled out and amply exemplified:

a. For any phenomenon one should have objective observations as well as introspective reports.
b. Case studies should be properly combined with statistical information.
c. Contemporary information should be supplemented by information on earlier phases of whatever is being studied.
d. One should combine "natural and experimental data." By experimental, I meant mainly questionnaires and solicited reports, while

20. This paper, entitled "Principles of Sociography," was submitted in 1934 to the journal of the New School for Social Research. Its graduate faculty had become the exponent of European social sciences, and I thought the editors would be interested in a paper trying to link explicitly empirical work done in both countries. I suppose, however, that "sociography" was at that time not considered a real part of the European tradition. The original paper was refused and never published. On re-reading it for the present purpose, I find it, and especially the examples contained in it, characteristic of the state of affairs in the early 1930's. Incidentally, the term "integrating construct" was originally called "leitformel," and was first translated as "matrix formula." However, the term matrix has become identified with its use in algebra. I therefore prefer the present translation. Sometime later, a more extended treatment of integrating constructs was published in Allen H. Barton and Paul F. Lazarsfeld, "Some Functions of Qualitative Analysis in Social Research," Sociologica, 1 (1956), 321–351.

by natural, I meant what is now called "unobtrusive measures"—data deriving from daily life without interference from the investigator.

Mere description was not enough. In order to get "behind" it a variety of data had to be collected on any issue under investigation—just as the true position of a distant object can be found only by looking at it from different sides and directions. It is unlikely that I was entirely aware of the rules underlying the Viennese research tradition as it developed. But its structure was close enough to the surface so that I could articulate it fairly easily when I had leisure to reflect on our work here in this country.

The efforts to develop a theory of integrating constructs, their logical nature, and how they are arrived at were part of a need to legitimize empirical work. At that time, I was not familiar with various papers by Tönnies in which he tried to introduce the idea of sociography into the tradition of German sociologists. It would be interesting today to compare these two developments in more detail. Some critics today oppose survey research as restrictive and one-sided, pointing to the Columbia tradition as an evil influence.[21] It is useful to point out that, from its beginning, this tradition stressed the importance of a diversified approach. Legitimation, like woman's work, seems never to be done.

3. *The personal equation.* The personal element cannot be avoided. What made me so convinced that a combination of "insight" and quantification was crucial for the social sciences? In the introduction to *Marienthal* I made such a combination appear almost a moral duty. Thus, I had expressed dissatisfaction with unemployment statistics, as well as with casual descriptions of the life of the unemployed in newspapers and belles lettres. Then I stated:

Our idea was to find procedures which would combine the use of numerical data with the immersion [*Sich einleben*] in the situation. To this end the following is necessary: we had to gain such close contact with the population of Marienthal, so that we could learn the smallest details of their daily life; at the same time we had to perceive each day so that it was possible to reconstruct it objectively; finally, for the whole a struc-

21. Arthur Vidich, Joseph Bensman, and Maurice Stein, eds., *Reflections on Community Studies* (New York, 1964).

ture had to be developed so that all the details could be seen as expressions of a minimum number of basic facts.

It is worth noting the formulation of these sentences—they imply an imperative to carry out this methodological mission. Like all missionaries, we did not feel a need to justify further what the voices ordered us to do. Still the position was pervasive. In an appendix to the Marienthal book on the history of sociography, Hans Zeisel includes a six-page review of the "American Survey." He pointed out that the Chicago studies "for some strange reason did not pursue the statistical analysis of their material." From his reading, he could only find a few examples of the quantification of complex patterns. His review ends with the following remarks, which echo the program just mentioned before:

American sociography has not achieved a synthesis between statistics and a full description of concrete observations. In work of impressive conceptualization—for instance, in *The Polish Peasant*—statistics are completely missing; inversely, the statistical surveys are often of a regrettable routine nature.

I cannot trace this urge to quantify complex experiences and behavior patterns to any outside influences prevailing at the time. Under such conditions, the historian is forced to look for idiosyncratic elements; and they are abundantly available. I remember my excitement when, around 1925, I saw in the window of a bookstore a scatter-diagram in one of the first German monographs on correlation analysis. A few years later, the German sociologist Andreas Walter showed me an ecological map he had just brought back from a visit to Chicago— and I had the same reaction. Most consequential was the following episode. At the age of about twenty-four I listened to a leader of the Young Socialist Workers Movement, who read from questionnaires he had distributed. He used individual quotations to describe the misery of factory life. Immediately I asked myself why he did not make counts; he was surprised at the idea, and turned the questionnaires over to me. I did a statistical analysis, which later formed the base of one of my first papers. I also gave a report in one of the first Bühler seminars, which brought me to their attention.[22]

22. When I was approximately fifteen, I read the memoirs of Lili Braun. She describes an election evening in Germany in the early 1900's, where everyone was waiting for the returns, and then celebrating the Socialist victory. I found this extremely exciting, and

My subsequent work for Mrs. Bühler reinforced this whole tendency. Her major studies in child psychology took a middle position between the American, Gesell, and the Swiss, Piaget. The latter made his famous semi-experimental observations on a few children only, drawing from them the far-reaching developmental theories; Gesell made minute statistical observations without drawing any generalizations. Mrs. Bühler's fame was based on a theory of phases, which she "underpinned" with statistical observations. At one point her position influenced me in a way which had rather far-reaching consequences. For my *Jugend und Beruf*, I coordinated a large amount of data from various sources into a rather coherent system of concepts. She was pleased, and also accepted my position on the need to distinguish between middle-class and working-class adolescents. But she objected strenuously to the tone in which my section on proletarian youth was written. I was, indeed, full of compassion, talking about exploitation by the bourgeois society, and the hortative style of this section was quite different from the rest of the manuscript. I could not deny this fact, and finally rewrote it. None of the argument was omitted, but the whole tone became descriptive and naturalistic, instead of critical. I have no doubt that this episode affected my subsequent writings and is a contributing factor to the debate on the role of sociology that was later led by C. Wright Mills.

III. The Organization of Social Research

TODAY, the main features of a research bureau are well-known. There is a division of labor in the essential work: writing and pretesting questionnaires, analyzing tables, and drafting reports. Coordinating and guiding this work is an administrative as well as an intellectual

---

in the summer of 1916, when I was living in the custody of Rudolf Hilferding, the Socialist leader, I asked him to explain to me what this election business was all about. He found my attitude rather childish, and said I should rather first know what the Socialist program was all about. We made a compromise that I would read a book by Kautsky if, at the same time, I also got a book on elections. How seriously I read Kautsky at the time I do not know, but as for the little book explaining elections, more than fifty years later I still remember the name of the author: Poensgen.

challenge. A bureau director is probably a new kind of professional for whom recently the name "managerial scholar" has been created. The nature of the work requires a more hierarchical relation among the participant professionals than is habitual in an academic department.

In the context of this memoir, the question is how we hit upon this type of organization in the late 1920's. In part it was due, I believe, to the fact that I and many of my collaborators had team experience in the Socialist Party and in the youth movement; in my case, I would guess that this style of work was partly a psychological substitute for political activities. But the example of Charlotte Bühler certainly also played a role. She had a Prussian ability to organize the work activities of many people at many places. Some felt exploited by her, but I always appreciated her good training and help.

The problem of financing such institutes is also well-known today. The money has to be begged from public institutions and private industry. This was much more difficult forty years ago, because there were then no foundations, no tax deductions, and, all in all, the idea of research was not widely accepted. One depended on a few individuals and was in a perpetual financial crisis. I created a board for the Center which consisted of representatives from all political and industrial groups in Vienna.[23]

While today all this seems rather obvious, at the time it was watched with some surprise. This can be seen from a document which is interesting in a number of respects. The leading journal of sociology at the time was edited in Cologne by Leopold von Wiese. In 1934, in its last issue before it was halted by the Hitler government, von Wiese wrote a rather extensive review of *Marienthal*. He, like other professors of sociology and economics, used the long German Easter vacations to take students on short field trips to factories or villages (a monograph of von Wiese's, called "The Village," resulted from such a trip). In his review he stressed, with approval, the difference between this tradition and our more organized enterprise.

23. The 1967 meeting of the World Association of Public Opinion Research was held in Vienna, and a day was given to commemorating the fortieth anniversary of the Vienna Center. Hans Zeisel gave a description of its beginning, which is published in the *Revue Française de Sociologie*, 2 (1968).

My own efforts are forced to be of a merely deductive nature; we can only assume that the students who live for a few days with the local population get stimulation and some instructions which, I hope, will be useful later on when they do more extended work. The Vienna enterprise had a different structure where more advanced and theoretically better-trained observers could devote themselves to their task for a longer period of time (the participation of medical doctors was helpful) so that scientifically valuable results were achieved, which went well beyond the mere purpose of training students.

Von Wiese suspected that funds available to the Bühlers through their American connections made this broader system possible. Actually that played only a very small role. The respondents were paid for their time by the donation of second-hand clothes we had collected in Vienna. The supervision and the analysis were done by colleagues most of whom contributed their time. We had a small subsidy for expenses from the central trade union council.

Von Wiese raised two methodological objections. He disapproved of using the term psychological for work which he considered essentially sociological; he was not aware of the Vienna University structure, to which I have alluded above. And on our basic position, expressed in the introduction to *Marienthal*, he commented as follows:

I consider it too great a concession to statisticians that the authors propose "to reject all impressions for which they cannot find quantitative evidence." Fortunately they were not too strict in the application of this principle.

Von Wiese's complex reaction seems to me a particularly clear indication that German sociology was beginning to take a new turn at the time when it was, for all practical purposes, suppressed by political events.

The Vienna Center was a sequence of improvisations, and the basic elements of a research organization developed only slowly. In spite of a number of external formalities it never fused into a stable organization. It was only when I came to the University of Newark that the different components, all concurrently in my mind, could be integrated into some kind of an institutional plan. Even so, the beginning in America was chaotic.

In the summer of 1935, I was obliged to return to Vienna to exchange my student permit for an immigration visa. In October, a few weeks after my arrival, I received word from Robert Lynd that the New Jersey Relief Administration had collected ten thousand questionnaires from youngsters between fourteen and twenty-five as a project of the National Youth Administration, and needed someone to analyze the material. They had turned to Frank Kingdon, who had just been made president of the University of Newark, a small institution which he was expected to develop into a place of higher learning for underprivileged students of Essex County, New Jersey.[24] Kingdon had the intelligent idea that someone paid by the NYA to analyze the questions could, at the same time, teach some research courses at his university. Lynd had recommended me for the job, and I gratefully accepted it.

Kingdon and I got along well with each other from the start. At the first talk, I suggested that the plan should be extended, and the NYA project should be made the beginning of a "Research Center of the University of Newark," which I proposed to create at the same time. Obviously, the University could not contribute financially, except indirectly in the form of working space. It was up to me to keep the Center alive by contracts, though Kingdon was later able to help by assigning relief money for the large number of unemployed students for whom I could invent work.

After a few months the situation was formalized. On June 19, 1936, Kingdon wrote me, in the name of the Trustees, an official letter of appointment. In it he said,

> It is understood that we are offering you the position of Acting Director of the Research Center of the University of Newark for a twelve-month period beginning May 21, 1936, and continuing until May 21, 1937.
>
> It is understood that the basic salary for this position is $4,800, but that the University is obligated to pay you only one-half of this sum, the remaining part of your salary to be derived from other sources. It is understood that your salary will be paid in equal monthly installments of $200.
>
> It is also understood that a portion of this half-time that is to be made available to

---

24. The plan never succeeded, because the very able Kingdon became involved in politics and neglected the institution. Caught between two stools, he ended rather tragically. Today, the building on Rector Street houses a local branch of Rutgers University.

the University of Newark may be assigned to teaching. It is further understood that the University will not ask you to teach in excess of eight hours.

I suppose that this is the first document proposing a split appointment for a bureau director. Unfortunately, even today it is assumed in many universities that the director is partly responsible for his own salary.[25]

There were many unemployed students, and I had continuously to think of work topics to occupy them. With the help of my market contacts, I obtained the circulation figures for some twenty magazines in the hundred largest cities of the United States. By combining this with census data and various economic information, we wrote a paper characterizing the cities in terms of their magazine profile. This was published later on in one of the first issues of the newly created *Public Opinion Quarterly* (1937).[26] At the same time, I began to build up contacts with other agencies. The superintendent of schools for Essex County subsidized a study of local school problems, from which we published several small statistical monographs. The WPA started a large project on technological unemployment, with headquarters in Philadelphia, and I prevailed upon them to let me study the glass manufacturing town of Millville, New Jersey, which had become almost totally unemployed as a consequence of the introduction of glass-blowing machinery and the transfer of the main company to Ohio. Though this study was never completed because of the discontinuance of funds, it made it possible for me in 1935–36 to build up the first elements of a staff. And the Horkheimer Institute came to my help by locating some of their work at the Newark Center and paying for supervision. The best-known result of this collaborative effort is the book by Mirra Komarovski, *The Unemployed Man and His Family* (1940).

In the spring of 1937, I wrote an official report to the Newark trustees in which I attempted to explain the whole idea of such a Center, to show that it would be of value to the University, and to prove that it

25. The very low salary level may be explained by the economic situation of the time. Still, eight hours a week of teaching for $200 a month was, even then, probably a rather poor way to make one's academic living.

26. Paul F. Lazarsfeld and Rowena Wyant, "Magazines in 90 Cities: Who Reads What?" *Public Opinion Quarterly*, 1 (1937), 29–41. At one point, I computed the average of all these figures to develop the profile of the typical city; it turned out to be Muncie, Indiana, Lynd's *Middletown*.

was financially viable. The aims of the field studies of the Research Center of the University of Newark, I wrote, were:

to give research training to students
to develop new methods of research
to publish finished studies
to help the City of Newark to a better understanding of its social and economic problems
to act as a consulting service to social and business agencies in the city
to give students the opportunity for gainful employment
to accumulate funds for the perpetuation and enlargement of the Center's activities
to make the University, as a whole, better known locally and nationally.

Its utility, I argued, could be justified in a variety of ways. Salaries up to the amount of $1,500 were paid every month to students and graduates of the University; this did not include relief money and could therefore be said to be exclusively due to the existence of the Center. About a thousand newspaper articles contained references to its work. "The Center and hence the University of Newark is represented through its Director on a variety of regional and national committees." I then listed ten studies in progress. Into this catalogue I put everything with which I was myself associated, including a number of articles I had published and commercial studies that I, as a personal consultant, was connected with.[27]

By 1936 the Newark Center had become known as something of a curiosity. One day Everett Hughes and Robert Park came to look at it, an honor which I did not fully appreciate at the time. George Lundberg (Bennington) and John Jenkins (Cornell) sent me students for training, among them Edward Suchman, who stayed with me until he joined Samuel Stouffer in the War Department. But the main indicator of a growing public interest is the fact that by the spring of 1937 I was con-

27. Included also was my work for the Social Science Research Council on the effects of the Depression. Thirteen monographs were planned (and carried out) on various aspects based on the collection and integration of available studies. Stouffer was made research director, and asked Lynd to recommend someone for the monograph on the family. On Lynd's suggestion, Stouffer invited me to Chicago, and this first meeting lasted practically the whole day. Within a few hours, we had laid out a joint plan, and from there dates my continuous collaboration with him, to which I will come back repeatedly. See Samuel Stouffer and Paul F. Lazarsfeld, *Research Memorandum on the Family in the Depression* (New York, 1937).

sidered a possible choice for director of the first major research project on mass communication, which the Rockefeller Foundation was about to sponsor.[28]

Throughout the entire course of this institutional development, research methodology was a characteristic feature. Partly, of course, this resulted from my own interest in "explications," mentioned above, but I am convinced that there is an intrinsic relation between research organization and methodology. In my presidential address to the American Sociological Association I expressed this point in a way which was perhaps a little exaggerated but which contains, I believe, the essential truth. Supervising even a small research staff makes one acutely aware of the differences between various elements of research operation and of the need to integrate them into a final product. Some assistants are best at detailed interviews, others are gifted in the handling of statistical tables, still others are especially good at searching for possible contributions from existing literature. The different roles must be made explicit; each has to know what is expected of him and how his task is related to the work of the others. Staff instruction therefore quickly turns into methodological explication. The point is perhaps akin to the kind of sociology of knowledge that Marxists employ when they argue that new tools of production are often reflected in new ways of intellectual analysis.

All of this still leaves open the question of how it happened that an organizational form developed in Vienna was relatively easily accepted and diffused in this country. For an interpretation I have to turn back to the two years of my fellowship, 1933 to 1935.

28. By then, it had become fairly clear that a research director required a new type of skills for which few people had yet been trained. The specifications and preparation for this job have been, for many years, a matter of great concern to me. In my Presidential Address to the American Association, "The Sociology of Empirical Social Research," *American Sociological Review*, 27 (1962), 757–767, I discussed the matter in great detail. The problem still seems to me important and as yet unresolved. I am, therefore, adding the corresponding sections of that address as an appendix to this essay.

iv. Atlantic Transfer—Directional Cues

THE impact of European intellectuals on the United States can be studied in a variety of ways. One approach is to examine a certain field before and after the arrival of specific individuals. Another is to trace the contacts which the immigrant had and the references that Americans made to him either in their own publications or in communications solicited especially for that purpose. A third approach to the transfer phenomenon is to examine how the immigrant himself saw the situation. What was his strategy and experience? Since most of the men with whom this volume deals are no longer living, it seems incumbent upon the few survivors to provide some information on how such a sequence of events looks from within.

The idea of an "expert witness" described in the Introduction is especially useful in this third approach. He reports his concrete experiences and at the same time tries to conceptualize them, to discuss episodes within coherent patterns. But the reader should be reminded that in this case the other participants may be considered expert witnesses too.[29] Historians could unearth additional documents, interview the other participants, and come to conclusions quite different from mine. There are no final verdicts here, only an interpretation of what might be called "strategy": the moves which the actor made more or less consciously and intentionally; the general motivations that guided his

29. The reader may compare, for example, Adorno's and my reports on the same events. To broaden the view, I want to add a few lines on Kurt Lewin, whom I knew and admired both abroad and here. Lewin had acquired fame in Germany through a series of papers written partly by him and partly by his students. These appeared over the years under the general title of "Psychology of Action." The notion of action, which enjoyed high prestige in Germany, was unacceptable here because of the dominance of behaviorism. When Lewin finally came to this country, he shifted to the topic for which he became famous here, namely "group dynamics." J. L. Moreno claims that it was he who advised Lewin to adopt this term. In 1938, I was visited by a recent Viennese refugee, Gustav Bergmann, who asked me for help. I remembered that he was a very good mathematician with great interest in psychology. By then, Lewin was already in Iowa. I phoned him and suggested that he give a job to Bergmann, who could help him to bring his topological ideas in harmony with prevailing procedures in mathematical topology. Lewin did, indeed, invite him, but the venture ended in a disagreement between the two men. Bergmann still teaches logic and philosophy of science in Iowa, and has repeatedly published on the nature of psychological theory.

reactions and choices; and the character of the total situation, even if the actor was not aware of what this was at the time. Perhaps the term "latent strategy" will serve best.[30]

The beginning of such analysis is found in what might be called *directional cues*. What did the person know about the country to which he came before his arrival? Where did he turn first? What antecedent experience guided his first moves?

I can summarize my experience along three lines, which at first were quite distinct but which ultimately converged: the continuation of my interest in research on unemployment; my interest in finding out more about American research techniques; and my desire to help the Vienna Research Center by establishing contacts for it with relevant organizations in this country.

The Marienthal study had received some attention in the United States through two channels. A visiting American psychologist had seen some of the material in Vienna and, on his return, wrote an article in the *Nation* called "When Man Eats Dog." At the International Psychological Congress in 1932, held in Germany, Mrs. Bühler arranged for me to be on the program; I reported on the first findings, and a number of prominent Americans, including Gordon Allport, Otto Klineberg, and Goodwin Watson, visited me to obtain more details. These were also some of the first people I saw when I came to the States.[31]

At the time my fellowship began, the Federal Emergency Relief Administration (FERA) had just established its first research unit. The Rockefeller Foundation arranged for me to work there as a volunteer. To do so, I moved to Washington and while there met several sociologists working as government consultants. They belonged to the then insurgent group of empiricists who soon thereafter created the Sociological Research Association as a spearhead for their position in the American Sociological Society. These men worked mainly with broad census-type data. Because of the following episode, I acquired some-

30. Elsewhere, I have stressed that such a general notion of strategy should be considered more seriously in sociological analysis: "Innovation in Higher Education," in *Expanding Horizons of Knowledge About Man* (New York, 1966).

31. My Congress presentation was published in English translation as "An Unemployed Village," in the journal *Personality and Character* (1933).

thing of a reputation in this group as a different kind of technician. The FERA was about to publish a monograph showing a marked correlation between unemployment and education. I suggested that the result might be the spurious effect of age, an idea which today would be commonplace. A cross-tabulation was made and indeed it turned out that the role of age was more important: older people were less educated and had a higher unemployment rate. This impressed the FERA research staff. When I spent some time in Chicago in the spring of 1934, they established a small tabulating unit for me so that I could help there on the multivariate analysis of their unemployment surveys.

During this early period I spent some time at the few places in which empirical social research was taught. I went to the University of Rochester to become acquainted with Luther Fry, who had written the first book on techniques of social research. I took over one of his classes for several weeks and organized a study of how people decide which movies to attend.[32]

At this time I did not think of myself at all as a sociologist. I went to no national or regional conventions of sociologists, although my fellowship would have provided the necessary funds. As a matter of fact I had only a vague notion of the state of sociology in the United States. I visited Chicago for a few weeks, but primarily to work with Arthur Kornhauser, a prominent applied psychologist. I have no recollection of any memorable meetings there, except for a respectful lunch with L. L. Thurstone. I am sure that I did not meet Samuel Stouffer during the first year. My strongest memory of the visit is an investigation of the University of Chicago faculty that the state legislature held at the time; and I recall being much impressed by Robert Hutchins.

My main sociological contact at this time was with Robert S. Lynd. Because of *Middletown* he was one of the first people I looked up. He was extremely generous with his time and advice. The important role he played in the first ten years of my professional life in the United States will become abundantly clear in the remainder of this essay.[33]

32. Later the questionnaire served as the model for the Decatur study that resulted in Elihu Katz and Paul F. Lazarsfeld, *Personal Influence* (Glencoe, Ill., 1955).

33. As far as my own work went, I began a program which never was carried through to completion. Starting from my own ideas on "The Art of Asking Why" and my interest in the German literature on the "will," I set out to study the American literature

Throughout this period, my main concern was with the Research Center in Vienna. I had left it in precarious financial condition. The situation deteriorated after the putsch of the Dollfuss government which considered the Center's activities and personnel subversive, probably with reason. My great hope was to get American research organizations or commercial firms interested in subsidizing some of the work in Vienna. I therefore spent a good part of my time with people who worked in the field of market research. I never succeeded in mobilizing help for Vienna, but my efforts had important consequences for me personally. It all began when some of the psychologists I met told me that I would be especially interested in a new development.

Around 1930, a group of prominent American psychologists, including E. L. Thorndike and J. M. Cattell, created a non-profit organization called the Psychological Corporation (PSC). Their plan was, on the one hand, to promote the use of applied psychology among businessmen and, on the other hand, to provide academic psychologists with research opportunities and, I suppose, additional income. When I heard about this I immediately got in touch with the research director of the PSC and volunteered my time.

At the time, American market research was based mainly on rather simple nose-counting. Nonetheless, I expected the PSC, because of the academic status of its founders, to take about the same research position as our Viennese group. But in fact I did not find this to be the case. The PSC had to fight for its existence, and its research activities consisted of simple consumer surveys, in competition with other commercial agencies. I considered it almost a mission to help the PSC do pioneering rather than routine work. Toward this end I proposed a number of projects, always along the line of why people did this or that, but nothing came of these efforts. The PSC's director, who combined radical behaviorism with the desire to have the organization stay solvent, objected that my questionnaires were too long. I used to counter with

---

on "motivation" and to write a monograph on the subject. I still have many folders of extracts and notes on the pertinent publications. I also visited William McDougall in North Carolina to learn more about his theories of sentiments. In retrospect, I believe it was the drift toward American sociologists as a new reference group that accounts for my having let this earlier plan peter out. This drift will become apparent as the story unfolds.

the anecdote of a woman who wanted to buy a dog; she was shocked to learn that the smaller the dog the more expensive it was, and finally asked what she would have to pay for no dog at all. Understandably, after a while my relations with the Psychological Corporation diminished to the vanishing point.[34]

Such were the main directional cues which guided my first activities. They were accompanied by a number of personal contacts, which were an important part of the process of transfer I am trying to describe. These can only be understood in terms of mutual interaction. Indeed, it will be necessary to shift back and forth between what I think were prevailing tendencies in this country and certain patterns of conduct I had brought with me.

v. Atlantic Transfer—Latent Strategies

A NUMBER of younger psychologists were consultants to the Psychological Corporation, and together we formed a sort of Young Turk movement. The member of this group I saw most often at that time was Rensis Likert, then an assistant professor at New York University. He became interested in the Viennese type of complex market studies, and I cherish an English translation of a tea study which Likert

34. This might be a good place to recall an anecdote characteristic of misinterpretations of norms and roles, which obviously do not happen only to Polish peasants. When I came to offer my collaboration to the director of the PSC, he asked me whether I knew how to use a slide rule. Upon a positive answer, he assigned me to computing percentages on his main study, called the Brand Barometer. It consisted of reports of what food brands American housewives used based on a national sample. Understandably, I found it boring to compute percentages for days on end. But I thoroughly "understood" the situation: American culture requires that everyone works his way up from the bottom; I was being put to the test before being admitted to true professional work. After a few days, I timidly asked the director whether I had sufficiently proved my endurance. Only then did he understand what a European Rockefeller Fellow is. He had just taken my work as labor for which he did not have to pay, and probably classified me as being supported by WPA. Similarly, on quite a number of my first trips I traveled by coach, even overnight. One day a Rockefeller accountant asked me why I did not use Pullman, to which I was entitled. I had not realized that Pullman cars existed; I had learned in Europe that in the democratic U.S.A. there is nothing like the European distinction between different classes of railroad cars.

made for his students. Finally, Likert became an ardent advocate of the exclusive use of unstructured interviews, which we in Vienna combined with statistical data.[35]

Another encounter was with an applied psychologist from Cornell, John Jenkins. He became interested in the complex kinds of cross-tabulations we incorporated in our studies. In Vienna I had worked up a mimeographed manual for my students, under the title "How to Get Along with Figures" (Umgang mit Zahlen;[36] the title was taken from a famous eighteenth-century book by Adolf von Knigge: Über den Umgang mit Menschen). Jenkins made an English translation for his students. I spent the summer of 1934 with him in Ithaca, and we discussed the idea of a "new look" in applied psychology. He later created a department specializing in this field at the University of Maryland.

Simultaneously, the small fraternity of commercial market research experts got interested in my work. Largely through the efforts of Percival White, who wrote an early textbook on market research, I was invited to talk at meetings and to participate in committees of the recently created American Marketing Association. The Association was about to publish an official textbook, The Techniques of Marketing Research, and commissioned me to write four chapters. One of these, on interpretation, contained references to depth psychology and is generally considered the beginning of "motivation research." The book was widely used in business schools and helped me later on when I needed cooperation for our radio research work.

35. A paradoxical situation developed during World War II: Likert was then research director of the Department of Agriculture which conducted morale studies among farmers. I was a consultant to the OWI, which did corresponding studies in urban areas. The research director of OWI was Elmo Wilson, who favored highly structured interviews. Rather heated battles developed between the OWI and the Likert group. I was asked to study the matter and write a report; it was later published in condensed form under the title "The Controversy Over Detailed Interviews—An Offer for Negotiation," Public Opinion Quarterly, 8 (1944).

36. When Hans Zeisel came to the United States in 1938, I suggested that he enlarge this text, and the Columbia Bureau arranged for the first publication. I wanted very much to find a good American title. One day in a flower shop I saw a promotion slogan then much in vogue: "Say It With Flowers." I immediately decided that the title of the book should be Say It with Figures, and under that title it appeared in 1947. In social theory, this is called functional equivalence. Zeisel has meantime greatly enlarged the scope of the book; it has been translated into several languages, and is now in its fifth U.S. edition.

It was at that time that the first political questions were included in commercial market studies. Around 1935 polling had become an independent commercial activity, with results of interest to sociologists as well as to psychologists. While the former were quite hospitable, the latter were not, because the enterprise partook too much of the low academic status held by "applied psychology."[37] My sociological acquaintances listened with interest to my adventures in the market research world.

By the end of my first fellowship year, I had developed a network of personal and institutional contacts woven around a rather narrow range of professional activities. It had grown from an effort to help the Vienna Center, to which I intended to return. But the political events in Austria slowly nurtured the idea that I remain in the United States. I began to look at people with a view to possibilities of work here in the fall of 1937. Only a position connected with a university was conceivable. But the fact that I had a foot in both the commercial and the academic camps made for a certain amount of maneuverability, of which the following is a typical example.

At the University of Pittsburgh there was a research center which had been created by a man well-known in educational research: W. W. Charters. I spent two months at this Retail Research Institute which, by the time of my visit, was under the direction of David Craig. With him, I organized a number of studies on topics such as "How Pittsburgh Women Decide Where to Buy Their Dresses," or, "How Pittsburgh Drivers Choose Their Gasoline."[38] (The first study once made me a house guest of a local Pittsburgh tycoon, Edgar Kaufman, and the second brought me into repeated contact with Paul Mellon.) At that time a large trade association of the major retail stores was established in Washington; its president consulted me as to who should be research

37. In the fall of 1933, Gordon Allport invited me to talk to his seminar on the problem of motivation. After a few introductory remarks, I said: "Let me give you a first example from a study of mouthwash." There was a roar of laughter, and I answered: "I don't quite see why 'lifted weights' are so much more dignified then 'mouthwash.'" I think that Edwin Boring was present and that might have suggested the remark.

38. These and other unpublished studies mentioned in this section are available in mimeographed form at the Archives of the History of Psychology, Akron University, Akron, Ohio.

director, and appointed Craig upon my suggestion. Toward the end of my fellowship, Craig resigned from Pittsburgh and moved to Washington. Before leaving, he arranged for me to get a temporary appointment at his Institute. The necessary meeting of the trustees had not yet taken place, but Craig wrote me a letter on official stationery, which was sufficient for me to obtain an immigration visa from the American consul in Vienna.

I subsume all these mechanisms of the transfer process under the broad notion of *latent strategy*. It would obviously be wrong to restrict it to a conscious manipulation. All of it has, rather, the character of an underlying vigilance which connects accidental situations to a latent goal. But not even this is enough of an explanation. One has to add a kind of "libidinal" element which makes all these things pleasurable within their own right. I was almost obsessed with the idea that I wanted to be connected with as many studies as possible, and used every occasion to add another one. So I soon obtained funds to study the adjustment of our immediate group, the nine European Rockefeller fellows; the questionnaires I used on that occasion thirty years ago are still available, and might be of some historical interest.[39]

Latent strategies and directional cues involve the interactions that always prevail between dispositions and situations. Latent strategies lead to selective perception of the environment, and they also become crystallized, more precise, more self-conscious as they meet success in an extending sequence of episodes. But what makes for a relatively high proportion of successes? Here I must take recourse to a term like *structural fit*. Both the environment and the life style of the immigrant are patterned in a certain way. The elements of these two patterns may complement each other, and to some degree they did in my case. Thus in Section II I gave examples of my quantitative interests, controlled by strong conceptual training, fitting well into some nascent trends in the American community. Let me give two more examples of such structural fit. The first shows the protective role of a personal idio-

39. In retrospect, I am aware of the costs involved in my style of life. All during the two years I saw hardly anything of the country except for research offices, and I also formed few personal social contacts. At that time, there was not much research going on in the West Coast, and I am probably the only one of the nine foreign fellows who came here at that time who did not exercise his right to a trip to California.

syncrasy; the second shows the usefulness of a tangential approach to conventional rewards.

In a letter to Vienna, of which I happen to have a copy, I reported during my first fellowship year that "I find it more interesting to meet with what you might call second-string people; whenever I come to a new place, I pay a respect visit to the big shots and then stay with the people who accept me and make me feel comfortable."[40] Without my knowing it, that helped me escape a certain uneasiness regarding foreigners, which, in my opinion, was quite prevalent at the time; foreigners were rare, and it is understandable that people had ambivalent feelings about them. In 1935, when Lynd began to help me look for a job, he seems to have written one correspondent that I do not look very Jewish; I have the answer from the other man, who writes Lynd that he has heard nice things about me, but he wants to correct Lynd on one point: "Lazarsfeld shows clearly the marks of his race." In 1936, Hadley Cantril wrote Lynd that they were looking for a research director who would have my kind of training but not be so peculiarly "scattered." That the word reflected an image of foreignness would appear from his praise, somewhat later, of the first radio issue of the *Journal of Applied Psychology*:[41] "The two I especially liked," he wrote, "were those of Herr Director himself for they beautifully illustrate the trends one can discover if statistics are intelligently used." So, even at the moment when he approved of what I wanted to do, the notion of foreignness crept in.

When I appointed T. W. Adorno, newly arrived from Germany, to the radio project I repeatedly had to explain that he did not yet know his way around. I shall come back to this later; but for now let me note that my own reaction was characteristic. I have a memorandum of March 7, 1938, addressed to Cantril and Frank Stanton, the co-directors of the project, in which I report on my first week of experience with Adorno. I wrote:

40. In writing this, I realize that this habit has carried over to the last twenty years, during which I have stayed for considerable time in a variety of European countries. My serious contacts on these occasions are definitely not with my age and status peers, but with younger people.

41. Volume 23 (1939).

He looks exactly as you would imagine a very absent-minded German professor, and he behaves so foreign that I feel like a member of the Mayflower Society. When you start to talk with him, however, he has an enormous amount of interesting ideas. As every newcomer, he tries to reform everything, but if you listen to him, most of what he says makes sense.

As late as 1941, when I was appointed to Columbia, Samuel Stouffer had to fight this ghost. He wrote, in a letter to the appointment committee that is one of the most thoughtful documents of support I have read in twenty-eight years on the receiving end of such mail, that

In spite of the fact that he has lived in this country for seven years or more, he has a distinctly foreign appearance and speaks with a strong accent. This prejudices some people against him, and I think some are further prejudiced because they feel that there is occasional arrogance in his manner. Actually, Paul is one of the most modest of men, but he does have a rather heavy Germanic way of presenting a topic which tends to make some people feel that there is not as much in the topic as the difficulty in following him would suggest. I think such critics would be occasionally right, but I can testify from experience that there is plenty of pure gold in them thar hills.

Obviously Stouffer felt uneasy about bringing up the topic, and so at the end caricatures himself as a kind of hillbilly.

I offer these examples as a way of characterizing the atmosphere of the period, an atmosphere notably different from the present in which foreign-born intellectuals are a dime a dozen in academic and professional life.[42] But, even so, I was not seriously hampered, because it never occurred to me to aspire to a major university job. I took it for granted that I would have to make some move similar to the creation of the Vienna Research Center if I wanted to find a place for myself in the United States.

42. One should not overlook the fact that every person has unlikeable characteristics, and that some of them can feed a stereotype. In the quotation just mentioned, Stouffer says that some people are prejudiced against me. I have a letter from Craig, in which he wants to explain to me why he couldn't help me more after he left Pittsburgh; he implores me not to come to the United States, because I would have so many personal difficulties. (The letter reached Europe when I had already returned to the States.) Intermingled with his—certainly sincere—expression of friendship, are such sentences as, "People don't feel safe with you . . . you are too grand at all times and never sufficiently modest . . . you seem not to have made many fast friends. . . . It is for that I am miserable."

It is obviously impossible for me to judge the extent and concrete basis for this reaction. One thing I am aware of is that, in the first years, I was rather rude to assistants and students, barking at them when they fell down on an assignment. I like to think I changed my behavior at the same time as I learned to eat with the fork in the right hand.

This leads to the second illustration of the notion of structural fit. At about the time I arrived in the United States, the problem of how to introduce empirical social research into the university structure had become visible. It was obvious that a new type of research center was necessary, though none had successfully developed.[43] One reason for this was the lack of people whose experience and career needs equipped them to create and direct such centers. Missing from the scene, in other words, were *institution men*.[44]

I have always been interested in the type of men who played major roles in academic innovations. At various times I have tried to show that such innovations can often be traced to people who belong to two worlds but who were not safe in either of them. The best historical examples are Wilhelm von Humboldt who, as a hanger-on at Weimar, belonged to the lower Prussian aristocracy and created the University of Berlin in 1807. Another is Guillaume Budé, who was a hanger-on among the French humanists but who had access to the Court of Francis I and spent his life developing the Collège de France in opposition to the anti-humanistic Sorbonne (1515 to 1550).

The institution man is a special case of a well-known sociological notion: the marginal man who is part of two different cultures. He lives under cross pressures that move him in a number of directions. According to his gifts and external circumstances he may become a revolutionary, a surrealist, a criminal. In some cases his marginality may become the driving force for institutional efforts; the institution he creates shelters him and at the same time helps him crystallize his own identity. In my case there was a general convergence toward institutional innovation. Under the adverse economic circumstances in Austria and the strong current of incipient anti-Semitism, a regular academic career would have been almost impossible. When I came to the United States, I was neither individually known, like some of the immigrant physicists, nor connected with a visible movement, like the psychoanalysts and Gestalt

43. I described and documented one such abortive effort at the University of Chicago in my A.S.A. Presidential Address, referred to above, note 28.

44. Historians, remembering the *Gueux*, will understand the acceptance of a term which originally had pejorative overtones. Still there is a difference between the organization man and the institution man. The former is supposedly pushed around while the latter finds in the institution a field for creative self-expression.

psychologists. (The status of a Rockefeller fellow helped in the beginning; but after a while I did experience the proverbial transition from a distinguished foreigner to an undesirable alien.) On the positive side I did belong, marginally, to a number of areas between which bridges were bound to be built; social science and mathematics, academic and applied interests, European and American outlooks. It seems plausible that such a configuration would lead to a career detoured through an institutional innovation rather than routed directly toward individual mobility.

The form this took was the role of a bureau director, a role I have already touched on and will try to develop in the two sections that follow. One of the points I will come back to repeatedly is the need in this role to take reasonable risks, to try deviant innovations without coming into too much conflict with prevailing norms. And in this connection it seems fitting to end this section with the note of the risk I took in coming here. It will be remembered that I went to Vienna to apply for an immigration visa based on the promise of an appointment at the Retail Research Institute at the University of Pittsburgh. The day after I got my visa I received a cable from Craig telling me that he was leaving Pittsburgh because he had taken the job of research director of the Retail Federation; my appointment would have to be delayed until a successor could confirm it. In some way, then, my visa was of dubious legality, and, more important, I had no job waiting for me in the States.

I had intended to inform the Rockefeller Foundation of my decision to move to Pittsburgh. Their regulations required return to the home base at the completion of the fellowship, but in view of the Austrian situation I could rather safely count on their understanding. Now having no guaranteed job, however, I doubted very much that an American foundation would also cooperate on a move which went against governmental regulations. Either a job or an affidavit of support by an American citizen was required.

I remember, of course, every detail of the few days and nights during which I had to make up my mind. I still had one month of fellowship money left; traditionally, the European fellows spent their last month traveling in Europe, as a kind of decompression procedure. I finally decided not to inform anyone, and used this last $150 to buy a third-class ticket on a slow American boat. I thus arrived in New York as the classic immigrant, penniless. A few weeks later, I began the work which led to the establishment of the University of Newark Research Center.

VI. The Rockefeller-Princeton Radio Project

I SPENT most of the academic year 1936–37 on the tasks of raising money, supervising studies, and training staff at Newark.

Sometime during the spring I heard that the Rockefeller Foundation was prepared to set up a large project to study the effect of radio on American society. The reviewing officer was John Marshall, who was trained as a medieval historian. A project director was looked for, and the job was offered to a number of senior people. I was interested in such an appointment, but had no way to present my candidacy. I had had some previous experience in radio research. In 1930–31, our Vienna Center had done a large-scale survey of listener tastes for the Austrian radio.[45] One of my junior colleagues in the department of psychology, Herta Herzog, had written her dissertation under my supervision replicating an earlier English study. Persons of varied background had been asked to read a story over the radio, and questionnaires distributed to the listening public had made it possible to discover what social and other characteristics the audience could derive from voice and diction.[46]

During my fellowship years, I had visited the research departments of the major radio networks, and had established friendly relations with Frank Stanton, then a junior staff member of the Columbia Broadcasting System. I knew that he was somehow in touch with the Rockefeller plans, but I was not well enough acquainted with him to ask for his help. The main academic proponent for the idea was said to be Hadley Cantril, who, a few years earlier, had published a book with Gordon Allport on the psychology of radio. I had known Cantril in the first pe-

45. The sampling design and the questionnaire were very naïve, but for years afterwards our survey was cited as the first of its kind in Europe. I would not be surprised if it antedated such work in the United States.
46. Herta Herzog, "Stimme und Persönlichkeit," *Zeitschrift für Psychologie*, 130 (1933).

riod of my fellowship during visits to Harvard, and was very much impressed by him. However, we had seen little of each other, and in any case it would have been embarrassing for me to approach him directly.

As was so often the case during that period, my main avenue of communication was Robert S. Lynd. Cantril wrote to him asking whether he had a suggestion for the directorship; he indicated that it should be someone of my training, at the same time mentioning that he had reservations about me personally. Lynd tried to dispel Cantril's doubts, and recommended me.

In July 1937, I went for six weeks to Europe to visit my parents and to attend to a number of other personal matters. While sitting in a mountain village I received a cable from Cantril offering me the directorship at the rather fabulous salary of $7,000, "two years or possibly four, headquarters Princeton." I cabled back that I was very much interested, but that I wanted to raise a number of questions, which I would do immediately by following mail. I wrote Cantril a two-and-a-half page single-spaced letter dated August 8, 1937, which crossed with one of his to me of about equal length, dated August 9, 1937. Cantril's letter urged me to take the directorship and explained the project.

... Princeton University, more particularly the School of Public and International Affairs, was given a grant of $33,500 a year for a period of two years—or a total grant of 67,000 dollars. This was to carry out a project which Stanton and I designed to investigate certain problems in radio research. ...

The sum mentioned was large indeed. The substantive purpose of the project was described as follows:

Our idea was to try to determine eventually the role of radio in the lives of different types of listeners, the value of radio to people psychologically, and the various reasons why they like it. The Rockefeller Foundation, through John Marshall, felt it was a new type of project getting at some of the "why" questions so long neglected.

The letter stressed that the formulation of purpose was intentionally vague, so that it would be possible to carry out varied research under its charter. One can see in the preceding quotation a considerable affinity to the Vienna tradition; indeed, Cantril and his teacher Allport had always been attentive to the work of Mrs. Bühler. Another element in the description was an emphasis on methods.

We had thought that this would require two years of preliminary work on methods—
that is, methods which we hoped to work out that would eventually enable us or
others to get the final answers to the sort of questions that interested us.

The hope for a "final answer" was typical of the optimistic mood of the
period. Now, after thirty years of further research in mass communication, most of us feel that we are still just about at the beginning. Cantril's letter included the expectation that the project would be continued
for another period of two years, and on this point at least his confidence
was justified by later events.

From my point of view the content of the project was not the main
issue. I had created the Newark Research Center, and my problem was
how the new proposal would affect it. So I first explained to Cantril
what this center was about.

I invented the Newark Research Center for two reasons. I wanted to direct a rather
great variety of studies, so that I was sure that from year to year my methodological
experience could increase—and that is, as you know, my main interest in research.
And I tried to build up groups of younger students to be educated just in this kind of
research procedures I tried to develop. Now as to the first point I think that your
project would do splendidly. Radio is a topic around which actually any kind of research methods can be tried out and can be applied satisfactorily.

I quote this rather lengthy statement because it provides a check on the
retrospective report I made in the preceding section: the formulation I
made at the time hardly differs from my present point of view. Following this background information I raised two questions with Cantril.
The first was:

. . . would it be possible to set up at least part of your project in such a way that it
could be used as a sort of training institution?

The second question goes to the heart of what I described as the attitude
of the institution man. I told Cantril that it made me apprehensive to
contemplate the Newark Center's collapse, which in all probability
would come about if I took a leave of absence to direct the new project.
Here is how I explained my feeling:

I try to identify whatever I do with an institution which might after some time acquire
the dignity which I myself, for reasons of destiny and maybe of personality, can hardly
aspire to.

The remainder of my letter argues for the solution I proposed: the Rock-efeller Project should be handled as an additional undertaking of the Newark Center. Considering that the budget of this single study was more than three times the total budget of the Center, it is not surprising that Cantril found my proposal rather absurd. He answered me with a letter that was friendly, complimentary, and persuasive. But on the crucial issue it was quite firm.

Your suggestion about a tie-up with the Newark Research Center is, I fear, out. I'm sorry that you didn't get the money there, but it is one of these somewhat absurd American grants to an "institution" and it would be impossible to have the work carried on elsewhere.

On my return from Austria I immediately got in touch with Cantril to negotiate the institutional aspect. It is also characteristic of the institution man that I was not too impressed by the inviolability of rules. I do not recall the details of this meeting; but I can reconstruct it: Cantril and Stanton needed a director, and they probably realized that it would be too anxiety-provoking for me to give up the Newark Center as a base. In any case, Cantril was finally willing to change his mind. I have a copy of the letter I wrote to Lynd on September 9, 1937, at his summer residence explaining this development. Reading that four-page single-spaced letter over today I am amused by the Machiavellianism that I seem to have attributed to myself, at least by implication. In all likelihood, Cantril did not feel it worthwhile to bother much, once he had reassured himself that the interests of the project and Princeton would be properly taken care of. The substantive parts of the understanding, which marks the turning point for the rest of my story, I reported to Lynd at length. Cantril agreed, I wrote Lynd,

that the actual headquarters of the project would be at the Newark Research Center and that I would be expected to come down to Princeton only for incidental meetings. In addition to my presence in Newark, he agreed that any amount of project money that would be allocated for research in an urban area could be spent from Newark, which means that I could appoint a number of people here for special studies. In practical terms, the whole arrangement therefore means that the Research Center has a huge new job.

The concern to have all my personal activities funnelled into an iden-tifiable institution merits a brief digression. I later tried to persuade my associate directors to adopt this policy generally. In a memorandum to Cantril and Stanton, written on February 8, 1938, I urged them to identify their "other" activities with the Princeton Office of Radio Research:

I feel that all of us should, as much as possible, use our prior activities or activities outside the project to feed the project itself. . . . I use just everything on which I have worked for the past years and call it radio now. . . . Frank is a very good investment from the standpoint of the project because of all the material and connections he may put at our disposal. I am quite confident that Had's previous and present work could be utilized in the same way if he would agree with my philosophy expressed here. He and his students would still get all the credit here for the work. It will be published in the frame of the project instead of in a magazine.

Given the multiple involvements of my then associate directors, one of whom became the president of a highly endowed research foundation and the other the president of the Columbia Broadcasting System, my suggestion was met with little enthusiasm. Nothing further was heard of it.[47]

In the fall of 1937, then, the symbiosis between Princeton and Newark Universities was created. The link was formalized by my appointment as Research Associate at Princeton University. The liberal formulation of the Rockefeller program permitted me to do any kind of specific study as long as I gave it some nominal connection with radio problems, and as a result a slow shift in the whole situation took place. Increasingly the Princeton Office of Radio Research became the main frame for my activities and Newark only the place of its physical location. I still had only a small staff, accidentally assembled, and I therefore had to write many of the early papers myself. In order to conceal this fact I invented a pseudonym, Elias Smith, under which three or four of the early project studies appeared. By now it should not be surprising that I considered it more important to publicize the institution than to lengthen my personal list of publications.[48]

47. When Robert Merton became my main associate at the Columbia Bureau of Applied Social Research, he approved this philosophy and acted on it. The conditions under which such a strategy makes sense (either on a senior or a junior level) deserve further analysis and discussion. I can do no more here than raise the general problem.

48. The Elias Smith story has a sequel, which deserves mention because of its historical setting. During the McCarthy period I was invited to a UNESCO meeting in Paris. I received the usual questionnaire needed for my clearance, which contained the question whether I had ever used a pseudonym. Without thinking, I interpreted the question in a

By the spring of 1938, it had become clear to everyone concerned (although perhaps last to me) that the Office of Radio Research had become my main base of operations and that it had acquired an institutional life of its own. We accepted outside grants and made elaborate arrangements with various research agencies to obtain data for secondary analysis. This increasing functional autonomy of the Office was paralleled by a decline of the University of Newark, which soon thereafter collapsed. Sometime in the summer of 1938—and it is perhaps revealing that I can remember none of the details—Kingdon felt that he could use our space to better purpose and asked us to move. By then Edward Suchman had become the manager of our operations. It never occurred to us to move to Princeton; so many of our research contacts had been established in New York City. Suchman was commissioned to find appropriate space in New York, and in the fall of 1938 the Princeton Office of Radio Research moved to 14 Union Square where we rented a few rooms.

VII. The Office of Radio Research—Work and Policies

A DETAILED description of the activities of the Princeton Office of Radio Research would go far beyond the purpose of the present essay. Instead, I shall list a number of events and observations which influenced my subsequent work in this country. In the next section matters elucidating European-American research relations will be discussed.

1. Cantril and Stanton, my associate directors, met with me regularly every few weeks to plan and review current work. They allowed me full freedom of decision and provided many valuable contacts, and I kept them informed about everything through a steady flow of memo-

---

political frame and answered, "No." My clearance was held up; I had to answer a number of specific questions. One of them stated that it was known to the inquiring agency that I had used the pseudonym Elias Smith, and why did I deny it. I sent them the titles of the Elias Smith papers, which satisfied even the clearance agency. The amazing thing about this episode is that some federal agency had found out about this pseudonym in papers on radio research. Incidentally, from time to time we still get inquiries at Columbia from people who want to know where Elias Smith is.

randa. Copies of many of these notes are preserved and others should be found in their files; it might be worthwhile some day to analyze these documents to obtain a picture of the ways an early bureau director kept things going. I tried in every way I could to foresee and to forestall possible difficulties, and created the slogan that it is more important for a director to worry than to work. In addition, I was aware that, as a recent immigrant, much of the authority I had derived from the good will of my two associates, both of whom had much deeper roots in the American scene.

Cantril was correctly strict about budgetary arrangements, since the university held him accountable. I did not make life easy for him, because I often exceeded the Princeton budget, sure that I would cover the deficit with additional income from some other source. By and large, this worked out all right, but it might be appropriate here to point out one weakness in the image of the managerial scholar I had developed. As long as I handled situations myself I was somehow always able to balance the budget, though often I came in by the skin of my teeth. But in situations where I could not go on juggling or raising additional funds, the matter became more complicated. For instance, after I left Vienna for my American fellowship, many financial difficulties seem to have emerged. I received numerous letters, especially from the Bühlers, cursing me for the financial embarrassments I had created for them. Many of the concrete references in these letters I cannot understand today; but there can be little doubt that I had left behind a rather chaotic situation, even if the sums involved seem rather small by today's standards. In financial matters the doctrine of "reasonable risks" may involve special problems.[49]

2. While the budget of the project seemed very large at the time, it soon turned out that it did not permit the collection of much primary material. The original plan, as formulated by Cantril and Stanton, assumed that much time would be given to laboratory experiments, but perhaps because of my training, experiments played a small role once I became director. Almost by necessity much of the early work was based

49. Similarly, at the time when I turned over the directorship of the Columbia Bureau to my successor, Charles Glock, we had accumulated a moderate deficit, which I, as usual, counted on covering with funds from future studies. The change in directorship was taken as the occasion for a financial review, and the university preferred to cover the deficit from general funds, so that thereafter a stricter accounting system could be set up.

on what I later called *secondary analysis*. From Gallup we obtained polls in which he had asked comparative questions on newspaper reading and radio listening, and analyzed them further. One of our main sources was program ratings which at the time were only used to compare the drawing power of various programs; we re-analyzed this material with special emphasis on social differences, using then as we do now the letters A, B, C to describe the socio-economic status of respondents.[50]

The secondary analysis of program ratings formed a bridge to my long-standing concern with social stratification. In a memorandum to my associate directors (February 8, 1938), I developed a number of themes which kept recurring in much of our subsequent work.

In a report by the Cooperative Analysis of Broadcasting I find consistently that the different economic groups show different tendencies in listening. Listening rises from A to C and goes down with the D group. [Here tables were inserted.]

It may seem odd today that these differences were then a surprise. In good Viennese fashion I immediately offered some tentative explanations.

Probably the decline in listening from the C to A group is due to more education and more money for other kinds of entertainment in the higher groups. It might also be that in the C group the family spirit is more developed. The decline of listening from C to D might be due to bad housing conditions which drive people out of the home; there are still many ways in which this influence can work—for instance, by family discord or gang formation.

It interests me today that I was then aware of the continuity in my own work.

Systematic comparison might yield very important results. I am speaking from a concrete experience in another field. When I wrote my book on Adolescents and Occupation I did nothing for months but collect figures on vocational choices all over Germany and Austria; they looked quite silly by themselves but gave marvelous leads when compared and the circumstances of their collection considered.

This first "concordance" had been written ten years earlier but in this memo I still found some of the results "marvelous." And it all led to an administrative policy for which I requested the support of my associates.

I am deeply convinced that current business research still contains a great wealth of

50. One of our early products was a paper by H. M. Beville, then on the research staff of NBC, entitled, "The ABCD's of Radio Audiences," *Public Opinion Quarterly*, 4 (1940).

information which has important social implications. Therefore I am so concerned with having sources continually comb the agencies for such results, which, of course, we shall have to examine very carefully.

The emphasis on this type of material ultimately had considerable influence on my own publications. The Austrian phase of my research required a diversity of techniques applied to rather small samples. Now I was faced with the task of making sense of data from large samples, with relatively little information about each respondent. This led to my concern with multivariate analysis.[51]

My interest in methods of qualitative research also broadened. For a long time I had felt that in this area too methodological explications were needed and possible. In the introduction to Komarovsky's study of unemployed families I had written

The present study . . . endeavored to contribute a more careful analysis of those non-quantitative procedures which very often are left to the laziness of "common sense." An assumption is often made that only quantitative procedures can be communicated, whereas all other procedures (insight, understanding) must be left to the inspiration of the student and the exigencies of the problem at hand. The non-quantitative methods cannot be formulated as explicitly as an arithmetic computation. But these procedures, now clothed in ambiguous terms, still remain to be described and standardized.

But not much happened until Cantril introduced an important type of procedure into the activities of the project. He suggested that a small number of open-ended interviews be conducted with listeners who were fans of typical radio programs. His suggestion was taken up by Herta Herzog, who was a staff member for the first few years. The first and most widely-quoted result of this approach was her discussion of the then popular Professor Quiz program.[52] She later made a similar study of listeners to daytime serials, in collaboration with T. W. Adorno, which appeared in the journal of the Horkheimer group which at that time was published in the United States.[53]

The largely qualitative nature of these first two studies was carried over into two subsequent enterprises where a tie-up with small-scale

51. The most accessible summary is in the entry "Survey Analysis" in the new *International Encyclopedia of the Social Sciences*.

52. It appeared as a special monograph and also in *Radio and the Printed Page* (New York, 1940), pp. 64–94.

53. Herta Herzog, "On Borrowed Experience," *Studies in Philosophy and Social Science*, 9 (1941), 65–95.

statistics was worked out. One was *The Invasion from Mars*,[54] and the other was the study of the Kate Smith War Bond Drive, a study that was supervised by Robert Merton and formed the basis of his book, *Mass Persuasion* (1947). The two studies just mentioned are examples of what was later dubbed "Firehouse Research." In both cases I had phoned Stanton the morning after the event and he provided money from his CBS research budget for immediate preliminary work. Today the bureaucratization of research applications makes such improvisations difficult. I find this regrettable and wish that emergency research funds that could be quickly mobilized as the situation demands were available.

3. Some time during this period, Harold Lasswell created his well-known formula for research on mass communications: to investigate who says what to whom, with what effect. Content analysis and audience research deal with the second and the third elements in this formula. The study of effects, the fourth item, was continuously on my mind, and led to panel studies, to be discussed in Section VIII, below. The neglect of the "who" by the Princeton Project is conspicuous: we never made systematic studies of the kind that today would be called organizational research. I was certainly not oblivious to the problem. The study of the popular music industry referred to before was one early effort; at one point I also commissioned a summary of such available studies as Leo Rosten's analysis of Washington correspondents. This summary was carried out by Alexander George, who later became a distinguished research member of the Rand Corporation.

George's survey was to be part of a large compendium on communications research. Another section was to deal with content analysis, and later appeared as a book under the authorship of Bernard Berelson.[55] Joseph Klapper's dissertation on the effects of mass media, later devel-

54. The early interviews on the Orson Welles program were summarized by Dr. Herzog in a memorandum to Stanton which was subsequently published as a contribution to the literature, and that was later extended into the book-length study, *The Invasion from Mars*, by Hadley Cantril, Hazel Gaudet, and Herta Herzog (Princeton, 1940). Though at the time I had hoped Dr. Herzog would receive a major share of the credit for her imaginative work on that study, there is no doubt that the type of interviews used in this study was due to Cantril's initiative.

55. Bernard Berelson, *Content Analysis in Communication Research* (Glencoe, Ill., 1952).

oped into a well-known book,[56] was initially also a part of this enterprise. Still another section on institutions resulted in a number of special studies, most notably a dissertation on unions in the communications industry.

Sometime around 1939 or 1940 our publication policy had become fairly well known, and a number of people offered me studies they had undertaken on their own. One of these approaches came from the professor of government at Harvard, Carl Friedrich. He had done a descriptive analysis of the relations between Congress, the Federal Communications Commission, and the radio industry. His study was subsequently published in the *Political Science Quarterly*, and I consider it a very fine example of institutional analysis, showing a perception of an important problem and providing significant factual information. I declined to include this study as one of our publications. My argument was that the evidence was too anecdotal, and did not conform to the quantitative traditions of our project. I want to take this occasion to express my regret to Professor Friedrich. Today I suspect that I then had a more complex motivation characteristic of someone responsible for a new and struggling institution. The next point will provide the necessary background.

4. Communications research was, at the time, a new enterprise, and I gave speeches about it to rather high-level audiences such as the National Association of Broadcasters and the Association of American Newspaper Editors. On such occasions I faced a very difficult problem: the relation with the industry. In one of those speeches, later published in *The Journalism Quarterly*,[57] I formulated the issue as follows:

Those of us social scientists who are especially interested in communications research depend upon the industry for much of our data. Actually most publishers and broadcasters have been very generous and cooperative in this recent period during which communications research had developed as a kind of joint enterprise between industries and universities. But we academic people always have a certain sense of tightrope walking: at what point will the commercial partners find some necessary conclusion too hard to take and at what point will they shut us off from the indispensable sources of funds and data?

56. *The Effects of Mass Communication* (Glencoe, Ill., 1960).
57. "Some Notes on the Relationships between Radio and the Press," *Journalism Quarterly*, 18 (1941), 10–13.

I finally thought of a compromise formula. In a speech on "The Role of Criticism in the Management of Mass Media," I started out by saying that the mass media were overly sensitive to the criticism of intellectuals, while the latter were too strict in their overall indictment; there ought to be a way of making criticism more useful and manageable for those who offer it and for those who receive it. An effective way to achieve this might be to make the development of critical talents an accepted part of the training and daily work of anyone connected with the mass media.

Not only should the problems of criticism be thoroughly discussed at conferences such as this, but they also should be the subject-matter of systematic courses and training programs. Students and researchers should come to think of criticism as something being systematically studied; they should be persuaded to undertake critical examinations of the mass media and to produce material amenable to criticism. If the whole area were institutionalized in this way, then there would be less emotionalism connected with it.

I made essentially four suggestions with journalism schools in mind. First, crusading is a traditional and accepted function for the journalist; there should be more careful study of which crusades succeed, which fail, and why; in addition, the question of crusading over the radio should be considered. My second point was that managers of the mass media should attempt to understand better why criticism of their activities is bound to be part of the liberal creed.

The liberals feel betrayed. They hoped that the increased time and money which they fought for would be channelized in directions and activities which interested them; instead it was drained off by the mass media. The situation of the liberals is much like that of the high school boy who, after weeks of saving, accumulates enough money to buy a bracelet for a girl, and who then learns that the girl has gone out with another boy to show off her nice new trinket. You can very well understand why the liberals are angry, and perhaps you can almost sympathize with them.

As a third point I suggested more attention to the critical help which the mass media can give each other. I pointed out that most newspapers had book critics but little discussion of radio programs was available. In this connection, I also cited the close relationship between audience research and literary criticism. Finally, as the fourth point, I suggested that some kind of periodic reporting of the content of mass media should be made available, so that all criticism would have a factual base.

This country is rightfully proud of its many statistical services. But our social book-keeping lags woefully when it comes to cultural matters. Social research is probably not yet ready to give us monthly information on how many people are happy or unhappy. But nothing would be easier than to set up a service based on sound sampling techniques which would periodically report the content of newspapers, magazines, and radio programs. It is just a matter of developing the appropriate motivation and providing the appropriate machinery.

In all of the work of the Princeton Office I tried to relate the research to public controversies, but usually thought of our office as serving a mediating function. Thus, for example, we served as a channel for a project of the progressive chairman of the Federal Communications Commission, Clifford Durr. He had commissioned Charles Siepmann to develop ideas on how the FCC could better work for higher broadcasting standards. This assignment resulted in two documents, the FCC's "blue book" promulgating stricter licensing standards, and Siepmann's *Radio: Second Chance*. To both publications the industry reacted with violent antagonism, and I prevailed upon John Marshall of the Rockefeller Foundation to provide a special budget so that I could organize a two-day conference among the industry, the FCC, and prominent scholars in the research field to discuss the issues.[58] Nothing much came of it, but I think this was partly because the beginning of the Second World War and the approaching involvement of the United States eclipsed interest in this kind of topic.

Just before the war, the FCC opened hearings on the question of whether newspapers should be permitted to own radio stations. We received funds to set up punched cards providing, for every station, data on ownership and on the way news programs were handled. These funds were provided by a committee including all radio stations owned by newspapers. This was, at the time, an important source of income for us, but I made it a condition of our work that the FCC would have complete access to our data. In retrospect, I consider it likely that the radio-newspaper committee accepted this neutrality because it was known that the newspapers owning radio stations were careful not to

58. The minutes of this conference are still available and might one day deserve more detailed scrutiny.

use them as a monopolistic device against competing newspapers which did not own stations; they were amply rewarded by the increase of advertising revenue, which did not fall under the scrutiny of the FCC.

5. After one year of existence—in the fall of 1938—the project was in a peculiar position. On the one hand my all-eggs-in-one-basket policy had resulted in the collection of a great deal of material and an enthusiastic work atmosphere within a small but promising young staff. On the other hand, the "image" of the office was not good. No central theme was visible, and we began hearing rumors that important people questioned whether we knew where we were going.

Clearly, something had to be done. There was indeed no major study to which I could point; somehow I had to make acceptable my policy of research improvisation guided by available material and personal interests and contacts. It occurred to me that I might persuade a journal to let me serve as guest editor for an issue on radio research; by writing a general introduction I might be able to pull together the various studies into something that would look systematic. I remember vividly that both Cantril and Stanton told me that this was against the American tradition, that no editor would allow himself to be displaced by a guest editor. (It would be useful to check whether this was, indeed, the case at that time; today, certainly, guest editors are not at all rare.) I was not discouraged—partly because in Europe guest editors for scientific journals were well known.[59] Shopping around, I was told that the editor of the *Journal of Applied Psychology* might be amenable to such an arrangement. He was, and the norm that supposedly existed was broken. In February 1939 the first radio research issue under my guest editorship appeared.[60]

The issue well reflected the situation in which the project found itself after a year. In an introduction I tried to lay out the new field of radio research. From a policy point of view I had three tasks. First, I had to make it convincing that this newcomer was just as good as the older members of the family of applied psychology; this I defined as "a sum

59. I had assisted Charlotte Bühler when in 1931 she was guest editor on child studies for the main journal on general psychology.

60. This episode, involving the notion of reasonable risk, implies a certain optimistic belief in the malleability of the social environment. A Bureau director cannot afford to underestimate or ignore options.

total of techniques used by psychologists when they are called upon to collaborate with agencies empowered to perform specific social initiation." It was not difficult to show that, in this sense, radio research was a reasonable parallel to industrial or educational psychology. Second, I wanted to show that something new was developing. This was a movement from descriptive studies to more strictly interpretative work. I chose the following formulation:

We should not be surprised if a discipline of "action research" should evolve one day, bringing out more clearly the great methodological similarity of many studies which now are not connected because they are done under different headings, such as criminology, market research, or accident prevention.

I have since preferred the phrase "empirical study of action" because the term "action research" acquired a different meaning.[61] And finally, as always, I tried to place the new activity in a broader context:

The operation of radio certainly bears the imprint of the present social system and is, in turn, bound to have certain effects upon social institutions. . . . The study of radio could even serve as a way to a better understanding of some basic issues in our society. . . . Such problems call for study by sociologists, economists, anthropologists, and have at the same time their psychological side.

My prediction that the new field would partly belong to other social sciences, including sociology, certainly became true.

The contents of the issue reflect my efforts to make the improvisations of the first year appear coherent. The issue was divided into five sections: 1) index problems; 2) program research; 3) questionnaire techniques; 4) research in different fields of activities; 5) reports of other surveys, including a bibliography of "current radio research in universities." In section two I included a number of studies done by other people. One of them was by Charles Osgood, then at Dartmouth, on the separation of appeal and brand name in testing spot-advertising. Another, by Cantril, dealt with the role of familiarity in the selection and enjoyment of radio programs. This was a well-designed experiment in which several radio stations participated; it was clearly a carry-over from the pre-1937 plan for the project. Section four exemplifies the

61. Cf. the section in *The Language of Social Research* entitled "The Empirical Study of Action."

way we used material from seemingly unrelated spheres. From the Komarovsky-Newark cases we culled some of the examples to show the importance of radio for unemployed people, and since Suchman's family owned a taxicab company, we presented an effort to see whether the recent introduction of taxi radios increased accidents. Gerhard Wiebe wrote on ratings of popular songs, and the venerable Elias Smith had two papers on index construction. Papers which later became closely identified with my work were on "Interchangeability of Indices" and on repeated interviews.

As a holding operation the issue was a success. The second year of the project brought up new problems and led, in turn, to the final phase of my story. First, however, there is another, special aspect of our activities to explain.

VIII. The Office of Radio Research—Culture Contacts

IN the first years of the project I was still concerned with establishing connections between American and European research approaches. In the spirit of the present volume some of these early efforts to merge the research traditions may be worth recording.

1. Soon after the Princeton project began, I arranged a dinner meeting with several psychoanalysts to obtain from them ideas on what we should pay attention to in our program. The meeting was held on December 16, 1937, and, according to a somewhat defective record, at least the following people participated: Karen Horney, Harry Stack Sullivan, John Dollard, and Erich Fromm. Along with the invitation, I distributed a two-page, single-spaced list of questions I wanted to raise. Among these were the following: can Freudian theory elucidate the entertainment value of radio and account for some especially successful programs? Can the method of free association be used in our study of radio listening? In developing types of radio listeners, will we have to go back to early childhood experiences? Would a psychoanalytic developmental theory clarify the role of radio at different ages? The list of questions ended with the following paragraph:

I am sure that in many of the cases you treated, radio was somewhat connected with the troubles of your patients. It would be very helpful for us if you could try to remember examples of this kind and tell about them in our meeting. We feel that you might have observed situations and incidents which are quite beyond the reach of our usual experimental methods.

I had a preliminary session with Fromm, at which I gave him the necessary information for the initial statement he made at the meeting; a six-page summary of his statement has survived.

I had no special involvement with psychoanalysis. The episode was part of a general concern with combining humanistic and quantitative approaches. Since that time, the convergence of social research with psychoanalytical case studies has become more familiar. In 1937, however, our enterprise was probably quite novel. It would be necessary to study the minutes in more detail to decide whether the meeting really led to interesting ideas.

2. An historical orientation was another concern of this kind. When I submitted my first progress report to the Rockefeller Foundation in 1939 I pointed out that efforts to assess the effects of radio on American society fifteen years after this new medium had appeared seemed a rather hazardous enterprise. To stress the point I suggested the parallel of a professor who, in 1500, might have been asked to assess the effect of printing on medieval society. After much careful empirical study, he might have argued cogently that printing had not had much effect:

For one, printing would be so expensive that it could not compete with the copying done by monks in a monastery. Furthermore, hardly anyone knew how to read, so what is the advantage of being able to provide larger numbers of copies? Then, too, religion was the only problem which really mattered in 1500, but the question of religion is for the pulpit, or for the private thought of individuals; it is not a topic which can be conveyed in print. And so for all these reasons, it is quite clear that printing will not have any effect on society, and that settles the matter in 1500.

For many years I used to lecture on mass media of communication in modern society. One of these talks is preserved because it finally became a Borah Foundation lecture, presented in Moscow, Idaho, in 1954; it has a rather extensive section on "historical retrospect." There was one idea which I used to reiterate,[62]

62. As director of the Bureau as well as in my teaching, I kept developing and sharpen-

At the time of the American Revolution, there was a very simple two-sided relationship. On the one side were the citizens; on the other was the government. Anyone who had political theories or an interest in political activities was either an actual or potential publisher, so that the publisher shared common interests with other citizens. The citizen and the publisher together fought for their freedom to criticize the government. In the last century, however, the situation has become vastly more complicated. The simple two-sided relationship has been superseded by a complex three-cornered structure. The citizens still represent one corner, the government still represents another, but now there is also the communications industry. This leads to complicated and sometimes surprising alliances. *Occasionally the citizen forms an alliance with the industry against the government; occasionally with the government against the industry; occasionally he finds himself faced with an alliance between the government and industry.* Many questions about the mass media can be answered if this development from a two-sided to a three-cornered relationship is kept in mind; confusion results if the historical trend is lost from sight.[63] [Italics provided now.]

The idea of latent strategy is again pertinent. This type of historical analysis seemed to me helpful for the policy problems discussed above (Section VII). By stressing that controversial topics are eternal but at the same time variable in their implications, I could keep the Bureau maneuvering between the intellectual and political purist and an industry from which I wanted cooperation without having to "sell out."

At the same time my historical interest was quite genuine and remained a characteristic feature of my activities. While the debate about mass culture was particularly acute, I sponsored Leo Lowenthal's work on the history of criticism of the mass media.[64] A few years later, when I was president of the American Association of Public Opinion Research, my address dealt with "The Historian and the Pollster," a theme which has remained a topic of discussion.[65] And from time to time I have pub-

---

ing such formulae over many years; I quote them from accessible publications even though their dates in certain cases lag behind the period in which they originated and in which I place them in this essay.

63. Paul F. Lazarsfeld, "Mass Media of Communication in Modern Society," *Borah Foundation Lectures 1954* (Moscow, Idaho, 1954).

64. Leo Lowenthal, "An Historical Preface to the Popular Culture Debate," in Norman Jacobs, ed., *Culture for the Millions* (Princeton, N.J., 1959). The book is the report of a symposium organized jointly by the Academy of Arts and Sciences and the Tamiment Institute. I was chairman of the sessions and in the introduction to the book I tried again to stress the constructive role of criticism.

65. "The Obligations of the 1950 Pollsters to the 1984 Historians," *Public Opinion*

lished essays on such topics as the history of quantification, of concept formation, and of the empirical study of action.[66]

3. Still another convergence with the humanities was in the field of music; this deserves more detailed discussion. I had always been interested in music, and when I became director of the Princeton project I immediately set up a special music division. The first two studies set the stage for the general program. To begin with, we started an institutional study of the popular music industry which, until then, had received little serious attention. At the same time, we initiated a survey to trace the effect of the New York City transmitter, WNYC, one of the first radio stations to broadcast large amounts of classical music. This was prior to the popularity of records, and interest in serious music was still quite rare; we wanted to know whether WNYC contributed to diffusion of such interests.[67]

But I had more general plans for this division. I had known about the work of T. W. Adorno on the sociology of music. He is now a major figure in German sociology, and represents one side in a continuing debate between two positions, often distinguished as critical and positivistic sociology.[68] I was aware of these controversial features of Adorno's work, but was intrigued by his writings on the "contradictory" role of music in our society.[69] I considered it a challenge to see whether I could induce Adorno to try to link his ideas with empirical research. In addi-

Quarterly, 14 (1950), 618–663. For an up-to-date review see Lee Benson, "An Approach to the Scientific Study of Past Public Opinion," *Public Opinion Quarterly*, 31 (1967), 522–568.

66. "Concepts, Theory and Explanation in the Behavioral Sciences," Gordon J. DiRenzo, ed., *Concept Formation and Measurement in the Behavioral Sciences* (New York, 1966).

67. Edward Suchman, "Invitation to Music," and Duncan MacDougald, Jr., "The Popular Music Industry," in Paul F. Lazarsfeld and Frank Stanton, eds., *Radio Research 1941* (New York, 1941).

68. The first formula of which I am aware stems from Max Horkheimer. It can be found in volume 6 (1937) of the *Zeitschrift für Sozialforschung*: "Traditional and Critical Theory," pp. 245–295, and "Philosophy and Critical Theory," pp. 625–631. Contemporary presentations of the two positions can be found in the following two papers: Hans Albert, "Der Mythos der totalen Vernunft. Dialektische Ansprüche im Lichte undialektischen Kritik," *Kölner Zeitschrift*, 16, h.2 (1964), 225–256; Jürgen Habermas, "Gegen einen positivistischen halbierten Rationalismus," *Kölner Zeitschrift*, 16, h.4 (1964), 635–659.

69. "Zur Gesellschaftlichen Lage der Musik," *Zeitschrift für Sozialforschung*, 1 (1932), 103 ff., 356 ff.

tion, I felt gratitude to the Frankfurt group led by Max Horkheimer, of which he was a member; they had helped support the work of the Newark Center, and I knew they wanted Adorno in this country. I therefore invited him to become part-time director of the music division of our project. To provide an expert on empirical data I appointed at the same time a former student of Stanton's, Gerhard Wiebe, who was a fine jazz musician, with a Ph.D. in psychology. Together, he and Adorno, I hoped, would develop a convergence of European theory and American empiricism.

The actual course of events was quite different from these expectations. Cooperation between the two men became difficult, and Adorno came to symbolize a more general problem. In a number of memos written in the spring of 1938 to my associate directors I explained the brilliance and importance of Adorno's ideas. This seemed to me necessary since his interviews with people in the radio industry had led to complaints of biased questions and distorted replies. This was the result, I explained, of misunderstandings common in encounters of this sort. To straighten out the situation, I asked Adorno to summarize his ideas in a memorandum which I planned to circulate among various experts to secure a broader basis of support for his work. In June 1938 he delivered a memorandum of 160 single-spaced pages, entitled "Music in Radio." But it seemed to me that the distribution of this text would only have made the situation more difficult, for in English his writing had the same tantalizing attraction and elusiveness that it had in German. The notion of "fetish" played—as could be expected from a neo-Marxist—a central role. He proposed to use it

wherever any human activity or any product of that activity becomes alienated from men so that they can no longer, so to speak, recognize themselves in it. Then they venerate it as something whose value is utterly divorced from the human activity which comprises it and from the function which it actually exercises upon other human activities. In any case (for instance, in the case of stars who have become fetishes) this is very close to the concept of suggestion by which people venerate something without quite knowing why . . . and without being immediately related to it. The scope of fetishes is larger, however, than that of suggestion and propaganda. In present day society, people are ready to throw the effects upon commodities because the commodity value is the fundamental value they acknowledge, even in cases where that value is not impressed upon them by any special propaganda for suggestion.

Critical theory scorns the use of definitions; but certainly Adorno was able to give vivid examples which helped to convey what he had in mind, as can be seen from another paragraph:

But the musical fetish-making goes far beyond the limits of the so-called "stars" which, on the surface, seem to be responsible for the features mentioned here. The fetish actually takes possession of practically every musical category in radio. Music in radio is thought of in terms of private property. As an illustration let us cite the cult of famous musical instruments, either Stradivarius violins (even though the average listener is definitely unable to make any distinction between a Strad and another ordinary good violin); or the piano once played by famous people like Chopin or Richard Wagner; or, last but not least, certain elements of the composition which are over-emphasized by radio technique and which, at the same time, seem to represent music as a commodity.

From the project's point of view the main problem was to see whether the phenomenon of fetishism could be described by a direct approach to a sample of listeners. (The same issue exists when Durkheim's structural notion of anomie is to be paralleled by the distribution of an individual characteristic now often called anomia.) Adorno and I agreed that he would establish a more discriminating typology; then a questionnaire might lead to a quantitative distribution of different types of music listeners. But no indicators for such a typology were developed because the direction he gave could hardly be translated into empirical terms. Thus, for instance, one of the types was described as follows:

Sometimes music has the effect of freeing hidden sexual desires. This seems to be the case particularly with women who regard music as a sort of image of their male partner, to which they yield without ever identifying themselves with the music. It is this sort of attitude which is indicated by weeping. The amateur's weeping when he listens to music (the musician will practically never weep) is one of the foremost tasks of the analysis of the emotional side of music.

I wrote Adorno a detailed criticism of his memorandum, and we finally agreed that he would write a much briefer document which could then be discussed at a meeting with several experts. This meeting took place sometime during the winter of 1938/39, but it was not profitable. John Marshall was present and probably felt that my efforts to bring Adorno's type of critical research into the communications field were a failure. The renewal of the Rockefeller grant in the fall of 1939 provided no budget for continuation of the music project.

I never regretted having invited Adorno to join the project. Soon after he left, the Horkheimer group devoted an issue of their journal to the problem of modern mass communication, and to this I contributed an essay in which I tried to explain the "critical approach" sympathetically to an American audience, and illustrated ways in which this basic position can lead to new research ideas.[70] I even tried to spell out "the operations into which critical communications research could be broken down." I used comparisons to highlight the main idea: the consumer movements fight misleading advertising and some economists deplore its wastefulness; but the critical approach thinks that any kind of promotion prevents people from developing their own standards of judgement. I ended the paper with the following sentences:

[The] Office of Radio Research has cooperated in this issue because it was felt that only a very catholic conception of the task of research can lead to valuable results. . . . The writer, whose interests and occupational duties are in the field of administrative research, wanted to express his conviction that there is here a type of approach which, if it were included in the general stream of communications research, could contribute much in terms of challenging problems and new concepts useful in the interpretation of known, and in the search for new data.

The defeat of this hope in the Princeton project has left a troublesome question in my mind. After the war Adorno was an active member of the Berkeley group that produced *The Authoritarian Personality*. Their basic concept of the fascistic character was developed by Adorno and was certainly no less speculative than what he wrote for us; nevertheless, his colleagues in California were able to convert his idea into the famous F-scale. I have an uneasy feeling that my duties in the various divisions of the Princeton project may have prevented me from devoting the necessary time and attention to achieve the purpose for which I engaged Adorno originally. As it was, the only product we were able to publish was a paper of his on the radio symphony; he himself later published an abbreviated version of the memorandum mentioned above.[71]

I take some comfort from the fact that not all contacts with German

70. "Administrative and Critical Communications Research," *Studies in Philosophy and Social Science*, 9 (1941), 2–16.
71. T. W. Adorno, "The Radio Symphony," in Lazarsfeld and Stanton, eds., *Radio Research 1941*: "On Popular Music," *Studies in Philosophy and Social Science*, 9 (1941), 17 ff.

experts on esthetic matters misfired. Rudolf Arnheim had written sensitive essays on movies as a form of art. I commissioned him to analyze the scripts of about fifty daytime serials, which he did brilliantly. One of his observations has often been quoted since: the so-called soap operas, which consisted of continuing stories in which families found themselves in trouble which they succeeded in resolving only to encounter new troubles, were broadcast during the day and were listened to mainly by housewives. Arnheim noticed, and developed the implications of the fact, that the troubles were always caused by men and the solutions provided by women. I remember the collaboration with him as enlightening for me and useful for the project.[72]

When the office moved to Columbia and my permanent appointment there became conceivable, the university became my main reference group and the concern with culture contacts began to weaken. It is quite likely that in many other respects the American component in my marginal position became increasingly stronger. But obviously my concern with the relation between the two social science traditions never subsided. In 1958 I was the rapporteur on methodology for the Stresa Convention of the International Sociological Association. The main theme of my report was how to avoid misunderstandings between European and American sociologists.

IX. From Princeton to Columbia

IN several respects the second academic year of the Princeton Office of Radio Research (1938/1939) was similar to the first, but a certain amount of consolidation became visible. The papers of this period were published in a second issue of the *Journal of Applied Psychology*, entitled "Progress in Radio Research."[73] In the introduction I wrote as guest editor, I stated:

72. Rudolf Arnheim, "The World of the Daytime Serial," in Paul F. Lazarsfeld and Frank Stanton, eds., *Radio Research 1942–43* (New York, 1944).

73. This issue appeared only in December 1940 because the regular editor did not want the two radio issues to be published too close together; the papers themselves, however, stem mostly from the Union Square period of the project.

At least three major trends in radio research have become noticeable. Studies on the effect of radio are moving into the foreground; material collected for commercial purposes is ever more frequently available for scientific analysis; and related areas such as reading research are developing so fast that the discipline of general communications research seems in the making.

The reference to the study of printed mass media deserves some comment. Circulation figures of magazines seem small compared to the size of radio audiences, but each copy of a magazine is read by several people; such readership figures are comparable to the audience rating. From our point of view, this opened a new area of secondary analysis: studying the structure of magazine "audiences" and drawing conclusions from a comparison with the distribution of radio listeners.[74]

Two activities moved into the foreground. One was what later became known as the Lazarsfeld-Stanton Program Analyzer. I had always been interested in popular music, and while still in Vienna devised a technique by which one could relate the musical structure of a song to the emotional reactions of listeners. Now at the Princeton project I was able to extend the idea to all kinds of radio programs and finally to films. Stanton greatly improved the technical aspects of the device. We published a number of technical studies of this program analyzer[75] but it was too expensive a procedure to use ourselves. It was doubtful that we could patent it, but two commercial groups, CBS and the McCann-Erikson advertising company, paid us a fee for the right to use the device in their own research departments. Since then program analyzers have found a variety of commercial applications. I hope that one day the whole idea will become again an object of academic inquiry.

While the critical importance of the program analyzer faded after a time, panel studies became increasingly central in our activities. In going over the early files of the Princeton project, I was surprised to see how soon after our start we began to experiment with repeated interviews to

74. I was a member of the magazine audience research program. It was ably guided by Neal DuBois, then research director of *Life*. Most of the major magazines were represented in the group. A summary of the many audience studies done at the time can be found in my paper, "Communications Research and the Social Psychologist," in Wayne Dennis, ed., *Current Trends in Social Psychology* (Pittsburgh, 1948).

75. See, for example, Tore Hollonquist and Edward Suchman, "Listening to the Listener," and Adolf Sturmthal and Alberta Curtis, "Program Analyzer Tests of Two Educational Films," both in Lazarsfeld and Stanton, eds., *Radio Research 1942-43*.

study the effect of radio. Though I can find now no full reports on the subject,[76] there are memoranda to the staff and to the associate directors from 1938 indicating that we spent much of our project money on small pilot studies tracing the effect of various local campaigns in New Jersey.

Administratively, the main innovation in the later part of the Princeton period was a series of Rockefeller fellowships which John Marshall established for graduate students who wanted to specialize in communications research; we integrated the work of these fellows into our general program, and I was charged with supervising their work. The policy was to assign them to concrete media activities, such as a public affairs program emanating from the University of Chicago or a radio station serving a largely rural population and managed by the State University of Iowa. A number of these specialized studies were published by the Federal Educational Radio Commission. It might be worthwhile to trace the origin and demise of that commission as part of the history of early efforts in educational radio and television.

Toward the spring of 1939, the problem of renewal of the Rockefeller grant became urgent. John Marshall, who had followed our work closely, was in favor of it. He appointed a review committee that included Charles Siepmann, Harold Lasswell, Robert Lynd, and Lyman Bryson. They gave a favorable verdict,[77] but for people less directly informed about details, the lack of a central theme after two years seems to have made a poor impression. During a trip to Iowa I received a wire from John Marshall that the foundation officers required more solid evidence of achievement before they would approve our application.

The problem for us was to review the available material and to select a theme around which a good part of it could be organized. For a variety of reasons, a comparison between radio and printed media seemed the most promising choice. This is how *Radio and the Printed Page* (1940), was born, a book that appears to have played a considerable role in consolidating the field of communications research. It was a gruelling task to assemble the manuscript in a short period of time; we worked day

76. The only exception is a staff paper (1939) by Hazel Gaudet which was later included in *The Language of Social Research*.

77. I find in the files a number of memoranda in which I suggested to the associate directors the proper strategy that should be followed and the roles they should play—a fine illustration of the typical behavior of the "worrying director."

and night literally, in relays, to accomplish it. I mobilized all conceivable resources, and I remember with special gratitude the help of Lloyd Free who volunteered to see us through this crisis. We had data from a Gallup poll on preferences for news reports, but they were not properly analyzed, and I therefore induced Samuel Stouffer to come to New York to supervise this part of the work. On his own initiative he added a clever analysis of newspaper circulation figures to trace the probable effect of radio; the two sections he contributed to the book are now properly included in his collected papers.[78]

We submitted the report on the morning of the deadline, which, if I remember correctly, was July 1, 1939. John Marshall was satisfied and considered it as an appropriate basis on which to propose continuation of our project officially to the Foundation.[79]

Meanwhile, internal difficulties had developed between Cantril and me. During the negotiations with the Rockefeller Foundation for a renewal of the grant, it became clear that an administrative decision had to be made. Either the project would stay at Princeton with Cantril as the main figure but with a new director, or, if I were to remain, the project would have to look for another institutional base. The Foundation naturally turned to Stanton as a third insider to arbitrate the situation; from the outcome I gather that Stanton put his weight on my side. Lynd prevailed on President Dodds of Princeton to release the project. In the fall of 1939, the Office of Radio Research was turned over to Columbia University, and at the same time I was appointed a lecturer there.[80] The Foundation gave us a temporary grant to prepare a proposal for a three-year continuation to begin March 1940.

The crucial part of the proposal we then wrote—from the point of view of further developments—was the following passage:

It is proposed, by utilizing the panel technique developed in the first two years of the project, to locate those individuals who do change their habits in response to a con-

78. *Social Research to Test Ideas* (New York, 1962).

79. The question of publication was troublesome because at the time the market that is now provided by the numerous courses on communications research did not exist. Robert Lynd devised the successful strategy: a friend of his wrote a story for the *Readers' Digest* taken from the manuscript. On the basis of this, Duell, Sloan and Pearce published the book. Since then there have been no difficulties in finding outlets for our studies.

80. A year later I was made a permanent member of the Department of Sociology. This made finally effective my classificatory change from psychologist to sociologist.

tinuous sequence of broadcasts; and then to study in detail the circumstances surrounding the listening and subsequent changes in these individuals. The plan involves the selection of two basically comparable but contrasting panels of some 200 persons each, and the interviewing of them six or eight times at intervals throughout the course of a continuous program sequence to which they listen.

I originally proposed that we carry out our test on "a program of the Department of Agriculture, since its innovations made major changes in American behavior and, it so happens, this Department has developed the most extensive use of the radio in support of its policies." I do not remember how this proposal was altered so that the November 1940 election became the focus of the first panel study. But such a change was carried out, and the result was *The People's Choice*.[81] The third edition of the book (1968) contains an extensive introduction that traces the impact of this first elaborate election study on subsequent political analysis both here and abroad.[82]

As far as work and administration were concerned, the move to Columbia made very little difference. We were located in a condemned building, the former site of the medical school on 59th Street and Amsterdam Avenue—a neighborhood then called "Hell's kitchen." (It is now part of the Lincoln Center area.) The financial core was the Rockefeller grant which had been renewed for three years. It was supplemented by a large number of commercial contracts. Often the fees were paid in checks made out to me personally, which were then redistributed as staff salaries. I was still rather uninformed about Internal Revenue regulations and in retrospect consider myself lucky not to have gotten into trouble handling funds in this way. The office had a supervisory board consisting of four Columbia professors and Frank Stanton. Somewhere along the line the organization acquired its present name, the Bureau of Applied Social Research.[83]

At about this time the United States prepared for and finally entered

81. Paul F. Lazarsfeld, Bernard Berelson, and Hazel Gaudet, *The People's Choice* (New York, 1944; 2nd and 3rd eds., New York, 1948 and 1968).

82. We did not have enough funds for a panel of six hundred respondents, and therefore solicited additional contributions. The most important one came from *Life* magazine through the intervention of Elmo Roper. Immediately after the 1940 election, *Life* published two feature stories based on our first tabulations.

83. The Bureau dates its origin properly to the beginning of the radio project, and celebrated its twentieth anniversary in 1957.

the war. In our little world this had two consequences. Stouffer had become research director for the United States Army and used the Bureau and its personnel for a variety of services. The fees provided by these assignments were turned over to the Bureau and were an important financial help. (We had a similar arrangement with the Office of War Information.) Robert Merton worked for a short while with Stouffer in Washington but returned to New York and channeled his work through the Bureau. He has remained an associate director and has played a crucial role in its subsequent development.[84] In our wartime work we concentrated on the testing of films and radio programs devised to maintain the morale of various sectors of the civilian and military populations. The main record of this effort is reported in the third volume of *The American Soldier*, which records, among a great many other things, the contribution to the war effort of the program analyzer, thinly disguised, on the advice of the editor of the volume, Carl Hovland, as the polygraph.[85]

By 1944 the need for a firmer organization became obvious. Columbia had a Council for Research in the Social Sciences, and for two years we received from them a subsidy of $5,000; they probably also assumed some financial supervision. My memory of the administrative details of this transitional period is as hazy as were the actual arrangements. Finally the Columbia Council, which up until then just dispensed small grants for faculty projects, commissioned its chairman, the economist Frederick Mills, to study the research efforts of the various departments in the Faculty of Political Science. A questionnaire was sent out; apparently only the Department of Sociology reported any form of organized activities. So Mills recommended to the Council in August 1944:

that a special committee of the Council be created to supervise the Office of Applied

84. The origin of this collaboration is vividly and correctly reported in a *New Yorker* profile on Merton by M. M. Hunt (January 28, 1961). My collaboration with Merton in the Columbia Department of Sociology transcends the frame of this essay.

85. Publications resulting from this work include: Paul F. Lazarsfeld and Robert K. Merton, "Studies in Radio and Film Propaganda," *Transactions of the New York Academy of Sciences*, 6 (1943), 58–79; Paul F. Lazarsfeld and Patricia L. Kendall, "The Listener Talks Back," in *Radio and Health Education* (New York, 1945), 48–65; Robert K. Merton and Patricia L. Kendall, "The Focussed Interview," *American Journal of Sociology*, 51 (1946), 541–557.

Social Research and other agencies of the same sort that may operate under the auspices of the Council. This supervising committee should give particular attention during the present academic year to an evaluation of the work of the Office of Applied Social Research, and to means by which the work of this office might be more effectively related to other Columbia research activities.

The committee thus appointed was clearly aware that something new was taking place; but its positive recommendations were more in the nature of acquiescence than of leadership. In October 1944 it made a number of recommendations of which the following two were most pertinent to the Bureau's existence:

Emphasis will be on research and training for research. Conducting work under contracts with commercial or other organizations will not be considered inconsistent with this condition provided the research emphasis be maintained.

Accounts of research agencies operating under the supervision of the Committee on the Administration of Social Research Agencies should be established and administered by the Bursar, under the general provisions proposed by the Committee on Patents and the Committee on Industrial Research.

The great innovation was the decision that contract work would be permitted. Today, when 50 percent of Columbia's operating budget comes from contracts, this does not seem like a major revolution, but it marks, I believe, a real turning point in the history of American universities. Even so, the committee missed the main point we were trying to make. We did not—using a saying by Anatole France—look for freedom to sleep under the bridges of the Seine; we wanted Columbia to accept the positive duty of integrating into its general instructional program training in empirical social research.[86] We protested the committee's failure to respond to this possibility, and, as a result, the Coun-

86. During the period of the Princeton project the staff consisted of employees without academic connections. The problems were simple: they wanted higher salaries and I wanted to spend more money on research. When the office moved to Columbia a shift slowly came about. Increasingly the staff was recruited from graduates of the Sociology Department for whom status in the academic community was important. Obviously the committee had been informed about this aspect of the Bureau-Department relation. Its report stated that it would be necessary to "frame regulations relating to the appointment of staff members of research agencies and to the responsibilities of the university toward such employees." The matter was not followed up for at least three reasons. The administration was mainly concerned with the contract problem; I fought mainly for recognition and financing by the university; the staff probably was not too insistent because they were a new breed and very much in demand by all major universities. For today's staff, problems of status and tenure are an issue of top priority.

cil appointed a special committee to decide on the role of the Bureau within the structure of the university. The chairman of this crucial committee was Elliot Cheatham, Professor of Legal Ethics in the School of Law;[87] one of its members was Arthur MacMahon. The group met frequently between December 1944 and May 1945, and finally recommended the status which the Bureau has today, "a research unit of the Graduate Faculty of Political Science of Columbia University," with space on the campus and about ten percent of its operating budget provided by the university. A large amount of correspondence and memoranda resulting from the work of the Cheatham Committee has fortunately been preserved, and I hope one day to analyze these documents in detail. I note, in reviewing the files quickly, a detailed fifteen-page memorandum written to Cheatham on his request that describes the operation of a social research center in terms that are quite literally applicable to the Bureau as it is today and to the whole range of similar institutions that sprang up since then throughout the country. An initial letter of mine to Cheatham telescopes all the issues we faced at the time:

It has almost become a commonplace that sociology is, at this moment, in a difficult stage of transition. The student in the field realizes that empirical research has become an integral part of sociology, but the universities have not yet developed budgetary and personnel provisions for such work. What one might call an institutional lag between the needs of the discipline and the administrative institution appears in practically all universities. The administrative problems with which your Committee is concerned at this moment can best be understood as deriving from the anomaly of having a division of the University which is essentially self-supporting.

I then conjured up a different way in which this problem could have been solved:

I could have spent all my energies in promoting the idea that the University administration should provide the necessary minimum budget of $25,000 to establish such a social research laboratory. Had I succeeded, this laboratory would have been set up as an integral part of the University from the outset, and its work would have proceeded in familiar, academic form.

I did not believe then, nor do I believe today, that there was the slightest chance that this would come about. As if I had known that one day I would write the present memoir I put on record my strategy and my confidence in it:

But because I was too impatient, or too pessimistic, or too sharply aware of how new institutions develop, I took a different course. The present Bureau was built up around an original Rockefeller grant, without budgetary assistance from the University. Service jobs for commercial and governmental agencies were the main sources of income. Practically all of these studies had scientifically valuable aspects, but only surplus time and money could be devoted to completely scientific purposes. Nevertheless, the Bureau now exists as a social science laboratory and is at the full disposal of the Department.

I then played my final gambit. Can a modern university really do without something like our Bureau? If not, could I take a chance on something very close to blackmail? I tried, along the following line:

Perhaps the unorthodox operation of the Bureau creates problems which outweigh its advantages. It seems to me perfectly legitimate to consider whether it might not be better to close it and wait until the time is ripe for it to be resumed on the basis of full support by the University. If, on the other hand, one agrees that new institutions are often created first and then legalized, the work of your Committee might be looked at as part of this process.

This letter was written in January 1945. Twenty-three years later I find myself chairman of a board of sixteen distinguished representatives of professional schools and graduate departments at Columbia—a board which the Cheatham Committee, when it legitimized the Bureau, set up to keep close watch on its risky director. It would be nice if this symbolized the final victory of an idea born in Vienna almost half a century ago. But it does not. Today scores of such bureaus exist throughout the country, many of them directed by alumni of the Columbia prototype, but they are not yet really integrated into the university structure. The effort continues. This year I induced the Columbia administration to appoint a new committee to see how the position of our Bureau could be improved. To bring them up to date I distributed to the members of this body copies of the letter from which I just quoted.

APPENDIX

THE SOCIAL RESEARCH INSTITUTE IN THE AMERICAN UNIVERSITY*

You are all aware of the controversies which have grown up around these institutes. On the positive side, we may note the following. They provide technical training to graduate students who are empirically inclined; the projects give students opportunities for closer contact with senior sociologists; the data collected for practical purposes furnish material for dissertations through more detailed study, or what is sometimes called secondary analysis; the members of a Department with an effective institute can give substance to their lectures with an enviable array of actual data; skills of intellectual cooperation and division of labor are developed; chances for early publications by younger sociologists are enhanced.

On the other side of the debate, the argument goes about as follows. Students who receive most of their training on organized projects become one-sided; instead of developing interests of their own, they become mercenaries of their employers; where institutes become influential, important sociological problems are neglected because they do not lend themselves to study by the "research machinery"; people who work best on their own find themselves without support and are regarded as outsiders.

The situation, as I see it, is promising but confused. We allow these institutes to develop without giving them permanent support, without integrating them into the general university structure, without even really knowing what is going on outside our immediate academic environment. As a bare minimum it is imperative that a more detailed study of the current situation be carried out. This would hopefully lead to recommendations for university administrators, for members of our own Association, and for all others concerned with the basic problem of how the avalanche of empirical social research can be fitted into current educational activities without having careless institutional improvisations destroy important traditional values or hinder creative new developments. True, we have no perfect formula for incorporating institutes into our graduate education. But pluralism is not the same as anarchy, and it is anarchy with which we are faced at the moment. Some form of permanent core support, assimilation of teaching and of institute positions, a better planned division of the students' time between lectures and project research, a closer supervision of institute activities by educational officers, more explicit infusion of social theory into the work of the institutes— all this waits for a systematic discussion and for a document which may per-

* Reprinted with permission from *American Sociological Review*, 27 (1962), 763–765.

form the service which the Flexner report rendered to medical education fifty years ago.

In such a report the role of the institute director will have to figure prominently. Let me place him in a broader framework. We are confronted nowadays, in our universities, with a serious problem which can be classified as an "academic power vacuum." When graduate education in this country began, no one doubted that the university president was an important figure. Gilman at Johns Hopkins and White at Cornell were intellectual as well as administrative leaders. Stanley Hall at Clark was impressive both as a president and as a psychologist. Inversely, individual professors were deeply involved in organizational innovation. John W. Burgess forced the creation of a graduate faculty upon the Columbia trustees. In his autobiography he describes movingly what this meant to him as a teacher and scholar. Silliman sacrificed his private fortune to establish a physical laboratory in his home and finally convinced the trustees at Yale that natural sciences were not a spiritual threat to young Americans.

Today, however, we witness a dangerous divergence: academic freedom is more and more interpreted in such a way as to keep the administration out of any truly academic affairs; and the faculty, in turn, has come to consider administration beneath its dignity. But educational innovations are, by definition, intellectual as well as administrative tasks. And, so, they have fallen into a no-man's land: the President and his staff wait for the faculty to take the initiative; the professors on their side consider that such matters would take time away from their true scholarly pursuits. As a result, many of our universities have a dangerously low level of institutional development.

One institutional consequence of research institutes is that they inevitably train men who are able and willing to combine intellectual and administrative leadership. An institute director, even if his unit only facilitates faculty research, must train a staff able to advise on important research functions. It is not impossible that, on specific topics, the collective experience of the institute staff exceeds the skills of the individual faculty member. One who has lived with scores of questionnaires can help write a better questionnaire on a subject matter in which he is not expert. Having helped to dig up documents and sources of data on many subjects makes for greater efficiency even on a topic not previously treated. In an autonomous unit this is even more pronounced. Here the staff carries out a self-contained work schedule. A hierarchy is needed, proceeding often from assistants to project supervisors, to program director, and, finally, to the director himself. The latter is at least responsible for reports and publications. But the director is also concerned with maintaining what is sometimes called the "image" of his operation. Its prestige, its attraction for staff and students, and its appeal for support are self-generated, not derived only from the reputation of the teaching departments. The professional staff sees its future career closely bound up with the destiny of the unit, a fact which sometimes makes for challenging problems in human organization.

At the same time, the director must develop the coordinating skills so necessary in a modern university. Often the place of his unit in the organization chart is not well defined. The novelty of the whole idea makes for instability and requires considerable institutional creativity. And, finally, we should frankly face the fact that in our system of higher education the matching of budgetry funds with substantive intellectual interests is a characteristic and enduring problem. The institute director knows the skills and interests of the faculty members, and he brings men and money together. This is not badly described as the role of "idea broker." Often he will have to work hard to obtain funds for a more unusual research idea suggested to him; at other times a possible grant looks so attractive that he will try to discover, among some of his faculty colleagues, what he would diplomatically call a "latent interest."

I am afraid this is not the appropriate forum for reforming university presidents. But I can at least try to convince some of you that directing a research institute is no more in conflict with scholarly work than is teaching. The director is faced with a variety of research problems which permit him to try out his intellectual taste and skills, while the individual scholar might find himself committed to a study prematurely chosen. The multitude of data passing through the director's hands considerably broadens his experience. Staff conferences provide a unique sounding board for new ideas. Even negotiations for grants open vistas into other worlds which a sociologist can turn to great advantage in his own work. Undoubtedly not every personality type is suited for this role, and even the right type of man needs proper training. But the opportunities for self-expression and for intellectual growth are considerable, and sociologists, in particular, should not be misled by the prevalent stereotype of administration.

SCIENTIFIC EXPERIENCES OF A EUROPEAN SCHOLAR IN AMERICA

by THEODOR W. ADORNO

translated by Donald Fleming

COMPLIMENTARY and friendly as the invitation was to write something about my contribution to American science and American intellectual life, I have asked to modify the subject somewhat. For it is not for me to say anything about that contribution, if any—only Americans could do that. Nor would I really be capable of it right now, for I have not been in America for fourteen years and have no proper perspective. Instead, I ask for the freedom to attempt something that I may be able to do—to formulate something about the scholarly, and more generally intellectual, experiences that I had in and of America. From this perhaps something can be indirectly deduced concerning the direction of my aims in the long years when I was working first in New York, then in Los Angeles. Perhaps I shall not be too great a burden upon the American public by such an attempt; for I represent an extreme case, which, because it is extreme, sheds a little light on something seldom expounded. I consider myself European through and through, considered myself as such from the first to the last day abroad, and never denied it. Not only was it natural for me to preserve the intellectual continuity of my personal life, but I quickly became fully aware of it in America. I still remember the shock that a housemaid, an emigrant like ourselves, gave me during our first days in New York when she, the daughter of a so-called good home, explained: "People in my town used to go to the symphony, now they go to Radio City." In no way did I want to be like her. Even if I had wanted to, I wouldn't have been capable of it. By nature and personal history, I was unsuited for "adjustment" in intellectual matters. Fully as I recognize that intellectual individuality can only develop through processes of adjustment and socialization, I still consider it the obligation and

338

at the same time the proof of mature individuality to transcend mere adjustment. Through the mechanisms of identification with images of authority, one must emancipate one's self from this very identification. This relationship between autonomy and adjustment was recognized by Freud long ago and has since become familiar to American scholarship. But for a refugee going to America thirty years ago, this was not yet true. "Adjustment" was still a magic word, particularly for those who came from Europe as persecuted people, of whom it was expected that they would prove themselves in the new land not to be so haughty as to insist stubbornly on remaining what they had been before.

The direction prescribed for my development up to the age of thirty-four was thoroughly speculative in the ordinary pre-philosophical sense of the word, though in my case inseparable from philosophical endeavors. I considered it to be my fitting and objectively proffered assignment to *interpret* phenomena—not to ascertain, sift, and classify facts and make them available as information. That corresponded not only to my idea of philosophy but also of sociology. To the present day I have never rigorously separated the two disciplines, although I well know that the necessity for specialization in one or the other cannot be annulled by a mere act of the will. The article "Zur gesellschaftlichen Lage der Musik," which I published as a privatdozent at Frankfurt in the *Zeitschrift für Sozialforschung* in 1932 and which was related to all my later researches in the sociology of music, was already thoroughly theoretical in orientation. It was founded on the conception of an inherently contradictory totality, whose contradictions also "appear" in art and by which art is to be interpreted. A type of sociology, for which such a mode of thought could at best supply hypotheses but never knowledge, was utterly alien to me. On the other hand, I hope at any rate that I went to America completely free from nationalism and cultural arrogance: I was much too much aware of the dubiousness of the traditional (particularly German) conception of culture in the sense of *Geistesgeschichte*. The spirit of enlightenment also in relation to cultural problems, in the American intellectual climate a matter of course, had the greatest attraction for me. Moreover, I was full of gratitude for deliverance from the catastrophe that was looming up as early as 1937; as determined to do my part, on the one hand, as I was not to give up my own individuality. The tension between these two impulses may in some degree define how I related to my American experience.

In the fall of 1937 I received a telegram from my friend Max Horkheimer, since pre-Hitler days director of the Institut für Sozialforschung at the University of Frankfurt, which was now being continued in connection with Columbia University in New York. There was a possibility for my speedy emigration to America if I were prepared to collaborate on a "radio project." After a brief deliberation, I agreed by telegraph. The truth was that I didn't know what a "radio project" was; the American use of the word "project," which is now translated in German by *Forschungsvorhaben*, was unknown to me. I simply thought that my friend would not have made the proposal unless he was persuaded that I, a philosopher by calling, could handle the job. I was only slightly prepared for it. In three years in Oxford, I had learned English autodidactically but fairly well. Then in June 1937, on the invitation of Horkheimer, I had been in New York for a couple of weeks and gained at least an initial impression. In the *Zeitschrift für Sozialforschung* in 1936 I had published a sociological interpretation of jazz, which to be sure suffered severely from a lack of specific American background but at any rate dealt with a theme that could pass as characteristically American. It was likely that I could quickly and intensively gain a certain knowledge of American life, particularly musical conditions; that presented few difficulties.

The theoretical core of the article about jazz was fundamentally related to later socio-psychological investigations that I undertook. Much later I found that many of my theories were confirmed by American experts such as Winthrop Sargeant. Nevertheless, that article, though closely tied to the musical facts of the case, had the defect according to American conceptions of sociology of being unproven. It remained in the realm of materials acting upon the listener, the "stimulus," with no possibility that I could or would have proceeded to the "other side of the fence." I thereby provoked the objection that I was not to hear for the last time: "Where is the evidence?"

A certain naïveté about the American situation was more important. I certainly knew what monopolistic capitalism and the great trusts were; yet I had not realized how far "rationalization" and standardization had permeated the so-called mass media and thereby jazz, in whose production they had such a great role. I actually still considered jazz to be a spontaneous form of expression, as it so gladly represented itself, and did not perceive the problem of a calculated and manipulated pseudo-spontaneity, a second-hand kind, which then dawned on me in my American experience and which I later, *tant bien que mal*, endeavored to formulate. When I had the paper "Über Jazz" reprinted almost thirty years after its first appearance, I was very far removed from it. I was therefore able to note, apart from its weaknesses, what merits it possessed. Precisely because it did not perceive an American phenomenon with the obviousness that it had for Americans, but rather, as one says a little too glibly in Germany nowadays, approached it from an "alienated" point of view, the article "Über Jazz" pointed out features that are all too easily lost sight of owing to familiarity with the jazz-idiom, yet may be essential to jazz. In a way, this lack of involvement on the part of an "outsider" and freshness of judgment are maintained in all of my writings on American themes.

When I moved from London to New York in February 1938, I worked half-time for the Institut für Sozialforschung, and the other half for the Princeton Radio Research Project. The latter was directed by Paul F. Lazarsfeld, with Hadley Cantril and Frank Stanton, then research director of the Columbia Broadcasting System, as co-directors. I myself was supposed to direct the so-called Music Study of the Project. Because of my membership in the Institut für Sozialforschung, I was not subjected to the unmitigated competitive struggle and the pressure of externally imposed demands as was then customary. I had the possibility of my own goals. I sought to do justice to my twin commitments by a certain combination of activities. In the theoretical texts that I then wrote for the Institut, I formulated the points of view and experiences which I then wanted to employ in the Radio Project. In the first instance, this applies to the essay "Über den Fetischcharakter in der Musik und die Regression des Hörens," which had already appeared in the *Zeitschrift für Sozialforschung* in 1938, and can now be read in the little volume *Dissonanzen*; and also to the end of a book begun in London in 1937 on Richard Wagner, of which we put several chapters in the *Zeitschrift für Sozialforschung* in 1939. (The whole book was published in

1952 by Suhrkamp Verlag.) The gulf between this book and orthodox publications in the empirical sociology of music may appear very considerable. Nevertheless, it belonged in the general framework that then occupied me. The *Versuch über Wagner* undertook to combine sociological, aesthetic, and technical analyses of music in such a fashion that analyses of Wagner's "social character" ("*Sozialcharakter*") and the function of his work would shed light upon its internal structure. On the other hand, and this seemed to me more essential, the internal technical findings should be interpreted as hieroglyphs of social significance. The paper on musical fetishes, however, was intended as a draft of the concept of the new musico-sociological experiences I had in America and to sketch something like a "frame of reference" for the specific researches to be carried out. At the same time, the article represented a sort of critical reply to an article of my friend Walter Benjamin, published in our periodical, on the work of art in the age of technical reproducibility. The problems of production in the culture-industry and the related behavioral patterns were critically underscored, whereas Benjamin seemed to me to take an all too positive attitude toward cultural industry, due to its technological potentialities.

The Princeton Radio Research Project had its headquarters at that time neither in Princeton nor in New York, but in Newark, New Jersey, and indeed, in a somewhat pioneering spirit, in an unoccupied brewery. When I travelled there through the tunnel under the Hudson I felt a little as if I were in Kafka's Nature Theater of Oklahoma. I was very much taken by the lack of embarrassment about the choice of a site that would scarcely have been conceivable by the lights of the European academic community. My first impression of the researches already in progress there was not exactly marked by any great understanding. At Lazarsfeld's suggestion, I went from room to room and spoke with colleagues, heard words like "Likes and Dislikes Study," "success or failure of a program," of which at first I could make very little. But this much I did understand: that it was concerned with the collection of data, which were supposed to benefit the planning departments in the field of the mass media, whether in industry itself or in cultural advisory boards and similar bodies. For the first time, I saw "administrative research" before me. I don't now recall whether Lazarsfeld coined this phrase, or I myself in my astonishment at a practically oriented kind of science, so entirely unknown to me. In any event, Lazarsfeld later defined the distinction between such administrative research and critical communications research in the sense of our Institut. He did this in an article that introduced a special volume of our *Studies in Philosophy and Social Science 1941.*

Naturally there appeared to be little room for such critical social research in the framework of the Princeton Project. Its charter, which came from the Rockefeller Foundation, expressly stipulated that the investigations must be performed within the limits of the commercial radio system prevailing in the United States. It was thereby implied that the system itself, its cultural and sociological consequences and its social and economic presuppositions were not to be analyzed. I cannot say that I strictly obeyed the charter. This was not in the least motivated by the desire to criticize for the sake of criticism, which would have been unbecoming in a person whose first task consisted in familiarizing himself with the cultural climate in which everything that it was incumbent upon him to study had its place. I was disturbed, rather, by a basic methodological problem—understanding the word "method" more in its European sense of epistemology than in its American sense, in which methodology virtually signifies practical techniques for research. I was perfectly willing to go to the famous "other side of the fence," and still recall how pleased I was and how much I learned when I personally, for my own orientation, conducted a series of certainly very random and unsystematic interviews. On the other hand, it appeared to me, and I am still persuaded today, that in the cultural sphere what is regarded by the psychology of perception as a mere "stimulus" is in fact, qualitatively determined, a matter of "objective spirit" and knowable in its objectivity. I oppose stating and measuring effects without relating them to these "stimuli," *i.e.*, the objective content to which the consumers in the cultural industry, the radio listeners, react. What was axiomatic according to the prevalent rules of social research, namely, to proceed from the subjects' reactions as if they were a primary and final source of sociological knowledge, seemed to me thoroughly superficial and misguided. Or, to put the matter more prudently: research had still to determine how far the subjective reactions of the persons studied are actually as spontaneous and direct as the subjects suppose; and how far not only the methods of dissemination and the power of suggestion of the apparatus, but also the objective implications of the material with which the listeners were confronted, are involved. And finally, it had still to be determined how far comprehensive social structures, and even society as a whole, came into play. But the mere fact that I proceeded from art as from something objective in itself, instead of from statistically measurable listener-reactions brought me into a certain conflict with prevailing habits of thought.

Furthermore, something specifically musical impeded my progress from theoretical considerations to empiricism—namely the difficulty of verbalizing what music subjectively arouses in the listener, the utter obscurity of what we call "musical experience." I hardly knew how to approach it. A small machine which enabled a listener to indicate what he liked and didn't like by pushing a button during the performance of a piece of music appeared to be highly inadequate to the complexity of what had to be discovered; and this in spite of the seeming objectivity of the data supplied. In any event, I was determined before I took the field to pursue in depth what could perhaps be called musical "content analysis," without confusing music with program music. I still recall how bewildered I was when my late colleague Franz Neumann of the Institut für Sozialforschung, the author of *Behemoth*, asked me whether the questionnaires for the Music Study had already been sent out, when I still hardly knew whether the questions that I regarded as essential could be done justice to by questionnaires. To tell the truth, I still don't know. Of course, and herein lay my misunderstanding (as I didn't realize until later), insights into the relationship between music and society were not espected of me, but rather information. I felt a strong inner resistance to meeting this demand by turning myself inside out. As Horkheimer comforted me, I probably couldn't have done it even if I had wanted to more than my intellectual orientation made possible.

Certainly that was all determined in considerable degree by the fact that I approached the specific field of sociology of music more as a musician than as a sociologist. Yet a genuine sociological impulse came into play, which I could not account for until much later. In having recourse to subjective attitudes toward music, I came up against the question of *spontaneity*. This concern was awakened by the fact that the apparently primary, spontaneous reactions were insufficient as a basis for sociological knowledge because they were themselves conditioned. On this score, one could point out that in the so-called motivation-analysis of the form of social research primarily concerned with subjective reactions and their generalization, a means is at hand for correcting this appearance of spontaneity and penetrating the pre-conditions of the subjective reactions through additional detailed, qualitative case studies. Yet aside from the fact that empirical social science was not as intensively concerned with the techniques of motivation research as later, I felt and still feel that even such a procedure, however much it appeals to "common sense," is not entirely adequate. For it still remains necessarily in the subjective realm: motivations exist in the consciousness and unconsciousness of individuals. It could not be established through motivation-analysis alone whether, and how, reactions to music are determined by the so-called cultural climate and over and above this through structural factors in society. Of course, objective social factors also become evident indirectly in subjective opinions and behavior. Moreover, the opinions and behavior of subjects themselves are always something objective, are "given." They are important for the tendencies of development of the entire society, if not in the same degree as in a sociological model that absolutely equates the rules of parliamentary democracy, the *volonté de tous*, with the reality of the living society. Generally, objective social factors illuminate subjective reactions, even in their concrete details. From the subjective material one can argue backwards to the objective determinants. The exclusive claims of empirical methods find support insofar as subjective reactions are more easily determined and quantified than the structures of the total society, which resist direct empirical treatment. It is plausible that one could proceed from the data derived from subjects to the objective social factors, as well as vice versa, except that, in the measure that sociology begins with the determination of these data, one feels on firmer ground. In spite of all this, it remains unproven that one can really proceed from the opinions and reactions of individuals to the social structure and the social essence. Even the statistical average of these opinions is still, as Durkheim already perceived, an epitome of subjectivity:

Moreover, there is another reason for not confusing the objective response and the average response: it is that the reactions of the average individual remain individual reactions. . . . There is no essential difference between the two propositions "I like this" and "a certain number of us like this."[1]

It is hardly an accident that the representatives of a rigorous empiricism impose such restrictions upon the construction of theory that the reconstitution of the entire society and its laws of action is impeded. Above all, however, the choice of the frames of reference, the categories and techniques employed by a science, is not as neutral and immaterial with respect to the content of the object to be studied, as a philosoply might suppose whose essential ingredients include a sharp distinction between method and object. Whether one proceeds from a theory of society and interprets the allegedly reliably observed data as mere epiphenomena upon the theory, or, alternatively, regards the data as the essence of science and the theory of society as a mere abstraction derived from the ordering of the data—these alternatives have far-reaching substantial consequences for the conception of society. More than any specific bias or "value judgment," the choice of one or the other of these frames of reference determines whether one regards the abstraction "society" as the most fundamental reality, controlling all particulars, or on account of its abstractness considers it, in the tradition of nominalism, as a mere *flatus vocis*. These alternatives extend into all social judgments, including the political. Motivation-analysis does not go much beyond the impact of selected factors upon subjective reactions; but those factors, in the overall context of the cultural industry, are only more or less randomly isolated from a totality that not only operates upon people from without but has long been internalized.

Behind this lie far more important issues for communications research. The phenomena with which the sociology of the mass media must be concerned, particularly in America, cannot be separated from standardization, the transformation of artistic creations into consumer goods, and the calculated pseudo-individualization and similar manifestations of what is called *Verdinglichung*—"reification"—in German. It is matched by a reified, largely manipulable consciousness scarcely capable any longer of spontaneous experience. I can most simply illus-

1. Emile Durkheim, *Sociologie et Philosophie* (Paris, 1963), pp. 121–122.

trate what I mean, without resorting to any detailed philosophical explanation, by drawing upon an actual experience. Among the frequently changing colleagues who came in contact with me in the Princeton Project was a young lady. After a few days she came to confide in me and asked in a completely charming way, "Dr. Adorno, would you mind a personal question?" I said, "It depends on the question, but just go ahead." And she continued, "Please tell me: are you an extrovert or an introvert?" It was as if she was already thinking, as a living being, according to the pattern of the so-called "cafeteria" questions on questionnaires, by which she had been conditioned. She could fit herself into such rigid and preconceived categories, as one can often observe in Germany when, for example, in marriage advertisements the partners characterize themselves by the signs of the Zodiac that they were born under: Virgo, Aries. Reified minds are in no way limited to America, but are fostered by the general tendency of society. But I first became aware of this in America. Contemporary Europe, in harmony with the economic-technological trend, is following close behind. In the meantime the complex has long since penetrated the general consciousness in America. In 1938 one met with strong resistance for daring to use even the concept of reification which has since been worn out by use.

I was particularly disturbed by the danger of a methodological circle: that in order to grasp the phenomenon of cultural reification according to the prevalent norms of empirical sociology one would have to use reified methods as they stood so threateningly before my eyes in the form of that machine, the program analyzer. When I was confronted with the demand to "measure culture," I reflected that culture might be precisely that condition that excludes a mentality capable of measuring it. In general, I resisted the indiscriminate application of the principle "science is measurement," which was then little criticized even in the social sciences. The prescriptive right-of-way given to quantitative methods of research, to which both theory and individual qualitative studies should be at best supplementary, precisely postulates that one must tackle that paradox. The task of translating my reflections into research terms was equivalent to squaring the circle. I am certainly not the right person to decide how much of this is to be laid to my personal equation. But the difficulties are certainly of an objective nature also.

They have this basis in the inhomogeneity of the scientific conception of sociology. No continuum exists between critical theorems and the empirical procedures of natural science. They have entirely different historical origins and can be integrated only with the greatest effort. Much later, back in Germany, I dealt with this discontinuity, opposing the views of Talcott Parsons in methodological articles of which I may mention "Soziologie und empirische Forschung." It is now in *Sociologica II* by Horkeimer and myself, in the series *Frankfurter Beiträge zur Soziologie* edited by the Institut für Sozialforschung. My doubts on this score piled up thirty years ago to such an extent that I immersed myself in observations of American musical life, especially the radio system, and set down theories and hypotheses about it; but I could not construct questionnaires and interview-schemes that would get to the heart of the matter. Of course, I was somewhat isolated in my endeavors. The unfamiliarity of the things that concerned me had the effect of inducing skepticism rather than cooperation from my colleagues. Interestingly enough, the so-called secretarial workers were immediately attracted to my ideas. I still remember most gratefully Rose Kohn and Eunice Cooper, who not only copied and corrected my numerous drafts but also encouraged me. But the higher up in the scientific hierarchy the more unpleasant the situation became. Thus I once had an assistant of Mennonite lineage, whose ancestors had come from Germany long before, who was supposed to help me, particularly in research on popular music. He had been a jazz musician, and I learned a great deal from him about the technique of jazz as well as the phenomenon of "song hits" in America. But instead of helping me to transfer my formulations of the problem into strategies for research, however limited, he wrote a sort of protest memorandum in which he contrasted, not without emotion, his scientific conception of the world with my idle speculations (as he regarded them). He had hardly grasped what I was after. A certain resentment in him was unmistakable: the type of culture that I brought with me and about which I was genuinely unconceited, critical of society as I already was, appeared to him to be unjustifiable arrogance. He cherished a mistrust of Europeans such as the bourgeoisie of the eighteenth century must have entertained toward the émigré French aristocrats. However little I, destitute of all influence, had to do with social privilege, I appeared to him to be a kind of usurper. Without in the least glossing over my own psychological difficulties in the Project, particularly the inflexibility of a man who was already set in his purposes, perhaps I may cite several recollections demonstrating that these difficulties did not arise entirely out of my own limitations. A colleague who was highly qualified in his own field, which had nothing to do with the sociology of music, has long since achieved high office and esteem. He asked me to make several forecasts for a survey on jazz: whether this form of light music was more popular in the city or the country, with younger or older people, with those affiliated with a church or with "agnostics" and the like. I answered these questions, which lay well within the bounds of the problems I dealt with in the sociology of jazz, with simple "horse sense," just as an unprejudiced person, unintimidated by science, might answer them. My prophecies, not exactly profound, were confirmed. The effect was surprising. My young colleague did not attribute the conclusion to my common sense, but rather to a sort of magical capacity for intuition. I thereby earned an authority with him which I certainly hadn't deserved for knowing that jazz fans are more commonly found in big cities than in the country. The academic training which he had completed had obviously had the effect of eliminating for him any considerations that were not already covered by strictly observed and recorded facts. Indeed, I was later confronted with the argument that if too many ideas are developed as hypotheses before empirical investigations, one may succumb to a bias that might endanger the objectivity of the findings. My very friendly colleague preferred to regard me as a medicine man rather than make room for something that lay under the taboo of speculation. Taboos of this nature have a tendency to spread beyond their original sphere. Skepticism toward the unproven can easily turn into a veto upon thought. Another equally qualified but already established scholar considered my analyses of light music as "expert opinion." He entered these on the side of the reactions rather than of the analysis of the actual object (*i.e.*, the music), which he wanted to exclude from analysis as a mere stimulus.

I met this argument time and again. Obviously it is very difficult in America, outside the special sphere of the liberal arts, to comprehend the notion of the objectivity of anything intellectual. The intellect is unconditionally equated with the subject who bears it, without any recognition of its independence and autonomy. Above all, organized scholarship scarcely realizes to how small a degree works of art can be understood in terms of the mentality of those who produce them. I once observed this carried to a grotesque extreme. For a group of radio-listeners, I was once assigned the task, I forget why, of giving a musical analysis in the sense of the structural elements to be heard. To begin with something familiar and corresponding to the popular taste, I chose the famous melody that forms the second main theme of the first movement of Schubert's B-Minor Symphony, and demonstrated the chain-like, interwoven nature of the theme which accounts for its particular impressiveness. One of the participants in the meeting, a very young man whom I had noticed because of his extravagantly colorful dress, raised his hand and said roughly the following: what I had said was all very well and convincing. But it would have been more effective if I had put on a mask and costume of Schubert's, as if the composer himself was giving information about his intentions and developing these thoughts. Something emerged in experiences of this sort that Max Weber had diagnosed almost fifty years ago in the prolegomena to his theory of bureaucracy, and which had already fully developed in America of the 1930's—the opposition between the expert technician and the European "intellectual," the "*gebildete Mensch.*" Whether and to what extent the division between intellectual and expert still exists and whether the latter has in the meantime become more open to self-reflection would be worthy of sociological analysis in itself.

I received my first real help in connection with the Princeton Radio Research Project when Dr. George Simpson was assigned to work with me. I gladly take the opportunity to thank him publicly. He was thoroughly informed theoretically and familiar as a native American with the sociological criteria observed in the United States and with the European tradition as well, as the translator of Durkheim's *Division du travail*. Time and again I have observed that native Americans were more open-minded, above all more willing to help, than European immigrants. The latter, under the pressure of prejudice and rivalry, often showed the tendency to be more American than the Americans and were also quick to consider every newly arrived fellow European as a kind of threat to their own "adjustment." Officially, Simpson functioned as "editorial assistant." In fact, he did a great deal more by making the first attempts to transform my distinctive efforts into American sociological language. This process was accomplished in a way that was very surprising and instructive for me. Like the burnt child that dreads the fire, I had developed an exaggerated caution and hardly dared to formulate my ideas as undisguisedly and emphatically as required to make them stand out. But it appears that such caution is not appropriate to a philosophy as remote from trial and error as my own. Now Simpson not only encouraged me to write as radically and uncompromisingly as possible, he also gave his all to make it succeed.

In the Music Study of the Princeton Radio Research Project from 1938 to 1940, I completed four larger treatises in which Simpson collaborated; without him, they would probably not exist. The first was called "A Social Critique of Radio Music." It appeared in the *Kenyon Review* for Spring 1945. It was a lecture that I presented in 1940 to my colleagues in the Radio Project, and which developed the basic viewpoints of my work—a bit crudely, perhaps, but clearly. Three concrete studies applied these insights to the data. One, "On Popular Music," printed in the communications volume of the *Studies in Philosophy and Social Science*, presented a sort of social phenomenology of hit tunes, particularly the theory of standardization and pseudo-individualization, and the sharp differentiation between serious and light music to be inferred from this. Perhaps it would not be entirely without interest if I point out that the discovery of the phenomenon of pseudo-individualism foreshadowed the concept of personalization that later played a significant role in *The Authoritarian Personality*, and indeed attained some importance for political sociology in general. Then there was the study of the NBC Music Appreciation Hour, whose extensive English text unfortunately remained unpublished at the time and certainly today would be too outdated in many respects to have any effect in America. What I regarded as essential, I later inserted in German, with the kind permission of Lazarsfeld, into the chapter "Die gewürdigte Musik" of *Der Getreue Korrepetitor*. It had to do with critical content analysis, with simply and strictly demonstrating that the "Damrosch Hour," highly regarded and widely listened to as a non-commercial contribution promoting musical culture, was propagating false information about music as well as a deceptive and untrue conception of it. The social bases of such inaccuracy were sought in conformity to the views of those who were responsible for this "appreciation hour." Finally, the text of "The Radio Symphony" was completed and printed in the volume *Radio Research 1941*. The thesis was that serious symphonic music, as transmitted by radio is not what it appears and that consequently the claim of the radio industry to be bringing serious music to the people is spurious. This essay immediately met with strong resistance. Thus the well known music critic B. H. Haggin polemicized against it and labelled it as the kind of nonsense that foundations fell for—a reproach which certainly did not apply in my case. I incorporated the gist of this paper also in the *Getreuen Korrepetitor* in its last chapter "Über die musikalische Verwendung des Radios." Certainly one of the ideas has become obsolete: my thesis that the radio symphony was not a symphony at all, a thesis derived from the technologically produced alterations in sound, the prevailing distortion, in radio at that time, which have since been overcome by the techniques of high fidelity and stereophonics. Yet I believe that this does not affect either the theory of "atomistic listening" nor that of the peculiar "image" of music on the radio, which have survived the actual distortion of sound.

In contrast to what the Music Study actually should have accomplished at least in outline form, these four papers were fragmentary, or in American terms, the result of a "salvaging action." I did not succeed in presenting a systematically executed sociology and social psychology of radio music. To what extent the later German book *Einleitung in die Musiksoziologie* meets such a need is not for me to judge. Examples were supplied rather than the plan of the whole that I felt called upon to produce. This shortcoming may have derived essentially from the fact that my transfer to audience research was unsuccessful. Such research would have been absolutely essential, if only for the refinement and revision of my propositions. It is an open question, to be answered only empirically, whether and to what extent the social implications observed in the content analysis of music are understood by the listeners themselves, and how they react to them. It would be naïve to take for granted an identity between the social implications to be discerned in the stimuli and those embodied in the "responses." It would certainly be no less naïve to consider the two things as totally uncorrelated with each other in the absence of conclusive research on the reactions. If in fact, as was deduced in the study "On Popular Music," the standards and rules of the popular music industry are the congealed results of public preferences in a society not yet fully standardized and technologically organized, one can still conclude that the implications of the objective contents do not completely diverge from the conscious and unconscious awareness of those to whom they appeal—otherwise the popular would hardly be popular. Bounds are set to manipulation. On the other hand it should be considered that shallow and superficial material which from the beginning is supposed to be received as a form of entertainment leaves relatively shallow and superficial reactions to be anticipated. The ideology projected by the music industry need not necessarily be the same as that of its audience. To cite an analogy, the popular press in many countries, including America and England, often propagates extreme right-wing views without any great consequences to date for the shaping of the popular will in those countries. My own position in the controversy between empirical and theoretical sociology, so often misrepresented, particularly in Europe, I may sum up by saying that empirical investigations are not only legitimate but essential, even in the realm of cultural phenomena. But one must not confer autonomy upon them or regard them as a universal key. Above all, they must themselves terminate in theoretical knowledge. Theory is no mere vehicle that becomes superfluous as soon as the data are in hand.

It may be noted that the four articles on music from the Princeton Project, along with the German article on music as a fetish, also contained motifs of the *Philosophie der neuen Musik*, not completed until 1948. The viewpoints that I had brought to bear in the American essays upon the reproduction and consumption of music were to be applied to the sphere of production itself.

The work on the Music Study was by no means entirely confined to what appeared under my name. There were two other investigations, one strictly empirical, which could at least be regarded as stimulated by my work without my having the direction of them—I was not among the editors of *Radio Research 1941*. Edward Suchman, in "Invitation to Music," has made the only attempt to date to examine a thesis of the "Radio Symphony" on listener reactions. He established the difference in capacity for musical appreciation between people familiar with live serious music and those who were only initiated by radio. The nature of the problem was related to my own in that mine also concerned the difference between live experience and the "reified" experience gained from mechanical means of reproduction. My thesis may have been confirmed by Suchman's investigation. The taste of people who had heard live serious music was superior to that of those who were acquainted with serious music only through the New York station WQXR that specialized in it. The question certainly remains open whether this difference was really attributable entirely to the modes of apprehending musical experience set forth in my theory and probably implicit in Suchman's conclusions, or whether, as seems probable to me now, a third factor entered in: that those who generally go to concerts already belong to a tradition that makes them more familiar with serious music than the "radio fans" and indeed have a more specific interest in it than those who confine themselves to listening over the radio. Furthermore, in this study, with which I am understandably satisfied, my reluctance to treat the problem of the reification of consciousness by methods reified themselves became fairly concrete. In keeping with the familiar technique of the Thurstone Scale, a panel of experts decided on the quality of the composers who were to serve for discriminating the standards of those who had become acquainted with music through live performances and through radio. These experts were largely chosen for their prominence and authority in the musical world. In this connection, the question arose whether these experts were not themselves imprinted with the same conventional notions included in the reified consciousness that really constituted the object of our researches. The high ranking of Tchaikowsky in the scale seemed to me to justify such misgivings.

The study by Malcolm McDougald on "The Popular Music Industry" in *Radio Research 1941* helped to demonstrate the theory of the manipulability of musical taste. It was a contribution to a knowledge of the conditioning of the seemingly spontaneous, in that it described in detail how "hits" were made. By the methods of "high pressure" publicity, the most important outlet for the popularization of song hits—the bands—were cultivated, so that certain songs were so often played, particularly on the radio, that they had a chance of being taken up by the masses through the sheer power of incessant repetition. Thus McDougald had the merit of giving the first circumstantial demonstration of such mechanisms in the musical world. Yet even here I did not feel entirely at ease. I would suggest that the facts on which he insisted belong to an earlier era than that of the centralized radio technology and the great oligopolists in the mass media. In this study, the manipulation of the popular taste still appears to be essentially the work of frantically eager "agents," if not indeed the result of bribery and corruption. In fact, however, the objective system and in considerable measure the new technological conditions had long since taken this work over. To this extent, McDougald's investigation needs to be repeated today, to inquire into the objective mechanisms for popularizing the popular, rather than the machinations and intrigues of the garrulous types whose "spiel" McDougald described so vividly. In the light of the present social reality, it easily stands out as old-fashioned and therefore, as it were, appealing.

In 1941 my work at the Princeton Radio Research Project, from which the Bureau of Applied Social Research developed, came to an end and we moved to California, where Horkheimer had already gone. He and I spent the next years almost entirely in Los Angeles with our joint work on the *Dialektik der Aufklärung*. The book was completed in 1944 and the last additions were made in 1945. Until the fall of 1944 my contact with American research was interrupted, and only then resumed. While we were still in New York, Horkheimer, under the impress of the gruesome things happening in Europe, got investigations under way on the problem of anti-Semitism. Together with other members of our Institut, we had outlined and published the program of a research project to which we often reverted. It contained among other things a typology of anti-Semites, which then recurred, substantially modified, in later studies. Just as the Music Study at the Princeton Radio Research Project was conditioned on the theoretical side by the article "Über den Fetischcharakter in der Musik und die Regression des Hörens," written in German, so the chapter "Elemente des Antisemitismus" in *Dialektik der Aufklärung*, which Horkheimer and I collaborated on in the strictest sense, literally dictated together, anticipated my later investigations with the Berkeley Public Opinion Study Group published in *The Authoritarian Personality*. The reference to *Dialektik der Aufklärung*, which has not yet been translated into English, does not seem superfluous to me, because that book most readily obviates a misunderstanding that *The Authoritarian Personality* encountered from the beginning and in some degree invited because of its emphasis—namely, that the authors had attempted to account for anti-Semitism and beyond that fascism in general on a purely subjective basis, thus subscribing to the error that this politico-economic phenomenon is primarily psychological. What I pointed out concerning the conception of the Music Study of the Princeton Project may suffice to show how little that was intended. "Elemente des Antisemitismus" theoretically placed racial prejudice in the context of an objectively oriented, critical theory of society. To be sure, we did not, in contrast to a certain economic orthodoxy, put up a stiff-necked resistance to psychology, but assigned it a proper place in our scheme as an explanatory factor. Nevertheless, we never questioned the primacy of objective factors over psychological. We adhered to what I believe to be the plausible consideration that in contemporary society the objective institutions and trends of development have achieved such dominance over individuals that the latter in ever-increasing numbers become mere agents of the tendencies developing over their heads. Less and less depends upon their own conscious and unconscious being, their inner life. In the meantime, the psychological as well as the socio-psychological explanation of social phenomena has become in many ways an ideological camouflage: the more people depend on the entire system the less they can do about it, hence the more they are intentionally and unintentionally led to believe that everything depends on them. "Man is the ideology of dehumanization." Therefore the socio-psychological questions that have been raised in connection with the Freudian theory, above all those concerning depth psychology and characterology, are by no means inconsequential. As early as the long introduction to the 1935 volume of the Institut für Sozialforschung, *Autorität und Familie*, Horkheimer had spoken of the "cement" that held society together, and had developed the thesis that in view of the discrepancy between what society promises its members and what it actually gives them, the machinery could hardly function unless it remade the people inwardly to conform to itself. Once the bourgeois epoch, with the growing need for free labor, produced men who corresponded to the demands of the new methods of production, these men, generated, as it were, by the socio-economic system, later constituted the additional factor that ensured the continuation of the very conditions that had shaped the inner man after themselves. Social psychology as we now knew it dealt with the conditioning of the subjective by the objective social system, without which the subject could hardly have been held to the task. In these theories, a certain affinity manifested itself between our views and subjectively oriented methods of research as a corrective for the rigidity of abstract thought, in which invoking the supremacy of the system becomes a substitute for insights into the concrete relationship between the system and its components. On the other hand, the subjectively oriented analyses have their value only within the objective theory. In *The Authoritarian Personality*, this is repeatedly emphasized. It was probably owing to the intellectual situation that the fact that that book focussed upon subjective impulses was construed to mean that social psychology was being employed as the philosopher's stone. The book was simply trying, according to a famous formula of Freud's, to add something new and complementary to what was already known. I welcome another opportunity to make this point perfectly explicit.

Horkheimer had made contact with a group of investigators at the University of California at Berkeley, above all Nevitt Sanford, Else Frenkel-Brunswik, now dead, and Daniel Levinson. I believe the first point of contact was a study initiated by Sanford of the phenomenon of pessimism, which then recurred in a greatly modified form in the wide-ranging investigations in which the destructive impulse was shown to be one of the decisive dimensions of the authoritarian character, only no longer in the sense of an "overt" pessimism but oftentimes as reaction formation to it. In 1945 Horkheimer took charge of the Research Division of the American Jewish Committee in New York, and thereby made it possible for the scientific resources of the Berkeley group and of our own Institute to be pooled, so that we were able over a period of years to conduct extensive researches connected with our common theoretical reflections. Horkheimer is not only responsible for the overall plan of the contributions that were collected in the series of *Studies in Prejudice* published by Harper's, but without him the specific content of *The Authoritarian Personality* is also unthinkable. For his philosophical and sociological reflections and my own have long been so thoroughly integrated that it would be impossible for us to say what came from one and what from the other. The Berkeley Study was so organized that Sanford and I served as directors, with Mrs. Brunswik and Daniel Levinson as our principal associates. But from the beginning, everything was done by perfect "team work" without any hierarchical restrictions. The fact that the title *The Authoritarian Personality* gives equal credit to all of us thoroughly expresses the actual state of affairs. This kind of cooperation in a democratic spirit that does not get bogged down in formal political procedures and extends into all details of planning and execution, I found to be not only extremely enjoyable but also the most fruitful thing that I became acquainted with in America, in contrast to the academic tradition in Europe. The current efforts to democratize the inner life of the German university are familiar to me from my American experience, and I truly feel it to be the continuation of a tradition to which I belonged in America to work as hard as I can for a similar democratization in Germany. The cooperation in Berkeley knew no friction, no resistance, no rivalry among scholars. At a great sacrifice of time, Dr. Sanford edited stylistically all the chapters written by me in the kindest and most meticulous way. Of course, the reason for this easy cooperation had to be not only the American atmosphere of "team work" but also an objective factor—our common theoretical orientation toward Freud. The four of us were agreed in neither tying ourselves inflexibly to Freud nor in diluting him after the manner of the psychoanalytical revisionists. A certain measure of deviation from him was indicated by the very fact that we were pursuing a specifically sociological concern. The inclusion of objective factors, above all those of the cultural environment, was not entirely compatible with the Freudian conception of sociology as merely applied psychology. There was also a certain contrast to Freud in our postulating quantification as a desideratum, since for him the essence of research consists in qualitative investigations, "case studies." Nevertheless we took the qualitative factor seriously throughout. The categories that underlay the quantitative researches were themselves of a qualitative character and derived from an analytical characterology. Furthermore, we had intended from the beginning to compensate for the danger of the mechanistic element in quantitative investigations by supplementary qualitative case studies. The deadlock that purely quantitative determinations seldom arrive at the genetical depth mechanisms, whereas qualitative results can easily be accused of being incapable of generalizations and thereby lose their objective sociological value, we sought to surmount by employing an entire series of different techniques, which we only related to one another in terms of the underlying categories. Mrs. Brunswik made the remarkable effort to quantify the findings of strictly qualitative clinical analysis attained in the area reserved to her, against which I raised the objection that through such quantification one could only lose again the complementary advantages of qualitative analysis. Through her early and tragic death we were never able to pursue this controversy. So far as I know, the issue is still open.

The investigations of the authoritarian personality were widely dispersed. While the center was in Berkeley, where I went once every fortnight, a study group was organized simultaneously in Los Angeles, by Frederick Pollock, in which the social psychologist C. F. Brown, the psychologist Carol Creedon, and several other people participated. At that time contact had already been established with the psychoanalyst Dr. Frederick Hacker and his collaborators, and discussions of a seminar type frequently took place among interested scholars in Los Angeles. The idea of a major literary work comprising the individual investigations only slowly emerged, and almost involuntarily. The heart of the common achievement was the F-scale, which of all parts of *The Authoritarian Personality* seems to have had the greatest influence. Applied and revised countless times, it later supplied (adapted to local conditions) the foundation for a scale used to measure the authoritarian potential in Germany, on which the Institut für Sozialforschung, re-established in Frankfurt in 1950, hopes to publish a report in 1969. Certain tests in American magazines, as well as unsystematic observations of several acquaintances, suggested to us the idea that without expressly asking about anti-Semitic and other fascistic opinions, one could indirectly determine such tendencies by establishing the existence of certain rigid views, of which one can be fairly certain that in general they accompany these particular opinions and constitute with them a characterological unity. Thus we developed the F-scale at Berkeley in a spirit of freedom of invention that deviated considerably from the conception of a pedantic science carefully scrutinizing its every step. The explanation for this is what might be called the "psychoanalytic background," particularly the familiarity with the method of free association, among the four persons responsible for the study. I emphasize this, because a work like *The Authoritarian Personality*, which, though much criticized, has never been charged with lacking familiarity with American materials and American procedures, was published in a fashion that did not attempt to conceal itself behind the customary facade of positivism in social science. The conjecture is scarcely too far-fetched that *The Authoritarian Personality* owes to that freedom whatever it has to offer that is original, unconventional, imaginative, and directed toward fundamental issues. The playful impulse that I would like to regard as necessary for all intellectual productivity was certainly not lacking in the development of the F-scale. We spent hours thinking up entire dimensions, variables, and syndromes, including particular questionnaire items, of which we were all the prouder the less they betrayed their relationship to the main theme, anticipating as we did for theoretical reasons correlations with ethnocentrism, anti-Semitism, and reactionary politico-economic views. Then we checked these items in standard pretests and thereby achieved the technically requisite limitation of the questionnaire to a length that would still be reliable, eliminating those items that proved to have insufficient "discriminatory power."

Of course in the process we had to water our wine a bit. For a number of reasons, among which the impact of educational factors played no small role, we often had to abandon precisely the items that we ourselves regarded as the most searching and original, and to give the preference to those that owed their greater discriminatory power to lying closer to the surface of public opinion than factors grounded in depth-psychology. Thus we simply had to abandon the dimension of the hostility of authoritarian types toward modern art, because this hostility presupposed a certain level of culture, namely that of actually having encountered such art, which the vast majority of our subjects had been denied. While we believed that by a combination of quantitative and qualitative methods we could overcome the antagonism between that which lends itself to generalization and that which is specifically relevant, this problem caught up with us in the midst of our endeavors. It seems to be the defect of every form of empirical sociology that it must choose between the reliability and the profundity of its findings. Nevertheless, we could still work with the Likert form of operationally defined scales in a fashion that often enabled us to kill several flies with one swat, that is, to get simultaneously with one item at several dimensions, which in our theoretical scheme of the authoritarian personality were characteristic of the "highs" and their opposite numbers, the "lows." In view of Gutmann's critique of the previously conventional methods of scaling, the conception of our F scale would be hardly conceivable. It is difficult for me to avoid the suspicion that the increasing precision of methods in empirical sociology, however impeccable the arguments for them may be, often restrains scientific productivity.

We had to prepare the work for publication relatively fast. It came out almost exactly at the time when I returned to Europe at the end of 1949, and I was not a witness to its impact in the United States in the next years. The pressure for time under which we found ourselves had a paradoxical result. The English joke is well-known about the man who began a letter by saying that he did not have the time to be brief. It was that way with us: simply because we could not arrange for a complete overhaul of the work, in order to shorten the manuscript, the book became as bulky and capacious as it now stands. Nevertheless, this deficiency, of which we were all aware, may be compensated for in some degree by the variety of more or less independent methods and the materials gained by these. What the book loses by a lack of disciplined rigor and unity may perhaps be made good in some degree by the fact that a great many concrete insights converge from many directions upon the same principal themes, so that what is unproven by the strictest criteria gains in plausibility. If *The Authoritarian Personality* made a contribution, this is not to be sought in the absolute validity of the positive insights, even less in statistics, but above all in the posing of the issues, which were motivated by a genuine social concern and related to a theory that had not previously been translated into quantitative investigations of this sort. What is essential is not that which is measured but the development of methods, which, after being improved, permit measurement to take place in areas where this had hardly been possible before. Since that time, surely not without the influence of *The Authoritarian Personality*, people have often tried to test psychoanalytical theorems by empirical methods.

It was not our main intention to determine present opinions and inclinations, and their distribution. We were interested in the fascistic *potential*. On this account, and to counteract it. we included in the investigation, as far as possible, the *genetic* dimension, the development of the authoritarian character. We all regarded the work, in spite of its considerable size, as a pilot study, more an exploration of possibilities than a collection of irrefutable findings. Yet our results were significant enough to justify our conclusions: not just as prejudices but as simple statements of fact. Else Frenkel-Brunswik paid particular attention to that in her part.

As in many other investigations of this sort, a certain difficulty lay in the nature of the sample, and we did not gloss it over. It used to be a chronic ailment of empirical sociology in American universities, and not only there, that they have to make do with students as subjects far more than could be justified according to the principles of a representative sample of the entire population. Later, in Frankfurt, we tried to obviate this difficulty in similar researches by experimenting with the organization of "contacts" expressly designated for this purpose, test-groups arranged by quotas from the most varied segments of the population. Nevertheless, it must be said that we were not aiming at really representative samples in Berkeley. We were interested instead in key groups: not so much as might perhaps have been desirable in the "opinion leaders" that have been so much discussed in later years, as in groups that we assumed to be particularly "susceptible," like prisoners in San Quentin—they were actually "higher" than the average—or inmates of a psychiatric clinic. From knowledge of the pathological, we anticipated information about the "normal."

A more substantial objection, particularly raised by Jahoda and Christie,[2] was that of circularity: that the theory, which was presupposed by the means of research, had to be confirmed by them. This is not the place to go into this objection. Only this much may be said: we never regarded the theory simply as a set of hypotheses but as in some sense standing on its own feet, and therefore did not intend to prove or disprove the theory through our findings but only to derive from it concrete questions for investigation, which must then be judged on their own merit and demonstrate certain prevalent socio-psychological structures. Of course, the criticism of the F-scale is not to be gainsaid, that to establish tendencies indirectly that cannot be got at directly owing to fear of censoring mechanisms coming into play, presupposes that one has first confirmed the existence of the tendencies that one assumes the subjects hesitated to proclaim. To this extent, the charge of circularity is justified. Yet I would say that one should not push one's challenge on this score too far. After a connection between the overt and the latent has once been established in a limited number of pretests, one can pursue this connection in the main tests in entirely different people who are undisturbed by any overt questions. The only possible difficulty was that, since people who were consciously inclined toward anti-Semitism and fascism hesitated to express their opinion in 1944 and 1945, the original correlation of the two types of questions could have led to excessively optimistic results, and overestimation of the potential of the "lows." Yet the criticism that was made of us pointed in the opposite direction: we were reproached for using techniques that were biased toward the "highs." These methodological problems, which are all structured on the model hypothesis-proof-conclusion, later helped to elicit the philosophical criticism of the scientific concept of the absolutely Primary that I employed in my books on the theory of knowledge (*Metakritik der Erkenntnistheorie*, 1956).

As in the case of the Radio Project, other investigations crystallized out of *The Authoritarian Personality*: for example, the "Child Study" that Mrs. Brunswik and I paved the way for, and whose execution actually fell to her. Unfortunately, this study remained uncompleted: only partial results have been published. A certain mortality of individu-

2. Richard Christie and Marie Jahoda, eds., *Studies in the Scope and Method of "The Authoritarian Personality"* (Glencoe, Ill., 1954).

al studies in large-scale research projects is unavoidable. Nowadays, since social science is so much given to self-consciousness, it would be well worth while to investigate systematically why so much that is started is never completed. The Child Study applied the fundamental categories of *The Authoritarian Personality*. Remarkable and totally unexpected results were achieved thereby. They refined the conception of the distinction between conventionality and the authoritarian temperament. It emerged that precisely the "good," *i.e.*, conventional, children are *freer* from aggression and therefore from one of the most fundamental aspects of the authoritarian personality, and vice versa. In retrospect, this appears to be quite obvious; but not *a priori*. From this aspect of the Child Study I began to understand for the first time wherein, quite independently, Robert Merton discerns one of the most important justifications for empirical research—that virtually all findings can be explained theoretically once they are in hand, but not conversely. Seldom have I experienced so profoundly the legitimacy and necessity of empirical research that really answered theoretical questions.

Even before the collaboration with the Berkeley group began, I myself wrote a larger monograph on the socio-psychological technique of a fascist agitator who had recently been active on the American West Coast, Martin Luther Thomas. This was completed in 1943. It was a content analysis of the more or less standardized and by no means numerous stimuli that fascist agitators employ. Here again the conception that lay behind the Music Study of the Princeton Research Project came into play— to treat types of reactions as well as objective determinants. No further reconciliation and unification of the two "approaches" was achieved in the framework of the "Studies in Prejudice." It certainly remains to be said that the calculated influence of agitators on the "lunatic fringe" is by no means the only and probably not even the most important objective factor promoting a fascistically inclined mentality among the masses. This susceptibility reaches deep into the structure of society itself and is generated by society before demagogues deliberately come to its aid. The opinions of the demagogues are by no means as restricted to the lunatic fringe as one may at first, optimistically, suppose. They occur in considerable measure in the utterances of so-called "respectable" people, only not as succinctly and aggressively formulated. The analysis of Thomas supplied me with a good deal of stimulation for items that were useful in *The Authoritarian Personality*. The study must have been one of the first critical and qualitative content analyses to be carried out in the United States.

In the late fall of 1949 I went back to Germany and was completely absorbed for an entire year in the reconstruction of the Institut für Sozialforschung, to which Horkheimer and I then devoted our whole time, and by my teaching activity in the University of Frankfurt. After a short visit in 1951, I finally returned in 1952 for about a year to Los Angeles as scientific director of the Hacker Foundation in Beverly Hills. The situation which I faced there was entirely different from that of the Princeton Project or *The Authoritarian Personality*. From the beginning it was established that I, neither a psychiatrist nor a therapist, must focus my endeavors upon social psychology. On the other hand, the workers in Dr. Hacker's Clinic, to which the Foundation was attached, were psychiatric social workers. Whenever we collaborated, it went well. But my colleagues had little time for research, and I for my part, as research director, did not have the authority to involve the clinicians in investigations. The upshot was that the possibilities for accomplishment were necessarily more limited than either Dr. Hacker or I had anticipated. I saw myself forced into the situation of a "One Man Show"—to use a good Americanism—obliged to carry out the scientific work of the Foundation, as well as the arrangement of lectures and a certain amount of publicity, almost single-handed. Thus I again found myself thrown back upon the analysis of "stimuli." I got two content studies well under way. One was on the astrology column of *The Los Angeles Times*, which was actually published in English under the title of "The Stars Down to Earth" in the *Jahrbuch für Amerikastudien* for 1957 and then later formed the basis for my German article "Aberglauben aus zweiter Hand" in *Sociologica II*. My interest in this material dated back to the Berkeley investigations, particularly to the socio-psychological significance of the destructive impulse that Freud had discovered in *Civilization and Its Discontents* and which at any rate so far as the masses are concerned seems to me to be the greatest potential danger in the present political situation. The method which I adopted was that of putting myself in the position of the popular astrologer, who by what he writes must supply his readers with a kind of personal satisfaction and finds himself continually confronted with the difficulty of giving to people whom he knows nothing about apparently specific advice adapted to each individual. The result is a strengthening of conformist views through commercialized and standardized astrology, as well as the appearance in the columnist's technique, above all in his "biphasic approach," of certain contradictions in the mentality of the audience, traceable to social contradictions. I proceeded qualitatively, though not failing to count at least in a very crude way the frequency of the basic devices that recurred in the material that I had chosen (stretching over a period of two months). It is a justification of quantitative methods that the products of the culture industry, second-hand popular culture, are themselves planned from a virtually statistical point of view. Quantitative analysis measures them by their own standard. Differences in the frequency with which certain "tricks" are repeated arise out of a semi-scientific calculation of the effect on the part of the astrologer, who in many respects resembles the demagogue and agitator, although avoiding openly political themes. Moreover, in *The Authoritarian Personality* we had already run into certain tendencies of the "highs" to accept superstitious statements eagerly, particularly of a threatening and destructive nature. Thus the astrology study linked up with what I had done in America earlier.

That also applies to the study "How to Look at Television," published in the *Hollywood Quarterly of Film, Radio and Television* for Spring 1954, later also used for the German article *"Fernsehen als Ideologie"* in the volume *Eingriffe*. It required all of Dr. Hacker's diplomacy to obtain for me a certain number of television scripts, with which to analyze their ideological implications, their intended ambiguities. Both articles belong to the realm of research on ideology.

In the fall of 1953, I returned to Europe and in addition to my activity in the Institut für Sozialforschung received a full chair of philosophy and sociology in the University. Since then I have not been back to the States.

I should like to summarize briefly what I hope I learned in America.

The first thing to be mentioned would be something sociological in itself and infinitely important for me as a sociologist—that in America, and even to a certain extent during my English stay, I was constrained no longer to regard as natural the circumstances that had developed historically in Europe— "not to take things for granted." My now departed friend Tillich once said that he was first de-provincialized in America; he probably had something similar in mind. In America I was liberated from a certain naïve belief in culture and attained the capacity to see culture from the outside. To clarify the point: in spite of all social criticism and all consciousness of the primacy of economic factors, the fundamental importance of the mind—"Geist"—was quasi a dogma self-evident to me from the very beginning. The fact that this was not a foregone conclusion, I learned in America, where no reverential silence in the presence of everything intellectual prevailed, as it did in Central and Western Europe far beyond the confines of the so-called educated classes; and the absence of this respect inclined the intellect toward critical self-scrutiny. This particularly affected the European presuppositions of musical cultivation in which I was immersed. Not that I renounced these assumptions or abandoned my conceptions of such culture; but it seems to me a fundamental distinction whether one bears these along unreflectingly or becomes aware of them precisely in contradistinction to the standards of the most technologically and industrially developed country. In saying this, I by no means fail to recognize the shift in the center of gravity of musical life effected by the material resources of the United States in the intervening period. When I began to concern myself with the sociology of music in America thirty years ago, that was still unimaginable.

More fundamental, and more gratifying, was my experience of the substance of democratic forms: that in America they have penetrated the whole of life, whereas in Germany at least they were never more than formal rules of the game and I am afraid are still nothing more. In America I became acquainted with a potential for real generosity that is seldom to be found in old Europe. The political form of democracy is infinitely closer to the daily life of the people themselves. There is an inherent impulse in American life toward peaceableness, good-naturedness, and generosity, in the sharpest contrast to the dammed-up malice and envy that exploded in Germany between 1933 and 1945. America is certainly no longer the land of unlimited possibilities, yet one still has the feeling that anything would be possible. If one encounters time and again in sociological studies in Germany expressions such as "We are still not mature enough for democracy," such expressions of the lust for power coupled with self-contempt are scarcely conceivable in the allegedly much "younger" New World. By this I do not mean to say that America is entirely immune from the danger of an upset in the direction of totalitarian forms of domination. Such a danger is inherent in the trend of modern society *per se*. But probably the power of resistance to fascistic currents in America is still greater than in any European country, with the possible exception of England, which in more respects than we are accustomed to recognizing forms a link between America and continental Europe.

We Europeans are inclined to see the concept of "adjustment" as a purely negative thing, an extinction of the spontaneity and autonomy of the individual. But it is an illusion sharply criticized by Goethe and Hegel that the process of humanization, of becoming civilized, necessarily proceeds from within out. Basically it is accomplished precisely through what Hegel calls "alienation." In this view, we do not become free human beings by realizing ourselves in isolation but rather by transcending ourselves, entering into relations with others, and in a certain sense surrendering to them. We do not first define ourselves as individuals by watering ourselves like plants in order to become universally cultured personalities. A man who under external constraints or through his egotistical interest behaves in a friendly manner may achieve genuine humanity in his relationships with other people easier than a person who, in order to preserve his own identity—as if this identity were always desirable—pulls a nasty glum face and gives one to understand from the outset that one doesn't exist for him and has nothing to contribute to his own inwardness—which oftentimes doesn't even exist. We in Germany, in venting indignation upon American superficiality, must be careful not to become superficially and undialectically rigid in turn.

To such general observations must be added something that concerns the specific situation of the sociologist or, less technically, that of anybody who regards the knowledge of society as central for and indivisible from that of philosophy. Within the total development of middle-class civilization, the United States has undoubtedly arrived at one extreme. She displays capitalism in a state of almost complete purity, without any pre-capitalistic remnants. If one accepts, in contrast to a very widely held opinion, that the other non-communist countries outside the so-called "Third World" are moving toward the same condition, then America precisely offers the most advanced observation post for anybody who would escape from a naïve posture toward either America or Europe. Indeed, the returnee finds many things confirmed in Europe, or sees them in the process of coming to pass, that first struck him in America. Whatever a serious cultural criticism might have to say when confronted with American conditions since Tocqueville and Kürnberger, one cannot avoid in America the question whether the concept of culture, in which one was brought up, has not itself become obsolete. One is further led to wonder whether this is not the result of the general tendency in contemporary culture toward self-castigation for its failures, the guilt it incurred by holding itself aloof in a separate sphere of the intellect, without manifesting itself in social reality. Certainly this did not happen in America either but the prospect of such effectiveness is not as obstructed there as in Europe. With respect to quantitative thinking in America, with all of its dangers of lack of discrimination and apotheosis of the average, Europeans must raise the deeply disturbing question how far qualitative differences matter in the present social world. Already the airports are interchangeably alike in all parts of Europe, America, and the countries of the Third World; already it is hardly a matter of days but of hours to travel from one country to the remotest reaches of the world. The differences not only in living standards but in the distinctive character of peoples and their forms of existence assume an anachronistic aspect. To be sure, it is still uncertain whether the similarities are decisive and the qualitative differences merely recessive, and above all whether it might not be that in a rationally ordered world the qualitative distinctions, which are today suppressed by the unity of a technologically oriented spirit, would again come into their own. Yet reflections of this sort are hardly conceivable without American experience. It is scarcely an exaggeration to say that any contemporary consciousness that has not appropriated the American experience, even if in opposition, has something reactionary about it.

In conclusion, perhaps I may add a word about the particular significance of scientific life in America for me personally and for my thinking. My speculations deviate considerably from "common sense." But Hegel, thereby displaying his superiority to all later forms of irrationalism and intuitionism, laid the greatest emphasis upon the principle that speculative thought is not absolutely distinct from the so-called healthy common sense but consists essentially in its critical self-reflection and self-scrutiny. Even a mind that rejects the idealism of the total Hegelian scheme must not stop short of this insight. Anybody who goes as far in criticizing common sense as I have done must meet the simple requirement of having common sense. He must not claim to have transcended something whose discipline he was never able to satisfy. In America I truly experienced for the first time the importance of what is called empiricism, though I was guided from youth on by the conviction that fruitful theoretical knowledge is impossible except in the closest contact with its materials. Conversely, I had to recognize with respect to the form of empiricism applied in scientific practice in America, that full scope of experience is fettered by empirical rules excluding anything that is inherent in the concept of direct life experience. By no means the worst characterization of what I had in mind would be a kind of vindication of experience against its translation into empirical terms. That was not the least important factor that led me to return to Germany, along with the possibility of following my own purposes without hindrance for a time in Europe and contributing something toward political enlightenment. This, however, did not in the least alter my gratitude, including intellectual gratitude, toward America, nor do I ever expect to forget as a scholar what I learned there.

THE DIASPORA OF
EXPERIMENTAL PSYCHOLOGY:
THE GESTALTISTS AND OTHERS

by JEAN MATTER MANDLER and GEORGE MANDLER

A S we began to write an account of the experimental psychologists who came to the United States up to the beginning of the
American involvement in the Second World War, we were
painfully aware of the impossibility of doing justice to such a task in
1967. The presumption of nonhistorians to write history of science is
compounded by the lack of perspective about the effects one is trying to
describe. A few years ago, we outlined some historical trends in the history of the psychology of thinking, and we were aware then, as we are
now, that the closer we came to the twentieth century, the more confusing the lines of influence became, and the more difficult it was to be
either objective or wise.[1]

The dean of American psychology and its most eminent historian,
Professor E. G. Boring, wrote in 1929 that "the beginning of the twentieth century is too close for a just historical evaluation," and "the last
two decades are not yet history at all."[2] To attempt, some forty years
later, a historical evaluation of events that had not yet taken place when
those words were written is surely foolhardy. When we add our beliefs
that broad historical developments in a science are not discernible at
first, that historical, cultural, psychological, and social forces are operative over and above the influence of individuals, we are forced to abandon all pretense at objectivity or wisdom and present what follows as a
personal document. We trust that as such it may be useful to a historian

1. Jean M. Mandler and George Mandler, *Thinking: From Association to Gestalt* (New
York, 1964). We have also discussed there the intellectual ancestry of the Gestalt movement as it affected the psychology of thinking.
2. Edwin G. Boring, *A History of Experimental Psychology* (New York, 1929), p. 645.
See also the second edition for a history of German psychology and the Gestalt movement in particular.

of psychology in the twenty-first century, when he writes a history of this century.

In what follows, we have restricted ourselves to the field of experimental psychology broadly conceived. Others have written and will write, both in this volume and others, about how psychoanalysis crossed the ocean, how clinical and other applied aspects of psychology were molded and influenced by the immigrations of the twentieth century, how developmental psychology was formed by immigrants and visitors from Central Europe, and how social psychology assimilated European social theory. Since we are too close to discern movements, we shall talk primarily about individuals. In a sense, there were few truly influential immigrants, just as the total number of immigrants in psychology was very small. The story we have to tell deals very largely with Gestalt psychology. It deals with the transformation of a movement from Germany to the United States. We shall sometimes roam over areas that are not strictly in experimental psychology, and we shall be able to give some space to psychologists who were not strictly members of the Gestalt movement. In the main, however, this is the story of Gestalt psychology and of some of its ancillary friends and foes. Many important psychologists were omitted because they were peripheral to our concerns.

The source of what follows is varied. We have corresponded with some thirty or forty psychologists, we have talked with some dozen at length, we have intruded our preoccupations into many conversations with colleagues to develop a feeling for the effects of the immigration on American psychology. We are particularly grateful to Mrs. Elinor G. Barber, biography editor of the *International Encyclopedia of the Social Sciences*, for making available biographies in galley form prior to publication of the *Encyclopedia*.[3] The Archives of the History of American Psychology kindly made their files available to us.[4] Most important are

3. David L. Sills, ed., *International Encyclopedia of the Social Sciences* (New York, 1968), hereinafter cited as *Encyclopedia*.

4. We are grateful to Dr. John A. Popplestone, Director, and Dr. Marion W. McPherson, Associate Director, of the Archives for their cooperation not only in providing us with available material but also in searching their files and the oral history records for relevant material. The correspondence and communications received in connection with our work will be deposited with the Archives at the University of Akron. Further reference here will be to *Archives*.

the dozens of letters we received recounting personal reminiscences, biographical details, and evaluations. To all those psychologists who felt that this chapter should be written as a reminder of an important period in the history of American psychology, we are most grateful. In particular, we are grateful for the many new friends we found in the process. Finally, we were most fortunate to be able to persuade Dr. Alfred Marrow to let us read the first draft of his important biography of Kurt Lewin.

1. The Situation in the United States

TO set the stage for the arrival of the immigrant German and Austrian psychologists, we must essay a characterization of the state of American psychology in the decade between 1925 and 1935. To the extent that German psychology, as represented by its immigrant scholars in the United States, affected the American scene, its influence must have been the result of interactions between two very different and essentially disparate intellectual traditions.

If, in 1910, somebody had told a group of American psychologists that twenty-five years later the arrival of some of the major representatives of German experimental psychology would create a collision between two different intellectual forces, he would have been ridiculed. In 1910, American psychology was an outpost of German experimental psychology. The promising young psychologist who wanted to make his way was practically guaranteed recognition, or at least acceptance into the establishment—small though it was at the time—if he spent some time at one of the major German laboratories, particularly Wundt's in Leipzig. Pilgrimage to Germany was necessary for any American psychologist who could afford it financially or intellectually. German experimental sensationism and atomism, as exported through the returning travelers, or by the sheer intellectual force of the grand old man of American psychology, E. B. Titchener (a German-trained Englishman), was the dominant force. William James had ably and eloquently fought against the German tradition, but though James was partially successful at Harvard, the major thrust of American psychology was German in origin and method.

By 1930 the situation had changed radically. During the first quarter of the century, behaviorism under the leadership of John B. Watson not only challenged the philosophical traditions prevalent in the non-experimental departments, it also overwhelmed experimental psychology that depended on introspectionist evidence, and subverted the functionalist school, which was intellectually indebted to John Dewey and developed in Chicago under the leadership of James Rowland Angell and Harvey A. Carr. The alliance among behaviorism, functionalism (with its comparative, evolutionary, pragmatic, and empirical emphases), and the remnants of British empiricism (i.e., associationism) dominated philosophical conceptions of the structure of the mind. The new Pavlovian rumblings from Russia also helped to create in America an experimental psychology which not only rejected introspective evidence as an empirical basis for a scientific psychology, but also emphasized comparative (animal) research, and reinstated a naive empiricism and associationism which had already been rejected by some of the more sophisticated associationists in England and Germany, such as Alexander Bain and G. E. Müller. In addition, or as a result of these tendencies, the investigation of complex human thought and perception was postponed. What was in fact an actual rejection was frequently represented as a postponement, with the claim that the investigation of complex human mental events must be relegated to the future when the basic elements of behavior, i.e., the conditioned reflex, and other simple responses in simple animals would be understood. These responses were to be the building blocks for an eventual science of the higher mental processes. This promissory note, or rubber check, dominated American thinking. It did not exclude other trends, and we do not claim that countervailing forces did not exist.

It has been suggested that the prevailing atmosphere was antitheoretical in its stance. The statement needs some elaboration. One might point to the paucity of theoretical thought in the early behaviorists, or one can point to the sorry joke of functionalism which started as a grand enterprise designed to accommodate psychology to Darwin and which used "function" in his sense, but which ended up as a label for dustbowl empiricism, narrowly concerned with some limited set of response variables operating as a "function" of an even more limited set of environmental events. In the area of human thought and language American psychology continued Hermann Ebbinghaus' tradition of the late nineteenth century in Germany, again betting on the eventual understanding of complex language and thought through the investigation of simple learning of simple events. Explicit theory was absent, and years of diligent research dealt with the effects of easily manipulated environmental variables. The complexity of language, the complexity of thought were rarely approximated or even admitted. When theory was attempted in the behaviorist camp, *e.g.*, the ambitious and grand theoretical attempts of Clark L. Hull, there was always the injunction that theoretical constructs must never again lead one to mentalism and complex mental structures. Even Hull, when building a theoretical model, reminds himself that it is not theory that is dominant but the observable, and he creates theoretical constructs which are internal representations of the cornerstones of behaviorist psychology, the Stimulus and the Response written small, s and r. We do not have the space or the motivation to look further into the effects of a transplanted operationism, advocated by the physicist, Percy Bridgman, on the model of his own precise and highly theoretical science, and deposited intact in an undeveloped empirical science like psychology.[5]

Thus the decade around 1930 finds in America an antimentalistic, comparative, pragmatic psychology. German hegemony had died with Titchener, and American psychology was to a very real extent American. To that extent, it was also xenophobic. The economic conditions which we will briefly refer to below certainly were one stumbling block for the settlement and placement of refugee psychologists, but there is no doubt about an attitude, expressed time and time again in our interviews with witnesses of the period, that the German psychologists and, in particular, the Gestalt group, were seen as intruders, alien to the prevailing psychological atmosphere.

American empiricism rejected the nativism of the Gestalt school,

5. See George Mandler and William Kessen, *The Language of Psychology* (New York, 1959) for a discussion of the conceptual background of psychology.

American functionalism rejected the frequently obscure theorizing of the Gestaltists, and American behaviorism neither wanted to nor could handle complex problems of cognitive processes. On the whole, the American establishment in psychology, firmly based at Harvard, Cornell, Princeton, Yale, Chicago, rejected the new psychology from Europe, particularly a psychology which had taken as one of its aims a determined opposition to behaviorism. Behaviorism was too new, too successful, too exciting an enterprise not to fight back spiritedly against the foreign invaders.

11. The German Background

BY the middle of the third decade of the century, Gestalt psychology had become one of the leading forces, if not the dominant theme, in German psychology. To a very large extent, it was the latest and most successful development in experimental German psychology. It must be remembered that the experimental, empirical tradition in psychology was only about fifty years old by then, and that even today much of European and particularly German and Austrian psychology is still committed to a philosophical, anthropological approach to its subject matter.

The birth of Gestalt psychology proper can be dated fairly precisely to Max Wertheimer's investigations of apparent movement in 1910, first published in 1912.[6] There had been previous attacks on the analytic, atomistic position of German experimental psychology and its ideological cousin, English empiricism and associationism. However, these attempts did not go as far as Wertheimer did. Wertheimer not only questioned the atomistic assumptions but also proposed alternative conceptions, specifically by denying the reality of sensory elements as part of perceptual experience.[7] He showed that the perceptual experience of motion was not some additive result of successive sensations of position,

6. Max Wertheimer, "Experimentelle Studien über das Sehen von Bewegung," *Zeitschrift für Psychologie und Physiologie der Sinnesorgane*, 61 (1912), 161–265.
7. Solomon E. Asch, "Gestalt Theory" in Encyclopedia. An excellent discussion of the theoretical issues involved in the Gestalt revolution.

but rather that perceived movement produced a new unitary outcome which could not be split up into successive stationary sensations. This insight was to revolutionize the experimental investigation of visual perception, but it also, in the wider forms of the Gestalt movement, changed the conception of the unit of psychological analysis. Sensationism, structuralism, the stress on the analysis of elements in psychophysics as the basis of psychology receded into the background, and the new analysis of the functional units of thought and perception, units not analyzable or definable in terms of their constituents, preoccupied the experimental psychologists in Germany.

To say that Gestalt psychology was successful in this revolution is to say too much and too little. Many of the specific theoretical notions that accompanied the insight that higher order units of perception and thought are important in psychology failed to survive beyond the field of visual perception. However, the acceptance of the notion that these higher order units are the psychological events that must be investigated is the success that Gestalt psychology has had and that no psychologist after the 1930's in Germany and after the 1940's in America and elsewhere was able to ignore. In that sense, current psychology has relived the Gestalt revolution at a different level and with different emphases. It might be noted that the so-called production theory of the Austrian psychologists that preceded the Gestalt movement probably better represents current attitudes. The production school insisted that Gestalt qualities result from complex mental operations imposed on sense data. In the same way, it is Karl Bühler's emphasis on the learning of rules and Otto Selz's notion of mental operations that are recognizable today. But what made today possible was the dynamic influence of the Gestalt school which posed the proper questions.

Wertheimer at Frankfurt first excited Kurt Koffka's interest, and in 1915 Koffka, then at Giessen, wrote an article which recorded what Wertheimer then and subsequently was hesitant to commit to public print—the principles of Gestalt psychology. Koffka and Wolfgang Köhler, at Berlin, were fascinated by Wertheimer's work, and just at a point when further collaboration might have developed, Köhler went to Tenerife in the Canary Islands to study chimpanzees. Köhler was forced by the war to stay in Africa for more than six years, and during that time continued his research, then under the influence both of Wertheimer's ideas and those of Max Planck. This wedding of the psychology of perception and physical field theory was to influence all of Köhler's subsequent work.

It is frequently believed that Köhler's position on Gestalt psychology represented its core. He was, by all means, the most prolific and, from an American point of view, the most forceful agent of the movement. However, a triumvirate representing the intellectual aegis of Gestalt psychology came into being after Köhler's return to Germany, and of the three leaders of the movement, Wertheimer, Koffka, and Köhler, it was understood that Wertheimer was the intellectual father, the thinker, and the innovator. In part, Wertheimer's influence then and later in America was due to his charm but also due to his mystic and romantic philosophical preoccupation with his subject matter. Koffka was the salesman of the group and, in fact, was probably more responsible than anybody else for the fact that America became the home of German Gestalt psychology. As we shall see below, his early departure for America set the ground for later developments. Köhler was the inside man, the doer, the writer.

In any case, Gestalt psychology had developed to an important internationally known movement in German psychology by the early 1920's. American psychologists came to study in Berlin as did many other Germans, Austrians, and Europeans. The close relationship among the triumvirs, their attraction for the best brains in psychology, and their obviously superior ability to attract thought and disciples, created a nucleus of psychology in Berlin, much of which eventually emigrated to the United States. Not only were the three great men there at one time or another, but Kurt Lewin also became part of the group, Fritz Heider spent some time there, as did George Katona from Hungary, and some of the younger generation who were all to come to the United States later, such as Rudolf Arnheim, Hans Wallach, and Karl Duncker. German atomism, sensationism, and associationism had been supplanted as a source of inspiration in psychology. However, the remnants of nineteenth-century German experimental psychology were still central to psychology in the United States, particularly in association with the peculiarly American revolution of behaviorism.

How did the German psychologists react to the American scene? A nonpsychologist, Franz L. Neumann, writing about the difference in the two atmospheres noted that "the German exile, bred in the veneration of theory and history, and contempt for empiricism and pragmatism, entered a diametrically opposed intellectual climate: optimistic, empirically oriented, ahistorical, but also self-righteous."[8]

In the same book in which Neumann made this observation, Köhler wrote about his experiences in coming to America on a permanent basis.[9] He notes that when physicists arrived in the United States there was no doubt about the essential direction, facts, and procedures of physics. However, in psychology, the infant science, "premises of individual or national origin are bound to have a strong influence upon scientific contact."

Köhler points out that the history of American psychology necessarily had European ancestry so that the new European influx and influence were in line with previous American experiences, but at the same time he demonstrates the superciliousness with which many of the German immigrants were charged, when in describing the background of various American psychological trends he notes: "The behaviorists, too, held convictions which had arrived from Europe; but these convictions had far less illustrious sources." (p. 127) But he also pays proper respect to the important American influence on psychological science in the twentieth century, the development of experimental procedures, and a much stricter attitude about experimental proof than had been present before. And he notes that it must be possible "to combine the American insistence upon precise procedures with the European tendency first of all to get a good view of the phenomena which are to be investigated with so much precision." (p. 135) In describing the impact of behaviorism on American psychology, he talks about traditional German experimental psychology and its fate: "The part of the imported science which dealt with the inspection of mental data collapsed in a surprisingly short time; even former students of Titchener were gradually

8. Franz L. Neumann et al., *The Cultural Migration: The European Scholar in America* (Philadelphia, 1953).
9. Wolfgang Köhler, "The Scientists and their New Environment," in Neumann, *The Cultural Migration*. All quotes of Köhler in this section are taken from that chapter.

converted to the new religion. When I first came to this country a young psychologist would hesitate to confess that he was not yet entirely convinced. Whichever way he turned, all around him the Joneses in psychology were now talking Behaviorese." (p. 121)

III. American Psychologists and the Immigration

THERE is little evidence that psychological organizations, either in Germany or in the United States, took immediate cognizance of the threat to academic and scientific freedom or of the threat to the individual livelihoods and lives of psychologists. Wellek's protestations to the contrary,[10] despite individual acts of political protest, organized German psychology, like most organized German science, did not protest its role in the new Germany. Publicly, German psychology accepted with equanimity both the dictum that this "Jewish" field was in for major upheaval and the removal of its leaders.

Some of the major figures in our story, such as Wertheimer, Lewin, and Köhler reacted with an immediate awareness to the events of 1933. The active flight from Germany started that year; in many cases, that flight was made easier by prior, primarily nonpolitical departures for America, by such men as Koffka and Heider.

When did the American psychological community formally take cognizance of the fact that what was happening in Germany and in Austria required more than personal political awareness, that concerted action was necessary for the defense of individual dignity and possibly lives?

In the United States, there is little evidence of any concerted action for the first five years of the Nazi regime. To be sure, nonprofessional organizations and individuals in the profession worked hard and long,

10. Albert Wellek, "The Impact of the German Immigration on the Development of American Psychology," *Journal of the History of the Behavioral Sciences*, 4 (1968), 207–229; previously published as "Der Einfluss der deutschen Emigration auf die Entwicklung der nord-amerikanischen Psychologie," *Jahrbuch für Amerikastudien*, 10 (1965), 34–58.

and sacrificed time, money, and effort to provide a haven for their colleagues. But America was riding out the Depression, and America was
preoccupied, understandably so, with its own problems.

It is not unreasonable to suppose that the mounting international
threat of Germany contributed to an increasing awareness in this country of events going on within the German borders. In 1937, the International Committee of the International Psychological Congress awarded the Twelfth International Congress to Vienna. In March of 1938,
Austria was occupied by German troops, and the following month the
Midwestern Psychological Association, meeting in Madison, Wisconsin, passed a resolution[11] requesting the International Committee to select a meeting-place "in a country which permits the unhampered development of psychology and of other sciences," and requested the
Executive Committee of the International Committee to add Karl
Bühler, who had been briefly arrested in Vienna, as an associate of the
Committee.[12] The resolution condemned "the Nazi dictatorship, which
has subordinated the integrity of science and of scientists to a political
creed, which has caused the dismissal of many scientists and scholars
from their positions," and is "thus in the process of reducing Vienna and
the rest of Austria to the same anti-intellectual, anti-scientific status that
is now Germany's official position."

Similar resolutions were passed by the Western Psychological Association and other groups. The Twelfth Congress was to be held in 1941,
but the cascade of events overtook those plans before then.

Whether influenced by an awareness of the political significance of a
Congress to be held in the Third Reich or generally driven by the pressure of events, in the fall of 1938, the American Psychological Association appointed a committee "to survey the problem of psychologists
displaced from their positions and livelihoods in other countries and
seeking asylum and professional opportunities elsewhere." This committee, the Committee on Displaced Foreign Psychologists, operated

11. Correspondence and documents relevant to this resolution and to the work of the
Burks committee were obtained from the *Archives*.

12. It might be noted that the resolution unequivocally made its political points. The
request for Bühler's appointment to the Committee was an act similar to the appointment
of the Spaniard, Emilio Mira, to the Executive Committee when the Eleventh Congress
had been moved in the previous year from Madrid to Paris.

most effectively under the leadership of Barbara S. Burks from 1938 until Dr. Burks' death in 1943. At the time of her death, most of the work of the Committee had been done and the Committee was disbanded.

For most of the five years of its existence, the Committee consisted of some ten members, one of whom was a "displaced foreign psychologist" himself, Max Wertheimer. From the beginning, the Committee was faced with the fact that it was operating in a depressed labor market. Its first statement in 1939 says that the Committee "has endeavored to find 'noncompetitive' positions for foreign psychologists." And throughout its history, it was faced with the difficult problem of trying to import psychologists into a country where many American psychologists were unable to find positions. In June 1939, Dr. Burks wrote to the Secretary of the American Psychological Association that the "work for displaced foreign psychologists should be coordinated with work for unplaced American psychologists." However, the Association decided to maintain an independent committee on foreign psychologists.

Within a surprisingly short time after its establishment, the Burks Committee, in March 1939, issued a list of "displaced foreign scholars," which included 111 names and descriptive data, including previous training and professional connections, family situation, current location and professional connections, languages spoken, fields of work, main publications, and professional references. This confidential list, kept confidential because of possible difficulties for those who had not yet been able to emigrate or for relatives remaining inside the German borders, was circulated to five hundred members of the APA and to other interested individuals and agencies. Most of the displaced psychologists who reached the United States were interviewed by one or more members of the Committee. Thus, by the end of its first year of operation, the Committee had interviewed some seventy-six individuals, including about a third who were not strictly psychologists but had had medical or philosophical training. Most of the placements that the Committee was able to secure were temporary internships in schools and institutions, temporary research and teaching positions, and in some cases volunteer positions. A total of thirty individuals was placed during the 1938–39 year of operation. Much of this work was done with the only resource available being the effort and dedication of Dr. Burks and other Committee members. The funds available to the Committee were pitiful. APA donated fifty dollars, and various other organizations and private individuals raised the total to some $580. Other national organizations provided funds for the support of the displaced psychologists, but the only funds available from psychologists themselves helped in very minor aspects of the work of this Committee.

By June of 1940, the Committee had been in touch with some 269 displaced scholars. About half of these were in the United States; the other half were still seeking entry. The Committee still had to be concerned with the unemployment problem and stressed in its Annual Report in the fall of 1940 that it was "supporting a policy of cultivating new opportunities in psychology, rather than increasing competitive pressure through partiality toward refugees."

In the following year, the Committee noted that "only a small proportion of the group either in this or other countries are in jobs commensurate with their training and experience." During 1940–41, some twenty emigré psychologists reached the United States, as compared with thirty in the previous year, and the total number in the United States reached 159. The last formal report of the Committee covers the year 1941–42, when "only a handful of refugee psychologists" arrived. During that year, the Committee had a $200 appropriation of which it spent $80. Its work was coming to an end, and Barbara Burks met her own untimely end in May 1943. In a letter in August 1943, Gordon W. Allport submitted a resolution to the Council of the American Psychological Association which characterized her "modest and generous efforts in behalf of refugee members of the profession," and in the letter calls her successes "not numerous [but] they were occasionally brilliant. There are a few instances . . . where her efforts surely turned the tide from disaster to success."

In retrospect, it seems ludicrous to talk of the influence of some hundred-odd psychologists, assisted by an organization that spent less than one thousand dollars over a period of five years in helping to integrate them into American psychology, and to assess the influence this handful of people had on a profession that today has some twenty thousand members and a yearly budget of over $2,000,000. When it is remembered that one-third of the psychologists who were in touch with the Burks Committee were either medically or philosophically trained, it becomes even more puzzling how the notion that American psychology in the forties was overrun by European immigrants ever gained credence. The puzzlement persists even if one grants the confusion between psychology and psychoanalysis, between psychology and psychiatry, and that the general identification of psychology with clinical psychology somewhat muddied the public perception of the field. It is not our intent here to discuss the quantitative impact of the refugee psychologists and psychoanalysts in such fields as clinical practice and training, developmental psychology, or applied psychology. However, what must become obvious is that the influence of the immigration on American experimental psychology was an influence of quality and not of quantity.

We have mentioned only collective efforts by psychologists and obviously very little can be said in the present context about the large number of public organizations and the devoted individuals who spent time, effort, and financial resources to help the European refugees. But one organization must be mentioned briefly because of the impact it made on American academic life and psychology—the New School for Social Research, and particularly its Graduate Faculty. As Clara W. Mayer, the then dean of the New School, pointed out to us: "The New School practically determined the receptivity of the intellectual world of America to the scholars from abroad." The Rockefeller Foundation had approached Alvin Johnson, the first president of the New School, with the offer to bring one hundred scholars to the United States. But the Rockefeller Foundation failed to reach that figure even though, through the facilities of the New School and many other foundations, two hundred scholars and their families did arrive at the New School during the period of immigration. Alvin Johnson selected the first group to come to the "University-in-Exile," and, throughout the thirties and early forties, was involved in the recruitment and selection of faculty. Among the experimental psychologists who taught or studied there were Max Wertheimer, George Katona, E. M. von Hornbostel, Rudolf Arnheim, Kurt Goldstein, Hans Wallach, and Martin Scheerer. Wolfgang Köhler visited frequently and taught there occasionally, and one semester Kurt Koffka substituted for Wertheimer in his seminar. The Graduate Faculty of the New School for Social Research was the first foothold for German experimental psychology in this country, and without it, much of what we have to tell might never have happened. This small group of psychologists is only one indication of the valuable work the New School did in fields other than psychology. As a major scholarly organization out of the mainstream of the American academic establishment, and often hostilely regarded by it, it made the transition to America possible in some cases, bearable in others.

In the preceding pages we have tried to sketch the intellectual background of German and American psychology and some of the specific interactions between American psychology and the immigration. We have used "America" and "United States" interchangeably and actually the distinction is difficult to maintain. Canadian psychology was then and has continued to be generally part of the same intellectual atmosphere as psychology in the U.S. Few European psychologists and none of the major figures in experimental psychology found their way to Canada. The effect of the immigration on Canada and its eminent psychologists —such as Donald O. Hebb—was parallel to that in the United States. Finally, as far as Latin America is concerned, the effect of the immigration in experimental psychology was negligible.

iv. The Gestalt School

FOREMOST in the migration of the Gestalt school to the United States was the move of its leading triumvirate—Max Wertheimer, Wolfgang Köhler, and Kurt Koffka. We shall deal with them in order of their arrival in the United States.

Kurt Koffka

Koffka was born in 1886 and received his degree of Doctor of Philosophy at Berlin in 1908.[13] His early work was in the classical tradition

13. See Grace M. Heider, "Kurt Koffka," in *Encyclopedia* for a more extensive biography.

of German psychology, first, with Carl Stumpf, then at von Kries's laboratory in Freiburg, and finally at Würzburg with Oswald Külpe and Karl Marbe. Würzburg was the center of the new psychology which had criticized associationism and questioned the elementarism of German psychology at the turn of the century. In 1912, Koffka wrote a book on the analysis of images and their laws which stemmed directly from the Würzburg tradition.[14] It might also be noted that he spent from 1904 to 1905 in Edinburgh where he not only learned English but became a committed Anglophile.

In 1910, he went to Frankfurt where he and Köhler were working as assistants when Wertheimer arrived. Both Koffka and Köhler were subjects for Wertheimer's first Gestalt experiments on apparent movement. In 1911, Koffka moved to Giessen where he became professor in 1918. In 1924, he accepted a professorship for one year at Cornell, and in the spring of 1925, he and Köhler, representing the Gestalt school, participated in a conference at Clark University. In 1926–27, Koffka went to the University of Wisconsin, and in 1927 was appointed for a five-year period to the William Allan Neilson Chair at Smith College, where he remained until 1941 and his death.

Why did Koffka come to the United States and settle here? We have already mentioned his Anglophilia. There are indications that he would have very much liked to move to England, a country, however, with an academic and ideological structure that essentially prevented a German professor from achieving a reasonable position. There were also personal reasons for his departure in the twenties, but we must note, that even prior to the impact of the political situation (and Koffka was half Jewish), Koffka's position in Germany had become at least difficult. He had been the major, most bitter, and sometimes vituperative exponent of the Gestalt school. It was Koffka who attacked its opponents in print and by word of mouth, and it was Koffka against whom much of the bitter hostility to Gestalt psychology in Germany was directed. Koffka was apparently in part responsible for the appointment of Köhler to the major German chair in psychology at Berlin, but there was little possibility that he himself might move from the professorship at Giessen—a minor provincial university. He had an excellent command of English,

14. See Mandler and Mandler, *Thinking*, for translated excerpts from this work.

and America offered him an opportunity for a personal career that may have been closed to him by then in Germany.

In assessing Koffka's influence, it is useful to quote from Grace M. Heider's biography of Koffka which describes the interrelated character of the Gestalt school. She writes:

> It is impossible to treat Koffka's contribution without taking into account the unique collaboration that produced the Gestalt movement. The men whose names were originally connected with it formed a close-knit triumvirate, and to some extent it is impossible to attribute particular aspects of the theory to one rather than another.[15]

However, some of his personal influence was specific and of some interest. When he was at Wisconsin, Clark L. Hull sat in on his seminar, and it is reported that on several subsequent occasions Hull noted that his opposition to Gestalt psychology and commitment to behaviorism was solidified by his negative reaction to Koffka's pronouncements at Wisconsin. On the other hand, E. C. Tolman, the other giant of the behaviorist learning theory movement, corresponded with Koffka, and they frequently discussed Tolman's book on purposive behavior,[16] which although behaviorist, was anti-associationist and deeply in debt to the Gestalt movement.

Koffka directly affected one important contributor to the American scene: Harry Helson was moved, in part by Koffka's article in the *Psychological Bulletin* in 1922,[17] to embark on an extensive exposition and critique of Gestalt psychology. Helson's work, his doctoral thesis, published in four articles between 1925 and 1926, made it possible for Americans to learn about the movement in detail. Helson was at Cornell when Koffka came in 1924–25 and tells of Koffka's impact in his autobiographical article.[18] That effect apparently was entirely on the personal level since the expected confrontation between Titchener and Koffka in Titchener's seminar never was allowed to develop. Helson's own work reflects clearly his early contact with the movement.

---

15. Heider, "Koffka."

16. Edward C. Tolman, *Purposive Behavior in Animals and Men* (Berkeley, 1932).

17. Kurt Koffka, "Perception: An Introduction to the Gestalt-Theorie," *Psychological Bulletin*, 19 (1922), 531–585.

18. Harry Helson, *A History of Psychology in Autobiography*, v (New York, 1967). The Gestalt articles were published in: Harry Helson, "The Psychology of Gestalt," *American Journal of Psychology*, 36 (1925), 342–370, 494–526; 37 (1926), 25–62, 189–223.

Apart from the passing contacts at Wisconsin and Cornell, Koffka's home base was at Smith College. James J. Gibson comments about those years:[19]

> Koffka had been brought to Northampton by William Allan Neilson, who installed him in an old house off the campus, permitted him to import assistants from Russia, Poland, Germany, and elsewhere, and let him experiment to his heart's content. Neilson had not consulted his department of psychology in making this research appointment, and the teaching staff did not quite know whether to be honored or offended. But Koffka promptly set up a weekly seminar to which we were cordially invited.
>
> Koffka did most of the talking, and I listened regularly from 1928 to 1941. I sometimes reported my own work and I occasionally ventured to argue with him, for my bent was skeptical and pragmatic. Koffka hated positivism. The emerging doctrines of Gestalt theory seemed to me tenderminded, but I learned a great deal, for the seminar was centered on evidence and the analysis of evidence. In 1933, after the original research funds had been exhausted, Koffka became a member of the department, teaching one course. He then began to put together the *Principles of Gestalt Psychology* (1935), requiring his undergraduates to summarize sections of his manuscript in class as he went along. This strange method of teaching, you might suppose, would soon bring his course enrollment to zero (the worst of all fates at a college), but, on the contrary, the girls were dazzled. He chose the brightest. It was a serious book, dedicated to difficult problems, and there was no compromise with difficulty.

One of the undergraduates with whom Koffka discussed the manuscript of the *Principles* was Mary Henle, who commented to us that she considers Koffka one of the stimulating and influential figures in her education. Among the psychologists Koffka had brought from abroad were Fritz Heider, Alexander Mintz, Tamara Dembo, and Eugenia Hanfmann. In general, however, he had no trained followers as Wertheimer and Köhler did. Apparently, Molly Harrower was the only student at Smith to take a Ph.D. with him.

At most times, Koffka was the slightly condescending European bringing "the word" to the Americans. He influenced the people with whom he interacted, although sometimes the interaction had more the character of a reaction. Gibson comments that Koffka was a major influence on his thinking but it took him a long time to fully appreciate the worth of Koffka's book.

Koffka's most important contribution was through his comprehen-

19. James J. Gibson, in *A History of Psychology in Autobiography*, v (New York, 1967), 130.

sive and systematic application of Gestalt principles, first in the *Growth of the Mind* in 1921 and later in 1935 in the *Principles of Gestalt Psychology*.[20] And it was primarily through his books rather than through personal contact that he influenced the psychological community. Most of our correspondents point to the 1921 book as Koffka's major contribution. It clearly prepared the American community for Gestalt ideas, although the dominant influence of the Gestalt school on America was via Wolfgang Köhler.

Finally, we should mention Koffka's somewhat peripheral relation to the psychological establishment. He gained the chair at Smith—which had first been offered to Köhler—largely through the influence of R. M. Ogden who had translated the *Growth of the Mind* and brought Koffka to Cornell. But Ogden was head of the School of Education at Cornell, and it was the Education group at Smith College that persuaded the president of Smith College to appoint one of the Gestalt group to the William Allan Neilson Research Chair. Similarly, Lewin was connected with the School of Home Economics at Cornell and the Institute of Child Welfare at Iowa. The Gestalt school certainly entered into American psychology, as Koffka was the first to do, but they came through the back door. On the practical side, the German professors just were not the type to take care of day-to-day work of an American professorship. Koffka was very much the European professor abroad. He rarely could be bothered to handle bookkeeping on grades and course work, and when he encountered conflicts at Smith he carried his case over the heads of the department to his friend, the president of the College. This was more German than American professorial behavior. But American or not, he taught and persuaded.

Max Wertheimer

Wertheimer was at least the godfather and certainly one of the most influential and powerful of the creators of Gestalt psychology. He was, of the triumvirate, the founder, almost the mystic, whereas Köhler was the natural scientist, the thinker, and Koffka was the systematizer, who also handled the public relations. Wertheimer was a powerful intellect.

20. Kurt Koffka, *The Growth of the Mind* (New York, 1924), originally published in German, 1921; *Principles of Gestalt Psychology* (New York, 1935).

Some saw him as "impatient, dogmatic, but very powerful." Others describe him as "charming, almost retiring." N. R. F. Maier, in his Oral History,[21] tells of his visit to Berlin and relates the impression that Wertheimer was the high priest, although Köhler seemed to be. Wolfgang Köhler was the director of the laboratory, but he always listened to Wertheimer, and if Wertheimer disagreed with something, Köhler would back down. Of the three, Wertheimer was the most philosophically and romantically oriented.

Wertheimer was born in Prague in 1880, and thus was, by some six or seven years, the oldest of the triumvirate.[22] His early interests were in poetry, literature, and music, and his enduring musical interests extended to composition. In the United States, practically all those who had contact with him recounted his charming preoccupation with providing musical portraits of friends and acquaintances, and playing guessing games with these portraits. His music also brought him, while in the United States, into contact with Albert Einstein, with whom he played chamber music.

After an early and brief attempt at the study of law, Wertheimer went to the University of Berlin where he studied psychology with Carl Stumpf and Friedrich Schumann, ending up at the University of Würzburg where he received his Ph.D. with Külpe in 1904. His early work on testimony and criminal investigation and on *alexia* could not have predicted the birth of formal Gestalt psychology. That event happened in Frankfurt in 1910. Wertheimer had been mulling over the inadequacies in the associationist analysis of psychological phenomena, and had been searching for a perceptual example to demonstrate his new ideas. He was traveling through Frankfurt when the idea of using a stroboscope occurred to him, and using Köhler and Koffka as his subjects he demonstrated the Phi phenomenon of apparent movement. The report of the experiment at the 1911 meeting of the *Gesellschaft für Experimentelle Psychologie* and the working out of a structural and dynamic analysis of the phenomenon by the three experimenters launched Gestalt psychology as a new movement.

21. In the *Archives*, and made available by permission of Dr. N. R. F. Maier.
22. Abraham S. Luchins, "Max Wertheimer," in *Encyclopedia*, from which following quotes are taken.

During the First World War, Wertheimer served in the German army, and from 1916 until 1929, the period that was to become the high point of the development of Gestalt psychology, he worked at the University of Berlin.

We might note that one of the important influences on American psychology was initiated during the period, again with Wertheimer as the spiritual leader. In the early twenties, American psychologists still found it desirable, and in contrast with today, necessary, to read the German literature in psychology. Thus the creation of a new journal, the *Psychologische Forschung*, was an important event not only in Germany but throughout the psychological world. The journal was started by Wertheimer, Koffka, and Köhler, together with Kurt Goldstein and Hans Gruhle. Wertheimer was editor of the journal for its first twenty volumes, from 1922 to 1935.

In 1929, Wertheimer accepted the chair at the University of Frankfurt, where he stayed until his departure from Germany. His career at Frankfurt was again marked by renewed interest in philosophical questions, and he not only taught psychology but participated in philosophical seminars with, among others, Paul Tillich. Wertheimer left Germany secretly the day before Germany voted Nazi in March 1933. He had listened to one of Hitler's speeches at a neighbor's, and Abraham Luchins reports: "The speech so disturbed Wertheimer that on the way home he decided to depart secretly the next morning. Leaving all their possessions, he and his wife and their children went to the summer resort of Marienbad in Czechoslovakia."

While in Czechoslovakia Wertheimer received an invitation from Alvin Johnson to join the faculty of the New School for Social Research and went to the United States in September 1933. He was the first eminent psychologist to come to the New School, establishing it as a center for Eastern activities of the Gestalt movement.

As in Europe, Wertheimer's influence in New York was through personal contact, through discussions, through the openness of his time and home to anybody who wanted to talk and listen. He published little, and there is a story, perhaps apocryphal, that at one time a possible appointment at Harvard was quashed in its early stages because Wertheimer had not published enough. His influence *had* to be through personal contact rather than through books. Where Koffka's influence was largely through his first, and partly through his second book, Wertheimer's was practically completely personal. All those who had contact with him remember with warmth and gratitude Wertheimer's conversations and his seminars at the New School. To quote Luchins:

> He had many new ideas about experiments and theories, most of which he did not publish, but some of which became the basis of research conducted and published by the participants in the seminars. This group includes the following: Rudolf Arnheim, Solomon Asch, George Katona, Abraham S. Luchins, Abraham H. Maslow, David Rapaport, Martin Scheerer, and Herman Witkin.

Wertheimer died suddenly in 1943, having left unfinished his work that became most influential in American psychology, *Productive Thinking*.[23] Wertheimer's book, and the studies of his former student in Berlin, Karl Duncker, laid the foundation for much of the later American work on creative thinking. Another aspect of Wertheimer's work, although peripheral to experimental psychology, may have in the long run a more important influence on American intellectual life. Wertheimer was one of the pioneers in the study of teaching students to attack problems creatively and with understanding of structural characteristics. His work, and that of his student, Catherine Stern, on structural arithmetic, presaged the change in teaching methods in mathematics and science which has revolutionized elementary and secondary education in recent years. Although it appears that some of the new ideas about teaching methods can be traced to Wertheimer and his students, the history of this movement has not yet been written and it is too early to estimate the overall effect the new methods will have on the character of American thought.

Karl Duncker was one of the students whose research Wertheimer directed in the Berlin years. Out of this research came Duncker's brilliant study on thinking, *Zur Psychologie des productiven Denkens*, published in Berlin in 1935 and posthumously translated into English in 1945 as "On Problem Solving."[24] At about the time of the Berlin publication, Duncker, a political liberal whose family also were suspect, was

23. Max Wertheimer, *Productive Thinking* (New York, 1945, 2nd ed. 1959).

24. Karl Duncker, *Zur Psychologie des produktiven Denkens* (Berlin, 1935); "On Problem Solving," *Psychological Monographs*, 58, No. 5 (1945), 1–112.

forced to escape to England. In 1938 he was invited to come to Swarth-more, at least temporarily, as a member of the teaching staff. It is doubly tragic that Duncker, depressed by the outbreak of the war, com-mitted suicide there early in 1940. Apart from the personal tragedy, there is reason to believe that he may have been the most brilliant of the Gestalt group. This is high praise indeed, but it comes from so many different sources that it is difficult to believe that Duncker was anything less than a man of unusual intellectual brilliance and capacity. His main contribution has made a continuing impact on the psychology of think-ing, both in the United States and elsewhere, and wherever serious work is done in the area of complex human thought, Duncker's mono-graph appears as a touchstone of theoretical insight and empirical thoroughness.

Probably the most influential student of Wertheimer's is Solomon Asch. He has expanded classical Gestalt thinking into social psychology, is an active and effective proponent of the Gestalt view in the psychol-ogy of memory, and has influenced both social psychology and experi-mental psychology of thinking, probably in no small part due to the influence of Max Wertheimer.

In the same area of the experimental psychology of thinking, mention must be made of George Katona, also a member of the immigrant group, but a man whose influence has primarily been out of the pur-view of this chapter, namely in industrial psychology. However, in 1940, Katona published a book on memory,[25] which is probably the best description of the Gestalt view during its heyday as it affected the phenomena of the experimental investigation of human memory. Though of little influence during the decade or two following its publi-cation, it is now recognized as an important milestone in the history of the field. Katona had been a personal friend of Wertheimer's while studying in Berlin, and he attended Wertheimer's first seminar at the New School in 1933. We might note here that during that first year at the New School Wertheimer was still lecturing in German, switching to English in 1934.

Another important influence on the American scene through Wert-heimer is Rudolf Arnheim. Arnheim did his dissertation with Wert-

25. George Katona, *Organizing and Memorizing* (New York, 1940).

heimer in Berlin and was in constant contact with him between 1940 and 1943. Together with Solomon Asch, Arnheim helped Wertheimer complete large parts of the book on productive thinking.

While Arnheim exerted his influence on American psychology primarily outside of experimental psychology, mention of that influence should be made here. It should be evident that the American psychology of the 1930's had little interest in problems of aesthetics. Arnheim's investigations in the psychology of art within the Gestalt framework, in part because of the sin of omission by the mainstream of American psychology, became the dominant influence in the psychology of art. His work has been central and seminal and is certainly one of the milestones in the contribution of Gestalt psychology to American culture.

In summarizing Wertheimer's influence, we must again remind the reader of two facets of Wertheimer's career: he published little and yet he was the undisputed leader of the movement. For a man who had probably more difficulty being assimilated into academic life in America than did Köhler or Koffka, his formal influence is not commensurate with his visible activities. Americans, probably dismayed and discouraged by Wertheimer's often mystical style, never really saw Wertheimer as the leading genius of the triumvirate, but American psychologists in contact with the group accepted what Köhler and Koffka told them, that Wertheimer was the leader and the originator of the movement. Perhaps his major distinction lay in his ability to provide the leadership and to provide cohesiveness for the Gestalt group. For a theory that never produced a unified statement, that had little in the way of formal theory, and that was diffuse and sometimes confusing, it was Wertheimer who provided it with a common direction. Somewhat as a paradox Wertheimer had more personal influence and more disciples than did Köhler and Koffka. Asch, in particular, fulfilled that role, but all Wertheimer's students spread the word of his ideas.

Wolfgang Köhler

If the mythical average American psychologist, or student of psychology, were to be asked what single man represented the Gestalt movement in the United States, he would undoubtedly answer Wolfgang Köhler. Köhler wrote more and influenced more people in the

United States than any other member of the triumvirate. Of all the immigrant psychologists only Kurt Lewin made more of a general impact on academic psychology in the United States. Köhler, of course, outlived all the major figures that came to the United States in the twenties and thirties by more than twenty years. He alone reached his seventies, and still active, although retired, died at the age of eighty.

Wolfgang Köhler was born in 1887, and received his doctoral degree at Berlin in 1909.[26] From 1909 until 1913, he was at Frankfurt, where we have already noted the beginnings of formal Gestalt psychology. Between 1913 and 1920, as has been recounted, he was at Tenerife in the Canary Islands. That period produced some of his most influential work—his research on problem-solving in apes, on perception, and theoretical work in Gestalt psychology. In 1920, he became acting director of the Psychological Institute at Berlin, went briefly to Göttingen, and, in 1922, assumed the chair at Berlin previously held by Carl Stumpf. He remained in Berlin until 1935. He was thus at Frankfurt at the beginning of the movement, in Berlin during its flowering, and was the last of the big four (if we are to include Lewin) to come to the United States.

Köhler was active in many aspects of Gestalt psychology during the Berlin years and gradually assumed the role of its major spokesman. He was becoming known in America both by visits of American students to Berlin and by his own trips to the United States. He visited Clark University[27] and Harvard in 1925–26 and made another trip to the United States in the spring of 1929. He was invited to give the 1934 William James Lectures at Harvard (published in 1938).[28]

McDougall had vacated his chair at Harvard in 1927, and Köhler was one of the leading candidates for the position. There is reason to believe that Köhler would have affected American psychology quite differently from within a university which was part of the establishment than from a smaller college on its periphery. E. G. Boring notes[29] that a permanent

26. Carl B. Zuckerman and Hans Wallach, "Wolfgang Köhler," in *Encyclopedia*.

27. It was there that he gave the exposition of Gestalt psychology later published in *Psychologies of 1925* (Worcester, Mass., 1926).

28. Wolfgang Köhler, *The Place of Value in a World of Facts* (New York, 1938).

29. Edwin G. Boring in *A History of Psychology in Autobiography*, IV (New York, 1952).

appointment to McDougall's chair was delayed for some years, but with the succession of J. B. Conant to the presidency of Harvard in 1933, the decision was finally made in favor of Karl Lashley, an exponent of a biological point of view. Köhler was closely associated with the philosophers at Harvard; he was a good friend of Ralph Barton Perry, living at his house while he prepared his William James lectures. The philosophers seem to have pushed for his appointment but the evidence suggests that the attempt to dissociate psychology from philosophy, as well as Köhler's aloofness, led others at Harvard, among them Boring, to be less than enthusiastic about a Köhler appointment.

In the spring of 1935, Köhler lectured at the University of Chicago. He was still on leave at this time from the University of Berlin. Köhler was one of the few German psychologists who had publicly taken issue with the Nazi regime, one of the few "Aryans" for whom an "inner immigration" was not enough. Hans Wallach has informed us that Köhler had made it known in Berlin that he would stay on at the university if there was no interference from the Nazis in the *Psychologische Institut*. Wallach reports that during 1933–34, when Wallach was doing his thesis, there was no interference. However, the Nazis took over the Institute in 1935, and, although Köhler could have kept his professorship, he resigned in the summer of 1935. That same year he was appointed at Swarthmore College.[30]

In 1933, Robert B. MacLeod had gone to Swarthmore College to develop a new department. MacLeod had had prior associations with the Gestalt group when, in 1928, he did some of his graduate work in Berlin at a time when Köhler was director of the Institute, and both Wertheimer and Lewin were there. In the spring of 1929, Wertheimer went to Frankfurt and MacLeod followed him there, later returning to the U.S. to complete his graduate work at Columbia. After teaching for three years at Cornell, MacLeod went to Swarthmore, and having appointed Edwin B. Newman as an instructor, he was ready for a third appointment. He reports a conversation with Frank Aydelotte, the president of Swarthmore College, in which he said, when asked whom he would

30. We are indebted to Professor Robert B. MacLeod for giving us a most informative historical account of the early days of the department at Swarthmore and to Professor Hans Wallach for adding reminiscences and personal evaluations and recollections of the Gestalt movement in the early days.

pick, "Obviously, Köhler, but I don't think we could get him." Ayde-lotte bristled and said, "Why not?" Köhler was in the United States at the time and to MacLeod's surprise, he was interested in the Swarth-more appointment. He joined the faculty in the fall of 1935 as a profes-sor, and stayed there until his retirement in 1958.

Köhler not only helped create at Swarthmore one of the major centers of psychological research and scholarship in the United States for some twenty years after his appointment there, but he also contributed to the reputation of the Department of Psychology at Swarthmore College for producing some of the outstanding young American psychologists of those two decades. In addition, he attracted a large number of post-doctoral and predoctoral research associates. Among them were David Krech, Claude E. Buxton, Richard Crutchfield, W. D. Neff, J. C. R. Licklider, H. Witkin, Mary Henle, Richard Held, Jacob Nachmias, and Ulric Neisser.

In 1936, one of Köhler's most eminent students, Hans Wallach, was increasingly under pressure to leave Germany, and that year, MacLeod went to Berlin, interviewed Wallach, and offered him an appointment as a research associate at Swarthmore. Wallach accepted, and subse-quently became a faculty member at Swarthmore, where he has re-mained. Wallach's collaboration with Köhler significantly influenced and changed the field of visual perception, and his own contributions to perception are among the important contributions made by the German immigration.

With Wertheimer at the New School for Social Research, Koffka at Smith College, and Köhler at Swarthmore, the Gestalt triangle in the East became a center of intense activity. Swarthmore and the New School formed the hub of Gestalt psychology, with Koffka's group at Smith and Lewin's at Iowa being satellites. Koffka, Wertheimer, and Lewin would frequently visit Swarthmore, and Köhler developed a continuing relationship with the New School for Social Research.

Between 1935 and the beginning of the war, which restricted the movement and availability of the principals, Gestalt psychology de-veloped most fruitfully on the East Coast. Major figures of American psychology would visit Swarthmore, the New School, Smith, and Iowa, and MacLeod and Wallach recall visits of such notables as R. H.

Wheeler, Karl Lashley, Edward C. Tolman, Karl Muenzinger, Egon Brunswik, Donald Adams, and Karl Zener. At Swarthmore itself, Köhler, Asch, and Wallach carried on the traditions of the Gestalt movement.

In all these considerations, one should not lose sight of the fact that much of the impact of Gestalt psychology as a new movement had been made prior to the arrival of its major figures in the United States. Many American psychologists had spent some time in Berlin in the late twenties and early thirties. Harry Helson's articles on Gestalt psychology had been widely circulated, Koffka's book had been translated, and Köhler's work was certainly well known in the United States by the late twenties. Thus, in a sense, the influence of Köhler and others was a continuation of a trend well established by the time Köhler himself came to the United States for permanent residence. As a matter of fact, his own work in the United States tended away from the major focus of Gestalt psychology in the area of visual perception to an increasing preoccupation with physiology. Köhler's physicalistic interpretation of the brain processes underlying perception tended to decrease his own influence. There is no doubt that in the area of neurophysiology Köhler's influence was much less pronounced, or to put it another way, those ideas were found to be much less acceptable or useful to the development of psychology. As one of our correspondents put it, "At the time of his death, Köhler was a historical figure only." And yet, much of his formal recognition came in the twenty years following the Second World War. He received the Distinguished Scientific Contribution Award of the American Psychological Association in 1957, was elected to the National Academy of Sciences, and became president of the American Psychological Association in 1958.

Formal recognition came late, but informally he was the leader of the Gestalt movement. He was probably the least accessible, the most "German" of the triumvirate. One "couldn't get easily to Köhler." During his early years, there was a certain disdain for American psychology as we saw in his derogatory comment on behaviorism. At one point he referred to his 1929 book on Gestalt psychology[31] as having been writ-

31. Wolfgang Köhler, *Gestalt Psychology* (New York, 1929). Other influential American publications of Köhler's were: *Dynamics in Psychology* (New York, 1940); and with Hans Wallach, "Figural After-effects: An Investigation of Visual Processes," *Proceedings of the American Philosophical Society*, 88 (1944), 269–357.

ten for "the American children," meaning the college professors and graduate students in America. While it affected all members of the triumvirate, the clash of cultures was probably most pronounced for Köhler. But like most of the immigrants, he truly became an American, and not just in the formal sense of becoming an American citizen; he identified with the country and with his American students. He settled down in his last years on a farm in New Hampshire, having been given the highest honors American psychology could bestow, and he was not drawn back to Europe despite repeated visits there, many honorary degrees, and many honors. Even for the Europeans looking across at the most viable product of German psychology of the twentieth century, Gestalt psychology by 1950 had become an American movement.

Kurt Lewin

The rule of the Gestalt movement by the triumvirate was unquestioned, but there was a fourth member of the Berlin group, who while not strictly a Gestalt psychologist, was one of the major figures to come out of Berlin in that period. Kurt Lewin was the youngest of the four, born in 1890.[32] He did his doctoral work in Berlin under Carl Stumpf and received his Ph.D. in 1915. Another one of his teachers was G. E. Müller and, much like the rest of the group, he was a product of classical German experimental psychology. At no time could Lewin be called an orthodox Gestaltist, but he was part of the movement and influenced it as much as he was influenced by it. From the beginning his interest was not strictly in the experimental laboratory but rather in social variables, social events, and the world beyond the ivory tower. His early work was on the role of the worker in agriculture and industry and on the organization of work. In 1921, he was appointed to the University of Berlin and taught there until 1933. He and Duncker were two of the four junior appointments under Köhler, closely associated with him, and probably furthest in their application of Gestalt principles, Duncker in the area of complex thought, Lewin in the area of dynamic and social psychology.

32. Ronald Lippitt, "Kurt Lewin," in *Encyclopedia*. Also see Dr. Alfred Marrow's forthcoming biography of Lewin. It contains a wealth of personal and unpublished material, evaluations, and reminiscences, none of which we can touch on here.

Lewin's years as a teacher are important for our purposes because he attracted a large group of very able graduate students. Some of these later came to the United States and became prominent psychologists in their own right. Among them were Maria (Rickers) Ovsiankina and Tamara Dembo.

Throughout this time Lewin was deeply involved with what would now be called dynamic psychology, and less with introspective experiments than his Gestalt colleagues. In that sense he was much better prepared for the objective experimentation of American psychology than were the other major figures. His concepts, specifically in opposition to the atomism of association theory, dealt with energies, tensions, and needs. The loose theoretical structure that integrated his work is generally referred to as field theory, even though Lewin's love for diagrammatic representations and his topological preoccupations suggest that topological theory was his preferred way of labelling it.

Lewin's identification with the Gestalt group is probably best underlined by the fact that the majority of his important experimental investigations appear in the *Psychologische Forschung*. During the late twenties, most of the experiments were concerned with problem-solving, interruption and completion of tasks, and related topics. These series of experiments easily adapted to the American tradition and are to this day fruitful starting points for experimental investigations of the level of aspiration, effects of success and failure, and environmental effects on problem-solving.

In the latter half of the twenties, American visitors became more frequent in Berlin. Probably Lewin's first impress on American psychology was the publication of a paper by J. F. Brown in the *Psychological Review* on Kurt Lewin's methods.[33] Thus, in 1929, the groundwork was laid for the influence of the most important immigrant to remodel American psychology in the subsequent thirty years. In addition to Brown, other visitors were Donald MacKinnon, Karl Zener, Donald Adams, and Norman R. F. Maier. Donald Adams translated several of Lewin's papers, and he relates the difficulty of dealing with Lewin's neologisms. Another observer of Lewin through the years has com-

33. J. F. Brown, "The Methods of Kurt Lewin in the Psychology of Action and Affection," *Psychological Review*, 36 (1929), 200–221.

mented that Lewin's German was as complicated and difficult to understand as his English, both coming from a man whose primary mode of
communication was visual, filling blackboard on blackboard with diagrams while talking with students and visitors.

In 1929, Lewin attended the International Congress of Psychology at
Yale, and in 1932, he was invited to spend six months as visiting professor at Stanford University. There followed a long series of meetings
with psychologists, including Gardner Murphy, all of whom were
deeply impressed by the new word from Berlin. In 1933, Kurt Lewin
and his family were on their way back to Germany. Lewin returned
home from California by way of the Pacific and through the Soviet
Union while the rest of the family who were visiting the Heiders at
Smith, sailed from New York. On January 30, Hitler came to power
and by the time Lewin arrived in Moscow he was certain that there was
no room for a Jew in Nazi Germany. He cabled to Fritz Heider from
Moscow, asking that he start looking for a job for him. He resigned
from the University of Berlin before he was removed by the new regime, and shortly thereafter R. M. Ogden, urged by Ethel Waring of
the School of Home Economics, offered him a position at Cornell,
where he went in August 1933. We note again that Lewin, the experimental psychologist, the social psychologist, the theoretician, was invited by the School of Home Economics at Cornell for a two-year appointment subsidized by the Emergency Committee on Displaced
Scholars. At Cornell, he pursued a previous interest in child development and worked extensively at the Nursery School.

Throughout this time Lewin's influence avalanched. Donald K.
Adams and Karl Zener translated a number of his articles and published
these in 1935, and Fritz and Grace Heider translated his manuscript on
topological psychology which was published in 1936.[34] Throughout
this early period Lewin seriously considered a final move to Palestine
and was a central figure in soliciting support for a psychological institute at the Hebrew University in Jerusalem. In 1935, he spent a brief
period in Palestine, and there were fears among his friends in the United
States that he would move there permanently. Lawrence K. Frank was

34. Kurt Lewin, *Dynamic Theory of Personality* (New York, 1935) and *Principles of
Topological Psychology* (New York, 1936).

influential in efforts to keep him in the United States and in persuading George Stoddard, the director of the Iowa Child Welfare Research Station at the University of Iowa, to offer him an appointment there. Lewin moved to Iowa in 1935. Again, one of the major figures of psychology moved from a post in a school of home economics to a child welfare installation. But it was primarily a research appointment and Iowa became one of the exciting centers of Lewinian studies. His longtime associate, Tamara Dembo, went with him, as did his postdoctoral fellows Roger Barker and Herbert Wright. It was at Iowa that a long stream of American students began to gather around Kurt Lewin. Among the Americans at Iowa, either permanently or on a visiting basis, were Dorwin Cartwright, Alvin Zander, Robert Leeper (visiting from Cornell College), J. R. P. French, Alex Bavelas, Leon Festinger, Sybille Escalona, Ronald Lippitt, and Erik and Beatrice Wright.

Lewin's interactions with his students, his time given freely, and his insatiable interests, made him one of the central figures of American psychology. In 1938, Kenneth W. Spence came to Iowa, and Iowa became one of the centers of American behaviorist learning theory, a movement diametrically different from Lewin's interests. However disparate Spence's and Lewin's interests, they had great respect for each other and Lewin, never letting his prejudices against associationist theory interfere, became deeply involved in discussion of Hullian theory. Spence related some time before his death that he was for a time a transmission station between Kurt Lewin and Clark L. Hull on suggested variations and changes in Hullian theory.

Starting in 1934, Lewin and his friends and associates in psychology formed a continuing group, the Topology Group, that would meet yearly around Christmas time. The group had no formal organization, and the number at the meetings varied from thirty to forty, with visitors coming and going, but the central group continued the meetings until Lewin's death and for some years thereafter. The first meeting was held at Smith, the home of Koffka and of the Heiders, old friends of Lewin's. In 1935, the meeting was at Duke and in 1936, at Bryn Mawr, and so forth. New ideas were generated and exchanged, and some of the most important interactions with the leaders of experimental psychology occurred in these meetings.

Again, during the thirties, Lewin's concern with the role of the Jew, not just in Europe but also in America, was reflected in a number of articles on such problems as the minority group and Jewish upbringing. Increasingly his interests and the interests of his students veered toward social psychology as, for example, in Lippitt's studies on authoritarian and democratic groups.[35] Lewin's personal influence spread beyond Iowa. In 1938 and again in 1939, he spent some time at Harvard primarily at the urging and invitation of Gordon W. Allport and Henry A. Murray. The summer of 1939 he spent at the University of California at Berkeley.

When war came, Lewin's preeminence as a social psychologist and his social conscience projected him directly into whatever support he could give to psychological problems in the war effort. He was a consultant for the Office of Strategic Services, the Office of Naval Research, and the Public Health Service. Much of this work was related to his interest in group dynamics which had begun in the late thirties. And in the early forties, Lewin was ready to start an institute to deal with problems of group dynamics, to go further into what he termed "action" research. The final two possibilities for institutions that might support such an institute were the University of California at Berkeley, and the Massachusetts Institute of Technology. MIT was the successful bidder, and in 1944, Lewin moved from Iowa to Cambridge, where he founded the Research Center for Group Dynamics, the crowning glory of his career in the United States. At the same time, he was instrumental in establishing a Commission on Community Interrelations, primarily to deal with the problem of the minority group central in Lewin's concern—the Jews. But both the work of C. C. I. and its goals went far beyond the question of anti-Semitism. The C. C. I. took hold in a loft in New York, at 50th Street and Broadway, remodeled by Lewin's old Berlin friend, Marcel Breuer.

The group at MIT became the central training center for the mainstream of American social psychology. But the work at C. C. I. and at MIT soon took its toll, and Lewin's life became more and more fran-

---

35. See for example Kurt Lewin, Ronald Lippitt, and R. K. White, "Patterns of Aggressive Behavior in Experimentally Created 'Social Climates'," *Journal of Social Psychology*, 10 (1939), 271–299.

tic. In the midst of strenuous activity, Lewin died in February 1947.

Lewin had moved far from his initial work on associationism under Stumpf and his work with the Gestalt group in Berlin to the leadership of American social psychology in 1947. His topological theories never really became a central aspect of his students' work or of the field at large. But his brilliant approach to an experimental investigation of social phenomena, his opening up of dynamic psychology, his work on the influence of personality and complex psychological factors on problem-solving, his field theoretical approach, and his bubbling enthusiasm for all of psychology left their impact, an impact that was much greater than that of any of the other immigrants.

Lewin's interests and methods of tackling problems fitted in with traditional American interests and methods, not so much in the limited field of experimental psychology itself as in the characteristic social temper of American life in the twentieth century. His interest in social problems, action research, the dynamics of personality, and his creative methods of attacking these problems experimentally, guaranteed him a wider audience for his ideas than was available to the more European viewpoint of the Gestalt triumvirate. His studies with Lippitt and White on the nature of authoritarian and democratic group leadership provided, in Wellek's words "an experimental proof of the superiority of democracy."[36] Certainly in a broad sense America was ready for Lewin when he arrived.

American social psychology, developmental psychology, and experimental psychology all changed significantly because Kurt Lewin wrote, because Kurt Lewin taught, and because Kurt Lewin was in the United States. Without him, vast areas that had been previously untouched would not have been subjected that early to experimental investigation. Experimental approaches to level of aspiration, interrupted tasks, substitution, group dynamics, frustration and regression, and personality and motivation can all be traced directly to Lewin's influence. But most important, he influenced people. His major efforts were not within the framework of the Gestalt school, even though Lewin was a product of that school. To list his students and associates at MIT at the Research Center in Group Dynamics is to list an honor roll of current social

36. Wellek, *Impact*.

psychology. Among them were Dorwin Cartwright, Ronald Lippitt, Leon Festinger, Marion Radke (all of whom went to MIT with Lewin in 1944), Alex Bavelas, and then Harold H. Kelley, Stanley Schachter, Kurt Back, Morton Deutsch, John Thibaut, and Albert Pepitone. Until 1947, MIT was the center of the new look in American social psychology, and when the Center under the leadership of Cartwright, Festinger, French, and Lippitt moved to the University of Michigan in 1947, so did the center of gravity of the field.

But the influence was not just in social psychology. E. C. Tolman, one of the central figures in the heyday of American learning theory in the forties and fifties, gives credit for the development of his ideas to Gestalt theory, but especially to Lewin, "whose ideas I have borrowed time and again and absorbed into my very blood."[37]

In his oral history, N. R. F. Maier stresses Lewin's influence on him in industrial psychology. Maier at one time tried to get Lewin to come to Michigan but was unsuccessful. Gordon Allport tried to get him to come to Harvard but his efforts failed because of lack of enthusiasm on the part of E. G. Boring and others. In many ways Lewin never really communicated with the members of the establishment, but it is fascinating to note that his life, spent at the periphery of the American academic psychological establishment, transformed the scene more than any of its major figures. Indeed, we must say this about all of the four idea makers to come out of Berlin. None of them was accepted into any of the major American universities in the thirties. They were visiting professors in the heartland of American academia, but their work was done at Smith, at Swarthmore, at Iowa, at MIT, and at the New School for Social Research. America's indifference to them and its preoccupation with behaviorism prevented the Gestalt school from becoming a formal part of the establishment. But the students came to the Gestaltists and the change was brought about even though most of the major universities stood passively by.

Fritz Heider

If the influences of the men we have discussed up till now were to a very large extent established before they came to the United States,

37. Edward C. Tolman, *A History of Psychology in Autobiography*, IV (New York, 1952).

Heider's influence on American psychology was practically wholly due to his activities in the United States. Heider was born in Vienna in 1896, and grew up in Graz where he received his Ph.D. with Meinong in 1920. Graz had long been a center of concern with the *Gestaltqualitäten*, the precursors of the Gestalt movement as such. Heider's thesis was on the subjectivity of sense qualities, but even prior to that he had made contact personally with the mainstream of German experimental psychology when in 1917 in Munich he met Karl and Charlotte Bühler. He took courses with them in child and experimental psychology and grew to admire Karl Bühler's contributions. From 1921 to 1924, Heider lived in Berlin where he had some contact with Köhler and Wertheimer and also extensive contact with Kurt Lewin. This association was completely informal, though the contact with the Gestalt movement shaped Heider's subsequent intellectual development. After a period of travel, Heider returned to Berlin in 1926, and worked part-time as an assistant at the University. In 1927, he went to the University of Hamburg with William Stern and Heinz Werner. He recalls the impression at the Bonn Congress of Psychology in 1927, when G. E. Müller and Wolfgang Köhler met head-on in a public confrontation of Gestalt and associationism.

In 1929 Koffka contacted Stern concerning an opening at Smith which Heinz Werner had turned down, and which was then offered to Heider. In 1930, Fritz Heider came to the Clarke School for the Deaf with a nominal appointment at Smith, where he started teaching on a part-time basis in 1931. In December of 1930 he married Grace Moore, and, partly as a result of this union of Austrian and American psychology, never again left the United States permanently.

Heider stayed at Smith until 1947, and during that period developed one of the most crucial theoretical conceptions in current social psychology—balance theory. The philosophical background of balance theory stems from the early influence of Meinong and from Spinoza's work on emotions, as well as the general Gestalt attitude. Heider's stress was on the centrality of mental attitudes which produce consistencies of behavior and thought.

In 1941, following Koffka's death, Heider took over Koffka's course in Gestalt psychology. In the early period at Smith, Tamara Dembo and

Eugenia Hanfmann were at Smith, as was Alexander Mintz. In 1947, Roger Barker asked Fritz Heider to join the reorganized Psychology Department at the University of Kansas, and he has remained there since.

During his years at Smith, Heider worked with Grace Moore Heider at The Clarke School for the Deaf, where he published two monographs on the psychology of the deaf, including work on social interaction of young deaf children without language. In that highly specialized field, Heider's work still is an important milestone.

Heider's impact on social psychology developed at first through his attendance at the Topology Group meetings of which he was a charter member. The first talks on balance theory were given in 1945 at Smith and at the 1948 meetings of the Topology Group. The first important publication was the 1946 paper on attitudes and cognitive organization[38] which was discussed by Heider at MIT and Harvard during that year.

From the thirties on, Heider had been working on his magnum opus which was finally published in 1958.[39] At the suggestion of Alfred Baldwin at Kansas, several chapters were mimeographed in the early fifties and became some of the most widely quoted unpublished documents in American psychology.

Balance or consistency theory is recognized as one of the important underpinnings of social psychological theory, in particular reference to social interactions and social perception. Leon Festinger, whose theory of cognitive dissonance is one of the approaches influenced by consistency notions, remembers Heider talking about balance theory as early as 1940 and 1941, and describes being influenced by Heider's notions through the availability of the mimeographed chapters of the book. He considers Heider's most important influence to be the formalization of cognitive structures. In any case, the consistency notions in Heider's theory have influenced every current consistency theory, including those of Cartwright and Harary, and Abelson and Rosenberg.[40]

38. Fritz Heider, "Attitudes and Cognitive Organization," *Journal of Psychology*, 21 (1946), 107–112.

39. Fritz Heider, *The Psychology of Interpersonal Relations* (New York, 1958).

40. D. Cartwright and F. Harary, "Structural Balance: A Generalization of Heider's Theory," *Psychological Review*, 63 (1956), 277–293; R. P. Abelson and M. J. Rosenberg, "Symbolic Psycho-logic: A Model of Attitudinal Cognition," *Behavioral Science*, 3 (1958), 1–13.

Undoubtedly, there were individuals personally affected by Heider, among them Alfred Baldwin, but in contrast to Lewin, Heider's influence was not through people but through his writings, specifically through his major work. Heider's influence was delayed by some twenty years after his arrival in the United States, but next to Lewin's contributions his theories today are the most alive of those stemming from the German and Austrian immigration.

Another though somewhat peripheral member of the Gestalt school was *Kurt Goldstein*, who was born in 1878 and died in New York City in 1965.[41] Goldstein had a medical degree from Breslau in 1903, and after various medical appointments was appointed Professor of Neurology at the University of Frankfurt where Wertheimer was a colleague. In 1930 he moved to the University of Berlin, but was forced to leave the country in 1933. The Rockefeller Foundation supported him for a year in Amsterdam, during which time he wrote his major book, *The Organism*.[42] In 1934 he reached New York where he was appointed Clinical Professor of Neurology at Columbia. In 1938–39 he gave the William James Lectures at Harvard,[43] and during his stay there also conducted a graduate seminar (with Sylvan Tomkins as teaching assistant) at the Harvard Psychological Clinic. In 1940, he became Clinical Professor of Neurology at Tufts College Medical School, a position underwritten (on Leonard Carmichael's suggestion) for five years by the Rockefeller Foundation.[44]

During his years in the Boston area he had close contacts with Gordon Allport and Karl Lashley, and collaborated with Eugenia Hanfmann and Maria Ovsiankina on concretization of behavior.

Goldstein's holistic position was very close to the Gestalt school, and his work on the effects of brain injury and on abstract and concrete behavior were highly regarded both in the United States and abroad.

---

41. See Marianne L. Simmel, "Kurt Goldstein," in *Encyclopedia* for a more extensive biography and evaluation of Goldstein's work.

42. *The Organism: A Holistic Approach to Biology Derived from Pathological Data in Man* (New York, 1939).

43. *Human Nature in the Light of Psychopathology* (Cambridge, Mass., 1940).

44. Marianne L. Simmel, "Kurt Goldstein, 1878–1965," *Journal of the History of the Behavioral Sciences*, 4 (1966), 185–191.

However, his work was tangential to the province of experimental psychology even though he was one of the editors of the *Psychologische Forschung*.

Werner Wolff was a direct product of the Gestalt school. Born in 1904, he received his doctorate in Berlin in 1930. From 1933 to 1936 he lived in Spain, and spent 1940 to 1942 at Teachers College, Columbia, and at Vassar College, but without a regular faculty appointment. In 1942 he went to Bard College, where he died in 1957. His work, not in experimental psychology, was devoted primarily to problems of expressive movement, which had been one of Wertheimer's particular interests.

v. Other Major Influences of the Immigration

The Vienna School

Psychology in Vienna in the twenties and thirties, led primarily by Karl Bühler, was to some extent a self-designated school. It never had any formal recognition as a school outside of its own circle, and it stood in the shadow of two other important and influential movements to come out of Vienna in that period—psychoanalysis and the Vienna Circle of logical positivists. It was these two movements that made the major impact of the Austrian immigration on American intellectual life. Furthermore, within psychology proper the more visible effects were in such areas as developmental psychology, particularly under the leadership of Charlotte Bühler, a topic not within our purview, but certainly of significant impact and importance.

Within academic psychology, and again excluding developmental psychology, two men represent the primary influence of the immigration from the University of Vienna. They were *Karl Bühler* and *Egon Brunswik*.

Karl Bühler was born in Germany in 1879, and started his academic career with an M.D. degree in 1903, doing a dissertation on color vision. He received his Ph.D. from the University of Strassburg in 1904. In

1906, he went to Würzburg and followed the leader of the Würzburg School, Oswald Külpe, to Bonn in 1909, and to Munich in 1913. In 1918, he went to the University of Dresden, and in 1922, was appointed to the professorship at Vienna. He stayed there until 1938, when he was arrested by the German government for a brief period. In 1939, he came to the United States. His first position was at St. Scholastica College in Duluth, and from 1940 to 1945, at the College of St. Thomas in St. Paul. Then, at the age of sixty-six, he moved to Los Angeles where he held appointments at the University of Southern California Medical School and at Cedars of Lebanon Hospital. He died in 1963.

Bühler, whose major contributions to psychology all predate his arrival in the United States,[45] was truly one of the casualties of the immigration. A man who had been considered for McDougall's chair at Harvard in 1928 and who in 1927–28 was a guest professor at Harvard, Stanford, Johns Hopkins, and Chicago, he was never given due recognition when he came to the United States on a permanent basis. As Bugental and his colleagues observed: "He had risen to great eminence in psychology and suffered a cruel and unwarranted displacement with a later coldness from those of whom he might have expected greater warmth. Yet I never heard him complain or dwell on the past." Bühler suffered from the fact that none of his major works written prior to his immigration was translated into English. It is only now that his influential books, one on the crisis in psychology and the other on theory of language,[46] are being translated and are about to be published in English. The recognition of Bühler in the American period was for a man whose work had been done, since he published nothing here until the early fifties. These publications were removed from his major concerns and influence, treating orientation and navigation in man and lower animals. Shortly before his death his final book was published in German.[47]

As one of the important contributors to the Würzburg development,

45. His career has been given full and deserved recognition in: James F. Bugental, ed., "Symposium on Karl Bühler's Contributions to Psychology," *Journal of General Psychology*, 75 (1966), 181–219. See also Albert Wellek, "Karl Bühler," in *Encyclopedia*.

46. *Die Krise der Psychologie* (Jena, 1929); *Sprachtheorie: Die Darstellungsfunktion der Sprache* (Jena, 1934).

47. *Das Gestaltprinzip im Leben des Menschen und der Tiere* (Bern, 1960).

as a man who foresaw the importance of rule learning and cognitive transformations decades before these ideas became popular,[48] Bühler influenced American thought primarily through the many Europeans and Americans who had studied with him in Vienna, such as Egon Brunswik, Edward C. Tolman, René Spitz, Else Frenkel-Brunswik, and others. It is possible and even likely that Bühler's fundamental contribution to psychology may be recognized in the near future. He was certainly one man whom America did not welcome with open arms. We have noted that his wife, Charlotte Bühler, fifteen years his junior, was much more influential in developmental psychology and had a major impact on that field.[49]

Egon Brunswik, born in 1963 in Budapest, started out in engineering but completed his formal studies as a student of Karl Bühler's in Vienna, where he received a Ph.D. in 1927. He received an appointment to the University in 1934. In 1933, Edward C. Tolman spent a year at the Psychological Institute in Vienna, and partly through his good offices Brunswik received a fellowship to come to the University of California at Berkeley in 1935–36, where he remained, joining the faculty in 1937 and attaining a full professorship in 1947. He died in 1955. Brunswik was the only major figure in the immigration who followed a more or less traditional career in American academics, but then, of course, he was the youngest of the men we are discussing here.

Else Frenkel, another student of Bühler's in Vienna, became Brunswik's wife in 1937, and her contributions to personality and social psychology, having a strong emphasis on psychoanalysis, are well known and fully recognized but do not fall under our present coverage.

It is very difficult, and probably too early, to assess adequately Brunswik's effect on contemporary American psychology. His most important notion, the probabilistic view of the environment, the uncertain flux of the organism's environment which affects its behavior and mental processes, is present in much of modern American psychology. It is difficult to say to what extent this was due to direct influence of Brunswik, though he certainly had contact with many of the important fig-

48. Mandler and Mandler, *Thinking.*

49. Charlotte Bühler, "Die Wiener psychologische Schule in der Emigration," *Psychologische Rundschau*, 16 (1965), 187–196.

ures in psychology while he was at the University of California at Berkeley. From the first there was a fruitful interaction between Tolman and Brunswik, with Tolman moving Brunswik toward the objective American methodology and Brunswik leading Tolman to stress the achievement character of motivation. His notion of representative design[50] has puzzled and stimulated American psychologists. And his brilliant, though sometimes obscure, work on the conceptual history of psychology[51] has both challenged and intrigued recent generations of psychologists. Certainly his experiments on probability matching were, as Tolman remarked, "a new sort of experiment," and have become a central feature of current experimental work. His students have continued to represent whatever they could glean from Brunswik's complex ideas, and in 1966, Kenneth R. Hammond published a *Festschrift* in honor of Brunswik.[52] In his introduction to the book, Hammond comments that Brunswik's legacy differed from that of other contemporary "heroes" in American psychology.

Whereas Tolman, Hull, and Lewin left their ideas and doctrine to a sturdy and determined second generation, there were, in effect, no heirs present at the reading of Brunswik's intellectual will.

This is a fact worth reflecting upon. It makes one wonder how Brunswik's influence could have been so large . . . During his lifetime he found not a single prominent psychologist who actively supported his views as a whole. True, there were some like Campbell, for example, who found their work touching upon areas that Brunswik had already explored, and who made their indebtedness to Brunswik clear. But there was never a prominent psychologist who frankly declared himself to be a "Brunswikian," as there were "Hullians," "Lewinians," and the like. The edifice that Brunswik erected became a significant landmark—but it was virtually empty; there were visitors, it is true, but no one stayed.

In summary, it seems likely that Brunswik's influence was more extensive than it appears on the surface. More than most of the other immigrants, Brunswik's ideas have become part of the American *Zeitgeist*. He published relatively few experimental articles but most of them were seminal. He did early work on probability learning and concept forma-

50. *Perception and the Representative Design of Psychological Experiments* (Berkeley, 1947).
51. *The Conceptual Framework of Psychology* (Chicago, 1952).
52. *The Psychology of Egon Brunswik* (New York, 1966).

tion with probabilistic cues, social perception, and the influence of values on perception. Other studies in these areas cite Brunswik's precedence, but it is difficult to untangle the threads of influence. He seems to have played an important role in the interchange within the Gestalt and quasi-Gestalt group, and certainly Lewin, Tolman, and Heider acknowledge significant intellectual debts to Brunswik. Many of the students at Berkeley were profoundly moved by him, among them, Donald T. Campbell, Kenneth Hammond, Jane Loevinger, Murray E. Jarvik, Julian Hochberg, and Max Levin. Others, like Roger Barker, explicitly indicate their debt to Brunswik. Over the years, Brunswik's name may disappear from the explicit history of psychology, but his ideas are certainly in its fabric.

The Hamburg Group

Mention should be made about the group of psychologists that came to the United States from the University of Hamburg. We have already discussed one of them, Fritz Heider, and his effect on American social psychology. Three others, though not strictly experimental psychologists, were William Stern, Heinz Werner, and Martin Scheerer.

William Stern, born in 1871, was a student of one of the founders of experimental psychology, Hermann Ebbinghaus, under whose direction he received his doctorate in 1892 at Berlin. In 1897, he followed Ebbinghaus to Breslau. In 1916, he was appointed director of the Psychological Laboratory and professor at Hamburg. In 1933, he left Germany, spending some time in Holland, and in 1934, went to Duke University to the department then headed by William McDougall. He died in 1938 at the age of sixty-seven. Even though originally an experimental psychologist, Stern's primary interests were in personality theory and in individual differences. His work has received some attention in the United States, and his major influence has been on Heinz Werner, also at Hamburg, and on Gordon W. Allport. Stern himself did not live long after his arrival in this country and it is primarily through these men that his influence has been felt in American psychology.

Heinz Werner was born in Vienna in 1890, and received his doctoral degree from the University of Vienna in 1914. From 1915 to 1917, he worked at the University of Munich, and in 1917, was appointed to the

Psychological Institute at Hamburg, where he worked under William Stern. He was appointed to the Hamburg faculty in 1921, and in 1933 was dismissed by the Nazi regime. Walter Pillsbury invited him to come to the University of Michigan where he stayed from 1933 until 1936, though not on a regular faculty appointment. In 1936, while still at Michigan, he was appointed as senior research psychologist at the Wayne County Training School where he stayed until 1943, with an intervening year as a visiting professor at Harvard during 1936–37. He received his first regular faculty appointment at Brooklyn College as an instructor in 1943. Several of our informants remember the attempts in those days to obtain regular faculty appointments for the European immigrants. It is noteworthy that a man of Werner's stature was not able to get an appointment at better than the instructor level. Finally, in 1947, Clark University invited him as professor in the Department of Psychology and Education, and in 1949, he became chairman of the independent Department of Psychology. Under his leadership, Clark University again attained the high reputation it had achieved some years earlier under G. Stanley Hall. He died in 1964, and Clark University renamed the Institute of Human Development at Clark as the Heinz Werner Institute of Developmental Psychology.

Heinz Werner's influence on American psychology can be measured by the *Festschrift* published on the occasion of his seventieth birthday in 1960.[53] Both in that volume and in a memorial volume published in 1966, his contribution has been evaluated by a distinguished and grateful group of students, collaborators, and admirers.[54]

While Werner was part of the tradition that developed Gestalt psychology in Germany, his interests, going back to his days in Munich, were in developmental psychology, and as such were in contrast to the ahistorical position of the Gestaltists, and particularly, Lewin. However, like the Gestaltists, his accommodation to America was easy in the one respect that made all of them respectable, they were—in contrast to the main body of German psychology—experimentally oriented and con-

53. Bernard Kaplan, ed. *Perspectives in Psychological Theory: Essays in Honor of Heinz Werner* (New York, 1960).
54. Seymour Wapner and Bernard Kaplan, eds., *Heinz Werner 1890–1964: Papers in Memoriam* (Worcester, Mass., 1966).

cerned with empirical investigation. His later research in this country was concerned with language and with perception. In the latter sphere he collaborated primarily with Seymour Wapner while in the area of language he worked primarily with Bernard Kaplan.[55]

Throughout all this work ran Werner's general concern with developmental principles, with processes of development regardless of the subject matter or the age of the subject. Under his direction the Clark laboratories developed the microgenetic method, the observation of sequences of structures that mimic ontogenetic development. The sensory-tonic theory of perception has become one of the important positions in contemporary American psychology, concerned with interactions between perceptual phenomena in the traditional sense and feedback from body movements and positions. Thus, after an essentially cold reception, Werner's influence, though not as extensive as that of the senior figures in Gestalt psychology, became part of the heartland of American psychology, at least in part because of his ability to create his own environment at Clark University.

Martin Scheerer, who was born in 1900 and died in the United States in 1961, received a Ph.D. at Hamburg in 1931, and though not an experimental psychologist, was important in the development of cognitive theory and symbolic processes. He was at Montefiore Hospital from 1936 to 1939, working with Goldstein, at Wells College for the year 1939–40, lectured at Columbia University, then was an instructor at Brooklyn College and at City College, New York, and after some time at the New School, became a professor at the University of Kansas in 1948, where he was an important member of the quasi-Gestalt group there.

55. Heinz Werner and Seymour Wapner, "Sensory-tonic Field Theory of Perception," *Journal of Personality*, 18 (1949), 324–338; Heinz Werner, *Comparative Psychology of Mental Development* (rev. ed., New York, 1957); Seymour Wapner and Heinz Werner, *Perceptual Development* (Worcester, Mass., 1957); Heinz Werner and Bernard Kaplan, *Symbol formation: An Organismic-Developmental Approach to Language and the Expression of Thought* (New York, 1963).

VI. Epilogue

IF the total effect of the German immigration on American psychology is at times problematical, if the best one can sometimes say is that a powerful individual exerted powerful influence on people, there is no doubt that the German immigration did leave German psychology denuded. To this date, German experimental psychology has not effectively recovered from the exodus of the twenties and thirties, nor from the blood bath which included those non-Aryan psychologists who were left behind or with whom the German war machine caught up in the forties. Today, German psychology in the West is—when being experimental—frequently a weak imitation of its American mentors; in the East, it is an equally weak imitation of its Russian mentors. Certainly few German psychologists, with several important exceptions such as Köhler, significantly protested the Nazi regime. In his evaluation of the impact of the German immigration on American psychology, Albert Wellek overemphasizes the effect of the German immigration on American psychology as much as he overemphasizes the resistance to Nazism of those who remained behind. The full force of a statement such as "American psychology of the present would not be what it is and could not become what it yet promises to be, without the ferments and instigations of the German emigration," dramatically overstates the case.[56] There is too much of current, live, exciting, and important American psychology that was untouched by the German and Austrian immigration and that represents the major nuclei of American psychological thought. One need only think of men and movements like B. F. Skinner, S. S. Stevens, current research on behavior modification, the psycholinguistic movement, and information theory, to realize how many aspects of American experimental psychology did in fact come out of a tradition that was not European in our current sense. As a matter of fact, probably the most influential name in one area of American experimental psychology—psychoacoustics—is Georg von Békésy, a postwar immigrant from Hungary.

But significant parts of American psychology were touched deeply,

56. Wellek, *Impact.*

personally, and conceptually by the German immigration. Donald O. Hebb has suggested to us that the Gestalt influence was deeper than the journal articles and other publications of the time would indicate, and that their influence must be judged as much by what the behaviorist establishment stopped saying as a result of Gestalt arguments as by the intensity of the counterarguments. Boring coined the phrase that Gestalt psychology died of its success, but it is difficult to know whether that success was a personal or a programmatic one. Gestalt psychology probably never existed as a school in the United States; it lived as a set of ideas unifying an immigrant group which might have fallen apart much faster had it not been held together by the common experience of the immigration. The Gestalt group stayed together because they were friends; they were often lonely, they were isolated, and they needed each other for support.

There was also the language problem, conquerable of course, and sooner or later conquered by all the immigrants, but a difficulty nonetheless in communication and adaptation to the new land. Early lecturing was usually done in German or postponed. These difficulties were possibly more acute for psychologists than for some of the natural scientists arriving in this country. Any scholar used to sophisticated thought must find it painful to struggle with a newly learned vocabulary, necessarily limited and lacking the familiar overtones and connotations of use, but further there was no extranational vocabulary which could help overcome disparities of language. It is difficult to estimate the toll that was taken in energy and meaningful communication with the American community.

The German movement did produce a leavening of American psychology by reminding it of its philosophical past. As such it often solidified behaviorism, but it maintained an underground movement stressing mental organization and structures so that in the sixties many American psychologists within or outside the Gestalt tradition can come back to the problem of mental structure, a problem originally stressed by an American—William James.

By thinking the unthinkable, by saying things that outraged the behaviorists, the German immigrants maintained a point of view which said that despite the behaviorist rejection of complex mental organization and cognitive processes, perhaps there was something to such ideas after all. The reaction to theoretical behaviorism, the rejection of naive associationism, whether in Pavlovian or Watsonian guise, was made easier because these men were in our midst. Methodological behaviorism, the commitment to objectivity, was an American movement that had strong roots in pragmatism and in American philosophy. That part of behaviorism survived and survived to the point of successfully infiltrating the methods of the Gestaltists. Theoretical behaviorism went and it went in part because the Gestaltists proved able foils.

There is no doubt about the lasting impact of the Gestalt movement on theory and research in visual perception, an impact which extended to those theorists whose primary orientation came from a perceptual point of view. D. O. Hebb, for example, explains how completely convinced he had been by the Gestalt arguments. Apparently his commitment was such that at first he was most reluctant to make his own theoretical arguments in opposition to the Gestalt notions.[57]

Aside from perceptual studies, Gestalt psychology remained the not so loyal opposition in the area of thinking and complex human behavior. As such it collected converts and allies as the locus and frequently the only alternative to the behaviorist position. While the Gestalt view did not prevail in these areas, current research on human thinking and information processing uses concepts and attitudes which are not far removed from the Gestalt position in the thirties and forties. The extent of a direct influence on such contemporary psychologists as George A. Miller and Wendell R. Garner is difficult to evaluate. One expression of the contemporary mood, a recent book by Ulric Neisser, does indicate a linkage.[58]

By becoming part of the American scene in the long run, the German immigrants pushed a young science to greater maturity, in an atmosphere conducive to such development, where behaviorism, pragmatism, and the open marketplace of ideas made it possible for psychology to become respectable. The fact that the immigrants were assimilated into the American scene is important for the history of psychology, and

57. Donald O. Hebb, "A Neuropsychological Theory," in Sigmund Koch, ed., *Psychology: A Study of a Science*, 1 (New York, 1959).
58. *Cognitive Psychology* (New York, 1967).

it was done despite opposition and xenophobia. It must be remembered that the United States was the one country that significantly opened its doors to these strangers. If it was sometimes hostile toward them once they arrived, it did, after all, make it possible for them to arrive. As one of our correspondents noted, "foreigners have not been too popular over here." The fact that the Gestalt psychologists and the other German immigrants had any influence, in spite of their exclusion from the prestigious establishment institutions, attests to the power of their ideas. The fact that Gestalt psychology is no longer recognized as a school attests either to its inadequacy as a system or to the fact that we have adopted its ideas into the fabric of American psychology.

THE MIGRATION OF
PSYCHOANALYSIS: ITS IMPACT
ON AMERICAN PSYCHOLOGY*

by MARIE JAHODA

IN October 1933 psychoanalysis was banned from the Congress of
Psychology in Leipzig as a "Jewish science"; soon after that psychoanalytic literature was burned, and the community of practising
psychoanalysts, mostly centered in Berlin, dispersed rapidly to save
their lives and their livelihoods. Some went directly to the United States,
but many were reluctant to leave the continent of Europe while Freud
was still alive and where their cultural, intellectual, and professional
roots were deep; or they preferred to ignore the danger signs. Vienna,
or rather Freud living in Vienna, was a strong attraction, but it provided
a troubled haven for a few years only. Then, in 1938, Freud, old and ill,
was compelled to leave with his daughter Anna, colleague and nurse to
her father, and went with the rest of his family to London. He had been
an Anglophile all his life and had never been tempted to settle in the
New World; but in those days even Freud's preferences did not count
as much as the ready availability of a refuge. Some other psychoanalysts,
among them Ernst Kris, also settled in England, many went to the
States just before the outbreak of war, but a few stayed in Europe—like
Heinz Hartmann, who remained in France first, then in Switzerland,
and went to the States only in 1941, where Kris and others soon joined
him.

On the continent of Europe Freud is now honored as a genius of a
past epoch; psychoanalysis is largely ignored. In England there are few,
if any, bridges between psychology and psychoanalysis. But America
has become the world center of psychoanalysis, as it is the world center

---

* This paper develops in a different context certain themes of an earlier essay, "Some
Notes on the Influence of Psychoanalytic Ideas on American Psychology," in *Human Relations*, 16, no. 2 (1963), 111–129.

of psychology, and the only country where Freud's ambition to make psychoanalysis the basis of a general psychology has any chance of realization.

It is tempting to assert that the quality of the men and women who emigrated to the States and the quality of the psychoanalytic system of thought which they brought with them fully explain this state of affairs. But this would be a gross oversimplification. Some first-rate psychoanalysts survived in Europe, mainly in England; the works of Freud and his students are available in many languages all over the world and are international intellectual property. The emigration of men and ideas can never be adequately understood in terms of their own attributes only; it is the intricate interplay between what they bring and what they find in the new host culture that decides their fate.

I

IN the 1930's American psychology was already a flourishing academic field. Most universities and colleges had psychology departments equipped with laboratories in which generations of rats and some humans were eagerly studied with rigorous experimental procedures and an ever increasing statistical sophistication. At that time American psychological publications were just about beginning to outnumber publications in German: according to the Psychological Index the percentage of American and German publications in the world were 30 per cent and 52 per cent respectively in 1910; in 1930 these proportions were 35 per cent and 38 per cent; in 1933 the reversal was dramatic with 52 per cent and 14 per cent; and from then on the growing American dominance in the field has never been challenged.[1]

Behind these figures lies the history of the relation between German and American universities, and in particular that of German and American psychology. Psychology as a science was born in Germany; its year of birth is generally reckoned to be 1879 when Wilhelm Wundt founded the first psychological laboratory. American scholars in all fields were

1. J. B. Maller, "Forty Years of Psychology," *Psychological Bulletin*, 31, no. 8 (October, 1934), 533–559.

accustomed to go to Germany, and German universities were often taken as the model of American institutions. Up to the first quarter of this century there is hardly an American psychologist of note who did not go to Germany to complete and enlarge his education. Originally, they came to study with Wundt; of the first nineteen noted psychologists who received Wundt's doctorate thirteen did their major work in America.[2] After the First World War Vienna began to rival the German universities as an attraction to American psychologists; there the University offered the psychology of Karl and Charlotte Bühler and the positivism of the Vienna Circle. But outside the University Freud and his students formed an at least equally powerful attraction.

It is in keeping with the deep split characteristic of Austrian culture between the two world wars in many fields—Vienna and the rest of the country, the two political parties, the German and the international tradition—that Bühler, the professor of psychology at the University, and Freud, the originator of the most powerful psychological theory till then invented, never met in person, even though they lived for seventeen years in the same city.[3] Bühler lectured on the shortcomings of psychoanalysis. Freud took no notice of academic psychology, though both Bühlers were actively involved in empirical studies of human development, an area to which Freud made major contributions. This curious situation put university students in psychology, native and American alike, into a quandary. Many wanted to have the best of both worlds, even if that forced them to lead intellectually double lives, "fluctuating between the academic and official nutriment and the revolutionary nutriment of Berggasse" (Freud's address), as Rudolf Ekstein, who got his Ph.D. at Vienna and is now in Los Angeles, working at the Psychoanalytic Institute, put it.[4] Ekstein regarded this double life as a symptom of the creative and intellectual ferment in Vienna between the wars. Two of the Bühlers' leading assistants who made a name for themselves in the effort to integrate American psychology and psychoanalysis after their emigration to the States—Käthe Wolf and Else

2. Samuel W. Fernberger, "Wundt's Doctorate Students," *Psychological Bulletin*, 30, no. 1 (January, 1933), 80–83.

3. Rudolf Ekstein, in James F. T. Bugental, ed., "Symposium on Karl Bühler's Contributions to Psychology," *Journal of General Psychology*, 75 (1966), 205.

4. *Ibid.*

Frenkel-Brunswik—were in analysis while working at the Bühler Institute; and—to speak now unavoidably in personal terms—so was I.

The contact which the younger generation of psychologists and psychoanalysts maintained in Vienna, surreptitiously in part, was matched in the United States by the attention which many leading psychologists paid to Freud's work long before the emigration. Probably the earliest reference in the American psychological literature to psychoanalysis was made by William James, who in an article in the *Psychological Review* in 1894 referred to a paper by Breuer and Freud. William James was not exactly *persona grata* with the German psychologists of that day because of his delightfully flippant remark that laboratory psychology of the type then practised was possible only in a country that didn't know the meaning of boredom. Only in recent years has it been pointed out by several psychologists that James's great *Principles* anticipated Freudian thought in several ways. Certainly his opening remark to a Harvard class, "Why is it that a perfectly respectable man may dream that he has intercourse with his grandmother?"[5] demonstrates not only his open-mindedness but also that the phenomena he included in his psychological thought ranged as widely as life itself.

James may have been the greatest but he was neither the only nor the earliest American to anticipate ideas and concepts normally credited to psychoanalysis. Henrik Ruitenbeek in his recent book *Freud and America* finds among early psychiatrists traces of a dynamic interpretation of mental disturbances; among them Dr. Benjamin Rush (1746–1813) and Dr. Samuel White (1777–1845); a generation later Dr. Edward H. Clarke, professor at the Harvard Medical School, who took dreams seriously as a concern for psychiatrists; and Dr. Andrew J. Ingersoll (1818–1893) who saw a causal relationship between hysterical symptoms and the voluntary suppression of sexual life.[6] These remarkable insights from early psychiatric practice, and even James's dynamic approach to psychology, recall Whitehead's statement: "But to come very near to a true theory, and to grasp its precise application, are two very different things, as the history of science teaches us. Everything of importance

5. Hutchins Hapgood, *A Victorian in the Modern World* (New York, 1939), quoted in David Shakow and David Rapaport, *The Influence of Freud on American Psychology* (*Psychological Issues*, 4, no. 1, Monograph 13, 1964), 41.

6. Hendrik K. M. Ruitenbeek, *Freud and America* (New York and London, 1966).

has been said before by somebody who did not discover it." Freud did discover psychoanalysis; and many American psychologists and psychiatrists early in the century had discovered Freud. Freud's one and only visit to the United States at the invitation of G. Stanley Hall for the celebration of the twentieth anniversary of Clark University in 1909[7] and the subsequent publication of his lectures there were certainly a major impetus to the spread of interest in psychoanalysis.

But apart from a few exceptions the American academic world was not ready to embrace Freud's ideas without question. Abraham Kardiner who was in college in 1909—in 1921 he went to Vienna to be analyzed by Freud—reports that if Freud's name was mentioned during his college days the response was invariably, "Oh, he's crazy."[8] Yet in 1918, Gardner Murphy says, "a large-scale invasion . . . by psychoanalytic modes of thinking" had already taken place, and he attributes this to the consequences of the war and to the mental hygiene movement.[9] In 1923 the American Psychological Association organized a symposium under the title, "The Current Impact of Freud on American Psychology."[10] But Edwin Boring, for example, had not been "invaded"; in the first edition of his *History of Experimental Psychology* (1929) he could find some justification in the criticism of psychology as "relatively sterile, that it set out to study mind by the experimental method, and that it has gained a mass of knowledge about sensation (which the physiologists might have gained), a little else, and nothing of great amount about the rational mind, the personality, and human nature." And Boring added his own regret that "Psychology has never had a great man to itself. Wundt was not a great man of the order of Helmholtz or Darwin." He was to change his mind later on. In the 1950 edition of his *History* he named Freud as the great man of psychology.[11] But in the first third of the century he and many others were ambivalent.

7. Ernest Jones, *The Life and Work of Sigmund Freud* (New York, 1953–1957), II, 54. For a more detailed documentation of the response of American psychologists to Freud see, *e.g.*, Shakow and Rapaport, *Influence of Freud*.

8. Abraham Kardiner, "Freud—the Man I Knew, the Scientist and His Influence," in Benjamin Nelson, ed., *Freud and the Twentieth Century* (New York, 1958), p. 47.

9. Gardner Murphy, *An Historical Introduction to Modern Psychology* (rev. ed., London, 1949), p. 329.

10. Quoted in Nelson, *Freud and the Twentieth Century*, pp. 117–118.

11. Edwin G. Boring, *A History of Experimental Psychology* (2nd ed., New York, 1950), p. 743; cf. 1929 ed., quoted *ibid*.

One reason why American psychologists were so obviously split in their reception of psychoanalysis is that their concerns and interests, and even their fighting spirits, were otherwise engaged. James, who had turned from psychology to philosophy before his death, soon fell into respectful and affectionate disregard, and his place as a central figure in the new self-consciously scientific field of psychology was taken by a brilliant young man, J. B. Watson, the founder of behaviorism.

Behaviorism, as Watson developed it first in his Columbia lectures in 1912, later at Johns Hopkins, and finally, after he left the academic world and became an advertising executive, in numerous popular magazine articles, had the flavor of a manifesto in support of science. It attacked right, left, and center the psychology of his day for its introspective methods, its use of terms such as "sensation," "perception," "memory," "consciousness," "imagery," "feeling," and "thought." What remained was stimulus and response. In a simple and readable, if somewhat crude, style Watson revolutionized the methodology of American psychology. In doing so he promised that "behavioristic psychology . . . will prove of inestimable benefit to society," that behaviorism could "almost remake an intelligent individual in a few weeks' time," and, most famous of all, that if he were given a number of healthy infants he would know how to make each into an artist, a scientist, or a thief, at will. Nobody took up this offer, as far as is known, but Watson's work created a storm which he himself likened to the "type of resistance that appeared when Darwin's *Origin of Species* was first published." In his *Behaviorism* he contemptuously brushed aside psychoanalysis: ". . . all the elaborate nonsense the Freudians have written . . ."; he blames Freud "for much of the confusion we have today," and "venture[s] to predict that 20 years from now an analyst using Freudian concepts and Freudian terminology will be placed upon the same plane as a phrenologist."[12]

And yet, Watson, too, was at least ambivalent about psychoanalysis. In an autobiography which appeared at about the same time and reveals him as a man frustrated in his academic ambition and surprisingly unaware of his influence on American psychology, he says that when he read Freud he could accept much of it, and he explains this acceptance

12. J. B. Watson, *Behaviorism* ([1924] 4th ed., Chicago, 1962), p. 297.

with reference to a breakdown he had suffered in his student days.[13] This ambivalence about psychoanalysis penetrates much of his style. So when he wishes to illustrate the possible application of behaviorism to the understanding of adult life he concocts a "case study" which reads like a vulgar popularization of psychoanalysis: ". . . a girl attached from infancy to her father, lives on until the age of 24 and does not marry. She finally marries. Because she has, of course, never had sexual relations with her father, she will not have them with her husband. If she is forced to, she breaks down. She may commit suicide or become insane to escape." *Sic*![14]

These examples are not meant to detract from Watson's influence and research approach. Indeed, there are more compatibilities between behaviorism—minus its excesses—and psychoanalysis than the frequent habit of assigning them to opposite poles would lead one to suspect. But Watson, just because of his far-reaching influence on American psychology, is a particularly suitable illustration of the general ambivalence toward psychoanalysis. There are other examples. In the series of studies, *A History of Psychology in Autobiography*, published between 1930 and 1965, a large group of leading American psychologists have described their intellectual development. Many of them had been to Germany or Austria; all of them were, of course, familiar—more or less—with psychoanalysis. This they indicate frequently in self-conscious introductory remarks to the effect that writing an autobiography feels like "psychoanalyzing" oneself. But with this acknowledgment to the popular version of psychoanalysis they proceed—with a few exceptions such as Gordon Allport or Gardner Murphy—to describe their lives' work as if psychoanalysis did not exist.

The most serious intellectual efforts among psychologists to come to terms with Freudian ideas were made at Yale. There, as David Shakow and David Rapaport describe in considerable detail, Clark Hull, the leading learning theorist of his day, organized between 1936 and 1942 a series of seminars with the aim of "achieving a synthesis of conditioning theory and psychoanalysis." These seminars were attended by a number of psychoanalysts and analyzed psychologists, including John Dollard,

13. Carl Murchison, *et al.*, eds., *A History of Psychology in Autobiography* (Worcester, Mass., 1930–1965), III, 274.
14. Watson, *Behaviorism*, pp. 294–295.

who had been analyzed by Hans Sachs in Berlin, and Neal Miller, who had been analyzed by Heinz Hartmann in Vienna. Hull, the great proponent of the hypothetico-deductive approach in psychology, wanted the seminars to formulate clear-cut psychoanalytic postulates from which theorems could be deduced in a rigorously logical fashion, but the participants struggled in vain. Neither in Freud's writings nor in those of any other analysts were such formulations contained. Indeed, the psychoanalytic literature of the time was anything but systematic. When the seminar realized the sisyphean nature of their undertaking, they changed course. Dollard and Miller, Sears and Mowrer began to formulate within the terms of their own theories analogues to psychoanalytic concepts. There can be no doubt that the effort was genuine; years later, in 1950, Dollard and Miller dedicated their book *Personality and Psychotherapy* to Pavlov and Freud. But Shakow and Rapaport conclude their description of this monumental effort as follows: "Thus Freudian terms and crudely analogous observations invaded the experimental literature on a scale never before attained, but the price paid was that Freud's concepts were turned into vague conceptions, barely related, and at times actually contradictory, to their original forms . . ."[15]

Perhaps the most interesting feature of this episode is the tremendous effort which the experimental psychologists put into it. Apparently they "did not tire of reiterating the idea that there is something important in that theory." A few years before the Yale seminars, a small group in Vienna consisting of some positivists and some psychologists influenced by psychoanalysis had engaged in a similar effort, similarly abortive: they attempted to translate Freud's *Group Psychology and the Analysis of the Ego* into positivist language. No record remains of this highly educational and totally frustrating endeavor.

Thus in the peak years of the European immigration just before the outbreak of war many American psychologists were in a curious state of mind about psychoanalysis: they were in many ways impressed by it, they could not let go of it, "there was something important in that theory," but neither could they come to terms with it in their scientific work. And there were always some in the profession who attacked and derided Freudian thought as unscientific and metaphysical.

15. Shakow and Rapaport, *Influence of Freud*, p. 142.

II

INTO this atmosphere of ambivalence the European psychoanalysts came, many of them brought over under emergency conditions. There is no doubt that their numbers, their personal ability, and the professional contacts they were able to establish in American academic life deepened the penetration of psychoanalysis into the field of psychology.

It is not easy to form an estimate of how many persons were involved. The American Psychological Association, for example, established a Committee on Displaced Foreign Psychologists, but it dealt also with professional persons with a medical background, with philosophers, and various other types of scholars. By June 30, 1940, the Committee was in touch with 269 displaced scholars, of whom 134 were in the States.[16] It operated on a budget of three hundred dollars. The American Philosophical Association established a Committee on Exiled Scholars, to whose care some of those registered with the psychologists were apparently transferred. In the turmoil of those days clear-cut classifications were not possible; checking of credentials was out of the question for humanitarian as well as political reasons, and the overlap or double counting must have been considerable. At best, one can guess only at the order of size, and this was surprisingly small, as the figures quoted above show. An estimate of the number of European immigrants who brought with them psychoanalytic training and ideas is doubly difficult because they included not only psychoanalysts proper but many psychologists—Paul Bergmann, Bruno Bettelheim, Else Frenkel-Brunswik, David Rapaport, Fritz Redl, and Käthe Wolf, for example. Perhaps one hundred to two hundred professional psychoanalysts and thirty to fifty psychologists with a psychoanalytic orientation were involved in the migration.

Most of the younger professionals found their feet quickly and learned to appreciate the American hospitality and generosity that was lavished on them, even if others who waited anxiously in American consulates all over Europe for the coveted quota place failed to realize these virtues of the American national character. At least one, Bruno Bettelheim,

---

16. *Psychological Bulletin*, 37, no. 9 (November, 1940), 715–718.

waited in a concentration camp; the article he wrote about this experience has justly become a classic.[17]

But even safe arrival in the States was, of course, no guarantee of finding professional satisfaction in the new world. A few scholars who were beyond the peak of their working life had bitter experiences, as the tragic course of Karl Bühler's professional career in America illustrates. Charlotte Bühler attributes to several factors the fact that Karl Bühler never found in the States the recognition to which he was entitled by his outstanding contributions to psychology. This sensitive and gentle scholar was crushed by his experiences in an Austrian prison, and even though this experience was short by the standards which then prevailed, his arrival in the States in 1939 did nothing to alleviate his depression. The earlier offer of a chair at Fordham had been canceled because Bühler, a Catholic, was married to a Protestant and had educated his children as Protestants. Other opportunities commensurate with his position at the University of Vienna were rare, and earlier arrivals had understandably been given preference.[18] Bühler finally accepted a minor position, but his working power was broken.

Yet for a variety of reasons, the fate of the psychoanalysts was by and large less tragic. Psychoanalysts were to a large extent, even in the pre-Hitler world, outsiders in their own countries; the academic world of Central Europe had never admitted them. The sect-like character of the psychoanalytic movement which has so often been ascribed to Freud's character was undoubtedly a response to the hostile climate of opinion that surrounded it. They had, as it were, experienced premature training in the psychological condition of being émigrés, and this must have stood them in good stead when they had to become émigrés in the full sense of the term. In addition, to their American colleagues they were no strangers; in the decades prior to immigration the international congresses of the psychoanalytic movement had brought people from all over the globe together. And finally, the psychoanalysts presented at least no financial problems to their hosts. Psychoanalysis is an urban

17. Bruno Bettelheim, "Individual and Mass Behaviour in Extreme Situations," *Journal of Abnormal and Social Psychology*, 38 (1943), 417–452.

18. Charlotte Bühler, "Die Wiener Psychologische Schule in der Emigration," *Psychologische Rundschau*, 16, no. 3 (1965), 187–196.

profession; in the great American cities the demand for practitioners of the art was high among people who could afford to pay the inevitably high costs of psychoanalytic treatment. The newcomers settled in New York, Boston, Chicago, Philadelphia, Detroit, Los Angeles, and San Francisco and were soon busily engaged in private practice, as teaching members of their local psychoanalytic training institutes, and as supervisors of a generation of young American psychiatrists.

These men and women carried prestige not only because of their personal achievements in Europe but also because they had belonged to the inner circle of "the Professor," as Freud's students used to call him, and because they were after all Viennese in culture if not by birth. For even though the immigrant group included also German and Hungarian analysts, Vienna had so unquestionably been the European capital of psychoanalysis that they all profited from the extraordianry reputation of that city, and conveyed not only European culture but also the proverbial Viennese charm. Whether Vienna's cultural reputation was ever deserved in the past is debatable. In 1938 the matter was beyond debate; the city itself demonstrated to the world how thin the veneer of civilization had been. Vienna quickly sank into barbarity. Those who escaped because they were Jews or because of their convictions, or because of both, remained the only symbol of what Vienna had once stood for in the eyes of the world.

In this prestigious and highly civilized group of men and women, Heinz Hartmann stands out both as the leading intellectual influence on the development of psychoanalytic thought in its convergence with general psychology, and as a person. His friends think of him as a man whose major challenge in life must have been to protect his integrity and creativeness against an overflow of good fortune. I remember well another leading young Viennese intellectual saying about Hartmann in a mixture of admiration and envy: he has everything. Indeed, he had. In the recent *Festschrift* for Hartmann, Ruth and Kurt Eissler describe his family background.[19] He was born into one of the leading scholarly families of Vienna, comparable to the Huxleys in England; in the generations before him there were scientists, philosophers, poets, historians,

19. Rudolf M. Lowenstein, Lottie M. Newman, Max Schur, and Albert J. Solvit, eds., *Psychoanalysis; A General Psychology* (New York, 1966), pp. 3–15.

social reformers, ambassadors. In his father's house an international, cultural, and intellectual élite met, and the growing boy was exposed to everything that was best in European civilization. His own gifts matched in their variety the many-sided influences to which he was exposed. He played the violin and the piano, he painted, and he wrote poetry; he used his university years not only to study medicine but to attend lectures in a variety of fields, particularly philosophy, psychology, and (when Max Weber was a guest professor in Vienna) sociology. It must have been difficult for so gifted and privileged a young man with this renaissance-like scope to find a center for his creative work; but he did, in psychoanalysis. He is one of the two persons known to have been invited by Freud to take their training analysis with him.

In contrast to the lack of relation between Freud and Bühler, Hartmann and his friend and colleague Ernst Kris had established, while still in Vienna, contact with academic psychology. Hartmann particularly had demonstrated quite early in his career that the still popular but spurious assertion that psychoanalysis was antithetical to the experimental method was wrong. In 1924 he published an experimental study on the use of symbols by patients suffering from Korsakoff psychosis; in 1933 he published an experiment, using Zeigarnik's method, on the memory for uncompleted tasks in obsessive-compulsive neurotics; in 1934 and 1935 he presented empirical work on the study of twins, which shows full familiarity with the work of academic psychologists in that area. Hartmann also occasionally attended the Bühlers' famous Wednesday evening colloquium and participated in an interdisciplinary seminar established by the young intellectuals at the University; Paul Lazarsfeld and Rudolph Carnap in addition to Hartmann were leading lights of that group.

Hartmann was in his late forties in 1941 when he arrived in New York, a few years after the height of the immigration; and his intellectual leadership within the psychoanalytic community was securely established, even for those who had not yet read his then untranslated earlier contributions. He quickly settled down to private practice, to a leading role in psychoanalytic education, and above all to the production of a large series of theoretical papers—many of them in collaboration with Ernst Kris and Rudolf Loewenstein—which extended the boundaries of psychoanalysis as Freud had left it into what is now known as psychoanalytic ego psychology.

Yet the special impact of psychoanalysis on psychology in America cannot be attributed only to the initial, partial receptivity of American psychologists to Freudianism, nor to the personal influence of even so remarkable a group of men and women as the émigrés. An explanation of this influence must reach deeper, into the character of the society into which the émigrés came, and, ultimately, into the subtle relationship between the general goal of psychology and the peculiar structure of psychoanalytic thought.

III

LONG before J. K. Galbraith popularized the phrase, America was an affluent society in which the belief that everybody could reach the top was widespread, almost universal. Many tried, but in the nature of things only few could succeed. This type of society creates its own peculiar human problems which are different from those in a society that knows itself to be class-ridden. In England before the war the ambitious working-class youngster knew that the class structure was holding him back. He could join a labor movement and find satisfaction in collective experience; though his individual fate was frustrating, he did not need to lose self-respect. Society was at fault, not he. His counterpart in the States, even in the relatively rare instance in which he joined a political movement, was confronted with the powerful ethos of his society: he believed in his heart that he had nobody to blame but himself.

But the power of the Horatio Alger myth in that society was not just a working class phenomenon. On all levels of society the less successful were undermined in their self-respect. Arthur Miller's salesman vainly tried to escape from the reality of failure into a dream of success; in the end he knew he had failed as a person. The middle-class men and particularly their wives were haunted by unachieved goals and ambitions, which conspicuous consumption could hardly alleviate. If it is possible that America's wealth was at least in part created by its emphasis on individual effort as the way to material success, then it would follow that the psychological price for her greatness was paid by the many millions who could blame neither the social structure nor the color of their skin for not reaching the top.

The great Depression multiplied this experience many times; the very anonymity of the culprits behind the economic disaster must have intensified the soul-searching and the fundamental doubts of many businessmen, professional people, and intellectuals, even if their own economic plight was as a rule less severe than that of the unemployed workers or of the youngsters who left school or university and could not find a job.

Such a society, geared in times of good fortune and bad to individual self appraisal, to the search for understanding of one's own fate, and no longer fully supported by the faith of its puritan forefathers, is ready for any system of thought that explains man to himself. Psychoanalysis affected American society generally not because of the originality and power of its scientific structure, but because it filled that need. However vulgarized and distorted the popular version was, it was a psychology that dealt with individual experience and explained events and feelings as no academic psychology had ever seriously done. The popular version of psychoanalysis took away from the individual the full responsibility for his success in life. Something might have happened to him during early childhood, his mother may not have loved him, or loved him too much; it led him to believe that there were reasons for failure beyond his control.

The impact of psychoanalysis on the popular culture was profound. According to Ruitenbeek the first popular article on psychoanalysis appeared in *Good Housekeeping* in 1915; its title was "Diagnosis by Dreams," and it carefully avoided any allusion to sex.[20] Such reticence was soon abandoned. Journalism, television, plays, films, musicals, and jokes made sex, libido, oedipal complex, defense mechanism, and the unconscious the common vocabulary of urban society to such an extent that Lionel Trilling could rightly call psychoanalysis "the slang of our culture."

But psychoanalysis was not alone among the various schools of psy-

20. Ruitenbeek, *Freud and America*, p. 61.

chological thought to capture the imagination of the American people as fitting their psychological situation. Watson's behaviorism had done it too. When in 1930, the year after the economic collapse, Watson's *Behaviorism* appeared in a new edition, the *New York Times* wrote, "This book marks an epoch in the intellectual history of man"; and the *Tribune*: "Perhaps this is the most important book ever written. One stands for an instant blinded with hope."[21] The public responded eagerly to a psychology that was simple and promised to solve all human problems via the formula of stimulus, response, and conditioning.

Both of these popularizations succeeded because the psychological ideas had a meaningful bearing on the lives of men and women; Freud dealt, and Watson promised to deal, with the real subject matter of psychology—man's experiences and behavior in their full complexity.[22] The degree of their success forced the attention of the academics, for not only were they exposed to the general stresses and strains of their culture, and not only were they pressured by their students and the general public to pronounce on these ideas but they saw in them a means of clarifying the major purposes of psychology. However useful and important experiments with rats, or with human memory for nonsense syllables may be, there are few if any psychologists who would seri-

21. Quoted in Robert S. Woodworth, *Contemporary Schools of Psychology* ([1936], rev. ed., New York, 1948), pp. 92–93.

22. The relationship between the two schools is subtle and revealing. In 1919 Watson published his *Psychology from the Standpoint of a Behaviorist*, in which his openness to Freudian ideas is clearly demonstrated though unacknowledged. Speaking of the attachment of small children to the parent of the opposite sex, he says ". . . as children grow older they learn from one or another source that such ways of reacting are either 'wrong' or unusual, then the process of discarding or replacement is necessary . . . we do not put [childish things] away—but they never for us lose their impulsive power . . ." Watson's later popular writing on childrearing made a large segment of American parents "behaviorists"; his *Psychological Care of Infant and Child* (1928) became the basis of publications of the United States Children's Bureau and through this medium conveyed to an enormous audience the doctrine of a "hands off" policy in childrearing. In an interesting article Ernest Hilgard has traced the manner in which Watson arrived at this basic idea on childcare through a misunderstanding of Freud: "Watson believed that the danger inherent in the Oedipal situation arose through the excessive emotional attachments of parents to their children, through their excessive fondling of them"; and Hilgard adds, "It is an odd coincidence that the child-rearing practices that later Freudians, such as Ribble and Spock, have tried to correct had themselves become established by one much impressed by Freud." Ernest R. Hilgard, "Freud and Experimental Psychology," *Behavioral Science*, 2 (January, 1957), 74–79.

ously wish to identify the aims of their specialized laboratory work with the general tasks of psychology. Freud, like Watson, offered general ideas on the whole field of human behavior and experience. But Watson's larger promises are today all but forgotten, and so, almost, is he, notwithstanding the spectacular initial success of behaviorism and the lasting impact of B. F. Skinner. To understand the sustained interest in Freudianism, so dramatically developed by the émigrés from Europe, requires a closer examination of its substance—its doctrines and method.

IV

THREE distinct aspects of psychoanalysis help account for the intense interest it has generated on the part of American psychologists: first, certain similarities with American academic psychology in the approach to psychological problems; second, the impressive temerity of psychoanalysis in dealing with problems that are clearly psychological in nature but not easily encompassed by academic psychology; and third, certain characteristics in psychoanalytic procedure.

Psychoanalysis and American academic psychology have a common intellectual ancestry. Both came of age in the wake of physiology and Darwinism. Freud's first scientific work was physiological research and, notwithstanding his well-known Lamarckian aberration, his thought was deeply influenced by Darwin. His early training in Brücke's laboratory led him to think of himself throughout his life as above all a scientist, much in line with the scientific aspiration of American psychology. Accordingly, his psychology was to be a *Naturwissenschaft* rather than a *Geisteswissenschaft*. Both psychoanalysis and American psychology aimed at a scientific pyschology which, in Hilgard's words, "would be pleasing to Helmholtz—a deterministic world, a world of energy-interchanges, a lawful world in which such principles as conservation of energy will hold."[23] Both schools also rejected the reliance on introspection as a method. Both take what a person says about himself as a datum toward an answer, not as the final answer itself.[24]

23. *Ibid.*, p. 77.
24. Vulgarized accounts of Freudian thought have often distorted this point. Hartmann

Because of these similarities and parallels American psychologists assumed that these new ideas would serve as a source of hypotheses that could be verified or disproved by their usual methodological techniques. But any such efforts were complicated by the fact that psychoanalytic thought had not as yet been systematically codified. Freud himself did not leave behind a comprehensive theoretical statement; up to the very end of his long life he was engaged in new discoveries involving reformulations of earlier ideas and changes in terminology, and did not take the time to spell out implications of later statements on previous ones. Hartmann has provided systematic accounts of many psychoanalytic ideas—the conflict-free ego zone, the reality principle, sublimation— but not of the entire system of thought. The most ambitious attempt to provide a comprehensive theoretical statement was made by David Rapaport; it resulted in an identification of the various basic principles of psychoanalytic thought but not in their integration.

Yet despite this difficulty, a host of empirical studies were made. In them psychologists took isolated aspects of psychoanalytic theory, reformulated them to fit the requirements of measuring techniques, and used the results as "confirmation" or "rejection" of the theory. The value of the ordinary run of such studies has proved to be dubious, as Rapaport has clearly seen: "The overwhelming majority of the experiments designed to test psychoanalytic propositions display a blatant lack of interest in the meaning, within the theory of psychoanalysis, of the propositions tested. Thus most of them certainly did not measure what they purported to; as for the rest, it is unclear whether they did or not. Even where the findings appear to confirm a relationship posited by psychoanalysis, the experiments usually tested only an analogous relationship on a high level of the hierarchy of psychological organization. It is not that all these experiments are useless as confirming evidence, but rather that at this stage of our knowledge it is not clear what—if anything—they confirm."[25]

---

in an essay written in 1927 said that what has been "carefully ascertained by introspection represents the connection in a patchy way, and ignores what is obviously most essential." Hartmann, *Essays on Ego Psychology* (London, 1964), p. 392.

25. David Rapaport, *The Structure of Psychoanalytic Theory* (*Psychological Issues*, 2, no. 2, Monograph 6, 1960).

Some of the psychologists' efforts to come to terms with psychoanalysis, however, were more sophisticated, especially those made by a number of learning theorists following the Yale seminars mentioned above. Their effort was to translate the theoretical and conceptual propositions of psychoanalysis into the established terms of learning theory. The outstanding work in this area was done by Dollard and Miller, and by Mowrer. Dollard and Miller found ingenious ways of dealing with some of the complexities of psychoanalysis. They interpreted changes occurring in the psychoanalytic interview as a function of the therapist's creating a situation in which "new conditions permit new learning." Even the unconscious finds room in this learning theory under the name of "the unverbalized." Conditioning remains the major mechanism by which all the phenomena with which Freud was concerned came into existence.[26] Mowrer's rather different position is that neurosis must be understood as a learning deficit consisting in a lack, or insufficient incorporation, of superego forces or social mores.[27] Hartmann has followed these efforts at translation, and by and large has welcomed them even where he disagrees with the formulations or conclusions.[28]

The results of even the most effective of these efforts were not always earthshaking, but they demonstrate dramatically how seriously psychoanalysis was taken by American psychologists. Robert Sears concluded his review of over a hundred such studies: "In some instances Freud's views have been supported and his principles importantly extended. In others, the new techniques have failed to cast much useful light on the behavior in question. All the work, however, serves to emphasize the increasing significance attached to psychoanalysis by non-analysts, as a guide to the planning of research on personality."[29]

26. John Dollard and Neal E. Miller, *Personality and Psychotherapy; an Analysis in Terms of Learning, Thinking, and Culture* (New York, 1950).

27. O. H. Mowrer, *Learning Theory and Personality Dynamics* (New York, 1950); O. H. Mowrer, "Motivation," *Annual Review of Psychology*, 3 (1952), 419–438.

28. Hartmann, *Essays*, particularly, "Comments on the Scientific Aspects of Psychoanalysis" (1958), and "Psychoanalysis as a Scientific Theory" (1959).

29. Robert R. Sears, *Survey of Objective Studies of Psychoanalytic Concepts* (New York, 1947), p. ix. The general conclusion of the survey is, however, "that other social and psychological sciences must gain as many hypotheses and intuitions as possible from psychoanalysis but . . . the further analysis of psychoanalytic concepts by non-psychoanalytic techniques may be relatively fruitless so long as those concepts rest in the theoretical framework of psychoanalysis." (p. 143) Another survey of experimental studies claiming

The second aspect of the psychoanalytic style of thought—its boldness in attacking the most elusive and fundamental problems of the human personality—was even more challenging. Psychoanalysts appeared to think on a larger scale about problems which ordinary psychologists, even when they recognized them as important, could not easily translate into experimental variables and which they therefore regarded as not amenable to scientific inquiry. Psychoanalysts knew no such limitations. Methods had to be devised to fit the problems, and not vice versa. The problems of psychoanalysis arose concretely out of the medical problems it faced. "Psychoanalysis was born of medical necessity":[30] Freud's patients presented him with problems through the solution of which he created a general psychological theory. His entire work was problem-centered; the American psychologists wanted to create a science, and inevitably their work became method-centered.

Freud clearly distinguished psychoanalysis as a theory from psychoanalysis as a therapy; he expected the former to have a longer life than the latter. But the creation of his theory is inconceivable without his practice which, as is well known, started with hypnosis and was succeeded by catharsis supported by placing a hand on the patient's forehead. Eventually the orthodox psychoanalytic interview, with a patient on the couch engaged in free association, emerged as the most fruitful method Freud could discover for minute observation over hundreds of hours of the full complexity of psychic life. Nothing short of this difficult, unorthodox, systematic observational procedure seemed to him to do justice to the problem he was tackling, which was the understanding of a total human personality rather than that of artificially isolated partial functions. It is this concern with the entire human being that enabled psychoanalysis to take note of phenomena academic psychology was forced to overlook or disregard as uncontrollable chance occurrences incapable of being investigated through laboratory enquiries.

---

to test psychoanalytic propositions was made by Orlansky, who feels after examining about 150 experimental contributions that there is not much in the Freudian ideas of the impact of early events on personality formation that stands up to experimental scrutiny. H. Orlansky, "Infant Care and Personality," *Psychological Bulletin*, 46, no. 1 (January, 1949), 1–48.

30. Freud, Preface to Theodore Reik, *Ritual: Psychoanalytic Studies* (London, 1931).

The meaning of symbols and dreams, the information value of slips of the tongue, and, above all, the fundamental role of the unconscious in determining human actions could be identified because the problem of finding a key to the understanding of patients predominated in the approach of psychoanalysts.

As a consequence the time perspective of psychoanalysts extended well beyond what most academic psychologists could encompass within the range of the here-and-now samples of their experiments. Psychoanalytic time perspective goes from birth to death, or, more realistically, from birth to the date at which a person lies down on the analytic couch. With this goes a rather different concept of the unity of personality that includes apparently discontinuous events.

This time perspective for psychological data is inextricably related to the genetic approach in its emphasis on events in infancy and childhood which are inferred from adult personality. While the predictions of the experimentalists were time-less, on the basis of the presumably necessary though unrealistic assumption that time stands still (they claimed their generalizations to be true "other things being equal"), psychoanalytic predictions are actually turned backwards to the past of the individual. That is to say, they start with knowing a patient's current state of affairs; they discover by the laborious and painstaking procedures of psychoanalytic treatment his early history, and then trace a meaningful relation of the past to the present—a procedure which left the new scientists in psychology cold, bent as they were on prediction rather than "post-diction" as a necessary element in their canon of operations.

Psychoanalysis formalized these approaches to the understanding of man in a variety of concepts concerning the structure and the development of the mind, the role of defense mechanisms, and the nature of neurosis. From the point of view of many academic psychologists, these concepts were important, even though they did not share the styles of thought which had permitted their original formulation. No wonder, then, that many psychoanalytic ideas entered American psychology in an anonymous fashion. Indeed, a scrutiny of text books reveals this to have been a frequent occurrence,[31] demonstrating the genuine diffi-

31. Hans Herma, Ernst Kris, and Joseph Shor, "Freud's Theory of the Dream in American Textbooks," *Journal of Abnormal and Social Psychology*, 38 (1943), 319–334.

culty of coming to terms with a system of thought which had so much to offer and yet seemed in important aspects so alien.

If again, in this second area, frustration and fascination seem to have come into precarious balance, the third aspect of the psychoanalytic style of thought—its characteristic procedure—would appear to have been fated for an unequivocally negative reception. The psychoanalytic literature is almost entirely untouched by efforts at measurement. Its concepts are not precisely defined, and its language encourages concrete imagery rather than scientific abstractions. For these reasons alone one might well have expected American academic psychology to turn away from the ideas of Freud and from the immigrant psychoanalysts, after having given them hospitality and a trial period.

Yet, if one surveys the psychological literature around 1950, it is clear that this did not actually happen. Psychoanalysts such as Ernst Kris and René Spitz, psychoanalytically oriented psychologists such as Else Frenkel-Brunswik and Käthe Wolf, were engaged with colleagues in various universities in empirical research which was based on psychoanalysis but used the methods and measurements of the academicians. Perhaps the best-known work demonstrating that the two styles of thought were, after all, not incompatible is the *Authoritarian Personality*.[32] The problem of this work was the study of anti-Semitism; its theoretical orientation was the psychoanalytic theory of personality; and its methods were largely quantitative, based on questionnaires, interviews, and tests of the "objective" and "projective" type. While both its conception and its methods have been attacked—with and without justification—it remains an outstanding example of the fact that concern with method need not lead to trivial problems and that major, meaningful problems need not defy efforts at quantification.

Empirical developmental studies based on a similar orientation were also progressing around 1950 at various universities, utilizing Hartmann's theoretical development of ego psychology and Erik Erikson's efforts in the same direction.[33] A whole field of personality tests—pro-

32. T. W. Adorno, Else Frenkel-Brunswik, D. J. Levinson, and R. N. Sanford, *The Authoritarian Personality* (New York, 1950).

33. Erik H. Erikson, *Childhood and Society* (rev. ed., New York, 1963). A particularly striking example is Edwin Bokert's study of the dream's power to gratify wishes: subjects thirsty when they went to sleep were wakened to report dream content, and permitted to

jective tests—grew out of increasing familiarity with psychoanalytic thought. The rapidly expanding area of clinical psychology, both in its practice and research efforts, was profoundly influenced by psychoanalytic ideas.

Has the mutual adaptation then been completed? Has psychoanalysis been absorbed by academic psychology in spite of divergencies in style of thought? Is the controversy a matter of the past? There is no simple answer to these questions. For there is one basic issue which keeps the debate alive and prevents complete adaptation: the nature of psychological explanation. On this issue the large majority of American academic psychologists are uncompromisingly mechanistic. A minority, whose voice is now heard with increasing volume, rejects the mechanistic model of the natural sciences for psychological explanation; the humanistic and existential psychologists—the "third force" psychologists who now replace psychoanalysis in the limelight of popular acclaim—do exactly this. The position of psychoanalysts is less consistent on the issue of explanation than either the majority or the minority view in American psychology. Freud set the pattern decades ago and contemporary psychoanalysts continue it in their current work: when it comes to the explanation of human behavior and experiences they speak a double language, the language of causes and the language of purposes. Some would call it the language of science and the language of fiction. However disparagingly the term "fiction" may be meant to be in this context, its connotation is echoed in Freud's own resentment when he felt reluctantly compelled by his data to talk of meaning and purpose, of crisis and conflict; he said it made him sound more like a novelist than a scientist. However, he invented at least a respectable terminology for the dual pattern of psychoanalytic explanation which is still in use: he talked of psychoanalytic theory which encompassed the teleological concepts without which he could not understand his patients, and of

---

drink as much as they liked in measured quantities in the morning. Those who had had gratifying dreams during the night drank less than those who had dreamed frustratingly. E. Bokert, "The Effects of Thirst and a Related Auditory Stimulus on Dream Reports" (unpub. Ph.D. Diss., New York Univ., 1965, as reported by George S. Klein, "Peremptory Ideation," in Robert R. Holt, ed., *Motives and Thought: Psychoanalytic Essays in Honor of David Rapaport* [*Psychological Issues*, 5, no. 2–3, Monograph 18/19, 1967]).

psychoanalytic metatheory which encompassed the physiological super-structure he erected in order to appease his conscience as a natural scientist. The function of the physiological metatheory is to "explain" in terms of energy and neurophysiology the other theory.

Even a cursory glance at current psychoanalytic writings reveals that both theories are still in the saddle; however uncomfortable their close partnership, however dangerously one or the other may be slipping, neither has been thrown off. In other words, psychoanalysis contains the body-mind problem as a problem; it has no clear solution for it.

This is not, of course, the place to enter into the substance of the debate on the nature of psychological explanation, even though chapter and verse could be cited to document the fact that the attitude of American psychologists to psychoanalysis depends to a large extent both on their own position in this ongoing debate and on whether they confronted psychoanalysis as a whole or addressed themselves to that aspect of it which was compatible or incompatible with their own view.[34] Yet this issue must at least be mentioned here since neither the intensity of nor the ambivalence in the reactions of American psychologists to psychoanalysis can be fully understood without it. In the last resort psychoanalysis made its intellectual contribution to psychology in the United States because it attempted to have the best of both worlds in matters of explanation. Wherever one stood on this core problem of all psychological inquiry, psychoanalysis was relevant. It combines in one school of thought approaches which outside it separate psychologists so deeply that they are hardly on talking terms with each other.

Now that cybernetics and computer simulation of behavior have made it possible for many psychologists to come to terms with the concepts of purpose and intention,[35] the road is open for a convergence of

34. The nature of psychoanalytic explanation is discussed in a vast number of publications. The following references are pertinent to the point made here: Sigmund Freud, "Project for a Scientific Psychology" (1895), posthumously published in *The Origins of Psychoanalysis: Letters to Wilhelm Fliess, Drafts and Notes, 1887–1902* (New York, 1954); Karl H. Pribram, "The Neuropsychology of Sigmund Freud," in Arthur J. Bachrach, ed., *Experimental Foundations of Clinical Psychology* (New York, 1962); Holt, *Motives and Thought*; Hartmann, *Essays*; Philip Rieff, *Freud: The Mind of the Moralist* (London, 1959); and George S. Klein, "Perspectives to Change in Psychoanalytic Theory" (mimeographed paper, Research Center for Mental Health, New York Univ., 1966), p. 11.

35. See, *e.g.*, George Miller, Karl H. Pribram, and Eugene Galanter, *Plans and the Structure of Behavior* (New York, 1960), a book that made a tremendous impact on American

psychoanalysis with general psychology. Perhaps by the end of this century it will have fulfilled its constructive function of providing an intellectual irritant to more consistent but oversimplified forms of psychology; then it may well disappear as a separate entity, rendered redundant by its very success.

V

HOW much of this influence was the result of the historical fact of the intellectual migration of the thirties? Would it have happened in any case? No exact answer can be given if only because history cannot engage in experiments to test alternative conditions and developments. Yet experimental modes of thinking are not altogether alien to the premises of historical thought just as they are not altogether alien to psychoanalytic thought. The complexity, at least, of the explanation of the psychoanalysts' impact can be derived from a comparison of the fate of associated groups of ideas in the United States which were or were not accompanied by the migration of "carriers" from Europe.

Two groups of schools suggest themselves for this task: on the one hand, Gestalt psychology, and on the other hand, the psychodynamic schools that split off from Freudian psychoanalysis before the migration, in particular the schools of Jung and Adler. The attempt here is not, of course, to appraise the scientific validity of these schools, just as no attempt was made to appraise the substantive scientific contributions of psychoanalysis. The analysis will remain within the context of what Peter Berger calls "the root platitude of the sociology of knowledge," namely, that "ideas do not succeed in history by virtue of their truth but by virtue of their relationship to specific social processes."[36]

Both Gestalt psychologists and Adlerians provided a fair contingent in the European intellectual migration; the Jungians, centered in Switzerland, did not. Many American psychologists were familiar with these

psychologists, even though it has not—so far—led to empirical work at the frontiers of psychological knowledge.

36. Peter L. Berger, "Toward a Sociological Understanding of Psychoanalysis," *Social Research*, 32, no. 2 (1965), 32.

three schools, thanks to their habit of completing their professional education on the continent of Europe during the period in which German psychology was dominant. Gestalt psychology, largely based on experimental work, fitted well methodologically into the native academic psychology, and was carried directly to this country by Köhler, Koffka, Wertheimer, and Lewin. Not that it did not give rise to controversy; it did. But the controversy remained within and between university departments which operated on the same wave length, as it were. Questions of scientific style and epistemology simply did not arise. Accordingly, it quickly became part of American psychology, gave rise to much empirical work, underwent several reformulations, and in the end ceased to be a separate branch of psychology; it achieved an unambiguous place in the history of this subject, but no longer plays a role in its advancement. This type of psychology did not, of course, gain public acclaim since its problems were far removed from public needs. To be sure, Lewin, one of its outstanding representatives, did more probably than any other psychologist to awaken the social conscience of his professional colleagues. But his influence did not transcend academic circles.

The situation was very different for Adler's individual psychology, which too was carried to this country by able and active disciples. Indeed, his concepts of inferiority complex and his emphasis on the power drive as a basic factor in motivation rivaled outside the university the popularity of Freudian terms with which they were often confused. This is not surprising as Adler's concerns were as relevant to the American situation as those of psychoanalysis. It too contrasted sharply in style and method with academic psychology. But unlike Freud, Adler and his students were never concerned with the problems of general psychology, nor did they acquire Hartmann's familiarity with contemporary developments in psychology. Furthermore, Adler had already in Europe abandoned the creative epistemological confusion of psychoanalysis. His psychology was free from mechanistic concepts and explanations. Hence it is hardly surprising that he did not provoke academic psychologists to translate him into their idiom; he and his work were left to be recognized by practitioners in the art of helping others.

The fate of Jung's ideas represents yet another pattern. Before the days of the migration Jung had his share of visiting American psychologists, among whom Henry Murray became probably the best known. But the vicissitudes of history saved him and his followers from having to make the journey to the States, and few in fact came. Jung's style of thought spans an even wider range than the others, from philosophical, metaphysical, and religious speculations to the invention of the word association test. The latter, one might have assumed, would have brought him intellectually near to the test-conscious Americans. And in addition he provided popular language with new terms—extroversion and introversion—and dealt with fundamental aspects of human experience. He may even have wished to influence general psychology—he wished to influence all thought about man—but if so, it was on the basis of a one-way traffic in ideas. He did not take much notice of academic psychology. And there is little trace, if any, of his contribution in the work of American psychologists.

If a comparison with Jung leads one to believe that the migration was an important factor in the convergence of psychoanalysis and general psychology, the comparison with the fate of Gestalt psychology and Adler's work demonstrates that it certainly was not the only factor. It is a combination of this historical event, the receptivity of the host culture, the intention of some leading psychoanalysts, and the resistance to oversimple solutions of psychological problems which altogether distinguished psychoanalysis from the other psychological schools, and which explain jointly the profundity of the impact of the émigré psychoanalysts on American psychology.

FRANZ NEUMANN
BETWEEN MARXISM
AND LIBERAL DEMOCRACY

by H. STUART HUGHES

TODAY most American students of sociology, history, or political theory are only dimly aware of who Franz Neumann was. A half generation ago, in the late 1940's and early 1950's, he ranked as a major force in social science, a man who from the start had given leadership to the intellectual emigration from Germany and had subsequently become one of the most respected professors in one of America's most prestigious universities. This contrast epitomizes what we may call in appropriately Germanic fashion "the Neumann problem." If Franz Neumann was enormously influential in his own time and began to suffer neglect very shortly after his death, the explanation lies only partly in the fact that the corpus of his published writing was small and that his powers of persuasion were exerted primarily through the spoken word; the change was also due to the ambiguity of the intellectual inheritance he left behind him. Beneath the force and clarity of his polemical style, his intimates had increasingly detected a profound hesitation and uncertainty. So long as Neumann himself was in charge of his theoretical output, he managed—at least in public—to impose order on his contradictions through the application of an inordinately powerful mind and a strict sobriety of method. After his death, all the ambiguities came to the surface, and it was difficult for his younger readers to find the thread of ideological and emotional consistency that held them together.

Thus the career of Franz Neumann suggests both what was tragic and transitory in the emigration experience and the fashion in which that experience passed into the wider currents of American intellectual life. While he may be read less today than he was a decade or two ago, his indirect influence persists—and persists largely through the work of

men who considered themselves his students, whether or not they were
ever formally enrolled under his direction. It is for this reason that it is
urgent for one of those in his intellectual debt to set down the record
before another half generation goes by and memories grow blurred.
Even in our century of unmanageable documentation, there are some
events of the mind that remain almost entirely unrecorded. The influence of Franz Neumann was one of these: it should not be lost to the
history of ideas.

The events of Neumann's life can be briefly told. Their relevance to
his development as ideologist and theoretician is readily apparent. Born
in Kattowitz (now Katowice) in 1900 of Jewish parentage, Neumann
grew up in a border area contested between German and Pole and
which was to change from the hands of one to the other on three occasions in his own lifetime. For Neumann's family, as for most of Germany's eastern Jews, the preference for the Reich was clear; they were
also more markedly Jewish than their highly assimilated co-religionists
in the western part of the country or in Berlin. Neumann was never
religiously observant; at the same time he never denied his Judaic origin.
The fact that he entertained no doubts about and saw no contradiction
in being both a German and a Jew may help to explain the self-confidence with which he adapted to American life and acquired American
citizenship. However his external circumstances might change, he always knew precisely who he was.

As an adolescent, Neumann did military service at the end of the
First World War, receiving his first ideological education in the Soldiers' Councils which sprang up in the wake of the armistice of 1918.
After that he studied labor law in Frankfort, and in 1927 settled in Berlin as a labor lawyer. Life in the capital evidently suited his tastes: for the
rest of his life he spoke both German and English with the harsh tones of
a Berliner, to which his increasing deafness gave an even more metallic
character.

Had German democracy been preserved, there seems no doubt that
Neumann would have attained a position of major political influence.
In the last years of the Weimar Republic, he was simultaneously teach-
ing at the Hochschule für Politik and serving as legal adviser to the

executive of the Social Democratic party. In the latter capacity, he acted as an ideological gadfly, contemptuous of the routine-mindedness of the official leadership. It was only natural, then, that when the Nazis came to power, Neumann should have been one of the first they deprived of German citizenship and drove into exile.

On the road of emigration, his initial stop was London. Here, with his characteristic practical-mindedness, realizing that a knowledge of German law was of no use to him abroad, he converted himself into a scholar by taking a degree in political science with Harold Laski. Soon, however, in equally practical fashion, he saw that permanent residence in England would not do. He had, as he recalled two decades later, originally gone there "in order to be close to Germany and not to lose contact with her." Yet "it was precisely in England" that he "became fully aware that one had to bury the expectation of an overthrow of the [Nazi] régime from within . . . The . . . régime, far from becoming weaker, would grow stronger, and this with the support of the major European powers. Thus a clean break—psychological, social, and economic—had to be made, and a new life started." But England, with its tight, homogeneous society, "was not the country in which to do it . . . One could . . . never quite become an Englishman . . . The United States appeared as the sole country where, perhaps, an attempt would be successful to carry out the threefold transition: as a human being, an intellectual, and a political scholar."[1]

Neumann arrived in the United States in 1936—at the high point of the New Deal—and he was frank to recognize that after the timidity of English politics, what he called "the Roosevelt experiment" made the same favorable impression on him that it did on Albert Einstein and Thomas Mann and so many of his émigré countrymen. But his interest or participation in American political life remained marginal to his chief concern. This was to assault Nazism with his lawyer's talents and the new intellectual skills he had acquired in London. Settling down with the left-oriented Institut für Sozialforschung which had migrated from Frankfort to Columbia University, he began work on the massive study of Hitler's system entitled *Behemoth* for which he is now chiefly

1. "The Social Sciences," in Franz L. Neumann *et al.*, *The Cultural Migration: The European Scholar in America* (Philadelphia, 1953), pp. 17–18.

remembered. After America's entry into the war, he moved to Washington, serving as principal expert on Germany for the Office of Strategic Services and subsequently for the Department of State; in the last years of the conflict his was widely recognized as the most authoritative analysis of the Nazi regime. And in a military sense the war followed the course he had predicted: Nazism was destroyed utterly, by the massed might of the Soviet and Anglo-American forces.

After 1945, however, Neumann's hopes for the post-fascist world were disappointed all along the line: the Cold War destroyed whatever lingering chance remained for the international order and the German society based on socialist principles which he had sketched in his war-time memoranda. For the West Germany that was emerging under Adenauer's guidance, Neumann never bothered to conceal his contempt. Toward Berlin, his former home, he was more indulgent: on repeated trips to the divided city he gave generously of his advice and encouragement to the Social Democratic leadership, the trade unions, and the newly-established Free University. To the end of his life, Neumann never ceased to feel the emotional pull of Germany and of traditional European culture.

In the United States there was only one career that both appealed to him and was open to him—university teaching. He disliked his office chores as a State Department expert, and after shuttling for a while back and forth between Washington and New York, he decided for the latter without hesitation as soon as a full-time professorship of political science at Columbia became available to him. By the late 1940's Neumann seemed to be fully absorbed in American life: for more than a decade he had made the United States his home; he was married and had two young children; he lived in a prosperous suburb, to outward appearance thoroughly *embourgeoisé*.

Yet the new fit was never complete. Whatever Neumann's academic success—and it was very great—however warmly he might speak of the openness of American social and university life, he remained curiously detached from his surroundings. And by the same token he became increasingly melancholy. When roused to action, his old vigor and combativeness would return; when alone or with his intimates, he would lapse into silent meditation. He was evidently groping for a new life and a new style of thought—and he was beginning to think he could find them when on vacation in Switzerland in the summer of 1954 he was killed in an automobile accident.

A career such as Neumann's cut off in mid course necessarily poses the question of what he would have said and done if he had lived another twenty or thirty years. And in Neumann's case the problem is complicated by the fact that his natural temperament was thwarted by events at two decisive points. The first was when the advent of Nazism forced him to transform himself from a political activist into a scholar; the second was when the Cold War frustrated the vision which had inspired both his politics and his scholarship. It is only if we bear these two enormous disappointments in mind that we can properly assess the writings he left behind him.

Like his Italian counterpart Gaetano Salvemini—whom he resembled in the verve with which he attacked the fascist system that ruled his homeland—Franz Neumann detested everything which was empty or false. He was first and above all a critic of established institutions and structures. "A conformist political theory is no theory,"[2] he once declared, and this statement—characteristically brief and cutting—might serve as an epigraph for his entire published work.

In *Behemoth*, the book that first established his reputation, such ruthless incisiveness marked the tempo of both the analysis and the marshalling of fact. Neumann remained faithful to the Marxist tradition in his insistence on "unmasking" as the political scientist's primary concern. "In analyzing the structure and operation of National Socialist economy," he contended, "we must never rest content with the legal and administrative forms. They tell us very little."[3] Yet one could not expose the irrelevance of these forms until one had fully understood their complexities. Thus Neumann felt obliged to plunge his powerful lawyer's mind into a morass of legislation and administrative decrees in

2. "The Concept of Political Freedom" (first published 1953), *The Democratic and the Authoritarian State: Essays in Political and Legal Theory* (ed. Herbert Marcuse, Glencoe, Ill., 1957), p. 162.

3. *Behemoth: The Structure and Practice of National Socialism* (New York, 1942), p. 227. The second edition, published in 1944, differs from the first only in including an appendix covering the developments of the two intervening years.

which someone less endowed with self-confidence and *Sitzfleisch* would soon have foundered, and he emerged triumphantly with what he regarded as a sure key to the workings of Nazi society.

The key, predictably enough, was economic. This was the first and more compelling of two parallel lines of analysis whose connection was not always apparent. Here Neumann aimed to demolish the facile explanations of Nazism currently in vogue—those which described Hitler's regime in terms of a "managerial" society, or, possibly, as one whose anti-capitalist intent was evident in its effort to reconcile class antagonisms—by charting the links between big business and the Nazi leadership. Far from being directed against business interests, he maintained, National Socialist economics was "an affirmation of the living force of capitalistic society." But it would be wrong to claim, as doctrinaire Marxists were doing, that the regime was merely a front for monopoly capital. The relationship was more subtle than that: "The German ruling class" in fact consisted of "four distinct groups" whose interests were overlapping and mutually reinforcing—"big industry, the party, the bureaucracy, and the armed forces." And among these the relations between the first two gave the cue to the functioning of the entire system:

National Socialism could, of course, have nationalized private industry. That, it did not do and did not want to do. Why should it? With regard to imperialist expansion, National Socialism and big business have identical interests. National Socialism pursues glory and the stabilization of its rule, and industry, the full utilization of its capacity and the conquest of foreign markets. German industry was willing to cooperate to the fullest. It had never liked democracy, civil rights, trade unions, and public discussion. National Socialism utilized the daring, the knowledge, the aggressiveness of the industrial leadership, while the industrial leadership utilized the anti-democracy, anti-liberalism and anti-unionism of the National Socialist party, which had fully developed the techniques by which masses can be controlled and dominated. The bureaucracy marched as always with the victorious forces, and for the first time in the history of Germany the army got everything it wanted.[4]

Within the framework thus established, Neumann subjected each aspect of Nazi society to unsparing dissection. He traced the steady advance in the cartellization of German business and how the officially-recognized regional or functional groupings had come to be dominated

4. *Ibid.*, pp. 305, 361.

by the large concerns. He exposed the sham of the German Labor Front and the "atomization" of the working classes; in this, the most expert of his individual analyses, he returned to his old profession as labor's advocate, systematically dismantling the National Socialist showpiece of class reconciliation. He further demonstrated that the so-called party sector of the economy was the product of little more than legalized "gangsterism" on the part of the Nazi chiefs, and that these latter were more and more entering into a state of symbiosis with the great capitalists themselves. "The practitioners of violence tend to become businessmen," he concluded, "and the businessmen become practitioners of violence."[5] Such was the final shape of the National Socialist ruling class as defeat drew near.

In subsequent years, Neumann's interpretation was frequently criticized as Marxist and simplistic. And it is true that he had occasionally let fall an expression—such as a passing reference to an "iron law of capitalistic concentration"—which showed the hold that his original intellectual allegiance still exerted over his thought.[6] But in fact Neumann's argument was far from simple-minded. It was flexible and often hard to follow, and it spared no variety of Marxist politician—whether Social Democratic or Communist—in its analysis of how Weimar democracy had gone wrong. It never claimed that fascism was the sole or necessary political expression of monopoly capitalism. Moreover, it closely paralleled what Salvemini was simultaneously writing about the fraudulent character of Mussolini's "corporative" institutions. It is curious that Neumann, who certainly knew of Salvemini's work, never referred to it in his Behemoth. It is still more curious that the latter's interpretation of Italian Fascism has remained standard and scarcely questioned—whether in Italy or abroad—down to the present time, while Neumann's similar reading of the German fascist experience has been repeatedly called into question.

Postwar research did indeed suggest that the number of German businessmen who remained free of Nazi involvement was greater than Neumann had supposed. But the same postwar years also demonstrated that the major German capitalists had ridden through the Hitler years virtually unscathed. And it was difficult to understand how they could

5. Ibid. (Appendix to 1944 edition), p. 633.   6. Ibid., p. 272.

have accomplished such a feat without substantial accommodation with the regime. This Neumann's critics or the defenders of German big business never satisfactorily explained.[7]

Unquestionably the postwar denigration of Neumann's work reflected the Cold War mentality in the United States. *Behemoth* did not fit the clichés of the late 1940's and early 1950's. Its line of analysis jarred the comfortable conviction that Soviet "totalitarianism" was substantially the same thing as the Nazi menace which had just been destroyed. Neumann did in fact use the word "totalitarian"—but he resorted to it sparingly and only when the context was clear.[8] He never exploited it, as the Cold War apologists did, to blur the distinction between fascist and Communist society. Neumann insisted that the Soviet Union (even under Stalin) operated on different principles from those of Nazi Germany, and that to lump them together made only for terminological confusion.

It was partly for this reason that he pursued a second line of argument parallel to his major economic and social one. This subsidiary analysis was implicit in the book's title, with its Hobbesian reference to an eschatological monster. It was more formal and legalist than the first— and less relevant to the main matter at hand. In brief, Neumann maintained that Nazi Germany—as opposed, in their different fashions, to both Soviet Russia and Fascist Italy—could no longer be described as a state in the traditional meaning of the term: it had sunk to a level of ethical and legal dissolution in which the distinction between state and society, along with every other customary norm, had been absorbed in a mass politicization of existence.[9]

Although Neumann admired the author of the *Leviathan* and owed much to his influence, the effort to attach his own work to the Hobbesian inheritance was excessively abstract and in part artificial. Here once again the postwar years revealed the shape of reality, and in this case national and middle-class norms proved more tenacious than Neumann

---

7. The latest (and most ambitious) of Neumann's would-be revisers, David Schoenbaum, in *Hitler's Social Revolution* (Garden City, N.Y., 1966), after doing his best to set up an alternative scheme, succumbs to internal confusions and contradictions and in the end is obliged to admit (p. 272) that his predecessor gave "a generally accurate reflection of the basic social situation."

8. *Behemoth*, pp. 49–50, 67, 261.   9. *Ibid.*, pp. vii, 470.

had imagined. Along with so many of his counterparts in the emigration, he had been generous to a fault in his judgments on the ordinary German. He had depicted the mass of his former countrymen as pulverized by a combination of economic and psychological pressures and incapable of expressing their sentiments of common decency. He had minimized the strength of popular anti-Semitism and had gone so far as to refer to the German people as "the least Anti-Semitic of all." (Even in the second edition of his book, when Hitler's decision to exterminate the Jews had become known in Washington, he had dealt with the "final solution" only in passing.)[10] In similar vein, Neumann had simultaneously branded racist or "social" imperialism as the "most dangerous formulation of National Socialist ideology" and denied that it had seriously infected the German working classes. As his book drew to its close, it was apparent that for all his hardheadedness and skepticism, he retained a faith in spontaneous indignation, a conviction that in the end the Nazi regime would be overthrown not only by the armed power of the victorious coalition, but by the "conscious political action" of Germany's "oppressed masses."[11]

That this was not the scenario which unrolled in the spring of 1945 was enough in itself to explain Neumann's subsequent disillusionment. Still more, the cement that held German society together through the prostration of the next four years was the traditional middle-class ethos whose dissolution *Behemoth* had announced. After the collapse of Nazism, Neumann had predicted, the middle classes would have "ceased to exist as a stratum out of which a democratic society" could "be rebuilt."[12] Yet such a reconstruction was precisely what happened during the era in which the spirit of Konrad Adenauer rather than that of the intellectual emigration presided over Germany's return to the Western community.

If *Behemoth* was mistaken in its specific predictions, the fault may be ascribed to the fact that Neumann's formulations had been either legalist or economic and had left too little room for emotional considera-

10. *Ibid.*, pp. 121, (Appendix) 551–552.
11. *Ibid.*, pp. 215–217, 476.
12. *Ibid.* (Appendix), p. 629.

tions. It is in this sense and this alone that the charge of narrow-minded Marxism directed against his work can be accepted. Neumann himself was unquestionably aware of the insufficiencies of his analysis, which he never revised for postwar publication. In his years at Columbia University he began to subject his earlier certainties to critical scrutiny. He expressed a new respect for the achievement of Max Weber.[13] He found intellectual refreshment in studying as unlikely a precursor as Montesquieu. Above all, he reflected on what it meant for his thought to be a citizen of a country where democracy was a living reality rather than the precarious web of compromise it had been in Weimar Germany. Yet Neumann found no substitute for the faith in Marxism and economic explanation that he had lost. Nor did he succeed in writing the comprehensive study of dictatorship that he had projected. Understandably enough, his postwar output was slight and fragmentary. Neumann's scrupulous and self-tormenting search for a new vision of the social world can be documented in the collection of essays entitled *The Democratic and the Authoritarian State* which Herbert Marcuse, who was Neumann's closest friend and was to marry his widow, edited for publication after his death.

What most clearly distinguished the Neumann of *Behemoth* from the later Neumann of the postwar essays was a new insistence on liberty as the condition *sine qua non* of all rational or humanist action, as of all political theory. Where earlier, no different from other Germans in the Marxist tradition, he had been concerned with unmasking the pieties of conventional liberalism, he now quite consciously joined the liberal-democratic current stemming from England and France. He wrote a perceptive and laudatory introduction to Montesquieu's *Spirit of the Laws*, locating the crucial distinction in the French theorist's writings in the "sharp dividing line" he drew "between despotism and all other forms of government," while limiting the latter's celebrated theory of the separation of powers to its "irreducible minimum" of an independent judiciary. He similarly associated himself with John Stuart Mill's "classic formulation" of the doctrine of political liberty.[14] These new—

13. "The Social Sciences," *The Cultural Migration*, pp. 21–22.

14. "Montesquieu" (first published 1949), *Democratic and Authoritarian State*, pp. 126, 142; "Intellectual and Political Freedom" (speech delivered at Bonn in 1954, translated by Peter Gay), *ibid.*, pp. 208–209.

or better, rediscovered—ideological affiliations highlight the dilemma with which he was contending in the postwar years: he never found a way to reconcile the passionate devotion to liberty that his belated Anglo-American education had given him, with the harsh Germanic conviction, which he refused to abandon, that most of what passed for liberty in the contemporary world was a disgusting fraud.

Thus Neumann's "Notes on the Theory of Dictatorship" remained an unfinished and disappointing fragment. And in his published writings he felt compelled to argue that constitutional guarantees, however desirable in themselves, were inadequate to check the abuse of political power. Nor did he discover any formula which would clearly define the citizen's right of resistance to tyranny: the decision to disobey constituted authority, he concluded, was one that each man was obliged to make in the loneliness of his own conscience. Moreover, the remedies commonly proposed for the failings of liberal democracy were in themselves of questionable value: "social rights," corporatism, attempts to "spiritualize" labor—all these palliatives failed to take sufficient account of the fact that modern industrialism was "politically ambivalent." Industrial society, Neumann found, simultaneously intensified "two diametrically opposed trends in modern society: the trend toward freedom and the trend toward repression."[15] Much as he might have liked to share the faith of a Sorel or a Veblen in industrialism's potential as a liberating force and a school of cooperation, he was far too conscious of its stultifying effects to harbor any comforting conviction that twentieth-century urban culture contained its own built-in correctives.

The dominant trend, Neumann knew, was toward political apathy and acceptance. And this he combatted with all the intellectual weapons at his command. But here again he never found a formula which brought him satisfaction. His unremitting attack on the tendency of professors and writers to remain "above" the political battle suggested how sorely he himself was tempted to adopt what he called an "Epicurean" attitude of detachment. Even more strenuously than Weber,

15. "Approaches to the Study of Political Power" (first published 1950), *ibid.*, p. 16; "On the Limits of Justifiable Disobedience" (first published 1952), *ibid.*, p. 159; "The Concept of Political Freedom," *ibid.*, pp. 189–193; "Notes on the Theory of Dictatorship," *ibid.*, p. 251.

he argued the intellectual's moral obligation to take a stand.[16] Yet he
could provide neither himself nor his readers with any fully convincing
reason for resuming the ideological battles of his youth in the disappointing and ambiguous circumstances of his middle age.

The Cold War exacerbated these doubts and scruples. From the beginning of the confrontation between the United States and the Soviet
Union until his death, Neumann never ceased protesting against the
distortion of intellectual and moral values that had resulted from it. He
assailed in turn the newly-fashionable Machiavellianism among American sociologists and political scientists, the perversion of independent
thought through propaganda and vilification, and the "loyalty" program in Washington, with the irrational fear and distrust it engendered
of those defined as ideological enemies.[17] Neumann's own passionate
revulsion was clear to those who conversed with him and who could
discern the emotion under the surface of his dry, clipped prose. Yet in
his public style he remained restrained and judicious. This was not
through any shallow conformism or fear of the consequences of speaking out. It was rather a manifestation of the tragic dilemma of American
(and émigré) intellectuals in the half decade from 1948 to 1953 when
the Cold War was at its height: how was one to perform one's essential
role as a critic of Western democracy without playing into the hand of
either Stalinism or political reaction, or possibly of both at the same
time? In Neumann's case this agonized self-questioning was raised to
maximum intensity by his previous experience of Nazism and his total
lack of illusion.

Neumann died too early to find a way out of what had become a
classic impasse—in the very year when with the passing of Stalin and
the end of the Korean War, a glimmer of hope for the future was appearing. Meantime he had felt obliged to act as the defender of a democracy of whose weakness and degeneration he was fully and unhappily aware. It was fitting, then, that his last major public appearance
should have been a lecture on the political implications of anxiety. In
the summer of 1954, only a few weeks before his death, the Free University of Berlin, which he had so notably aided, awarded Neumann an

16. "Intellectual and Political Freedom," *ibid.*, p. 215.
17. See particularly the statements in "The Concept of Political Freedom," *ibid.*, pp.
161–162, 188, 194.

honorary doctorate. He took the occasion to outline a new view of politics that had been slowly maturing in his mind. The lecture subsequently published under the title "Anxiety and Politics" marked the fact that Neumann had at last caught up with Freud and the psychoanalytic current; by the same token it showed how far he had advanced beyond the boundaries of law and economics within which he had earlier confined his thought; and it demonstrated his thorough understanding of the manipulation by despots such as Adolf Hitler or by demagogues such as Joseph McCarthy of the anguish and the sense of guilt that afflicted the contemporary world.[18]

"Anxiety and Politics" revealed that Neumann had finally recognized and rectified the insufficiencies in his earlier writing. But in itself the lecture was not notably original; at fifty-four Neumann was too old and too well fixed in his intellectual patterns to make a major contribution to the psychoanalytic study of politics and history on which so many others, younger and better qualified than he, were about to enter. It is far from certain that had he lived a decade or two longer, his new interests would have significantly altered the character of his intellectual legacy.

This legacy was at least as much oral as it was written. The great difficulty in arriving at an assessment of Neumann's career is that his published work gives no adequate sense of his range and influence. Like most of the émigrés from Central Europe, he never learned to write English with literary ease; but he wrote clearly and directly and without the Teutonic portentousness which so many of his countrymen carried with them across the Atlantic. The trouble with Neumann's prose was almost the opposite: it was so compact and schematic, it made so few concessions to rhetoric or anecdote, that it conveyed little of its author's personal power. Moreover, it was burdened with scholarly paraphernalia and historical citations which were unnecessary to his argument and foreign to the very special combination of practical-mindedness and abstraction that was his natural temperament. To cite merely one example: although a central contention of his *Behemoth* was that the intellectual rationalizations of National Socialism could be dismissed as

18. Translated by Peter Gay for *ibid.*, pp. 270–295.

"pure eyewash," he nonetheless felt obliged to rehearse them at tedious length.

Those who had never met Neumann in person could scarcely be expected to find the human being behind the aridity of his prose style. Those who knew him well recognized the familiar figure—the bald head, the metallic voice, the hearing aid which he switched off with a beatific smile when he sensed that someone was about to embark on a pompous or boring exposition, the thick, heavy-rimmed glasses framing a face that was both ugly and radiating sexual attraction. One of his younger friends concluded that Neumann's mind was like an incandescent bulb which, although it had burned away his hair, his sight, and his hearing, continued to exert a fascination on all it encountered. And another who saw a great deal of him during his years at Columbia named Neumann without hesitation as his "most extraordinary teacher":

It was not simply that he was a European intellectual on an American campus. He would have had an equally startling impact on a European university, as in fact I saw him have at the Free University. Nor was it simply his erudition, great and varied though it was. What struck all, I think, was that he embodied in his own person the vitality and the drama of intellectual life ... He had a dazzling power of incisive analysis and critical judgment, and students were overwhelmed by the rapidity and certainty with which he imposed logical meaning or order onto a set of facts or problems. His habit of subsuming various phenomena under logical or historical categories and of seeing things as orderly and clear where to others they had appeared ambiguous or blurred might have been Hegelian-Marxist in origin and might have been practiced in lawyer's briefs and political arguments, but the results were always new and strikingly unpredictable. . . . By his own intellect he belied any crude notion of the social determinism of ideas; he communicated to his students his interest in the social origins and relevance of ideas, and he surprised students and friends alike by his precise and intimate knowledge of so much of European literature. Finally what impressed his students—because rare in any age—was his simultaneous and reciprocal function as philosopher and political man. . . .

The students' admiration was aroused by more than a brilliant mind. There was something in this seemingly austere man, with his brusque manners and his relentless seriousness, that awed students. He was often hard on them. His critical comments were likely to be curt and devastating, and it took little acumen to realize that he did not suffer fools gladly. But there was a magnetism of character and intellect that many students could not withstand. They became disciples and critics, admirers and rebels by turn. . . .[19]

19. Letter from Fritz Stern to H. Stuart Hughes, August 21, 1967.

Neumann's own estimate of his role was more modest. He saw himself in the mediating capacity of on the one hand telling his German friends that they cared too little for empirical research while simultaneously counselling his American colleagues to balance their empiricist enthusiasm with a greater concern for history and theory.[20] Within his chosen discipline of political science, Neumann's advice was rarely heeded: the quantitative and behavioral approaches which became so influential in the United States immediately after his death were in large part responsible for the neglect into which his work began to fall. And the excessive legalism of his own method frequently gave it an old-fashioned air. It was on historians, rather more than on political scientists, that Neumann's precepts left their most lasting impression.

During his war years with the Office of Strategic Services, Neumann had gathered about him an informal circle of younger men, all American-born, but concerned with German affairs and destined a decade or two later to receive professorships of modern European history at some of America's most influential universities. This wartime group included Carl Schorske, Leonard Krieger, Franklin Ford, and myself. Later on, at Columbia, Neumann attracted into his orbit two sons of émigrés from Germany, Peter Gay and Fritz Stern. Of these six, Gay was the only one who was directly Neumann's student—and it was symptomatic of the latter's postwar shift in emphasis that after writing a Ph.D. thesis which treated the revisionist Social Democrat Eduard Bernstein in sympathetic terms (something that the earlier Neumann could scarcely have stomached), Gay transferred his field of interest from political science to history. Toward his younger associates, Neumann was in turn an ideological mentor, an initiator into the realities of European society, and a friend who never ceased inspiring a certain amount of awe. In the informal seminars he conducted in Washington or New York—and a conversation with Neumann seldom failed to turn into a seminar—he refrained from trying to impose any formal Marxian concepts on his listeners. And none of the young historians closest to him in fact became a Marxist. What Neumann imparted to them was something less specific and more pervasive—a conviction that the study of history must begin with economic and class relationships, and that one

20. "The Social Sciences," *The Cultural Migration*, p. 25.

understood little of politics or ideology unless one was aware of the pressure of interest groups that lay behind them.

Today such precepts have become the common coin of graduate instruction in history. A quarter century ago, when Neumann first made the acquaintance of his young admirers, they were far from being generally accepted. The study of contemporary European affairs was still dominated by Ranke's notion of the "primacy of foreign policy"—a conviction reinforced by the tendency of so many American scholars in the post-Versailles years to focus their attention on diplomatic history. Neumann took up the challenge that the most talented of Social Democratic historians, Eckart Kehr, had thrown down: he asserted the "primacy of domestic policy,"[21] in the sense that foreign affairs should be understood not in terms of an abiding and consensual "national interest," but rather as an expression of the economic and ideological forces currently dominant in a given society, and this interpretation his American friends brought with them into the universities at which they subsequently taught. It was characteristic of them that they gave only passing attention to war and diplomacy. What was more surprising—and suggested how much independence they combined with their loyalty to Neumann's memory—was that they directed their attention to intellectual rather than to social history. In the way they defined such study, however, the spirit of their mentor was readily apparent: as opposed to the older "history of ideas" which dealt in abstract terms with great thoughts perceived as protagonists in their own right, Neumann's heirs wrote what one of them has called a "social history of ideas," setting those thoughts in the full context of historical circumstance out of which their creators had given them form.[22]

Thus although Neumann himself did not succeed in resolving his perplexities, his grapplings with them had a clarifying effect on the minds of his younger friends. Never having been sectarian Marxists, they were untroubled by feelings of ideological betrayal when they found Marx in error. And as native-born citizens of the United States or as bilingual Americans who had come very young to this country,

21. See the references to Kehr in *Behemoth*, pp. 203–204, 206.
22. See the preface by Peter Gay to *The Party of Humanity* (New York, 1964), pp. ix–xii, and my own definition in *Consciousness and Society* (New York, 1958), pp. 9–12.

they saw no contradiction between a non-doctrinaire socialism and the liberal-democratic tradition. For Neumann it had been a wrench to recognize that political power or deep-running sentiments might on some occasions be divorced from any visible economic base. His young American friends had never been tempted to think otherwise.

Neumann's influence, then, lived on after his death in a diffused form which it was difficult for the non-initiated to recognize. Besides the work of his intellectual heirs, he left behind him a superb series of individual critiques of politics and society. Neumann's "all pervasive conviction," his friend Otto Kirchheimer has written, was that "critical analysis of established social structures and . . . institutions" was "the political scientist's only worthwhile job. . . . His late writings no less than his early ones" were "impregnated with the belief in the rational propensities of man" and in the "feasibility and urgency of a cooperative society."[23] In this sense his work had an underlying unity and coherence. In comparing Neumann's aspirations with his published writings, one might easily conclude that his professional life was a noble failure. But to do so would be to suggest that he eventually succumbed to despair. This Neumann never did. Although the abiding ambiguities in his thought made it harder for him to put his reflections on paper than to deliver them orally, he kept on trying to give rational, persuasive form to what he had understood about modern society. "Throughout Neumann's essays runs the struggle against temptations to surrender; pessimism and Epicureanism were his personal devils."[24] To say that these devils never conquered him is the final tribute one can pay to his living memory.

23. "Franz Neumann: An Appreciation," *Dissent*, IV (Autumn 1957), 386.
24. David Kettler in *ibid.*, p. 392.

TWO *ROMANISTEN* IN AMERICA: SPITZER AND AUERBACH

by HARRY LEVIN

I

T HE literary event to which I owe my acquaintance with Erich Auerbach happens to have been the birth of Cervantes. In the fall of 1947, four hundred years afterward, it was being commemorated at Harvard University by a series of lectures and conferences. Américo Castro, whom I likewise had the privilege of meeting on that occasion, was naturally among the presiding spirits. One of the private receptions took place at the home of Amado Alonso, who himself had twice become an emigré. As a young Spaniard, trained at the Centro de Estudios Históricos in Madrid, he had emigrated to Buenos Aires, where he had been placed in charge of the Instituto de Filología. As a leader in the academic opposition to Perón, he had lately been compelled to leave Argentina a year before. His decision to settle in the United States signalized a revival of Hispanic studies at Harvard—though his leadership of it would, alas, be cut short by his premature death in 1952. From the hospitable Don Amado I gathered that Auerbach, of whose work I then had barely heard, was present by a happy accident. He had just come for the first time to America, where he would be spending the rest of his career, and was here in Cambridge to visit a son who was studying chemistry at the Harvard Graduate School.

The man I met was slight and dark, gentle to the point of diffidence, yet lively and engaging in conversation, speaking mostly French at that time, and looking not unlike one of those kindly ferrets in the illustrations of children's books. Though he had recently published *Mimesis*, and would shortly have his Swiss publisher send me a copy, he was not sanguine about its impact on either side of the Atlantic. Though he was on leave of absence from his chair of Romance philology at the Turkish State University in Istanbul, he spoke with candor and modesty about his possible willingness to accept an American professorship. Finding that we had much to talk about, both on a theoretical and on a practical plane, we agreed to lunch together a few days later. Our lunching place deserves at least a footnote in the annals of cultural migration. The Window Shop was started during the nineteen-thirties, by a group of Harvard faculty wives, as a means of finding employment for German and Austrian refugees. Having flourished, it had moved along into a well-known habitat on Brattle Street, which had formerly been a New England tearoom and originally the smithy of Longfellow's Village Blacksmith. Where the spreading chestnut tree had stood, *Sacher Torte* was now the specialty of a Viennese menu.

Regularly favored by the patronage of the stately Hellenist, Werner Jaeger, and of other scholarly expatriates, this was our local Cantabrigian symbol of the great American melting pot. Auerbach seemed pleased to be taken there, and our dialogue opened with a polite exchange about the tenor of life in Cambridge, Massachusetts. Prompted by his questions, I found myself repeating an old byword about the Galata Bridge at Istanbul: that, if you sat there long enough, all the world would pass by. Auerbach, whose penetrant eyes had been inspecting the situation, did not immediately respond. Instead he rose, excused himself, and walked to a neighboring table. Its occupant, who warmly greeted him, was—as Auerbach explained on his return—an American with whom he had been acquainted in Istanbul. Coincidence had reinforced my groping parallel. In the ensuing discussion he made it clear why he no longer wished to sit and wait at his Turkish bridge. Whether, by crossing the seas, he had come to another Byzantium, worthier of Yeats's ideals for a holy city of the arts, might well have been in doubt. But America, at any rate, had niches ready to be filled by wandering sages. Belatedly yet wholeheartedly, Auerbach joined that throng of European intellectuals who passed by the transatlantic bridge, to the vast enrichment of our culture.

Born in 1892 at Berlin, Erich Auerbach had proceeded through his earlier studies to a doctoral degree in law at Heidelberg. After his military service, he shifted his interest to Romance philology, taking a second doctorate at Greifswald in 1921 with a thesis on the Italian and French *novella* of the early Renaissance. For several years thereafter he was employed by the Prussian State Library, while publishing a number of translations from the Italian—notably a German version of Vico's *Scienza Nuova*, which was to be a main guidepost in the development of his own thought. In 1929, when he was named professor at the University of Marburg, he brought out his compact study of Dante, which characteristically emphasizes the earthly aspects of the *Divina Commedia*. After six years, he was forced out of his appointment by the Nazi government. Like so many German intellectuals, he took the path of exile that led to Turkey. He was appointed to his new university post in 1936, and served for the next eleven years. One of the by-products of his teaching was a small handbook, prepared for the orientation—or, perhaps we should say, the occidentation—of his Turkish students.[1] This introductory sketch of the Romance languages and literatures offers no hint of those special insights which he was even then beginning to generate.

One of his anecdotes casts a comic light upon the sense of disconnection from which he must have suffered. On taking up his official duties at Istanbul, he was introduced to various Turks with whom, it was presumed, he would have much in common. One of them, understandably, was the Turkish translator of Dante, whose rendering of the *Commedia* had been accomplished in less than two years; indeed it would have been completed sooner, he boasted, had he not also been translating potboilers during the same interim. When Auerbach congratulated him on his presumable grasp of the language, this colleague blandly confessed that he knew no Italian at all. His brother did; but that was scarcely a help, since the brother had been away at the time. To Auerbach's obvious question, his informant replied that he had worked from a French translation. Auerbach, doing his best to keep his eyebrows from twitching, asked which one. "I don't recall the name," said the Turk, "but it was a large brown book." What could be expected, under these circumstances, from so highly qualified a *Gelehrter* as Auerbach? He would be working, as he liked to put it, "*dans un grenier*." After he had used up his backlog of notes, he would have to

---

1. Erich Auerbach, *Introduction aux études de philologie romane* (Frankfurt a M., 1949). This is the original text of which a Turkish translation was published at Istanbul in 1944. The English translation by Guy Daniels, *Introduction to Romance Languages and Literature* (New York, 1961), is abridged and not entirely accurate.

suspend his medieval researches. In the absence of learned journals, compilations, and commentaries, how could one continue to be a scholar?

To be sure, there was a fair collection of the major authors of the West. And it is true that, in countries where seminars were grinding out professors and bibliographical tools were being multiplied, critics had begun to wonder whether all the philological apparatus was not obscuring the literary artistry. A certain correlation was suspected between the short-sightedness of footnote-scholarship, *Anmerkungswissenschaft*, and the acquiescence of the German universities to the Hitler régime. Auerbach, at all events, could never be deprived of his own learning and training. His artistic perceptions, innately keen, had been broadened by historical perspectives acquired from Vico and from Vico's modern apostle, Benedetto Croce. He found himself perforce in the position of writing a more original kind of book than he might otherwise have attempted, if he had remained within easy access to the stock professional facilities. There is not a single footnote in the English edition of *Mimesis*, and the only ones in the German edition are simply Auerbach's translations of the texts already cited in foreign languages.[2] Each of these is the theme of a chapter devoted to its stylistic interpretation. But the sequence of twenty chapters also comprises an anthology—or, better, an imaginary museum—of European civilization extending, across three millennia and eight languages, from Homer to Virginia Woolf.

Ever since Aristotle expostulated with Plato over the imitation of nature, *mímesis* has been the central and most problematic concept of esthetics and criticism. Auerbach's subtitle pins it down to the representation of reality by means of words, so that textual explication becomes the key to a concrete understanding of the occidental past. Realism in the explicit sense, as practised by the French novelists, is telescoped into two dense chapters toward the end of the book.[3] Equally real, for Auer-

2. Erich Auerbach, *Mimesis: Dargestellte Wirklichkeit in der abendländischen Literatur* (Bern, 1946). The excellent English translation by W. R. Trask, *Mimesis: The Representation of Reality in Western Literature* (Princeton, 1953), contains an additional chapter on *Don Quixote*, originally written for the Spanish edition.

3. *Cf.* the remark of René Wellek, "Auerbach's Special Realism," *Kenyon Review*, XVI, 1 (Winter, 1954), 301: "it concerns not realism but man's attitudes toward the world in general."

bach, are a mob scene under the Roman Empire and the stream of Mrs. Ramsay's consciousness in *To the Lighthouse*. The selection of passages to be chronologically analyzed is always interesting and often surprising. The recognition of Odysseus by Euryclea, Eve and the serpent in a mystery play, Manon Lescaut and her lover at supper, Pantagruel's mouth viewed as a microcosm—these are privileged moments if not epiphanies. We are plunged into particularity without any introduction. Auerbach shies away from generalization, though a brief epilogue draws together the guiding threads of his approach.[4] His starting point is the canonical assumption of traditional rhetoric, the separation it maintained between grand and humble styles, plus the subsequent conditions of their intermixture, so deliberate in the Bible and elsewhere, with an effect of elevating the commonplace which has social as well as esthetic implications.

His other key idea, which more peculiarly bears the stamp of his thinking and derives from his work as a medievalist, is the exegetical device of *figura*. That rhetorical term of the ancients had been utilized by the early Christians, when they saw the personages and events of the Gospels prefigured in the narratives of the Old Testament. In the Middle Ages it was invoked to show how a particular manifestation could express a transcendental reality. Thus it illuminates the vivid concreteness of Dante's otherworldly allegory. Auerbach had traced and formulated this conception through an article first published in Italy at the outset of the Second World War.[5] (A decade afterward I sat next to him at a meeting of the Modern Language Association, watching his weary smile and hearing his wry comment, as an American colleague made effective but unacknowledged use of his method.) Since *mimesis* is realistic by definition, and *figura* is a symbolic mode, one of the contributions of Auerbach's book is to demonstrate precisely how they conjoin and enmesh. He wrote to me that his European reviewers, though they were friendly, looked upon *Mimesis* as no more than "an amusing series

---

4. Auerbach found occasion to amplify and clarify his position in "Epilegomena zu Mimesis," *Romanische Forschungen*, LXV, 1/2 (1954), 1–18.

5. Erich Auerbach, "Figura," *Archivum Romanicum*, XXII (October–December, 1938), 429–489; reprinted in *Neue Dantestudien* (Istanbul, 1944) and translated into English by Ralph Manheim in *Scenes from the Drama of European Literature* (New York, 1959).

of analyses [in?] of style."[6] Having hoped that his integrating ideas would be noticed and discussed, he transferred his hopes to the English edition, which was laboriously being prepared under the sponsorship of the Bollingen Foundation.

Meanwhile he had received his first American appointment from Pennsylvania State College, where—in addition to his teaching in Romance languages—he taught a course in Goethe for the German Department. After a mutually satisfactory year he would have been given tenure, but for a technicality which arose when the prerequisite medical examination revealed a heart condition. He was enabled to spend a congenial interlude at the Institute for Advanced Study in Princeton, where he also gave one of the Christian Gauss Seminars. In 1950 he was called to Yale, and he passed his last years on that distinguished faculty which includes such cosmopolitan figures as Henri Peyre and René Wellek. His position there he described as "almost ideal."[7] He had occupied the transitional years in "filling up the enormous lacunae in bibliography, and western life in general, caused by the eleven years in Turkey—adaptation to academic and literary life in USA . . ." He was delighted to have generous hours for reading and writing, along with a few courses wholly devoted to medieval subjects. His essay applying the stylistic theories of *Mimesis* to Baudelaire and modern poetry, he declared, would be his farewell to modernity.[8] My feelings of loss were all the more poignant, when he died in the fall of 1957, because he had accepted an invitation to teach the course in Dante at Harvard that year. "Had we but world enough and time . . ."

Marvell's line is quoted on the title page of *Mimesis*, whose dates of composition are given on the verso: "*Mai 1942 bis April 1945.*" Partly to fill in temporal gaps from the resources of American libraries, Auerbach's later investigations were again specialized and concentrated on more distant periods. They are vivified by a percipient reader's concern with the nature of the reading public, manifested earlier through a study of the role the audience had played in French classicism.[9] His illumina-

6. Letter from Erich Auerbach to Harry Levin, December 15, 1951.
7. Letter from Erich Auerbach to Harry Levin, October 21, 1951.
8. Letter from Erich Auerbach to Harry Levin, January 12, 1949.
9. Erich Auerbach, "La Cour et la Ville," in *Vier Untersuchungen zur Geschichte der Französischen Bildung* (Bern, 1951), a volume dedicated to Leo Spitzer. Manheim's English translation of this article appears in *Scenes from the Drama of European Literature*.

tion of the dark ages before the invention of printing should counter-
balance the postliterate sociology of Marshall McLuhan. The introduction
to Auerbach's final volume harks back to his earliest mentor, Vico, and
reaffirms the commitment to historicism they shared.[10] In contrast to the
medievalism of Ernst Robert Curtius, Auerbach stresses changes rather
than continuities. History, as he conceives it, is recorded consciousness,
to be interpreted by continual scrutiny of the surviving records. For the
questionable absolutes of *Geistesgeschichte*, he would substitute a relativ-
istic perspective, which seeks realities in those different places where our
differing predecessors have found it.[11] What confers a unity on this outlook is a vision of Europe intensified by successive expatriations to the
east and west. A posthumous collection is entitled *Scenes from the Drama
of European Literature*. Now and then an elegiac tone hints to us that the
drama is a tragedy which has entered its last act.

II

ONE of Leo Spitzer's favorite words—which, of course, he brilliantly elucidated—was *ambiente*. Though I was more casually acquainted with him than with Auerbach, I had the chance to meet Spitzer in
his American ambiance, at a time when he had comfortably settled into it.
The scale of the Johns Hopkins University, and its emphasis on its graduate program, evidently brought out the personalities of its professors in a
way which must have been comparable to the German universities before the war. I had been invited in 1950 to read a paper to the Hopkins
seminar in literary criticism. To my surprise and embarrassment I perceived in my audience the very man to whom I should have been listening, probably the greatest living virtuoso of the *explication de texte*.

10. Erich Auerbach, *Literatursprache und Publikum in der Lateinischen Spätantike und im Mittelalter* (Bern, 1958); translated into English by Ralph Manheim as *Literary Language and its Public in Late Latin Antiquity and the Middle Ages* (New York, 1965), with a full bibliography of Auerbach's writings.

11. For a differing opinion on this point, registered by a close colleague, *cf.* René Wel-lek, "Erich Auerbach (1887–1957)," *Comparative Literature*, X, 1 (Winter, 1958), 94. See also Dante Della Terza, "Erich Auerbach," *Belfagor*, XVIII, 3 (May, 1963), 306–322, and W. B. Fleischmann, "Erich Auerbach's Critical Theory and Practice: An Assessment," *Modern Language Notes*, LXXXI, 5 (December, 1966), 535–541.

I felt some slight protection in the fact that my subject was a contemporary American writer, though I was unprepared for Spitzer's analogy between Ernest Hemingway's metaphors and those of the Church Fathers. Still, it was flattering to have a commentator who had produced so impressive a body of commentary himself; and, on the whole, he was much kinder to me than I deserved. As it happened, he had only one criticism to offer, and he offered it with some urbanity. But, as those who knew him better could have predicted, it was sufficient to cast doubts on whatever I had been attempting to demonstrate.

Though the substance of my remarks proved somehow acceptable, I had been proceeding in methodological error. Having started properly enough by analyzing a passage, I had then gone astray, and had sought to illustrate the range of my author's style with brief quotations gathered here and there throughout his work. Spitzer fervently believed, and I should have remembered, that the explicator's task is to extract the quintessence of an author from a single text, selected with care for the purpose. Thus the choice is the strategic step, and the process is like plucking the flower in the crannied wall, whose immanent secret could teach us the knowledge of God and man. That this was a highly mystical conception Spitzer admitted, when he summed up explication as "a theodicy in a nutshell."[12] There was something rabbinical, an austerely patriarchal dedication, about the truly leonine figure he cut. His mode of writing reveals him as a secular Talmudist, sometimes almost a Kabbalist, a high priest amid the hieratic mysteries of literature. In any case, after scoring his point and setting me straight, he showed his warmly sociable side. We had a long walk and a good talk next day. I got a glimpse of his Faustian study—described by his gifted colleague, the Spanish man of letters Pedro Salinas, as an alchemist's laboratory.[13] Its emblem was a portrait of the philologist's patron, Saint Jerome, with the lion very much in evidence.

Leo Spitzer was born at Vienna in 1887. He took his doctorate at the university of his native city in 1910, working chiefly under Wilhelm

12. Leo Spitzer, *Linguistics and Literary History: Essays in Stylistics* (Princeton, 1948), p. 128.

13. Pedro Salinas, "Esquicio de Leo Spitzer," printed as an introduction to Spitzer's *Essays in Historical Semantics* (New York, 1948), p. xvii.

Meyer-Lübke, the redoubtable etymologist of the Romance languages. Spitzer was fond of recollecting his master, with praise for his rigor and blame for his rigidity. So vivacious a pupil was bound to rebel against a positivistic philology, which altogether divorced linguistics from literature. Moreover, he had another Viennese master, more dynamic if unofficial, in Freud; Freudian psychoanalysis was to have a marked influence on Spitzerian stylistics, which in turn would help to bridge the gulf between linguistics and literature. For a trial lecture that he was asked to give, in qualifying for the post of *Privatdozent*, Spitzer hazarded the disapproval of his medievalistic seniors by holding forth upon a contemporary novelist, Matilde Serao. This avid interest in the present would not decline with his own advancing years; one of his unfinished projects was to have been devoted to *le nouveau roman*. He was always intensely concerned with the word—not merely *la langue* but *la parole*— as the vital link in the chain of human intercourse. Out of his experience as an Austrian censor during the first World War came a study of circumlocutions for hunger among Italian military prisoners. Again, a mother's pet-name for a child provided him with material for a psycho-linguistic inquiry.

He managed to bring his solid training in *Wortbildungslehre* to the service of literary art at its most creative, by centering his doctoral dissertation upon the techniques of word formation used by Rabelais. The contributions that came after this one in such dazzling profusion, and on so ubiquitous a variety of subjects, assured him quick advancement in the hierarchy of learning. He taught at the University of Bonn from 1920 to 1925, when he was appointed to the professorship at Marburg. Auerbach succeeded him in that chair, when Spitzer was called to Cologne in 1930. Three years later National Socialism began to decimate the German faculties, and—again preceding Auerbach—Spitzer found a temporary position at Istanbul. The relative inadequacy of the Turkish libraries—which would turn out to be a blessing in disguise for Auerbach —made a long sojourn unthinkable for Spitzer, who gladly accepted the call from Johns Hopkins in 1936. The two scholars kept in touch from a distance, and followed each other's work with mutual esteem. They would be brought into closer relations when Auerbach eventually came to America, and one of his later volumes is dedicated to Spitzer. But

Istanbul represents a parting of the ways, insofar as its lack of scholarly paraphernalia drew a sharp line between the two approaches within the same field: the para-scholarship of Spitzer and the infra-scholarship of Auerbach.

Both men were aware of their divergence. Spitzer considered Auerbach's emphasis, in contrast with his own, to be socio-historical rather than strictly stylistic.[14] Auerbach, while praising Spitzer for his tenacious pursuit of individual forms, acknowledged a more general intention: "My purpose is always to write history."[15] Spitzer had begun by reacting against an old-fashioned school of literary historiography, based narrowly upon biographical data, in favor of an esthetic and psychological approach. Since style is the unique use that the individual makes of a common language, it discloses itself in deviations from norms; hence its analyst, emulating the psychoanalyst, looks for verbal *tics* and tries to account for them. Spitzer's monograph on Henri Barbusse, for example, lays bare the persistent imagery of violence in the vocabulary of that ardent pacifist. "The Style of Diderot," under Spitzer's investigation, appears to be regulated by sexual rhythms. The diction of Charles Péguy reflects his assent to the metaphysics of Bergson. In the slang of Charles-Louis Philippe, an obsessive repetition of one phrase, "*à cause de*," betrays a subconscious determinism. But Spitzer was no less concerned with form than with psychology, and some of his critical concepts are useful tools. The concept of chaotic enumeration clarifies the structure of Claudel's poems—or, for that matter, Whitman's. The principle of linguistic perspectivism helps to explain the oscillations of viewpoint in *Don Quixote*.

Problems of meaning were ultimately philosophical, to one who believed in speech as a reflection of *Weltanschauung*. Social tensions were illuminated when Spitzer traced such expressions as *Schadenfreude* or *Gentile*. His arrival in Baltimore brought about a stimulating conjunction, since the Hopkins—through the learned and lucid endeavors of Arthur Lovejoy—had become a center for the history of ideas. Insofar

14. Leo Spitzer, "Les Etudes de style dans les différents pays," in *Langue et littérature: Actes du VIIIe Congrès de la Fédération Internationale des Langues et Littératures Modernes* (Paris, 1961), p. 28.
15. Auerbach, *Literary Language*, p. 20.

as that discipline might reduce literature to a handmaid of philosophy, Spitzer had and voiced his reservations.[16] But the intellectual cross-fertilization inspired him to his farthest ranging studies in semantics: the related pair of monographs on the terms *milieu* and *ambiance* and on the long tradition of cosmic order subsumed by *Stimmung*. Auerbach's reorientation was limited by the circumstance that he spent no more than a decade in the United States, whereas Spitzer lived among us for twenty-four years. René Wellek reports a conversation in which Spitzer complained that he was now *"echolos"*;[17] yet his writings reverberated when they were published in English; and, furthermore, his adopted country had some impact on him. Along with elucidations of Poe and Whitman, his English essays include the acute and amusing *tour de force*, "American Advertising Explained as Popular Art," which explicates a pictorial advertisement for Sunkist Oranges.[18] The second sentence of his first American book reads as follows:

I dedicate this first book of mine printed in America, which is to continue the series of studies in stylistics previously published in Germany—*Aufsätze zur romanischen Syntax und Stilistik*, Halle (Niemeyer) 1918; *Stilstudien*, I–II, München (Hueber) 1928; *Romanische Stil- und Literaturstudien*, I–II, Marburg an der Lahn (Elwert) 1931—to Assistant Professor ANNA GRANVILLE HATCHER who is an outstanding American scholar in the too little cultivated field of syntax—which in her case, is expanded into stylistic and cultural history—and who could thus teach me, not only the intricacies of English syntax and stylistics, but some of the more recondite features of American culture and of its particular moral, logical, and aesthetic aspirations: a knowledge without which all endeavors of the philologist to explain poetry to an American public must fail completely.[19]

To explicate this remarkable piece of syntax would require the insight of Spitzer himself, plus a self-detachment to which he laid no particular claim. Stripped of its relative clauses and appositions, of what a classical rhetorician would call *epergesis* and *anacoluthon*, and of an al-

16. Leo Spitzer, "History of Ideas versus Reading of Poetry," *Southern Review*, VI, 3 (Winter, 1941), 584–609.

17. René Wellek, "Leo Spitzer (1887–1960)," *Comparative Literature*, XII, i (Fall, 1960), 310, an admirable appraisal with a selective bibliography. See also the well-informed tribute of Spitzer's co-worker Helmut Hatzfeld, "Léon Spitzer et la littérature française," *Etudes Françaises*, II, 3 (October, 1966), 251–253.

18. Leo Spitzer, *Essays on English and American Literature* (ed. Anna Hatcher, Princeton, 1962).

19. Spitzer, *Linguistics and Literary History*, p. v.

most Shandyan sequence of dashes, it would be a simple gesture of gratitude and acknowledgment to that colleague who would become his successor at Johns Hopkins. But the personal declaration is rounded out, to the extent of 135 words, by professional afterthoughts at both ends. At his end a bibliographical footnote, parenthetically assimilated into the sentence, advertises the continuity with his publications in German. At her end the professional compliment leads, through a moving personal excursus, into an affirmation of scholarly faith and an attestation of national loyalty. Editors who received his manuscripts can recall the visible traces of how he wrote: the accumulation, the stratification, the interlineation, addenda, and more last words. Footnotes were his *genre par excellence*, sometimes outrunning the text in Venetian fashion, and containing observations on everything in the manner of Montaigne. The intensive focus he brought to bear on an abstruse point, the polyglot outpouring of related facts and ideas, did not leave much room for a sense of proportion. On a paper read at a meeting and subsequently printed in *Comparative Literature* Auerbach commented:

Et ce que Spitzer a dit sur la Peregrinatio est peut-être un peu trop poussé, comme tout ce qu'il fait—mais au fond c'est tellement vrai et neuf que vous ne vous repentirez certainement d'avoir pris l'article pour Compar. Lit.[20]

This tendency to overstrain the evidence at times, to hinge his arguments on supersubtleties which no one else had ever noticed, was calculated to draw more vocal and sharper criticisms. His reading of *Phèdre* stressed the key word *voir* in the concluding monologue of Théramène; but Jean Hytier has pointed out that the word was unavoidable at that moment in any neoclassical tragedy, since the offstage dénouement had to be reported by an eyewitness.[21] In such interchanges, which were the breath of Spitzer's life, he was the challenger more often than not. He met a Hopkins colleague in English on his own ground, by challenging his interpretation of Keats's "Ode on a Grecian Urn." The consequent overreading is too erudite to be quite convincing; it mainly proves that Spitzer knew more than Keats about Greek archeology. His polemical

20. Letter from Erich Auerbach to Harry Levin, January 1, 1949.
21. Jean Hytier, "La Méthode de M. Leo Spitzer," *Romanic Review*, XLI, 1 (February, 1950), 42–59.

stance was robed in righteousness. Not for nothing did his name mean "sharpener." Fellow scholars, especially younger Americans, had to be castigated for their own good. He was here to set an example, to teach us a lesson. One of his most punitive review articles, on Stephen Gilman's *Art of "La Celestina,"* concludes (though Spitzer characteristically appended a postscript, eulogizing the late Ernst Robert Curtius):

I have often been asked why I devote so much of my efforts to "destructive criticism." The answer is that I believe that, in the discipline of Philology as in the sciences, the ultimate goal, however more arduous in its attainment or approximation, must be Truth; and that the failure to expose contentment with half-truths or non-truths would amount to a conspiracy of silence against that noble discipline.[22]

Professor Gilman could scarcely be expected to accept this pharisaical answer, since every scholar seeks the truth according to his lights and few today believe themselves so uniquely privy to it. A rejoinder, in probing for the animus that had carried the reviewer so far beyond the legitimate occasion of the review, suggested that Professor Gilman's sin—in Spitzer's eyes—had been to write a book. Spitzer, for all his penetrating intelligence and formidable learning, had never come to grips with the problem of synthesis.

His sharp-edged atomistic mind, a mind which has divided Juan Ruiz into his sources, his own "*obra*" into a thousand and one articles, and his articles into a myriad of footnotes, has been baffled by the fact of composition itself.[23]

It would be hard to compile an exhaustive bibliography of Spitzeriana, written as they were in five different languages and scattered across the world in periodicals of limited circulation. There would be at least a thousand entries; and, if we did not count miscellaneous collections, monographs, or pamphlets, there would be no books among them. Many, which are not explicit reviews, were touched off by the efforts of other writers to discuss subjects about which Spitzer had deep knowledge and strong opinions. If he needed to be provoked into writing, perhaps it is fortunate that he was so infinitely provokable. His reaction to six pages by Grace Frank on a Provençal poem took the form of a

22. Leo Spitzer, "A New Book on the Art of 'The Celestina', " *Hispanic Review*, XXV, 1 (January, 1957), 24.
23. Stephen Gilman, "A Rejoinder to Leo Spitzer," *Hispanic Review*, XXV, 2 (April, 1957), 120.

seventy-four page monograph.[24] Increasingly and somewhat defensively, during his American period, he would talk about his methodology. It was more easily demonstrated than formulated, with autobiographical cross-reference to earlier demonstrations. Whenever he directly confronted the literary object, he was more interested in beauties than faults, believing as he did that the details he scrutinized were organic parts of a perfect whole. His critics accused him of knowing well in advance what he claimed to arrive at empirically. Spitzer replied that such reasoning was inherent in "the philological circle," the continuous movement of the interpreter's mind from the text at hand to the contexts of widening awareness and back again.[25] His hypotheses might be no more than shrewd hunches, but so were the scientist's.

In a politely devastating critique of the phenomenological critic, Georges Poulet, Spitzer maintained that the "chameleonic" approach of the philologist was more germane to literature than the systematic approach of the philosopher.[26] Spitzer's own procedures resisted formulation because, in the last analysis, they were based upon a rare combination of intuition and erudition. One of his attempts to set them forth takes its departure from a dictum of Friedrich Gundolf, "*Methode ist Erlebnis*," and repeats a scholastic adage which Spitzer loved to quote, "*individuum est ineffabile*."[27] His method was his very exceptional self. An essay of mine had the good luck to please him because it cited an instance where the lifelong devotion of a single humanist had done more to clarify certain exacting problems than the heavily organized enterprises of a modern team. In this connection he wrote:

Choosing from your own words, I would say that the "new frontiers of knowledge" consist in the gigantically increasing *information* we get in our times while a unified Weltanschauung or wisdom, is disappearing. Just open any of our journals and you witness the anarchy of values while the learning displayed is (sometimes) stupendous.[28]

In September 1960, two weeks before his sudden death at the Italian

24. Leo Spitzer, *L'Amour lointain de Jaufré Rudel et le sens de la poésie des troubadours* (Chapel Hill, 1944).

25. Spitzer, *Linguistics and Literary History*, pp. 19ff.

26. Leo Spitzer, "A propos de la 'Vie de Marianne'," *Romanische Literaturstudien, 1936–56* (Tübingen, 1959), pp. 248–276.

27. Spitzer, *Linguistics and Literary History*, pp. 1, 11.

28. Letter from Leo Spitzer to Harry Levin, August 17, 1951.

resort he frequented, I spent a week in close contact with Spitzer at Liège. As the two Americans invited to address plenary sessions at the congress of the Fédération Internationale des Langues et Littératures Modernes, we were lodged at the same hotel, and took a number of walks and meals together. Only once, when we had to climb a steep hill on a visit to a local professor, did he show the hesitations of age. But I found him constantly mellow and sparkling, benign and fatherly. What was to be his farewell address, *"Les Etudes de style et les différents pays,"* appropriately terminated the congress and received a standing ovation. Possibly because he was speaking in urbane French, which lends itself less readily to polemics than German or even English, he seemed to have come to terms with himself, his fellow men, and his field. His final statement was a proclamation of open-mindedness, a far cry from the doctrine he had been propounding at Baltimore ten years before:

> Ainsi beaucoup de chemins mènent vers la Rome de la stylistique, et la stylistique elle-même n'est pas la porte d'accès unique au paradis de la bonne critique littéraire.[29]

Shortly before we parted, he agreed to give some lectures at Harvard the following year. That my own university so narrowly missed the opportunity of hearing both Spitzer and Auerbach is one of my lasting regrets.

III

CONVERSING with Auerbach at—of all places—the site of the Village Smithy, I had been reminded of Longfellow walking down Brattle Street from his home to the Harvard Yard a hundred years before. He had been the first professor of modern languages at his *alma mater*, Bowdoin College, and one of the first in the country. During his undergraduate days, the college had offered no instruction in that area. He had picked up some French from a church organist at Portland, and he prepared himself for his teaching duties by a grand tour of Europe which lasted three years. Another such *Wanderjahr* preceded his arrival at Harvard, where he held the Smith Professorship of the French and Spanish

29. *Langue et littérature*, p. 38.

Languages from 1836 to 1854. When he resigned, in order to devote full time to his literary activities, notably his verse translation of Dante, he broadened his role as a cultural mediator between the hemispheres. His predecessor, the first Smith Professor, George Ticknor, belonged to that early and eager band of American students who had sought to quaff the cup of knowledge at its German academic source. After studying at the University of Göttingen and travelling widely in Spain and elsewhere, he had laid out the program of instruction in the modern languages at Harvard. His resignation widened his scope by permitting him to concentrate upon his pioneering history of Spanish literature.

Longfellow's successor, James Russell Lowell, was also a respected man of letters rather than a professional scholar. Yet it should not be forgotten that, at the fourth meeting of the Modern Language Association of America in 1886, Lowell—whose teaching career had been interrupted by his ministries to Spain and Britain—was elected president. During the next generation the M.L.A., reinforced by the establishment of graduate schools and the introduction of the Ph.D., saw itself consolidated into a citadel of philological scholarship. By and large, it emulated the methods of Germany, with a special American zeal for the sheer accumulation of facts; and, since it was farther removed from the springs of its subject-matter, it was even drier than its model. Its standard products were textbooks of historical grammar. English studies were allowed somewhat more leeway, since they had long functioned within the framework of rhetoric and have always attracted the part-time writer. But there too the history of literature hardly looked beyond the Middle Ages, while the language requirements were overburdened with such extraneous matters as Gothic. In the departments of foreign languages, so much of the pedagogical effort went into elementary chores that advanced research was the exception more often than the rule. By the opening decades of our century, the severance between philology and *belles lettres* was all but complete.

Of course, it is the exceptions who prove worth remembering, particularly among scholars, and we have had our share. If C. H. Grandgent seems more typical of the M.L.A. than his forerunners at Harvard in Romance Languages, he must be credited with what is still a standard edition of the *Divina Commedia*. But it is significant that, before Grand-

gent took over Harvard's course in Dante, it had been taught by
Charles Eliot Norton, whose prose translation is so frequently cited;
for Norton, though he pointed the way to more technical approaches in
the history of art and archeology, prided himself on remaining a gentle-
manly amateur. By the nineteen-thirties the *Publications of the Modern
Language Association* had become such a catchall for encrusted profes-
sionalism that a younger generation of college teachers was able to stage
a successful revolt. This was the New Criticism proclaimed by John
Crowe Ransom. Though its strategic exponents had come from southern states, they recognized two Anglo-American forerunners: T. S. Eliot,
a British subject since 1927, and I. A. Richards, who was translated from
Cambridge University to Cambridge, Massachusetts, in 1939. The consequent rediscovery of literature as an art, through emphasis upon its
structures and textures, had a wholesome influence in the classroom. A
concomitant disregard of historical and linguistic contexts threatened
serious misconstruction at the scholarly level.

There was some danger lest the pendulum swing too far in the new
direction: toward a concern with texts which lacked the background to
understand them fully, an assumption that the critic's and the scholar's
interests were mutually exclusive. This attitude had been exacerbated
by the dryasdust philistinism of a good many elder scholars, who made
a point of choosing detective stories when they were reading for pleasure. Such, then, was the *impasse* which the example of Europe could
resolve and the European migration would help to correct. The traditional *explication de texte* had been reduced to a perfunctory exercise
since Gustave Lanson, but it could be reanimated by informed percep-
tivity on the part of the *explicateur*. Poets like Andrei Bely, critics like
Victor Shklovsky, and philologists like Roman Jakobson had joined
forces under the aegis of Russian Formalism. The Centro de Estudios
Históricos at Madrid, the Cercle Linguistique de Prague, the *Ideali-
stische Philologie* of Munich—what these varying schools had in common
was a focus on stylistics as the middle ground between linguistics and
literary criticism. The timely presence in the United States of Spitzer
and Auerbach—the one so active a controversialist, the other so influential through his book—was a reassurance, for some of us caught in the
cross fire, that our discipline embraced both erudition and esthetics.

When the history of the twentieth-century diaspora is fully chronicled, we should be able to test the parallel it implies with the fifteenth-century influx of catalytic knowledge to western Europe after the fall of Constantinople. Meanwhile, given the scale of events precipitating the latter-day exodus, the number of countries whence the refugees took flight, the brilliance of their talents and the variety of their fields, we make a modest start wherever we can by trying to follow the fortunes of those whose paths have crossed our own. Those losses to European faculties, which have meant such gains for ours, have completed the maturation of American higher learning. A touch of the medieval Sorbonne, with its "nations" of students, has been internationalizing our universities. To be sure, they had previously imported some of their professors, especially for the purpose of language teaching. Witness such colorful figures as Mozart's librettist, Lorenzo da Ponte, who was briefly the first professor of Italian at Columbia University, or the Norwegian-born novelist, H. H. Boyesen, professor of Germanic literatures at Cornell and Columbia. But, until so many distinguished *savants* were expatriated by the political conflicts of our time, the majority of our foreign-born college teachers of languages were what Dr. Johnson would have termed harmless drudges, who would not have achieved substantial positions by staying at home.

Within the more recent movement, the pattern of adaptation has varied according to nationality. Thus the French have tended to be emissaries rather than expatriates. Their viceroy among us, Henri Peyre, admits that his compatriots "have proved more stubborn than most other Europeans in withstanding assimilation."[30] However, they have thrown light on Franco-American relations, notably through the contributions of Gilbert Chinard. The Spaniards, moving to a hemisphere still rich in Hispanic associations, turned their exile into a perspective on the historic uniqueness of Spanish culture. Spitzer, who waxed impatient over what he called "national tautology" ("*die irgendweise implizite Behauptung, dass ein spanisches Kunstwerk gross ist, weil echt spanisch, und echt spanisch, wenn gross*"), provoked a controversy with Américo

---

30. Henri Peyre, "The Study of Literature," in *The Cultural Migration: The European Scholar in America* (ed. W. R. Crawford, Philadelphia, 1953), p. 37.

Castro over that battleground.[31] In the widespread dispersion of Russian intellectuals, comparatively few were accomplished literary scholars, among whom Gleb Struve stands out as the historian of Russian emigré literature. The American undertakings of Roman Jakobson have combined more effectively with Slavic and general linguistics than with literary studies. Some of the most adaptable émigrés have been those who were trained, in their homelands and by earlier travels, to be experts on cultures other than their own. The Slavicist from Italy, Renato Poggioli, and the Anglicist from Czechoslovakia, René Wellek, arriving almost simultaneously at Harvard and Yale, guaranteed a realization of the protracted American hopes for comparative literature.

It is worth noting that the *Journal of Comparative Literature*, undertaken by G. E. Woodberry at Columbia University in 1903, did not survive that year; whereas the journal sponsored by the University of Oregon, with the cooperation of the M.L.A., *Comparative Literature*, has been appearing regularly since 1949, and there are now three additional periodicals in this sphere. A glance at their tables of contents will reveal the extent to which they have thriven upon the collaboration of our European-American colleagues. To the first six volumes of *Comparative Literature* Spitzer contributed five articles. Auerbach had promised an article; but, since he seldom wrote directly for publication in English, he decided to publish it elsewhere in German; and he did contribute three reviews. It could be reciprocally said that such contributors were happy to find so close at hand "a forum for those scholars and critics who are engaged in the study of literature from an international point of view."[32] Spitzer had continually chafed against the barriers set by specialization and departmentalism: "The splitting up of a field which knew in former times of no international boundaries is, to say the least, anachronistic."[33] Auerbach acknowledged a sense of European "mission," which he attributed to his own formation—not as a Romance philologist nor indeed

31. Leo Spitzer, "The Mozarabic Lyric of Theodor Frings," *Comparative Literature*, IV, 1 (Winter, 1952), 1–22. *Cf.* Américo Castro, "Mozarabic Poetry and Castille: A Rejoinder to Mr. Leo Spitzer," *Comparative Literature*, IV, 2 (Spring, 1952), 188–189. The quotation is from Spitzer's review of Dámaso Alonso's *Poesía española* in *Romanische Forschungen*, LXIV, 1/2 (1952), 215.

32. From the editorial statement appearing on the inside cover in each issue of *Comparative Literature*.

33. Spitzer, *Essays in Historical Semantics*, p. 11.

as a German, but as a combination of both, a *Romanist*, with the good German's feeling for the civilizing traditions of that Latin world which stretched from the Rhine to the Mediterranean.[34]

Similarly Ernst Robert Curtius would affirm: "*Ich wusste mich gebunden an die* Roma aeterna."[35] That vision of the monuments attesting the continuity of Europe itself, systematized by the monumental investigations of Germanic scholarship into Romanic matters, made the *Romanisten* more consistently humane than their more nationalistic colleagues, the *Germanisten*. The *doyen* of their last great generation was Karl Vossler, friend of Croce and founder of idealistic philology, who studied Dante as a mirror of medieval culture and the French language as a mirror of French civilization. A liberal, he was morally fortified by his trans-European outlook; a study of the poetry of solitude in Spain is characteristic of his work during the Nazi period; and he was enabled to resume the rectorship of the University of Munich during the postwar occupation.[36] Curtius, at Bonn, had been undertaking his own internal migration. Hitherto he had best been known as a searching and sympathetic interpreter of modern French literature. Motivated by his "concern for the preservation of Western culture," he returned to medieval Latinity, retracing its tropes and conventions from Vergil to Dante in his *magnum opus*.[37] To judge from his conversation with Stephen Spender in 1946, he felt that the war had not left much worth preserving.[38] On his brief visit to America, for the Goethe bicentennial in 1949, he seemed gracious but quite incurious.

Whether Spitzer and Auerbach would have produced comparable works of synthesis, if it had been possible for them to go on working in Germany, is a question which does not lend itself to belated speculation. As Jews, they had no choice but to emigrate; possibly they adjusted more readily to a new environment because of their migratory ancestry. But other *Romanisten*, coming for other reasons, have brought with

34. Auerbach, *Literary Language*, p. 16.

35. E. R. Curtius, *Kritische Essays zur Europäischen Literatur* (Bern, 1954), p. 439.

36. See Helmut Hatzfeld, "Karl Vossler (1872-1949)," *Comparative Literature*, I, 2 (Spring, 1949), 189.

37. E. R. Curtius, "Author's Foreword to the English Translation," *European Literature and the Latin Middle Ages* (tr. W. R. Trask, New York, 1953), p. viii.

38. Stephen Spender, "German Impressions and Conversations," *Partisan Review*, XIII, 1 (Winter, 1946), 7-13.

them their skills and talents. Helmut Hatzfeld, who was a pupil of Vossler, is now their *doyen*. Teaching at the Catholic University of America, he has focused his researches upon literary manifestations of the baroque and of mysticism and upon comparative stylistics. Herbert Dieckmann, once a student of Curtius, may be the youngest of the tribe. Taking his doctorate at Bonn in 1933, he came to the United States via the Turkish detour, and has taught at Washington University, Harvard, and Cornell. Though his intellectual range is wide, his discovery of important manuscripts has centered most of his energies on the reediting of Diderot. By the mid-century, with the reconstruction of Europe, it was clear that fewer and fewer emigrés would be candidates for our professorships. Much is to be hoped for, however, from a younger generation of European-born scholars trained in America, such as Paul De Man, Peter Demetz, Victor Erlich, W. B. Fleischmann, Claudio Guillén, Juan Marichal, Georges May, Alain Renoir, and Walter Strauss.

Spitzer summed up his unstinting advice to young American scholars with an address at a general meeting of the M.L.A. in 1950, "The Formation of the American Humanist." Reminiscing about the ideals and rigors of his Viennese education, he reaffirmed his commitment to scholarship as a way of life. He was unsparing in his censure of those distractions and pressures which make it something less than a *modus vivendi* for most of us. His twin targets were administration and overproduction, and he aphoristically footnoted: "The telephone of the organizer is the deadly enemy of the desk of the scholar."[39] The broad solution he proposed was the establishment of a scholarly élite, which—he urged in his concluding plea—should not be incompatible with the highest aims of a democracy.

You may have decided that, given my criticism of the life actually led by our young scholars in our university system, a system so intimately connected with national ideals, I am criticizing these ideals themselves and that, consequently, as the phrase goes, "I should go back where I came from." But I do not wish to go back, I wish to stay in this country which I love. Is it not understandable that a relationship deliberately based on choice may inspire, at the same time, more passion and more criticism

39. Leo Spitzer, "The Formation of the American Humanist," *Publications of The Modern Language Association of America*, LXVI, 1 (February, 1951), 44n.

than an inherited relationship? It is just because I find in American democracy the only air in which I could breathe, because I am convinced that the average American is more decent, less selfish, and more human than the average of any other nation where I have lived, that I would wish the American university system to possess all the advantages of the best systems of the old world![40]

Elsewhere, with the same extra measure of passion and criticism, Spitzer voiced his specific objections to current practices: to the sort of capricious reinterpretations, by ill-informed reinterpreters questing for novelty, that abound in our learned journals as well as our literary quarterlies. He feared lest the Americans outdo the Germans in such willful and subjective misreading.[41] He found himself reverting, on a second recoil, to historicist and positivistic assumptions which he had previously been reacting against.[42] One of his marginal admonitions is a "negative reading-list," a warning against certain thinkers who have befuddled many an aspiring scholar-critic.[43] The full roster includes some *mauvais maîtres* whom he himself had once esteemed more highly: Bergson, Buber, Dilthey, Freud, Heidegger, Ortega, Sartre, Scheler, Spengler, Unamuno. But Spitzer's precepts had less effect than the striking example he set, while Auerbach was content to go his own way, leaving the paperback edition of *Mimesis* to play an exemplary role before an ever widening audience. The lesson they propounded to us was reading, the most elementary subject in the curriculum pressed to its most advanced stage through the sharp and disciplined perceptions of incomparably well-stored minds. Nor should it be overlooked, in our faltering effort to carry on their endeavors, that—in Spitzerian terms— "they are the results of talent, experience, and faith."[44]

40. *Ibid.*, p. 47.
41. Spitzer, "The Formation of the American Humanist," p. 23.
42. "History of Ideas versus Reading of Poetry," p. 608.
43. Spitzer, "A New Book on the Art of 'The Celestina'," pp. 19, 23.
44. Spitzer, *Linguistics and Literary History*, p. 27.

THE AFTERMATH OF THE BAUHAUS IN AMERICA: GROPIUS, MIES, AND BREUER

by WILLIAM H. JORDY

I N architecture and design the German émigrés who most profoundly influenced American developments were former teachers
at the Bauhaus. Their impact on American culture may well be
considered to have been the most direct legacy of the Bauhaus—not its
continuation, but its postscript.

Three of its former faculty members have played major roles in
American architecture: Walter Gropius, Ludwig Mies van der Rohe,
and Marcel Breuer.[1] Their contributions were buttressed by those of
three other Bauhaus teachers who were close to Gropius: the graphic
designer Herbert Bayer, and especially Josef Albers and László Moholy-
Nagy, both of whom had taught the introductory courses in vision and
design at the Bauhaus and helped bring some of these ideas to the United
States. As Gropius asked Breuer to join him at Harvard, so two of the

---

* For information in this article I am especially grateful for interviews with Walter
Gropius and Marcel Breuer. For insights on Gropius' and Breuer's teaching at Harvard, I
am indebted to John McL. Johansen and to Richard G. Stein, architects who were among
their early students at Harvard. For insights into Mies's teaching and early career in
Chicago, I am similarly indebted to Peter Carter of Mies's office, and to the following
architects who taught, studied or worked with Mies shortly after his arrival in the United
States: Charles Dornbusch, Charles Genther, Myron Goldsmith, Alfred Mell, and John
B. Rodgers. Comments attributed to any of these individuals and not otherwise noted
were gained from these interviews.

1. For basic coverage of the work and careers of these architects, and on Mendelsohn
mentioned below, see the following. On Gropius: Sigfried Giedion, *Walter Gropius: Work
and Teamwork* (Zurich, 1954); James Marston Fitch, *Walter Gropius* (New York, 1960).
On Breuer: Peter Blake, *Marcel Breuer* (New York, 1949); Breuer, *Sun and Shadow* (ed.
Peter Blake, New York, 1955); *Marcel Breuer 1921–1961: Buildings and Projects* (introd.
Cranston Jones, New York, 1962). On Mies van der Rohe: Philip C. Johnson, *Mies van
der Rohe* (2nd rev. ed., New York, 1953); Arthur Drexler, *Mies van der Rohe* (New York,
1960); Werner Blaser, *Mies van der Rohe: The Art of Structure* (New York, 1965). On
Mendelsohn: Arnold Whittick, *Eric Mendelsohn* (New York, 1956); Wolf von Eckardt,
Eric Mendelsohn (New York, 1960). Most of these works contain additional bibliography.

teachers on Mies's staff when he briefly directed the Bauhaus, Walter Peterhans and Ludwig Hilbersheimer, joined Mies at the Illinois Institute of Technology. To this list of transplanted designers, three names at least should be added. Among the architect émigrés, Erich Mendelsohn should be included as one of the German leaders in the modern movement of the twenties (and, incidentally, the only one of the group whose "race" as well as his ideas were degenerate by Nazi standards). His impact on American architecture, however, in no degree matched that of Gropius, Mies, and Breuer. The Austrian, Frederick Kiesler, should also be mentioned, although the influence of his speculative sweep across the entire spectrum of the visual arts, including architecture, scene design, sculpture, and painting, remained seminal and restricted rather than decisive during his lifetime. At least one more German artist, also outside the Bauhaus group, Hans Hofmann, deserves mention for his extraordinary influence in American painting of the forties and fifties. This minimal roster in itself suggests the impact of the German émigrés on the visual arts in the United States.

It is the architects who will principally, though not exclusively, concern us. Three factors account for the nature and extent of their influence. One was the mere circumstance that the architects (except Kiesler) arrived late in the thirties. Thus a number of years separated the apogee of their European work in the late twenties from the commencement of their American lives. The interval is vexatiously important because it complicates generalization about the "American" aspects of their oeuvre. Some qualities in their American work, temptingly attributable to "American" conditioning, are at least partially the result of a changed situation in modern architecture between the beginning and end of the thirties. A second factor accounting for their influence is their teaching. The teaching of Gropius and Breuer at Harvard and of Mies at the Illinois Institute of Technology marked the beginning of systematic training in modern principles in American architectural education. Mendelsohn, who lectured widely in American universities, eventually taught at the University of California at Berkeley, but with less impact than the others. The far-ranging Kiesler headed an "architectural laboratory" in the School of Architecture at Columbia from 1936 until 1942, intended for experimental rather than for specifically professional studies. A third factor in their influence, especially that of Gropius, Breuer, and Mies, was their immense success as practicing architects. Thus the world situation in architecture at the time of their arrival, their teaching, and their actual designs all require examination in any assessment of the impact of the German émigrés on American architecture, and of American conditions upon them.

By the late thirties the polemical phase of the European development in modern architecture during the twenties was unmistakably past. The revolutionary ardor that had marked the pronouncements on modern architecture had diminished by the early thirties. Although still considered radical, the rationale for the community style developed in Europe was by then well established. Its principal exemplars were built. No fresh impetus in the thirties dislodged the supremacy of the movement to which most referred during the thirties when they spoke of "modern architecture." Hence American architects or would-be architects of progressive inclination, who had been mere bystanders during the European episode of the twenties and pretty much continued in this state throughout the better part of the next decade, sustained themselves while they waited more on what *had* happened in the immediate past than on what *was* then happening.

To these Americans, Le Corbusier's *Vers une architecture* of 1922, which they for the most part read in the English translation of 1928 with its altered title *Towards a New Architecture*, was a cardinal document of the movement. For them it served anomalously as at once a call to arms and a historical document for a familiar point of view. *Towards a New Architecture* was supplemented at irregular intervals by installments of the *Oeuvre complète* in which Le Corbusier chronicled his buildings, his projects, and his further speculations. "There exists a new spirit," *Vers une architecture*, in its awkward English translation, informed the world. Look around you, Le Corbusier in effect urged architects who designed with "eyes that do not see," in the trumpery of neoclassical columns and pediments and entablatures. Look at those objects that "move us" by their modernity: at liners, airplanes, and automobiles; at the naked force of factory buildings flaunting their skeletal structure in reinforced concrete; at the "pure" cubic and cylindrical shapes of grain elevators.

The future is *now*, in these objects waiting to be seen, waiting to be used.

Although the group endeavor which resulted was variously (and often opprobriously) termed the Functional Style, the Machine Style, the Bauhaus Style, and finally, the International Style, none of the labels conveyed its essence. This lay in a comprehensive objectivity charged with optimism about the possibility of creating a humane physical environment consonant with and expressive of modern technology.[2] The largeness and force of its vision rather than the complete success of its achievement accounted for its enormous influence, not only as an incident of its own decade, but as a sustaining ideology for the subsequent development of modern architecture. As Mies would say of the influence of the Bauhaus on the occasion of Gropius' seventieth birthday, "You cannot [exert such influence] with organization, you cannot do it with propaganda. Only an idea spreads so far."[3]

The modern movement of the twenties dared to confront the modern situation unequivocally, to create a self-consciously "modern" architecture from essentials believed to be rigorously objective. The new architecture would be *technologically* objective in utilizing modern techniques of building and in searching for ideal standards or norms that might be mass produced. It would be *esthetically* objective in the elemental, "pure" forms it used. It would be *sociologically* objective in its quest for an architecture consonant with the metropolitan culture of the modern world, which included a commitment to mass housing previously unparalleled in the history of the profession. It would be *psychically* and *symbolically* objective in accepting the clarity, lucidity, tautness, and dynamism assumed to be the qualities of modern life, and celebrating these in an esthetic at once concrete and visionary. Thus Le Corbusier's "*esprit nouveau*" would challenge the overemphasis on naturalism, individualism, historicism, and sentimentality which had characterized nineteenth-century architecture. Architects and designers would no longer exist on the fringes of society, producing *objets d'art* for an elite. They

2. See my "The Symbolic Essence of Modern European Architecture of the Twenties and Its Continuing Influence," *Journal of Society of Architectural Historians*, 22 (October, 1963), 177–187, which discusses this theme as central to the movement in opposition to some other interpretations.

3. Cited in Paul Heyer, *Architects on Architecture: New Directions in America* (New York, 1966), p. 202.

would advance to the center of their world and both appropriate and shape it. To use the description which Le Corbusier came to prefer for his metropolises of crystal skyscrapers, he and the group of architects who shared his beliefs would create the Radiant City of the modern world.[4] To interested Americans, as bystanders experiencing this exhilarating episode from a double distance of time and geography, Le Corbusier became the fervent apostle of the modern movement. Gropius' Bauhaus was its collegium.

America's role in this development had been secondary: it consisted partly of the example of Wright, but mostly of such unique phenomena as skyscrapers and mass production, appropriated in the propaganda of the movement for cues to the future. The first extensive publication of Wright's work had actually appeared in Germany in two works confusingly similar in their titles, *Ausgeführte Bauten und Entwürfe von Frank Lloyd Wright* of 1910 and *Frank Lloyd Wright Ausgeführte Bauten* of 1911. (The first comprehensive American study of Wright's work, Henry-Russell Hitchcock's *In the Nature of Materials*, appeared as late as 1942, and even then did not cover the most significant buildings in Wright's early work in such detail.) In 1940, on the occasion of an exhibition of Wright's work at the Museum of Modern Art, Mies remarked on its impact among the young liberal-minded architects in Berlin.

The work of this great master presented an architectural world of unexpected force, clarity of language and disconcerting richness of form. Here, finally, was a masterbuilder drawing upon the veritable fountainhead of architecture; who with true originality lifted his creations into the light. Here again, at long last, genuine organic architecture flowered. The more we were absorbed in the study of these creations, the greater became our admiration for his incomparable talent, the boldness of his conceptions and the independence of his thought and action. The dynamic impulse emanating from his work invigorated a whole generation. His influence was strongly felt even when it was not actually visible.[5]

Whatever the influence of Wright, it had been subsumed by the early twenties. The conspicuous American contributions to European modernism during the twenties were more fragmentary. Even before World War I, Gropius had called attention to American factories and grain

4. *Le Corbusier Talks with Students* (New York, 1961), p. 27.
5. Reprinted in Philip Johnson, *Mies van der Rohe* (New York, 1953), p. 201.

elevators.[6] It was *Vers une architecture*, however, which popularized these artifacts among architects. Le Corbusier's tract also lauded Frederick Winslow Taylor and Henry Ford for establishing "standards" for mass production, while it of course dwelt on the American skyscraper, as much to chide its anachronistic veneer as to recommend its urban usefulness. But in the mid-thirties, after Le Corbusier had finally visited the United States (toward which he eventually acquired a paranoia of De Gaulle-like proportions), he came away complaining of "the country of timid people."[7] So much potential with which to realize the world of the new spirit! So little courage for the job!

Le Corbusier's Americana was poetic and visionary. In the twenties, the architects with soundest appreciation of American technology in structures and building methods were the Germans. This conditioning went far toward accounting for their congeniality to the American environment, and their eventual achievement in it. Mendelsohn visited the United States in 1924, to prepare a picture book of his sightseeing in New York, Buffalo, Detroit, and Chicago.[8] The book was somewhat in the Corbusian vein of mingled ecstasy and taunts. Mendelsohn, however, studied the American situation more specifically, noted the building technology of skyscrapers, and looked at Sullivan's Schiller Building, Root's Monadnock, and at half a dozen buildings by Wright before making a pilgrimage to Wright at Spring Green. There Richard Neutra, then apprenticing with Wright, served as translator.[9] Neutra had emigrated from Vienna in 1923. During the decade he prepared two remarkable books on American building methods and processes. *Wie Baut Amerika?* appeared from a Stuttgart publisher in 1927; *Neues Bauen in der Welt: Amerika*, one of a series, from a Vienna publisher in 1930. Gropius himself made a trip in 1928, visiting New York, Chicago, Los Angeles (Neutra's adopted home city), and San Francisco for the purpose of studying American building technology.

It was not merely structures but building methods, not merely the

6. Walter Gropius, "Die Entwicklung moderner Industriebaukunst," *Jahrbuch des deutschen Werkbundes*, (1913), 17–22.

7. Le Corbusier, *When Cathedrals Were White: a Journey to the Country of Timid People* (New York, 1947).

8. Erich Mendelsohn, *Amerika: Bilderbuch eines Architekten* (Berlin, 1926).

9. Von Eckardt, *Mendelsohn*, p. 19.

engineer's business but the contractor's, that interested the Germans. Both Gropius and Breuer have remarked on American efficiency in building operations as among their first and most enduring impressions of the United States. Breuer, for example, never ceased to be amazed at what he termed the "loneliness of American building," on which (to use his figures) thirty or forty workmen would be doing the work of three hundred in France, whose building problems he knew well. "The American has an instinct for efficiency. I don't say 'know how,' and I don't like the phrase. American efficiency goes deeper than 'know how.' You see this quality in the smallest contractor. It's the way he plans every move; the way he orders materials; the way he stacks them and places them around the job. Americans have an instinct for building. Every housewife in America knows what a two-by-four is. European women don't know such things. Only a few days ago some young English architects visited my office to study our organization. They were astonished at the amount of work we turn out in a day, and the quality and detail of the drawings. We produce twice as much as they are accustomed to do in a day. And you can see for yourself," he shrugged ruefully, "that this is no high-powered operation. Everyone is always taking a coffee break."

"Americans are efficient," Breuer concluded; "Germans are systematic." Gropius has said much the same thing, "The American attitude is 'go and do it.' The European can contribute method." System and method wedded to efficiency: this reciprocity substantially accounted for the success of the Germans in the United States. Even the artist teachers who most profoundly influenced American students, Albers and Hofmann, linked system and method to the American penchant for "action"—to use the word loosely, with reference not only to the painting of improvisatory gesture of Pollock and de Kooning but to the fluxant dazzle of Op as well as to the strident presence of Pop. Surely, system applied to efficiency characterizes Mies's teaching, or rather the start of it.

> Technology is far more than a method,
> it is a world in itself.
> As a method it is superior in almost every respect.
> But only where it is left to itself as in

the construction of machinery, or as in the
gigantic structures of engineering, there
technology reveals its true nature.
There it is evident that it is not only a useful means,
that it is something, something in itself,
something that has a meaning and a powerful form—
so powerful in fact, that it is not easy to name it.
Is that still technology or is it architecture?
And that may be the reason why some people
are convinced that architecture will be outmoded
and replaced by technology.
Such a conviction is not based on clear thinking.
The opposite happens.
Wherever technology reaches its real fulfillment,
it transcends into architecture.[10]

To understand the extension of the European movement in modern architecture to the United States from the twenties through the thirties, one must keep in some sort of balance conditions which in part braked its creative momentum, in part enlarged its influence, and in part insinuated competing possibilities.

As for the braking conditions, these were in the first instance external to the movement. The rise of political dictatorships saw the dissolution of the idealism of that democratic socialism which had especially informed the most creative aspects of German culture, but had also played a role in Italy and Russia. (In the latter countries, the radical cultural movements had been more specifically committed to the existing political structures, Fascism or Communism; but in these countries, too, freedom for creation in the arts began to be curtailed before the end of the twenties.) Gropius' resignation from the Bauhaus in 1928, and the accompanying resignations of Breuer, Moholy-Nagy, Bayer, and Alexander (Xanti) Schawinsky, portended events to come. Aside from such personal reasons as he may have had for leaving, Gropius has stated that he resigned in the hope that his action would save the school against mounting pressure from conservative opposition, much of which he

10. Reproduced in Johnson, *Mies van der Rohe*, p. 203, from an address on the occasion of the celebration of the addition of the Institute of Design to the Illinois Institute of Technology in 1950.

believed was personally directed at him.[11] Then, of course, on top of this political repression, the gathering Depression brought practically all building to a halt.

Had these outside forces not interfered with the modern movement in architecture, would its course in the thirties have been radically different from what it actually became? Or had the movement as a movement achieved its creative peak as a cooperative achievement before the thirties? Without disruption from outside, might it not have fragmented as a group endeavor, or alternatively congealed into uncreative dogma? Answers to these questions are obviously impossible; but what did happen is suggestive. With some exceptions for work in Finland and the Scandinavian countries, the immediate aftermath of the most intense achievement of the movement in the years from about 1926 through 1931 occurred for the most part outside the countries in which it had been centered—that is, outside of Germany, France, and Holland. Further developments in the thirties, with considerable diminution of intensity, occurred in a somewhat desultory fashion in England, and, eventually, with more energy, in the United States. What did happen in the thirties was of course overwhelmingly conditioned by the flight from Hitler's Germany, in many instances by stages, first to England, then to the United States—the "diaspora," as Sibyl Moholy-Nagy has termed it, of the leading German proponents of the modern movement.[12]

For the American bystander, as we have observed, the thirties were a decade of catching-up; but catching-up with an achievement which, if new, was already so well established that the act of absorption could be united with that of popularization. The situation at the beginning of the decade appears most clearly in an event of cardinal importance in the history of the movement. It was accorded a comprehensive exhibition at the Museum of Modern Art in 1932, as one of a series of exhibitions during the thirties by which this newly established institution brought the American public up-to-date on modern art in what must stand as one of the most breathtakingly successful educational enterprises of the twentieth century. Henry-Russell Hitchcock, the first American histo-

11. See, for example, Sibyl Moholy-Nagy, *Experiment in Totality* (New York, 1950), pp. 45ff.

12. Sibyl Moholy-Nagy, "The Diaspora," *Journal of the Society of Architectural Historians*, 24 (March, 1965), 24–26.

rian to have become seriously interested in the progressive aspects of contemporary architecture, and Philip Johnson, the initial curator for architecture and industrial design at the Museum (a post that was innovative in itself) organized the exhibition. They called it "The International Style."

The catalogue bearing this title was destined to become another cardinal document in the movement. It tended to fix the label on the movement, in part because of its very neutrality as opposed to more specific but controversial tags, in part because of the comprehensive and authoritative quality of the presentation. Of course many styles have been international in scope, so whoever would defend as a historical label what came into being as a timely expedient could ultimately justify it only by maintaining that what he meant by the "International Style" had either appeared in *The International Style* or was comparable to what had appeared in this volume. In any event the title indicated the stage of the movement, which Alfred Barr, then the Director of the Museum, underscored in his preface: "there exists today a modern style as original, as consistent, as logical, and as widely distributed as any in the past."[13] There exists a *new spirit*, Le Corbusier had proclaimed in 1922. Ten years later, it was a *new style*. The fact that the movement could be formulated as a "style" suggested that the phase of initial discovery was past; the work of assimilation, diffusion, variation, and popularization had begun.[14]

Two aspects of *The International Style* inadvertently underscored the change of phase.[15] In the first place, the authors could not then know the degree to which all the major works in the "new" style as they defined it had already been realized between roughly 1926 and 1931, the year in

---

13. The most convenient edition of *The International Style* is the paperback edition (New York, 1966), in which Barr's statement appears on p. 11. This edition is especially valuable because it contains a reappraisal of his book and the style it defined, written by Hitchcock in 1951, and also a foreword giving further thoughts on the original volume *and* the reappraisal.

14. The "principles" were pretty much a reworking of such formulations as Le Corbusier's "5 points" in his *Oeuvre complète 1910–1929* (Zurich, 1956), pp. 128ff.

15. For parallel discussions of the situation of modern architecture during the thirties, see my "The International Style in the 1930's," *Journal of the Society of Architectural Historians*, 24 (March, 1965), 10–14; also in the same issue "The Diaspora" by Sibyl Moholy-Nagy (see note 12), and Vincent Scully, "Doldrums in the Suburbs," pp. 36–47.

which they completed their research. What they had intended as an interim report looking toward future glories for the style was more of a summing up. To be sure, the International Style continued at the heart of what was considered to be "modern architecture" throughout the thirties and into the decades following World War II, and many buildings from these decades continued the Style. Yet any historian who used the "three principles" enunciated in the volume would not really have had to go outside their illustrations for his key examples. Indeed, the inadvertently historical quality of the volume contributed to its eventual authority. As time went on, its readers were increasingly justified in feeling that the volume presented, not what the International Style was *as of 1932*, but simply what it was in the timeless present. Meanwhile, the economic freeze on building in the thirties acted to fix the corpus.

The International Style had another inadvertent effect stemming from the esthetic emphasis that Hitchcock and Johnson gave to their definition.[16] They did not fail to link their esthetic principles with certain conditions, primarily technological and practical, that justified these tenets. But they went out of their way (and justifiably for the time) to point out that the Style was not really a Functional or a Machine Style, as it had been either narrowly praised by those of a materialistic mentality, or narrowly condemned by those who saw architecture as a something more than the mere matching of the building to its practical program. Like all important Styles, the authors maintained—and at the time they were prepared to rank the International Style as *the* modern style beside the great styles of the past[17]—this too possessed esthetic significance. True (or at least true enough) and wise (as far as they went); but *The International Style* insufficiently explored the deeper social, psychic, cultural, and symbolic aspects of the movement, which had given it urgency during the twenties. By this omission the Style was reduced to a particular appearance—to a mere "look"—justified in an off-hand manner by some practical observations on function and convenience. In this respect, too, the historical flavor of the book was emphasized, since the "look" had already been achieved, its esthetic principles

16. Specifically emphasized by Barr, in Hitchcock and Johnson, *International Style*, p. 13.

17. *Ibid.*, pp. xiii, 11, 19ff.

already staked out; whereas the idealism that informed the movement during the twenties, the themes from the modern situation which
it confronted, had continuing validity, and called for continuing creativity. But from a strategic point of view, for the education of those
who were catching up, the suggestion in *The International Style* of a
ready-made esthetic, with down-to-earth reasons for employing it, was
surely calculated to spread the doctrine. So much was this the case by
the time Gropius arrived in the United States that he felt called upon in
his initial statement of his intentions at Harvard to assert with some heat
that he meant to teach no "Style," but a "method."[18] To this Hitchcock and Johnson might have replied that any such group endeavor *is* a
style, and that a creative conception of style provides the very "method"
for further development that Gropius advocated.

The thirties also saw challenges from within the modern movement
to the hegemony of the International Style. Nowhere was the confrontation more direct than in the United States, because it was during the
thirties that Frank Lloyd Wright emerged from a period of obscurity
to the professional and popular fame that he maintained for the rest of
his life. He detested what he termed the "cardboard style" of modernism. Although the greatness of his work would have created a counter-
weight to the International Style whatever his nationality, he was especially difficult to ignore in the United States. The nature of his work
and the depth of his understanding of his environment made him *the*
"American" architect. His agrarian bias as opposed to metropolitan
concerns; his individualistic emphasis as opposed to community endeav-
or; his regional and national commitment as opposed to their internationalism: these attitudes, in the context in which he exemplified them,
took on a specifically "American" coloration, abetted by the Song of
Himself as the "democratic" architect. The formal qualities of Wright's
architecture seemed diametrically opposed to those of the International
Style: in his emphasis on the physical properties of materials as opposed
to the abstract qualities of the International Style; on weighty architectural elements intimately bound to the earth as opposed to membranous
boxes lightly stilted above the ground; on complexity of light and

18. See, for example, Walter Gropius, "Architecture at Harvard," *Architectural Record*,
81 (May, 1937), 8–11.

shadow as opposed to the lucid clarity of primal shapes; on the hearth-core for space as opposed to the center-less tension and counter tension of all elements visually tugging at one another in big box-like spaces; on complex perimeters where the building meets its environment as opposed to razor-edge limits. Although Wright's position did not directly influence the Germans, it was impossible, especially in the suburban houses with which Gropius and Breuer began their American careers, to be oblivious to indigenous conditions and attitudes that informed Wright's work.

In the thirties, moreover, tendencies within the International Style itself altered the stereotyped image of the seamless, membranous white box on stilts. A few of these indications appeared in Hitchcock and Johnson's book, among them a vacation house on the Riviera for Madame de Mandrot that Le Corbusier completed in 1930, and the first of several of this kind that he did in the thirties (figs. 1 and 2). Hitchcock and Johnson noted important aspects of dissimilarity between the de Mandrot House and most of the other buildings in their exhibit, although they quite legitimately brought it within the purview of their "principles," and indeed used its example to demonstrate that the "principles" were not narrowly restrictive.[19] The de Mandrot House is an L-shaped box, enclosed in a combination of bearing masonry walls arranged as panel-like entities around the perimeter of the box, and of non-bearing in-fill comprised of rough plaster panels and windows rudely framed in timber. The box, in turn, was solidly set on a stone terrace. Here, the lightness of Le Corbusier's previous boxes gave way to a weightier appearance, the machined look to rusticity, and the metropolitan vision to the regional vernacular. Le Corbusier eventually developed the implications of the de Mandrot House into the massively rough, sculptural qualities characteristic of his architecture after World War II.

Meanwhile, during the thirties, the esthetic of the de Mandrot House was widely exploited by other architects, usually without Le Corbusier's feeling for rugged austerity of form. On the whole, they used the ingredients of Le Corbusier's house to soften the harshness of the International Style by sentimental recall of reassuring textures and traditional image-

19. Hitchcock and Johnson, *International Style*, pp. 48ff.

ry. Rather belatedly, in 1948, the editors of the English *Architectural
Review* could speak of current developments in Scandinavian architecture as the "New Empiricism," which they defined as "the effort to
avoid the stylization of modern forms or formalist theory [of the International Style] by widening the modern idiom to re-include sensible
practices even when they are traditional ones."[20] The article specifically
discussed modern houses in Denmark, where the editors noted that
traditional building had prevailed during the twenties, and the International Style effected changes only by compromising with tradition.
The *Architectural Review* further contrasted the situation in Denmark
with that in Sweden. In Sweden, where the International Style had
been enthusiastically received from the start, with Swedish architects
like Sven Markelius making important contributions to its formulation,
the trend in the forties seemed to be working in the other direction:
from strong prior commitment to modern architecture toward its vernacular modification. In both instances, the editors of the *Review* saw a
happy rapprochement between modern and traditional building. In
Finland, too, where the work of Alvar Aalto was especially familiar to
Americans, substantially because of an exhibition at the Museum of
Modern Art in 1938,[21] a similar movement could be observed in modern architecture. Even in the last years of the twenties Aalto had begun
to rely less on concrete surfaces for his buildings and more on the wood
and plywood indigenous to Finnish building. As early as 1929, moreover, Aalto had employed bentwood in furniture designs (fig. 3), welcomed by many as a relief from the chrome metal finishes that had become a hallmark for the furnishings of the International Style.

In the years immediately following World War II, this rapprochement of modern and traditional vernacular building came to a head.
Sigfried Giedion could speak of the "New Regionalism" in attacking
the very idea of an International Style.[22] He not only pointed to certain
developments of a regional nature then current in modern architecture.
He even indicated regional qualities in the very developments of the

20. "New Empiricism," *Architectural Review*, 103 (1948), 236ff.
21. The catalog of the show appeared as, *Architecture and Furniture: Aalto* (New York, 1938).
22. Sigfried Giedion, "The State of Contemporary Architecture: The Regional Approach," *Architectural Record*, 115 (January, 1954), 132–137.

twenties that Hitchcock and Johnson had considered to be "international"—a *volte face* that indicated as clearly as any evidence could the extent of the attitudinal shift within the movement. In the United States, the New Regionalism was especially congenial. It meant a more popular, less doctrinaire approach to architecture. Moreover, it implied that even the Johnny-come-latelys to modern architecture might make some contribution. This regional point of view came to focus in an exhibition in 1949 at the San Francisco Museum of Art of the redwood modern that was omnipresent on the hillsides surrounding the Golden Gate. The so-called Bay Area Style enjoyed brief popularity in the late forties and early fifties for many who saw it as a portent for the creative development of modern architecture.[23]

If the regional bias became emphatic immediately after the war, the trend was evident at the end of the thirties when the German émigrés reached the United States. Cultural points of view with a regional bent were, moreover, particularly congenial in the United States during the Depression period as a result of widespread poverty and the isolationism fostered by concern with domestic problems. Although much of this regional idealism had its genesis in the preceding decade, the thirties marked the peak of its impact. Southern agrarianism, intense interest in regionalism among sociologists, Steinbeck's *Grapes of Wrath*, Borsodi's ideal of subsistence farming, Wright's Broadacre City, the Tennessee Valley Authority: these are random manifestations of regional enthusiasm during the decade. For present purposes it is especially relevant that Gropius and Breuer participated in this enthusiasm for regional values by adapting the modern idiom to the carpentered vernacular of New England and to the fieldstone masonry of its boulder-bounded fields. But it is equally important to realize that Breuer had visited the de Mandrot House shortly after its completion, even before its owner had moved in.[24] A few years later, in 1936, he had essayed a comparable treatment for the small Ganes exhibition pavilion in England (figs. 4 and 5). In the middle thirties, too, he had followed Aalto's lead in designing

23. The catalog for the show is entitled, *Domestic Architecture of the San Francisco Bay Region* (San Francisco, 1949). Lewis Mumford, who, among others, contributed to the catalog, did much to popularize the Bay Area Style by allusions in various articles praising the regional point of view. See also *Architectural Record*, 106 (September, 1949), 119–126.

24. Interview with the author.

furniture of bentwood and curved plywood (fig. 6). Ten years earlier it was Breuer who had pioneered in the design of the chrome-plated tubular furniture when inspired one day by the handlebars of his bicycle.

If, then, the influential house designs of Gropius and Breuer done shortly after their arrival in New England were "American" in quality, they were far from being the products of an abrupt conversion on stepping on to American soil. And since the Bay Area Style is substantially indebted to Gropius' and Breuer's assimilation of regional influences in New England, it, too, requires more than provincial explanation.

Finally, another kind of transformation in the International Style, occurring less conspicuously in the thirties, warrants brief attention: the tendency to return the Style toward a neoclassical monumentality, austerely stripped. Even as Beaux-Arts academicism was dying in the democratic countries like the United States and Great Britain, it reemerged in the simultaneous retreat from modernity in the Fascist countries.[25] Insofar as modern buildings had been "monumental," this quality occurred integrally in their being "of their time" rather than in any specific endeavor to attain grandiose effects.[26] Whether or not Mendelsohn was influenced by the reactionary trends of the decade, it is ironical that of all the work done by the former leaders of the International Style it should be his series of stone-surfaced buildings in Israel that most nearly resemble the monumentality favored in the Fascist countries. But Mies's major projects of the thirties, designed while he was still in Germany, also show some of the same qualities. The change was less abrupt than in Mendelsohn's work, however, since Mies's lifelong feeling for the great German neoclassicist of the early nineteenth century, Karl Friedrich Schinkel, had inclined him to a graver, more monumental approach even in the twenties.

25. Hellmut Lehmann-Haupt, *Art under a Dictatorship* (New York, 1954), provides an excellent account of the situation in Nazi Germany.

26. The most significant attempt to create a monumental building within the International Style was Le Corbusier's project of 1927–1928 in the competition for a building to house the League of Nations. Even more impressive was his design of 1931 for a similar competition for the Palace of the Soviets, where the building shells are in the International Style (strictly defined), but the roofs of the major halls are hung from a parabolic arch and from structural bends left exposed in an expressive manner which is closer to Constructivism than is typically the case in the predominantly Purist geometry of the International Style.

Mies did not leave Germany until 1938, and then only after some persuasion from Stanley Resor, an American advertising executive who asked him to design a house in Jackson Hole, Wyoming. He has been criticized for his delayed departure; but his apolitical posture, coupled with his loyalty to Germany[27] and a phobia against travel which taxed all of Resor's powers of persuasion, account at least in part for his reluctance to leave. Surely his career has been so unflinchingly dedicated to a quest for truth as to redeem the sense of dismay that he should have acted more falteringly with respect to Nazism than most of his German colleagues of equal stature in the modern movement. In any event, he completed the designs for two major projects while he continued to live in Hitler's Germany, neither of which were built. One was a design for the Reichsbank (completed in 1933); the other, an administrative center for the silk industry (1937) in Krefeld (fig.7) which foundered upon the claims for steel and concrete made by preparations for war.[28] Although without the reactionary flavor of Mendelsohn's contemporaneous buildings, their symmetry and ponderous mass seem to have absorbed the chill of the environment. And in England, Gropius, too,

27. In 1926, Mies had designed a monument in Berlin to the memory of Karl Liebknecht and Rosa Luxemburg which was destroyed by the Nazis. Throughout the twenties he was associated with the socialist aspirations of the modern movement. John B. Rodgers, in an interview with the author, recalled that he had only just arrived in Berlin in 1933 to study at the Bauhaus with Mies when he found the school one morning cordoned off by police under orders from the Nazis to hunt the premises for documentary evidence against Dr. Fritz Hesse, the former socialist mayor of Dessau who had welcomed the Bauhaus to his city in the mid-twenties when reactionary pressures forced its removal from Weimar. After Mies decided eventually to close the Bauhaus in the face of Nazi opposition, he left Germany to set up quarters in the house of a friend on Lake Lugano, inviting some of the architectural students to follow him. There he assigned problems which the students brought once a week to Mies's house. With the first of the plebiscites Mies felt it his duty to return to Germany to vote. Some of the students at Lugano returned with him to Berlin, to maintain the arrangement. Inevitably, some of his former colleagues were bitter that Mies remained in Germany. See comments by Sibyl Moholy-Nagy during the course of a discussion reproduced in the *Journal of the Society of Architectural Historians*, 24 (March, 1965), 83ff. Howard Dearstyne is presently completing a book covering the years of Mies's directorship of the Bauhaus that will throw more light on Mies's career in Germany during the Nazi regime.

28. Again Rodgers supplied the information that Mies accepted his teaching post at what was then the Armour Institute with the stipulation that he be permitted to meet the commitments of his Krefeld commission. He made a trip to Germany for this purpose only to learn of the impossibility of going further with the building, and fortunately returned immediately to the United States.

designed with a heavier hand than had been the case in his work of the previous decade.[29] Such buildings as these by Mendelsohn and Mies and Gropius in the thirties foretell the demands for monumentality in modern architecture that erupted in the fifties, as architects increasingly received commissions for public buildings, churches, university facilities, and corporate headquarters buildings for which varying degrees of grandeur seemed appropriate.

These widespread demands for a self-conscious monumentality, evident in the thirties, only came to a head in the plush days for modern architecture just over the horizon of our essay. At the time, regional concerns and the emergence of Wright's prestige were more conspicuous signs that the International Style had already undergone significant changes in the course of the decade when, belatedly, those Germans who would be particularly influential in the future of American architecture eventually reached their new home.

They came as teachers. Some were called to teaching positions; others almost immediately found themselves in this situation. Teaching was their bridgehead to a new life. But it was also in their blood. Gropius, Breuer, and Mies especially transformed professional training in the United States.

Arriving so late in the decade, they found a receptive climate for their points of view. The battle between ancients and moderns had dragged on in the American professional magazines throughout the decade, with the space devoted to modern architecture, or what passed as such, steadily increasing. Through the middle of the decade, up to about 1937, when the editorial balance seems to have tipped decisively, the magazines reflected the ambiguous attitudes of the profession toward modern architecture. Books, too, other than Le Corbusier's and Hitchcock and Johnson's acquainted Americans with European modernism of the twenties, thereby increasing understanding and, among liberal-minded students, increasing impatience as well for the kind of instruction that Gropius, Mies, and Breuer eventually offered. The authors of those books most influential in the serious popularization of

29. See especially his complex for Impington College in Cambridge (1936), for which Maxwell Fry served as his collaborator.

modern architecture in the United States during the thirties were to a surprising degree German or culturally German. Consider the list, without the culling that would exaggerate the German contribution. It begins with a flurry of publications occurring within a few years of the English translation of *Vers une architecture*. Bruno Taut's *Modern Architecture* and Sheldon Cheney's *The New World Architecture* (both published in 1930) were the popular surveys at the beginning of the decade. Henry-Russell Hitchcock's *Modern Architecture, Romanticism and Reintegration* (1929) studied the modern movement of the twentieth century in relation to its background in a volume admirable for its critical and scholarly acumen. László Moholy-Nagy's *The New Vision* (1928) brought the basic visual education of the Bauhaus to Americans by one of the teachers responsible for its formulation. As the decade unfolded, other influential books appeared. *Machine Art* (1934), with a foreword by Philip Johnson, provided a permanent record of another influential exhibition at the Museum of Modern Art. Walter Gropius' *The New Architecture and the Bauhaus* (1935) was immediately followed by Nikolaus Pevsner's *Pioneers of the Modern Movement* (1936) and by Walter Curt Behrendt's *Modern Building* (1937), both remarkable surveys, with a revised version of Pevsner's work still a standard treatment of its period. The next year, 1938, saw yet another in the notable series of exhibitions prepared by the Museum of Modern Art. *Bauhaus: Weimar Dessau 1919–1928* celebrated Gropius' arrival at Harvard the previous year by presenting a comprehensive showing of the work of the school during the term of his directorship. Herbert Bayer, who only reached the United States in 1938, designed the exhibition and the catalog to which he also contributed editorially, along with Gropius and his wife Ise. (Bayer's work, in turn, eventually became the focus for Alexander Dorner's seminal *The Way Beyond "Art"* published in 1947.) Meanwhile, a series of books made evident the American contributions of the late nineteenth and early twentieth centuries to the modern movement: Lewis Mumford's *Brown Decades* (1931), Hugh Morrison on Sullivan (1935), Hitchcock on Richardson (1936) and later on Wright (1942). Wright's own publications, especially the Kahn lectures at Princeton (1930–31) and *The Disappearing City* (1932), spread his gospel.[30] The

30. Although Wright's buildings, projects, writings, and remarks received desultory

blending of American achievement into accounts of modern architecture made the assimilation of modern ideas the more congenial to Americans in that they could identify the movement with their own past.

Aside from the Americans on this list of authors, and the continuing influence of the writings of Le Corbusier, the rest are German or culturally German. Most of them (Moholy-Nagy, Gropius, Pevsner, Behrendt, Bayer, and Dorner) either had become émigrés by the time their books appeared, or would eventually become such. To this impressive evidence of German influence in the books most important for American understanding of modern architecture in the thirties must be added the most spectacularly influential work in the series, although its publication postdates Gropius' arrival. This is of course Sigfried Giedion's *Space, Time and Architecture*, the first edition 1941, and still going strong, five editions, sixteen printings, and twenty-seven years later. Swiss, but from the German-speaking section of Switzerland, Giedion was especially close to German developments (except that the first edition of *Space, Time and Architecture* contains almost no mention of Mies). A friend of Gropius and Breuer (Breuer had designed a combination house and apartment complex for him in Zurich), and secretary of the influential Congrès Internationaux d'Architecture Moderne,[31] Giedion gave the Charles Eliot Norton Lectures at Harvard in 1938–39, largely at Gropius' instigation. From these lectures, the book emerged. Merely to leaf through the pages is exhilarating, the text euphorically racing along with the illustrations, like the slides with a lecture; but with something of the jolting surprise from image to image that Le Corbusier provided in *Vers une architecture*. The layout by Herbert Bayer makes the most of Giedion's juxtapositions. The sweep of the book, too, is exciting and (perhaps a little unconsciously) epic in its organization. Giedion appears in a heroic quest through space and time for the golden fleece of mod-

------

consideration in the professional press throughout the decade, the major turning point in his professional recognition did not come until "New and Unpublished Work of Frank Lloyd Wright," *Architectural Forum*, 68 (January, 1938), 1–102—a full issue devoted to Wright's work of the thirties.

31. The most recent (fifth) edition of *Space, Time and Architecture* (Cambridge, Mass., 1967), pp. 696–706 include a section on the history and importance of the now-disbanded C.I.A.M.

ern architecture. Departing, with suitable fanfare, from the palatial splendors of the Renaissance and Baroque, he wanders a tortuous path through the difficult terrain of the nineteenth century, finding clues along the way in the most unlikely places (many of them American, to the satisfaction of his American readers), before finally attaining the prize. By the beginning of the forties, American students had added Giedion to Le Corbusier and Hitchcock and Johnson as touchstones of their comprehension of the International Style. For Americans the grandiloquent epic took its place beside the rousing polemic and the didactic corpus.

Even without Giedion's capstone, by the time Gropius, Breuer, and Mies had arrived in the United States the ground had been well prepared —for restless students, indeed, overprepared. Dissension and discontent in professional schools were widespread; student petitions to school administrators were common. How frustrating to "lay down" careful washes in china ink when the headlong scrawl of Le Corbusier's sketches (which served as the modern standard for draftsmanship at the end of the thirties) was immediately at hand! How galling to labor over Renaissance details when those illustrations of Acquitanias, Caproni Explorers, and Sports Torpedos beckoned from his pages—and these liners, airplanes, and automobiles already among the antiques of modernity! It would be callous simplification to say that the three German émigrés who would play the most substantial role in American architecture entered upon their new roles without difficulties; but, in fact, the lateness of their arrival did mitigate the anguish of transition.

Their new situations were wholly different from the circumstances surrounding their teaching at the Bauhaus, as both Gropius and Breuer have remarked. From a school with a precarious hold on resources they came to a massively established university. Although the Harvard students were idealistic in embarking on a program with a modern emphasis after years of a Depression that had affected the architectural profession particularly, they came for the most part from a relatively affluent segment of society with the specific purpose of learning a profession. The same circumstances did not hold for the Bauhaus. The Bauhaus had been a school for general instruction in visual design, where, because of limited funds and the brevity of its existence, the department of architecture was relatively weak despite Gropius' commitment to architecture as the center of his educational philosophy. As a school, the Bauhaus was less an institution than a community infused with an idea and the spirit that went with the idea, both maintained at high pitch by the desperate precariousness of a situation that fostered the extremes of idealism and despair.

"The Bauhaus was starting at zero," Breuer has said. "Everyone knows about the basic design course, and that was important. It changed visual education. But the basic design approach wasn't the Bauhaus. The Bauhaus belonged to its society, and to its time. It was made for a destroyed society. Germany had lost the war. The inflation was terrible. Uncertainty was everywhere. The Bauhaus student was no professional. When I came to the Bauhaus [this was in 1920, the year after Gropius had established the Bauhaus from the merger of two regional art schools] I had no idea what I would become. In those conditions you didn't think about what you would become. The Bauhaus student was nobody. The Bauhaus ideal was starting from zero."

To start from zero was the educational ideal of beginning from fundamentals. Starting from zero was also undertaking what had not previously been done. Because it was so much an idea, so much a matter of spirit, despite its physical embodiment in the familiar building that Gropius provided at Dessau (figs. 20 and 21), the Bauhaus led a perilous existence in the force of its beliefs rather than in its stability as an institution. Starting from zero meant, finally, that the students sought, more than a career, a new world. Or rather, they sought a new world that careers might be possible.

Richard Stein, who went to Harvard during the first year of Gropius' teaching there, recalled talking with Alexander (or Xanti) Schawinsky, one of the former Bauhaus students who was briefly in Cambridge during the early years of Gropius' tenure. "In talking with him I felt that the Bauhaus could have gone in either of two directions: toward nonsense or toward creativity. Those pages in the book on the Bauhaus" (he was flipping the pages of the Museum of Modern Art catalog as he spoke) "that show the wild parties and celebrations, and the preparations the students made for them, seem to me to be more than student high jinks. They are part of the story—the other way that the Bauhaus might have gone." Constructive vision on the one hand, nihilism on the other: the "other way" was painfully close at hand as the void against which the school and its idea must struggle, with the issue no less than the salvation of the modern world.

"The Bauhaus idea as it really existed," Breuer concluded, "could not be transplanted." It was tried in the United States. The Bauhaus catalog for the exhibition at the Museum of Modern Art mentions four attempts.[32] Two of them, the Design Laboratory (later the Laboratory School of Industrial Design) in New York and the Southern California School of Design, had fragile existences. Two others, more substantial, also failed eventually. The first, a rough equivalent at best, was the teaching of Albers and Schawinsky at Black Mountain College, an experimental liberal arts venture of the sort which the Depression period encouraged, with small groups living and working together with Brook Farm enthusiasm. This one initially operated in the columned ramble of a one-time resort and assembly complex near Asheville, North Carolina. It suggested the high-minded, Bauhaus community of young people and teachers finding not only an education but a way of life. The collegiate idea was different, however. So was the agrarian withdrawal from the center of society, and the emphasis on individual development and expression. But the dreams for the institution were large, and, in 1939, Gropius and Breuer even made a model of a grandly stilted and extravagantly glazed structure shaped in a broad curve for a ridge in the mountain. It was the largest single building of their collaborative designs, and the one most completely within the tradition of the International Style as this had been formulated by Hitchcock and Johnson.[33] Of course, nothing came of the scheme. Albers, however, made his initial American reputation in this mountain hideaway, influencing Robert Rauschenberg among others. (Is it going too far to speculate that Rauschenberg's subsequent career might give some inkling of that "other way" for the Bauhaus had circumstances gone differently?) In any event, Albers left Black Mountain in 1949 and, like his architect

32. Pp. 215–217.

33. Illustrated in Fitch, *Gropius*, figs. 103 and 104. Their nearly contemporaneous project for a building to house the visual and performing arts at Wheaton College, also unrealized, shows some of the "American" qualities discussed in the final section of this essay.

friends in Cambridge, entered into his influential career as a teacher of professionals at Yale.

In a genuine attempt to transplant the Bauhaus, László Moholy-Nagy established the New Bauhaus in Chicago in 1937. After its initial financial vicissitudes, it was reconstituted in 1939 as the School of Design (later the Institute of Design), at first through Moholy-Nagy's personal courage and efforts without the aid of the usual trustees. After a few wartime years of bare survival it did obtain more support and some promise of success before his untimely death in 1946. Sibyl Moholy-Nagy has written the sad account of her husband's idealism in the face of continuous fund raising, repeated renovations of dingy warehouse buildings for studios, and the unceasing foraging for gifts of equipment and furnishings. Finally, by the end of the war, the Institute found itself in desperate straits for faculty, at a time when colleges and universities were adding basic design programs (the fruit of The New Vision!) and designers with a Bauhaus stamp had begun to make their way in industry.[34] If the curriculum remained comparable to that of the Bauhaus, Moholy-Nagy's students were more interested in specific careers. As fund raising became difficult and problems mounted, trustees advised increased enrollment, intensified vocationalism, and affiliation with some recognized academic institution. The school eventually did meld into the Illinois Institute of Technology.

Moholy-Nagy held out stubbornly for his own school; but this stand in itself was exhausting. Had he lived, would his valiant efforts have been rewarded?[35] Or would he, too, have found that the more effective way of making an impact in the United States was within the "department"of a large educational establishment? Surely, whatever the strictures against the policy, the way in which the largest American educational institutions vie with one another in their eager embrace of experiment

34. S. Moholy-Nagy, *Experiment*, pp. 139–147. From his American experience Moholy-Nagy supplemented *The New Vision* (then in its third edition) with *Vision in Motion* (Chicago, 1947). On the teaching program in Chicago, as this extended Moholy-Nagy's idea after his death, and with special attention to architecture and industrial design, see also Serge Chermayeff's admirably cogent account: "L'Architecture au Bauhaus de Chicago," *L'Architecture d'Aujourd'hui*, 20 (February, 1950), 50–68.

35. Serge Chermayeff took over the presidency of the Institute of Design after Moholy-Nagy's death. He retained this position from 1946 to 1951, before going to the Harvard School of Architecture in 1953, which he left for Yale in 1963.

and in their concern with the teaching of present points of view is, on balance, a source of strength. This very receptivity of colleges and universities to new ideas, however, discourages alternate kinds of education, however beneficial they may be. Eventually, Sibyl Moholy-Nagy did go to Pratt Institute as an eloquent historian and sharp critic of architecture and design. If Josef Hoffmann succeeded in maintaining his own school of painting, it was because he could work as an individual, whereas education in architecture and design demands collaboration. That the two most successful ventures in architectural education by the German émigrés should have occurred under collegiate and university auspices is hardly surprising.

The two programs—Gropius' at Harvard and Mies's at Illinois Institute of Technology were very different in character. Gropius had made collaboration a central tenet of his architectural philosophy, in the sense that he not only believed in the "team" as a method for success in design and in teaching, but welcomed the competition of different points of view. This attitude had, indeed, accounted for the vitality of the Bauhaus under his directorship. It was a school that came to the position for which it ultimately stood as the result of the collision of varied and even hostile points of view, but guided by conviction about the role of the artist in the modern world and general ideals for his education. If the Bauhaus position never congealed into a dogma, this mainly resulted from the generosity of Gropius' outlook; it also depended to some degree on the circumstance that the Bauhaus only began to discover its position when Gropius left, as well as the changes in administration and the external difficulties that followed his departure. In any event, Gropius brought to Harvard not only his own philosophy but his openness to other progressive ideas.

Because of its fluidity, Gropius' program is more difficult to describe than Mies's.[36] His reputation and enthusiasm for collaboration, together

36. The best idea, although more impressionistic than definitive, of Gropius' teaching at Harvard appears in Paul Rudolph, ed., "Walter Gropius et son École," *Architecture d'Aujourd'hui*, 20 (February, 1950), 1–116. Gilbert Herbert, *The Synthetic Vision of Walter Gropius* (Johannesburg, 1959), is an impressive and succinct statement of Gropius' educational philosophy which Gropius himself endorses. Additional references will be found in William B. O'Neal, *A Bibliography of Writings by and about Walter Gropius* (Charlottesville, Va., 1966), in which references devoted to Gropius' role as an educator are specifically designated as such.

with the wealth and prestige of Harvard and the unsettled world situation, made Cambridge the world center from the late thirties through most of the forties for the exchange of ideas on modern architecture. The continuous coming and going by the stars of the movement, especially the Europeans, as lecturers, critics, and visiting faculty, provided a kaleidoscope of opinion. Even Mies occasionally visited Harvard. In the early years of Gropius' and Breuer's tenure, moreover, Mies's partisan, Philip Johnson, having abandoned his extraordinarily influential curatorship at the Museum of Modern Art to become an architect, enrolled as a student at Harvard. His fellow students were open-mouthed when he proceeded, while still a student, to build himself a Mies-inspired house inside a walled court within a few blocks of the School. The ferment of the school, and the current interests of the students, appeared in the student publication *Task*. Published from 1939 through 1941, it represented the first American student publication dedicated to the cause of modern architecture. Exchanges with the English and Australian student journals, *Focus* and *Smudges*, provided other contacts abroad.

Gropius and Breuer, like Mies, worked personally with the seniors, but principally with the candidates for master's degrees. If the program at Harvard varied at the lower levels depending upon changing interests and instructors, it was solidly grounded in the primary investigations of visual phenomena that had started the Bauhaus student on his way. From the first year to the last, Harvard training emphasized the development of design from the physiological and psychic effects of the basic properties of materials, of elemental shapes, of forthright structure and of simple spatial relationships, as these could be related to functional and community needs. Both Gropius and Breuer liked to take building elements—windows, doors, and stairs, for example—and consider their practical, esthetic, psychic, and symbolic functions, and the range of possibilities that these functions suggested.[37] Of the two, Gropius was more the theoretician, the "world figure" enunciating principle, although intensely interested in concrete detail, in structures, in building processes,

37. Eventually, after Chermayeff joined the teaching staff, he developed this analytical approach of deriving design from the primal elements of building and from systems of such elements as these embraced human needs. He anticipated this program while at the Institute of Design; see note 34. His approach also appears in a book on housing that he did with Christopher Alexander: *Community and Privacy; Towards a New Architecture of Humanism* (New York, 1963).

and in problems of building maintenance. Breuer, in his early thirties when he arrived in the United States and still a bachelor, was inevitably closer to the students. During his years at Harvard, indeed, they not only viewed Breuer as their teacher, but identified with him as the young professional with an international reputation whose achievement could be taken as an omen of the future. The more creative designer of the two as his subsequent American work amply demonstrated, Breuer's early work in furniture design had developed his gifts for designing elegant, yet laconic, building elements and their connections as basic structural systems. He insisted on clear drawings from his students, to show how their buildings went together. To him perspectives intended merely as pretty pictures with which to beguile clients were anathema. Each drawing must display a significant aspect of the total building, as a constructed entity, in space and making space.

Interested as both Gropius and Breuer were in structure and in building processes, it was hardly surprising that, together with their students, they began their American careers by studying American methods of carpentry and of metal framing. Because modest surburban houses comprised their own initial buildings in the United States they gave particular attention to indigenous balloon framing in wood. The lightly nailed, densely positioned two-by-four uprights of balloon framing contrasted with the widely spaced, more heavily timbered post-and-beam construction typical of European carpentry. Giedion's praise in *Space, Time and Architecture* of this midwestern vernacular invention of the nineteenth century was a by-product of their investigations. During at least the first years of their teaching there were many visits to building sites, including of course those on which the two teachers were building the wood and stone houses destined to exert great influence both in the United States and abroad during the immediate postwar years.

Gropius' deductive approach, and his zest for the collision between different points of view, was as happy for Harvard as Mies's inductive discipline for a technological institute little-known for architecture at the time that he joined the faculty.[38] The relative smallness of Illinois

38. On Mies's educational program, see Reginald F. Malcolmson, *Philosophy of Architectural Education* (mimeographed at Illinois Institute of Technology), a copy of a talk given in November 1959; also Howard Dearstyne, "Basic Teaching of Architecture," *Liturgical Arts*, 12 (May, 1944) 56–60.

Institute of Technology, compared to Harvard, made it easier for an individual to impose his point of view in a way that even Mies could hardly have done in a great university. The rigidity and precision of the Miesian discipline was also more readily effected in a technological institute than it might have been in the liberal arts environment of Harvard. In setting his stamp on the architectural program at Illinois Institute of Technology, moreover, Mies was charged by the young president of the Institute at the time, Henry Heald, with the complete design of a new campus.[39] These buildings rising on the south side of Chicago beginning in 1940 embodied his teaching in a vivid manner, its demonstration forcefully at hand for the students, with the impact of the individual buildings as they appeared all the greater because of their knowledge of the total plan to be realized.

John B. Rodgers, who had studied with Mies in Berlin, and in whose office Mies had worked on the Resor commission, has commented on the origin of the program. "Never having been through an architectural or engineering school, Mies simply asked himself what he had had to learn to get where he was. That was the program." The course of study began with elementary exercises designed to give the student control for the "honed" line, as Mies sometimes called it, that he sought in draughtsmanship, and then to teach some fundamentals of vision. In the beginning, Walter Peterhans taught the basic program. He had taught photography in Mies's Bauhaus in Berlin, but was also a gifted mathematician. If anything, this course in fundamentals started at a level more basic than most, with rudimentary problems in ruling lines in india ink, designed to obtain mechanical perfection while dividing the sheet into harmonious segments. The second year, originally Rodgers' province, was wholly devoted to simple structures. It typically began with the design of brick walls, where, in fact, Mies's own education in architecture had begun. His father was a mason, his mother was Dutch, and Mies has always had great feeling for brick. "Architecture begins when you place two bricks *carefully* together," Mies has said. Students had to calculate the brick pattern so that the rows of stretchers

39. President of Illinois Institute of Technology from 1940 to 1952, Henry Heald subsequently became chancellor of New York University in 1952, and president of the Ford Foundation in 1956. After he left, Mies was replaced by other architects for buildings at Illinois Institute of Technology. Hence he did not complete his scheme for the campus.

(bricks with their long dimension at the face of the wall) and headers (bricks with their ends to the face of the wall, to create a bond through its thickness) came out precisely without breaking a brick, and with maximum strength in bond. They built walls of building blocks scaled to brick. They drew these walls in isometric perspective, brick for brick, in the precise unshaded linear drawing for which Mies was famous—very different from the Beaux-Arts mode of quickly indicating a brick texture by means of a wash and a few penciled lines to suggest texture, with the label "brick, flemish bond," as a cue for the mason to go his way. Such problems not only perfected drawing ability and provided meticulous knowledge of structure, but taught the student to think in structural terms down to the brick. Mies always disliked the term "design." To him, buildings were not "designed," but "developed" from soundly conceived structure. Equally rudimentary problems and equally demanding drawings of structures in other basic materials followed. History, too, came to the students in terms of structure, with examples from the past (especially simple vernacular buildings) used to point up the various studies.

Proportion received steadily increasing attention, first in the structural problems; later, and especially in the third year (originally Ludwig Hilbersheimer's province), the study of proportion was more centrally pursued. Studies of proportion also developed from normative structural sections and spans. In his own work, Mies has never believed in ideal geometrical schemes, but rather in an empirical approach to proportion, with full-scale mock-ups of sections, moldings, and connections to see how they really looked—a practice for which his office became famous. A favorite exercise for students was alternate schemes for the proportioning of the same skeletal elevation, first in steel, then in reinforced concrete, such as Mies himself has published. The third year also saw investigations of space, beginning with problems characteristically simple, and treated with characteristic gravity. How could a table and some chairs be placed in a room? There were simple problems in function too. How should basic kitchen equipment be arranged in a given rectangle?

In this year and the next, Hilbersheimer also introduced the students to city planning as he had done with Mies in Berlin. Hilbersheimer typically started by erasing streets from the Chicago grid, until he had created a spinal road for major transport, with commercial and manufacturing facilities ranged along it. Widely spaced spur streets off this central spine—all that remained ideally, after the progressive eliminations—provided access for housing, with each residential salient separated from the next by a tongue of open space occasionally spotted with schools and other community facilities (fig. 8). The structural severity and purity of Hilbersheimer's scheme retained much of the rigidly rationalized organization of the *Siedlungen* or Central European housing developments of the twenties, with their long, narrow apartment buildings ruthlessly regimented for optimum conditions of light, air, and sun (fig. 9). Typically, in the American environment, Hilbersheimer loosened the rigidity of the *Siedlung*, allocated more space to single houses, and gave greater emphasis to the transportation spine. There was, moreover, an unbounded quality in Hilbersheimer's American schemes, as though the throughway with its vertebral branchings could be endlessly extended in the expansiveness of the prairie. The organization of the scheme was "organic" in the sense in which Mies uses the adjective, where design is utterly integral with structure and each part clearly articulated and defined in its working relation to all other parts within a harmonic order. The Miesian scheme contrasted markedly with that other kind of "organic" image in greenbelted loops, with building informally clustered around central business and shopping cores (fig. 10). The latter became the publicized norm for Harvard, although Harvard planning actually took various forms. The contrast characterized the different tempers of the two schools: Gropius rather more genially and casually adapting himself to the most progressive aspects of the American suburban tradition (at least through the war years);[40] Mies hewing to the more rigorous order of the commercial and factory framing associated with the big city and with the implacable grid of its streets.

40. Not until the fifties in his own work in the United States did Gropius (with The Architects Collaborative) venture into planning schemes for the central city. Then, in 1953, he did a scheme for the South side of Chicago, including the campus of Illinois Institute of Technology, which therefore invites direct comparison with Hilbersheimer's schemes, and a proposal, with other Boston architects, for the area now occupied by Prudential Center. Thin as the buildings were individually, the overall scheme was far superior to what was finally built from designs by other architects. See especially, S. Giedion, *Gropius*, pp. 84–90 and plates.

Despite differences in approach between Gropius' and Mies's programs, they both believed in a visual language of simple, clear, elemental forms as the "objective" basis for architectural education. They both emphasized structure and technology which was normative and standard rather than radical and extraordinary (in, say, the manner of Buckminster Fuller's geodesic domes). Both programs accepted what is laconically given in modern American society and made this the starting point for their programs.

These attitudes are general in architectural education today and create no stir. But this in itself testifies to the extent of the émigrés' achievement. Their educational methods and goals, in conjunction with comparable tactics in other areas of visual education also domesticated in the United States during the same decade under the same general auspices, have transformed professional training in the visual arts. The end result has been to transform lay education in the visual arts as well.

Had their teaching programs been the sole contributions of the émigré architects to the culture of their adopted country, they would have contributed handsomely. But there are their buildings too, especially those of Gropius, Breuer, and Mies. All three men have taught by examples as well as precept—Breuer more, ultimately, than Gropius, and Mies most of all.

As for the houses that Gropius and Breuer designed between 1939 and 1941, how tidy the generalization could be had it been a simple matter of their stepping ashore in New England, discovering its vernacular of carpentry and stone walls, and radically modifying the machine-like precision and austerity of their European style! Unfortunately, as already indicated, what happened was not that simple. The development of the two architects after their separation demonstrates that Breuer is more responsible than Gropius for the style of their collaborative works; and Breuer at least had tentatively picked up some aspects of his "New England" style prior to his arrival.

How easy, too, to make the comparable generalization about Mies's work. He came to Chicago and saw the straightforward use of metal skeletal construction, boldly in-filled with glass, that characterized the tall office buildings put up at the end of the nineteenth century—the buildings that Sigfried Giedion popularized as the group achievement of the "Chicago School." Here, unhappily, the neat generalization collides with Mies's own denial, in an interview with the critic Katherine Kuh.

I really don't know the Chicago School. You see I never walk. I always take taxis back and forth to work. I rarely see the city. In 1912 when I was working in the Hague I first saw a drawing by Louis Sullivan of one of his buildings. It interested me. Before I came to Chicago I also knew about Frank Lloyd Wright and particularly about the Robie House. . . . As to your question, no: living in Chicago has had no effect on me. When I first arrived, I immediately went to the campus of the then Armour Institute (now the Illinois Institute of Technology). I felt I ought to turn around and go home.[41]

The spectacle of Mies foiling the art historian's generalization by taking taxis has its ludicrous, and humbling, aspect. Whether or not the shell of a taxicab insulated Mies as completely from his environment as he asserted, in essence what he said is undoubtedly true. Mies has always been a fundamental thinker about buildings, engrossed in the study of theoretical buildings in ideal sites whenever he had no commissions, which in Europe was most of the time. His hatred of travel is in itself an indication that he might not be an enthusiastic sightseer. Rodgers, who often translated for Mies during his first years in Chicago, has underscored Mies's self-sufficiency in recalling that he remained perfectly content to wall himself in his native tongue for four years before making any effort to speak English, much as he walled himself in taxicabs in his travels through the Chicago streets.

Yet, though the generalizations that come first to mind are too crude, changes did occur in the work of the German architects after their arrival in the United States, changes that depended in some degree upon their new situation. During the period of their initial collaboration, Gropius and Breuer admittedly studied the vernacular building of New England, to which prior predilections in Breuer's work stemming from Le Corbusier's de Mandrot House (figs. 1 and 2), such as the Ganes pavilion (figs. 4 and 5), could only have predisposed them. Though Breuer while still in England had begun to use wood as a subordinate structural material in some of his buildings, he certainly had had no

41. Katherine Kuh, "Mies van der Rohe: Modern Classicist," *Saturday Review of Literature*, 48 (January 23, 1965), 61.

recourse to balloon framing. In his American houses done with Gropius in the years immediately following their arrival, wood was often the sole material or, where combined with stone, the main material. In this respect, these houses reveal the sea change that traditionally modified European masonry styles from the colonial period onward.

Yet to press the issue further: where Gropius and Breuer frequently mixed masonry with wood in these houses, did the use of stone indicate an enthusiasm for the stone walls of New England or a fond recollection of Europe? Breuer's Preston Robinson House (1946–1947) in Williamstown, Massachusetts (figs. 11, 12, and 13), is a case in point. It typifies on a luxurious scale the group of houses done during the period of their collaboration, even though the partnership had dissolved prior to this commission. The modest height of the masonry elements of the Robinson House in contrast to the ground-to-roof height in the de Mandrot and Ganes designs do evoke the fieldstone enclosures of the local pastures. More important, the low spread of the Robinson House, generously open to its extravagant acreage differs markedly from the stringent boundaries of European boxes like the de Mandrot House or Breuer's own Harnischmacher House (figs. 14 and 15). To be sure, the box made of planes, disposed freely in space instead of along the perimeter, had previously appeared in the Ganes pavilion, but timidly, with the planar elements arranged to make a compact whole. Here the emphatic spread of the walls, and even their low parapeted quality suggest Wright (fig. 19). So does the relative prominence of the stone hearth and the roof with its extravagant overhang vaguely reminiscent of the roof tilts of Taliesin West.

In the days of their purist enthusiasm for "modernity," architects working in the International Style would generally have scorned as sentimental archaisms the ground-hugging spread of the Robinson House, its fireplace and sloping roof, let alone its candid use of traditional materials. All violations of *l'esprit nouveau*. But another influence shows itself in the Robinson House—a general reminiscence of Mies's project for a country house done as early as 1923 (figs. 16 and 17). Mies conceived his theoretical project as a construction of discrete panels, partly of brick, partly of plate glass, tensely distributed in right-angled opposition to one another across varied intervals of space. Sliding beneath a horizontal roof plane, the primal elements come together as a configuration of equilibrated tensions within a continuous field of force to make a house. It is perhaps the best echo in modern architecture during the twenties of the contemporary demonstration in physics of the equivalence of energy and matter. Mies, in turn, has admitted the influence of Wright and of the Robie House in particular[42] on his own work of the early twenties. The way in which the planes of the Robie House slide past one another in space (figs. 18 and 19) especially applies to the project of 1923 as one of the few buildings by architects working in the International Style to emphasize the open spread of the building rather than its containment. In the Robinson House, therefore, the right-angled dichotomy of the planar composition of elements precisely and abstractly organized with respect to the ground as a flat plane recalls the very project of Mies's from the twenties which is most akin to Wright's feeling for form. This rediscovery of Mies's early project, occurring at a time when both Mies's work and Wright's assumed fresh relevance for a younger generation, is here so organized by Breuer as to create a Corbusian-like box in the manner of the de Mandrot House. Breuer assimilates all of these influences into his design, but they come together as part of the accumulated potential of the modern movement, to result in a work that only Breuer could have done.

Hence the impossibility of distilling the "international" from the "American" influences in the work of the émigrés. The American ingredients in the situation are less specific than catalytic. The apparent finesse with which Breuer combined diverse approaches from the earlier development of modern architecture into a new statement may of course represent a phenomenon common to that stage in any movement when a period of consolidation follows a period of rapid and varied innovation. In this instance, however, there is reason to believe that the American situation was particularly congenial to the kind of synthesis apparent in the Robinson House. The impatiently receptive temper and headlong tempo of the American assimilation of the International Style fostered

42. See notes 5 and 41. It is also worth mentioning that Mies's Barcelona Pavilion of 1929, which grew out of his project of 1923, seems to have influenced Wright's work of the early thirties, so that ideas from these two architects are during the thirties to a degree pre-assimilated for those like Breuer who would borrow from both. See Vincent Scully, "Wright vs. the International Style," *Art News*, 53 (March, 1954), 32–35.

the tumbling together of *all* that had happened in Europe, while increasing the mix by confronting the European achievement with native traditions and circumstances. This generous, even heedless, embrace of so many possibilities, coupled with the circumstance that Europe was in no position to effect any synthesis at all meant that the phase of consolidation and eclecticism concluding a period of innovation had to occur in the United States.

After World War II current building in the United States for the first time made an immediate impact on international developments in architecture, as compared to its fragmentary and peripheral influence during the twenties. Histories of the modern movement which had begun, in the thirties, to interweave the account of American contributions with those of Europe, acknowledge the steadily expanded role of American accomplishment and influence after the war. Whether as architects, teachers, or historians, the German émigrés played an important role in shaping America's new and decisive position in modern architecture around 1950.

If the American situation in the late thirties and forties favored assimilative forces within the modern movement, it favored as well the concomitant trend toward popularization of what had been an *avant garde* movement. Americans felt none of the ideological urgency which had brought the International Style into being as a quest for a comprehensive objectivity consonant with the facts and aspirations of the modern world. For them, it was a ready-made Style with an established esthetic conditioned by certain practical considerations that made it appropriate for its time, and hence "modern" in a prosaic and universally acceptable rather than ideological or spiritual sense.

In an environment which would fold Wright into the International Style, the folkish virtues of his point of view, agrarian, democratic, and "native," inevitably sped and conditioned the process of popularization. Surely, Breuer's Robinson House, beautifully abstract as it is, is intrinsically more popular in its appeal than the Harnischmacher House. Even those who might feel it too extreme could readily imagine ways to dilute the abstractness still further toward a more conventional "hominess."

Sophisticated architecture of the sort represented by the Robinson

House thus lent itself to progressive degradation toward the entropy of "picture windows," "storage walls," "pass throughs," "carports," and "decks" that speedily became by-words—or buy-words—for developers and editors of the popular "homemaking" journals. Fired by the immense resources for consumption and the American passion for novelty, the suburban and commercial emphasis in modern architecture in the United States until after 1950 served to accelerate the process of popularization. So did a diminution of its earlier utopian fervor with respect to urban design and housing, with the result that greenbelt schemes and Le Corbusier's skyscraper city of 1922 remained the only visions of community design until well into the sixties. So, finally, did the vast development in the technological sophistication of modern buildings which also claimed the architect's time and imagination. It was principally American technology during the forties that made feasible, for example, the persistent vision of the glass skyscraper in modern architecture. Only the invention of the mechanical equipment, the tinted glass, the surfacing materials, the sealants, made this "functional" image functional, this "machine for living-in" fully inhabitable.

    Whatever the benefits of this popularization, its inevitable cost was a blandness of both visual qualities and theoretical commitment in most modern architecture. Thus, for all its quality, the Robinson House does not possess the rugged force of Le Corbusier's de Mandrot House. As Vincent Scully has pointed out in further comparisons with Le Corbusier, the same may be said of Breuer's subsequent work, admirable, inventive, and influential as this has been.[43] The blandness of most architecture by the late forties is more evident in Gropius' work, as in the mildness of the Harvard Graduate Center (completed 1949; figs. 22 and 23) compared to the tautness of the Bauhaus (figs. 20 and 21). Whereas Breuer's American work is informed by a coherent philosophy of architectural form based upon an inventive constructivist esthetic and a superlative building craftsmanship, Gropius' work loses a sense of commitment. Pleasant enough as a student domicile, would the Graduate Center occa-

    43. V. Scully, "Doldrums in the Suburbs," *Journal of the Society of Architectural Historians*, 24 (March, 1965), 39–43, and John Jacobus, *Twentieth-Century Architecture: The Middle Years 1940–65* (New York and Washington, 1966), pp. 35–62 *passim*. I shall also be discussing Breuer in my forthcoming *Buildings in American Architecture: Rockefeller Center to the Sixties*.

sion much comment except that it is by Gropius? How does one relate the Pan-Am Building in New York, on which Gropius and Pietro Belluschi were consultants, with the Graduate Center, or either with Gropius' intrinsically finer, but hardly profound, building for the American Embassy in Athens, which melds the International Style with the image of the Parthenon? These buildings are not without quality, but they are essentially without personality and without the intense social and philosophical commitment of his work of the twenties. Although appropriate solutions for specific problems (if in fact the Pan-Am Building meets this test), they lack the inner imperative for being what they are that marked the Bauhaus.

As for Mendelsohn, he fared the worst. In a series of synagogues that comprise his principal American achievement, and influenced much subsequent synagogue design, he attempted to return to the expressionism of his first works around 1920. Of those he was able to complete, his Synagogue in Cleveland is the most impressive (fig. 24). A single image suffices to raise disturbing questions: does the massing make a coherent composition? Where the expression of monumentality might have depended on the weighty quality of the forms, or alternatively on the opposite expressive extreme of soaring lightness, do they here positively assert themselves either way? Do dome and windows relate to one another? Or the materials of the dome and the wall? Is the detailing of the windows anything but confused and heavy?

For present purposes the relevant question is the degree to which this blandness represents the cost of success in the American situation. Again assessment is complicated because evidences of lessened force in design appeared in the work of Gropius and Mendelsohn in the thirties before they reached the United States, and even in the work of Mies. In fact, Gropius' weakest works, like Mies's, occurred then. (Since Breuer's first completed building, the Harnischmacher House, dates from 1932, comparison with earlier achievement is impossible in his case.) A diminution in the intensity of expression appears to have been another of those tendencies in modern architecture that were world-wide in the thirties, a let-down in the creative impetus of the International Style, and not specifically attributable to the American environment in which the Germans came to work. As if to clinch the point, the thirties marked a period of great achievement for Wright. Perhaps the best formulation would be that the turbulence of the American development resulting from the efforts of assimilation and popularization, together with the profusion and variety of commissions that suddenly came the architect's way, did little to counter the relaxation that customarily accompanies the success of any radical venture.

On the other hand, the very turbulence of the American situation forced innovation to the point of distraction, encouraged facile novelty with bewildering rapidity. In this forcing environment, to which the German émigrés themselves contributed substantially, they fared differently. In the case of Mendelsohn, if his new environment did not destroy him neither did it help. Gropius has been successful, but in no consistent way; his fame secure, his work at the close of his career blurs his former "position" to that of the merely distinguished professional. Breuer, and especially Mies, who remained most faithful to the old cause amid the distractions of their new environment, have pursued the steadiest careers.

For both of them the source of their strength has been the long-standing German admiration for American technology. The principal change effected by their actual transfer to America was their greater emphasis on the discrete unit and its assemblage to make the building. The American structural tradition favored the frame rather than the wall and depended on a high degree of prefabrication of building parts that could be assembled rapidly and easily by a labor force that, by European standards, was at once scarce and expensive, in part specialized and in part ill-trained. Throughout the history of the modern movement in the United States, from Sullivan through Wright to the American adaptation of the International Style, this expression of the frame and the prefabricated part marks a difference (not absolute but decisive) from characteristic European practice.[44] Mies's concern with the frame and the prefabricated part in his American work is obvious. But a comparison of the Robinson with the Harnischmacher House reveals the same tendency in Breuer. Whereas the membrane-enclosed box dominates the earlier work, the later design appears as a structure of parts, with the frame especially evident. The same transformation occurs in

44. See my "PSFS: Its Development and its Significance in Modern Architecture," *Journal of the Society of Architectural Historians*, 21 (May, 1962), 47–83.

schemes for prefabricated housing on which Gropius had worked while at the Bauhaus and again with Konrad Wachsmann beginning in 1943 while at Harvard. Although all his experiments with prefabrication depend on jointed panels, Gropius did whatever he could to minimize the separateness of the units in his German work, whereas in his American experiments he intensified the sense of their discreteness to make visible their coming together to build the building.[45] In short, the emphasis on the container in Europe becomes an emphasis on the component in America.

Yet Breuer was interested in the Constructivist movement while in Europe, as the mast and the guy wires supporting the pipe frame for the sundeck of the Harnishmacher House display. Hence what may be termed the constructivist tendencies in his American work, *i.e.*, the use of structure in the quasi-sculptural manner typical of furniture design, cannot automatically be labelled as "American." It might also be argued that modern architecture in Europe during the thirties was slowly moving toward a greater use of prefabricated parts (for example, the precast concrete slabs and other units that Le Corbusier began to have moved to the site and derricked into position). Given Breuer's interests, his architecture would surely have reflected this development had he remained in Europe. Yet in this event his constructivism would surely have differed from that which he absorbed from his study of American building. Additionally, it is probably true that the constructivist innovation in his work would have occurred more gradually, perhaps in a more piecemeal fashion, and possibly not have gone as far. In coming to the United States Breuer had to rethink his architecture completely. In the early houses he did with Gropius, he had literally to work through his previous building experience, to redesign detail by detail, in a confrontation of different technologies, different modes of life, and different images. The completeness of the "shake-up" accounted for the change, while the coherence of Breuer's own architectural philosophy enabled him to withstand the shaking. Acceptance of the new situation, but resistance too: this is usually the fruitful formula if the displaced creator continues to be creative.

45. S. Giedion, *Gropius*, pp. 74–78, and especially the plates 193–200, conveniently demonstrate the point.

This applies to Mies too, with the difference that he seemingly maintained a greater aloofness from his new environment. At least he did not deliberately set out to explore it in the manner of Gropius and Breuer. But would he have developed elsewhere his steel skeletal esthetic visibly assembled of discrete components which are either standard structural elements or custom designed in their image (figs. 25 and 26)? He might have. After all, use of discrete components to make the building appears more vividly in his work of the twenties than in that of any other leaders who worked in the International Style. The clearest examples of this interest, his project of 1923 (figs. 16 and 17) and the Barcelona Pavilion, are widely spaced episodes. The components, moreover, are not only custom designed but conceived more as visual entities—that is, as linear and planar constructions in space—rather than as the frankly *technological* entities that he employed in his American work.[46]

But the argument that Mies *might* have come to something like the Lake Shore Apartments had he remained in Germany can be pushed further. He had the example of his old master, in the exposed metal framing of Peter Behrens' Turbine Plant (1909) in Berlin (fig. 27). With Mies's awareness of all kinds of structures, this image from the past might have returned to him had he continued to live in Germany. There was surely the steel with which to have built it. Moreover, in his final project in Germany, that of 1937 for the administration building for the silk industry in Krefeld (fig. 7), he had used the exposed skeletal frame (in this instance in reinforced concrete rather than in steel) as the elevational esthetic for the building. Since this was his final design prior to his departure for America, it suggests that, even had he remained in Europe, he might have moved toward a more overtly structural esthetic. As in his American work, this structural image opposed itself to the typical building in the International Style, with its supporting frame enclosed within the membranous wall, partly glass, partly a seamless concreted surface and stretched as a container around it.[47] Even here,

46. Of all Mies's projects of the twenties the one that most closely approaches his American structural esthetic is his project for a reinforced concrete office building of 1922.

47. That the Krefeld project might have represented an altered point of view for Mies with long-range possibilities whether or not he had gone to America is underscored by its contrast with the immediately preceding project for the Reichsbank where the treatment of the wall remains very much within the canonical International Style. With respect to

however, Mies used the frame to emphasize the overall volume of the building—the box of space enclosed rather more than its structural matrix. Insofar as one can tell from photographs of the model, the volumetric emphasis of the Krefeld project appears partly because the structural grid maintains the surface of the enclosing skin, instead of asserting its independence, partly because the skeleton appears as a homogeneous grid rather than as an opposition of horizontals against verticals and of one component against another. In both respects Mies's American work develops the structural image beyond the Krefeld project. But the start was there; and this in the project that immediately precedes his departure for America. Had circumstances been different would the "American" style have emerged in due course in Berlin?

Whatever Mies *might* have done had he stayed in Europe with respect to the creation of a straightforward, structural esthetic, he did it in the United States. And tightly as he may have incarcerated himself in taxicabs, he nevertheless immediately sensed that steel framing was the standard means of construction for commercial and large-scale buildings in the United States. At least it was on his arrival, although the war and the subsequent rise in steel prices immediately thereafter made reinforced concrete technology competitive with steel construction for standard framing for the first time in American building history. Mies also consulted with American engineers in designing his buildings. It is important to underscore what has already been mentioned: how very different Mies's first American buildings in his skeletal esthetic comprised of prefabricated components were from the Krefeld project, where the skeleton existed as a monolithic poured entity. To combine the image of structure and assemblage in an esthetic that made straightforward use of standard construction and standard components, both of which had been regarded as in themselves anti-esthetic, gave the structural image a force of wholly new magnitude. The conjunction of circumstances that made Mies's contribution seem so natural in the

---

the Krefeld skeleton as a partial anticipation of Mies's work in the United States, it is at least marginally interesting that Gropius and Meyer submitted just such a skeletal project in the competition of 1922 for the Chicago Tribune tower as though they would acknowledge the dominance of this kind of structure in the United States. In his subsequent work of the twenties, however, Gropius did not further develop the exposed skeleton.

American environment might possibly have been forced in Germany. This, however, is doubtful, though not as improbable as that Breuer should have produced his wooden and fieldstone houses with Gropius had he remained in Germany.

A final question needs asking. Had both of these kinds of building somehow appeared in Europe, would they have appeared to such effect? Would they have seemed as appropriate to the European as to the American situation; and if not, would they have made their way as they did in this country? To produce a Barcelona Pavilion as a set-piece in the modern movement, to produce a Harnischmacher House as an exceptional example: this is one thing. To put up building after building, to develop an esthetic with the opportunity to work on variations and to explore possibilities is another matter. Breuer, a young man when he reached the United States, had built but three houses (or at least house-sized buildings) in a ten-year period. Philip Johnson's study of Mies reveals but seventeen completed buildings during his European practice of roughly twenty-five years—eight of these being displays for exhibitions, the largest of them four-story apartment houses. Except for furniture design, for both architects everything else was a project. In the United States they found full careers. The affluence of the society and the congeniality of their work to the new environment were cardinal factors in their success, both economic and architectural. But something would also seem to be owed to the willingness of Americans to take risks, to their enthusiasm for innovation and experiment. At least the American record with respect to the émigré architects from Germany shines by comparison with the French response to Le Corbusier, and makes one wonder how differently his career might have ended if he could have tolerated an environment in which the Germans thrived.

The émigré architects, like the German émigrés in other professions, richly repaid the generous response of their new country.

G. 1. Terrace elevation.

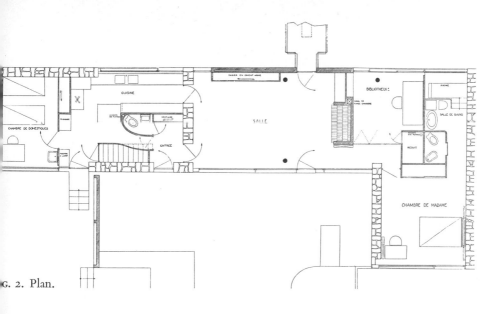

G. 2. Plan.

Corbusier: De Mandrot House, Le Pradet, France, 1930–31 (*Oeuvre complète*, permission of itions Girsberger, Zurich).

FIG. 3. Alvar Aalto: Chair with bent plywood frame, 1929 (Museum of Modern Art, New York)

FIG. 4. Exterior view.

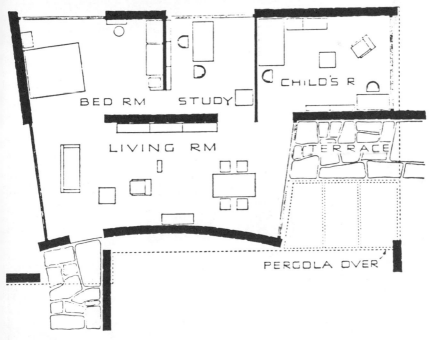

BED RM STUDY CHILD'S R

LIVING RM TERRACE

PERGOLA OVER

FIG. 5. Plan.

Marcel Breuer, with F. R. S. Yorke: Ganes Pavilion, Bristol, England, 1936 (courtesy of the architect).

FIG. 6. Marcel Breuer: "Isokon" chair in bent plywood, 1935
(courtesy of the architect).

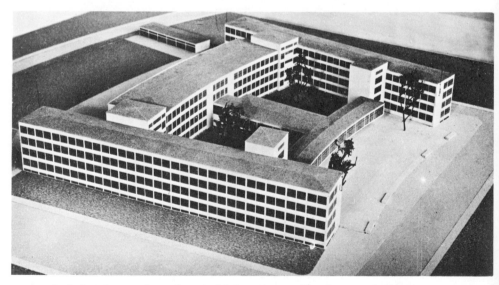

FIG. 7. Ludwig Mies van der Rohe: Model for a projected headquarters building
for the silk industry, Krefeld, Germany, 1937 (courtesy of the architect).

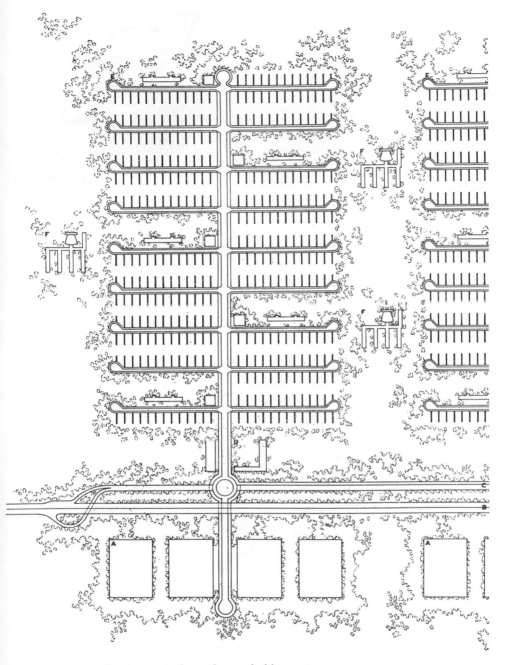

FIG. 8. Ludwig Hilbersheimer: Scheme for an ideal linear city
from *The New City*, 1944 (permission of Paul Theobald & Co.).

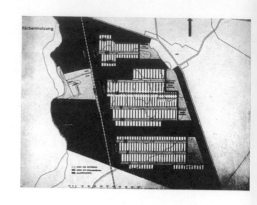

FIG. 9. Walter Gropius: Site plan for Siedlungen, Berlin, 1929 (courtesy of the architect).

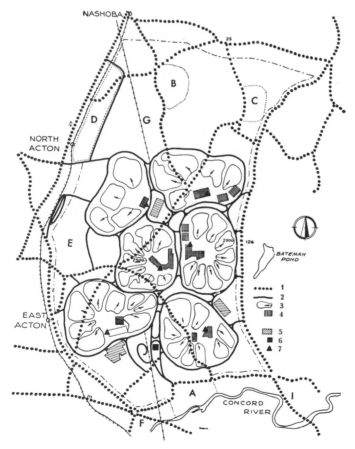

FIG. 10.
Walter Gropius,
with Martin Wagner
and John Harkness:
Scheme for six
townships near
Boston, Massachusetts,
with loop roads
and greenbelts, 1942
(courtesy of
the architect).

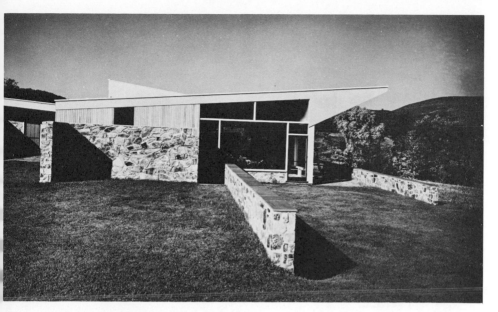

FIG. 11. Exterior of the living room from the entrance side.

FIG. 12. Interior of the living room.

Marcel Breuer: Preston Robinson House, Williamstown, Massachusetts, 1946–47 (copyright Ezra Stoller; plan courtesy of the architect).

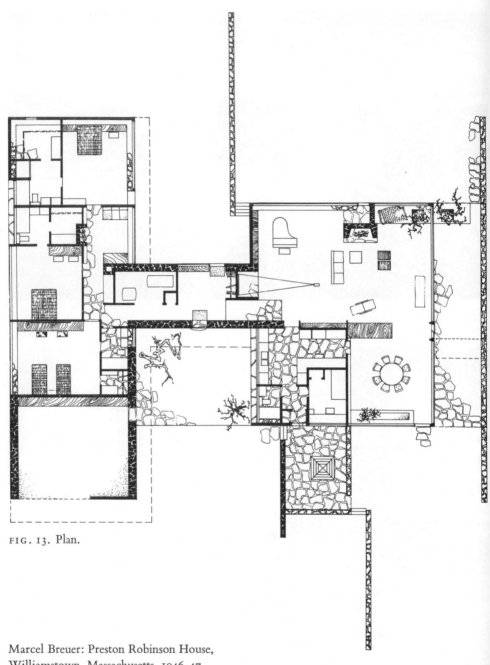

FIG. 13. Plan.

Marcel Breuer: Preston Robinson House,
Williamstown, Massachusetts, 1946–47
(copyright Ezra Stoller;
plan courtesy of the architect).

FIG. 14. Exterior from the garden.

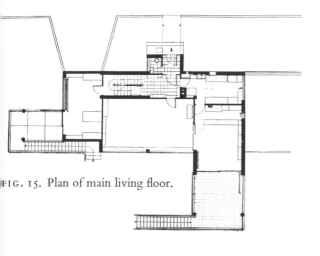

FIG. 15. Plan of main living floor.

Marcel Breuer:
Harnischmacher House,
Wiesbaden, Germany, 1932
(courtesy of the architect).

FIG. 16. Elevation.

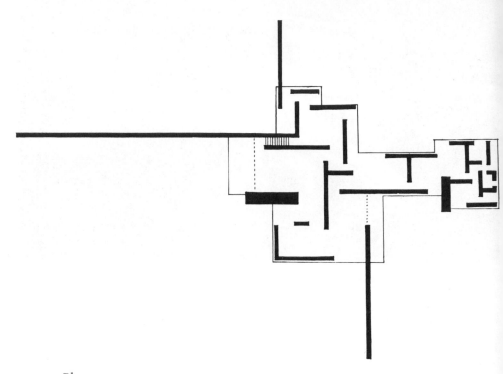

FIG. 17. Plan.

Ludwig Mies van der Rohe: Project for a brick country house, 1923 (courtesy of the architect).

FIG. 18. Front elevation.

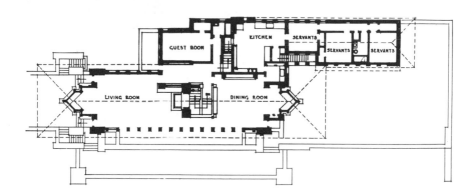

UPPER FLOOR

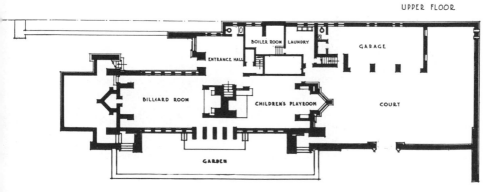

LOWER FLOOR

FIG. 19. Plans of ground and principal floors.

Frank Lloyd Wright: Fred Robie House, Chicago, 1908 (Chicago Architectural Photo Company; plans from H.-R. Hitchcock, *In the Nature of Materials*).

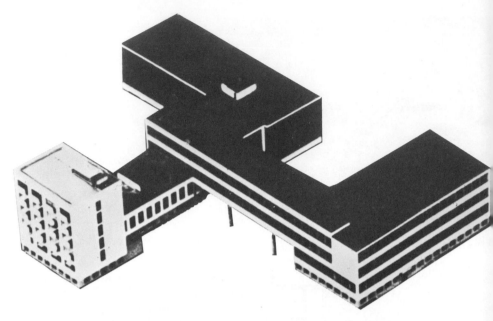

FIG. 20. Air view.

FIG. 21. View of the buildings, northwest elevation showing, left to right,
workshop block, classrooms and community facilities, and dormitory block.

Walter Gropius: Bauhaus, Dessau, Germany, 1925–26 (Museum of Modern Art, New York).

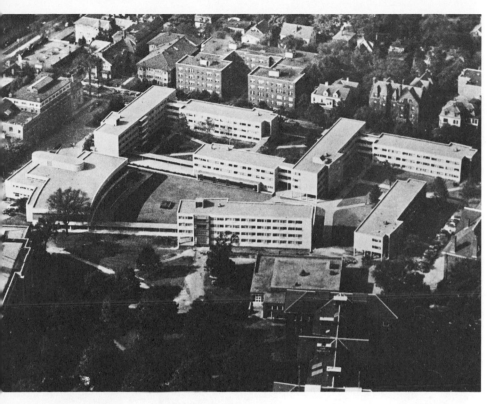

FIG. 22. Air view (Roger M. Burke).

FIG. 23. View of the campus (Fred Stone).

Walter Gropius: Graduate Center, Harvard University,
Cambridge, Massachusetts, completed 1949.

FIG. 24. Erich Mendelsohn: Synagogue and Community Center,
Cleveland, Ohio, 1946–52 (Hans Schiller).

FIG. 25. General view (Hedrich–Blessing).

Ludwig Mies van der Rohe: Apartments at 860 Lake Shore Drive,
Chicago, Illinois, 1948–51.

FIG. 26. Structural cross section
          (courtesy of the architect).

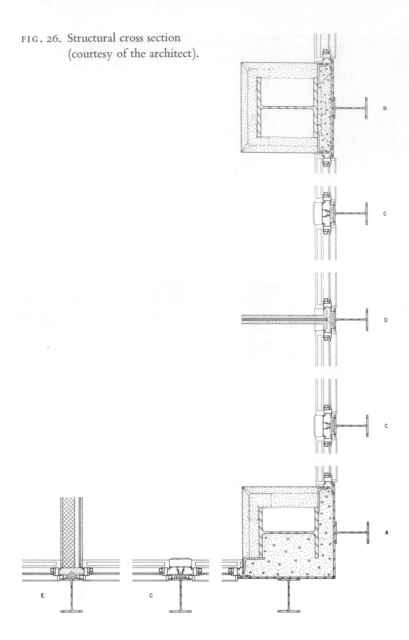

Ludwig Mies van der Rohe: Apartments at 860 Lake Shore Drive,
Chicago, Illinois, 1948–51.

FIG. 27. Peter Behrens: Turbine Plant for Allgemeine Elektrizitäts Gesellschaft, Berlin, 1908.

KUNSTGESCHICHTE AMERICAN STYLE: A STUDY IN MIGRATION

by COLIN EISLER

I shall not die without a hope that light and liberty are on steady advance. We have seen, indeed, once within the records of history, a complete eclipse of the human mind continuing for centuries. And this, too, by swarms of the same northern barbarians, conquering and taking possession of the countries and governments of the civilized world. . . . And even should the cloud of barbarism and despotism again obscure the science and liberties of Europe, this country remains to preserve and restore light and liberty to them.[1]

I

WRITING to a friend in 1864, Jakob Burckhardt, the great Swiss master of the new academic study of art history, observed:

One of the veritable truths of our time is the disproportionate suffering in store for the author whose work is planned in terms of long periods of years. A hundred years ago all the conditions of life were far simpler and more stable. You knew your house belonged to you, that you could fill it as you pleased with books and collections, and that

* Written in loving memory of Edith Weinberger (d. 1967), whose beneficent presence and German tuition to Institute of Fine Arts students contributed so much to *Kunstgeschichte* in America.

The writer is indebted to the following, who were so kind as to complete a long questionnaire: Mirella Levi d'Ancona, Margarete Bieber, Frances Grey Godwin, Edith Porada, Gertrude Rosenthal, Kate Steinitz, Justus Bier, Helmut von Erffa, Richard Ettinghausen, Julius S. Held, George M. A. Hanfmann, Hans Huth, Horst Janson, Pál Kelemen, Richard Krautheimer, José López-Rey, Ulrich Middledorf, Alfred Neumeyer, John Rewald, Guido Schoenberger, Heinrich Schwarz, Peter Selz, Otto von Simson, Wolfgang Stechow, Emmanuel Winternitz, and Herbert Weissberger. He would also like to thank Rosemarie Garipoli, Barbara Giella, Phyllis Williams Lehmann, Ann Plogsterth, Jane Sebersky, James Ackerman, John Coolidge, J. LeRoy Davidson, H. von Erffa, Philipp Fehl, Alfred Frazier, Thomas B. Hess, George Kubler, A. Hyatt Mayor, James McCredie, Donald Posner, Christopher Tietze, and George S. Wittenborn.

1. Letter from Thomas Jefferson to John Adams, September 12, 1821, reprinted in *The Writings of Thomas Jefferson* (ed. Albert Ellery Bergh, Washington, 1907), XV, 333.

if nothing unusual happened you would die in that same house in thirty or forty years' time. Therefore you could tell yourself to make a sensible start. But who can say that nowadays? Frequent moving days, confined living quarters, the variety of excitations with which our charming century is so richly spiced, the hurry and rush and all the rest—in the face of these conditions even literary labors must be Americanized.[2]

The succeeding, less charming century was to see large numbers of scholars, including many of the best of Burckhardt's heirs to art history in Germany and Austria, uprooted and forced to flee from their homes to a new land, where their citizenship as well as their labors were quite literally "Americanized."

Thousands of German and Austrian architects, lawyers, artists, doctors, businessmen, craftsmen, manufacturers, film-makers, journalists, and publishers came to the United States throughout the 1930's and the early 1940's, often making their way to this country over a tortuous route with lengthy involuntary stops in South America or Asia. Often highly trained and specialized, these men and women made their presence and abilities felt in almost every aspect of American life. Of all the many branches of academic inquiry on which the immigrants settled, that of the history of art was among the most popular.[3] As Erwin Panofsky, perhaps the most distinguished of them all, has written in a masterful study, "Three Decades of Art History in the United States: Impressions of a Transplanted European," the most spectacular manifestation of this expansion of art historical studies taking place in the 1930's was due to "the providential synchronism between the rise of Fascism and Nazism in Europe and the spontaneous efflorescence of the history of art in the United States."[4]

The same country which rejoiced in the expulsion of all art historical scholars linked to Jewish birth or ancestry was also the birthplace of their discipline in the preceding century when "A full professorship was established . . . , [in] 1813, at Göttingen, its first incumbent being the excellent Johann Dominic Fiorillo (in spite of his name a native of

2. Translated and quoted by Oswald Goetz in *Essays in Honor of Georg Swarzenski* (Chicago, 1951), p. 5.

3. For an excellent characterization and description of his approach to art history, see Erwin Panofsky, "The History of Art as a Humanistic Discipline," *The Meaning of the Humanities* (ed. Theodore M. Greene, Princeton, 1940), pp. 89–118, especially pp. 108–109; reprinted in Erwin Panofsky, *Meaning in the Visual Arts* (New York, 1955), pp. 1–25.

4. *Meaning in the Visual Arts*, p. 332.

Hamburg)."[5] According to Nikolaus Pevsner, "the first man whom we can call an art historian, and who was Professor of the History of Art, was Franz Kugler at the Academy of Art in Berlin. He was appointed in 1833 and wrote a *History of Painting* in 1837 and a *Handbook of the History of Art* in 1841–1842. At that time Jakob Burckhardt was a student of history at Berlin, under Ranke; and with Burckhardt the history of art, in our sense, begins."[6]

In the 1840's, just when German art history was established as a flourishing discipline, it was still among the fields which Jews were forbidden to teach according to Prussian law. The University of Berlin, founded in 1810 and destined to have an outstanding art history department, fell under this ruling. In these years thousands of liberal Germans left their repressive homeland for America, where the richest immigrants and their descendants were to be distinguished for their interest in art and art history in the latter part of the century, contributing to the expansion of this field through their own patronage.

The position of the Jew in German society was always an especially complicated one. The conflicts between identity and career, integrity and opportunity were often ennervating and deleterious. Treitschke's encomium for Felix Mendelssohn, which appeared in the fourth volume of his *Deutsche Geschichte im neunzehnten Jahrhundert*, declares, "In this way a German of Jewish descent led our cultured society back to the tradition of its own national art . . . Mendelssohn's great and noble influence proved for all time that the German Jew can achieve real distinction only when he enters completely and without reservation into German life."[7] The liberation to pursue higher studies, won with the great Humboldt's aid, continued to be paid for at an often intolerable price—that of "proving oneself as a German."

Throughout much of the nineteenth and early twentieth centuries, the American world of scholarship and art was drawn to Germany. This was due, in the first place, to what Germany was not—not the hated England, which for all its linguistic and traditional accessibility

5. *College Art Journal*, 9.

6. Nikolaus Pevsner, "An Un-English Activity? Reflections on Not Teaching Art History," *The Listener* (October 30, 1952), p. 715.

7. (Leipzig, 1889), IV, 454–455; the translation by Edward Yarnall Hartshorne, *The German Universities and National Socialism*, appeared in London in 1937.

had been the enemy of the Republic, and not, as far as higher learning was concerned, predominantly Catholic.

Walter Agard has pointed out:

From 1850 to 1890 the ablest classical students in this country completed their training in Germany. It is not surprising that they were captivated by their experience in the German universities. Here they came into contact with a new type of scholar and a new system of training: the critical analyst of language and literature and the collector and organizer of factual material in every field of classical life and the seminar type of instruction and co-operative research, culminating in the dissertation on a highly specialized individual project.[8]

The whole idea of postgraduate education in the humanities on a relatively large scale—a commonplace in Germany—was a considerable rarity in England, where it was long viewed as a somewhat risible, vulgar concept, while in America such research remained unknown until 1861, when the first Ph.D. in a field other than theology or medicine was given to Morris Wheton of Yale, who deserves immortality for his peculiarly appropriate dissertational subject, "Ars longa, vita brevis."[9] Fifteen years later, a new university—Johns Hopkins—"was founded expressly for the providing of graduate instruction on the German model," with Gildersleeve directing Classical Philology.[10] With the ever-dubious zeal of a convert, America intensified some of the rigors of her German academic model. One tends to forget that German doctoral training was in one sense far less confining than its American equivalent. Although there may have been a stiflingly hieratic milieu— still much in evidence—German students were free to come and go and pick and choose until making their final commitment as to where they would write their dissertations, spending years in travel from one academic environment to another. Their theses always tended to be much shorter and less of a monumental stumbling block than the American equivalent, more of a maiden voyage than a tombstone.

8. Walter R. Agard, "Classical Scholarship," *American Scholarship in the Twentieth Century* (ed. Merle R. Curti, Cambridge, 1953), p. 148.

9. Paul Shorey, "Fifty Years of Classical Studies in America," *Transactions of the American Philological Association*, 50 (1919), 40–41. See William M. Calder III, "Die Geschichte der klassischen Philologie in den Vereinigten Staaten," *Jahrbuch für Amerikastudien*, 2 (1966), 213–240, especially p. 217.

10. René Wellek, "Literary Scholarship in the Twentieth Century," *American Scholarship in the Twentieth Century*, p. 112.

Since all American higher education was cast in an increasingly Teutonic mold toward the middle of the nineteenth century, it is hardly surprising that this should be true for art—not only for its history, but also for its practice, with the academies of Düsseldorf, Dresden, and Munich (no doubt deemed "safer" than those of Paris) receiving throngs of students from the United States.

Just as American teachers of Greek were translating German Greek grammars for the benefit of their students in colleges throughout the United States, so were their colleagues in art departments welcoming the translation of art historical texts which appeared in American or English publications and far outstripped the popularity of French works in the field. Winckelmann's *History of Ancient Art*, translated by G. Henry Lodge, was published in this country in 1849, 1856, 1871, 1872, and 1880. The Teutonic approach was favored for the relative objectivity and lack of flag-waving with which the author approached his subject. Like his American counterpart, the German art historian felt the subsidiary role that the land of his birth played in the development of the major phase of art history, producing texts which, in their day, were far less biased than the chauvinistic scholarly literature of France and Italy.

II

SINCE the incorporation of art historical studies was really only firmly established in Germany toward the middle of the nineteenth century, it cannot be said that America lagged far behind, with lecturers in this field first appointed at the University of Michigan in 1852, Vermont in 1853, the College of the City of New York in 1856, and Princeton in 1859. New York University had appointed the "American Leonardo," Samuel F. B. Morse, Professor of the Literature of the Arts of Design in 1835, but he had few occasions within the university framework to give art historical lectures. One year earlier Yale College, with the aid of the Connecticut State Legislature, had taken over the paintings of the seventy-four-year-old John Trumbull, in exchange for an annuity, and built a handsome neoclassical building after the "Patriot-Artist's" design. The Trumbull Gallery, partially in the Wunderkammer tradition of Tradescant's museum at Oxford, included natural as well as artistic wonders and marks the building-up of American university art museums—a most important, largely indigenous educational adjunct.[11]

More important than the academic developments of the mid-nineteenth century toward a broadening of America's knowledge of past art was the series of contemporary, almost casually made acquisitions of great art of the Ancient Near East, the Orient, and Pre-Columbian South America. To complete the influx of ancient masterpieces, James Jackson Jarves, an American diplomat and distinguished writer on art, was forming a most important collection of early Italian painting, which, failing to find a suitable buyer in the United States, was deposited at Yale University in 1868. This was largely a didactic collection, based upon the evolutionary lines promulgated by Italian amateurs of the preceding century, designed according to Jarves to show "the chronological and historical sequence of Italian art from its revival in the thirteenth century to its decadence in the seventeenth."[12]

German rather than French texts loom large in the early bibliographies offered in the fairly popular survey courses in art history given toward the middle of the century. Teaching at the very distinguished Art School at Yale (founded in 1866), Daniel Cady Eaton was one of the most dynamic and vociferous protagonists of an enlarged art historical curriculum. He called for "a chair for art history in every college" in 1881, noting, "Even text-books are obtainable. Lübke's *History of the Fine Arts* has been translated into English and may be memorized with as little injury to the student as any book of the typical course." This influential text, *Grundriss der Kunstgeschichte* (1860), was published in England in translation in 1868 and in America in 1871.[13]

The magnificent torrent of writings on art flowing in endless pro-

11. Wilmarth S. Lewis, *The Yale Collections* (New Haven, 1946), pp. 15ff.

12. *Ibid.*, p. 17. See also Francis Steegmuller, *The Two Lives of James Jackson Jarves* (New Haven, 1951).

13. Priscilla Hiss and Roberta Fansler, *Research in Fine Arts at the Colleges and Universities of the United States* (New York, 1934), pp. 26, 50.

fusion from Ruskin turned American art thought to England once again. The great stylist was also a great moralist, and Ruskin's tormented conscience, his sense of socialist obligations, made him an especially attractive figure in New England, where the addition of ethics to art history and aesthetics often seemed not only palatable but essential for the legitimacy of the field. Ruskin's interests were also of the moment as far as both industrial and architectural developments in America were concerned, since the most original and powerful building was couched in a medieval vocabulary close to Ruskin's heart. His greatest American apostle, Harvard's Professor of History of Fine Arts as Connected with Literature, Charles Eliot Norton, may also have been drawn to the splendid English writer, nine years his elder, as a reaction against the somewhat indiscriminately pro-German sentiments of his father's generation. Norton regretted the enduring American pilgrimages to those universities, from which students returned "Germanized pedants . . . ill-taught in Germany by the masters of the art of useless learning,"[14] whose expository style had already been noted by Basil L. Gildersleeve as following a "misty, tortuous and muddy path."[15]

Much as he loathed Teutonic erudition, Norton stated in 1874, "No student who is unable to use a German text-book will be admitted to Fine Arts 2 or 3," and texts by von Reber, Schnaase, Burckhardt, Michaelis, and other Germans far outnumber the few works by Viollet-le-Duc and his compatriots in Norton's lists. Charles Eliot Norton not only succeeded in restoring scholarly rapprochement in the arts between the United States and England, but he also expanded the American cultural domain by encouraging ancient research *in situ*. He founded the Archaeological Institute of America in 1879, from which the American School of Classical Studies in Athens sprang in 1881, followed in turn by the establishment of the American Academy in Rome in 1895. Norton may also have been a pioneer in the admission of an American Jew of German descent to the Establishment of advanced art scholarship, choosing Charles Waldstein to be director of the American School at Athens from 1888 to 1892.

14. Letter from Norton to Godkin, December 31, 1901, reprinted in Kermit Vanderbilt, *Charles Eliot Norton, Apostle of Culture in a Democracy* (Cambridge, 1959), p. 83.
15. Quoted by Agard, "Classical Scholarship," p. 148.

The apogée of German-American cultural links came with the founding of Harvard's Germanic Museum in 1912 (later named Busch-Reisinger after the Saint Louis beer baron and his son-in-law who were responsible for raising funds in 1908 and 1914 for a new building) designed by a Dresden architect, for which ground was broken in the inauspicious year of 1914. The Museum's first quarters were opened by Carl Schurz in 1903 on Schiller's birthday. Bewailing the gift of a series of huge plaster casts of sculpture to the Museum, presented by Prinz Heinrich, Norton wrote, "What are we to do with them? We cannot even burn them for lime as the barbarians burnt even greater masterpieces. The mission of German erudition is bad enough—but of German art—."[16] The gift so much deplored by Charles Eliot Norton was a first installment of the vast numbers of casts after major monuments of German sculpture which were to fill the special museum devoted to Teutonic culture that was to function as a New England Trocadero of reproductions of the art of Germany.[17]

By the 1880's, sons of the second and in some cases third generation of German Jewish mercantile and banking fortunes were attending American colleges, no longer sent back to German universities as had been the custom among so many of their families in previous decades. Harvard's early receptivity to Jewish students, whose attendance no doubt increased when compulsory chapel was abolished in 1886, continued the steady trend away from a conservative religious direction that had been taking place for a century. The rapid diminution of Orthodoxy among the German Jewish immigrants must also have facilitated their going to college away from home. The sons of Solomon Loeb—Morris and James—both went to Harvard and into academic life. James, frustrated by parental objections to a scholarly career and to a promised appointment at the Boston Museum of Fine Arts in the field of ancient art, endowed that great publication project, the Loeb Classical Library. His foundation of the Charles Eliot Norton Fellowship at Harvard for study at the newly founded School at Athens and that of the great Loeb

16. Letter from Norton to G. S. Ward, March 10, 1902, reprinted in *Letters of Charles Eliot Norton* (eds. Sara Norton and M. A. de Wolfe Howe, Boston and New York, 1913), II, 319–320.

17. Kuno Francke, *Handbook of the Germanic Museum* (7th ed., Cambridge, 1927).

Library of classical authors were first inspired by Charles Eliot Norton's magnetic and magnanimous personality.[18]

Jacob Schiff was in correspondence with President Charles W. Eliot by the turn of the century. There seems to have been considerable rapport between the most proper Bostonians and the Jewish aristocracy of New York who in so many ways resembled one another in their thrift, love of Germany and music, mild liberalism, dislike of flamboyance, and interests in cultural activities, education, and philanthropy.

Germany and Switzerland were not only the homeland of the founders of the first generation of huge fortunes—the Seligmans and the Loebs—but of the group toward the end of the nineteenth century as well, including Meyer Guggenheim, Philip Lehman, Adolph Lewisohn, Jacob Schiff, his son-in-law Felix Warburg, and the latter's younger partner Otto Kahn. Their approach to what used to be known as culture was still quite firmly rooted in the *fin-de-siècle* milieu of Hamburg and Frankfurt. At the turn of the century the involvement of this group with American institutions of learning and art had already become quite pronounced—Jesse Seligman as major donor to the Metropolitan Museum of Art; Adolph Lewisohn and Philip Lehman were accumulating splendid galleries of paintings, while Felix Warburg was building up a fine print collection.

American museums—the largest established in the seventies and eighties in New York, Boston, and Philadelphia—were beginning to draw upon German scholars to curate their collections, just as the National Gallery of England, formed in the first half of the century, depended upon the genius of Mündler to locate great paintings for purchase. As might be expected, Boston was in the forefront with its accession of German curatorial skills, first with S. R. Koehler, who helped build up the outstanding print department at the Museum of Fine Arts. He was responsible for bringing together a remarkable series of reference and source books on the history of graphic techniques, writing his own study on the development of color printing. Koehler seems to have had as a model for the Boston Museum the great scholarly libraries as well as galleries, and succeeded in bringing over this complex amalgamation

18. Louis E. Lord, *History of the American School of Classical Studies at Athens 1882–1942* (Cambridge, 1947), p. 3.

of visual and literary references and incorporating it within the American museum.[19]

III

ALTHOUGH scholars of many European nations were making invaluable contributions to the study of art, German-speaking countries, on a quantitative and quite frequently qualitative basis, outstripped the rest of the Continent for their activities in this field. Two different approaches to art emerged—the close study of the meaning of images and investigation of various esoteric sources, seen in Giehlow and Schlosser, and on the other hand the equally intense exploration of stylistic change in a descriptive, visually analytical way, inaugurated by Wölfflin and his circle. The latter approach became especially popular in America, probably due to the fact that it had a seemingly scientific, objective ring.

Drawn to so many fields of advanced study, Germans and Austrians of Jewish descent in the 1860's and 1870's seem to have been attracted in very considerable numbers to academic careers in art history or related pursuits. This long-lived generation may have been among the first to be able to enter universities with relative ease. Outstanding among its art historians were Paul Frankl (1878–1962), Max J. Friedlaender (1867–1958), Walter Friedlaender (1873–1966), Gustav Glück (1871–1952), Adolph Goldschmidt (1863–1944), Georg Swarzenski (1876–1957), Hans Tietze (1880–1954), Aby Warburg (1866–1929), Werner Weisbach (1873–1953), and Heinrich Wölfflin (1864–1945). It was largely due to Alexander von Humboldt, whose life and writings were extraordinarily influential in American as well as German art and educational institutions, that the repressive anti-Semitic legislation of 1812, forbidding Jews to teach anything other than medicine and "*Sprachwissenschaftlichen Lehrfacher*," was partially repealed in the 1840's. As late as 1847, the Prussian ministers of education were adamant in their refusal to let any Jews

19. I am indebted to Egbert Haverkamp-Begemann for acquainting me with Koehler's achievements.

become Professor Extraordinarius of history, classical mythology, and Oriental languages.[20] Those born in the last two decades of the nineteenth century showed the tendency toward the humanities gathering considerable momentum, with large numbers of intellectually gifted young men eschewing careers in the more traditional areas of commerce, law, medicine, or scientific research for the arts. Germany and Austria, which abounded with museums and universities as well as many other educational institutions such as the Hochschulen and special research and government organizations for advanced art studies, also provided considerable employment opportunities in these fields.

Paralleling, or perhaps preceding this wave of interest in art history among young Jewish intellectuals, was the development of splendid art collections among German and Austrian Jews. Outstanding among these were the Goldschmidt, Oppenheim, von Pannwitz, Pringsheim, Rothschild, and von Simon collections. It was also in the second half of the nineteenth century that such amazingly active Jewish art-dealing firms in Germany, Austria, and France were founded as Cassirer, Heinemann, Seligmann, Wertheim, and Wildenstein. In the relatively benevolent and prosperous climate of Germany and Austria prior to the First World War, the Kaisers both ennobled and occasionally consorted with the affluent or otherwise distinguished or useful subjects of Jewish descent, and intermarriage, with or without baptism, was not uncommon.

Art history, with its curious fusion of intuition and erudition, the incommunicable vibrations of connoisseurship, the constant interpenetration of the tangible and the intangible, the factual and the theoretical, often seems to parallel the intellectual and applied exercises that are so densely interwoven within the Jewish experience. It seems an especially appropriate field of interest for a people to whom religious imagery had been largely forbidden, whose renunciation of the opportunity for visual expression—such a basic aspect of human experience—must in itself have created a heightened awareness of the effectiveness of art, an awareness which could have contributed to the Second Commandment in the first place. Predominantly mercantile, Jews were long confined to eval-

---

20. Adolph Kohut, *Alexander von Humboldt und das Judentum: ein Beitrag zur Culturgeschichte des neunzehnten Jahrhunderts* (Leipzig, 1871), pp. 33–34.

uations, money lending, and the jewelry trade, all concerns in which a feeling for authenticity, rapid appraisal, and close observation was necessarily highly developed. A keen diagnostic and analytical sense, applied for thousands of years in the practice of medicine, long among the few professions allowed, also led to a predisposition to art. Sensitivity to expression; to the significance of appearance and attribute; to physiognomy, was necessarily heightened in the process of relative survival during the past several thousand years. Purveying the sumptuary arts for centuries—jewelry, furs, tailoring, textiles—also brought out an awareness of style in a very basic and tangible sense. Straying into the murky depths of motivation, art history may perhaps have afforded a singular safety valve, permitting those who were otherwise excluded to participate with intimacy and impunity in the private realms of religious and personal experience, a journey into foreign faiths and lives that is far more immediate than those afforded by literature or history. Needless to say, the propriety of art history made it a desirable choice for students of many different backgrounds who might otherwise have preferred a more creative, less vicarious aspect of the arts. The subject provided a heaven-sent niche for the sons and daughters of German Jewish families of some prosperity, who, interested in art, wanted an academic as opposed to commercial or creative career in that field, while retaining the approval of their occasionally still devout families. Americans, excluded by nationality from any direct claim to a European heritage, may have been drawn to art history for the same reasons.

Colin Wilson's glib "Outsider" theory of intellectual achievement seems to work especially well for Jewish art historians, and it is tempting to see its applicability to both Bernard Berenson (1865–1959) and his junior, Richard Offner (1890–1965), who, with the most important exception of James Jackson Jarves, were the first American scholars to achieve an international reputation in the field of early Italian painting. Both were born in central Europe—Berenson in Vilna and Offner in Vienna—and both, as soon as their early years at Harvard were completed, gravitated toward the quality of art historical scholarship linked with Northern European universities. Berenson was drawn to the approach of Morelli, whose writings were all in German, while Offner went straight to the University of Vienna for doctoral studies, completed in 1914. Neither of these men seemed at home in the United States, where they came as children. They may have viewed the Old World rather than the New as paved with streets of gold, which, in the case of Berenson, proved quite true. Both spent most of their lives in Florence; Berenson establishing himself as the squire of I Tatti, while Offner divided his year between a term of teaching or research in the United States, first at Chicago, then at Harvard as a Sachs Fellow, and after 1923 at New York University. Both died and were buried in Florence, Berenson with Catholic rites.

Contemporary with the meteoric rise of Berenson in the first years of the twentieth century, American art history was making itself established on every major campus in the Northeast and many in the Midwest as well. Robert Goldwater has estimated that between 1900 and 1910 the number of offerings in the history of art had jumped more than 50 percent.[21]

The first German art historian to come to America to teach after World War I was Adolph Goldschmidt, who gave a seminar in German Medieval sculpture at Harvard in 1921 and 1927, coming to this country once again in 1930 to teach at New York University. Goldschmidt, with his mistrust of the generalization, his suspicion of the German penchant for elaborate theorizing, while not viewed in the Fatherland as one of the crown princes of art history, was an especially happy choice for instruction in America, since, as Panofsky pointed out, he won all hearts for his rare combination of authority and modesty, his distinction tempered with a sense of irony and distrust for the doctrinaire. His enthusiasm for America included Hollywood, of which he was a devoted fan.[22]

Goldschmidt was followed in 1922 by Gustav Pauli, the outstandingly liberal director of the art museum in Hamburg, who conducted a seminar in the field of early German print-making and delivered a public lecture series on German painting from Classicism to Expressionism.

21. Robert J. Goldwater, "The Teaching of Art in the Colleges of the United States," *College Art Journal*, 2, Part 2, Supplement (May, 1943), 17–18.

22. Quoted by Udo Kultermann, *Geschichte der Kunstgeschichte: der Weg eine Wissenschaft* (Vienna, 1966), p. 344. For recollections and biographical data concerning Goldschmidt, see the entry by Hans Kauffmann in the *Neue Deutsche Biographie*, VI (Berlin, 1964), 613–614.

Both scholars worked in conjunction with Harvard's Germanic Museum. The Orientalist Alfred Salmony also came for a lecture series in 1926–27 and again in 1932.

Long before Hitler, in the 1920's and very early 1930's, several German scholars came to the United States to teach on a permanent basis. These include the Orientalist Ludwig Bachhofer at the University of Chicago, Oscar Hagen, a prominent scholar of early German painting, who headed the art history department at the University of Wisconsin, Rudolph Meyer Riefstahl who joined the faculty of New York University, Helmut von Erffa who went to Rutgers, William S. Heckscher, who went to Iowa, and Walter Horn, to the University of California. Wilhelm Köhler, whose equally distinguished psychologist brother Wolfgang was to take a solitary academic stand against Hitler in the mid-1930's, came to teach medieval art at Harvard earlier in the decade.

In the 1920's and early 1930's Harvard had achieved a unique fusion of art history with studies in conservation and technique, possibly the world leader in the latter. There was a creative vibration between the intensely qualitative pole of connoisseurship and the equally concentrated pole of methods and preservation, which under Edward Forbes, Arthur Pope, and Paul Sachs produced excellent work and fine students. This valuable but relatively short-lived combination soon drew apart, with each pole ossifying in isolation. Subsequent attempts have been made to revive the good work achieved at Harvard, there, at the Institute of Fine Arts, and elsewhere, but the reciprocal relationship between the aesthetic and the technical, which promised to be a permanent and especially appropriate fixture in American art scholarship, has never been wholly recaptured. The entrance of many émigrés with totally different interests at just the time that the fruitful movement was disintegrating may have hastened its already rapid decline. In recent years new collaboration between American, Belgian, and Florentine institutions has revived the promising scholarship of earlier times, with the participation of Eve Borsook, Lawrence Majewski, Millard Meiss, the late Paul Coremans, and Leonetto Tintori.

Erwin Panofsky, after characterizing the distinguished achievements of earlier twentieth-century art history in America, the Della Robbia studies of Marquand (1912–1922), Clapp's two Pontormo studies (1914,

1916), E. Baldwin Smith's work on Early Christian ivories in the Provence (1918), the founding of the Princeton Index of Christian Art (1917), the Frick Reference Library (1920), and the Medieval studies of A. Kingsley Porter, A. M. Friend, and Charles Rufus Morey, pointed out, "No European scholar—least of all the Germans and Austrians who, whatever may be said against them, were less afraid of foreign literature than most Italians and nearly all Frenchmen—could remain blind to the fact that the United States had emerged as a major power in the history of art; and that, conversely, the history of art had assumed a new, distinctive physiognomy in the United States."[23]

Millard Meiss, a student of Richard Offner's and among the earliest Ph.D.'s in the very new graduate program in art history at New York University, was much in touch with the new European iconographical research as well as with the approach of *Geistesgeschichte* which admirably complemented his teacher's stylistic orientation and caused the latter to invite Panofsky to teach at his new department in 1931. Meyer Schapiro's acquaintance with German and Austrian scholarship in the Medieval field, as well as his early interest in the recently evolved psychoanalytic approach, also attest to contact with the most advanced currents of Northern European thought.

In 1931 both London and New York were generating major independent centers for art historical specialization on a graduate level. England, long less interested in this study than America, received large funds from a great textile manufacturer and art collector of Huguenot descent, Samuel Courtauld, to establish the institute named after him that was affiliated with the University of London, just as in New York the art department associated with New York University suddenly strove to expand its resources and goals; the outstanding manifestation of this new outlook was Offner's invitation to Erwin Panofsky of the recently founded (1920) University of Hamburg.

Intertwined in origin, subject, and approach, art historical and classical studies often illuminate or depend upon one another. Discussing the years of American classical scholarship between 1919 and 1935—the

23. *Meaning in the Visual Arts*, pp. 325–326. For another fairly recent appraisal of art history in America, see also Alfred Neumeyer, "Victory without Trumpet," *Frontiers of Knowledge* (ed. Lynne White, Jr., New York, 1956), pp. 178–193.

dates approximately equivalent to the initiation and completion of the first mature, independent era of art history in America, just before the influence *in situ* of émigré scholars—William M. Calder III has characterized that period as "A very very American epoch, practical, drawn to the purely objective, above all to archaeological or inscribed data (*steine*). Those who interested themselves in stones were completely satisfied. Those who interested themselves in facts, possibly; those who were interested in ideas, certainly not."[24] The art historical parallel to this relentlessly objective, factual trend in classics might be found in the concern with techniques and conservation at Harvard, the tendency toward the list and the corpus started by Berenson extended and deepened by Richard Offner and Chandler Post. The competent Wölfflinianism, the absorption of Riegl, Schlosser, and others, showed cognizance of the European approach, but, as John Coolidge observed, "By the early 1930's, after a decade of brilliant contributions, art history in America remained sporadic and provincial. It was the task of the refugees from Germany to establish it as a unified discipline and to bring it abreast of continental practice. This required dedication and a clear sense of direction."[25]

IV

1923, the year often selected as the coming of age of art history in America, with the new eminence of the College Art Association and its *Bulletin* and with the publication of A. Kingsley Porter's *Romanesque Sculpture of the Pilgrim Roads*, also saw the printing of Josef Strzygowski's *Die Krisis der Geisteswissenschaften*. The author, famous for his elaborate theories concerning the Eastern origins of Christian architecture belonged to the generation of the Grand Old Men of art history, born in the 1860's. He had just completed a tour throughout the United States as Norton Lecturer, selected by the Archaeological Institute, and had also given the Lowell Lectures in Boston. With the inscription "Opus

24. "Die Geschichte der klassischen Philologie," p. 225.
25. "Walter Friedlaender, 1873–1966," *Art Journal*, 26 (Spring, 1967), 260.

178" alongside the author's signature, the introduction dedicates *Die Krisis* to Strzygowski's colleagues at Harvard and Princeton, whose acquaintance he had made in America. What follows is in part a turgid manifestation of the intensified anti-Semitism of Germany and the author's native Austria, arising after the defeat of the First World War. Strzygowski claims he writes for the benefit of his "Jewish friends," since the greatest danger to the history of art is now to be found in the rise of the Jews and their "Geistesverwandten," who, seeking world supremacy, heedlessly trampled across the benevolent, protective borders of Northern nationalism in their pursuit of dominion.[26]

This bizarre fusion of hysterical, racist thought and an ostensibly academic frame of reference—Strzygowski's book is subtitled *Ein grundsätzlicher Rahmenversuch*—was not entirely novel, but heretofore racial thought had been applied to the genesis of art rather than to its

---

26. "*Wenn ich anfange, Sache und Beschauer auseinanderzuhalten, so wird auch jenem Geiste ein Riegel vorgeschoben, der sich infolge der Schwäche der Menschheit nach dem Kriege immer mehr ausbreitet, jenem mit spitzfindigen Einfällen und geistreichen Auslegungen wuchernden Judentum und seiner arischen Gefolgschaft, die beide aller folgerichtig vorgehenden Sachwissenschaft ebenso gefährlich werden, wie die Ausbeutung dem gesunden wirtschaftlichen Leben. Ich weiss mich mit einigen meiner jüdischen Freunde, die zur Einfachheit und dem selbstlosen Hingegebensein an die Sachen zurück wollen, eins, indem ich die Judenschaft selbst zur Hilfe in dieser Säuberung aufrufe. Wenn es so weiter geht wie im Augenblicke, dass Einfälle und Ausbeutung zur Weltmacht zu werden drohen, so steht eben alles auf dem Spiele.*

"*Die grosse Gefahr liegt zudem darin, dass die Juden und ihre Geistesverwandten heute nach dem Kriege die ganze Welt durchsetzen und überall Herrschaft ausüben. Bedenkt man dabei, dass sie über alle staatlichen Grenzen hinaus geeinigt vorgehen, so ist klar, dass zu fürchten ist, die Herrschsüchtigen unter ihnen würden eine neue Art von Weltmacht aufrichten. Das sollten sich die Völker gesagt sein lassen und ihre trennenden Gegensätze endlich vernünftig über Bord werfen, um geeinigt an die stetige Entwicklung des Gedankens der Menschheit herantreten zu können. Nur so würde das Judentum als wichtige treibende Kraft, die ihr niemand absprechen wird, zum Segen werden.*

"*Allerorten treten unter den Juden immer offensichtlicher führende Geister auf, die im Wege der jüdischen, von Land zu Land fliegenden Ausbreitung rasch Weltruf gewinnen und durch die Presse allein schon alles in Schatten stellen, was sich daneben an tüchtigen, nichtjüdischen Kräften regt, ja diese ganz natürlich überflügeln, weil die Menschheit ja noch immer, das heisst jetzt sogar erst recht wieder ihre Volksverschiedenheit zu unzähligen hemmenden 'nationalen' Grenzen aufbauscht. Wenn Natur-, Geistes- und technische Wissenschaften sich nicht auf übervölkischen in meinem Sinne sachlichen Boden stellen, wird sich die Eigenart des Judentums als Beschauer derart hemmungslos ausleben, dass für alle Teile Unsegen aus einer Bewegung herauskommt, die in ein grosses Ganze und Allgemeine eingeordnet und zu stetiger Entwicklung gebracht, der gesamten Menschheit zum Nutzen sein könnte. Die Kunstgeschichte weiss von diesen Dingen ein Lied zu singen.*" Josef Strzygowski, *Die Krisis der Geisteswissenschaften* (Vienna, 1923), p. 29.

historians. Long before the time of Gobineau and Taine there had been vaguely anthropologically-oriented explanations of the origins of style in terms through much of the nineteenth century.[27] Even Jakob Burckhardt teeters on the brink of excess in this area, and Wölfflin was no stranger to scientifically dubious distinctions of *Kunst* and *Rasse* to account for various factors in German and Italian art.[28]

The Teutonic compulsion to explain the inexplicable came to a head with one of the silliest books in the history of art, written by the great Holbein connoisseur and Ordinarius at Karlsruhe, Alfred Woltmann. Entitled *Die Germanen und die Renaissance* (1905), the publication went about proving that each and every genius of the Renaissance in Italy—Alberti, Leonardo, Raphael, and the rest—were necessarily of "nordisch-germanisch" origin on the basis of their rather large noses, shown in portraits whose authenticity was often as dubious as the author's hypothesis.[29] Following Woltmann's only too prophetic lunacies, a racial approach to *Kunstgeschichte* was to be "developed" throughout the next decades. Even such a profound scholar as Henry Thode, the author of pioneering studies correlating Giottesque Naturalism with Franciscan thought, and of major Michelangelo research, became a member of a fanatically racist organization known as the Werdandi Bund.[30]

27. For a helpful résumé of Taine's works, see the anthology by Jean-François Revel, *Taine: philosophie de l'art* (Paris, 1964).

28. Paul Ortwin Rave, *Kunstdiktatur in Dritten Reich* (Hamburg, 1949), p. 20.

29. "*Fassen wir die Ergebnisse zusammen:*

"*1. Die nachrömische Kulturgeschichte Italiens ist keine Renaissance des Altertums, wenn auch antike überlieferung und Zurückgriefen auf antike Vorbilder eine Rolle gespielt haben. Sie ist vielmehr im wesentlichen eine eigenartige Leistung der eingewanderten germanischen Rasse, die in einheitlichem Zusammenhang mit der germanischen Kultur in ganz Europa steht. Von Norden her, namentlich von Frankreich und Flandern, hat Italien wichtige Anregungen und Beeinflüssungen erfahren, besonders in Architektur, Musik und Dichtkunst, weniger in Plastik, Malerei und Wissenschaft.*

"*2. Die Germanen haben in Italien die meisten und grössten Genies hervorgebracht, abgesehen von einer geringen Zahl von Mischlingen, die teils mehr der nordisch-germanischen, teils mehr den brünten Rassen sich nähern.*

"*3. Diese Leistung der Germanen ist nicht die Folge günstiger wirtschaftlicher Bedingungen oder einer zahlenmässigen Überlegenheit, sondern der Ausfluss ihrer höheren natürlichen Begabung.*

"*4. Die Kulturentwicklung Italiens vollzeit sich auf Kosten der blonden Rasse, die von Jahrhundert zu Jahrhundert an Zahl abnimmt. Das Schicksal Roms wiederholt sich.*" Ludwig Woltmann, *Die Germanen und die Renaissance in Italien* (Leipzig, 1905), p. 150.

30. Hellmut Lehmann-Haupt, *Art under a Dictatorship* (New York, 1954), p. 66.

By 1921, Ottmar Rutz, in his *Menscheitstypen und Kunst*, published in Jena, "tried to explain works of art as the result of certain definable temperamental and psychological human categories and as an emanation of the physical characteristics resulting from their character traits," which was soon followed by a study by Hans K. F. Günther, *Rasse und Stil* (Munich, 1926), in which a more overtly racist basis was given to Rutz's circular "reasoning."[31] To provide but one example of this new school—"Was it the dinaric blood in the Nordic-dinaric Dürer which opened up in him the southern art will, the dinaric blood, which is inclined to facilitate the transition of the soul across the Alps to Upper Italy?"[32]

Exploring and integrating its cultural history with that of the mainstreams of the classical tradition, German scholarship, long before resorting to the racist maneuvers of Woltmann, sought to explore the links between North and South in a reasonable and revealing fashion. This approach was first clearly manifested in such a sensible chapter as Anton Springer's "Das Nachleben der Antike im Mittelalter" in the first volume of his history of art of 1867, a publication revolutionary in its scope. The apogée of this productive concern with exploring the "half-life" of antiquity as it radiated through Medieval and later art was achieved by Aby Warburg, scion of a Hamburg Jewish banking family who renounced his share of the family fortune for the subsidy of a private research library in 1901. Among the causes for Warburg's inspired, fruitful studies concerning the survival of the ancient gods and that of the mystical and scientific thought of antiquity throughout the Middle Ages and the Renaissance was the desire to rediscover and perpetuate through publication the fugitive bonds between North and South. Warburg's equally valuable discovery of the influential presence of Northern art in Italy during the Renaissance provided a valid, reassuring link between what had long, and in the main mistakenly, been viewed as mutually exclusive as Snow's *Two Cultures*.

Through meticulous yet imaginative scholarship, Warburg and his associates showed the intricate web of thought and faith that linked Europe after the fall of the Roman Empire, providing a resilient, closely-

31. *Ibid.*, p. 38.
32. *Ibid.*, p. 39.

reasoned skein of arguments for the grain of truth in the overblown, chauvinistic claims made by the racist, demagogic elements in German art history. A great patriot, Warburg never reconciled himself to German defeat in the First World War; he long refused to revisit his beloved Italy in view of its defection from the German cause. A man of genius, Warburg was to be the victim of madness, six years in duration. He once said that this insanity was punishment for his revelation of the significance of astrology and the occult upon Western thought, which clouded his own reason in retribution. An oddly prophetic mania of Warburg's, in which he blamed himself for Germany's defeat in the Great War, was soon to be shared by his countrymen, who, blaming the Jews for all their misfortunes, sought their destruction.[33]

Among the many ironies of Nazism was its projected destruction of Warburg's lifework, the irreplaceable "studio" of 65,000 volumes, used by Saxl, Wind, Panofsky, Cassirer, and others in the 1920's for a series of brilliant studies, often in collaboration with the Univeristy of Hamburg, which provided a new amplification and enrichment of art history as significant as the sweep of Burckhardt's brilliance and the approach of *Geistesgeschichte* by Dvorak and his school in Vienna. The library, research institute, and most of the staff were exported to London in 1933, where, affiliated with that city's university, the scholarly achievements of its founder have been continued under Saxl, Frankfort, and Gombrich.

Many scholars, including Cassirer, Frankfort, Heckscher, Panofsky, Stechow, Wind, Winternitz, and Wittkower, who had been associated with Warburgian studies in Hamburg, and others linked with the London center, were to come to this country at a later date. The Wölfflinian approach (long popular in America but made even more so by the American residence of such an eloquent disciple as Jakob Rosenberg) together with the Warburgian, represent the two poles of German art historical scholarship to which most émigré scholars were to belong.

33. See Kultermann, *Geschichte der Kunstgeschichte*, pp. 380, 464, n. 1. The observations on Warburg have also benefitted from discussion of this writer with his friends.

The Warburg Library was, in fact, an American institution in terms of financial support, since Aby Warburg's brothers in the United States were the chief contributors to its maintainance. "In 1931, the Institute's budget was halved from one day to the next owing to the American Depression." Gertrude Bing, "Fritz Saxl (1890–1958)," *Fritz Saxl: a Volume of Memorial Essays* (ed. D. J. Gordon, London, 1957), p. 22.

Among the most effortless of the many easy victories of the Nazis was the conquest of all the universities of Germany. The notion that advanced education could contribute to political virtue was certainly dealt a death blow by the usually less than massive resistance to Hitler's thought or action by the academic community, where few joined the courageous protest of Edward Spranger and Wolfgang Koehler. German anti-Nazi thought and conduct was far more clearly asserted by professional soldiers than by professors. Unsurprisingly, it was the German Catholics—fellow victims of Nazi enmity—rather than the more secure Protestants, who were most courageous and uncompromising in their assistance to Jewish colleagues. The largest number of these, not including museum employees, were in the field of medicine (412), followed by social sciences (173), law (132), physics (106), philology (95), chemistry (86) and technology (85), history and mathematics (60 each), biology and chemistry (53 and 52), psychology (51), art and art history (50), philosophy (33), theology (32), and so on down.

The sentiments of Francis Henry Taylor, director of the Metropolitan Museum at the end of the Second World War, commenting on the role of teachers and curators, "Our job is to deal straightforwardly in human values. Had our German colleagues been more concerned with these in teaching their Nazi pupils, they might not now find themselves in their present situation,"[34] fall very flat in view of the situation actually confronting German professors in the early 1930's.

Twenty-eight directors of German museums, often of major importance, were to lose their jobs, not because they were themselves insufficiently Aryan, but because they were considered partisans of degenerate art—*Entartete Kunst*—the category in which all avant-garde painting was placed, and therefore, necessarily, of Jewish devising.[35] Protesting against the last large show of contemporary German art without Nazi sponsorship held in Berlin in 1933, Nazi journalists claimed, "*Was uns in diesem Kronprinzen-Palais als junge deutsche Kunst vorgeführt wird, sind Juden, nicht als Juden,*"[36] when actually only five out of the 173 exhibitors belonged to that group.

34. Francis Henry Taylor, *Babel's Tower: the Dilemma of the Modern Museum* (New York, 1945), p. 50.
35. Rave, *Kunstdiktatur*, p. 28.   36. *Ibid.*, p. 92.

This in the long run flattering but generally mistaken identification of artists of Jewish descent with modern trends was probably due to the deserved prominence of such able and advanced dealers as Cassirer, Flechtheim, Neumann, Seligmann, Valentin, and many others. They, rather than the artists whose careers they advanced, were Jews, as were many of the influential teachers, journalists, publishers, architects, collectors, and officials, sympathetic to new art forms.

Expressionism met with the unmitigated scorn of Nazi officialdom, which sold the masterpieces of Marc, Lehmbruck, Klee, Beckmann, and many others after the large exhibition of *Entartete Kunst* held in Munich in 1937. Many of these works came to the United States, where several of their artists—Beckmann, Grosz, and Moholy-Nagy, among others— were to find refuge. Scholars and museum directors were "exported" together with the outstanding art of their time. Just as many of the refugee scholars went to the centers where they received support from Americans of similar background and interests, so did the German works of art, most of them flocking to New York, Saint Louis, or Minneapolis. In several cases, the exiled curators were actually reunited in America with exported art that they had purchased first in Germany and then again in America for the museum of their employ.

In the main, the art scholars who left Germany in the 1930's were rejected and expelled by their compatriots, not for what they did or thought or felt about themselves, their faith, their country, or their discipline, but simply because they or their wives were to some ascertainable extent of Jewish descent. There were a very few, who, although totally devoid of Jewish ties, chose to leave in the midst of an established career; most preferred to jettison or silence their conscience for academic survival or other personal considerations.

Although most of the exiled scholars were "non-Aryan," those who left comprised a diverse group, even among one of the same general professional interests, including members of the aristocracy whose families had been ennobled in the late nineteenth century or who had married into that class; others were sons of prosperous manufacturers, or prominent professional men; many were veterans of the First World War, some war heroes, others officers in the Weimar Republic. Several had been brought up as Catholics or Protestants, the children of a mixed marriage or of converts; others, such as Alexander Dorner, descendant of a long line of Lutheran pastors, preferred voluntary exile to a life of compromise and persecution in Germany. Still others, without any particular religious or communal affiliations, were the sons of similarly inclined parents, one of whom may have been of Jewish descent. Most of the above were helpless before the new German laws enacted in 1933, since, on the basis of their advancement of "degenerate art," or their ancestry, they were automatically unfit to retain their posts as teachers or officials of research institutes, state agencies, or museums. There were, for the time being, certain exceptions—"*Wer ein Jud ist, das bestimme ich*" was the proud and far from empty assertion of Karl Lueger.

Among the leading art scholars in America are many who left Germany in the 1930's before the completion of their undergraduate or graduate studies, which were brought to a conclusion in the United States, where they received their first appointments as teachers or curators. Some, like Lorenz Eitner, Philipp Fehl, and Peter Selz, were forced to leave at an early age or were sent abroad by families who knew what was coming. Others, such as Frances Godwin, left as early as 1931 to study under an American scholar in the field of their special interest and then decided to stay; Gertrude Achenbach Coor and Horst W. Janson came as exchange students or on special fellowships from Germany in the later 1930's and elected not to return. Dietrich von Bothmer, after receiving a Rhodes Scholarship to Oxford, chose further graduate work at the University of California (Berkeley) to going back to a dictatorship; his brother Bernard, already working at the Berlin Museum, had, as an anti-Nazi, his doctoral work thwarted at the University and came to America a few years later. Otto von Simson came to America in 1939, aged twenty-six, near the time of the completion of his doctoral studies, so that his professional life as a teacher was almost entirely in this country. Other German scholars prominent in America, such as William S. Heckscher, Walter Horn, and Ulrich Middeldorf, under no "racial" obligation to leave Germany, chose to come to this country in the 1930's, their departure without any strict correlation to political events. To these names could be added several more, indicative of the large numbers of able, interested, and well-trained art scholars produced by the many scholarly centers in Germany and Austria specializing in art historical and allied research, who left the then depressed and extremely competitive European economy to find jobs elsewhere.

Far from uninterested in their religious heritage, such prominent German scholars as Richard Krautheimer and Guido Schoenberger made it an object of important art historical research, most notably in the former's *Mittelalterliche Synagogen*, published in Berlin in 1927. As though aware of his own and Austria's eventual fate, the great scholar Hans Tietze turned toward both the future and the past in 1933, when, in addition to all his administrative duties, he found time to translate James Truslow Adams' *March of Democracy* for a Viennese edition and to publish his own *Die Juden Wiens: Geschichte, Wirtschaft, Kultur*. He appears to have made an American trip around 1932, and wrote numerous articles on American museums and art collections as well as a more searching study, "Das amerikanische Kulturproblem," for *Zeitwende*.[37]

V

G UARANTEED utility or financial independence were usually the price of American or other sanctuary to refugees from Germany's "solution to the Jewish problem." Special committees and councils were established in the mid-1930's to expedite the evacuation of scholars from Germany. These organizations included the Academic Assistance Council in London, since many refugees came to America by way of England, where the Committee on Displaced Scholars acted as a clearing house, helping those who registered to find a guarantee of employment in the United States which was usually a prerequisite to receiving a permanent entry visa. At least one art scholar, Guido Schoenberger, was snatched from imminent death by his call to teach in America. An inmate of Buchenwald in 1939, following a distinguished museum career in his native Frankfurt, his appointment to the Institute of Fine Arts in 1940 saved Dr. Schoenberger's life.

It was legally, as well as professionally, far easier to get a teaching than a museum appointment in the 1930's, since entry visas often stipu-

37. 8 (1932), 181–190.

lated that instructive duties were to be the field of employment. Though most émigré scholars found jobs reasonably suited to their special interests within a remarkably short time, their salaries appear, in the main, to have been low even for the Depression era. At the most hospitable, recently founded New School or "University in Exile" and the Institute of Fine Arts, new funds had to be found for increasing numbers of refugee appointees, who were rarely free from financial worry and a nagging insecurity which was less acute among their American colleagues.

With the expulsion of hundreds of scholars from Europe, many prosperous American families of German Jewish descent—the Lehmans, Schiffs, Speyers, Warburgs, and others—played a major role in providing funds and temporary or permanent appointments. The Rosenwald Family Fund devoted much of its resources to the aid of art scholars; Lessing Rosenwald was then starting the great print and drawing collection now presented to the National Gallery. Solomon Guggenheim and Hilla Rebay's Museum of Non-Objective Art made available an important showcase for the work of many artists banished from Germany, while Peggy Guggenheim's Art of This Century gallery and collection did the same in the 1940's for other outstanding painters and sculptors, many fugitives from Germany and from the German invasion of France.

None of this is to say that there were not hundreds, perhaps thousands of generous Americans whose background was neither German nor Jewish, both charitably inclined and interested in art scholarship, whose solicitude saw to it that many were provided with visas, shelter, and temporary and permanent appointments throughout the United States. Since Hitler's policies first took effect in Germany, it was, quite naturally, American citizens of German Jewish descent who were among the earliest to appreciate what was happening and to be among the initiators and contributors toward the relief of the scholarly victims of Nazism.

That New York city with its huge Jewish population should have been able to assist and employ the largest number of refugee art scholars, for the most part Jewish victims of German persecution, is hardly surprising. In addition to being the cultural as well as the financial center of the country, New York has the largest number of museums, art libraries, galleries, and research institutes and was the home of many families of German Jewish descent who had been outstanding for their philanthropy and their interest in art. Several of these families had been concerned with scholarly research in the arts long before the rise of Hitler. Like their scholar brother in Hamburg, Paul and Felix Warburg in New York were interested in art research as well as collecting, and the latter had subsidized the important and costly inquiries in the print field by Fitzroy Carrington. Robert Lehman, who has continued to study, catalogue, and enlarge his father Philip's great collection, was also to be a most generous patron of art history, endowing a chair at the Institute of Fine Arts and another at Yale, in addition to devoting much time to his appointment as trustee of the Metropolitan Museum. One branch of the mercantile Straus family underwrote the massive *Corpus of Florentine Painting*, Richard Offner's life work, while another subsidized the foundation of the Institute of Advanced Study, where the history of art has played a most important role since the appointment of Erwin Panofsky in 1935. Previously a distinguished associate of the Warburg Library in Hamburg, Panofsky was appointed to the University there in 1926, before coming to the Institute of Fine Arts in New York in 1931 at the invitation of Richard Offner.

New York University's Fine Arts Graduate Center was to develop into the department in the United States where the largest number of refugee scholars were to teach advanced courses together with American colleagues. Relatively little had come of the University's plans for instruction in the arts between its appointment of the "American Leonardo," Samuel F. B. Morse, in 1835 and the time of the tenure of the distinguished architect, art historian, and future director of the Philadelphia Museum, Fiske Kimball, who came as Morse Professor of the Arts of Design in 1922. Kimball established the important precedent of close collaboration with the Metropolitan Museum and other collections in New York to supplement the new department's need for classroom space and instructors, enlisting the aid of museum curators, valuable adjuncts to his staff. It was Kimball, in the late 1920's, who brought over Goldschmidt and P. T. Sarre from Berlin as visiting lecturers. Richard Offner, the cornerstone of the faculty, and A. Philip

MacMahon joined the department, as did Meyer Rudolph Riefstahl, who had come from Germany in the late 1920's and became Kimball's successor, to be succeeded in turn by John Shapley following Riefstahl's early death. Under Shapley, Byzantine studies were developed with the aid of Thomas Whittemore.

Two administrators, General Sherrill, chairman of the New York University Council Committee on the Fine Arts, followed by Walter W. S. Cook, were largely responsible for establishing an unusually cosmopolitan, Europe-oriented faculty in the history of art in the late 1920's and early 1930's, in the years just before Hitler presided over German education.

Colonel Michael Friedsam, the heir to his bachelor uncle Jacob Altman's fortune, presidency of the family department store, and taste for art collecting, gave important financial support to what was to become the Institute of Fine Arts in the late 1920's, when General Sherrill planned a dramatic expansion of the art historical faculty. Sherrill's advanced ideas included advocating "research professors" and espousing the idea of a faculty "who spend half a year in research abroad in their respective fields," planning courses to be held for New York University students at the École du Louvre, Berlin, and Munich in 1930. Indicative of the scholarly calibre of the fledgling Institute was one of its first Ph.D.'s, Millard Meiss, who, working under Richard Offner, received his degree in 1933, the same year that the Nürnberg Decrees were promulgated and all Jewish or otherwise "undesirable" professors were summarily fired from German universities. Walter W. S. Cook had decided to spearhead the group headed by Offner, MacMahon, and Panofsky to build up an entirely separate faculty for the history of art on a graduate level at New York University. Panofsky recalled that

It grew out of the small graduate department which it was my good fortune to join in 1931, and which, at that time, had about a dozen students, three or four professors, no rooms, let alone a building, of its own, and no equipment whatsoever. Both lecture and seminar courses were held in the basement rooms of the Metropolitan Museum, commonly referred to as "the funeral parlors," where smoking was forbidden under penalty of death and stern-faced attendants would turn us out at 8:55 p.m., regardless of how far the report or discussion had proceeded.

. . . In the course of the next few years no fewer than five distinguished German refugees were called to permanent positions at what had now become the Institute of Fine

Arts. Considerable funds were raised in mysterious fashion. And today this Institute, so far as I know the only independent university organ exclusively devoted to graduate instruction in the history of art, is not only the largest but also the most animated and versatile school of its kind. . . . All of which, however, would not have been possible had not . . . the chairman, Walter Cook, shown an unparalleled combination of foresight, doggedness, business sense, self-effacing devotion, and lack of prejudice ("Hitler is my best friend," he used to say; "he shakes the tree and I collect the apples"), and had he not been given his chance by the providential synchronism between the rise of Fascism and Nazism in Europe and the spontaneous efflorescence of the history of art in the United States.[38]

The first "American" manifestation of Warburgian scholarship appeared in 1933 with Erwin Panofsky and Fritz Saxl's *Classical Mythology in Mediaeval Art*, published in the Metropolitan Museum Studies, the outgrowth of a lecture given by the authors at Princeton and based in large part on research done in Hamburg.[39]

Coming to the Institute as a graduate student in 1936, and now Avalon Professor of Medieval Art, Harry Bober remembers the roster of scholars drawn to the Institute, then known as the Graduate Center:

From Paris there were Henri Focillon, Marcel Aubert, and Eustache de Lorey. Key chairs and museum posts in Germany were represented by Erwin Panofsky (Hamburg); Adolph Goldschmidt, Ernst Herzfeld, and Richard Ettinghausen (Berlin); Karl Lehmann (Münster); Otto Homburger (Marburg); and Martin Weinberger (Munich). In addition, leading scholars in American universities, in an unusual display of academic brotherhood, brought their special gifts eagerly to the Center. The program might well be compared with a new kind of planetary system. It had a small but centrifugally-controlling force at the center, its planets not yet in settled orbits or even determinable in number. Its most unusual feature lay in its capacity to attract splendid comets from afar and synchronize their periodicity with its own rhythms . . . and of the influx of German refugee scholars, two were chosen as Visiting Professors—astute choices that were to prove fruitful indeed. Karl Lehmann, who had been Professor of Classical Archeology at Münster, created, single-handed, a division of classical art, while Walter Friedlaender from Freiburg put the department on the map in the field of baroque painting.[40]

Commenting on Walter Cook's desire to keep as many émigré scholars at the Institute as he could, Professor Bober recalled that since "he could

38. *Meaning in the Visual Arts*, pp. 331–332.
39. IV, 193–217.
40. Harry Bober, "The Gothic Tower and the Stork Club," *Arts and Sciences* (Spring, 1962), p. 1.

never hope to keep all he liked, he ran an unofficial but highly selective placement bureau. Every scholar soon learned that he could count on transient accommodations, at least, in the Graduate Center. When the new Institute for Advanced Study in Princeton offered Panofsky a permanent professorship in 1935, he could scarcely refuse. But, characteristically, he accepted only on condition that he might continue to teach at New York University."[41]

Even though Paul Warburg was not himself responsible for his home becoming that of the Institute of Fine Arts, it seems particularly appropriate that this should have taken place, since so many members of the Institute faculty had been associated with or inspired by the research institute and library founded by his oldest brother Aby in Hamburg.

Cook's great contribution to the sympathetic reception and placement of scholars from Europe can hardly be exaggerated. A genial, hearty gentleman of the Old School (Harvard 1913, Ph.D. 1924), Cook was the most generous and helpful of men, working selflessly to find appropriate jobs for the floodtide of displaced art scholars. Because he was himself in many ways so different from his protégées, Cook with his ruddy, clubby manner made an especially eloquent and irresistible champion, who managed to assemble and sustain a distinguished faculty with few financial resources other than those that he could himself muster. "I just passed the hat around" was his characteristically modest way of describing the way in which he managed to assemble the funds needed to keep the Institute afloat. A leading professor's salary was pieced together from no less than twenty-four different sources, including foundation and individual contributions of fifty dollars or less.

No doubt Walter Cook's ebullient, assuring aura persuaded many a nervous department chairman or Americans First-minded dean to find room in his ranks for foreign talent that would have been spurned without so authoritative and seemingly Establishment-oriented a sponsor. Not only responsible for the hiring of many German and Austrian art scholars throughout the country, Cook's continued interest in their welfare, and that of his graduate students at the Institute, saw to it that they managed also to find jobs teaching in the New York city colleges

41. *Ibid.*

where so many talented undergraduates were to be found, who, in turn, often chose the Institute for further study.

The Institute's roster of refugee and native American scholars continued growing. Both Julius S. Held and Richard Krautheimer taught at times during the 1930's and the early 1940's. A prominent leader of the Spanish republicans, José López-Rey, who had come to Smith to teach, joined the Institute in 1944. In addition to purely historical courses, the Institute also continued the museum training program begun by New York University in the 1920's, following those of Wellesley and Harvard. Rudolph Berliner, Hans Huth, and Martin Weinberger, all outstanding museum men in Berlin and Munich, participated in this course, which has prepared many of the major museum curators and directors in the United States and Canada.

The climate of the Institute during the 1930's and 1940's was one of intimate and intense scholarship—as far removed from the affluent, museum-oriented milieu of Harvard's art history department, ensconced in the Georgian splendors of the Fogg, as from the cloistered, masculine fastnesses of Princeton. Its students could not count upon the cachet of an Ivy League degree or setting, nor the promise of a good job associated with admission to a more exclusive, long-established institution. Although the director, Walter W. S. Cook, and first, leading professor Richard Offner, were fixed stars in the American academic firmament, students found a largely refugee faculty to whom the New university and museum World was often baffling, and whose standards and methods frequently differed from those the students had been led to expect. Having made the commitment to come to the Institute, most students were diligent and productive, accepting the great demands and rewards which the extremely independent, erudite, and sometimes unusually possessive faculty had to offer.

From this bubbling kettle of art historical endeavor came many students with M.A.'s and Ph.D.'s who had tackled far thornier and less tailor-made research subjects than their young colleagues elsewhere. Moreover, several students with M.A.'s from Halls of Ivy were prepared to face the somewhat Byzantine doctoral requirements of the Ph.D. degree at the Institute, rather than continue the bland, regimented diet previously their due.

Like most blessings, the young American graduate student's life at the Institute of Fine Arts must have been a somewhat mixed one, surrounded as he was by a host of distinguished European scholars, most of whom would normally have enjoyed supreme authority as sole full professor, department chairman, planner of the curriculum, and supervisor of graduate research. These professors, many of them the Grand Old Men of their fields, while deriving comfort from one another in terms of a shared past, occasionally found such proximity exasperating, cooped up in various improvisational housing arrangements—the basement of the Metropolitan Museum, a few rooms at the Croydon Hotel —until permanent sanctuary was found in the Gothic Warburg townhouse, prior to their apotheosis in the marble halls of the Duke House in 1960, by which time several of the Old Guard had died or retired. Some engaged in a certain rivalry for students, lining them up in their own ranks, but such exactions of loyalty rarely left lasting scars on the young, who, for the most part, probably preferred such benevolent despotism and passionate concern to the relative indifference of a graduate career elsewhere.

In the midst of a great Depression-beset city, with an extraordinarily heterogeneous student body, many working part-time, others with full-time jobs, taking courses in the evening over a long period of time to complete degree requirements, the Institute had little of the conventional *esprit de corps* of the neat clusters of graduate students clocked in and out of most of the larger universities on an efficient if somewhat mechanical basis. Small scholarship funds also precluded, in large part, the attraction of gifted students from far-away places who needed financial support. The Institute tended to be inclusive rather than exclusive, willing to wait and see if the student could pull through rather than pre-rating him with the appraising battery used by other graduate schools. Thus the student body was a mixture, including recent, excellently prepared college graduates attracted by the names of scholars with whose works they were already familiar, while others, often considerably older, had rather unorthodox academic backgrounds and might not have been admitted elsewhere. Themselves the victims of oppression and discrimination, many of the Institute faculty were unusually sympathetic to those whose education had been interrupted or thwarted, yet who were willing to make great sacrifices to work in the field of their choice. What other institutions would have viewed as great laxity if not excessive lenience in the Admissions Department often proved to bear fruit. Much excellent work came from a category known as "the late bloomers" who would never have been countenanced, let along allowed to flourish, at any of the other graduate departments.

VI

IN a very few cases, scholars who came to this country at a relatively advanced age seemed rejuvenated by the stimulus of a new land and a new language. Some elderly savants thrived under the sudden requirement to teach after decades of primarily independent, isolated research, revived through renewed contact with a much younger generation, benefitting from the immense efforts made to cope with the alien if friendly society in order to function within a totally novel although academic milieu. This American renaissance is seen most dramatically in the case of Walter Friedlaender and only a little less so with Paul Frankl. Survivors from the genial, fertile intellectual climate in Germany well before the First World War, from the days of such prolific, magnificent scholars as Schmarsow and Schlosser, both Friedlaender and Frankl had a certain *belle époque* expansiveness, endowed with unusual and deserved confidence in their own wide realms of interest.

The major miracle among refugee scholars was Walter Friedlaender (1873–1966). Already sixty-three when he arrived in this country in 1935, he was like some great solitary sea turtle washed up on a foreign shore, afflicted with indifferent health and poor hearing and eyesight. His long, creative life in America was to be a triumph of the spirit and the flesh. Voracious, inexhaustible, meddlesome, lovable, witty, and hugely intelligent, Friedlaender was obviously a giant among men. Reminiscent of both Rabelais and Voltaire, he was most interested in the art of the sixteenth through the early nineteenth centuries, embracing the oeuvre of Caravaggio, Poussin, and the Neo-classic and Romantic generations in France. His lust for life and art, the breadth of his interests, and the depth of his understanding were phenomenal. He brought to his teaching an endless font of intuitive brilliance, good sense, and good humor. As he grew still older, with no family of his own, Friedlaender's dependence upon his students grew; they "adopted" him, passing on their distinguished and demanding charge from one generation to the next.

Passionately interested in people—"I never stick my nose in my own business"—endowed with a gallic understanding of the Human Comedy, the grand old man's huge curiosity to know all about those he cared for may have driven away some superior students who wanted to share their minds but not their lives, but all in all, possessive though he may have been, Friedlaender could always give far more than he received.

His endless zest for art—only teaching what he loved—brought an element of pure pleasure into academic investigation which must have come as a welcome surprise to American graduate students who had been brought up in a rather tiresomely objective, impersonal manner. Friedlaender loved art, but he certainly did not put it on a pedestal, approaching his subject with an inimitable combination of delicacy and directness.

In this country he produced the major monograph on Caravaggio (1955) and a study of Poussin (1964), a new work on his old love, as well as volumes on Poussin drawings (1939–1953) and many important articles which included the art of the sixteenth, eighteenth, and nineteenth centuries as well as that of the baroque. Like several European scholars of the 1910's and 1920's, Friedlaender had been especially interested in Mannerism, whose psychological complexity seemed to parallel the states of mind then being investigated by Freud and his associates. Friedlaender was also concerned with the long equally unfashionable art of neo-classicism and early romanticism, and his pursuit of these areas has been followed with great productivity by young American scholars for almost thirty years.

The gifts which flowed from him in such prodigal fashion until almost the day of his death were so enveloping and so catching that even the less talented of his disciples shared in the old man's riches. Many somewhat timid, intellectually hesitant students suddenly bloomed from their association with Friedlaender, who found qualities in them that less interested, less generous or inspiring minds had not brought out. As though by an act of will, Friedlaender could produce promise, insight, and even subtlety in those where such attributes seemed absent. John Coolidge, one of his first students in America, director of the Fogg Art Museum from 1948 to 1968, has said of Friedlaender: "He was the skeptic, the gentle anarchist. In a world where Berensonian appraisals were largely unchallenged, even by his fellow émigrés, his interests were off-beat—Mannerism, Caravaggio, the painters of Napoleon. One vivid tribute to the effectiveness of his teaching is how orthodox these interests now seem."[42]

First trained as an architect, Paul Frankl built only one home, his own. Fortunately for future scholarship, it proved an almost total functional failure, so he turned to the history of architecture and art theory, enjoying an illustrious career until 1934, when he was dismissed from a professorship at Halle. Frankl remained in Germany until 1938, when his mammoth book *Das System der Kunstwissenschaft* was published—then seemingly his life work. All copies except Frankl's own were burned by the Nazis; the author inscribed his thousand-page *unikum* with the words, "It took courage to write this book; it may take even more courage to read it."

Coming to the United States at the age of sixty, he taught for two years at City College in a volunteer seminar organized by Julius S. Held between 1938 and 1940. One of his students, now a tycoon in the publishing field, cherishes memories of Frankl's inspired teaching and applies his views to art books. Becoming a member of the Institute for Advanced Study, Frankl was characterized by great modesty and simplicity. Working away day after day in the Marquand Library, he seemed like a blue-eyed baby hippopotamus, tenderly pleased with his own powers of physical and mental locomotion as he produced his vast definitive study *The Gothic: Literary Sources and Interpretations through Eight Centuries*, published in 1960. Typically, his contribution to Panofsky's *Festschrift* was a delightfully informative and gay study, "Bou-

42. "Walter Friedlaender, 1873–1966," p. 260.

cher's Girl on the Couch." Frankl's volume for the Pelican History of Art, *Gothic Architecture*, was completed at the age of eighty-two, on the very day of his death in 1962.[43]

With the stellar exceptions of Friedlaender and Frankl, few of the oldest émigrés who came to America could find the sort of stimulating contact with students that is often so beneficial to both master and pupil. The most glaring example of a failure to utilize a brilliantly endowed scholar is found in Hans Tietze's American years. His erudition and almost infinite field of competence in the field of Western art, coupled with unparalleled industry and drive, made his professional history unique. Born in Prague in 1880, Tietze came to Austria where he was first the student and then the assistant of Franz Wickhoff, among the finest scholars at the turn of the century. In 1906 he joined the Austrian Commission for Historical Monuments and produced innumerable articles and many monographs in this field. Tietze's ever increasing interest in contemporary art caused certain conflicts in his governmental work, and he joined the Department of Education in 1918, where he was much concerned with the distribution and incorporation of the Hapsburg collections; suggestions made by him at this time were only fully appreciated and followed after the Second World War. He helped found the fine Barockmuseum at the Upper Belvedere, but by 1925, thwarted by the Austrian bureaucracy, he resigned and became a professor at the University of Vienna. Despite Tietze's countless government and other duties, he wrote important articles ranging from medieval art and architecture to the painting of his own time and was a passionate advocate of many avant-garde artists including Schiele and Kokoschka whose splendid double portrait of Hans Tietze and his prodigiously scholarly wife Erica Tietze-Conrat now graces the Museum of Modern Art.

As Ernst Gombrich pointed out, "Exile overtook him at the age of 58, cutting deeper into his roots than it did with most other scholars." Unlike most of his émigré colleagues in America, Tietze found the transition from German to English a painful one, comparing his new language to the enforced use of a sieve which caused all subtle shadings and inflections to drain away. A visiting one-year professorship, fi-

43. For obituaries of Paul Frankl, see Richard Krautheimer, *Art Journal*, 22 (1963), 167–168; and Ernst C. Hassold, *Journal of Aesthetics and Art Criticism*, 21 (1962), 112.

nanced by the Carnegie Foundation, was arranged for Tietze at Toledo in 1938, but it is hard to imagine that that less than fascinating city, despite its fine museum, could have been an appropriate setting for him. Coming to New York, the Tietzes wrote many books and articles together, working into extreme old age with dazzling productivity and good sense, partially sustained by royalties and retainers for research from the National Gallery in Washington. Only shortly before his death in 1954 was Hans Tietze given a chance to teach in this country, conducting a course at Columbia on the Venetian painting he knew and loved so well. The aged, exiled scholar may have been a hugely unwieldy cog to fit in the often little wheel of American academic life. That Tietze should have led such a lonely and unused existence in America seems all the more unjust since he was perhaps the only art historian, apart from Hans Huth, to have interested himself deeply in American society and its special problems long before permanent residence in the United States, showing great familiarity with the literature and history of this country in his article "Das amerikanische Kulturproblem" of 1930.[44] Deprived of the support of a regular appointment and a sense of being needed, Tietze's isolated last years form the least happy ending in the tale of émigré art scholars in this country. His bibliography requires fourteen pages of fine type; it is no doubt incomplete.[45]

Endowed with almost total visual recall, Erica Tietze-Conrat's long memory included visits of Brahms to her father, whose Hungarian poems he set to music. As Gombrich wrote, "Forthright and fearless in the face of adversity, she cared for truth." Hard at work until the very end, she had a freezer and hotplate at her desk-side so that she could do the requisite cooking with a minimum of fuss. Her last, unfinished work was an iconographical reflection of her triumph of scholarly art over adversity, an essay on the motif of suicide in literature and art.[46]

Younger men than Friedlaender or Frankl often found the adjustment

44. *Zeitwende*, 8 (September, 1932), 181–189.

45. See Ernst H. Buschbeck, "Hans Tietze and His Reorganization of the Vienna Museums," *Essays in Honor of Hans Tietze* (eds. Ernst H. Gombrich, Julius Held, and Otto Kurz, Paris, 1958), pp. 373ff. For a bibliography of Tietze's works, see pp. 439–453. See Gombrich's obituary in *Burlington Magazine*, 96 (1954), 289–290; and Held's obituary in *Art Journal*, 14 (1954), 67–69. For Erica Tietze-Conrat's obituary, see Gombrich, *Burlington Magazine*, 101 (1959), 144.

46. Her bibliography is included in *Essays in Honor of Hans Tietze*, pp. 454–459.

to this country far harder. These "senior non-citizens" belonged to a more secure generation than their juniors as they were rooted in a relatively magnanimous past, in the era so unforgettably described in Sibyl Bedford's *The Legacy* (1956). Having won their laurels with far less blood, sweat, and tears, the elder refugees sacrificed less of themselves in attaining museum or university appointments and may have viewed their loss with more stoicism than could their younger colleagues, who were forced to leave academic or museum appointments of real authority and power in their peak years. Scholars in their late thirties, forties, and early fifties could not help being more than momentarily stunned by the loss of position as they struggled with a new language and an exotic society which was as different from Europe as that of Japan and all the more baffling for its fleeting, deceptive resemblance to aspects of the Continent from which they came.

With few exceptions, the children, if any, of the older scholars were already financially independent, so that the parents needed only minimal subsistence to permit them to round out the works of a lifetime, or to undertake research for museums, publishers, or dealers. The younger men, with families to support, often found the pressures and demands agonizing. Far from ready to sing their swansong, they were in the midst of their research, their lives savagely interrupted, often unable to work as productively and consistently as their elder fellows for years to come since they were young enough to be saddled with the large teaching and administrative demands of the American campus.

Outstanding among the younger generation was the late Karl Lehmann (1894–1960), who at the early age of thirty-eight was Professor Ordinarius at the University of Münster when the decrees of 1933 forced him to leave his appointment and enter Italian exile. Born into an academic family—his father was a professor of law at Rostock—Karl Lehmann's life was devoted to the study of classical art, which he taught at the Institute of Fine Arts from 1935 until his retirement in 1958.

He was also director of the Archaeological Research Fund of New York University and William Allan Neilson Research Professor at Smith College in 1958–59. In addition to a productive American career as teacher and scholar and director of the rich finds excavated at Samothrace (where he set up the museum that was given to Greece),

Professor Lehmann found time to write the important monograph entitled *Thomas Jefferson, American Humanist*, published in 1947.

A lecturer of unparalled eloquence, Karl Lehmann brought to his subject the breadth of knowledge of a late nineteenth-century humanistic-philological training, which caused Lehmann to call himself a "fossil of the nineteenth century." Frederick Hartt wrote:

The doctrine and the influence of Karl Lehmann transcended the immediate limits of his courses and his writings. In his lectures he presented in brilliant detail the complex drama of interacting forces that characterized the artistic civilizations of ancient Greece and Rome. Yet from this kaleidoscopic spectacle there emerged imperceptible in the mind and memory of the student a sense of the enduring structure of classical humanistic values on which subsequent cultural achievements have largely been based.[47]

A regal, occasionally even imperious man, Lehmann inspired awe as well as admiration; the cozy veneer of American academic life was not cut to his measure. Independent and complex, the less happy facet of Lehmann's personality may have been cut by his isolation from a stellar, centrifugal position in a great German university in which the full spectrum of his erudition and authority could have been most fully exercised. The fact that few if any of the American classical societies availed themselves of his extraordinary abilities must have also contributed to a certain defensiveness which would have quite naturally arisen in the course of exile.[48]

Another distinguished émigré scholar in the field of ancient art, Professor Otto Brendel of Columbia University, spent many years at Washington University in Saint Louis, where he shared an astonishingly broad range of erudition, combining special interests in Roman art with Picasso studies.

A new area in art historical research, the art of the Central Asian migrations, was brought to the United States with the migration of Alfred Salmony (1890–1958). Active in museum work rather than teaching in Cologne, he became joint editor of *Artibus Asiae* from 1924 to 1932 and continued to edit the journal when he revived it in this country, from

47. Frederick Hartt, "Art and Freedom in Quattrocento Florence," *Essays in Memory of Karl Lehmann* (ed. Lucy Freeman Sandler, New York, 1967), p. 114.
48. For a bibliography of his works, see *Essays in Memory of Karl Lehmann*, pp. vii–xv. For his obituary by Phyllis Pray Bober, see *Gnomon*, 33 (1961).

1946 until his death. Dr. Salmony taught at Mills College and the University of Washington before coming to the Institute of Fine Arts, and his studies were sponsored by the Art Institute of Chicago, Vassar College, and presumably C. T. Loo, for whom he wrote several jade catalogs. His publications include *Carved Jades of Ancient China* (1938) and *Antler and Tongue* (1954). He died on the way to his sixth journey to Russia, where he had undertaken so much productive research. Professor Salmony's interests supplemented the study of an area long popular among American scholars and collectors—ancient Chinese bronzes and jades, of which such abundant collections are to be found in New York, Washington, Boston, Chicago, and Minneapolis.

The most celebrated of émigré scholars in America, Erwin Panofsky (1892–1968), first came to America to teach at the Institute of Fine Arts in the fall of 1931. He then arranged with the University of Hamburg to spend alternate terms there and in New York. Teaching and lecturing at many institutions such as Bryn Mawr, Vassar, Harvard, New York University, Northwestern, Princeton, and Yale, Panofsky brought his great scholarship to a wide academic audience, including St. Vincent College, sponsor of a lecture resulting in the publication of *Gothic Architecture and Scholasticism* (1951). Steeped in such ancillary fields as the history of science, literature, philosophy (especially Neo-Platonism), and theology, Panofsky brought any and all of these fields to bear upon whatever area in art or architecture happened to be the object of his fruitful scrutiny. His *Studies in Iconology: Humanistic Themes in the Art of the Renaissance* (1939) brought out, in English, a wealth of information related to the studies then being published by Panofsky and his colleagues Saxl, Wind, Gombrich, and Wittkower in the *Journal of the Warburg Institute*, making available to a wide audience a sense and understanding of the realms of inquiry that had first been opened by Giehlow, Schlosser, Borinski, Warburg, and himself earlier in the century in German and Austrian *Jahrbücher* and other scholarly journals, especially the *Vorträge der Bibliothek Warburg*.

Panofsky's influence on American historical scholarship, especially in the realms of literature and musicology, is almost as noteworthy as that upon younger art historians. He was one of the few great scholars who could teach a method, impart a sense of special approach, and communicate a certain utilization and employment of cultural resources through his lectures and writings in such a way that the significance of his *oeuvre* extended far beyond the particular subject to which he had addressed himself.

The Life and Art of Albert Dürer (Princeton, 1943) has gone into four editions and, like the *Studies in Iconology*, brought together decades of Dürer scholarship by Panofsky and others which had previously been almost entirely in German. This book internationalizes a field long inaccessible to Americans without mastery of that language. The same may be said for *Early Netherlandish Painting*: *Its Origins and Character* (Cambridge, 1953), of still greater interest to this country since it possesses so many major works of art examined in the book. Most important of all, in terms of bringing Panofsky's studies to the widest audience, is the paperback anthology *Meaning in the Visual Arts* (Doubleday Anchor, 1955).

As first art historian at the Institute for Advanced Study, Panofsky shaped the selection of scholars who came there on a permanent or visiting basis, providing such outstanding men as Paul Frankl, Charles de Tolnay, Kurt Weitzmann, and many others with an invaluable opportunity to work uninterruptedly. Retiring from the Princeton Institute, where he was succeeded by Millard Meiss, Panofsky returned to the Institute of Fine Arts, where he was Samuel F. B. Morse Professor until his death early this year.

Jakob Rosenberg, Panofsky's junior by one year, came to Harvard's Fogg Art Museum in 1937 as print curator and professor specializing in Dutch and Flemish seventeenth-century art. His earlier professional life was spent in the Berlin museum, where he was Max J. Friedlaender's assistant, and active in the great print room there. A student of Wölfflin, and a painstaking, judicious, unusually temperate scholar, Dr. Rosenberg brought a welcome sense of quiet contemplation and sensitive yet forceful scrutiny to the study of the work of art, with a constant reminder that it *is* art, rather than an exercise in symbolism, propaganda, or literary allusion. The author of monographs of Rembrandt (1964) and earlier of Ruisdael (1928), Rosenberg is also much interested in the art of Rubens and that of the fifteenth-century master Schongauer. A man of gentle speech and calm, introspective demeanor, Dr.

Rosenberg has managed to impart, in deceptively effortless, seemingly understated fashion, much of the interest, sympathy, and understanding for the art of the Northern seventeenth century which is the subject of such renewed concern today.

Not narrowly restricted in scope, Dr. Rosenberg has long been a great admirer of the art of this century and has done a brilliant job of building up the Fogg's collection of the recent master print-makers of Germany and France. His clear gaze, encompassing the total achievement of the seventeenth century and many earlier and later fields, has enlightened these areas for many curators and teachers throughout the United States, whose privilege it has been to be his students.

A different, more dynamic approach characterizes Professor Richard Krautheimer (1897–   ) who came to this country from Marburg, where he had been Privatdozent, teaching at Louisville from 1935 to 1937 and then at Vassar and the Institute of Fine Arts. The breadth of his interests—from the Early Christian period through the Italian Baroque with special concern in the history of architecture and sculpture—has made him one of the most stirring teachers and scholars. An active archaeologist, he unites a refreshing awareness of actual problems in technique and construction with an equally profound knowledge of art theory and liturgy. Professor Krautheimer is the author of the great monograph on Lorenzo Ghiberti, written in collaboration with Trude Krautheimer-Hess; the Pelican *Early Christian and Byzantine Architecture* (1965); and is now Wrightsman Professor at the Institute. Charged with wit and excitement, Krautheimer's imaginative temperament is accompanied by a rigorous, exacting approach. He lectures with dramatic eloquence, in a fluent, somewhat British English, which carries the listener along an audacious, revealing journey into art. For all the erudition at his command, Krautheimer has never lost a sense of spontaneity and enthusiasm which encourages students to share and continue some of the more austere as well as the more immediately attractive of his many interests.

A curious meeting of art history, American history, and Early Christian archaeology took place when Richard Krautheimer was called in during the Second World War to advise the Air Force, then compiling a list of the most important monuments of Rome to be preserved from bombing. The only one on the list to be hit, S. Lorenzo fuori le Mura, revealed through war damage important aspects of its construction and early history that had been totally obscured over the centuries, which have been explored and published by Professor Krautheimer in various studies and will be included in his *Corpus Basilicarum Christianarum Romae.*

His concern with the latest Western architecture as well as some of the earliest has contributed to the building of one of the handsomest buildings in New York. Teaching at Vassar, Dr. Krautheimer led one of his students, Phyllis Bronfman Lambert, to work with Mies van der Rohe in an architectural career. When her father was planning to add yet another bleached ziggurat to the Manhattan skyline as headquarters for his Seagram Corporation, Mrs. Lambert prevailed upon him to select Mies, and the end of the story is architectural history.

Krautheimer's mastery of the history of architecture, a subject singularly attuned to the American temper, together with his gifts as a teacher, make him the most influential of his émigré colleagues in the United States, attracting and directing the best students to carry on his work.

A former colleague of Krautheimer's and past master of the major and minor arts, Martin Weinberger (1893–1965) came to the Institute of Fine Arts from a museum career in Munich. First teaching in this country, he brought to his work the scrutiny and skepticism of the museum man, with the breadth of interest and knowledge of the humanist. In addition to his concern with Italian sculpture from Pisano to Michelangelo, Dr. Weinberger was endlessly curious and knowledgeable in the field of decorative arts, including textiles and furniture. Among his first activities in America were the curatorship of the Robert Lehman collection and the cataloguing of the vast George Gray Barnard collection preparatory to its sale. Totally uncompromising, a loner and curmudgeon by fate, not inclination, Martin Weinberger was a lumbering wounded bear of a man. He spoke with extraordinary delicacy and elegance; his great sensitivity and purity were as much at odds with the Brave New World as with the Bad Old One. His monograph on *The Sculpture of Michelangelo* (1967) was published posthumously.

Another master of the art of Michelangelo, Charles de Tolnay (1899–), of Hungarian birth and German and Austrian training, has published extensively in the field of Netherlandish art as well as that of the Italian Renaissance. His earlier European studies of Campin, Van Eyck, and Bruegel are all milestones in the history of art. In America, in addition to his five-volume monograph on Michelangelo (Princeton, 1943–1960), Dr. de Tolnay published a study of *The Drawings of Pieter Bruegel the Elder* (New York, 1952). A Fellow at the Institute for Advanced Study and professor at Princeton and Columbia, Dr. de Tolnay had no opportunity to establish a following since all his academic appointments were on a visiting basis. He has returned to Europe, where he is now, most appropriately, director of Michelangelo's Casa Buonarroti in Florence.

Adolph Katzenellenbogen (1901–1965, Ph.D. Hamburg 1933), the prominent medievalist, left Germany in 1939, teaching at Vassar from 1940 to 1953 and at Smith from 1956 to 1958. His death cut short a most productive career at just the time when, as departmental chairman at Johns Hopkins, he was about to establish a major new graduate faculty. His studies such as *The Sculptural Program at Chartres* (1959) and those of Hans Swarzenski, another émigré scholar and curator at the Museum of Fine Arts, Boston, have brought new life to medieval scholarship in America, a field that never quite fulfilled the promise of the 1920's and 1930's.[49]

A fine musician as well as an outstanding art historian, Wolfgang Stechow (1896–) elected a somewhat quiet but far from retiring American academic life after coming to this country in 1936. Teaching at Wisconsin for four years, he then went to Oberlin where he was department chairman and director of the Allen Memorial Art Museum. Few other teachers in America have imparted such care and thought to their students. Stechow has developed several of the most responsible and enlightened museum curators in the country. His own numerous and uniformly excellent publications—most recently *Dutch Landscape Painting of the Seventeenth Century* (1966)—have also contributed to insights in the realms of both iconography and Dutch and Flemish painting. He has had emeritus *Wanderjahre*, teaching at Michigan and Williamstown and is now advisory curator of European art at the Cleveland Museum.

49. See his obituary by Harry Bober in *Art Journal*, 24 (1965), 347.

The forceful, original personality of Richard Bernheimer must certainly have made itself felt at both Bryn Mawr and Haverford, where the former Munich scholar was professor of art history from 1933 until his death in 1958 and wrote on such diverse subjects as *Wild Men in the Middle Ages: A Study in Art, Sentiment and Demonology* (1952), the Gothic Revival in sixteenth-century Italy, and the posthumously published *Nature of Representation: A Phenomenological Inquiry* (1961).

Professor Julius S. Held (1905–   ) received his Ph.D. from Freiburg in 1930. After two years of apprenticeship in the Staatliche Museum in Berlin, terminated by the decree of 1933, he came to this country the following year. Held started publishing in American journals prior to leaving Germany. He is on the faculty of Barnard College, where he has taught from 1937 to the present and has taught at the Institute of Fine Arts, also lecturing at Bryn Mawr, the New School, Yale, and the Metropolitan Museum. Held has done much to revive and maintain scholarly interest in this country in the field of Flemish and Dutch fifteenth-, sixteenth-, and seventeenth-century art, most outstandingly that of Rubens. Like Wolfgang Stechow, Held has been especially effective as a teacher in his ability to combine criteria of connoisseurship with those of historic and stylistic significance, breaking the barriers between the visual and the literary. His informed, refreshingly eclectic taste has contributed recently to the building of the most rewarding museum collection at Ponce, Puerto Rico, the donation of Luis Ferré, whose acquisition policy has been guided by Julius Held since its inception.

John Rewald (1912–   ) presents the example of an extraordinarily productive and successful scholarly career in America, without, until recently, any academic affiliation. Receiving his doctorate from the Sorbonne in 1936, Rewald published monographs in Paris and London before coming to New York in 1941. For almost three decades this German-born, French-educated authority in the field of Impressionism and related art has written the invaluable, fundamental studies on his subject—exhaustive, self-contained, admirably documented and ordered. Rewald has done for French nineteenth-century painting what Max J. Friedlaender did for that of the early Netherlandish painters—staked out a generous claim to a century and country of major achievement and mined it responsibly and comprehensively, sharing his finds with the United States, which is so unbelievably rich in the field. Rewald has been a professor at the University of Chicago since 1963 and has also worked with museums and galleries in the preparation of many important exhibits.

Dr. Margarete Bieber came to this country in 1934 in the midst of her most productive, distinguished career, leaving Giessen, where she was head of the Department of Archaeology and occupied the monumentally-entitled position of *Planmässiger ausserordentlicher Professor*. She had received an affidavit from Dean Gildersleeve at Barnard, teaching there for two years before joining the graduate department of Columbia, where she enjoyed an illustrious career. An indefatigable scholar, Dr. Bieber is still active in her field at the age of eighty-one, if one may divulge this most remarkable lady's age.

Another Athena at Columbia is Dr. Edith Porada, one of the most outstanding scholars in the field of Ancient Near Eastern art and archaeology. She left Vienna in the midst of her doctoral research in 1938. After tackling a variety of unacademic jobs in her first year and embarking on a lecture tour in the one following, Dr. Porada received a fellowship from the American Philosophical Society in 1940, continuing her studies for the next five years with temporary positions at the Walters Art Gallery and Pantheon Books. She was a Bollingen Fellow in 1947. Dr. Porada joined the Queens faculty in 1950 and Columbia in 1959. She was the Norton Lecturer at Harvard in 1967. Although her doctorate was completed in this country, Dr. Porada's personality was, happily, "completed" in Austria, bringing to her teaching and scholarship a most welcome warmth and grace.

Very few émigré scholars with German doctorates permitted much time to lapse between their arrival in this country and the continuation of their scholarly career. An exception is the brilliant scholar of the art of Hieronymus Bosch, Professor Lotte Brand Philip, of Queens College. She spent her first years in this country as a designer of costume jewelry and only returned to art history about a decade later. She has taught at Bryn Mawr and New York University and brings to her scholarship and her teaching a sense of life and broad understanding of the practical considerations of the artist's craft, most recently demonstrated in a revolutionary study of the Ghent Altarpiece where solutions to seemingly insoluble problems have come about through a searching investigation of the character and function of the frame of the work. One of the reasons for Dr. Philip's excellence as a teacher may stem from her long professional work in an unacademic field which has contributed to the unusually stimulating freshness and directness of her approach.

Perhaps the European art historian whose insight, vivacity, and informed approach to art influenced the most undergraduates is Professor Frances Gray Godwin, a student of Strzygowski, who came to New York University from Vienna in 1931 to complete her graduate studies under Richard Offner. Working since 1945 at a very large department of a very large college, Queens, through which thousands passed annually, it would be difficult to exaggerate her importance as an inspiring teacher. Numbers of excellent students have gone on to graduate school and courses in art history due to the unusually high level of instruction and infectious enthusiasm for scholarship that Professor Godwin has been able to maintain and impart with such matchless persuasiveness.

VII

THE American museum world, always delicately and ambiguously poised between the worlds of Art, Society, and the Commonweal, was one to which many refugees were drawn, since their entire working experience in Germany and Austria had been in this area. The major American art museums were, in the main, far less interested in availing themselves of refugee scholar-curators than the universities and colleges were in their professorial colleagues. One might bear in mind, as kindly noted by John Coolidge, that "the great museums never recovered from the depression, and the emergence of middle rank museums during the '30's and '40's (Toledo, Hartford, Worcester in the Taylor era, Buffalo) was based on the exploitation of local resources which precluded much dependence upon refugees."[50] The Boston Museum of Fine Arts, whose warm welcome for Georg Swarzenski as Fellow for Research in Medieval Art and in sculpture, and later his son Hanns (the present Curator of Decorative Arts) and Bernard Bothmer (now Curator of Egyptian Art at the Brooklyn Museum and on the faculty of the Institute of Fine Arts), is certainly the happiest exception to the rule. The same may be said for the Fogg, with its proud possession of the curatorial and educational talents of Jakob Rosenberg and George M. A. Hanfmann.

Since the main function of the American museum official is that of increasing the collection of art, money, or attendance, the refugee scholar-curator, with his specialized interests, academic orientation, and ignorance of the Social Register, was seen as an undesirable *rara avis*. Accustomed as he was to real independence, time for individual research, and the automatic acceptance of his suggestions for new acquisitions—their proposal a mere formality—the European museum man must have found himself utterly perplexed by the folkways of most of his sister institutions in America, where few of these activities were even remotely countenanced. Usually conservatively oriented, conducted with neo-Byzantine protocol, America's major museums have rarely welcomed Jews to their employ. In fairness to American museum officials, the didactic zeal and scholarly hauteur of several refugee curators must have been hard to take. Some directors with truly generous intentions may occasionally have had second thoughts in later encounters with the occasionally implacable subjects of their aid. All in all, this was certainly not a case of opposites attracting.

Considering the topic of the careers of the few émigrés from Germany and Austria who managed to penetrate the gilded Iron Curtain of most of this country's major museums' hiring policies, one must begin with the life of Paul J. Sachs (1876–1965), without whose generous advancement of refugee colleagues there would be very little to write of. Although entirely of American birth (New York), education (Harvard), and parentage, it is tempting to include Sachs as an émigré scholar since his background and career so often parallel those of the refugees of the 1930's. Trained for the family bank of Goldman, where he worked

50. Letter of August 1, 1967.

from 1904 to 1914, Sachs left after a decade to teach, first at Wellesley's art department and then at Harvard, where he brought a range of interests, especially in drawings, that had long been popular in Northern Europe. He sprang from the art-loving German Jewish mercantile milieu which had already contributed so much to the culture of New York, his family in some ways reminiscent of the activities and the interests of the Warburgs of Hamburg and New York. Both he, his brother Arthur, and his former associate Henry Goldman formed art collections of the first magnitude, now dispersed in museums and private ownership throughout America and Europe.

In addition to his importance as builder of the collections at the Fogg Art Museum through his own benefactions and the encouragement of such prodigious collectors as Grenville Winthrop in the drawing field (initially guided by Charles Eliot Norton, Winthrop bequeathed his works *in toto* to the Fogg), Paul J. Sachs continued the rapport between Harvard and the newer wealth of New York, initiated by Norton and Eliot. A passionate collector of drawings and masterful teacher of museum personnel—Sachs's Harvard course staffed the musems of America in the 1930's and 1940's—he was drawn to the scholarly world of the art connoisseur for its social as well as narrowly academic assets. Younger than Waldstein and Berenson, Sachs managed to lead the life of his liking in America, finding the official acceptance his elders probably missed. Sachs purchased Charles Eliot Norton's residence in Cambridge and may well prove to have been the first Jew to receive major appointments in the museum and art history field at a long-established American university. On countless committees, tireless and enthusiastic, a visiting lecturer at the Courtauld, Bonn, and Paris, Sachs was president of the American Association of Museum Directors and a trustee of Smith College, the Boston Museum of Fine Arts, Wellesley, Radcliffe, the Institute of Contemporary Art, and the Museum of Modern Art, whose founder, Alfred Barr, had been his student, as are the present directors of the Boston Museum and Art Institute of Chicago.

It was partially due to Sachs that the Meyers, Naumburgs, Warburgs, and Wertheims made their great donations to the Fogg Art Museum of Harvard University, but, even more important in terms of American scholarship was Sachs's most sympathetic role in the lives of a considerable number of the refugees of the 1930's, helping them secure what employment they could in an inhospitable field. Thanks to his double-barreled influence as prominent academician and multiple trustee, many distinguished émigré scholars and curators, including Otto Benesch, George M. A. Hanfmann, Hans Huth, Jakob Rosenberg, Georg and Hanns Swarzenski, Emmanuel Winternitz, and many others, received invaluable encouragement and support in often bitter and difficult times.

While the major American art museums have generally eschewed adding émigré scholars to their curatorial staffs, they have long assumed an educational role, albeit conducted on an extremely popular level. Most refugees were amazed by the emphasis upon instruction offered by art museums here, which include education as a department capable of curation. This sometimes relentless didacticism of the American museum differs markedly from the policy of European museums—largely "nationalized palace collections," they feel no need to justify their *raison d'être.* Whatever educational endeavors were undertaken by the great Berlin and Vienna, Frankfurt and Munich museums usually took the role of excellent, bulky annuals, largely the result of original scholarship undertaken by their own curatorial staffs and destined for a very limited audience, publications infinitely more elaborate and costly than the most lavish, generally lightweight American art museum bulletins.

Perhaps as a result of the merit and fame of such European museum publications, émigré European scholars have been permitted, in considerable number, to participate in the preparation of museum catalogs, work which, in the main, offered so little prestige to the American curators that they willingly consigned this seemingly arid, prosaic activity to the foreign-born newcomer.

Such exemplary catalogs as George Steindorff's work on the Egyptian collection of the Walters Art Gallery and Charles Sterling's for the Metropolitan Museum are important examples of special scholarship which would not have been undertaken in America had it not been for the availability of "foreign talent."

Urbane, sophisticated, a man of broad cultivation, the Metropolitan Museum's Francis Henry Taylor did bring in distinguished scholars—Olga Raggio, Charles Sterling, and Emmanuel Winternitz—but he and his successor James Rorimer were long reluctant to promote them, and the best known, Charles Sterling, returned to the Louvre, coming back to this country permanently to teach at New York University's Institute of Fine Arts.

A happy exception among refugee scholars seeking to continue museum careers in American was Georg Swarzenski, for many years the director of the Staedel Institut in Frankfurt until 1939, and a distinguished medievalist. Coming to America in late middle age, he found an appointment, with the help of Paul J. Sachs, as Fellow for Research in Medieval Art and Sculpture at the Museum of Fine Arts, Boston. In a charming account of his early years there, Georg Swarzenski recalled that one of the museum's trustees informed him that a suitable hour for special research was before 8 a.m. Nonetheless, his tenure at the museum was a rewarding one; some of the reasons for this were recalled by Edwin J. Hipkiss, the curator of the Department of Decorative Arts: "It is remarkable, as I see it, that the former Director of an important European museum, an art historian and a scholar of recognized accomplishments, should join the Director and Curators of an American museum and delight us with a versatile ability matched by tact, courtesy and even modesty. It is my pleasure to repeat: Here we call him the gentle doctor and we speak from the heart."[51]

There were, understandably, some to whom Hipkiss might politely have referred as Ungentle Doctors, embittered and intractable, used to the authority and deference which they had received for decades and therefore far less readily assimilable with the museum world. Such was the late Otto Benesch, former curator of the Albertina, to which he returned as director after the war. His years at the Fogg and Wellesley seem to have been stormy, chiefly remembered for Benesch's perpetual, unremitting insistence upon the inferiority of all things American. Nevertheless, his years of American residence saw the writing of his masterly *Art of the Renaissance in Northern Europe* (1945), an invaluable introduction to a highly complex subject, where most of the literature is in German. It may well be that such an unbiased work, traversing the borders of Germany, France, and the Netherlands with almost unprec-

51. *Essays in Honor of Georg Swarzenski*, p. 8. For Swarzenski's publications, see pp. 261–267.

edented objectivity, could only have been produced by a writer working in America. His teaching at Wellesley gave students the opportunity to learn about fields rarely included in the American art historical curriculum.

Among the most original, innovational personalities in art scholarship sent by Hitler to America was the late Alexander Dorner, from 1922 to 1936 director of the revolutionary Landesmuseum in Hannover, which, with the Bauhaus, was one of the finest manifestations of the Weimar Republic. There he had worked in collaboration with E. Lissitzky, the Russian Constructivist, to install the Abstract Cabinet, a gallery of contemporary art, also known as the Gallery of Our Time, containing a prophetic assemblage of synaesthesia, combining Moholy-Nagy's *Light Machine* (now at Harvard's Busch-Reisinger) with stage designs and films. No small compliment to Dorner's concern with contemporary, advanced currents in German art may be seen in the fact that his museum made the major "contribution" to the contents of the notorious *Entartete Kunst* exhibition held in Munich in 1937, 270 works in all. In 1928 he already advocated the provision of literature and audio-visual aids, introduced by him at the Museum of the Rhode Island School of Design and adopted by the National Gallery in Washington about twenty-five years later. Many of his exhibitions in the "Good Design" field, held in the 1920's, appear to have been the models for those at the Museum of Modern Art. Dorner was one of the very few to be entrusted with the directorship of an American museum, that of the Rhode Island School of Design. There he "bought back" two paintings by Franz Marc which he had originally purchased for Hannover, included among the *Entartete Kunst* in 1937 and sold to an American dealer. Dorner resigned from the museum, after considerable friction with the trustees in 1941, to lecture on art history and aesthetics at Brown University. His *Way Beyond "Art"* was published in 1947, and two years later Dorner joined the Bennington faculty, where he was the earliest to see the museum possibilities of Buckminster Fuller's architecture, first realized at Expo in 1967, a decade after Dorner's death.

In several instances, émigré scholars, pioneering in the advanced instruction in art history on campuses where this was a relatively new subject, laid the way for further development and employment of other

European specialists. When Richard Krautheimer, after teaching at the University of Louisville, left for Vassar in 1937, he was succeeded by Justus Bier, a specialist in German fifteenth-century sculpture and formerly director of the Kestner Gesellschaft in Hannover. At first changing from museum work to teaching, Bier became department head from 1941 to 1960 and director of the Allen R. Hite Institute of the University, also finding time to be art editor and critic of *The Courier-Journal* and to write copiously on German fifteenth-century sculpture. In 1961 he returned to the museum field when he became director of the North Carolina Museum of Art in Raleigh, the only state-initiated and state-subsidized art museum in the country, where his predecessor had been W. R. Valentiner. It seems appropriate that this museum, whose founding is far more in the European style than the general American pattern of building first and collecting later, should have had on its Art Commission another émigré scholar, the late Dr. Clemens Sommer, chairman of the Art Department at Chapel Hill.

Many important contributions to the museums of America have been made by Rudolph Berliner, Harold Joachim, Antonio Morassi, Guido Schoenberger, Heinrich Schwarz, William Suida, and Lionello Venturi. These men have brought a much needed deepening and broadening of the museum collections in America, sometimes combatting considerable opposition in order to explore and enrich the fields of their special interests for the museums so fortunate as to have them in their employ.

Among the happiest examples of the ability of a European with deep interest and ability but little previous professional experience to make scholarly contributions in America are Mrs. Kate T. Steinitz, working in Los Angeles, and Emmanuel Winternitz, in New York. Neither had been professionally active in the museum or art research fields prior to arriving in this country in the late 1930's. Mrs. Steinitz, who had worked as an artist in her native Germany, after some art historical studies on the East Coast following the death of her husband in 1942, found herself in the employ of Dr. Elmer Belt, a Los Angeles physician, then engaged in building up a library devoted to Leonardo da Vinci. She recalls, "I consulted Dr. Elmer Belt as a surgeon; he diagnosed my knowledge of art literature." With the understanding, interest, financial support, and enthusiasm of Dr. Belt behind her, Mrs. Steinitz has helped develop his Library of Vinciana into a research center of international importance, since 1961 donated to the University of California in Los Angeles. She has made new discoveries concerning the Renaissance genius, many of them in the most complex realm of textual matters, also finding time to teach at Pomona.

Appropriately enough, the other brilliant, initially amateur scholar, Emmanuel Winternitz, has also been involved in Vinciana, the author of several revealing articles on Leonardo and the relationship of his music to his art. A lawyer with enormous interest in the history of music in his native Austria, Winternitz also taught at the *Hochschule* and participated in a Cassirer seminar at the University of Hamburg. An active musicologist and scintillating lecturer, with all the wit and verve of Vienna, Emmanuel Winternitz has brought more advanced knowledge of music and art to a wider audience than any other scholar. A lecture that he gave at Paul Sachs's invitation at the Fogg resulted in Francis Henry Taylor's appointing him Curator of Musical Instruments at the Metropolitan Museum, where Winternitz has combined history of art, musicology, and curatorship.[52] In addition to his constant curatorial responsibilities at the Museum, Winternitz has taught at Yale, where he was Visiting Professor for eleven years, and many other institutions. Through his lectures, exhibitions, and articles, he continues to make a uniquely valuable contribution to art history and musicology in America. The fact that neither Mrs. Steinitz nor Dr. Winternitz have had to work within a rigid, pre-existing academic framework, largely shaping their careers to personal interests rather than formal requirements, may well have played an important role in letting them develop into the delightfully independent, vivacious, and authoritative scholars and curators they are.

An unusually active and productive career in the museum field has been that of Hans Huth, who came to this country at the end of 1938 from Berlin, where he worked as administrator of the former royal palaces and library of Prussia. Despite the aid of Paul Sachs, who knew of Huth's great knowledge in the field of the decorative arts, he was un-

52. See James Delihas, "Winternitz: Notes on a Well-Tempered Curator," *Metropolitan Museum Bulletin* (Summer, 1967), pp. 24–28.

able to secure a teaching appointment in this country, due to his lack of experience and what were viewed as his too *recherché* interests. His proposal for the improvement of historical museums, many of them under the supervision of the National Park Service, prompted the latter to hire him under a special grant from the Carl Schurz Foundation, and at the same time he conducted the Museum Training Course at the Institute of Fine Arts. Huth remained a consultant to the Park Service after leaving its employ in 1942 to join the curatorial staff in the decorative arts at the Chicago Art Institute, where he was to become curator of the department until retirement in 1965.

Hans Huth has long been interested in the American approach to natural conservation and the growth of parks and landscape design and had written on this subject prior to coming to this country, where his studies resulted in *Nature and the American*, published in 1958 by the University of California, where he has taught. His White House Inventory (done with the Park Service) culminated in the new scholarly approach brought to the care of the White House in the Kennedy years by a First Lady whose art history courses at Vassar may have contributed to her thoughtful stewardship. Huth's articles in the *Warburg Journal* and elsewhere have done much to familiarize Europeans as well as his new countrymen with an important yet much neglected aspect of their cultural heritage.

While the academically affiliated refugee art scholars have taught innumerable American students since the mid-1930's, one should not lose sight of another important, unsung educational institution in which German and Austrian émigré art specialists functioned informally, which might best be entitled the Free University of 57th Street and Madison Avenue. Countless American curators and collectors learned more about their special interests from visits to the galleries and antique shops run by European refugees than from lectures at their Alma Maters or the pages of learned journals. Although gifted and often erudite art dealers such as the fabulous Joseph Brummer (a Rumanian pupil of Rodin), the Samuels, Knoedlers, and Duveens were established in America long before Hitler, the rise of Nazism brought a flood of gallery people whose cultivation and knowledge were often far in advance of their American colleagues in the trade, whom they had, in fact, been supplying in happier years. Generally university-trained, the "new dealers" were widely traveled, highly literate, endowed with sophisticated taste and often at home with the latest scholarly publications. Unlike the most powerful of their American competitors, the refugees could not specialize in purveying an Instant Medici or Marie Antoinette milieu. They were free or forced to indulge in a more personal, and less expensive, less narrowly prescribed world, without the million-dollar masterpieces. Often interested in the then unfashionable fields such as Mannerism, the Italian Baroque, and the primitive, European dealers in America were able to provide a far more catholic selection, acquainting their clientele with a wider range than the Fifth Avenue galleries generally found profitable. Admittedly, few of the émigrés had the capital they might have liked and needed to buy the "gold chip" Old Masters of the moment, but their very necessity was the mother of invention which brought a vast range of fascinating and important art to the American market.

With the establishment of refugee artists and dealers in New York throughout the 1930's and early 1940's, that city became the center of the international art market. Georges Wildenstein came to reside in New York (where his family firm had long had a branch), where he published the *Gazette des beaux-arts* during the war years. Other famous galleries and dealers, such as Leopold Blumka, Rudolph Heinemann, Paul Rosenberg, Saemy Rosenberg, Germain Seligmann, and Erich Stiebel, came from Germany and France, bringing with them major works of art, many of which entered American museums and private collections. Among the best known of the smaller yet influential firms was the gallery of the late Hans Schaeffer, working closely with American museums, and those of Messrs. Drey, Lilienfeld, Mont, and Tannhauser.

Newer to America and therefore more important as a cultural influence were the large number of dealers concerned with contemporary art or with what was then known as Modern Art, for which, with a few early exceptions such as Alfred Stieglitz and later Julien Levi and Kirk Askew, American collectors and museum directors had always to go to Paris and Berlin. Dominating the modern market, New York's leadership was initiated by the brilliant activities of the late Otto Gerson, the

Perls, and especially the late Curt Valentin, whose sure taste and handsome installation and publication of the works of Calder, Moore, Lipschitz, and Picasso made a critical contribution to the American art scene. His authoritative yet charming personality influenced the taste and obviously the purchasing policies of many American museums and did much to continue the innovational and inspired work begun by A. Everett Austin, Jr. and Alfred Barr, Jr. in the early 1930's.

With the American residence of Breton, Chagall, Duchamp, Matta Echuarren, Max Ernst, Feininger, Gleizes, Grosz, Kandinsky, Lipschitz, Miró, Mondrian, Pevsner, Yves Tanguy, and many other of the major artists of the century, to say nothing of innumerable great musicians, musicologists, and composers of the stature of Stravinsky and Bartók, this country became, and in large part was to remain, the world center for all the arts. The prominent role of such men as Albers, Beckmann, Gleizes, and Moholy-Nagy, who were active as teachers as well as painters, also created new developments in the arts in America which had previously been largely dependent upon importing innovations.

It was mostly the émigré dealers from Germany, France, and Austria who took an interest in and facilitated the economic survival of the host of artists who came to this country but left most of their audience in Europe. The galleries, rather than the museums, were long responsible for keeping these artists before the American public, so that they could, at last, become what was often an acquired taste. The Museum of Non-Objective Art, run by Baroness Hilla Rebay and subsidized by Solomon Guggenheim, was perhaps the only Germanic modern art institution to survive the Hitler years unscathed for the obvious reason that it was designed and maintained in New York, largely as a showcase for the works of Kandinsky and Bauer. Although not without a certain silliness, the Museum was distinctly "life-enhancing" and provided America with the invaluable opportunity of seeing the Russian master whose genius is ever more apparent.

Great European architects in residence in America, such as Breuer, Gropius, Mendelsohn, Mies van der Rohe, and Neutra, and designers like Bayer, Kepes, Matter, and Rudofsky, almost all of whom taught as well as practiced, also contributed immeasurably to the new American sophistication in the arts, through such important, lamentably short-lived art schools as Moholy-Nagy's New Bauhaus in Chicago and Josef Albers' at Black Mountain. Albers' teaching at Cooper Union and Yale kept alive an approach to art which might otherwise have died.

Otto Kallir, the Austrian scholar and art dealer whose Galerie St. Étienne had presented the works of Klimt, Kokoschka, Kubin, Modersohn-Becker, Schiele, and others, is perhaps best known in America for his enthusiastic backing of the works of Anna Mary "Grandma" Moses, also editing her books and selling her works. That an Austrian rather than an American should have been the first to admire naïve paintings is not surprising in view of the huge interest in folk art and *Hinterglasmalerei* so characteristic of Continental circles in the 1910's and 1920's.

Earlier graphic arts were increasingly out of fashion in America since the 1930's, and such well established firms as Knoedler's closed out their print department over a decade ago. Were it not for a host of smaller European dealers, most notably Lucien Goldschmidt, Ferdinand Roten, William Schab, Walter Schatzki, Hans Wallach, William Zinser, and other German and Austrian émigrés of the 1930's, the American market would have collapsed long before the very recent inflationary spiral in this area.

Almost as great a dependence upon émigré dealers to keep the market afloat may be seen in the field of decorative arts, furniture, porcelain, and sculpture, where, with the exception of a few extremely restricted fields, relatively little interest was shown since the 1920's. Earlier works in these areas were less and less sought after in the 1930's and the 1940's, with extremely depressed prices until America again succumbed to European taste and started bidding them up in the last few years. Without a host of relatively small dealers in New York, willing to purchase what then often amounted to unsalable objects at auction, and prepared to hold onto them for years, the fickle taste of America might have resulted in the neglect if not actual destruction of many important works.

Most memorable of print and drawing shops was the modest, Left Bank-like establishment of the genial Frederick Rockman on Third Avenue, where thousands of prints and drawings were sorted in boxes according to price range and subject, providing an invaluable opportunity for students and collectors of modest means to choose between the ridiculous and the nearly sublime, and more than occasionally, to make purchases of real distinction, watched over by the scrupulous and benevolent proprietor.

Like their émigré colleagues in the Old Master field, refugee dealers in contemporary art were unafraid of a somewhat educational, literate approach which did much to prepare the American public for an art from which they had been so long removed. Kurt Valentin brought his superb judgment to bear in the field of publication as well as installation. Another art publisher and dealer who did much to propagate enthusiasm in America for recent European art was Karl Nierendorf, who published Klee's *Pedagogical Sketchbook* in translation as well as James Johnson Sweeney's monograph on the same artist and Voltaire's *Candide* with illustrations by the Swiss master. These generally unprofitable ventures were largely embarked upon as labors of love. Such German or German-influenced art dealers as Alfred Stieglitz and Emil Weyhe and the un-German Mitchell Kennerly had initiated similar publications decades before, but these had lapsed at just about the time that the new influx of émigré publishers and dealers were prepared to carry on the task.

A major service to art history in America was rendered by the publications of Wittenborn and Schulz, making available for the first time, in English translations, the writings of Apollinaire, Arp, Ernst, Kandinsky, Klee, Moholy-Nagy, Mondrian, and many others, in a paperbound series *Documents of Modern Art*, directed by Robert Motherwell. These appeared in the 1940's, long before such names were edged with gilt. Like the exemplary publication style of the Museum of Modern Art, the *Documents* were most attractively and inexpensively produced.

Accustomed to intelligently, handsomely printed art books, refugees from Germany and Austria tried to introduce the sort of scholarly publications long taken for granted in Europe but very rare in America, where they tended to require the subsidies and cachet of a university press. Herbert Bittner was one of the most courageous and inspired printers in what, for the United States, amounted to a new genre in publications. In a recent letter Hyatt Mayor recalls that

Bittner was able to make money by selling old books, for which he had nothing but contempt, so that he lost more than he made by publishing the kind of books that he respected. I loved working for him though he was not everybody's dish. He suggested the Bibiena and Piranesi books, cheered me on to work as no one had ever done before or since. We did the Bibiena book in the middle of the war, when no photographs could be got from abroad, and paper was scarce here, but he charged ahead with reckless courage, printing a thousand copies, of which nearly one hundred were spoiled by new clumsy hands at the bindery. The Piranesi came out in six thousand copies, many of which were on his hands when Henry Regnery in Chicago took over after Bittner's final bankruptcy. Poor Herbert never made a penny out. of these books, and I got enough almost to cover the cost of photos, but what a beautiful, difficult simplicity he introduced in the American art book!

Another important figure in New York art publishing is J. J. Augustin, scion of a firm established at Glückstadt in 1641. Through his dedication and taste, Augustin has produced many of the finest American art books since the 1930's, written by scholars such as the Tietzes, De Tolnay, von Hagen, and others.

The surprise encounters, the fruitful, accidental meeting of minds that often accompany the improvisational and result in a new and valuable development are largely absent in academic life. Just because so many of the émigré scholars of the 1930's found jobs in their fields of specialization within a reasonably short time, or were placed in an intellectual setting more or less consistent with their previous experience, their influence was perhaps less discernible in the mainstream of American art-thought than that of their peers in the livelier arts and commerce who were more directly involved with the unacademic hurly-burly of the later Depression years. The enforced purveyance of one's talents in some new medium economically viable for an alien society often produces far broader "influence" of personality and concept than is possible within the confines of Academe.

After suffering and tribulation, the refugee colony in the world of architecture, painting, sculpture, publishing, art-dealing, design, music, the theater, films, art publication, and fashion did, without doubt, bring to these fields in America new sophistication and often a change in attitude. That now delightfully quaint word "modern" is what American culture was often not in the mid-1930's. The refugees who made the most vital imprint on American life were, necessarily, those who brought the present, not the past. While this country was of course hugely innovational in techniques and manufacture, in the expeditive and communicational, and had produced individual key figures in the arts, there was, by the mid-1930's, an extraordinary "cultural lag" between advanced currents in America and Europe, with the latter about twenty years ahead. During the next decade, the combined forces of totalitarianism and the war years held Europe back, while America advanced with the aid of the imported European avant-garde, so that at the end of the Second World War, a stage of cultural equilibrium had been reached.

VIII

MANY European scholars in the United States have found liberating qualities in the atmosphere of the American campus. Professor Stechow, writing of the pleasurable atmosphere of teaching in America, has said, "The giving would never have been the joyful experience it has been had not the welcome, and willingness to take been as warm and inspiring as it actually has been."[53] The refreshingly breezy, irreverent interchange between student and teacher, so different from the frozen stratification of the German university, has also produced a more spontaneous and fresh approach in the work of foreign scholars in America. Several German and Austrian teachers have commented on the structure of the American university, generating a new vitality, benefiting from the interdisciplinary approach. Other professors noted the more open climate of inquiry in America, finding less fear of "having ideas stolen."

Professor López-Rey has observed: "To my mind, the most important contribution made by émigré art-historians as a whole, has been the sense of intellectual conviction that they have brought to the study and teaching of their subject. When they came here, in the 1930's, most of them realized, or at least felt, that they had to address themselves, in the lecture hall, in the classroom, or in writing, to audiences that, generally speaking, were less sophisticated than they were used to. This led them to examine and make explicit, even to themselves, the very roots of their knowledge—which, I think, had a healthy effect on everybody concerned."[54]

53. Questionnaire and letter to author. 54. Questionnaire.

The German tendency to have a single full professor to a department, with seemingly infinite and perpetual powers, functioning as both Mikado and Lord High Executioner, may prove less than beneficial for the man in question, his lesser colleagues, and his students. American fraternity on the faculty level, even when feigned, is certainly psychologically preferable, as is the common practice of a rotating chairmanship, which tends to squash the incipient megalomania lurking in the hearts of most mortals.

Émigré art historians often comment, in comparing their own education with that of their American colleagues and students, on the surprising, impressive breadth of their studies in such fields as pre-Columbian and Oriental art, areas rarely touched upon in Europe.

An expanded approach to research due to his American experience is to be found in the career of the outstanding scholar and archaeologist of Greek and Roman art, George M. A. Hanfmann, who came to this country in 1934 as a double refugee, first from Communism in Lithuania in 1918–1921, and then from Nazism in 1934. He notes: "In order to obtain my training I became a nearly philological classicist; exposure to art museums and the collector's point of view (via Paul J. Sachs) was something totally new and different. The love for a direct contact with the object, the idea one can be passionate rather than historical about art was something I had not come across in my archaeological or art historical training."[55]

Dr. Hanfmann has pointed out that Harvard's Society of Fellows, to which he was elected in 1938, also "made a point of intellectual communication in a great diversity of areas—via informal contact." Such free exchanges in a rather relaxed yet academic context, while they may have been possible within the German and Austrian university framework, seem to have been the exception rather than the rule. Similarly, Otto von Simson has observed a broadening of his own interests through the sociological stress in the structure of the University of Chicago.

Panofsky noted that:

. . . it was a blessing for him to come into contact—and occasionally into conflict—with an Anglo-Saxon positivism which is, in principle, distrustful of abstract specula-

55. Questionnaire, September 23, 1967.

tion; to become more acutely aware of the material problems (posed, for example, by the various techniques of painting and print-making and the static factors in architecture) which in Europe tended to be considered as the concerns of museums and schools of technology rather than universities; and, last but not least, to be forced to express himself, for better or worse, in English.

There are more words in our philosophy than are dreamt of in heaven and earth, and every German-educated art historian endeavoring to make himself understood in English has to make up his own dictionary. In doing so he realizes that his native terminology was often either unnecessarily recondite or downright imprecise.

Forced to express ourselves both understandably and precisely, and realizing, not without surprise, that it could be done, we suddenly found the courage to write books on whole masters or whole periods instead of—or besides—writing a dozen specialized articles; and dared to deal with, say, the problem of classical mythology in medieval art in its entirety instead of—or besides—investigating only the transformations of Heracles or Venus.[56]

The past forty or so years of art historical scholarship has, by and large, addressed itself to highly specific, narrowly defined issues, questions to which a "Right" or a "Wrong" answer can be found. We have moved away from Hegel and Riegl's neo-Hegelian *Kunstwollen*, from the murky depths of art theory into the unambiguous, but occasionally intellectually arid reaches of Who? What? Where? When? How? but with a minimum of Why? The latter is usually and necessarily completely speculative, and the recent questions of art historians have, by and large, reacted against the endless disputes in the realm of theory over which so many pages of ink were spilled in lengthy articles in the *Zeitschrift für Kunstwissenschaft* and other journals. The authors of some of these works, upon re-reading them, today claim that they are less than entirely sure what they meant when they were written.

The continuing exploration of German art by German and Austrian refugees—Benesch's general study of the Northern Renaissance, the work on Dürer of Panofsky, Schwarz, and the Tietzes, Jakob Rosenberg's sustained interest in Cranach and Schongauer, Bier's Riemenschnieder research, Neumeyer's investigation of Marées, Schoenberger's Grünewald studies, von Simson's work on Runge, Weinberger's Altdorfer investigations—all these served to keep alive and unpolluted an area of achievement, a sense of objectivity which might otherwise have been extinguished during the horrors of the Second World War.

56. *Meaning in the Visual Arts*, pp. 329–330.

The refugee scholars' renunciation of the polemic, of the insertion of propagandistic interpretations of art such as Émile Mâle's during the First World War, is another indication of the sad wisdom, at once old and new, perpetuated in American exile.

Scholars, selecting the *vita contemplativa*, cannot plunge themselves into the confusing hurly-burly of the American political scene, yet it is worth noting that almost all the émigrés have expressed real interest in that field, voting on every level and stating that they had become much more involved with politics in America than they ever had before. A few art scholars, such as Paul Zucker, had actually occupied responsible positions within the Weimar Republic.

Among the most "outer-directed" of studies, art history, with its universal, supra-national scope, is always, albeit often unconsciously, a reminder of the errors of provincialism. The refugee scholars in America's midst at just the time that Europe was being increasingly sealed off, brought to their teaching a sense of another world and other interests which must have been especially valuable in the atmosphere of impending and actual world war. Having learned at first hand the penalty of indifference or silence to rising totalitarianism, several art scholars have taken consistently courageous stands in the face of such trends in America—most notably Panofsky's address "In Defense of the Ivory Tower," reprinted countless times in American journals, and the uncompromising behavior of the late E. Kantorowicz in the face of academic outrages at Berkeley. One of the finest hours of scholarship in America was certainly Erwin Panofsky's stirring call to conscience in 1953 at the conclusion of his survey of art history in America, written at the height, if that is the proper term, of the McCarthy era.

All in all, the émigré scholars probably fared better in the United States than those who had specialized in other branches of the humanities or who were in professional fields, needing further studies for American accreditation. Some émigré lawyers and doctors, far from young upon arrival here, could not memorize vast amounts of data in a new language, lacking the necessary peace of mind for preparation and concentration. Scholars in the arts did not face this particular hurdle, working in a field long regarded as "foreign" and accepted as their birthright. Almost all wrote in English from the moment they came to this country;

while they sought instruction or help in editing their works, amazingly little time was lost in coming to terms with the challenge of a new language.

Beginning with Aby Warburg (who visited America near the turn of the century and was to write with characteristic prescience about American Chap Books and American Indian culture of the Southwest), a long list of art historians from Germany and Austria has shown a powerful response to the new culture in which these men and women found themselves. Goldschmidt's enthusiasm for the world of Hollywood was followed, in more restrained and scholarly fashion, by Panofsky's much reprinted essay "On Movies" for the *Princeton University Bulletin* of 1936, followed with another on the same medium for *Transition and Critique* in 1947. The same art historian wrote on Booth Tarkington for the Princeton University Library in 1946, and many of his publications have been enriched by their felicitous quotations from the works of Henry James. Not surprisingly, several German scholars have been drawn to American eighteenth- and early nineteenth-century culture, which is so close to that of Prussia in some of its aspirations for a way away from the provincial. Wolfgang Born's investigation of American landscape painting, Helmut von Erffa's work on Benjamin West, Hans Huth's exploration of the American and Nature, Karl Lehmann's important study on *Thomas Jefferson, American Humanist*, Alfred Neumeyer on Spanish colonial architecture, Rahel Wischnitzer-Bernstein's book on early synagogues in the United States, offer ample evidence of the substantial scrutiny which German and Austrian scholars brought to the art of their new land.

Inured to and yet shaped by the strongly nationalistic currents of early twentieth-century Europe, those very few art scholars exiled from Germany and Austria who managed to create careers for themselves in England made themselves more influential there than could their émigré colleagues in America. English culture, so much closer to the continent than that of America, was more manageable and explicable to many refugees than that of America, with its endlessly confusing mixture of the provincial with the inventive; the conventional with the independent; the snobbish with the egalitarian. Scholars like Antal, Pevsner, Saxl, Wittkower, and several others worked their way into the fiber of English art and literature in a way that their equivalents in America couldn't or wouldn't, perhaps because they did not have to. Although far fewer jobs were available in England than America, with fierce competition for the minuscule number of appointments in a country which still scarcely recognizes art history in its oldest universities, those German and Austrian refugees who succeeded in establishing themselves in the face of almost insuperable odds have, it must be said, had more impact on the intellectual climate of Britain than have their, on the average, far more affluent émigré colleagues in America.

One cannot point to an art historian-refugee or native American whose influential role in the country in the teaching of his subject parallels the creative, authoritative position of Ernst Gombrich in England. This may well be due to a purely individual breadth of interest and sympathy and to Gombrich's concern with psychoanalysis and philosophy (reflecting his Austrian origins and the *Wiener Schule*), going far beyond the bounds of conventional art history and netting a rich catch. Odd as it may sound, speculation is decidedly not in style on the American campus, and Gombrich's brilliance, his modest audacity, his almost limitless scope would not, thank goodness, have "fitted in" with the make-up of any Fine Arts Department in this country. Significantly, few adherents of the *Wiener Schule* came to America, where their complex approach, combining knowledge of art history, psychology, and often the decorative arts would have been far less at home in the campuses or museums than even the Warburgians. Those who did come, Berliner, Kris, Schwarz, the Tietzes, De Tolnay—excepting the latter—were primarily involved in museum work. Prior to their arrival and that of Rudolf Arnheim, some interest in psychoanalysis had been evinced by American art historians such as Meyer Schapiro, and the subject had received wide attention through such publications as Herbert Read's *Art and Society* (1937). That unclassifiable masterpiece, Adams' *Mont-Saint-Michel and Chartres*, already showed receptivity to psychology.

Such psychologists and psychiatrists as Viktor Lowenfeld and Kurt Eissler have given extensive consideration to art history and creativity, but these have not been integrated in academic art history. America has shown far less interest in this area than did Germany almost forty years ago, when Pinder was extremely receptive to the new psychological research of the late Kurt Lewin, who like Lowenfeld and Eissler came to the United States.

The analytical, symbolically oriented studies initiated by Aby Warburg and entitled iconology sprang from many of the same sources as those of Freudian thought. Warburg's omnivorous interests were often allied to those encompassed by anthropology and sociology, but he never succumbed to Scientism in the expression of his insights and discoveries in the role of ritual and the occult. In America, the impact of European psychoanalytical thought in the realm of art history has been about as silly as that of Freud on the movies. Years ago Hollywood was entranced with schizophrenia and related maladies in the *Three Faces of Eve* and *The Dark Mirror*, now more vigorously and originally represented in Warhol's split screen. As far as art history is concerned, apart from Rudolf Arnheim's and Ernst Kris's insights, the Freudian approach has not yet led to valuable American explorations; such studies as the relationship between Cézanne's masturbation and his art do not do much to illuminate either. Freud's own reliability as an interpreter of art has been called into question by Meyer Schapiro in "Two Slips of Leonardo and a Slip of Freud."[57]

One of the most brilliant Austrian art historians, Ernst Kris, turned completely to psychoanalytical practice and research in America. In his late twenties Kris completed catalogs for objects in precious metals and stone in the Kunsthistorisches Museum that suggested the culmination of a lifetime of advanced, intense, and specialized scholarship. His work on the Rustic Style, published in the *Wiener Jahrbuch*, remains among the outstanding studies of the century. Some of his concern with art continued in his later American studies, but these are clinical and not historical.

A dynamic scholar, from Germany, who became a giant in English art history before repeating that achievement in America, is Rudolf Wittkower, now chairman of the Department of Art and Archaeology at Columbia University. As acknowledged on the B.B.C., Wittkower's innumerable publications did so much "to elucidate British art and architecture to the British."[58]

57. *Psychoanalysis: Journal of Psychoanalytic Psychology*, IV (1955–1956), 3–8; "Leonardo and Freud: an Art-Historical Study," *Journal of the History of Ideas*, 17 (1956), 147–148.

58. Pevsner, "An Un-English Activity?" p. 716.

The subjects, contents, and references of art history are perhaps still more native to Europe than to America; there the people interested in it are far from limited to an academic milieu, so that a keen personality with something to say in the field of art may strike a more responsive and profound chord in the Old World than the New.

No European art historian in America has achieved the extraordinary eminence in the realm of connoisseurship that a man like the Austrian scholar Johannes Wilde realized in London where he is a sort of *éminence grise* among museum people and collectors as well as many scholars. Regrettably, no scholar comparable to the late Frederick Antal came to this country, since the far inferior but related economically-determined genre of the Swiss Arnold Hauser has been received with much American enthusiasm and huge commercial success. Closely linked to a Marxist interpretation of history, Antal was rarely blinded by theory when it came to making the most sensitive appraisals of Italian art of the fourteenth and fifteenth centuries as well as the eighteenth-century art of his new English home.

One of the reasons for Nikolaus Pevsner's huge and richly deserved success in England is the great ease and effect with which he transferred some of the nationalistically-oriented art historical approach of Germany to England. His famous address "On the Englishness of English Art" recalls Kurt Karl Eberlein's title of 1933, *Was ist deutsch in der deutschen Kunst*. The same is true for his publications—the paperback guides in the best tradition of Baedeker and Tauschnitz, and the *Pelican History of Art*, a vastly improved, textually enriched *Propyläenkunstgeschichte*.

A loss to art history in America was the return of the medievalist Otto von Simson to Europe. He left his professorship at the University of Chicago to work as cultural attaché for Germany in France, and is now on the faculty of the Free University in Berlin. Ulrich Middeldorf, another gifted German scholar also active at the University of Chicago, remained there until retirement as department chairman, continuing his career as director of the Kunsthistorisches Institut in Florence, where he was first active before coming to this country. Wolfgang Lotz, who came from Germany in 1953 to teach at Vassar and then at the Institute of Fine Arts, also returned to Europe to lead the German art historical research institute in Rome, the Bibliotheca Hertziana. Charles de Tolnay, the great historian of fifteenth- and sixteenth-century art of Europe, now resides in Florence as director of the Casa Buonarroti, long owned by the descendants of Michelangelo, whose art was so profoundly explored by de Tolnay during his American years and publications.

IX

THE history of art, a subject of considerable American interest since the mid-nineteenth century, made steady strides as an academic displine from the end of that century onwards, generally under very considerable Germanic influence. By the mid-1950's, this country had been producing scholars of international repute for five decades, most of whom were especially concerned with stylistic or archaeologically-oriented research, with considerable emphasis on connoisseurship. The influx of émigré German and Austrian scholars in the 1930's caused art historical studies in America to broaden in scope. Numbers of qualified teachers brought the field to campuses in the South and the Midwest and Far West where it had barely been adequately taught before. Since advanced art historical research in Vienna, Munich, Berlin, and Hamburg was known to American specialists through publications and the presence of visiting or permanently appointed European scholars in America, the sudden arrival of numbers of the most distinguished professors and curators of these centers did not in itself immediately alter the character of the field in this country.

With the establishment of special institutions where these émigrés could work and teach and their employment in museums, colleges, and universities throughout the country, their influence resulted in the deepening of the art historical endeavors, now conducted on a wider scale than ever before. Considerations of function and meaning became more important than before, with instruction and research moving away from an emphasis upon names and dates toward a more intellectually challenging approach. Three different generations of Germanic scholarship, represented by such men born in the 1860's and 1870's as Frankl, Friedlaender, and Goldschmidt, those at the end of the century—Krautheimer, Lehmann, Panofsky, Rosenberg, Stechow, De Tolnay, Weitzmann, Wind—and younger men just starting their careers at the time of the decrees of 1933 such as Julius Held—brought to this country a more intense, directly experienced concern with the history of art than was the American rule.

In addition to the many curators and professors of art history who came to this country, there were specialists in the history of literature, music, and philology who had worked together with art scholars in Germany and Austria. This co-operation and sharing of sources led to the rich, intricate scholarship more characteristic of Europe than of America. The rise of Fascism and Nazism brought such profoundly erudite, productive men as Herbert Diekmann, Ernst Herzfeld, Werner Jaeger, Ernst Kantorowicz, René Wellek, and Heinrich Zimmer here, almost all of them much interested in art or music as a manifestation of the culture or literature or history of Greece, India, Medieval Germany, Europe in the age of the Baroque or the Enlightenment. Unlike their American colleagues, who leaned toward either a very narrowly defined approach or usually fruitless interdepartmental promiscuity, these men utilized and contributed to art historical findings. Together with the émigré art historians themselves, the scholars contributed further understanding and prosecution of major areas of endeavor often neglected by their American associates. A sterling example of this sort of scholar is Paul Oskar Kristeller of Columbia University, who left Europe in 1939. His endless erudition in all matters pertaining to the philosophy, history, literature, and documentation of Renaissance Italy has made him invaluable to any scholar interested in that central period. Luckily, Dr. Kristeller's protean knowledge is matched by his Franciscan generosity. Similarly endowed in knowledge of Renaissance history is Hans Baron, now Research Fellow and Bibliographer at the Newberry Library, who also came from the University of Berlin to this country in 1939, teaching in Queens College. His study *The Crisis of the Early Italian Renaissance* (Princeton, 1955), together with Kristeller's innumerable publications in Italian philosophy, should provide the groundwork for further scholarship in America on the excellent model of Millard Meiss's *Painting in Florence and Siena after the Black Death* (1951). This new scholarly breadth has resulted in such a rewarding institution as the Columbia University Seminar on the Renaissance, where specialists in the history, literature, philosophy, art, political science, and science of that period convene for a productive exchange of findings.

Often more versatile than their American colleagues, willing to go back and forth between the art of varying centuries and in different media, European scholars tended to be exploratory on a wider scale without danger of dilettantism. Unafraid of value judgments, prepared to go out on a limb more readily than the cautious and accurate, factually oriented scholars in America, the European art historian tended to present his material in a speculative, sometimes more adventurous and stimulating manner than was the custom here. A certain amount of *panache* and dash accompanying a successful European academic career on the highest level, conducted with a breadth and freedom in approach absent in the more parochial yet democratic demeanor of his American counterpart; this could bring an often novel sense of excitement and interest to a field which America often linked to the edifying and the politely appreciative.

The major area to benefit from the teaching and scholarship of émigrés in America has been that of the later sixteenth and seventeenth centuries. Much of the oeuvre of these years is, with the exception of later Holland, very Catholic, very erotic, very inverted—all factors explaining American indifference if not neglect of Italian Mannerism and the art of the Counter-Reformation. While the Northern Baroque, because of its seemingly more Protestant nature, has long been immensely popular in America, the Flemish and French areas had been much ignored. Nowhere is native distrust of the Baroque made more clear than in the circumstances surrounding the very recent foundation in America of the two museums largely devoted to this area, brought to it by way of the circus and Fundamentalism. Drawn to the panoply of Catholic art of the seventeenth century through its resemblance to his own activities as master of the Ringling fortunes, the circus tycoon assembled the fine collection now known as the John and Mable Ringling Museum of Art in Sarasota, catalogued by Suida. Equally appropriately in a southern climate is the Bob Jones University College (Greenville, South Carolina), a Southern Baptist divinity school, which has accumulated an outstanding collection of works, mostly executed in the spirit of the Counter-Reformation, purchased in large part from émigré dealers and collectors, and used didactically to impart Fundamentalism!

With the teaching of Friedlaender in the field of Italian Mannerism and the anti-classical style, many American scholars have gone on from his stimulating discoveries to make important additional findings in this area. In Italian Baroque art, both Friedlaender and Richard Krautheimer have inspired numbers of distinguished followers in the United States in the field of sculpture and architecture as well as painting. The Northern Baroque, both Catholic and Protestant, has also been richly studied in America by Held, Rosenberg, and Stechow, all of whom have produced many fine scholars active in teaching or museum work with special competence in an area so splendidly represented in American collections. Early Netherlandish art, also brilliantly contained within the museums of this country, has received great scholarly attention from Held and Panofsky, both of whom have instructed several students who are carrying on further research in this area on a high level.

Among the areas illumined for American students by the émigré scholars was that of European decorative arts. Although Fiske Kimball and a few others had been masters in this field, all works other than paintings, prints, drawings, sculpture, and architecture tended to be viewed with disdain as less than minor because of their functional or sumptuary connotations. The curse of Interior Decoration and that dread category The Decorative often stifled any scholarly concern with metalwork, furniture, jewelry, tapestry, and innumerable related fields. Such specialists as Rudolph Berliner, Yvonne Hackenbroch, Hans Huth, Ernst Kris, Olga Raggio, Guido Schoenberger, Georg Swarzenski, Martin Weinberger, and many others brought to generally neglected fields new knowledge, interest, and stimulus which is now being felt in American colleges and museums. Several émigré scholars, formerly employed in museums specializing in the decorative arts, first started teaching in the United States.

One early and one late field of art history in which the United States has long shown especial interest are those of Byzantium and Impressionism. The elder, with its regal but remote splendor, has enjoyed particular appeal among the most aristocratic American collector's patronage for scholarly research, first drawn together by Thomas Whittemore for the Byzantine Institute and since enriched by the contributing studies of émigré scholars such as Richard Krautheimer, Kurt Weitzmann, and more recently Ernst Kitzinger and Hugo Buchtal, who have come over here after years of British residence.

Impressionism, combining some of the carefree charm of the art of the eighteenth century with a more conventional, rather bourgeois orientation, has also long been the mainstay of American collecting. Once again, émigré scholars have done much to place the abundant masterpieces of late nineteenth-century French art in America within a more scholarly setting. Outstanding in this area have been José López-Rey, John Rewald, and Lionello Venturi. Earlier French painting, also magnificently represented in American collections, has been studied by Klaus Berger, Lorenz Eitner, and Walter Friedlaender.

Lorenz Eitner has noted how:

With few exceptions, the triumphs of American art historical scholarship have been won through careful workmanship and method, rather than through fresh discovery or the formulation of new ideas. Their soundness and caution, their prudent specialization, have preserved American art historians from the sweeping speculations, the doctrinaire excesses and flagrant errors to which some of their European colleagues have been prone, but they have also dampened the spirit of their students and lessened their enthusiasm, and have made them look to Europe for a periodical renewal of stimulation.

Is there a connection between the two conditions which have just been noted? There would appear to be. The preoccupation with soundness, the over-emphasis on method, the caution and conservatism of American art history are qualities which are university-bred. They are academic qualities. Like the eclectic campus architecture which surrounds him, the American student and scholar in the humanities is profoundly conditioned by the economics of the academic market place and the bureaucratic patterns of university administration.[59]

This view is largely shared by James S. Ackerman, who wrote:

The typical American art historian is, like his fellow scientist and businessman, distinguished for his know-how. He has developed sensitive techniques for dealing with

59. In *The Visual Arts in Higher Education*, (ed. Andrew Ritchie), a study prepared for the College Art Association of America under a grant from the Ford Foundation (New Haven, 1966), p. 57.

historical data, and is singularly free of national or parochial biases. He does not twist facts to fit a theory, because for him facts are sacrosanct. He publishes only when he has new information to offer, and seldom writes vague and subjective books for sale at Christmas. Sparing no pains to thoroughly investigate his subject, he is characteristically reliable.[60]

Some of the factors in the American university system weighing against the successful addition of émigré scholars are to be found in the reports, from presidents of colleges and universities, as to why certain professors did not work out well in their midst; "I do not think that we can say they were readily absorbed," writes an administrator in a large Midwest university, in reply to a query sent him by the Emergency Committee in Aid of Displaced Foreign Scholars in the 1940's, concerning the four refugees sent to his campus, "for only one out of four became a member of the regular staff; furthermore it cannot be denied that they presented a problem in the sense that they caused apprehension on the part of other staff members, especially the younger ones, as to their seniority in the department concerned. On the other hand, it cannot be denied that they made a scholarly contribution to the institution, bringing new viewpoints and a considerable amount of ability." In all the unsatisfactory cases, the institutional official says that his new faculty member "has not been absorbed," meaning, in part, tossed into the melting pot but refusing to bubble into a state of appropriately functional anonymity.[61] Problems in the realm of the American administrative approach and the foreign scholar are elucidated by Professor Eitner's observation that: "The acceptance procedures of graduate programs and the hiring policies of departments, the world of committee action and deanly decree,—all these are designed to smooth out irregularity and to minimize eccentricity. One wonders how Berenson would have fared in the academic business, and one knows how some other scholars of independent turn of mind have in fact fared in the groves of Academe."[62]

The integration of a large number of refugee scholars and art specialists into the fabric of American academic life was, by and large, a success

60. "On American Scholarship in the Arts," *Art Journal*, 17 (1958), 359.
61. Stephen Duggan and Betty Drury, *The Story of the Emergency Committee in Aid of Displaced Foreign Scholars* (New York, 1948), pp. 155–158.
62. "The Visual Arts in Higher Education," p. 56.

story; amazingly few were passed over, wasted, or ignored. But it would be less than accurate to gloss over the fact that the great universities failed to take real advantage of the most challenging intellects to come to this country. Challenging intellects are often not easy to live with. Unfortunately Alma Mater American Style has tended to stress Togetherness and Tolerance at the price of brilliance. Since uncompromising individuality usually accompanies the incisive mind, several of the most outstanding art scholars to come to this country lived out their American careers in relative isolation.

The Institute of Fine Arts and the Institute for Advanced Studies, invaluable though they are, inevitably kept their distinguished faculty from the undergraduate and from much contact with younger colleagues and graduate students in other fields who might well have benefited from their approach. The American college student was rarely as short-changed as when the "specialists," generally by far the most inspiring lecturers, were kicked upstairs into exclusively graduate instruction or pure research, leaving the undergraduate at the mercy of the usual mealy-mouthed survey mentality.

The black-humored definition of a graduate student as "an undergraduate with his spirit broken" has more than a little truth to it. Few teachers would deny that the sense of awareness and intellectual excitement is rarely higher than in the first years of college. While the conventional graduate education allowed much valuable work to be produced uninterruptedly and helped shape future specialists, it did isolate the more adventurous and creative minds from their most fertile audiences. Before the "peacetime" draft, few of the brightest American undergraduates went on to graduate studies in the humanities. Much to the disadvantage of America, few of the major powers in American cultural life—the trustees, directors, and advisory committees—almost without exception social and financial leaders, had the privilege and stimulus of attending a lecture by Panofsky in their formative undergraduate years.

The Warburgian scholar was a novel element in the American academic scene. Seemingly equally at home in art, literature, history, and philosophy, his dazzling command of different disciplines and his pyrotechnical lectures sometimes caused considerable dismay among the departments whose spheres of special interest seemed threatened by such unclassifiable poaching. The impression of fairly rarified, iconographically-oriented scholarship upon undergraduates—students of Otto Benesch's at Wellesley and Harvard, Bernheimer's at Bryn Mawr and Haverford, Lotte Brand Philip's at Queens—has been characterized by a gifted student, Mrs. Daryl Hafter, who has gone on to an academic career in the field of European history:

Nothing gives me more pleasure than to reminisce about Edgar Wind on the Smith scene. His Hamburg ? accent and his puckish smile when he asked us a rhetorical question that could be answered only by Berenson remain the most delightful memories. I would say in general that his undergraduate students couldn't help being overwhelmed by his sophistication and erudition. I was in an undergraduate seminar of 10 or 12, some art majors, some in literature or, as in my case, history, and it must have been only the most advanced who could appreciate the sessions with discrimination. Those of us whose claim to expertise was that we had successfully passed Art 11 felt that we were in a kind of never-never land, where rare viands grew on ordinary trees; the question was not that this fare was unusual, but whether the dish were better spiced with myrrh or frankincense. I know that I went home for vacation, filled with very heady doctrines, and proclaimed them as gospel to anybody who would listen. When my father suggested that they might be controversial, I scoffed of course, having been thoroughly entranced by Wind and his, may I say it, charisma.

That is the quality which made the greatest impression. Wind led us by the hand through labyrinths in Renaissance art and iconography. His first question was "What is an icon?" Nobody knew. By the time we were through, he had convinced us that the most complicated theories he had were completely self-evident, taking each object in the picture and describing its significance in the simplest, most logical way. Of course we learned a lot about Renaissance thinking, and I dare say the faculty did too. Intellectual history *had* to expand with nasty little girls asking embarrassing questions. But the quality of mind and approach is what the non-specialist takes away. An esthetic sensibility of immediacy. For instance, he disabused us of the notion that it was a debasement of art for patrons and artists to direct a work—positive value of limits. And did you know it is poor form to write a paper in the library? The presence of books makes for stiffness and bookish expression!

I think that he and his wife made a warm addition to the social scene, and always, his utterly charming European manner, urbane, intellectual must have been stimulating and encouraging to those who taught Ren. and Ref. literature, history, art history. I wonder what the devotees of art for art's sake in the Art Department thought? If nothing else, I learned a most handy phrase, that I always trot out when my son is pushing me—"Festina lente." Don't you think the course was worthwhile, even for that?[63]

63. Letter of September 24, 1967.

The influence of refugee scholars may occasionally have accentuated some of the pitfalls of art historical writing in this country. The showers of footnotes, lengthy bibliographies, and free-wheeling references abounding in the European art historian's work seem sometimes to have produced a caricature of this approach in the American scholar—all Medium and no Message. Similarly, the Warburgian interest in subject matter, the study of symbolism, the role of the emblem, the significance of the allegory, although always presupposing familiarity with the style and the ambiance in which they were generated, tend in American hands to have been undertaken in isolation from the work of art. The last twenty years have seen unwitting parodies of symbolic research, especially in nineteenth- and twentieth-century art, take over considerable space in American scholarly journals. The acceptance accorded such fallacious, supposedly Warburgian studies may have inadvertently contributed to the rise of an aggressive, excessively involved American concern with "Pure Style." Some professors have deplored the role of the refugee scholars, which they view as too narrowly specialized, niggling, uncreative, and fact-bound. These critics have made German and Austrian academicians in America the whipping boys for the conventional orientation of art scholarship in this country, which, since the mid-nineteenth century, has been rooted in a somewhat Teutonic approach. "It is no longer the history of art but the history of an autopsy." Few have followed Panofsky's lead in producing an admirable monograph addressed to both layman and specialist, like the *Dürer*, which omits footnotes in the text and is, as he wrote in the preface, "addressed to a 'mixed audience' rather than to scholars," with notes accompanying catalogues at the end.

Now, in the *Spätstil* of some of the great art historians born in the late nineteenth century, one senses a certain mellowing, an occasional impatience with the elaborate scholarly structure which they themselves erected in order to look at, and in, the work of art. Panofsky's last works on Correggio and Titian and Stechow's recent book on Dutch landscape show a more open delight in the beauty of their subjects, which, while always present in the sensitive appraisal they never neglected to provide, seems more overt and less inlaid within the analytical apparatus. Similarly, Wind's frank appreciation for the achievements of the great nineteenth-century connoisseur Morelli in *Art and Anarchy* points to a congruent sympathy for a First Things First approach, which may, if these intimations bear such elaborate examination, point to a slow reopening of the creaking door to Appreciation.

The archaeological, the technical, the qualitative, the philological, the iconographical, the *catalogue raisonnée*, the psychological, the social and economic approaches to art—the myriad spy glasses, the nets, the traps of scholarly apparatus—all these have been explored, shared, and expanded by the teaching and research of the émigré scholars in America, bringing a new scrutiny, often in a foreign area, to the ultimate mystery of art.

Many refugee scholars, in the prime of life in the 1930's and 1940's, full of energy and ability which was not drained off in the administrative ranks of officialdom or in the rather dense, demanding social life of campuses, could give their students unprecedented amounts of undivided attention, which such scholars might have been unable to spare had they remained in Europe. Excluded as they largely were from the status-centered American equivalents of the prestigious life of the professor in German-speaking countries, émigré teachers could bring to their students an unparalleled concentration of Paideia, which came as a special shock and delight to graduate students from the more fashionable colleges. Such intense instruction was most productive in the cases of the brilliant students who rose readily to the occasion or for those who were willing, by sheer sweat, to meet the minimal requirements. But some of the most gifted and independent students, seemingly casual but actually highly dedicated, got lost along the way since their European teachers found it hard to sense within a somewhat passive, deliberately relaxed American manner the sort of attention to which they were accustomed.

In teaching American students, especially as a foreigner, it is easy to confuse their innocence with ignorance. Had it been possible to undertake a still more positive approach in the introduction of a new field to new students, letting art history develop toward a more indigenous discipline with the aid of European wisdom and perspective, an even greater educational achievement might have taken place. A student of émigré professors has noted, "They were so good they probably retarded our development in a way by making us struggle to make up all those language deficiencies in sheer volume of classical learning. I don't think they sensed the American style. They meant to make us like themselves."

Refugee scholars of the 1930's contributed toward the removal of a certain aura of preciosity and ever so upper-class dilettantism which had long been assiduously maintained or cultivated in the world of art scholarship in America. The bite and acumen of instructors sharpened by exile proved art history to be more than the scholarly fringe-benefit of gracious living. The increasing popularity of art on all fronts throughout the 1940's and 1950's, this "democratization" of art history, might well have taken place in any event, but it seems probable that the sense of commitment brought over with foreign scholars may have encouraged able but less conspicuously "social" or socially ambitious students to join a field which might otherwise have seemed uncongenial.

Comparing his college days to graduate years at the Institute of Fine Arts, John Coolidge recalls:

The great discovery I made at the Institute was that art history was a discipline. There was a standard method. There were several basic schools. By comparison, however high the individual achievement of my Harvard teachers, their approach had the virtues and weaknesses of the individual pioneer.

The second basic discovery was the importance of creativity. Perhaps because I was an undergraduate, nobody at Harvard suggested that one should consider scholarly publication. Nobody at New York University suggested that one should consider anything else, and the sooner the better. All of them were publishing all the time and their simple message was, "Now YOU get cracking."

The third point was the high intellectual seriousness of art history. My Harvard teachers were men of considerable personal culture but this seemed to have little relevance to their professional work. The New York University faculty taught art history as an integral part of modern intellectual life and, if they did not always think in terms of other humanities and sciences, that was a personal shortcoming. The link was there and had only to be discovered.

William M. Calder III has pointed out how the appointment of refugee scholars to classical professorships in the Ivy League broke an unspoken policy of not hiring candidates of Jewish descent for tenure posts.

One last point: the emigrants once and for all opened the way for the rise of Jews in the higher appointments in our discipline. The anti-Semitism of the upper classes in

America was strongly represented in the best East Coast universities, especially in the classical fields, in which the *"jeunesse dorée"* were carefully cultivated, where they let themselves be instructed in Horace by gentlemen. No Jew was an associate or full professor in classical philology in any well-known center of learning. Things are different today.[64]

Charles Waldstein's career in classics in the late nineteenth century is an exception that seems to prove Calder's "rule." Apart from Harvard's Paul Sachs, the same would in the main hold true for art history also. Whether or not "gentlemen's agreements" in hiring policy prevailed among several distinguished art historical faculties whose graduate admissions policies seem to have long been dictated by them, the influx of foreign Jewish scholars in the 1930's often changed their make-up.

In a rather pessimistic evaluation of the influence of the nineteen classical authorities who came to the United States in the 1930's—including the art scholars—Margarete Bieber, Dietrich von Bothmer, Otto J. Brendel, G. M. S. Hanfmann, and Karl Lehmann—Professor Calder wrote:

How great was the influence of these people? Astonishingly slight, largely because they were dispersed. Columbia was in the forefront with six (New York has the largest and richest Jewish community in the world and is, apart from Washington, the only American city of international character). Then came Harvard with three, the others had but one each. None of these scholars founded a school, as we have seen in the case of Ferguson, Gildersleeve, Oldfather, D. M. Robinson, M. Rostovtzeff, or Paul Shorey. If one makes a generous estimate, they, in the course of twenty years, produced two or three Ph.D.'s who then proved to be very good scholars.

Professor Jaeger often complained to me that, above all else, he missed "his school" in America.[65]

Although there is much truth to the somewhat negative tenor of Calder's remarks, his estimate of the number of students of Brendel and Hanfmann seems too low; Karl Lehmann is known to have supervised at least seven doctorates and about twenty Master's theses. In the case of history of art, through the expansion of the Institute of Fine Arts in the 1950's, such a *Schule*, collectively if not individually, was indubitably established. For the past thirty-five years large numbers of graduate

64. Calder, "Die Geschichte der klassischen Philologie," pp. 213–240, especially p. 236.
65. *Ibid.*, p. 234.

students have gone on from the Institute to teach or curate, whose approach has, in fact, been shaped by a scholarly disposition often geared to that of Northern Europe.

To evaluate the specific results of teaching by refugee scholars in terms of present-day art history in America would belabor the obvious, since their students are now numbered among the faculties of almost every good department throughout the country. One of the newest of these in America, at Brandeis, is largely staffed by Institute alumni. The junior members of the faculties of Columbia University and New York University are, as might be expected, often alumni of both these institutions, which include many émigré scholars in their midst.

With James S. Ackerman, John Coolidge, Sydney Freedberg, Frederick Deknatel, and Seymour Slive at Harvard, all of whom were largely trained or influenced by émigré scholars, it is abundantly clear that one of the largest and oldest art history departments in the country is closely determined by the German and Austrian émigrés who came to this country in the 1930's. Princeton, too, already disposed to German scholarship under Mather and Morey, is permeated by the quality of art historical scholarship of the émigrés. The presence of Panofsky at the Institute of Advanced Study, together with, over the years, that of Frankl, de Tolnay, Weitzmann, and many others who also taught at the University, shaped the thought of the departmental leaders, who were formerly among their disciples. Although they may not all have been his students, it is hard to imagine the works of David Coffin, Robert Koch, John Martin, and James Snyder without the enriching aura of Panofsky's proximity and availability. The late Gertrude Achenbach Coor, who completed her graduate studies at the Institute in New York, came to Princeton to work at the Index of Christian Art and stayed as a faculty wife, brought to the department (where she had no official appointment) a whirlwind of intellectual expertise, capacity for unflagging industry, and ingratiating verve. In addition to producing many articles and her monograph on *Neroccio de' Landi* (Princeton, 1961), Mrs. Coor's energetic pursuit of accuracy and mastery of detail is abundantly evident in a series of Princeton faculty publications in which her extensive editorial contribution is gratefully acknowledged by such scholars as George Rowley and Rensselaer Lee. At the University of

Chicago, John Rewald and Earl Rosenthal, a student of Cook and Weinberger, have a very active role in a department where Bachhofer, Huth, von Simson, and Middeldorf were long important members of the faculty.

Yale's art history department was firmly rooted in the fruit, the flower, and the shade of the French scholars Marcel Aubert and Henri Focillon, who brought to America a sensitivity and grace often absent in German art history. Focillon's disciplined yet profoundly imaginative mind provided a welcome sense for the wonder of art and creativity continued in the works of his many distinguished students there. This Gallic orientation at Yale was tempered by visiting German and Austrian refugee scholars of different interests who stayed just long enough to present another approach. Edgar Wind would come from Smith to release a barrage of artfully aimed iconographical insights in special lectures, often at the invitation of the Philosophy rather than the Art History department. Yale has had such a long trail of visiting émigrés, including Ettlinger, Krautheimer, Panofsky, Sterling, Wind, and Wittkower, that one of them jested about the "rabbinical succession" at Old Eli. Such luminaries as Auerbach, Cassirer, Holborn, Kris, Kristeller, Mommsen, Wellek, and many others were members of the Yale faculty; the French emphasis in the art historical and literary departments—Gustave Cohen was also there—may have provided "a delicate balance."

America can pride itself on a rich crop of full-fledged art historians now in their late thirties, forties, and early fifties, the products in large part of the teaching generation which included so many émigré art scholars, but it would be foolish to say that they are demonstrably superior in any way except quantitatively to the distinguished scholars formed here in the preceding decades.

Certainly no specifically "American School" of art history has evolved with any more definition in the 1960's than in the 1930's. Constantly refreshed by new currents generated here and in Europe, by differing emphasis in the history of art itself, without any uniform philosophical or psychological or political premise, art history is, perhaps fortunately, a rather shapeless conglomerate of individual interests and expertise.

As far as the vast majority of the émigré scholars are concerned, their life in America has clearly been a gratifying and rewarding experience. From the horrors of Germany they came to a country which was in the main receptive and accommodating, where those scholars who had already established themselves abroad often found suitable positions with rapidity and were able to continue their fields of special interest within an amazingly short time. Those who had just completed their European doctorates, or were in the process of so doing when they were forced to leave, found their first years in a Depression-beset America extremely difficult; without the Union Card of a Ph.D., some of them became secretaries, furniture painters, physical education instructors, even helping sell the huge Hearst art collection at Gimbel's, taking any one of the few available jobs for funds to complete their degree or to help establish a reputation through publication.

One cannot help but remark that had the émigrés come from less bigoted and destructive societies than those prevailing in Germany and Austria, already riddled with prejudice and rancor long before Hitler came to power, some might perhaps view their American experience in a slightly less kindly light. In large part, this country really needed the experienced scholars who came over; there was room in the slowly but steadily expanding areas of art studies, art publications, and art collecting to accommodate even the large numbers who came from abroad within such a short time. Few refugees, if any, would or could recognize that prejudice may have played a role in diminishing their potential in this country, since such prejudice was so immeasurably smaller and less mordant than the one America had freed them from. Clearly the American institution which proved the most hospitable and invaluable to the refugee art scholar—the New York University Institute of Fine Arts—was a very recent foundation and for the most part subsidized by Americans of strikingly similar background with the European scholars they helped maintain. Although almost all the émigré scholars received generally suitable employment soon after their arrival here, several of the most outstanding did not receive the recognition and opportunity that they merited, above all, access to the outstanding students. Nor in the main did they have access to curatorial roles in art collections which was their due. With very few exceptions, newly arrived scholars never penetrated the power-centers of academic life—the executive committees of the scholarly societies and consultant posts with foundations.

America continues to be voracious for European-trained art historians; since the Second World War many German, Austrian, and Swiss scholars have come over. These include Peter H. von Blankenhagen, François Bucher, Hugo Buchtal, Ernst Kitzinger, and Rudolph Wittkower; the late Ernst Büchner at the Samuel H. Kress Foundation; Ernst Grube, Helmut Nickel, Hubert von Sonnenburg, and Claus Virch at the Metropolitan Museum; Max Loehr at Michigan and Harvard; Wolfgang Lotz at Vassar and the Institute of Fine Arts (now the director of the Hertziana in Rome); Marcel Röthlisberger at Yale and the University of California at Los Angeles; Axel von Saldern at the Brooklyn Museum.

The whole question of influence, whether in the history of art or the history of refugee art historians in America, is often a somewhat circular one. One is influenced by whatever one wants or is prepared to be influenced by, with as little rocking the boat as possible. The most effective outside agent or source is usually as close to the internal demands and prescriptions as possible. America is now in an art boom which encompasses creation, instruction, history, publication, museum-going, collecting, social climbing, even the printing of postage stamps from Audubon's *Bluejays* to Baskin's *Thoreau*. Hungry for teachers, curators, books, articles, and objects, this country is prepared to snap up the pupils and literary products of the émigré scholars of the 1930's, together with those of their followers with far greater enthusiasm than ever before. The simultaneous maturation of the generation of students of the great émigré scholars of the 1930's and the present national art compulsion seem largely coincidental. Art history continues to boom, expanding day by day as new campuses mushroom from New York to the Pacific coast, new museums blossom in the deserts, and new galleries line the streets of every major and many minor city. Art and art history are subjects peculiarly suitable and sympathetic to a great power that is neither as great or as powerful as it was. England, losing her empire, has derived the most extraordinary comfort from her art and art historical domain since the Second World War—The Sun Never Sets on English Art History, and while America may have lost China, we certainly will never lose Chinese art. Retrospective, comprehensive, synthetic, primarily concerned with the beauty and the achievement and the meaning of the past—these are the aspects of art history which we cherish and perpetuate. The sales pitch for Time-Life's visual presentations of past cultures is "Civilizations pass away but the glory remains forever." Undesirable though it may be, our approach is far less deceptive and pretentious than André Malraux's meretricious *Musée Imaginaire*.

One of the happiest recent marriages between art historical scholarship and patronage may be seen in the Mellon and Wrightsman Lectures—where distinguished art scholars are invited to give talks in the fields of their specialization which then appear in published form. Such collaboration between the collector-patron, the scholar, the museum where the lectures are held—the National Gallery for the Mellon and the Metropolitan Museum and Institute of Fine Arts for the Wrightsman—is in the tradition of the Lowell and Norton series, but reaching a far wider audience. These lectures in New York and Washington point to a new breadth of interest in art beyond the confines of a campus or Boston—traditionally the American Athens. Looking over the names in the Mellon series—Blunt, Clark, Giedion, Gilson, Gombrich, Maritain, Pope-Hennessy—and the Wrightsman selections—Ashmole, Clark, Demus, Panofsky, Pope-Hennessy—the "foreign" character of the acknowledged stars of the art historical firmament show how clearly the supplementary wave of scholars whom Hitler lavished upon our shores were essentially needed, wanted, and used.

The American approach to art has become increasingly academic since the 1930's—"Appreciation" is out and "Seminars" are in; even contemporary painters think of their oeuvre in periods. A series born from a mystic marriage between the Book of the Month Club and the Metropolitan Museum of Art in whose title the word seminar looms large, locatable in the home, has proved to be one of the biggest bonanzas in art publishing. With the burgeoning of Harry Abrams, George Braziller, Frederick Praeger, and other publishers who can produce useful and affordable as well as attractive art books in the current paperback renaissance, America in the 1960's has really outstripped the high level of publications available to German middle-class culture of the early twentieth century which contributed so much to the formation of the work of the refugee scholars of the 1930's. Time-Life Books is now producing a handsome and thoughtful series of monographs entitled The Time-Life Library of Art under the consulting editorship of H. W. Janson, German-born chairman of the Art Department at Washington

Square College and professor at the Institute of Fine Arts. His clear-cut influence on the American and international concept of art history has already been manifested through his cosmically successful *History of Art* (1962). Dr. Janson has now provided America with as indigenous a Lübke as it may ever have. With millions of Americans studying Janson's *History of Art* (printed in Germany) and the Time-Life monographs edited by him, one can certainly write affirmatively of the influence of the German-born scholar on the thought of the United States, but this is a scholar with a Harvard Ph.D.

A correspondent, understandably resenting the necessarily impersonal yet equally necessarily prying questionnaire upon which this study is based, and fearing a quasi-sociological report written in Foundationese, wrote: "When the sorrow of the life of a victim of persecution and of exiles is touched upon, the *essay* can be the only vehicle of representation. Why not invite contributions for a kind of *Festschrift* in honor of those among our colleagues who died by those who made the 'impact' by surviving?" While this seems an admirable idea, one notes with satisfaction that it is almost impossible to examine any art journal published in America today without noting names of the men or their students who have been considered in this study. In a sense all American scholarly art publication will continue to be an enduring, self-perpetuating *Festschrift*, celebrating the development of a beautiful subject to which the migrants of the 1930's contributed so much.

There must be many scholars, such as the late Clemens Sommer, a disciple of Riegl, who regrettably remain largely unknown to this writer. A letter of Philipp Fehl's characterizes Sommer's achievement, which can stand for many émigrés who worked long and devotedly away from the major urban centers of American scholarship.

He was much beloved and did much to further the cause of history of art in the South. He was, I believe, the first art historian to come to North Carolina and, in many ways, as far as our field is concerned, a pioneer.[66]

Charles Rufus Morey once told an émigré colleague, "Your task is to train the men who will take your place."[67] This, the scholars individually and as a group have achieved.

66. Letter of July 19, 1967.
67. I am indebted to Richard Krautheimer for these last lines, from which only the modest "I think" has been removed from the final sentence.

APPENDIX

The following inevitably incomplete listing includes the names of European scholars, most of whom came to the United States in the 1930's to escape Fascist oppression and have continued their art historical interests in this country.

Ludwig Bachofer
Otto Benesch
Klaus Berger
Rudolph Berliner
Frederick A. Bernett (Bernstein)
Richard Bernheimer
Margaret Bieber
Justus Bier
Wolfgang Born
Bernard von Bothmer
Dietrich von Bothmer
Edgar Breitenbach
Otto Brendel
Leo Bronstein
George Caro
Alexander Dorner
Lorenz Eitner
Hans Engel
Richard Ettinghausen
Else Falk
Philipp Fehl
Paul Frankl
Walter Friedländer
Gustav Glück
Oswald Goetz
Adolph Goldschmidt
Carla Gottlieb
George M. A. Hanfmann
Julius S. Held
Hans Hesslein
Ernst Herzfeld
Hans Huth
Horst Janson
Adolph Katzenellenbogen
Emil Kaufman
Stephen Kayser
Ernst Kris
Richard Krautheimer
Trude Krautheimer-Hess

Karl Lehmann
Lotte Lenn
José Lopez-Rey
Antonio Morassi
Alice Muehsam
Günther Neufeld
Alfred Neumeyer
Leo Olschki
Erwin Panofsky
Lotte Brand Philip
Adolph Plazcek
Edith Porada
Liselotte Pulvermacher Egers
John Rewald
Gertrude Rosenberg
Jacob Rosenberg
Alfred Salmony
Guido Schoenberger
Heinrich Schwarz
Berta Segall
Otto von Simson
Clemens Sommer
Wolfgang Stechow
Kate Steinitz
Charles Sterling
William Suida
George Swarzenski
Hans Swarzenski
Hans Tietze
Erica Tietze-Conrat
Charles de Tolnay
Lionello Venturi
Kurt Weitzmann
Edgar Wind
Emmanuel Winternitz
Rahel Wischnitzer-Bernstein
Heinrich Zimmer
Paul Zucker

THE WIENER KREIS IN AMERICA

by HERBERT FEIGL

1. Origin and Development in Vienna

THE migration of a philosophical movement from Central Europe to America is the topic of this essay. Since I am not a trained historian, and since the data available to me are rather incomplete and uneven, I decided to write the story in a somewhat impressionistic manner. This, of course, involves in part an autobiographical perspective. Although I realize that I am a minor figure in the development of Logical Empiricism, I have known fairly intimately many of the major figures, and have been in more or less continual contact with most of them. I trust that my procedure of presentation—necessitated by unavoidable circumstances—will not be regarded as presumptuous. In extenuation I can only mention that I was (after Schlick's brief visits) the first "propagandist" of our outlook in the United States. I also happened to be, in 1930, the first of the group to enter the United States with an immigrant visa, and the first to acquire U. S. citizenship by naturalization, in 1937. Moreover, my friend Albert E. Blumberg and I were the ones who provided, in 1931, our philosophical movement with its international trade name, "Logical Positivism." For reasons to be sketched briefly later in this essay, most of us have preferred the label "Logical Empiricism" or "Scientific Empiricism" ever since about 1936.

The movement quickly aroused a great deal of discussion, criticism, and dispute. In retrospect I feel that we were most hospitably received in the United States, even by our most fervid opponents. It took me a while to realize how much we were indebted to our hosts for the generous and friendly treatment extended to every one of us. Several of our group arrived in the United States in a spirit of "conquest." We were deeply imbued with the conviction that we had found a "philosophy to end all philosophies." Naturally, we offended—especially the more tradition-bound thinkers in the new country. Nevertheless we met almost everywhere with very amiable and amicable philosophers. Our views were sharply criticized, in countless discussions and publications. Gradually we learned—or shall I say, we mellowed and matured. We realized that it is intellectually fruitful to "compare notes" with the various kinds of opposition. Lines of communication that we had never even dreamed of in Europe opened up in the New World. Among our early contacts were also a good many scientists and scientifically-oriented philosophers who greeted us as comrades-in-arms.

Before I review these varied reactions in detail, I must first relate, in outline, the origin, spirit, and organization of our movement in Europe.

Logical Positivism, or Scientific Empiricism, can be traced in its genesis to a number of factors and influences in European thought. The Vienna Circle (of which I was a member from its beginning in 1924 until 1930) and the Berlin Society for Scientific Philosophy had their roots in the views of the great scientist-philosophers of the second half of the nineteenth century and of the early years of the twentieth century. The most important influences came from the physicist-philosophers Hermann von Helmholtz, Ernst Mach, and Albert Einstein, and from the mathematician-philosophers Henri Poincaré, David Hilbert, and Bertrand Russell. In the period before World War I that we in the Vienna Circle called with affection and respect (and not at all with derision) "prehistoric," a group of young doctors of philosophy, with "major fields" in physics, mathematics, and the social sciences, and including most notably Philipp Frank, Hans Hahn, Richard von Mises, and Otto Neurath, met in an old Vienna coffee house on Thursday evenings for discussions, mainly of issues in the philosophy of science. At that time it was primarily the positivism of Ernst Mach that inspired this small group of scholars. Mach's historical and critical studies, as in his *Science of Mechanics*, *Wärmelehre* (Thermodynamics), *Optik*, and his epistemological and psychological investigations in *Analysis of Sensations* and *Erkenntnis und Irrtum* (Knowledge and Error) had engendered in a completely renewed and highly enriched form a positivistic philosophy that went far beyond the doctrines of Auguste Comte and John Stuart Mill. In its destructive aspects it was—after Kant's *Critique*—the most radically antimetaphysical philosophy of the nineteenth century.

In its constructive aspects it contained many important, though controversial, contributions to the philosophy of the empirical sciences. Philipp Frank and Richard von Mises were certainly the ones most deeply imbued with Mach's positivism. This did not prevent them, however, from disagreeing with Mach's opposition to the atomic theory. (Mach's doubts regarding the theory of relativity belong to his old age and a long period of illness; they played no role in those early days of Viennese Positivism.)

As far as I can ascertain, the ideas of Franz Brentano and his foremost disciples, Alexius Meinong and Edmund Husserl, though not entirely uncongenial had at best only a weak and indirect effect upon both the early as well as the later Vienna Positivists. Sigmund Freud's theories were on the whole more fully appreciated, though the more radical among the Viennese thinkers insisted that the psychoanalytic doctrines should be scrutinized very carefully. They felt that much in these doctrines was "metaphysical," *i.e.*, unverifiable. I shall return to this theme in connection with the later developments.

In 1924 under the direction of Professor Moritz Schlick, the Thursday evening gatherings of the "prehistoric" Vienna Circle evolved into the Vienna Circle of Logical Positivists that achieved world-wide attention, acclaim, and opposition. Schlick had come to the University of Vienna in 1922, having held teaching positions previously in the Universities of Rostock and Kiel in North Germany. The Viennese mathematician, Hans Hahn (above mentioned as a member of the "prehistoric" Circle) was influential in bringing Schlick to the famous "Chair in the Philosophy of the Inductive Sciences," which had been occupied by the great physicist-philosophers Ernst Mach and Ludwig Boltzmann and had been vacant for many years. Schlick was clearly a most worthy successor. He had earned his doctorate with a thesis in theoretical optics under Max Planck in Berlin, but his life work was in philosophy. Schlick was among the first academic philosophers (one should group with him C. D. Broad and Ernst Cassirer) who had an adequate understanding of Einstein's theory of relativity and who recognized its profound philosophical significance. His slender book *Space and Time in Contemporary Physics* was first published in Berlin in 1917. This was followed by his magnificent *Allgemeine Erkenntnislehre* (General Theory of Knowledge, first edition 1918, second, revised, edition 1925). This book appeared as the first in a series of outstanding monographs in the natural sciences published by Springer, Berlin. Not since the publications of Mach, Helmholtz, Boltzmann, and Poincaré had any book in the field of epistemology been as close to the outlook of modern natural science as Schlick's epoch-making work. The theory of knowledge and the philosophy of science were his major concerns. "*Naturphilosophie*," as it was then still called in German universities, had nothing in common with the obscure speculations of Schelling, Hegel, and others in the first half of the nineteenth century. "*Wissenschaftstheorie*," a designation that came to be used more frequently later, is a much better expression of the actual intent of these endeavors. S. S. Stevens, the Harvard psychologist, called it the "Science of Science," correctly indicating thereby that the aim of this reflective enterprise was the clarification of the basic assumptions, concepts, and methods of the sciences.

Schlick was a man of considerable erudition. In contrast to many other members of the Circle, he was well informed in the history of philosophy and the history of science. He was an extremely lucid thinker and writer, but not a brilliant lecturer. His students had the impression that he was slightly bored with lecturing to his usually large audiences. But he gave more of himself and went to much greater depths in his seminars. There he often proved immensely stimulating. His was a warm, kindly personality. He seemed extremely calm and unassuming in his self-effacing modesty.

As I recall, it was in 1924 that F. Waismann and I—we were favored students of Schlick's—approached him with the idea of forming a discussion group. Schlick consented, and the result was a Thursday evening colloquium—the beginning of the Vienna Circle. Among its initial members were the mathematician Hans Hahn, the sociologist-economist Otto Neurath and his wife Olga (she was Hahn's sister and a mathematician and logician), Felix Kaufman, then a lecturer in the philosophy of jurisprudence, and Victor Kraft, a philosopher well versed in history and much concerned with epistemology and the methodology of science. During that early period we were also joined by the German mathematician Kurt Reidemeister, who had just come from the University of Königsberg to an appointment at the University of Vienna.

There were several other scholars, all highly competent in their respective fields but less influential in the development of the ideas of the Circle. Friedrich Waismann and I, together with a handful of other advanced students, were among the junior members.[1]

It was Kurt Reidemeister who in 1924, or perhaps 1925, suggested to us a project that was to become decisive in the development of the Circle's philosophical outlook. We read and discussed at length Ludwig Wittgenstein's *Logisch-Philosophische Abhandlung* which later became famous in English under the title *Tractatus Logico-Philosophicus*. This earlier publication of Wittgenstein's appeared in the last volume (1921) of Wilhelm Ostwald's *Annalen der Naturphilosophie*. I had chanced to read this essay in the Nationalbibliothek of Vienna in 1922. I must confess that although I was struck with whatever I could understand of this aphoristic and cryptic work, I dismissed it as the product of an eccentric, though incisively brilliant, mind. In the Circle we began to penetrate Wittgenstein's ideas on the nature of language and its relation to the world, his repudiation of metaphysics (notwithstanding a few aphorisms toward the end of the *Tractatus* that had a mystical flavor), and his conception of logical and mathematical truth. We had been well prepared for this venture, especially by Hans Hahn, who in an extracurricular evening course had introduced us to the major ideas of the great work of Alfred North Whitehead and Bertrand Russell, *Principia Mathematica*. Hahn had done for us what would otherwise have been a most arduous task: he extracted the philosophical message from that veritable "cemetery of formulae." I still remember how Hahn, equipped with a long stick, pointed to the formulae, beautifully displayed on the many blackboards of the Mathematical Institute.

In 1925–1926 Schlick and Hahn were considering two candidates for the position of lecturer (Privatdozent) in philosophy. These were Hans Reichenbach and Rudolf Carnap. These two young but already outstanding scholars had partly similar backgrounds in mathematics, phys-

---

1. At the University of Vienna there was no distinction between undergraduate and graduate students. Waismann, about six years older than I, was already a lecturer at the People's Institute (*Volkshochschule Wien*). I attended several of his brilliant courses, which were mainly in the foundations of mathematics. I was just then beginning to work on my Ph.D. thesis, "Chance and Law," concerned with the problems of probability and induction in the natural sciences.

ics, logic, and epistemology. Both had been much concerned with the philosophy of space, time, and relativity. They also had a tinge of Neo-Kantianism due to their early training. Carnap, having been a student of Gottlob Frege's at the University of Jena, was especially interested in the formal-logical problems and techniques, whereas Reichenbach was at that time primarily a philosopher of physics. (In some of his earliest work he was also concerned with the theory of probability, a subject to which both he, and later Carnap, were to make immensely important contributions.) Schlick, who became personally acquainted with Carnap as well as with Reichenbach, was equally impressed by both of these young and productive thinkers. The fact that Carnap was finally offered the position at the University of Vienna can perhaps be explained by Hahn's strong influence, for Hahn, a great admirer not only of Mach but more especially of Russell, was convinced that Carnap would carry out in detail what was presented merely as a program in some of Russell's epistemological writings (notably in *Our Knowledge of the External World*). In fact, several of us in Vienna were reading a large typescript of Carnap's which was then entitled *Konstitutionssystem der Begriffe* (A System of the Constitution of [Empirical] Concepts). In this great work, later published under the title suggested by Schlick *Der Logische Aufbau der Welt* (now available in English as *The Logical Structure of the World*), Carnap attempted a logical reconstruction of the concepts of empirical knowledge. The logical form of this reconstruction was essentially the symbolic logic of Whitehead and Russell. In *Principia Mathematica* they had tried to show that all concepts of pure mathematics could be introduced by step-wise definitions on the basis of the concepts of a modernized logic. Similarly, Carnap sketched in considerable detail how the concepts of empirical knowledge could be defined on the basis of concepts pertaining to immediate experience. This seemed indeed the fulfilment of the original intentions of Mach's positivism, as well as a brilliant application of the tools of modern logic to some of the perennial issues of epistemology.

Carnap paid us a visit in Vienna in 1925. He presented a paper on the logic of space-time structure to the Circle. Everyone was impressed with his logical proficiency and scientific competence. Several of us felt that here was a very atypical (at the time!) philosopher who explained his logical reconstructions in the manner of an engineer describing the workings of a machine. Carnap—if psychological typing be permitted —was strongly introvert, Reichenbach strongly extrovert; but this character difference was much more noticeable in their attitudes and behavior than in their published work. Carnap and Reichenbach had become friends in the early twenties and kept up a lively correspondence on logical and philosophical issues long before they became coeditors in 1929 of *Erkenntnis*, the periodical which for ten years was to be the main organ of publication for the new outlook in philosophy. Reichenbach, after a spell of teaching physics at Stuttgart, had become in 1928 a lecturer in philosophy at the University of Berlin, where he formed his own Society for Scientific Philosophy. Outstanding members of that group led by Reichenbach and the mathematician Richard von Mises (originally a Viennese) were Kurt Grelling, Walter Dubislav, Alexander Herzberg, and, later, Reichenbach's students Carl G. Hempel and Olaf Helmer. The aims and activities of this Berlin group were very similar to those of the Vienna Circle. Strong connections between the two groups existed from the very beginning, partly because of the personal friendships between Carnap and Reichenbach, and between von Mises and Philipp Frank, then professor of physics at the University of Prague. Frank, never an actual member of the Vienna Circle, was a frequent visitor, and a friend of Hahn's and Schlick's. Frank and Schlick soon became editors of a series of notable books called *Schriften zur Wissenschaftlichen Weltauffassung* (Writings toward a Scientific World View). This series contained such important items as Frank's own book *Causality*; Carnap's *Logistics* and his *Logical Syntax of Language*; Neurath's *Empirische Soziologie*; and later, in 1934, K. R. Popper's *Logik der Forschung* (Logic of Scientific Discovery).[2]

Carnap's participation in the Circle discussions (1926–1931) brought

2. Schlick had invited me to publish my doctoral dissertation ("Chance and Law") in this series, but my thesis was completed in 1926, the very year of the revolution that quantum mechanics engendered in the determinism–indeterminism issue. And while in my work I had open-mindedly discussed that issue at length, I had not, and could not have, foreseen, let alone digested, the specific form that indeterminism was to take in the theories of Heisenberg, Born, Jordan, and Bohr. Thus I decided not to publish my thesis at that time, and except for a few articles on probability, induction, and causality, this work in which I had invested an enormous effort will remain unread in the library of the University of Vienna.

about rapid developments. Even outside the regular Circle sessions, Carnap engaged in a continual interchange of ideas with Neurath, Waismann, and myself. Carnap and Neurath also had a great deal in common in that they were somewhat utopian social reformers—Neurath quite actively, Carnap more "philosophically." Neurath, a man of great erudition, especially in history and the social disciplines, was also a powerful propagandist of the Viennese positivist outlook. He was of powerful physical stature, extremely energetic, full of "enterprise," with great talents for organization. He was also a very witty man, using sarcastic dialectics most effectively in discussions and controversies. I owe him a special debt of gratitude for sending me (I think as the first "emissary" of the Vienna Circle) to Bauhaus Dessau, then, in 1929, a highly progressive school of art and architecture. It was there in a week's sojourn of lectures and discussions that I became acquainted with Kandinsky and Klee. Neurath and Carnap felt that the Circle's philosophy was an expression of the *neue Sachlichkeit* which was part of the ideology of the Bauhaus. I don't know of any exact synonym in English for that German word *Sachlichkeit*. Perhaps the closest would be "fact-minded, sober attitude." This was indeed the basic mood of the Vienna Circle. In a pamphlet (*Überflüssige Wesenheiten*) in which Hans Hahn extolled the virtues of "Occam's Razor" (*entia non sunt multiplicanda praeter necessitatem*), he contrasted sharply the *weltabgewandte* with the *weltzugewandte* orientation in philosophy. This is essentially the distinction between "other worldly," transcendent speculation or mysticism, and the "worldly," secular scientifically enlightened types of philosophical attitude.

It was especially Neurath and Frank who envisioned and worked for a new era of enlightenment, propagating the Viennese form of positivism. In consonance with this idea, Neurath began the planning of the *International Encyclopedia of Unified Science*, modeled, though only distantly, on the ideas of the French *Encyclopédistes* of the eighteenth century. (Later an Institute for the Unity of Science would flourish in Boston, under the presidency and wise leadership of Philipp Frank.)

During Carnap's first year in Vienna (1926) the Circle took up a second reading of Wittgenstein's treatise. Wittgenstein himself, though he lived in Vienna from 1927 to 1929, never joined the Circle. He emphatically told the few of us (Schlick, Waismann, Carnap, and myself) with whom he occasionally met (either in cafés, at Schlick's apartment, or that of my fiancée, Maria Kasper, then a student of philosophy) that he was no longer interested in philosophy. He felt that he had said all he could in the *Tractatus*. Moreover, only on relatively rare occasions could we get him to clarify one or another of the puzzling or obscure passages in his work. He seemed himself rather unclear on the ideas he had developed during the First World War. During those Vienna years he was mainly preoccupied with architecture; he designed an almost palatial mansion for his sister in one of Vienna's most aristocratic and secluded districts. On occasion, he would read poetry to us (*e.g.*, that of Rabindranath Tagore). We encountered him also at symphony concerts, and I remember that he shared my enthusiasm for Anton Bruckner's music. Beethoven, Schubert, and even Johann Strauss (which surprised me then, but now no longer) were very dear to his heart. It was quite clear that the genius of Wittgenstein might well have expressed itself in art or music had the circumstances of his life been slightly different. All of us were deeply impressed with his fascinating personality. Schlick adored him and so did Waismann, who, like others of Wittgenstein's disciples, even came to imitate his gestures and manner of speech. Schlick ascribed to Wittgenstein profound philosophical insights that in my opinion were in fact formulated much more clearly in Schlick's own early work.

I recall Wittgenstein, on one occasion, precipitating a quarrel with Carnap, which, as Waismann and I interpreted it, was mainly an expression of diametrically opposite personalities. Carnap was always the tenacious, exact, thorough, painstaking logician, Wittgenstein a man of profound intuition and, at least in conversation, not very articulate. Hence Wittgenstein became impatient to the point of exasperation when Carnap, with the best intentions, asked him to "explain a little more fully" this or that point. "If he doesn't smell it, I can't help him. He just has got no nose!" Wittgenstein complained to me about Carnap. Indeed, for a time I had to suffer long harangues against Carnap before I was able to get some philosophical conversation going with Wittgenstein, and finally, sensing that I was closer to Carnap, Wittgenstein became inaccessible even to me. But I cherish the privilege of having known him, and of meeting him fairly frequently in 1927–1929.

I mention these matters because they reflect, at a personal level, the beginnings of a profound schism in modern analytic philosophy. Although I believe that Carnap's and Wittgenstein's basic substantive positions were fairly similar in the twenties, their manners of approach were radically different. Later, this led to the sharp divergence between the method of Carnap's rational reconstruction and the procedure of informal analysis of the "ordinary language philosophy," in England as well as in America, and that was inspired by Wittgenstein.

One more incident stands out in my memory. When the Dutch mathematician Luitzen Egbertus Jan Brouwer was scheduled to lecture on intuitionism in mathematics in Vienna, Waismann and I managed to coax Wittgenstein, after much resistance, to join us in attending the lecture. When, afterwards, Wittgenstein went to a café with us, a great event took place. Suddenly and very volubly Wittgenstein began talking philosophy—at great length. Perhaps this was the turning point, for ever since that time, 1929, when he moved to Cambridge University Wittgenstein was a philosopher again, and began to exert a tremendous influence. A veritable *bouleversement* took place in English philosophy, soon to spread to the United States and Australia as well. Bertrand Russell, dismayed at the new turn Wittgenstein's philosophy had taken, first was icily silent and later outspokenly opposed to it. Carnap, never very much disturbed by the fashions of the times, continued his constructive work in Prague and later in America.

I think it was by 1927 that we began to feel we had developed into a "movement" in philosophy. Despite some disagreements and of course great differences in emphasis, we had attained a predominantly common "platform." Visitors from other countries began to join the Circle for various periods of time. Among them were Eino Kaila, a brilliant Finnish philosopher, and Dickinson S. Miller, an American philosopher who, though elderly and rather silent, was a keen analytic thinker. One of the most outstanding members of the Polish group of logicians, Alfred Tarski came for a short visit in 1930, attracted primarily by Carnap's work. Carnap, a few months later, reciprocated with a visit to Warsaw where he continued discussions on logic and metamathematics with Tarski, and also with Lesniewski and Kotarbinski. This was the time when Carnap developed his ideas on the logical syntax of language, published in the Frank-Schlick series in 1934.

In the late twenties the Circle was greatly enriched by the attendance and participation of several advanced students, three of them primarily mathematicians: Gustav Bergmann, Kurt Gödel, and Karl Menger. Gödel, whose great abilities were quickly appreciated, had a lively exchange of ideas with Carnap (much of it outside the Circle) and began to develop extremely original ideas, culminating in 1931 in his famous proof of the essential incompleteness of a large class of mathematical systems. The proof itself was most ingenious, utilizing syntactical methods, *i.e.* an arithmetization of the syntax of mathematics. Gödel was a very unassuming, diligent worker, but his was clearly the mind of a genius of the very first order. Carnap immediately realized the importance of Gödel's discoveries and dealt with them later in various publications. On the personal side, I should mention that Gödel, together with another student member of the Circle, Marcel Natkin (originally from Lodz, Poland) and myself became close friends. We met frequently for walks through the parks of Vienna, and of course in cafés had endless discussions about logical, mathematical, epistemological, and philosophy-of-science issues,—sometimes deep into the hours of the night. Natkin, whose doctoral dissertation concerned causality, induction, and simplicity, was a brilliant thinker—thoroughly Humean in his positivism, but able to apply it to some of the most difficult and controversial issues in the logic of the empirical sciences. For personal and practical reasons he decided on a career in business, and left Vienna after his doctorate and settled in Paris. There he became one of the world's outstanding experts on photography.

I visited Natkin in Paris several times, and in 1957 he, Gödel, and I had a most enjoyable reunion in New York. The first of my Paris visits was in 1929, after I spent a few days with Neurath in Geneva, serving as his French interpreter at a conference. It was also in 1929 that I visited Reichenbach in Berlin for the first time. He had read my doctoral thesis, as well as my first book (*Theorie und Erfahrung in der Physik*), and generously gave me the benefit of his very helpful comments and criticisms.

In the early autumn of the same year, 1929, the Vienna Circle together with the Berlin Group held its first conference in Prague. I shall always remember the excitement of that meeting, as well as that of the second meeting in Königsberg the year after. A fairly large group of highly competent thinkers gathered on both occasions, and despite some divergencies, we felt that we all had basically a common orientation. This contrasted sharply with the situation among the more tradition-bound philosophers; they did not even seem to communicate effectively with one another. The Königsberg conference included among its personnel John von Neumann (who represented Hilbert's formalist philosophy of mathematics); the Dutch mathematician Arend Heyting (representing intuitionism); and Werner Heisenberg, the physicist and founder of quantum mechanics. Von Neumann's intellectual agility and genius was already quite noticeable in the public discussions and in the many private conversations that took place at Königsberg. At the preceding conference in Prague, Reichenbach, von Mises, Waismann, and I presented papers pertaining to the problems of probability and induction. Waismann, building upon some of Wittgenstein's ideas, formulated a logical concept of probability. This, much later, became the basis of Carnap's extensive work in this field.

There were two outstandingly brilliant minds in Vienna who, though close to us in philosophical orientation, never joined the Circle: Edgar Zilsel and Karl R. Popper. Both were convinced of their intellectual independence from us, and tried to preserve that independence by remaining outside the Circle. Indeed, I felt that both these men, each in his own way, were among our most valuable and helpful critics. Several of us met with them separately and privately—with Zilsel in the small discussion group that gathered at the house of Victor Kraft, in which Professor Heinrich Gomperz (son of Theodore) was a prominent member. Gomperz was a most stimulating lecturer, a highly erudite philosopher, and like his father an authority in the history of philosophy, especially of the classical Greek period. He was a man of great wit—and despite his occasional sarcasm, a kind and helpful teacher. (He moved to the University of Southern California in 1938 where he enjoyed a happy life and continued his highly effective teaching.) Gomperz, in his skeptical wisdom, viewed the Logical Positivist movement with severe reservations, but nevertheless with considerable understanding and sympathy.

Edgar Zilsel, who had been a student of Gomperz', had published several books—his earliest and perhaps most original being *Das Anwendungsproblem* (1916) (The Problem of Application, *i.e.*, problems of induction and probability, and more generally on the application of mathematics in the empirical sciences). This book, while severely defective in some respects, was extremely original, and certainly fascinatingly written. Zilsel, too, migrated to the United States—first settling in New York, working with the Horkheimer-Adorno group on social philosophy, later teaching at Mills College in Oakland, California. I met him only on a few occasions in the United States. It seems his was an unhappy and isolated existence in this country. We were deeply shocked to learn that his life ended in suicide.

Karl Popper's story is a very different one. He was a school teacher in Vienna. He was close to Gomperz and Kraft during his student years. I came to know him only shortly before my emigration. It must have been in 1929 that we spent a whole day and a large part of the night in discussion (in the apartment of my parents). Popper had read my doctoral thesis which dealt with problems to which he had already given much independent thought. His disagreements with my views, and also those of the Circle—especially with Carnap's epistemology (as in the *Aufbau*) —stimulated the further development of his thought. Schlick finally invited him to publish a monograph in the Frank-Schlick series. Many discussions with Schlick ensued; and as I know from Schlick's remarks (in Italy in 1935), Popper impressed him with his high originality and independence, and with all his characteristic "intensity" of discussion. To make matters worse, Reichenbach had criticized Popper's ideas severely (and perhaps unjustly), so that Popper remained on the whole quite critical, if not antagonistic, to our movement. In any case, his book, *The Logic of Scientific Discovery* (1934), was outstandingly successful. Carnap, despite some basic disagreements, appreciated deeply Popper's highly original approach to many issues of common concern. Thus it came about that I arranged for a few weeks of summer vacation (1932) in the Tyrol where Popper and I joined Carnap for many fruitful discussions and conversations. Popper later moved to New Zealand, and finally to England where he has been professor of philosophy at the University of London's School of Economics since 1946, and a knight since 1965. He also came to the United States quite a few times on visiting appointments. But more of this later.

11. Early Contacts with American Philosophers, and the Beginnings of our Migration

SEVERAL members of the Circle had a reading knowledge of English, but Schlick, whose wife was American, spoke English perfectly. Some of the conversations at Schlick's house were in English, notably with such visitors as Roger Money-Kyrle but occasionally even with Wittgenstein who also was fluent in English. Schlick was the first of our group to be invited to the United States. In 1929 he was visiting professor for a semester at Stanford University. At that time Paul A. Schilpp, also a German, who would later attain world-wide recognition with his Library of Living Philosophers, served as his assistant.[3] Schlick enjoyed his sojourn at Stanford, made many friends, and was promptly invited to another visiting professorship, this time (in 1931) to the University of California at Berkeley. Thus it came about that Schlick was the first to spread the Vienna "gospel" (with a strong emphasis on Wittgenstein's ideas) in America. My own first journey to the United States occurred in September 1930, when I was fortunate to obtain an International Rockefeller Research Fellowship. This allowed me to work at Harvard University for about nine months.

My interest in visiting and quite possibly even settling in the New World was motivated by various circumstances. To start with, there were my early contacts with two splendid American philosophers, Dickinson S. Miller and through him Charles A. Strong. Miller, as I have already mentioned, spent a year in Vienna attending the Circle sessions. About a year later I received from him a most amicable invitation to visit him and his good friend Charles Augustus Strong in Fiesole near Florence. He offered to cover all my expenses and to be his house guest. (It occurred to me later that it was Strong, a son-in-law of John D. Rockefeller, who must have financed my trip.) Both Strong and Miller were retired from their respective positions in American

3. Schilpp's general scheme, as realized in the Library's many volumes, was to have prominent philosophers (*e.g.* Dewey, Whitehead, Russell, Einstein, Carnap) write their intellectual autobiographies; to follow these writings with critical essays by about twenty-five writers; and then to conclude with the philosophers' replies.

universities, Strong from his chair in philosophy and psychology at Columbia University, Miller from a succession of posts, notably at Bryn Mawr, Smith, Harvard, and Columbia. Both of these gentlemen were wonderful hosts. Miller showed me the great works of art in Florence, and I enjoyed the Italian spring in the hills of Fiesole—it was indescribably beautiful. Both Miller and Strong knew German much better than I knew English at the time, so our conversations—mostly on epistemological issues—were in German. I reported and explained the views of the Vienna Circle to them. Nearly a year later they invited me to Fiesole once more—mainly to help Strong toward a better understanding of Einstein's theory of relativity. Strong was working on a metaphysical theory of space and time, and wanted to find out to what extent his views were compatible with those of Einstein. This again proved a most enjoyable experience for me. I was impressed with the erudition and the generosity and open-mindedness of these American scholars.

During the summer of 1929 I met a young American student in Paris, Albert E. Blumberg, who had come from Baltimore (Johns Hopkins University) and was interested in coming to Vienna. I encouraged him to do his thesis (on Emile Meyerson's philosophy of science) under Schlick's supervision. Blumberg and I soon became close friends, and I helped him, philosophically and linguistically, with the composition of his thesis. It was through Blumberg that I learned a great deal about the United States, its philosophers, its system of education, and its ways of life.

Most of us in the Vienna Circle were largely ignorant of American philosophy. We had, of course, read some of the work of William James and of John Dewey. But we had only a very vague idea of Charles S. Peirce.[4] We knew that James and Mach had some affinities and that they respected each other enormously. But for the rest, our ignorance was vast. We hardly knew anything about the American philosophical movements of Neo-realism and Critical Realism, though I personally had learned a bit about them from Miller and Strong, and later from Blumberg. I think it was through Bertrand Russell's books that our at-

4. This is partly excusable: Peirce's *Collected Papers* did not begin to appear until the early thirties.

tention was called to American Behaviorism, particularly as represented in the work of John B. Watson and his followers.

In any case, what I found out through the personal contacts mentioned above and through my reading of some of the American philosophical literature attracted me strongly. "Over there" I felt was a *Zeitgeist* thoroughly congenial to our Viennese position. It was also in 1929 that, I think through Blumberg's suggestion, we became acquainted with Percy W. Bridgman's *Logic of Modern Physics* (1927). Bridgman's operational analysis of the meaning of physical concepts was especially close to the positivistic view of Carnap, Frank, and von Mises, and even to certain strands of Wittgenstein's thought.

Thus encouraged, I applied to the Rockefeller Foundation in New York for a fellowship. I was "looked over" by one of their officials in Vienna in the spring of 1930, and about two months thereafter I was awarded a fellowship for research in the logic of scientific theories at Harvard. I arrived at Harvard in September 1930, shortly after the conference in Königsberg.

I was tremendously impressed by many things in the United States. New York was the first overwhelming experience. Soon afterwards there were the scholars at Harvard with whom I was fortunate to become acquainted: in short order, P. W. Bridgman, C. I. Lewis, Henry Sheffer, and of course A. N. Whitehead. In addition there was Susanne K. Langer, of German parents, the wife of the Harvard historian, William Langer. We had already known in Vienna her fine first book, *The Practice of Philosophy*. At her house a small group of scholars met occasionally for an evening's discussion. Then there were the "soirées" at Whitehead's house; most of them were long, rambling, but thoroughly captivating soliloquies—on all sorts of subjects—by the amiable, thoroughly British, philosopher. Whitehead had turned increasingly metaphysical (or "cosmological") after coming to the United States a few years earlier. His lectures were rather poetic ("the flickering, perishing flame of life . . ."), though when his students handed him term papers, he was dismayed with their imitations of his flowery style. (Returning the papers in class, he said, with that slight characteristic stammer of his: "You—you can't (cawn't) do that—I–I do that!"). Paul Weiss, then an instructor at Harvard and at that time still more interested in logic and epistemology than in metaphysics, was a most kind and helpful friend. George Morgan, who in 1927 had been secretary to Dickinson Miller in Fiesole, also aided me in my efforts of adaptation to the manners and intellectual climate of this new environment. (This gifted man later entered upon a career as diplomat; but there is a good book on Nietzsche by him.)

Among the graduate students at Harvard I was especially impressed with W. V. O. Quine, who later became one of the world's greatest logicians. Sheffer, an outstanding logician in his own right, remarked about Quine's first book, "Quinine logic—a bitter pill."

It so happened that Karl Menger was also at Harvard University for part of that year. He had by then achieved international recognition as a mathematician, especially through his work in topology and the theory of dimensions which he had begun in Vienna under Hans Hahn (stimulated by some of Poincaré's work). I was glad to have this reunion with a Circle member in the New World.

At Christmas, 1930, Albert Blumberg and I met in New York for a week's vacation, and for work on an article, "Logical Positivism; a New Movement in European Philosophy," that was published in the spring of 1931 in the *Journal of Philosophy*. It was this article, I believe, that affixed this internationally accepted label to our Viennese outlook. I should mention that previously, in 1929, a slender pamphlet, *Wissenschaftliche Weltauffassung: der Wiener Kreis*, had been composed by Carnap, Neurath, and Hahn, aided by Waismann and myself. This was, as it were, our declaration of independence from traditional philosophy. We presented this pamphlet to Schlick upon his return from Stanford. Schlick was moved by our amicable intentions; but as I could tell from his facial expression, and from what he told me later, he was actually appalled and dismayed by the thought that we were propagandizing our views as a "system" or "movement." He was deeply committed to an individualistic conception of philosophizing, and while he considered group discussion and mutual criticism to be greatly helpful and intellectually profitable, he believed that everyone should think creatively for himself. A "movement," like large scale meetings or conferences, was something he loathed. Yet the expansive spirit of Neurath and Reichenbach, and to some extent also of Carnap, had taken hold of us.

Blumberg and I felt we had a "mission" in America, and the response to our efforts seemed to support us in this. We had, indeed, "started the ball rolling," and for at least twenty years Logical Positivism was one of the major subjects of discussion, dispute, and controversy in United States philosophy. Among the early reactions were important articles by C. I. Lewis (Schlick replied to one of them), W. H. Werkmeister, V. C. Aldrich, and P. A. Schilpp; and a notable book by Julius Weinberg.

My own presentations at various meetings of the American Philosophical Association (especially those at Ann Arbor, Michigan, 1932; Chicago, 1933; and St. Louis, 1934), though concerned with specific issues such as induction, mind-body, and transcendence, were largely iconoclastic in regard to traditional metaphysics, and advocated the Viennese type of logical analysis. To some extent it was a "*succès de scandale*," perhaps somewhat similar to that of the early A. J. Ayer in England, whose aggressive and extremely well written book, *Language, Truth, and Logic* (1936) contributed greatly to the propagation of the Viennese views, especially those of Carnap, Wittgenstein, and Schlick, in the English-speaking world.

I remember well the national meeting of the American Philosophical Association in Chicago in which I was given the special privilege of an hour and a half for my lecture and subsequent discussion. My topic was "A Logical Analysis of the Psychophysical Problem." I tried to show that the notorious vexations of the mind-body puzzles in traditional philosophy could be solved (or dissolved!) by conceptual clarification. Fairly soon I came to realize that my ideas were rather half-baked, and that the problems involved were much more complex and intricate than I had thought at the time. My paper was published in the first volume of *Philosophy of Science*, a periodical for whose initiation I was in small part responsible. The reactions to my paper ranged from enthusiastic approval to devastating criticism. The California philosopher S. C. Pepper repudiated my entire approach, shrewdly spotting some inconsistencies of which I was then unaware. At the Chicago meeting I encountered, for the first time, Professor Charles Morris, who very generously supported me in the discussion.

Morris and I became better acquainted later. He invited me to give a colloquium lecture in Chicago in 1934, where I was also his house guest. Morris had grown up in the pragmatist movement and had high regard for the philosophies of John Dewey and George H. Mead. He had published a book, *Six Theories of Mind*, and was becoming increasingly interested in the theory of language. He had already formulated his general program of research. The broad discipline of *semiotic* was to combine studies in the syntax, semantics, and pragmatics of language. I encouraged Morris to visit Carnap in Prague, which he did in the summer of 1934. Morris, realizing what tremendous contributions Carnap could make on the American scene, mobilized those in power at the University of Chicago to invite Carnap. Thus it came about that Carnap started his American teaching career in the fall of 1936. He arranged also for assistantships for his young friends and disciples, Carl G. Hempel and Olaf Helmer.

Charles Morris was also instrumental in bringing Hans Reichenbach to the United States. Reichenbach had to leave Germany because of the increasing menace of the Nazi regime. He went first to Istanbul (Richard von Mises was also there at that time) where he taught first in French, and later even in Turkish. In 1938, the year in which Reichenbach's important book *Experience and Prediction* was published by the University of Chicago Press (Morris had arranged for this), he began teaching at the University of California at Los Angeles, where he taught until his untimely death in 1953. He soon established himself as one of the leading philosophers of science in America. He was a most productive scholar; he worked in many areas, and published several important books. Reichenbach was also a brilliant speaker and lecturer, beloved by his students. He and Carnap and I met occasionally at specially arranged conferences, or—as in 1951—at a combined meeting of the American Philosophical Association and the American Association for the Advancement of Science at Bryn Mawr and Philadelphia.

Kurt Gödel accepted a research position at the Institute for Advanced Studies at Princeton in 1938. There he collaborated during several periods with Einstein on problems of cosmology and continued his work on the foundations of mathematics, notably on the Continuum Problem.

C. G. Hempel, one of the most clear-headed thinkers and most effective teachers of the group, held positions at Queens College, New York, later at Yale University, and finally at Princeton University. His studies in the logic of scientific explanation were begun in collaboration with Paul Oppenheim, also an émigré from Germany, who was a close personal friend of Einstein's, a private scholar who, in his quiet way, stimulated a great deal of interesting work in the philosophy of science. In Oppenheim's magnificent house at Princeton there were many social gatherings of distinguished scientists and philosophers.

Also in 1938, Gustav Bergmann moved from Vienna—first to New York and later to the University of Iowa. When, in 1940, I was called from Iowa to a professorship at the University of Minnesota, Bergmann became my successor at Iowa and began a highly influential teaching career and a long period of scholarly production there. Olaf Helmer, after his brief spell with Carnap in Chicago, joined the research staff of the Rand Corporation in Santa Monica, California. Alfred Tarski, who proved to be one of the greatest logicians and mathematicians of our time, settled at the University of California in Berkeley. And Henryk Mehlberg, another outstanding Polish philosopher of science, taught first at the University of Toronto (1949–1956) but settled in 1957 at the University of Chicago.

Philipp Frank left Prague a year before the Nazis occupied Czechoslovakia and Austria. He was offered a position in the Physics Department of Harvard University, where he taught primarily philosophy of science courses and seminars. The teaching and the books of this wise and humorous man contributed greatly toward the empiricist outlook on the American scene. Frank's book *Philosophy of Science* (1957) bore the subtitle "The Link Between Science and Philosophy." Thus, shortly before C. P. Snow's ideas on the "two cultures" emerged in the limelight of public discussion, Frank had already pointed to one important bridge over the chasm.

Very much in the same spirit, and perhaps even more incisively written, was Richard von Mises' book *Positivism—A Study in Human Understanding* (1951). Von Mises, too, had found a haven at Harvard. His main work there was, however, in the fields of mathematical physics and aerodynamics.

Felix Kaufmann, until his premature death (in 1949), was a professor of philosophy in the New School for Social Research in New York City. Although he had been an active and cherished member of the Vienna Circle, his philosophical allegiance during those years was distinctly to Edmund Husserl's phenomenological approach. He had published books on the philosophy of law and the foundations of mathematics. During his American years he devoted a good deal of his work to the philosophy and methodology of the social sciences, and in this connection he was fairly close to the outlook of the Viennese positivists.

During the spring of 1931, while I was at Harvard University, it became clear to me that my chances for a teaching position in an Austrian or German University were extremely slim. True, the ever so optimistic and kindly Schlick was convinced that I would obtain a Privatdozentur (position as a lecturer) at the University of Vienna. But though I was Austrian by birth, I had become a Czechoslovakian citizen after the revolution in 1918. My home was then in Reichenberg (Liberec), in the Sudetenland, where I was born and grew up, and had attended primary and secondary schools. My parents, though thoroughly "assimilated," were of Jewish descent. More realistic than Schlick, I abandoned the idea of a teaching career in Europe, and began applying for a position in a number of American universities. I had been given generous recommendations by Einstein, Whitehead, C. I. Lewis, and Bridgman. I received very courteous replies from about thirty American universities (I had sent out forty-five applications), but most of them then had "no opening." Three universities, Rutgers, New York University, and the State University of Iowa, were the only ones that wanted to "look me over," and toward the end of May 1931 I visited all three places. Iowa seemed most strongly interested. The late Dean George Kay, a prominent geologist of Canadian origin, telephoned Professor Lewis long distance. As Lewis later related to me, Dean Kay asked him in detail about my qualifications, character, and personality. At the end of that (about twenty minutes!) telephone conversation, Kay finally asked: "Is he a Jew?" To this, Lewis, the noble New Englander, gave the—to me unforgettable—reply: "I am sure I don't know, but if he is, there is nothing disturbing about it." Thus it came about that a few days after my visit, to Iowa, I received a telephone call from Dean Kay offering me the position of a lecturer. That telephone call reached me just fifteen minutes before my departure for Europe. It was one of the most exciting moments of my life. I returned to Vienna, and married Maria Kasper (to whom I had been engaged for three years). We both obtained immigration visas for the United States and settled, in September 1931, at Iowa City.

The transition from cosmopolitan Vienna to the small town, then with a population of about fifteen thousand in the "Tall Corn State" required some effort. But we were young and eagerly interested in starting a "*Vita Nuova.*" Moreover, we soon acquired a number of wonderful and helpful friends—some of them typically midwestern, others of German, Austrian, French, or South African origin—all on the Iowa faculty. I had improved my fluency in the English language considerably at Harvard during the previous year. Within a few weeks, I managed to communicate effectively with my students. I shall relate my further experiences at Iowa, and return to my "propagandistic" activities, after the following section devoted to the "ideology" of Logical Positivism.

III. Logical Positivism; Logical Empiricism
—A Brief Sketch for Non-philosophers

IN order to make more intelligible the impressions, experiences, and influences of the European positivists in the United States, it is necessary to sketch, in brief outline, some of our basic doctrines and their early modifications. Logical Positivism (the position of the Vienna Circle) and Scientific Empiricism (the position of the Berlin Society), despite important differences, had much in common. Both ideologies were conceived as philosophies for our age of science. As a culmination of the empiricist tendencies in philosophy since the Renaissance, positivism attempted to retain from traditional philosophies the spirit of enlightenment and clarification. The opposition to obscurantist metaphysics and mysticism became the most conspicuous, and to some the most offensive, feature of positivism. The critique of metaphysics was directed essentially against two major traditional philosophical tendencies: first, the conviction that truths regarding matters of fact could be established by pure reason alone ("a priori"); the empiricist opposition to this position had already been clearly enunciated by David Hume in the eighteenth century. The second was the conviction that knowledge regarding "transcendent" reality could be justified by speculation, intuition, dialectics, or other non-empirical procedures. Thus limiting the scope of factual meaning to what is testable by observation and experience, many positivists drew a line of demarcation between the knowable and the unknowable even more narrowly than some of the earlier empiricists.

The designation *logical* positivism seemed required in order to mark an important difference between our position and that of such empiricists as Comte and Mill. Logical and mathematical truths were considered, for example by Mill, as a most general kind of empirical knowledge. In this regard, we favored the different attitude already adumbrated by Leibniz and developed much more fully by Frege and Russell. The truths of *pure* mathematics (*i.e.*, not including physical geometry or other branches of the factual sciences) are *a priori* indeed. But they are *a priori* precisely because they are *analytic, i.e.*, because they are validated on the basis of the very *meaning* of the concepts involved in the propositions of mathematics. Empirical certification of mathematical truths is neither required, nor indeed possible. The Vienna Circle regarded, for example, the identities of arithmetic as necessary truths, based on the definition of the number concepts—and thus analogous to the tautologies of logic (such as "what will be, will be"; "the weather will either change or remain the same"; "you can't eat your cake and not eat it at the same time"). With the formalists (*e.g.*, Hilbert) we would consider mathematical proofs as procedures that start with a given set of sign combinations (premises, postulates) and according to rules of inference (transformation rules) lead to the derivation of a conclusion (theorem). Russell (who was not a formalist himself) formulated this doctrine in his famous quip "Mathematics is the science in which we never know what we are talking about, nor whether what we say is true." With the logicists (*e.g.*, Frege and Russell) we regarded mathematics as a branch of logic. As we saw it, there were no insurmountable difficulties connected with the mathematical problems of the infinite (or its Cantorian levels). Our view appeared derogatory to the mathematicians. They understood us to say that mathematics is no more than a huge tautology. But this is derogatory only if "tautology" is taken as synonymous with "triviality." Far from maintaining anything so silly, we insisted that the proof of the very tautologicality of the implication that holds between the postulates (and definitions) and the theorems of mathematics often requires the intellectual powers of a genius.

In any case, we were convinced that there are only two kinds of genuine knowledge: the purely formal (logico-mathematical) and the factual (empirical). This distinction, already clearly drawn by Hume, but greatly refined and elaborated later, is also inherent in the two meanings of the word "proof" as used in common language. It is one thing to "prove" (by deductive derivation) a theorem in mathematics, and quite another thing to "prove" the truth (or rather the likelihood or credibility) of a factual assertion (hypothesis, prediction, theory) by inductive or hypothetico-deductive procedures and observational-experimental (or statistical) confirmation.

These are in essence the guiding principles of the epistemology of Logical Positivism. Schlick preferred the label *Konsequenter Empirismus* (Consistent Empiricism), but our designation, emphasizing as it did our view of logical truth, gained world-wide acceptance.

It became necessary to guard against misunderstandings of our main thesis. Our concern was not with the psychological origins or the social conditions of the cognitive enterprise. Our distinction was based on differences in the method of validation. In Reichenbach's terminology, we were analyzing knowledge claims in the "context of justification" and not in the "context of discovery." We always admitted that all sorts of intuitive processes (*e.g.*, "hunches," consciously or subconsciously discerned analogies), may well be extremely instrumental (heuristically) in the *genesis* of hypotheses and theories. We never claimed that great scientific theories could be constructed by a logic-machine. (This was long before the age of computers—and who knows what may yet be achieved by them?) We firmly held (with Einstein, and with Popper) that there is no straight logical path that leads from the data of observation to an explanatory theory. Great ingenuity, with all the risks of "guessing wrong," is the order of the day in theory construction. Many of us agreed with Popper that the procedure here is: bold conjectures, and their criticism through persistent and perspicacious attempts at refutation. If the theory in question survives such searching experimental challenges, it may "until further notice," be considered as corroborated, and as such be included in the corpus of science—as long as no refuting evidence turns up.

The Logical Positivists' most controversial tenet was their "principle of verifiability." This was intended as a criterion of factual meaningfulness. Actually, as formulated by Carnap as early as 1928, it was not verifiability but *testability-in-principle* (*Prüfbarkeit*) which we used as the distinctive mark of factually (not just scientifically) meaningful assertions. We used this criterion in repudiating any *transcendent*-metaphysical propositions. We thus continued and sharpened the critique of the *absolutes* (such as substance, space, time, vital force, soul, the deity) that had already been characteristic of the empiricist tradition.

Telling metaphysicians and theologians, not that they make false or unjustifiable statements, but that their verbal utterances make no sense, this was clearly the most iconoclastic and offensive challenge that could be put to them. Judging by the tremendous flood of polemical reactions, we had touched a sensitive spot here. To be sure, we had to modify and to mollify our attack, for we were soon confronted with pertinent and provocative questions regarding the very meaning, and the justification of our criterion. We explained that we were distinguishing the various functions of language, or (what amounts to the same thing) the diverse types of significance. While admitting that the cognitive and the non-cognitive uses of language are almost always combined, and psychologically fused, it seemed imperative to warn against confusing one with the other. The pictorial, emotional, or motivative functions of language must be sharply distinguished from the informative function. In metaphysical and theological assertions the emotive (*i.e.*, pictorial, emotional, and/or motivative) type of significance is often erroneously taken to be a genuinely cognitive-factual meaning.

Despite the many changes that have been made in the formulation of the criterion of factual meaningfulness, its basic intent has remained the same. Essentially it amounts to eliminating from cognitive discourse questions which can neither logically nor empirically be answered. Problems which are guaranteed unsolvable are *cognitively* meaningless. But as existentialist torments indicate, questions such as "the meaning of life," or "why is there something rather than nothing?" may be highly significant emotionally or motivationally; cognitively, however, they are absolutely unanswerable. The proffered answers or assertions are proof against disproof. They are beyond the limits of rational discourse. To put it yet another way: we tried to establish a clear line of demarcation between genuine problems and pseudo problems.

It is true that some of the early formulations were too drastic in that they eliminated difficult questions along with nonsensical ones. This was remedied by later more circumspect and more liberal formulations. Discussion and dispute concerning the very feasibility of an adequate formulation continues. It should also be noted that we never accused the metaphysicians or theologians of deliberately talking nonsense. Our diagnosis was rather that they were unwittingly mistaking pictorial or emotive significance for factual meaning.

Since the word "metaphysics" is used in a variety of ways, and thus designates several quite different philosophical endeavors, it is important to note that by no means all of them were "taboo" from our point of view. If "metaphysics" designates speculative extrapolations based on scientifically obtainable evidence, then such an endeavor, though risky, is not necessarily meaningless. Examples in various domains would be cosmology (essentially a branch of astrophysics) and psychoanalytic theory (an attempt to explain behavior and experience on the basis of speculative assumptions regarding unconscious motivation). Such types of "inductive" metaphysics are thus continuous with science, but its theories are more precarious because they are only very indirectly and incompletely testable. Another time-honored meaning of "metaphysics" may be characterized as categorial analysis, *i.e.*, an investigation of the basic concepts and conceptual frames used in our knowledge of reality. This is not fundamentally different from the sort of logical analysis pursued by the positivists themselves.

What we did repudiate as illegitimate was rather the use of "verbal sedatives," that is, high sounding phrases that may tranquilize scientific curiosity and thus impede the progress of research. We were convinced that the emotional needs of man can be fulfilled much more adequately in poetry, music, and the arts in general, if not in life itself. We pointed out that the word "belief" is quite ambiguous in that it may mean: (1) a cognitive attitude connected with testable propositions, or (2) the acceptance of transempirical (untestable) assertions, or (3) a commitment to certain values or ideals. We were convinced that transempirical assertions were devoid of cognitive meaning, and that their utterance (as in sermons, prayers, rituals) merely enhanced the motivative power of commitments. Thus our attitude toward theology and religion was that of the naturalistic or scientific humanists. Indeed, several of us found in the general position of the American Humanist Association an ideology that seemed very similar to our basic philosophical attitude. If, as most humanists prefer, "religion" is not connected with any theology whatever, then a deep commitment to such human values as basic and equal rights, the civil liberties, the ideal of a peaceful and harmonious world community, may well be said to be the religion of the humanists —and of the positivists.

We encountered strong opposition to some of our early provocative pronouncements in regard to the significance of moral judgments. We agreed (for example with G. E. Moore—though this important insight had already been explicit in Hume's work) that it is logically impossible to derive moral norms or imperatives from purely factual premises about human nature. But we disagreed with Moore's idea (and with many other philosophers, past and present) that moral judgments could be justified by "intuition." It is *familiarity* that breeds intuition (in many areas)—but this does not in any way validate the intuited judgment. What appears as intuitively cogent may well vary from person to person, or from culture to culture. But going beyond these observations, some of the positivists assimilated moral judgments to judgments of taste, and thus not only offended well intentioned moral philosophers but actually did not do justice to the nature of moral reasoning. Schlick's largely psychological approach to the problems of ethics found little attention. But A. J. Ayer's chapter on ethics in his *Language, Truth and Logic* aroused strong opposition. The important work of the American philosophers Charles L. Stevenson and Charles Morris in moral philosophy and value theory helped greatly in paving the way toward a less offensive (by no means purely "emotivist") position in ethical theory. The issues are logically delicate and intricate. Here, just as in epistemology and philosophy of science, our outlook has undergone considerable change and development.

At this point I should explain the reasons for the change in label from "Logical Positivism" to "Logical Empiricism." The original positivism of Auguste Comte, as well as that of the late nineteenth-century exponents, especially Mach and Avenarius, were often misunderstood as being yet another version of subjective idealism. Careful reading of all these authors reveals that this is indeed a misunderstanding. In any case, Carnap's work (especially in the *Logische Aufbau*) was similarly misinterpreted. Carnap had quite emphatically explained that his reconstruction of the empirical knowledge was phenomenalistic or solipsistic only in a methodological sense. That is to say, he chose as the basis for his particular reconstruction the data of immediate experience. But he pointed out that a reconstruction on a physicalistic basis was equally possible. Actually he later came to prefer this latter kind of reconstruction. Carnap was equally explicit on the "metaphysical neutrality" of either (or any other) type of reconstruction. He considered metaphysical interpretations as illegitimate intrusions of *Begleitvorstellungen* or of *Begleitgefühle* (accompanying imagery or emotions): an irrelevant surplus beyond the genuinely cognitive content.

Perhaps the most important and constructive aspect in the transition to Logical Empiricism was the element of empirical or scientific realism that became increasingly prominent in our views. Reichenbach and I had already opposed the phenomenalistic reduction during the twenties. In this regard we were closer to the views of Zilsel and Popper. We regretted that Schlick had abandoned his early critical realism, and we tried to reinstate it in a more defensible form. This was achieved through the liberalization of the empiricist meaning of criterion. Verifiability was replaced by (at least indirect and incomplete) testability; or, as we now usually put it, by confirmability or disconfirmability. On this basis it makes perfectly good sense to speak of the existence of theoretical entities—be they the particles or fields of modern physics or the unconscious mental processes in psychoanalytic theory.

The most important positive contributions by the individual members of the movement pertain to the philosophy of science. The foundations of mathematics and the structure and confirmation of the theories in the natural and social sciences have been among our major concerns. Carnap's work in syntax and semantics and in the logic of probability and induction, and Hempel's contributions to the logic of concept formation and scientific explanation, are outstanding examples. Most of these more technical endeavors are far too intricate to permit brief description. It should also be noted that even more than during the initial stages of the movement (in Vienna and Berlin) there have developed considerable divergencies in point of view as well as in method among the individual members of the group. In addition to our conspicuous preoccupation with the philosophy of science, there is one aspect of method that the movement as a whole still shares. It is the pursuit of formal logical reconstruction, and in this regard it is quite different from the neo-Wittgensteinian informal linguistic analysis. Some of us accept the informal procedures as a useful first step, *i.e.*, the sorting out of explicanda, and thus paving the way for exact explication. Others find the procedures of Oxford-type linguistic analysis completely uninteresting and fruitless. The need for formal reconstruction, it should be remembered, was already recognized by Aristotle. He could never have succeeded in codifying syllogistic inference had he not transformed the phrasings of ordinary-language sentences into standard patterns. Though this was only a first simple beginning, it is the prototype of all the reconstruction in terms of "ideal languages" pursued in our century. That some of these reconstructions deviate considerably from the patterns of the natural languages does not matter. Any sort of reconstruction is bound to appear "procrustean" from the point of view of ordinary language. Our answer here, as well as in all related issues, is the pragmatic one: "By their fruits ye shall know them."

IV. The Termination of the Vienna and the Berlin Society:
International Meetings, Expansion and Migration

THE rise of the Third Reich, and the invasion of Austria in 1938 and
of Czechoslovakia and Poland in 1939, put an end to the Continental phase of the Logical Positivist movement. As mentioned before,
two prominent members of the Berlin group, Reichenbach and Richard
von Mises, found a temporary haven in Turkey before they came to the
United States. The activities of the Vienna Circle had continued until
1936, the year of Schlick's tragic death. He was murdered by one of his
former students, in all probability not a political assassin but a paranoid
personality. All members of our now partly dispersed group were
deeply shocked and grieved. Schlick had been extremely kind to all his
students, even to the man who later committed that horrible crime.

There had been several international meetings of the Unity of Science
movement—in Prague, 1934, Paris, 1935, Copenhagen, 1937, and Cambridge, Massachusetts, 1939. I participated (coming from the University of Iowa) in the Paris congress where I had a happy reunion with my
erstwhile Vienna friends (Carnap, Neurath, et al.) but also met for the
first time Bertrand Russell and Alfred Ayer. Ayer, who had not known
Russell before this occasion either, and I introduced ourselves to Russell. I said, "In a manner of speaking, we are your [Russell's] intellectual
grandsons." In characteristic fashion Russell instantly asked, "And who
is your father?" "We have three of them," I replied, "Schlick, Carnap,
and Wittgenstein." (Laughter on all sides.) Charles Morris was one of
the American participants at the Paris meeting. Tarski (from Warsaw),
Jorgenson (from Copenhagen), and Ajdukiewicz (from Poznan) were
also present. For Carnap, the Paris meeting marked the beginning of his
work in semantics. Although Neurath was skeptical if not outright opposed, Carnap was persuaded of the importance of semantics by Tarski.

A year later, in the summer of 1936, Carnap was invited to participate
in the tercentenary celebrations of Harvard University. I joined Carnap
there for a few weeks. This was also the first occasion on which we met
Ernest Nagel, who was to become a good friend of both of us. Nagel
had by then been teaching at Columbia University for several years.

He had previously been a student of John Dewey at Columbia and Morris R. Cohen at City College. Cohen was an outstanding thinker and teacher, and perhaps the only prominent American philosopher of science after C. S. Peirce. Cohen's keen critical mind greatly influenced many of his students who were later to become notable philosophers in their own right. His own position was on the whole more rationalistic than empiricist. He opposed and criticized the positivists in many of his publications and lectures. Nevertheless Cohen, more than anyone else, brought Bertrand Russell's thought to the attention of the American scholars. When I came to America Cohen and Abram Cornelius Benjamin were the only really distinct representatives and teachers of the philosophy of the empirical sciences. Of course, there were also the philosophizing scientists, notably the physicist Bridgman and the psychologists E. G. Boring and S. S. Stevens (all three at Harvard) who were concerned with the logical and methodological aspects of their respective disciplines. The physicist Victor F. Lenzen, at the University of California at Berkeley, was another outstanding scholar in the philosophy of physics. The American intellectual climate, then, was not entirely unprepared for the tremendously accelerated upswing of interest in the philosophy of science that came about through the influx of the European positivists and empiricists. In 1939, just at the time of the outbreak of the Second World War, a Unity of Science conference took place at Harvard. This had been organized by Neurath (coming from Holland) and by Charles Morris (University of Chicago). A number of American sympathizers, and also friendly critics, participated in this conference. But the *Journal of Unified Science*, which was originated as a successor of *Erkenntnis*, was doomed to expire after publication of its first two numbers. The war and the dispersion of our groups temporarily impeded our collaborative efforts. Still, there was a sort of revival of the Vienna Circle in 1940. This was at the time when Bertrand Russell gave his William James Lectures (later published as *Inquiry into Meaning and Truth*) at Harvard. Carnap and Tarski were at Harvard as visiting professors. I spent part of my second Rockefeller research fellowship year at Harvard and thus was able to participate in the fascinating regular discussions that took place in the fall of 1940 and included, besides Russell, Philipp Frank, Richard von Mises, W. V.

Quine, E. G. Boring, S. S. Stevens, P. W. Bridgman, and I. A. Richards, among the more active members. Issues in the foundations of logic and semantics, as well as of the theory of probability, were extensively discussed. Carnap offered a seminar on semantics at that time. Although he and Tarski agreed on the basic principles of the (semantical) metalinguistic approach, there remained some differences (also with Quine) on the nature of logical truth. Tarski and Quine refused to draw a sharp line of distinction between analytic and synthetic propositions, and hence between logical and empirical truth. Carnap, except for some recent modifications, upheld the sharp distinction that was one of the main tenets (later called "dogmas" by Quine) of Logical Empiricism. Russell also was critical in other respects (especially in regard to the principles of inductive inference) of the original Vienna doctrine.

The closest allies our movement acquired in the United States were undoubtedly the operationalists, the pragmatists, and the behaviorists. The leader among the physicists was P. W. Bridgman. His tough-minded outlook, his generosity, and to some extent even his (as I think, misguided) subjectivism made him sympathetic to our ways of thinking. Bridgman was famous for his work in experimental physics; he was awarded the Nobel Prize for his investigations of the effects of very high pressures on the properties of metals. But he was also highly competent in theoretical physics. Unassumingly, he always protested against being considered a philosopher, and he did not like the label of "operationalist." All he claimed was that in order to understand the concepts of physics, the operational approach proves most useful. By that he meant a reflection upon, and analysis of, the procedures employed in the use of concepts in the various contexts of measurement, experiment, and theory. This is very close to one aspect of Carnap's and Wittgenstein's views. "Don't ask me for the 'meaning' of a concept, ask me about the *rules* according to which the concept is used." Although this is not an exact quotation, it reflects the attitude shared by all three (otherwise quite different) thinkers. Paraphrasing some of Bridgman's own formulations, he advised not to "fall into mystical bewilderment" about the nature of space, time, matter, or energy. Let us rather see according to what rules of "physical" (observational, mensurational, experimental) and "mental" or "paper and pencil" (logico-mathematical) operations we use the symbols (representing concepts) in the actual procedures of the sciences. Operationalism in this broad sense would indeed cover the entire range of cognitive "meaning." Bridgman himself was not a formalist, and I suppose he felt that Carnap and other logicians were doing a rather farfetched and artificial job of all-too-exact reconstruction. Bridgman, who was philosophically not too well informed, had perhaps not even known to what extent his ideas had been adumbrated by C. S. Peirce, the great American philosopher about fifty years before him. Indeed, reading Peirce's famous essay on "How to Make Our Ideas Clear" (1878!) one is impressed with how close Peirce came to anticipating the basic positivistic and operationalist outlook. To be sure, empiricists view Peirce as a "split personality." We were prone to disregard his profound metaphysical essays, but I don't think we ever managed to understand them.

The operational orientation soon became prominent in the methodological work, or pronouncements, of several distinguished American psychologists. E. G. Boring, S. S. Stevens, E. C. Tolman, C. L. Hull, and B. F. Skinner, anxious to make of psychology an "honest natural science" of the behavior of organisms, endeavored to provide operational definitions of the basic concepts of that discipline. This harmonized well with John Dewey's outlook and that of his disciples in their instrumentalistic view of science. According to that philosophy, concepts, hypotheses, theories are *tools* in the organization of empirical knowledge.

The quick response of these physicists and psychologists was, I believe, responsible for the friendly reception accorded to us, and our remarkable success in the early years of our American existence. We soon struck a responsive chord too with some of the American sociologists, notably G. A. Lundberg. Other scientists with whom we had a large measure of agreement were the physicists Victor Lenzen, Henry Margenau, and R. B. Lindsay.

Philipp Frank established very cordial relationships not only with Bridgman but also with a number of scholars outside the field of physics. His genial temperament and his interest in the socio–cultural–historical settings of the scientific enterprise attracted historians, linguists, social scientists, and philosophers. Similarly, Neurath—who had found a haven (after his escape in a small boat from Holland and his temporary internment on the Isle of Man) in England—visited the United States several times, establishing relations between our movement and leading representatives of the social sciences.

It was my good fortune to teach summer session courses in the University of California at Berkeley in 1946 and 1953 and also to spend a part of a sabbatical leave in Berkeley in 1948. There I had close contacts with the psychologists E. C. Tolman and Egon Brunswik and Brunswik's wife, Else Frenkel-Brunswik. The Brunswiks already were friends of mine (and of my wife) during our Vienna years. They were students of the great psychologists Karl Bühler and Charlotte Bühler; but they were also students of Schlick's. It was Tolman, truly a "prince of a man," who facilitated the immigration of the Brunswiks and who appointed Egon Brunswik to a position in the University of California Psychology Department. Brunswik and I organized a Unity of Science meeting at Berkeley in the summer of 1953. I also had very pleasant relationships with several of the California philosophers, especially with W. R. Dennes, Paul Marhenke, and David Rynin. These three had known Schlick during his sojourn in Berkeley in 1931. Later Stephen C. Pepper and I came to be good friends. His early (1936) sharp criticism of my first essay on the mind-body problem, though painful at the time, had stimulated my re-thinking of that baffling and perennial problem. When I presented (in 1954) a drastically revised paper on the same issues at the Meeting of the Pacific Division of the American Philosophical Association at Seattle, Pepper happened to be in the audience and expressed his enthusiastic agreement with my new outlook.

Most of the Continental scholars participated in various conferences of the American Philosophical Association, the American Physical Society, the American Psychological Association, and others. In the early thirties I defended Logical Positivism in discussions with such noted American metaphysicians as Charles Hartshorne, David Swenson, and Paul Weiss; and with the critical realist Roy W. Sellars. Later on, the entire atmosphere of the debate became different. Great changes had taken place in our own outlook, and, of course, American philosophy, too, underwent tremendous transformations, expansion, and diversification. Some of these developments can be gleaned from the contents of that remarkable book edited by P. A. Schilpp, *The Philosophy of Rudolf Carnap*.[5] There twenty-six philosophers, many of them American, are represented by their critical essays. Carnap's replies, but also his intellectual autobiography in the first part of that book, bear testimony to the changes that have taken place in the thought of one of the leaders in our movement.

My own experiences at the University of Iowa, and later at the University of Minnesota, reflect the rapidly growing influence of our scientifically oriented outlook in philosophy. The Iowa philosophy department had only three members when I arrived there. And while a general course on "Philosophy and Science" had been offered there, mine was the first course in the "Philosophy of Science." The situation was similar at Minnesota in 1941. On my suggestion the young and brilliant philosopher Wilfrid Sellars (son of Roy W. Sellars) was called to Iowa in 1938, and he joined the Minnesota department in 1946. Sellars was a most helpful collaborator. In 1949 we published the first anthology in analytic philosophy.[6] In this volume we included a good many of the now "classical" essays of the Logical Positivists, as well as those of their best critics. In the same year we began issuing, with May Brodbeck, John Hospers, and Paul Meehl as co-editors, the journal *Philosophical Studies*. This was, and still is, exclusively devoted to topics in analytic philosophy, and is thus the American counterpart of the British journal *Analysis*.

For a few years in the late forties and early fifties, Sellars and I, together with May Brodbeck, John Hospers, Paul Meehl, and D. B. Terrell, made up a discussion group in which occasionally visitors from other universities would participate. Gradually we came to think about organizing a more official center for research in the philosophy of science. Encouraged by the generous financial support of the Louis W. and Maul Hill Family Foundation in St. Paul, the Minnesota Center for Philosophy of Science was established in 1953. During the first few years the local staff members were Paul E. Meehl (an outstanding psychologist and philosopher), Wilfrid Sellars (who later left for Yale University and is now at the University of Pittsburgh), and Michael Scriven (originally from Australia and now at Berkeley). In the fourteen years

5. La Salle, Ill., 1963.
6. *Readings in Philosophical Analysis* (New York, 1949).

of its activities, the Center has enjoyed visits of various durations by many outstanding American, European, and Australian and New Zealand scholars. Our major publications (thus far three volumes of *Minnesota Studies in the Philosophy of Science* and one volume entitled *Current Issues in the Philosophy of Science*) have aroused considerable interest. Several of the younger generation philosophers of science have been our visitors, among whom have been Scriven, Adolf Grünbaum (Pittsburgh), Hilary Putnam (Harvard), N. R. Hanson (Yale), Wesley Salmon (Indiana), Karl R. Popper (London), Paul Feyerabend (Berkeley), Bruce Aune (University of Massachusetts), Henryk Mehlberg (Chicago), George Schlesinger (Australia, now North Carolina), and Arthur Pap (Yale). For shorter visits we had C. D. Broad, Gilbert Ryle, Antony Flew, Peter Strawson, Gavin Alexander, and a number of scholars from various other countries.

Partly stimulated by the Minnesota Center's success, other centers or departments were established by men who had been our visitors, most notably at Indiana University and the University of Pittsburgh. Parallel but largely independent developments occurred in other places—the Boston Symposium (with Robert S. Cohen and Marx Wartofsky leading), the Stanford University group (led by Patrick Suppes), and for a few years, the Delaware Seminar.

The Minnesota Center was established as a *research* department in the College of Liberal Arts of the University of Minnesota. Its staff members, in recent years primarily Grover Maxwell, Paul Meehl, and I, have continued to be active in the regular teaching departments of the University. A good many graduate students of philosophy, physics, and psychology, and a few from the biological and social sciences, have been regularly admitted to most of our Center colloquia. In view of the great demand for philosophers of the empirical sciences, this sort of training appears most helpful. There is hardly any university or college in the United States today in which philosophy of science is not represented. In fact, currently the demand for competent philosophers of science still exceeds the supply by far. The experience of my friends (Carnap, Reichenbach, Hempel, *et al.*) through the years has shown that many gifted young students prefer to become pure logicians concerned with relatively technical and advanced topics. On the other hand, anyone with strong interests and abilities in the empirical sciences is more likely to become a scientist, and thus pursue a career in pure science or in the various technologies. Nevertheless, there are now a number of outstanding philosophers of science in the younger generation. Some received their major inspiration from such scholars and teachers as Carnap, Reichenbach, Hempel, Nagel, Bergmann, Margenau, and Frank, or from the groups and centers mentioned above and their members.

Practically every one of the erstwhile Continental Logical Empiricists has been invited to visiting appointments in various universities inside and outside of the United States. Reichenbach gave a series of lectures at the Institut Henri Poincaré in Paris. Carnap and Hempel have been at Harvard, Carnap also at Princeton, Bergmann in Stockholm. I have been at Berkeley twice, once at Columbia University, and in 1964–1965 in Austria and Australia. It was most gratifying to note that after a long spell of neglect (if not of suppression) there was again a strong interest in the philosophy of science in Vienna. There, in the Institute for Advanced Study and Scientific Research (established by the Ford Foundation in 1963), I enjoyed a reunion with Karl Popper, Hilary Putnam, and Karl Menger. In the summer of 1964, Carnap, F. A. von Hayek, P. K. Feyerabend, and I joined forces in the European Forum (Austrian College) in the lovely Tyrolean village of Alpbach, where we were offering a seminar in the philosophy of science to an excellent group of advanced students, most of whom—like those in the Vienna Institute—had already obtained their Ph.D. degrees in Austrian or German Universities.

I was also especially pleased with the interest I encountered in Australia. American philosophy of science was well known there, no doubt through the influence of several very active and brilliant scholars: J. J. C. Smart (Adelaide), John Passmore (Canberra), Brian Ellis (Melbourne), D. M. Armstrong, and David Stove (Sydney). The Australian psychologist William O'Neil, who had often been a visitor to American universities, is one of the increasing number of scholars in his field who is also intensely interested and competent in the philosophy and methodology of science. Under his guidance several younger scholars did worthwhile work closely related to American Logical Empiricism in the foundations of psychology.

On my trip from Austria to Australia, I encountered strong interest in and familiarity with American philosophy of science in general and Logical Empiricism in particular: in Athens, in India, in Hong Kong.

It is gratifying to know that the Continental Logical Empiricists contributed so greatly to the worldwide developments in the philosophy of science and more generally in a scientifically oriented philosophy.

v. Some Personal Impressions and Reminiscences

AMONG the many scientists who welcomed and supported the "imported" outlook of the Logical Empiricists there is in my personal experience one man to whom much is owed: Carl E. Seashore. When I came to Iowa in 1931 he was the head of the Psychology Department. Having himself come from Sweden, he was a pioneer in American experimental psychology. At the time he was also Dean of the Graduate School of the University of Iowa. An energetic, forthright man, he was largely responsible for the important developments in experimental, theoretical, and child psychology. He was greatly loved and admired by faculty and students. But he was also somewhat feared for cracking down on questionable projects in the University. Thus it was with some trepidation that I asked him (I believe it was in 1932) whether he would approve of my offering a seminar in philosophical problems of psychology. I was afraid he would reply with his notorious and crushing "NO!", but to my pleasant surprise he slapped my shoulder and shouted "Good idea, Feigl!" Ever since then I have enjoyed the support and encouragement that came to me from many outstanding American psychologists, notably E. G. Boring, S. S. Stevens, C. C. Pratt, B. F. Skinner, C. L. Hull, K. W. Spence, E. C. Tolman, and from the Continental immigrants Kurt Lewin, Wolfgang Köhler, and Egon Brunswik. In 1958 I was the invited guest speaker of the American Psychological Association at its national meeting in Washington, D. C., where I spoke to about 3500 listeners on "Philosophical Embarrassments of Psychology." One of my friends remarked: "Aristotle never had it so good!"

On the whole I have found greater interest in our work on the part of psychologists and social scientists than among physicists, chemists, or biologists. But I have been invited for lectures or contributions to publications quite frequently by their societies, departments, or individual scholars. My immigrant confrères had similar experiences. Perhaps because of their great interest in methodology, the psychologists and sociologists are, by and large, more appreciative of philosophy of science than are the physicists. Some thirty years ago the great English astronomer and cosmologist Sir Arthur Eddington said that the physicists put up a big sign, "Reconstruction going on here; philosophers please keep out." This was understandable in view of the almost permanent revolution in theoretical physics, and because of the small number of philosophers properly trained and competent in that highly intricate domain. But the situation has changed greatly since the thirties. There are now a considerable number of well-equipped philosophers of science specializing in the logic and methodology of physics. In addition to the older generation of American physicist-philosophers such as Henry Margenau, Victor Lenzen, and R. B. Lindsay, a younger group has come to the fore. Among them are Hilary Putnam and Wesley Salmon (both formerly students of Reichenbach), Adolf Grünbaum (influenced by Reichenbach's work), N. R. Hanson (a brilliant American philosopher-physicist who had spent many years in England and tragically perished in an airplane accident in 1967), Henryk Mehlberg, Grover Maxwell, Richard Schlegel, and P. K. Feyerabend (originally from Vienna where he was a student of Victor Kraft's but later became closely associated with K. R. Popper).

I met Feyerabend on my first visit to Vienna after the war (my last previous visit was in 1935). This was in the summer of 1954 when Arthur Pap was a visiting professor at the University of Vienna. Feyerabend had been working as an assistant to Pap. Immediately, during my first conversation with Feyerabend, I recognized his competence and brilliance. He is, perhaps, the most unorthodox philosopher of science I have ever known. We have often discussed our differences publicly. Although the audiences usually sided with my more conservative views, it may well be that Feyerabend is right, and I am wrong.

Arthur Pap and Paul Feyerabend, concurring with Professors Victor

Kraft and Béla Juhos, the only two members of the Circle who had remained in Vienna, told me that the new spirit in the Philosophy Department of the University was quite hostile toward anything that even remotely reflected the ideas of the Logical Positivists. Peculiar alliances of Hegelianism and Existentialism, as well as Catholic Philosophy, were predominant in 1954. I found this still confirmed ten years later when I revisited Vienna (in 1964–1965) in connection with my appointment at the Institute for Advanced Study and Research. This Institute is administratively completely independent of the University. Its teaching staff, consisting mostly of visiting scholars, is truly international and thus includes a number of Americans.

As I reflect on my motivations in connection with the Minnesota Center for Philosophy of Science, it seems fairly clear to me that my formative experiences in the Vienna Circle, and again at Harvard in 1940, have encouraged me to endeavor collaborative teamwork in philosophical research. In this regard, I have found the intellectual atmosphere in American philosophy and science even more favorable than that of the continent in the twenties and early thirties. On the whole, I have found that American scholars are remarkably open-minded, willing to accept criticism as much as to proffer it. Of course, there is occasionally a rare "prima donna" who has to be handled with care, and to be exploited in "cafeteria style"—you take from them whatever valuable ideas they offer, but you don't have to accept whatever seems dogmatically rigid or narrow; nor should you expect to convert them to your own point of view.

Among the American philosophers who have left with me a lasting and deep impression are—in the early years—John Dewey, Ralph Barton Perry, C. I. Lewis, C. H. Langford, R. W. Sellars, and Morris Cohen. John Dewey came to Harvard as a visiting professor in 1931, and he offered a rather tedious seminar in the philosophy of logic. While one could not help being impressed with Dewey's personality, he was clumsy and diffuse as a lecturer. I saw him again in 1940 in New York, when (at the New School for Social Research) I was an invited participant, together with Paul Tillich and Herbert Schneider, on issues in the theory of values. Tillich was almost unintelligible to me. During the public discussion John Dewey, with extended threatening forefinger, asked whether I had absolute values in mind when I spoke of "terminal values." I reassured him that I meant nothing of the sort.

Morris Cohen and I had a rencontre in 1938 at one of the meetings of the American Philosophical Association. We were both, together with Evander McGilvary, panel members on a symposium on Universals. Cohen, always brilliant and challenging, took sharp issue with me—and we even continued our conversation at breakfast on the following day. I remember the "squelch perfect" he sometimes used in reply to students (or also his opponents): "As a matter of fact you are wrong; but supposing you were right, what of it?"

C. H. Langford and I for several years spent the first evening of association meetings together. It was on our first encounter (in 1932) that he challenged me with the problem of the logical analysis of contrary-to-fact conditionals, which we Viennese had neglected. Langford was certainly one of the keenest and personally most attractive and congenial American logicians and philosophers.

During my early years (in the forties) and later at Minnesota, I was very fortunate in having a number of interesting colleagues on the faculty, in as well as outside of the Philosophy Department. The brilliant psychologist B. F. Skinner and I became close friends. We disagreed sharply on philosophical issues of psychology, but this never disturbed our personal relations. In a small group of psychologists and philosophers, Skinner read to us, chapter by chapter, his utopian novel *Walden Two*.

During my first year at Minnesota I became acquainted with the man who probably was my best student, Paul E. Meehl. Although about twenty years younger than I, Meehl became one of my most cherished friends. He has been and still is, one of the two or three most helpful and contributive members of the Minnesota Center for Philosophy of Science. He is best known as a highly versatile psychologist, but there is no question in my mind that he is also one of the most penetrating philosophers and methodologists of science in our time. He has applied his tremendous intellectual powers not only to the psychology of learning, to clinical psychology and psychiatry, but also to the analysis of the basic concepts and methods of psychology. For several years (in the fifties) we gave seminars together on the philosophical problems of psychology, and were warmly rewarded by the response.

In 1962–1963 Professor Karl R. Popper was a visitor of the Center for a semester. He, Paul Meehl, Grover Maxwell, and I had many extremely fruitful private discussions, in addition to a regularly scheduled seminar on the philosophy of physics. In this memorable seminar we had five professors: Popper, Maxwell, Feyerabend, Edward L. Hill (University of Minnesota theoretical physicist), and myself, debating with each other before an audience of graduate students and some faculty members. One afternoon we were joined by the theoretical physicist Alfred Landé (then at Ohio State University, now retired). We discussed especially the philosophical issues of quantum mechanics and some of the fundamental problems of theory construction in physics. This was surely one of the occasions when I felt we had attained the high quality of discussion characteristic of the Vienna Circle or its equivalent at Harvard in 1940.

One of my most thrilling experiences was my visit with Albert Einstein at Princeton in 1954 (one year before his death). I had once previously visited Einstein—in Berlin in 1923, when my teacher Schlick had sent me to the great man. The visit at Princeton was made possible through the kind assistance of Dr. Paul Oppenheim. Oppenheim had told me that Einstein loathed "journalistic" interviews and also merely "socially pleasant" conversations. Einstein liked visitors who would come with questions for him. Naturally, I arrived with a long list of questions. Einstein, greeting me in the entrance hall of his home on Mercer Street, hardly indulging in any social amenities (though we had tea later), after a few minutes of ordinary conversation, asked, "And what shall we talk about?" At that point I pulled out my long list and began by asking him about the important changes that had taken place in his philosophical outlook throughout his long life. He admitted that in his early years he had been strongly influenced by the positivism of Hume and Mach, but that he had changed his views gradually toward a scientific realism. Of course, I had known about this from his publications. I wanted to hear some of the detailed reasons that motivated this transformation. I was immensely pleased to learn that there was a large measure of agreement in this respect with the development of Logical Positivism toward a more liberal Logical Empiricism. Einstein was in a very happy mood, and often laughed loudly when he said something slightly shocking or surprising. I remember that upon one of my questions regarding the mind-body problem he said (I translate from his forceful and somewhat coarse German phrase): "If it were not for the 'internal illumination' (that is, by consciousness) of the physical universe, the world would be no more than a mere pile of dirt!" Einstein also discussed with me his reasons for considering quantum mechanics (despite its admitted fruitfulness) to be incomplete. He was still hoping for some sort of deterministic and unified field theory.

In his autobiography Carnap relates some of his fascinating conversations with Einstein and his impressions of that genius. I think to many of us Europeans, the very presence of that revered scientist-philosopher in this country was a source of inspiration and encouragement.

For me, personally, it was also and primarily my frequent visits with Carnap (in Chicago, Princeton, Los Angeles, and for a while at his summer home in the hills outside Santa Fe, New Mexico) that I always found instructive, encouraging, and helpful. After Schlick's death, Carnap and Reichenbach were in my estimation the leading exponents of our philosophical approach. Thus I had the privilege of learning first hand of Carnap's developing ideas, be it in the field of semantics or in the field of inductive logic and the foundations of probability. Carnap also was a willing listener and an acute critic when I submitted to him my own ideas on scientific realism or on the mind-body problem. As I reflect on my more than forty years of frequent contacts with Carnap, I feel he is perhaps the most ametaphysical philosopher I have ever known. The metaphysical neutrality, already explicitly formulated in his early work (1928), pertains to all important traditional philosophical issues. For Carnap, such disputes as those between Nominalism and Platonism, and Realism and Phenomenalism, are not substantive issues of an ontological sort. In his reconstruction he considers them as questions regarding the linguistic frame of knowledge (in more traditional terminology, the basic "categorial" conceptual frame) whose acceptance or rejection is a pragmatic matter. By contrast, questions within the chosen frame are genuinely cognitive, and are susceptible of solution by deductive, inductive, or hypothetico-deductive methods.

All this was evident in our most recent meetings—a small-scale conference I had arranged at the University of California in Los Angeles in March 1966, and in a different context at the University of Hawaii, where both Carnap and I were invited for a week's seminars and colloquia in March 1967.

Both my sojourns at Hawaii—for a semester in 1958 (as Carnegie visiting professor) and the much briefer visit in 1967—were among the most pleasurable experiences of my life. The peerless hospitality of the friendly and excellent faculty of the University of Hawaii, the marvelous climate and scenery, make this indeed the "Paradise of the Pacific." I shall never forget the amicable Professor Charles A. Moore who, to my great sorrow, passed away in April 1967. When I arrived in my office at the University of Hawaii's Philosophy Department in February 1958, Moore appeared with a big stack of books and put them down on my desk. He said: "These are the best books on Oriental Philosophy. You will want to read them." Somewhat astonished, I replied: "I thought you wanted me to bring modern Western Philosophy of Science to Hawaii!" "Of course," he replied, "that's your obligation, but here is your opportunity to learn something different!" I shall always be grateful, and remember Professor Moore fondly, for I really achieved at least a smattering of information about (especially) Indian philosophies and religions at that time.

Many members of the Vienna and Berlin groups have been honored with distinctive positions in various scholarly organizations of America. Reichenbach, Hempel, Bergmann, and I were elected (at various times) to the presidency of the American Philosophical Association (Pacific, Eastern, and Western Divisions, respectively). I was elected a vice-president of the American Association for the Advancement of Science and chairman of Section L (for History and Philosophy of Science) in 1959. Carnap received an honorary doctorate from Harvard University in 1936 and from the University of Michigan in 1966. Most of us have been visiting lecturers at several United States universities at various times. All of us are deeply grateful for the splendid opportunities that have been ours in the New World, for the magnanimous friends, and many brilliant students it was our good fortune to find here.

300 NOTABLE ÉMIGRÉS

IN THE following list, as elsewhere in this volume, we have confined ourselves to members of the intelligentsia. The figure of 300 was chosen arbitrarily. We wished to indicate by its very arbitrariness that we are well aware that a much longer list of notable refugees could be assembled. Thus Colin Eisler has appended to his essay a list of art-historians, only some of whom are included below. We are confident that all the persons we have singled out here were truly eminent on at least one side of the Atlantic; but equally confident that names of the same importance have been omitted.

Our purpose has not been to circumscribe the community of notable refugees but to delineate in concrete terms the stages of the refugee experience. For this reason, we have deliberately included a substantial number of people, chiefly French by birth or adoption, who spent some years in America but returned to Europe immediately after World War II. Conversely, we have systematically excluded scores of men and women, now distinguished, who were brought to America by their parents and received all of their higher education here; for in terms of making their way professionally, they did not have the experience of beginning again in mid-career. We do not imply that their early lives left no mark upon them; merely that our present categories would throw little if any light upon the issue.

In listing notable publications of émigré writers, we have confined ourselves to works produced or completed in America. In singling out the honors and distinctions conferred upon émigrés, we have been highly selective.

We acknowledge with gratitude the assistance of Mrs. Helen Kessler in compiling the data.

ACKERKNECHT, Erwin (b. Stettin, Germany 1906). Historian of medicine. M.D. Berlin 1931. Asst. Univ. Clinic Berlin 1932–33. In Paris 1937–38; French Army 1939–40. To U.S. 1941; naturalized. Fellow Johns Hopkins Inst. Hist. Med. 1941–44; asst. curator Am. Mus. Nat. Hist. (N.Y.) 1945–46; prof. hist. med. U. Wisconsin Med. Schl. 1947–57. Director and prof. Inst. Hist. Med. Zürich from 1957. *Rudolf Virchow* (1953).

ADORNO, Theodor W. (b. Frankfurt 1903). Social scientist and philosopher. University student in Frankfurt; studied music with Alban Berg in Vienna.

Ph.D. Frankfurt 1931. Privatdozent Frankfurt 1931–33; associated with Institut für Sozialforschung. Expelled by Nazis. In Oxford 1934–38. To U.S. 1938. With musical section Princeton Office of Radio Research 1938–41. In Los Angeles 1941–49 directing research for *The Authoritarian Personality* (1950). Musical adviser to Thomas Mann for *Doctor Faustus*. Returned to Frankfurt 1949–52. Scientific director Hacker Fdn. Beverly Hills, Calif., 1952–53. Professor philosophy Frankfurt from 1953; now director Institut für Sozialforschung.

ALBERS, Anni née Fleischmann (b. Berlin 1899). Textile designer. Diploma Bauhaus (Dessau) 1930. Married Josef Albers 1925. To U.S. 1933; nat. 1937. Asst. prof. art Black Mountain College (N.C.) 1933–49. Free Lance work New Haven from 1950. *Anni Albers on Designing* (2d. ed. 1962).

ALBERS, Josef (b. Bottrop, Germany, 1888). Painter. Studied: Munich, Bauhaus (Weimar). Married Anni Fleischmann 1925. Prof. art Bauhaus 1923–33. To U.S. 1933; nat. 1939. Taught Black Mountain College (N.C.) 1933–49. Prof. art Yale 1950–60.

ALEXANDER, Franz (b. Budapest 1891; d. 1964). Psychoanalyst. M.D. Budapest 1913. Clinical asso. and lect. Inst. Psychoanalyse Berlin 1921–30. To U.S. 1930; nat. 1938. Vis. prof. psychoanalysis U. Chicago 1930–31; research asso. in criminology Judge Baker Fdn. Boston 1931–32; with Chicago Inst. for Psychoanalysis from 1932 (director); taught psychiatry U. Illinois 1938–56, prof. from 1943; clin. prof. psychol. USC; chief of psychiatric staff, director Psychiatric and Psychosomatic Research Inst. Mt. Sinai Hosp. Los Angeles. Pioneer of psychosomatic medicine.

APEL, Willi (b. Könitz, Germany, 1893). Musicologist. Ph.D. Berlin 1936. Taught Luisenstädtisches Gymn. Berlin 1928–36. To U.S. 1936; nat. 1944. Taught Longy Schl. Music Cambridge (Mass.) 1936–43. Lect. music Harvard 1938–42. Lect. music Boston Center for Adult Educ. 1938–50. Prof. music Indiana U. from 1950. Ed. *Harvard Dictionary of Music* (1944).

ARENDT, Hannah (b. Hannover, Germany, 1906). Political scientist. Ph.D. Heidelberg 1928. Social worker Paris 1934–40. To U.S. 1941; nat. 1950. Research director Conf. on Jewish Relations 1944–46; chief ed. Schocken Books (N.Y.); exec. director Jewish Cultural Reconstruction (N.Y.) 1949–52. Vis. prof. Berkeley (1955), Princeton (1959), Columbia (1960). Prof. U. Chicago 1963–67; New Schl. for Soc. Res. from 1967. *The Origins of Totalitarianism* (1951); *The Human Condition* (1958); *Eichmann in Jerusalem* (1963). Rockefeller Fdn. Fellow; Guggenheim Fellow 1952–53; Lessing Prize City of Hamburg 1959.

ARNHEIM, Rudolf (b. Berlin 1904). Psychologist of art. Ph.D. Berlin 1928.

Asso. ed. publs. Internatl. Inst. Educ. Films Rome 1933–38. To U.S. 1940; nat. 1946. Lect. and vis. prof. New Schl. for Soc. Res. 1943–68; fac. Sarah Lawrence Coll. 1943–68. Prof. psychology of art Harvard from 1968. *Film as Art* (1957); *Picasso's Guernica* (1962); *Toward a Psychology of Art* (1966). Fellow Rockefeller Fdn., Office of Radio Research 1941; Guggenheim Fellow 1942–43.

ARTIN, Emil (b. Vienna 1898; d. 1962). Mathematician. Ph.D. Leipzig 1921. Prof. mathematics Hamburg 1924–37. To U.S. 1937. Prof. Notre Dame 1937–38, U. Indiana 1938–46. Prof. mathematics Princeton 1946–62.

ASCOLI, Max (b. Ferrara 1898). Editor. LL.D. Ferrara 1920; Ph.D. Rome 1928. Taught jurisprudence, Italian universities, 1926–31. To U.S. 1931; nat. 1939. Married Marion Rosenwald 1940. Grad. fac. New Schl. for Soc. Res. from 1933, dean 1940–41. Founder and ed. *The Reporter* 1949–68. Rockefeller Fdn. Fellow 1931.

AUERBACH, Erich (b. Berlin 1892; d. 1957). Historian of literature. Ph.D. Greifswald 1921. Prof. Romance philol. Marburg 1929–35; prof. Turkish State U. Istanbul 1936–47. To U.S. 1947; nat. 1953. Vis. prof. Pennsylvania State U. 1948–49; member Inst. for Advanced Study Princeton 1949–50. Prof. Fr. and Romance philol. Yale 1950–57, Sterling prof. from 1956. *Mimesis* (1953).

AUGER, Pierre (b. Paris 1899). Physicist. Docteur ès Sciences Paris 1926. Prof. Paris 1932–41. To U.S. 1941. Research asso. U. Chicago 1941–44. Director higher educ. Paris 1945–48. Director natural sci. div. UNESCO Paris 1948–59. Director-general European Space Research Organization from 1964. Discovered Auger effect 1926; Auger showers 1938. Feltrinelli Prize 1961.

BAADE, Walter (b. Schröttinghausen, Germany, 1893; d. 1960). Astronomer. Ph.D. Göttingen 1919. Observator and privatdozent Hamburg 1929–31. To U.S. 1931. Astronomer Mt. Wilson Observatory 1931–47; Mt. Wilson and Palomar Observatories 1948–60.

BARON, Hans (b. Berlin 1900). Historian. Ph.D. Berlin 1922. Privatdozent hist. Berlin 1929–33. To U.S. 1938; nat. 1945. Asst. prof. hist. Queens Coll. 1939–42; member Inst. for Advanced Study Princeton 1944–48; with Newberry Libr. from 1949; professorial lect. Renaissance studies U. Chicago from 1963. *The Crisis of the Early Italian Renaissance* (1955). Guggenheim Fellow 1942–43; Rockefeller Fdn. grant 1961–63.

BARTÓK, Béla (b. Nagy Szent Miklos, Transylvania, now Rumania, 1881; d. 1945). Composer, pianist. Studied Roy. Acad. Music Budapest. After

World War I member with Dohnanyi and Kodály music directorate of Music Acad. Budapest. U.S. tour as pianist 1927–28. To U.S. 1940; few concert engagements. Appt. Columbia U. to prepare for publication a Yugoslav folksong collection. *Concerto for Orchestra* (1944) comp. in U.S.

BAYER, Herbert (b. Haag, Austria, 1900). Artist and designer. Studied design Linz, Darmstadt, Bauhaus (1921–23), wall-painting with Kandinsky. Engaged in advertising, typography, painting, photography, exhibition planning Berlin 1928–38. To U.S. 1938; nat. 1943. Designed Bauhaus Exhibit Museum Modern Art (N.Y.) 1938 (catalogue with Walter and Ise Gropius, *Bauhaus 1919–1928*). Instructor of design Am. Advertising Guild 1940–42; chm. dept. design Container Corp. Am.; designer various bldgs., Aspen Inst. for Humanistic Studies.

BENESCH, Otto (b. Ebenfurth, Austria, 1896). Historian of art, curator. Studied Vienna. Asst. later Keeper Albertina Sammlung (drawings) Vienna 1923–38. Dismissed by Nazis. In France and England 1938–40; lectured Cambridge U. To U.S. Research Fellow Fogg Art Museum Harvard. Member Inst. for Advanced Study Princeton. Guggenheim Fellow. Returned to Vienna 1947 as director Albertina; prof. U. Vienna from 1948. *The Art of the Renaissance in Northern Europe* (1947).

BERGMANN, Gustav (b. Vienna 1906). Philosopher. Ph.D., J.D. Vienna 1928, 1935. To U.S. 1938; nat. 1943. Fac. State U. Iowa from 1939, prof. from 1950. *The Metaphysics of Logical Positivism* (1954); *Philosophy of Science* (1957). Pres. Am. Philosophical Assn. 1968.

BERMAN, Eugene (b. St. Petersburg 1899). Painter and designer. Art educ. Russia 1914–18. Settled Paris 1919. U.S. resident from 1937; nat. 1944. Guggenheim Fellow 1947, 1949.

BERNHEIMER, Richard (b. Munich 1907; d. 1958). Art historian. Ph.D. Munich 1930. To U.S. 1933; naturalized. Fac. Bryn Mawr 1933–58, prof. art from 1951; Haverford 1942–58, prof. from 1951. *Wild Men in the Middle Ages* (1952).

BETHE, Hans Albrecht (b. Strassburg 1906). Physicist. Ph.D. Munich 1928. Taught theoretical physics Frankfurt, Stuttgart, Munich, Tübingen 1928–33. Manchester, Bristol 1933–35. To U.S. 1935; naturalized. Asst. prof. physics Cornell 1935, prof. from 1937. Director theoretical physics div. Los Alamos Sci. Lab. 1943–46. Member President's Science Advisory Com. 1956–64. Natl. Acad. Sci.; For. mem. Roy. Soc. London. Presidential medal of merit 1946; Henry Draper medal, Natl. Acad. Sci. 1948; Max Planck medal 1955; Enrico Fermi award, Atomic Energy Commn. 1961; Nobel Prize in physics 1967 for "his contributions to the theory of nuclear reaction, especially his discoveries concerning the energy production of stars."

BETTELHEIM, Bruno (b. Vienna 1903). Psychoanalyst. Ph.D. Vienna 1938. To U.S. 1939; nat. 1944. Research asso. Progressive Educ. Asso. U. Chicago 1939–41. Asso. prof. psychology Rockford Coll. (Ill.) 1942–44. Asst. prof. educ. psychology U. Chicago 1944–47, asso. prof. 1947–52, prof. from 1952, Rowley prof. educ. from 1963. *Love Is Not Enough* (1950); *Symbolic Wounds* (1954).

BIBRING, Grete Lehner (b. Vienna 1899). Psychoanalyst. Married Eduard Bibring, psychoanalyst, 1921. M.D. Vienna 1924; student of Freud. Asst. director Vienna Psychoanalytic Out-Patient Clinics 1926–30; training analyst and instructor Vienna Psychoanalytic Soc. 1933–38. To England 1938; training analyst Brit. Psychoanalytical Soc. and Inst. 1938–41. To U.S. 1941; nat. 1946. With Boston Psychoanalytic Soc. and Inst. from 1941. Fac. Harvard Med. Schl. 1946–65 (prof. clinical psychiatry from 1961). Psychiatrist-in-chief Beth Israel Hosp. Boston. Pres. Am. Psychoanalytic Asso. 1962–63.

BIEBER, Margarete (b. Schönau, W. Prussia, 1897). Classical archaeologist. Ph.D. Bonn 1907. Prof. and dept. head Giessen 1931–33. To England 1933; hon. fellow Somerville Coll. Oxford 1933–34. To U.S. 1934. Fac. Barnard Coll. 1934–54.

BJERKNES, Jacob A. B. (b. Stockholm 1897). Meteorologist. Ph.D. Oslo 1924. Prof. Geofysiske Inst. Bergen (Norway) 1931–40. Lect. MIT 1935–36; consultant U.S. Weather Bureau 1939–40. Settled in U.S.; naturalized. Prof. meteorology UCLA from 1940. Natl. Acad. Sci. Bowie Medal, Am. Geophy. Union.

BLOCH, Ernst (b. Ludwigshafen, Germany, 1885). Philosopher. Ph.D. Würzburg. Left Germany 1933; lived successively in Czechoslovakia, France, and U.S. Co-founder Aurora Press N.Y.C. Returned to Germany. Prof. philosophy Leipzig 1949–56. Prof. Tübingen from 1961.

BLOCH, Felix (b. Zürich 1905). Physicist. Ph.D. Leipzig 1928. Lect. theoretical physics Leipzig 1932. Left Germany 1933. Fac. Stanford from 1934, prof. from 1936, Max Stein prof. from 1961. War work Stanford, Los Alamos, Harvard. Director-General CERN Geneva 1954. Rockefeller Fdn. Fellow Rome 1933. Natl. Acad. Sci. Nobel Prize in physics 1952 with Edward M. Purcell for "their development of new methods for nuclear magnetic precision measurements and discoveries in connection therewith." Pres. Am. Physical Society 1965–66.

BLOCH, Herbert (b. Berlin 1911). Classicist, historian. Dott. Lett. Rome 1935; dipl. in ancient hist. Rome 1937. Excavated at Ostia 1938–39. To U.S. 1939; nat. 1946. Fac. Harvard from 1941, prof. from 1953. Guggenheim Fellow 1950–51; member Inst. for Advanced Study Princeton 1953–54.

BLOCH, Konrad (b. Neisse, Germany, 1912). Biochemist. Studied Chem. Eng. Technische Hochscule Munich 1934. To U.S. 1936; nat. 1944. Fac. U. Chicago 1946–54, prof. from 1950. Higgins prof. biochemistry Harvard from 1954. Natl. Acad. Sci. Nobel Prize in physiology or med. 1964 with Feodor Lynen for "their contributions to our knowledge of the complex pattern of reactions involved in the biosynthesis of cholesterol and of fatty acids."

BOCHNER, Salomon (b. Podgorze, Poland, 1899). Mathematician. Ph.D. Berlin 1921. Lect. Munich 1927–32. To U.S. 1933; nat. 1938. Fac. Princeton from 1933, prof. from 1946, Henry Burchard Fine prof. math. from 1959. *The Role of Mathematics in the Rise of Science* (1966). Internatl. Educ. Bd. Fellow 1925–27. Natl. Acad. Sci.

BORGESE, G(iuseppe). A. (b. Palermo 1882; d. 1952). Historian. Ph.D. Florence 1903. Prof. aesthetics and hist. criticism Milan 1926–31. Left Italy 1931. To U.S. 1931; nat. 1938. Vis. prof. Italian culture Berkeley 1931. Lect. New Schl. for Soc. Res. 1932. Prof. Smith Coll. 1932–36. Prof. Italian lit. U. Chicago 1936–48. Professorial rank at Milan restored 1948. *Goliath, the March of Fascism* (1937).

BOULANGER, Nadia (b. Paris 1887). Teacher of composition. Studied Conservatoire de Paris. Head of dept. of theory Ecole Normale de Musique Paris. To U.S. 1940. Taught Longy Schl. Music Cambridge (Mass.). Returned to Paris after war. Now director, hon. prof. Conservatoire de Paris. Maître de Chapelle to the Prince of Monaco.

BRECHT, Bertolt (b. Augsburg 1898; d. 1956). Writer. Married Helene Weigel. Emigrated to Denmark and Sweden 1933. Co-editor with Lion Feuchtwanger of anti-Nazi magazine *Das Wort* (Moscow 1936–39). To U.S. 1941; settled in Hollywood. Returned to Europe 1947; first in Switzerland, later in East Berlin as director Deutsches Theater. *Galileo Galilei* (1942); *Der Kaukasische Kreidekreis* (1944–45); *Furcht und Elend des dritten Reiches* (1945). Stalin Prize for literature 1954.

BRETON, André (b. Tinchebray, France, 1896; d. 1966). Writer on art. Participant in Dada and Surrealism. To U.S. during World War II. Organized Surrealist exhibition N.Y.C. 1942. Lect. Yale. Studied Am. Indian art Arizona, N.M. 1945. Returned to France 1946.

BREUER, Marcel (b. Pécs, Hungary, 1902). Architect. M.A. Bauhaus (Weimar) 1924. Master of Bauhaus (Dessau) 1925–28. Architect Berlin 1928–31. Commissions and travel in Spain, Switzerland, Germany, Hungary, England 1931–35. Architect London 1935–37. To U.S. 1937. With Harvard Schl. Design 1937–47, asso. prof. arch. from 1939. Partner Walter Gropius and Marcel Breuer, architects, Cambridge (Mass.) 1937–42. Now arch. in N.Y.C. Gold Medal Am. Inst. Architects 1968.

BRILLOUIN, Léon (b. Sèvres 1889). Physicist. Ph.D. Paris 1921. Prof. Coll. de France 1932–39. Gen. director French National Broadcasting System 1939–40. To U.S. 1941. Vis. prof. U. Wisconsin 1941–42; prof. Brown U. 1942–43; research sci. Natl. Defense Research Committee Columbia 1943–45. Fac. Harvard 1946–49, Gordon McKay prof. applied math. from 1947. Director research Watson Lab. IBM 1949–54. Natl. Acad. Sci.

BROCH, Hermann (b. Vienna 1886; d. 1951). Writer. To U.S. 1938. *The Death of Vergil* (1945). Guggenheim Fellow 1941–42. Rockefeller Fdn. Fellow for philosophical and psychological research Princeton 1942–44.

BRUCK, Eberhard (b. Breslau 1887; d. 1960). Legal scholar. J.S.D. Breslau 1904. Prof. Roman and civil law Bonn 1932–35. To U.S.; naturalized. Fac. Harvard Law Schl. 1939–52, emeritus 1952 with title "prof. legal hist., Roman and civil law."

BRÜNING, Heinrich (b. Germany 1885). Statesman, political scientist. Member German Reichstag 1924–33; leader Center party 1929–32. Reichskanzler 1930–32, forced out by Nazis. To U.S. 1933. Fac. Harvard 1937–52, Lucius N. Littauer prof. govt. from 1939. Prof. pol. sci. Cologne 1951–55.

BRUNSWIK, Egon (b. Budapest 1903; d. 1955). Psychologist. Ph.D. Vienna 1927. Married Else Frenkel-Brunswik. Privatdozent Vienna 1934. To U.S. 1934; nat. 1943. Fac. Berkeley 1937–55, prof. psychology from 1947. *The Conceptual Framework of Psychology* (1952). Rockefeller Fdn. Fellow 1935–36.

BÜHLER, Charlotte (b. Berlin 1893). Psychologist. Ph.D. Munich 1918. Married Karl Bühler. With Wirtschaftspsychologische Forschungsstelle U. Vienna; Asso. prof. psychology Vienna 1922–38. Prof. Oslo 1938–40. To U.S. 1940; naturalized. Taught Coll. of St. Catherine (St. Paul, Minn.) 1940–41; vis. prof. Clark 1941–42; clin. psychologist Minneapolis Genl. Hosp. 1942–45. In private practice in Los Angeles from 1945 (at Los Angeles Genl. Hosp. 1945–53). Asst. clin. prof. psychiatry USC from 1950. *Value Problems in Psychotherapy* (1961).

BÜHLER, Karl (b. Heidelberg 1879; d. 1963). Psychologist. M.D. Freiburg 1903; Ph.D. Strassburg 1904. Married Charlotte Bühler. Prof. psychology

Vienna 1922–38; created Wirtschaftspsychologische Forschungsstelle U. Vienna. Vis. prof. Stanford, Johns Hopkins, Harvard 1927–28. To U.S. 1940; naturalized. Taught Coll. of St. Thomas (St. Paul, Minn.) 1940–45. In private practice 1945–56.

BUSCH, Adolf (b. Siegen, Germany, 1891; d. 1952). Violinist. Formed Busch string quartet 1912; soloist throughout Europe. Vis. soloist with Toscanini (U.S.) 1931. Refused to play concerts in Germany from 1933. To U.S. 1939; nat. 1949. Refounded Busch Chamber Orch. 1941.

CARNAP, Rudolf (b. Wuppertal, Germany, 1891). Logician, philosopher. Ph.D. Jena 1921. Prof. natural philosophy German U. of Prague 1931–35. To U.S. 1935; nat. 1941. Prof. philosophy U. Chicago 1936–52. Prof. philosophy UCLA from 1954. *Foundations of Logic and Mathematics* (1939); *Logical Foundations of Probability* (1950). D.Sci. (hon.) Harvard 1936.

CASPARI, Ernst (b. Berlin 1909). Geneticist. Ph.D. Göttingen 1933. Asst. in zool. Göttingen 1933–35. Asst. in microbiology U. Istanbul 1935–38. To U.S. 1938. Asst. prof. Lafayette Coll. 1938–44; asst. prof. Rochester 1944–46. Fac. Wesleyan U. 1946–60, prof. from 1949. Prof. biology Rochester from 1960. Ed. *Advances in Genetics.*

CASSIRER, Ernst (b. Breslau 1874; d. 1945). Philosopher. Ph.D. Marburg 1899. Prof. philosophy Hamburg 1919–33 (Rector 1930–33). Left Germany 1933. At All Souls Coll. Oxford 1933–35; vis. prof. Göteborg 1935–41. To U.S. 1941. Vis. prof. Yale 1941–44. Prof. Columbia 1944–45. *An Essay on Man* (1944); *The Myth of the State* (1946).

CASTIGLIONI, Arturo (b. Trieste 1874; d. 1952). Historian of Medicine. M.D. Vienna 1896. Prof. hist. med. Padua 1922–38. Noguchi lect. Johns Hopkins 1933. To U.S. 1939; nat. 1946. Fac. Yale 1939–47, prof. hist. med. from 1943. Returned to Italy.

CASTRO, Américo (b. Rio de Janeiro, 1885). Literary scholar, historian. Ph.D. Madrid 1911. Prof. Madrid 1915–36. At Natl. U. Buenos Aires 1936–37. To U.S. 1937; naturalized. Prof. Spanish and comp. lit. U. Wisconsin 1937–39; prof. Romance langs. U. Texas 1939–40; prof. Spanish Princeton 1940–53. *España en su historia; cristianos, moros y judíos* (1948); trans. as *The Structure of Spanish History* (1954).

CHAGALL, Marc (b. Vitebsk, Russia, 1887). Painter. Left Russia 1910 for Paris; returned to Russia 1914; returned to Paris 1922. To U.S. 1941. Returned to France 1948.

CHARGAFF, Erwin (b. Austria 1905). Biochemist. Ph.D. Vienna 1928. Research fellow Yale 1928–30. Asst. in charge chem. lab. Inst. Hygiene Berlin 1930–33. Research asso. Inst. Pasteur Paris 1933–34. To U.S.; nat. 1940. Fac. Coll. Physicians and Surgeons Columbia from 1935, prof. biochemistry from 1952. Discoverer of principal empirical evidence for pairing of purines and pyrimidines in DNA. Guggenheim Fellow 1949, 1958. Natl. Acad. Sci. C. L. Mayer prize, Acad. des sci. Paris 1963.

CLAIR, René (b. Paris 1898). Motion picture director. To U.S. during World War II. Returned to France after war. Director *I Married a Witch* (1942).

COURANT, Richard (b. Lublinitz, Poland, 1888). Mathematician. Ph.D. Göttingen 1910. Prof. math. and director Math. Inst. Göttingen 1920–33. Lect. Cambridge U. 1933–34. To U.S. 1934, aided by Emergency Committee; nat. 1940. Prof. math. NYU 1934–58. Natl. Acad. Sci.; Acad. dei Lincei (Rome).

DALI, Salvador (b. Figueras nr. Barcelona 1904). Painter. Studied Schl. Fine Arts Madrid 1921–26. Designed Dali's Dream House, New York World's Fair 1939. In U.S. during World War II. Designed costumes, scenery for Metropolitan Opera 1939–42. Huntington Hartford Fdn. award 1957.

DAM, Henrik (b. Copenhagen 1895). Biochemist. Ph.D. Copenhagen 1934. Asso. prof. Copenhagen 1929–41. On lecture tour Canada and U.S. 1940–41; unable to return to Denmark. Research at Woods Hole Marine Biological Labs. 1941. Senior Research Asso. Rochester U. 1942–45. Asso. member Rockefeller Inst. 1945–46. Returned to Denmark 1946. Appt. prof. biochemistry Copenhagen *in absentia* 1941; prof. biochemistry and nutrition from 1950. Nobel Prize in physiology or medicine shared with E. A. Doisy 1943 for Dam's "discovery of the chemical nature of vitamin K."

DE BENEDETTI, Sergio (b. Florence 1912). Physicist. Ph.D. Florence 1933. Asst. prof. Padua 1934–38. Fellow Lab. Curie Paris 1938–40. To U.S. 1940; nat. 1946. Asst. Bartol Research Fdn. (Swarthmore) 1940–43. Asso. prof. Kenyon Coll. 1943–44; senior physicist Monsanto Chem. Co. 1944–45; principal physicist Clinton Labs., Oak Ridge Natl. Lab. 1946–48. Asso. prof. Washington U. (St. Louis) 1948–49. Professor physics Carnegie Inst. Tech. from 1949.

DE BRUYN, Peter P. H. (b. Amsterdam 1910). Anatomist. M.D. Amsterdam 1938. Asst. Histological Lab. Amsterdam 1936–39. Med. officer Dutch Army 1939–40. To U.S. 1941; nat. 1947. Instructor anatomy U. Chicago 1941, thence to prof. from 1952.

DEBYE, Peter Joseph William (b. Maastricht, The Netherlands, 1884; d. 1966). Physical chemist. Ph.D. Munich 1910. First professorial appt. Zürich 1911. Director Max Planck Inst. Berlin 1934–39. To U.S. 1940; nat. 1946. Prof. chemistry Cornell 1940–52. Natl. Acad. Sci. For. mem. Roy. Soc. London; Acad. Sci. USSR. Lorentz, Faraday, Rumford, Franklin, Willard Gibbs, Max Planck, Priestley medals; National medal of science 1965. Nobel Prize in chemistry 1936 for "his contributions to our knowledge of molecular structure through his investigations on dipole moments and on the diffraction of X-rays and electrons in gases."

DELBRÜCK, Max (b. Berlin 1906). Physicist, biologist. Ph.D. Göttingen 1930. Rockefeller Fdn. Fellow in physics Copenhagen and Zürich 1931. Asst. in Kaiser Wilhelm Inst. für Chem. Berlin 1932–37. To U.S. 1937; nat. 1945. Rockefeller Fdn. Fellow in biology Caltech 1937–39. Fac. Vanderbilt U. 1940–47. Prof. biology Caltech from 1947. Natl. Acad. Sci. Pioneer of phage genetics.

DEUTSCH, Helene (b. Przemysl, Galicia, Poland, 1884). Psychoanalyst. M. D. Vienna 1912. Founder and director Vienna Psychoanalytic Inst. 1924–33. To U.S. 1933. Member Boston Psychoanalytic Inst. from 1937. *Psychology of Women* (1944–45). Menninger Award 1962.

DEUTSCH, Karl (b. Prague 1912). Political scientist. Dr. Law and Pol. Sci. German U. of Prague 1938. To U.S. 1938; nat. 1948. Ph.D. Harvard 1951. Instructor MIT 1942, thence to prof. hist. and pol. sci. 1952–58. Chief various research sections OSS and Dept. State 1944–46. Prof. pol. sci. Yale 1958–67. Prof. govt. Harvard from 1967. *Nationalism and Social Communication* (1953); *The Nerves of Government* (1963). Guggenheim Fellow 1954. Pres.-elect Am. Political Science Asso. 1969–70.

DICHTER, Ernest (b. Vienna 1907). Psychologist. Ph.D. Vienna. To U.S. Research psychologist with J. Stirling Getchell Inc. advertising agency (N.Y.C.). Pres. Inst. for Motivational Research Inc. Consulting psychologist on programs CBS. *The Strategy of Desire* (1960).

DIECKMANN, Herbert (b. Duisberg, Germany, 1906). Literary historian. Ph.D. Bonn 1930. Fellowship Notgemeinschaft Deutscher Wissenschaft 1930–33; subvention from Dutch Emergency Council for Refugees 1933–34. Lect. Turkish State U. Istanbul 1934–37. To U.S. 1938; nat. 1945. Asst. prof. Washington U. (St. Louis), thence to prof. 1948. At Harvard 1950–65, prof. from 1952, Smith prof. Fr. and Sp. langs. from 1957. Prof. Cornell from 1966, Avalon prof. from 1967. Guggenheim Fellow 1948, 1949, 1951.

DÖBLIN, Alfred (b. Stettin 1878; d. 1957). Writer. M.D. Freiburg 1905. Practiced psychiatry. To France 1933; later to Palestine. To U.S. 1940.

Converted to Catholicism. Returned to Germany as French officer 1945; left Germany for Paris 1951. *Die deutsche Literatur* (in exile; 1938).

DRUCKER, Peter F. (b. Vienna 1909). Management consultant. LL.D. Frankfurt 1931. Economist with London banking hse. 1933–37. To U.S. 1937; nat. 1943. Prof. philosophy and politics Bennington Coll. 1942–49. Prof. management NYU from 1950. *The End of Economic Man* (1939); *The Future of Industrial Man* (1941).

EDELSTEIN, Ludwig (b. Berlin 1902; d. 1965). Classical philologist; historian of medicine. Ph.D. Heidelberg 1929. Lect. in philosophy Berlin 1933. To U.S. 1934; nat. 1940. Fac. Johns Hopkins Inst. Hist. Med. 1934–47. Prof. classical langs. and lit. U. Washington 1947–48. Prof. Greek Berkeley 1948–50. Leader in refusal to sign Calif. oath. Prof. humanities Johns Hopkins 1951–60. Prof. Rockefeller U. from 1960. Co-author with Emma J. Edelstein *Asclepius*, 2 v. (1945).

EDINGER, Tilly (b. Frankfurt 1897; d. 1967). Vertebrate palaeontologist. Ph.D. Frankfurt 1921. Curator fossil vertebrates Senckenberg Museum Frankfurt 1927–38. Asst. instructor neurology Frankfurt 1931–33. Translator in London 1939–40. To U.S.; naturalized. Research asso. in palaeontology Museum Comparative Zoology Harvard 1941–64. Vis. prof. Wellesley.

EINSTEIN, Albert (b. Ulm, Germany, 1879; d. 1955). Theoretical physicist. Ph.D. Zürich 1905. Prof. physics Berlin and director Kaiser Wilhelm Phys. Inst. 1914–33. Renounced German citizenship 1933. To U.S. 1933; nat. 1940. Prof. theoretical physics Inst. for Advanced Study Princeton 1933–55. Natl. Acad. Sci. Member Institut de France; For. mem. Roy. Soc. London. Nobel Prize in physics 1921 "for his services to Theoretical Physics, and especially for his discovery of the law of the photoelectric effect." Copley medal, Roy. Soc. London 1925.

EINSTEIN, Alfred (b. Munich 1880; d. 1952). Musicologist. Ph.D. Munich. Ed. *Zeitschrift für Musikwissenschaft* 1918–33; music critic *Berliner Tageblatt* 1927–33. Lived in London and Florence 1933–38. To U.S. 1939; nat. 1944. Prof. music Smith Coll. 1939–50. *Mozart* (1945).

EISENSTAEDT, Alfred (b. Dirschau, Germany, 1898). Photographer, journalist. Photo reporter Berlin office, Pacific and Atlantic Photos 1929–35. To U.S. 1935. Staff photographer *Life* from 1936. Pioneer of candid camera reporting. *Witness to Our Time*.

EISLER, Hans (b. Leipzig 1898). Composer. Studied composition with Arnold Schoenberg. To U.S. 1933. Lect. New Schl. for Soc. Res. Musical asst. to Charlie Chaplin 1942–47. Left U.S. 1948 under terms of "voluntary deportation." Settled in East Germany.

EPHRUSSI, Boris (b. Moscow 1901). Cytologist, geneticist. Sc.D. Paris 1932. Married Harriett Taylor, biologist. With Inst. de Biol. physicochim. Paris 1928–41, asso. director 1935–41. To U.S. 1941. Asso. prof. biology Johns Hopkins 1941–44. Prof. genetics Paris from 1946. F. H. Herrick Distinguished prof. biology Western Reserve U. from 1961. For. asso. Natl. Acad. Sci.

EPSTEIN, Fritz (b. Saargemünd, Germany, 1898). Historian, archivist. Ph.D. Berlin 1924. Asst. U. Hamburg 1927–32. Lect. in German, French Institute London 1933–36. To U.S. 1937. Research asso. Harvard 1937–43. With OSS 1944–46. Historian German War Docs. Project 1946–48. Curator Central Eur. and Slavic colls. Hoover Libr. Stanford 1948–51. Specialist USSR and Central Eur. area Libr. Cong. 1951–60. Prof. hist. Indiana from 1962.

ERIKSON, Erik Homburger (b. Frankfurt 1902). Psychoanalyst. Grad. Vienna Psychoanalytic Inst. 1933. To U.S. 1933; nat. 1939. Teaching and research Harvard Med. Schl. 1934–35; Yale Schl. Med. 1936–39; U. Calif. Berkeley and San Francisco 1939–51. Senior staff member Austen Riggs Center (Stockbridge, Mass.) 1951–60. Prof. human development Harvard from 1960. *Childhood and Society* (1950); *Young Man Luther* (1958).

ERNST, Max (b. Cologne 1891). Painter. Studied Bonn, left Germany for France, never to return, 1922. Leader in Dada and Surrealism. To U.S.; nat. 1948. Married 3d Peggy Guggenheim 1941; div. Returned to France; Fr. citizen 1958. Grand Prize Venice Biennale 1954. Retrospective exhibitions Museum Modern Art (N.Y.) 1961; Tate Gallery 1962.

ETTINGHAUSEN, Richard (b. Frankfurt 1906). Art historian, museum curator. Ph.D. Frankfurt 1931. To U.S. 1934; nat. 1938. Research asso. Am. Inst. Persian Art and Archaeology 1934–37. Member Inst. for Advanced Study Princeton 1937–38. Asso. prof. Islamic art U. Michigan 1938–44. Asso. Nr. Eastern art Freer Gallery of Art, Smithsonian, 1944–58, curator 1958–61, head curator 1961–66. Prof. Inst. Fine Arts NYU from 1967.

FAJANS, Kasimir (b. Warsaw 1887). Biochemist. Ph.D. Heidelberg 1909. Prof. and director Inst. Phys. Chem. Munich 1917–35. To U.S.; naturalized. Prof. chemistry U. Michigan 1936–57.

FEIGL, Herbert (b. Reichenberg, Austria-Hungary, 1902). Philosopher. Ph.D. Vienna 1927. Lect. People's Inst. Vienna 1927–30. To U.S. 1930; nat. 1937. Fac. U. Iowa 1931–40. Prof. philosophy U. Minnesota from

1940. Director Minnesota Center for Philosophy of Science from 1953. Rockefeller Fdn. Fellow Harvard 1930–31. Guggenheim Fellow 1947–48.

FELLER, William (b. Zagreb 1906). Mathematician. Ph.D. Göttingen 1926. In charge of applied math. lab. U. Kiel 1929–33. Research asso. U. Stockholm 1933–39. To U.S. 1939; nat. 1944. Asso. prof. Brown U. 1939–45. Prof. Cornell 1945–50. Prof. Princeton from 1950. Natl. Acad. Sci.

FELLNER, William John (b. Budapest 1905). Economist. Ph.D. Berlin 1929. Partner in mfg. firm Budapest 1929–38. To U.S. Fac. Berkeley 1939–52, prof. from 1947. Prof. economics Yale from 1952, Sterling prof. from 1959.

FENICHEL, Otto (b. Austria 1898; d. 1946). Psychoanalyst. With Berlin Inst. Psychoanal. To U.S. 1937. Training analyst Los Angeles from 1938.

FERMI, Enrico (b. Rome 1901; d. 1954). Nuclear physicist. Ph.D. Pisa 1922. Prof. theoretical physics Rome 1927–38. To U.S. 1939; nat. 1944. Prof. physics Columbia 1939–42. With Manhattan Project Chicago 1942–45. Prof. physics U. Chicago 1946–54. Hughes medal Roy. Soc. London 1942; Congressional medal merit 1946; Franklin, Rumford medals. Natl. Acad. Sci. For. mem. Roy. Soc. London. Nobel Prize in physics 1938 "for his demonstrations of the existence of new radioactive elements produced by neutron irradiation, and for his related discovery of nuclear reactions brought about by slow neutrons."

FERMI, Laura (b. Rome 1907). Writer. Student U. Rome 1926–28. Married Enrico Fermi 1928. To U.S. 1939; nat. 1944. *Atoms in the Family* (1954); *Mussolini* (1961); *Illustrious Immigrants* (1968). Guggenheim Fellow 1957.

FEUCHTWANGER, Lion (b. Munich 1884; d. 1958). Writer. Ph.D. 1907. To S. France 1933. Co-editor with Bert Brecht of anti-Nazi magazine *Das Wort* (Moscow 1936–39). To U.S. 1940; settled in Calif. 1941. *Josephus and the Emperor* (1942).

FRAENKEL-CONRAT, Heinz (b. Breslau 1910). Biochemist. M.D. Breslau 1933. Ph.D. Edinburgh 1936. To U.S. 1936; nat. 1941. At Rockefeller Inst. 1936–37; Inst. Butanton São Paulo 1937–38; Inst. Experimental Biology Berkeley 1939–42; Western Regional Research Lab. Dept. Agriculture 1942–49. Prof. virology Berkeley from 1951. Reconstituted tobacco mosaic virus. Lasker award 1958 with Gerhard Schramm and A. D. Hershey.

FRANCK, James (b. Hamburg 1882; d. 1964). Physical chemist. Ph.D. Berlin 1906. Prof. experimental physics and director 2d Inst. for experimental physics Göttingen 1920–33. Left Germany, vis. prof. Johns Hopkins, Copenhagen. Prof. physics Johns Hopkins 1935–38. Prof. physical chemistry U. Chicago 1938–47. Director chem. div. Metallurgical Lab. Manhattan District Chicago during World War II. Franck Report proposing open demonstration atomic bomb before military use 1945. Natl. Acad. Sci. For. mem. Roy. Soc. London. Max Planck, Rumford medals. Nobel Prize in physics with G. Hertz 1925 "for their discovery of the laws governing the impact of an electron upon an atom."

FRANK, Bruno (b. Stuttgart 1886; d. 1945). Writer. Ph.D. Heidelberg. To Switzerland 1933, then London. To U.S. 1937.

FRANK, Philipp (b. Vienna 1884; d. 1966). Physicist, philosopher of science. Ph.D. Vienna 1906. Prof. physics Prague 1912–38. To U.S. 1938, aided by Emergency Committee; nat. 1945. At Harvard 1939–54, research asso. physics and philos. 1939–41, lect. physics and math. 1941–54. *Einstein* (1947).

FRANKEL, Hermann (b. Berlin 1888). Classical philologist. Ph.D. Göttingen 1915. Taught classics Göttingen 1925–35. To U.S. 1935, aided by Emergency Committee. Fac. Stanford 1935–1953, prof. from 1937.

FRENKEL-BRUNSWIK, Else (b. Lemberg, Austria, 1908; d. 1958). Psychologist. Ph.D. Vienna 1930. Married Egon Brunswik. Instructor psychology Vienna 1930–38. To U.S.; naturalized. Research asso. Inst. Child Welfare Berkeley 1939–58, lect. from 1944. Co-author *The Authoritarian Personality* (1950).

FRIEDLAENDER, Walter (b. Berlin 1873; d. 1966). Art historian. Ph.D. Berlin 1900. Prof. Freiburg 1914 till dismissal by Nazis 1933. To U.S. 1935; naturalized. Prof. Inst. Fine Arts NYU 1935–42. *Poussin* (1966).

FROMM, Erich (b. Frankfurt 1900). Psychoanalyst. Ph.D. Heidelberg 1922. Married Frieda Fromm-Reichmann 1926; div. Lect. Psychoanalytic Inst. Frankfurt and Inst. für Sozialforschung Frankfurt 1929–32. To U.S. 1934. With Inst. for Social Research N.Y.C. 1934–39. Fac. Bennington Coll. 1941–50. Prof. Natl. U. Mexico from 1951. Prof. Michigan State U. 1957–61. Prof. NYU from 1962. *Escape from Freedom* (1941). Terry lecturer Yale 1949.

FROMM-REICHMANN, Frieda (b. Karlsruhe 1889; d. 1957). Psychoanalyst. M.D. Königsberg 1913. Married Erich Fromm 1926; div. Head private psychoanalytic hosp. Heidelberg 1923–33. Co-founder and teacher Psychoanalytic Inst. Frankfurt 1929–33. To U.S. 1935. Fellow William Alanson White Inst. of Psychiatry and Psychoanalysis 1943–57. Adolf Meyer award, Assn. for Improvement Mental Hosps. 1952.

GEIRINGER, Karl (b. Vienna 1899). Musicologist. Ph.D. Vienna 1922. Curator archives Soc. Friends of Music Vienna 1930–38. Vis. prof. Royal

Coll. Music London 1939–40. To U.S. 1940; nat. 1945. At Hamilton Coll. N.Y. 1940–41. Prof. Boston U. 1941–62. Prof. music U. Calif. (Santa Barbara) from 1962. *Haydn* (1946). Pres. Am. Musicol. Soc.

GERSCHENKRON, Alexander (b. Odessa 1904). Economist, economic historian. Dr. Pol. Vienna 1928. Research asso. Austrian Inst. for Bus. Cycle Research 1937–38. To U.S. 1938; nat. 1945. Taught economics Berkeley 1938–44. Staff mem. Bd. Governors Federal Reserve System 1944–48. Asso. prof. econ. Harvard 1948, prof. 1951, Walter S. Barker prof. from 1955. Guggenheim Fellow 1954–55. Pres. Econ. Hist. Assn. 1966–68. *Economic Backwardness in Historical Perspective* (1962).

GILBERT, Felix (b. Baden-Baden 1905). Historian. Ph.D. Berlin 1931. To U.S. 1936, aided by Emergency Committee; nat. 1943. At Scripps Coll. 1936–37; member Inst. for Advanced Study Princeton 1939–43; research analyst OSS 1943–45; with State Dept. 1945–46. Prof. hist. Bryn Mawr 1946–62. Prof. Inst. for Advanced Study Princeton from 1962. *To the Farewell Address* (1961; Bancroft Prize); *Machiavelli and Guicciardini* (1965).

GÖDEL, Kurt (b. Brünn, Austria-Hungary, 1906). Mathematician. Ph.D. Vienna 1930. Privatdozent Vienna 1933–38. To U.S. 1940, aided by Emergency Committee; nat. 1948. Member Inst. for Advanced Study Princeton from 1938; prof. from 1953. Discoverer of Gödel's Theorem. Natl. Acad. Sci.

GOETZE, Albrecht (b. Leipzig 1897). Assyriologist. Ph.D. Heidelberg 1920. Prof. Marburg 1930–33; dismissed by Nazis. To U.S. 1934; nat. 1940. Vis. prof. Yale 1933–36. Prof. Assyriology Yale 1936–65, Sterling prof. from 1956. *Old Babylonian Omen Texts* (1947); *Laws of Eshunna* (1956).

GOLDHABER, Maurice (b. Lemberg, Poland, 1911). Physicist. Ph.D. Cambridge 1936. Fellow Magdalen Coll. Cambridge 1936–38. To U.S. 1938; nat. 1944. Fac. U. Illinois 1938–50; prof. from 1945. Senior scientist Brookhaven Natl. Lab. from 1950. Natl. Acad. Sci. Morris Loeb lecturer Harvard 1955.

GOLDMARK, Peter (b. Budapest 1906). Physicist. Ph.D. Vienna 1931. TV engineer Pye Radio Ltd. Cambridge (England) 1931–33. To U.S. 1933; nat. 1937. Consult. engr. N.Y.C. 1934–35. Chief engr. TV dept. CBS 1936–44. Director engring. r. and d. CBS 1944–50. Pres. CBS Labs. from 1950. Zworykin award 1961.

GOLDSCHMIDT, Richard (b. Frankfurt 1878; d. 1958). Zoologist. Ph.D. Heidelberg 1902. Prof. Kaiser Wilhelm Inst. for Biol. Research Berlin 1914–36, director from 1921. To U.S. 1936. Prof. zoology Berkeley 1936–48. Natl. Acad. Sci. Silliman lecturer Yale 1939–40.

GOLDSTEIN, Kurt (b. Kattowitz, Poland, 1878; d. 1965). Neuropsychiatrist. M.D. Breslau 1903. Director Hosp. für hirnverletzte Soldaten Frankfurt 1922–23; also prof. U. Frankfurt. Rockefeller Fdn. Fellow Amsterdam 1933–34. To U.S. 1934. Fac. Columbia U. 1934–40. Head Neurophysiology Lab. Montefiore Hosp. (N.Y.) 1936–40. Prof. Tufts Med. Schl. Boston 1940–45. Vis. prof. psychology CCNY 1950–55. With New Schl. for Soc. Res. 1955–65. *The Organism* (1939). William James Lecturer Harvard.

GOTTMAN, Jean (b. Kharkov 1915). Geographer. Doctorate from Sorbonne 1934. Asst. geography Sorbonne 1937–40. To U.S. 1942. Member Inst. for Advanced Study Princeton 1942 and later occasions. Cons. to Bd. Econ. Warfare 1942–44. Fac. Johns Hopkins 1943–48, ult. asso. prof. Research in Paris 1948–51. Research director Megalopolis study, Twentieth Century Fund 1956–61. Prof. Ecole des Hautes Etudes Paris from 1960. *Megalopolis* (1961). Rockefeller Fdn. Fellow 1942–44.

GRAF, Oskar Maria (b. Berg am Starnberger, Germany, 1894). Writer. Voluntary exile to Austria 1933; deprived of German citizenship. To Czechoslovakia 1934. To U.S. 1938. *Unruhe um einen Friedfertigen* (1947); *Die Eroberung der Welt* (1948).

GROPIUS, Walter (b. Berlin 1883). Architect. Studied Technische Hochschule Munich. Married Alma Mahler 1916; div. United two art schls. as Bauhaus (Weimar) 1918; moved Bauhaus to Dessau 1925. In private practice Berlin 1928–34. To England; partner of Maxwell Fry, architect, London. Prof. arch. Harvard Schl. of Design 1937–52. Formed Architects Collaborative 1946. Grand Prix Internatl. d'Architecture; Royal Gold Medal, Roy. Inst. Brit. Arch.; Gold medal, American Inst. Architects.

GROSZ, George (b. Berlin 1893; d. 1959). Painter. Studied Roy. Acad. Dresden; Kunstgewerbeschule Berlin; Paris. To U.S. Guggenheim Fellow 1937–38. Gold Medal, Natl. Acad. Arts and Letters 1959.

GRUEN, Victor (b. Vienna 1903). Architect. Studied Tech. Inst. and Acad. Fine Arts Vienna. In private practice Vienna, projects in Austria, Germany, Czechoslovakia 1932–38. To U.S. 1938; nat. 1943. In architectural practice N.Y.C.; other offices Los Angeles, Chicago. Principal designer of large-scale shopping centers.

GUILLÉN, Jorge (b. Valladolid 1893). Poet. Prof. Spanish lit. Murcia, Seville. To U.S. Prof. Spanish Wellesley Coll. *Cántico* (3d enlarged ed. 1945).

HABERLER, Gottfried (b. nr. Vienna 1900). Economist. Ph.D. Vienna 1923; J.D. Vienna. Fac. Vienna 1928–36. Attached to financial sect. League of

Nations Geneva 1934–36. To U.S. 1936. Asso. prof. Harvard, prof. 1938, Paul M. Warburg prof. 1947, Galen L. Stone prof. Internatl. Trade 1957.

HADAMARD, Jacques (b. 1865; d. 1963). Mathematician. To U.S. 1940. At Columbia during World War II. Returned to France. Mem. Acad. des Sci. Paris. *Essay on Psychology of Invention in the Mathematical Field* (1945).

HAMBURGER, Viktor (b. Landeshut, Germany, 1900). Embryologist. Ph.D. Freiburg. Privatdozent zoology Freiburg 1927–32. To U.S. 1932, aided by Emergency Committee; nat. 1940. Research Fellow zoology U. Chicago 1932–33. Fac. Washington U. (St. Louis) from 1933; prof. from 1941. Natl. Acad. Sci.

HANFMANN, George M. A. (b. St. Petersburg 1911). Classical archaeologist. Ph.D. Berlin 1934. Ph.D. Johns Hopkins 1935. Society of Fellows Harvard 1935–38. Fac. Harvard from 1938, prof. from 1956. Curator classical antiquities Fogg Art Museum Harvard from 1946.

HARTMANN, Heinz (b. Vienna 1894). Psychoanalyst. M.D. Vienna 1920. With Psychiatric and Neurological Clinics U. Vienna 1920–34; denied appointment as privatdozent by Austrian government for declaring himself "*konfessionslos.*" In private practice as psychoanalyst Vienna 1934–38. Training analysis with Freud 1934–36. Left Vienna 1938 for Paris, Geneva, Lausanne. To U.S. 1941. In private practice as psychoanalyst N.Y.C. Director Treatment Center N.Y. Psychoanalytic Inst. 1948–51. *Essays on Ego Psychology* (collected 1964).

HEIDER, Fritz (b. Vienna 1896). Social psychologist. Ph.D. Graz 1920. To U.S. Fac. Smith Coll. 1930–47. Prof. U. Kansas from 1947. *The Psychology of Interpersonal Relations* (1958). Lewin Memorial Award 1959.

HEMPEL, Carl Gustav (b. Oranienburg, Germany, 1905). Philosopher of science. Ph.D. Berlin 1934. Private research and writing Brussels 1934–37. To U.S. 1937; nat. 1944. Research asso. U. Chicago 1937–38. Fac. CCNY 1939–40. Queens Coll. 1940–48; Yale 1948–55. Prof. philosophy Princeton from 1955, Stuart prof. from 1956. *Fundamentals of Concept Formation in Empirical Science* (1952); *Aspects of Scientific Explanation* (1965). Guggenheim Fellow 1947–48.

HERZOG, Herta (b. Vienna 1910). Psychologist. Ph.D. Vienna 1932. Asst. Wirtschaftspsychologische Forschungsstelle U. Vienna from 1932. Married 1st Paul Lazarsfeld; 2d Paul Massing. To U.S. 1935; nat. 1941. With Office of Radio Research Princeton 1938–41, DuPont Co., and Bureau of Applied Social Research Columbia 1935–43. With McCann-Erickson advertising agency 1943–61. Partner Jack Tinker and Partners advertising agency from 1962.

HESS, Victor Francis (b. Waldstein, Austria, 1883; d. 1964). Physicist. Ph.D. Vienna 1906. Prof. Vienna, Graz, Innsbruck 1919–38. Chief Physicist U.S. Radium Corp. N.Y.C. 1921–23. To U.S. 1938; nat. 1944. Prof. physics Fordham 1938–56. Nobel Prize in physics with Carl D. Anderson 1936 "for his discovery of cosmic radiation."

HINDEMITH, Paul (b. Hanau, Germany, 1895; d. 1963). Composer. Studied violin, viola Frankfurt. Prof. composition Berlin Hochschule from 1927. All works banned by Nazis. In Turkey 1935. To U.S. Toured U.S. as violist 1938. Prof. composition Yale to 1953. Prof. music theory Zürich 1953–63. Mus.D. (hon.) Oxford 1954; Sibelius Prize 1955; Balzan Prize for music 1963.

HIRSCHMAN, Albert (b. Berlin 1915). Economist. Ph.D. Trieste 1938. To U.S. Rockefeller Fdn. Fellow Berkeley 1941–43. Served in U.S. Army 1943–45. Chief West European and Brit. Commonwealth sect. Federal Reserve Bd. Washington 1946–52. Financial adviser Natl. Planning Bd. Bogotá (Colombia) 1952–54. Private econ. consultant Bogotá 1954–56. Research prof. econ. Yale 1956–58. Prof. internatl. econ. relations Columbia 1958–1964. Prof. pol. economy Harvard from 1964. *The Strategy oj Economic Development* (1958).

HOLBORN, Hajo (b. Berlin 1902). Historian. Ph.D. Berlin 1924. Carnegie prof. hist. and internatl. relations Berlin Schl. Polit. 1931–34. To U.S. 1934, aided by Emergency Committee; nat. 1940. Vis. prof. Yale 1934–38; permanent fac. from 1938, prof. from 1940, Sterling prof. from 1959. On leave with OSS 1943–45. *The Political Collapse of Modern Europe* (1951); *A History of Modern Germany*, 2 v. (1959, 1964). Pres. Am. Hist. Asso. 1967.

HOLTFRETER, Johannes (b. Richtenberg, Germany, 1901). Embryologist. Ph.D. Freiburg 1924. Asst. prof. Zool. Inst. Munich 1933–38. Research staff Zool. Inst. Cambridge (England) 1939–40. Fac. McGill U. 1942–46. Prof. biology Rochester from 1946. Natl. Acad. Sci. Deutsche Akad. Leopoldina.

HORKHEIMER, Max (b. Stuttgart 1895). Sociologist, philosopher. Ph.D. Director Institut für Sozialforschung Frankfurt till 1933. Migrated to Paris 1933; to U.S. 1939. Reestablished Institut für Sozialforschung in Paris and N.Y. Head Dept. Social Research Am. Jewish Committee 1944. Returned to Frankfurt as Rector 1949; director refounded Institut. *Eclipse of Reason* (1947); *Dialektik der Aufklärung* (with T. W. Adorno 1947).

HORNEY, Karen née Danielson (b. Hamburg 1885; d. 1952). Psychoanalyst. M.D. Freiburg 1913. Instructor Inst. for Psychoanalysis Berlin 1920–32.

To U.S. 1932; nat. 1938. Asso. director Chicago Inst. for Psychoanalysis 1932–34. Lect. New Schl. for Soc. Res. from 1935. Dean Am. Inst. for Psychoanalysis (N.Y.) from 1941. *The Neurotic Personality of Our Time* (1936); *Self-Analysis* (1942).

JAEGER, Werner (b. Lobberich, Germany, 1888; d. 1961). Classical philologist. Ph.D. Berlin 1911. Prof. classical philology Berlin 1921–36. To U.S. 1936; naturalized. Prof. U. Chicago 1936–39. University prof. Harvard 1939–59. *Paideia*, 3 v. (1939–46). Litt. D. Manchester U., Cambridge U., Harvard; D.Phil. (hon.) Athens.

JAHODA, Marie (b. Vienna 1907). Psychologist. Ph.D. Vienna 1932. Married 1st Paul Lazarsfeld; 2d Austen Albu, M.P. Asst. director then director Wirtschaftspsychologische Forschungsstelle U. Vienna 1933–36. In England 1937–45. To U.S. 1945; nat. 1950. Research asso. Am. Jewish Committee 1945–48. With Bureau of Applied Social Research Columbia 1948–49. At NYU 1949–58, becoming prof. psychology and director Research Center for Human Relations. Returned to England 1958; now prof. psychology Sussex U. *Current Concepts of Positive Mental Health* (1958). Co-author: *Anti-Semitism and Emotional Disorder* (1950); *Research Methods in Social Relations* (1951).

JAKOBSON, Roman (b. Moscow 1896). Linguist. Ph.D. Prague 1930. Research asso. Moscow U. 1918–20. Thereafter in Prague. To U.S. 1941. Prof. general linguistics and Czechoslovak studies École Libre des Hautes Etudes (N.Y.C.) 1942–46. Vis. prof. linguistics Columbia 1943–46. T. G. Masaryk prof. Czechoslovak studies Columbia 1946–49. S. H. Cross prof. Slavic lang. and lit. Harvard 1949–67; also prof. gen. linguistics 1960–67. Inst. prof. MIT from 1957. *Fundamentals of Language* (1956). Pres. Linguistic Soc. of America 1956. D.Litt. (hon.) Cambridge, Chicago, Oslo, Uppsala, Rome, Yale.

KAC, Mark (b. Krzemieniec, Poland, 1914). Ph.D. Lwów 1937. Teaching asst. U. Lwów 1935–37. To U.S. 1938; nat. 1943. Fellow Johns Hopkins 1938–39. Instructor Cornell 1939–43, asst. prof. 1943, prof. 1947–61. Member Inst. for Advanced Study Princeton 1951–52. Prof. Rockefeller U. from 1961. Andrew D. White prof.-at-large Cornell from 1965. Guggenheim Fellow 1946–47. Natl. Acad. Sci.

KAHLER, Erich (b. Prague 1885). Philosopher, historian. Ph.D. Vienna 1911. Left Germany 1933. In Czechoslovakia 1934, Switzerland 1935–38. To U.S. 1938; nat. 1944. Lect. New Schl. for Soc. Res. 1941–42. Prof. German lit. Cornell 1947–55. Member Inst. for Advanced Study Princeton 1949. Fellow Bollingen Fdn. 1947–50, 1960–62. *Man the Measure* (1943); *The Tower and the Abyss* (1957).

KANN, Robert A. (b. Vienna 1906). Historian. Dr. Juris. Vienna 1930. In practice Vienna 1931–38. To U.S. Member Inst. for Advanced Study Princeton 1942–45. Asst. prof. history Sampson Coll. (N.Y.) 1946–47. Fac. Rutgers from 1947, prof. from 1956. *The Multinational Empire: Nationalism and National Reform in the Habsburg Monarchy 1848–1914*, 2 v. (1950).

KANTOROWICZ, Ernst (b. Posen, Germany, 1895; d. 1963). Historian. Ph.D. Heidelberg 1921. Prof. hist. Frankfurt 1932–34. To England; vis. prof. Oxford 1934. To U.S., aided by Emergency Committee; naturalized. Fac. Berkeley 1939–51, prof. from 1945. Refused to sign Calif. oath. Prof. Inst. for Advanced Study Princeton 1951–63. *The King's Two Bodies: A Study in Mediaeval Political Theology* (1957). Haskins medal, Mediaeval Acad. Am. 1959.

KATZENELLENBOGEN, Adolf (b. Frankfurt 1901: d. 1964). Art historian. Dr. Jur. Giessen 1924; Dr. Phil. Hamburg 1933. To U.S. 1939; nat. 1946. Fac. Vassar Coll. 1940–58, prof. from 1953. Prof. fine arts Johns Hopkins 1958–64. *The Sculptural Programs of Chartres Cathedral* (1959).

KELSEN, Hans (b. Prague 1881). Jurist, philosopher of law. Dr. Juris. Vienna 1906. Drafted Austrian Const. 1920. Prof. internatl. law Cologne 1930–33. Prof. internatl. law Geneva 1933–40. To U.S. 1940; naturalized. Oliver Wendell Holmes lect. Harvard 1940–41; research asso. comparative law 1941–42. Fac. Berkeley 1942, prof. 1945–52. Renner Prize Vienna 1952; Feltrinelli Prize 1960.

KEPES, Gyorgy (b. Selyp, Hungary, 1906). Painter, designer. M.A. Roy. Acad. Fine Art Budapest. Exhibitions of paintings, Budapest, Berlin, New York, London 1930–37. To U.S. 1937. Head light and color dept. New Bauhaus (Chicago) and its successor Institute of Design 1938–43. Designed exhibitions Chicago, Paris 1944–45. Prof. visual design MIT from 1946. *The Language of Vision* (1944); *The New Landscape* (1956). Guggenheim Fellow 1960–61.

KESTEN, Hermann (b. 1900). Writer. Emigrated to France, then to U.S. Active in Emergency Rescue Committee. Settled in Rome 1949.

KITZINGER, Ernst (b. Munich 1912). Art historian. Ph.D. Munich 1934. Asst. British Museum 1935–40. To U.S. 1941; nat. 1948. With Dumbarton Oaks Center for Byzantine Studies Harvard 1941–67, prof. Byzantine art and archaeology from 1956. A. Kingsley Porter University prof. Harvard from 1967. Research analyst OSS 1943–45. *The Mosaics of Monreale* (1960).

KLEMPERER, Otto (b. Breslau 1885). Conductor. Studied conservatories Frankfurt, Berlin. Conductor Berlin State Opera and Philharmonic Choir

1927–33. To U.S. 1933. Conductor Los Angeles Philharmonic 1933–39. Principal engagements in Europe since 1946. Lifetime conductor Philharmonia Orchestra London and its successor the New Philharmonia from 1959. Now resident in Switzerland.

KOHN, Hans (b. Prague 1891). Historian. Dr. Juris. German U. Prague 1923. To U.S. 1933. Lect. New Schl. for Soc. Res. from 1933. Prof. hist. Smith Coll. 1934–49, Sydenham Clark Parsons prof. from 1941. Prof. CCNY 1949–62. *The Idea of Nationalism* (1944).

KOPAL, Zdenek (b. Litomyal, later Czechoslovakia, 1914). Astronomer. D.Sc. Charles U. Prague 1927. Dennis Fellow Cambridge U. 1938. Agassiz Research Fellow Harvard Coll. Observatory 1938–40. Research asso. Harvard Obs. 1940–46. Asso. prof. MIT 1947–51. Prof. astronomy Manchester U. from 1951. Now resident in England.

KORNGOLD, Erich (b. Brünn, Austria-Hungary, 1897; d. 1957). Composer, conductor. Studied Vienna. Conductor Opera Hse. Hamburg, Vienna State Opera. Collaborated with Max Reinhardt from 1929. To U.S. 1934; nat. 1943. Arranged Mendelssohn's music for Reinhardt's film *Midsummer Night's Dream* (1934). Motion Picture Academy Awards for original scores 1936, 1938.

KOYRÉ, Alexandre (b. Russia 1892; d. 1964). Historian of science and philosophy. Left Russia for Paris at time of Bolshevik Revolution. To U.S. during World War II. Later prof. Ecole Pratique des Hautes Etudes Paris and concurrently member Inst. for Advanced Study Princeton. *From the Closed World to the Infinite Universe* (1957); *Newtonian Studies* (1965): *Metaphysics and Measurement* (1968).

KRACAUER, Siegfried (b. Frankfurt; d. 1966). Theorist of films. Dr. engn. Berlin 1915. Ed. for cultural affairs *Frankfurter Zeitung* 1920–33. To U.S. 1941; nat. 1946. Special asst. film library Museum Modern Art (N.Y.) 1941–43. With Voice of America 1950–52. Senior staff member Bureau of Applied Social Research Columbia 1952–58. *From Caligari to Hitler* (1947); *Theory of Film* (1960). Rockefeller Fdn. Fellow 1941–43; Guggenheim Fellow 1943–45; Bollingen Fellow 1949–52.

KRAUS, H(ans). P(eter). (b. Vienna 1907). Rare book dealer, publisher. Studied Acad. of Commerce Vienna. Book dealer in Vienna till 1939. To U.S. 1939; nat. 1945. Partner H. P. Kraus Co. from 1940; pres. Kraus Periodicals from 1948; pres. Kraus Reprint Corp. from 1962.

KRAUTHEIMER, Richard (b. Fürth, Bavaria, 1897). Art historian. Ph.D. Halle 1923. Privatdozent Marburg 1928–35. To U.S. 1935; nat. 1942.

Fac. U. Louisville 1935–37. Prof. art Vassar Coll. 1937–52. Prof. Inst. Fine Arts NYU from 1952. *Lorenzo Ghiberti* (1956).

KRENEK, Ernst (b. Vienna 1900). Composer. Studied Acad. Music Vienna, Berlin. Music correspondent *Frankfurter Zeitung* 1928–37. His compositions widely performed in Europe and U.S. To U.S. 1937; nat. 1945. Prof. music Vassar Coll. 1939–42. Dean of fine arts Hamline U. (St. Paul, Minn.) 1942–47. Living in Hollywood from 1947; tours as lect. and conductor of own works.

KRIS, Ernst (b. Vienna 1900; d. 1957). Psychoanalyst. Ph.D. Vienna 1922. Member, training analyst, lect. Vienna Psychoanalytic Inst. 1927–38. With Inst. Psychoanalysis London 1938–40; research for BBC 1939–40. Project director New Schl. for Soc. Res. 1940–45. Vis. prof. CCNY 1946–51. With Child Study Center Yale Med. Schl. 1949–57.

KRISTELLER, Paul Oskar (b. Berlin 1905). Historian of philosophy. Ph.D Heidelberg 1928. Fellow Notgemeinschaft der Deutschen Wissenschaft 1932–33. Lect. in German U. Pisa 1935–38. To U.S. 1939; nat. 1945. Fac. Columbia from 1939, prof. from 1956. *The Philosophy of Marsilio Ficino* (1943); *Eight Philosophers of the Italian Renaissance* (1964). Serena medal for Italian studies, British Acad. 1958.

KRONER, Richard (b. Breslau 1884). Philosopher, theologian. Prof. Kiel from 1939; research prof. Berlin 1934. Refugee in Oxford 1938. To U.S. 1940. Prof. Union Theological Seminary N.Y.C. 1940–52. Prof. Temple U. Philadelphia 1944–64. Now living in Switzerland. *How Do We Know God?* (1942); *Culture and Faith* (1951).

KUTTNER, Stephan (b. Bonn 1907). Mediaevalist. J.U.D. Berlin 1930. Asst. law faculty U. Berlin 1929–32. Research asso. Vatican Library 1934–40. To U.S. 1940; nat. 1945. Vis. prof. canon law Catholic U. America 1940–42, prof. 1942–64. Riggs prof. Roman Catholic Studies Yale from 1964. Guggenheim Fellow 1956–59. Prize for distinguished achievement in humanities Am. Council Learned Societies 1959. Hon. doctorates Paris, Genoa.

LANDÉ, Alfred (b. Elberfeld, Germany, 1888). Physicist. Ph.D. Munich 1914. Prof. Tübingen 1922–31. Prof. Ohio State from 1931.

LANDOWSKA, Wanda (b. Warsaw 1879; d. 1959). Harpsichordist. Grad. Warsaw Conservatory Music 1893. To France; French citizen. Founded Schl. of Ancient Music (St. Leu la Forêt, France) 1927. Teacher of harpsichord in France 1927–40. To U.S. 1941. Many concerts.

LAZARSFELD, Paul F. (b. Vienna 1901). Sociologist. Ph.D. Vienna 1925. Married 1st Marie Jahoda; 2d Herta Herzog; 3d Patricia Kendall. Instructor psychology Wirtschaftspsychologische Forschungsstelle U. Vienna. To U.S. 1933 on Rockefeller Fdn. Fellowship; nat. 1943. Director Research Center U. Newark 1935–37. Director Office of Radio Research Princeton 1937–39. Fac. Columbia from 1939, later prof. sociology; Quetelet prof. social sciences from 1962. Concurrently director then chairman Bureau Applied Social Research. Co-author: *Radio and the Printed Page* (1940); *The People's Choice* (1944); *The Academic Mind* (1958); *Latent Structure Analysis* (1968). Pres. Am. Sociological Asso. 1961. Hon. doctorate U. Chicago.

LE CORBEILLER, Phillippe (b. Paris 1891). Physicist. Dr. Math. Sorbonne 1926. With French Ministry of Communications 1920–39; with French Govt. Broadcasting 1939–40. To U.S. 1941; nat. 1944. Fac. Harvard 1941–59, prof. applied physics and genl. educ. from 1949. Now resident of The Netherlands.

LÉGER, Fernand (1881–1955). Artist. To U.S. 1940. Returned to France 1945.

LEHMANN, Karl (b. Rostock, Germany, 1894; d. 1960). Classical archaeologist. Ph.D. Berlin 1922. Prof. Münster 1929–33. To U.S.; naturalized. Prof. classical archaeology NYU from 1935; director Archaeological Research Fund from 1938.

LEICHTENTRITT, Hugo (b. Pleschen, Poland, 1874; d. 1951). Musicologist. Ph.D. Berlin 1901. Taught music and wrote music criticism in Germany. To U.S. 1934. Lect. music Harvard from 1934.

LEINSDORF, Erich (b. Vienna 1912). Operatic and symphonic conductor. Studied Vienna. Asst. conductor Salzburg Festival 1934–37. To U.S. 1937; nat. 1942. Conductor Metropolitan Opera N.Y. 1937–43; Cleveland Orchestra 1943; music director Rochester Philharmonic 1947–56; director N.Y.C. Center Opera 1956; conductor Metropolitan Opera 1957–61; music director Boston Symphony Orchestra 1962–69.

LEMKIN, Raphael (b. Bezwodne, Poland, 1900; d. 1959). Lawyer. LL.D. U. Lwów, Sec. Court of Appeals Warsaw 1926–29; public prosecutor Warsaw 1929–34; law practice Warsaw 1934–39. Lect. U. Stockholm 1940–41. To U.S. 1941. At Duke U. 1941–42. Chief consultant Bd. Econ. Warfare Washington 1942–44; adviser on for. affairs Dept. War 1945–47. Member prosecuting staff U.S. Army Nuremberg trials 1945–46. Prof. law Yale 1948–59. Coined word "genocide" and launched internatl. treaty outlawing it.

LENYA, Lotte (b. Vienna 1905). Singer. Dancer in neighborhood circus; became tightrope walker at age 8. Corps de ballet Stadttheater Zürich. Married Kurt Weill 1926. Featured in Brecht-Weill *Dreigroschenoper* Berlin 1928; *Rise and Fall of the City of Mahoganny* Leipzig 1930. To U.S. 1935. Most recent performance in *Cabaret*.

LÉVI-STRAUSS, Claude (b. Brussels 1908). Anthropologist. Agrégé de philosophie Paris 1931. Docteur ès Lettres Paris 1948. Prof. sociology U. São Paulo 1935–38. With New Schl. for Soc. Res. 1941–45. Cultural counselor French embassy Washington 1946–47. Asso. curator Musée de l'Homme Paris 1948–49. Prof. Ecole des Hautes Etudes from 1950, Coll. de France from 1959. Hon. doctorates Brussels, Oxford, Yale, Chicago.

LEWIN, Kurt (b. Mogilno, Germany, 1890; d. 1947). Psychologist. Ph.D. Berlin 1914. Prof. philosophy and psychology Berlin 1926–33. To U.S. 1932. Vis. prof. psychology Stanford 1932–33; acting prof. Cornell 1933–35; prof. child psychology U. Iowa 1935–44. Prof. and director Research Center for Group Dynamics MIT 1944–47. Counselor U.S. Dept. Agriculture from 1942; with OSS 1944–45. *A Dynamic Theory of Personality* (1935); *Principles of Topological Psychology* (1936); *Resolving Social Conflicts* (1947).

LIPCHITZ, Jacques (b. Druskieniki, Latvia, 1891). Sculptor. Worked in Paris, became French citizen. To U.S. 1941. Gold medal for sculpture Am. Academy and Natl. Inst. Arts and Letters 1966.

LIPMANN, Fritz (b. Königsberg 1899). Biochemist. M.D. Berlin 1922; Ph.D. Berlin 1927. Research asst. to Otto Meyerhof 1927–30; to A. Fischer (Berlin) 1930. Rockefeller Fdn. Fellow laboratory of P. A. Levene Rockefeller Inst. N.Y. 1931–32. To Copenhagen with Fischer; research asso. Biol. Inst. of Carlsberg Fdn. 1932–39. To U.S. 1939; nat. 1944. Research asso. biochemistry Cornell Med. Schl. 1939–41. With Mass. General Hosp. Boston 1941–57. Prof. biological chem. Harvard Med. Schl. 1949–57. Prof. Rockefeller U. N.Y. from 1957. Natl. Acad. Sci. For. mem. Roy. Soc. London. Nobel Prize in physiology or med. 1953 with Hans A. Krebs "for his discovery of coenzyme A and its importance for intermediary metabolism."

LIPS, Julius (b. Saarbrücken 1895; d. 1950). Ethnologist. Ph.D. Leipzig 1919. Prof. anthropology Cologne 1930–33. Vis. prof. Columbia 1934–36. Prof. Howard U. 1937–39. Researcher in primitive law Oxford from 1939.

LOEWI, Otto (b. Frankfurt 1873; d. 1961). Physiologist, pharmacologist. M.D. Strassburg 1896. Prof. pharmacology Graz 1909–38. Franqui prof. Brussels 1938–39. To U.S. 1940; nat. 1946. Research prof. pharmacology

NYU Coll. Med. from 1940. For. mem. Roy. Soc. London; Acad. dei Lincei (Rome). Nobel Prize in physiology or medicine 1936 with Sir Henry Dale "for their discoveries relating to chemical transmission of nerve impulses."

LONDON, Fritz (b. Breslau 1900; d. 1954). Physicist. Ph.D. Munich 1921. Privatdozent Berlin 1928–33. Research for Imperial Chemical Industries England 1933–36. With Inst. Poincaré Sorbonne 1936–39, director 1938–39. To U.S. 1939. Prof. Duke U. from 1939.

LOPEZ, Robert S. (b. Genoa 1910). Historian. Litt.D. Milan; Ph.D. Wisconsin 1942. Asst. prof. Genoa 1936–38. To U.S. 1939. With Office of War Information N.Y.C. 1942–43. Lect. hist. Brooklyn Coll. 1943–44. For. news ed. CBS 1944–45. Lect. hist. Columbia 1945–46. Asst. prof. hist. Yale 1946, prof. from 1955, Durfee prof. from 1962. *Medieval Trade in the Mediterranean World* (1955); *The Birth of Europe* (1961).

LORENTE DE NÓ, Raphael (b. Zaragoza, Spain, 1902). Physiologist. M.D. Madrid 1923. Asst. Inst. Cajal Madrid 1921–29; head dept. otolaryngology hosp. Santander 1929–31. To U.S. 1931. Neuro-anatomist Central Inst. Deaf (St. Louis) 1931–36. With Rockefeller Inst. from 1936; member from 1941. *A Study of Nerve Physiology* (1947). Natl. Acad. Sci.

LOWENTHAL, Leo (b. 1900, Berlin). Prof. of Comparative Literature; sociologist. Ph.D. Frankfurt 1923. With Institut für Sozialforschung, Frankfurt, ed. *Zeitschrift für Sozialforschung* from 1926. To U.S. 1934; nat. 1940. With Inst. for Social Research, Bureau of Applied Social Research, and Columbia U. to 1949. Research director Voice of America, 1949–53. To U. Calif. Berkeley 1955, now prof. sociology. Co-author, *Prophets of Deceit* (1949); author *Literature and the Image of Man* (1957), *Literature, Popular Culture, and Society* (1961). Co-editor, *Culture and Social Culture* (1961).

LÖWITH, Karl (b. Munich 1897). Philosopher. Ph.D. Munich 1923. Privatdozent Marburg 1931–34. Rockefeller Fdn. Fellow Rome 1934–36. Prof. Sendai U. Japan 1936–39. To U.S. 1939. Lect. Bryn Mawr, Swarthmore 1939–40. Prof. Union Theological Seminary 1941; also Hartford Theological Seminary from 1941. Returned to Germany after war. Now prof. philosophy Heidelberg.

LURIA, Salvador (b. Turin 1912). Virologist. M.D. Turin 1935. Research Fellow Curie Lab. Inst. Radium Paris 1938–40. To U.S. 1940; nat. 1947. Research asst. surg. bacteriol. Columbia 1940–42. Fac. U. Indiana 1943–50, ult. asso. prof. Prof. bacteriol. U. Illinois 1950–59. Prof. microbiology MIT from 1959, now Sedgwick prof. biology. Guggenheim Fellow 1942–43. Natl. Acad. Sci.

MACHLUP, Fritz (b. Wiener Neustadt, Austria, 1902). Economist. Dr. rer. pol. Vienna 1923. Lect. Volkshochschule Vienna 1929–33. To U.S. 1933; nat. 1940. Rockefeller Fdn. Fellow 1933–35. Prof. Buffalo 1935–47; prof. Johns Hopkins 1947–60. Prof. Princeton from 1960.

MAETERLINCK, Maurice (b. Ghent 1862; d. 1949). Writer. To U.S. 1940; returned to Belgium at close of war. Member Institut de France 1937. Nobel Prize for literature 1911.

MAHLER-WERFEL, Alma (b. 1879). Writer. Married 1st Gustav Mahler; 2d Walter Gropius; 3d Franz Werfel. With Werfel to France 1938. To U.S. 1940. *And the Bridge Is Love* (1958).

MANN, Golo (b. Munich 1909), s. of Thomas Mann. Historian. Ph.D. Heidelberg 1932. Lect. French universities 1933–37. Ed. lit. review *Mass und Wert* Zürich 1937–40. Prof. hist. Olivet Coll. (Mich.) 1942–43. Served in U.S. Army 1943–46. Prof. hist. Claremont Men's Coll. 1947–58. Prof. Münster 1958–60; Stuttgart 1960–64. Now resident of Switzerland.

MANN, Heinrich (b. Lübeck 1871; d. 1960), br. of Thomas Mann. Writer. In France 1933–40. To U.S. 1940; settled in Calif. and died there. *Jugend und Vollendung des Königs Henri Quatre* (1935–38); *Ein Zeitalter wird besichtigt* (1945–56).

MANN, Thomas (b. Lübeck 1875; d. 1955). Writer. Left Germany for Switzerland 1933. Settled in U.S. 1939; nat. 1944. In Calif. from 1941 where he wrote *Doctor Faustus* (1948). Settled near Zürich in 1952 and died there. Nobel Prize for literature 1929.

MARCUSE, Herbert (b. Berlin 1898). Philosopher. Ph.D. Freiburg 1922. Asst. to Husserl and Heidegger 1928–33. To U.S. 1934, aided by Emergency Committee; nat. 1940. With Inst. Soc. Research Columbia 1940–41. With OSS and State Dept. 1941–50. Prof. politics and philosophy Brandeis 1954–65. Prof. philosophy U. Calif. (San Diego) from 1965. *Reason and Revolution* (1941); *Eros and Civilization* (1954); *One-Dimensional Man* (1965).

MARCUSE, Ludwig (b. 1894). Writer, drama critic. To France 1933. To U.S. 1939. Prominent in émigré literary circles.

MARK, Herman F. (b. Vienna 1895). Polymer chemist. Ph.D. Vienna 1921. Prof. chemistry Vienna 1932–38. Research mgr. Canadian Internatl. Paper Co. Hawkesbury, Canada. To U.S. 1940; nat. 1945. Prof. organic chemistry Brooklyn Polytechnic Inst. from 1940; director Inst. Polymer Research from 1944. Natl. Acad. Sci.

MARSCHAK, Jacob (b. Kiev 1899). Economist. Ph.D. Heidelberg 1922. Instructor econ. and statistics Heidelberg 1930–33. Director Inst. Statistics and All Souls Coll. Oxford 1933–39. To U.S. 1939; nat. 1945. Prof. economics New Schl. for Soc. Res. 1939–42; prof. U. Chicago 1943–55; prof. Yale 1955–60; prof. econ. and bus. adminis. U.C.L.A. from 1960.

MARTINU, Bohuslav (b. Policka, Austria-Hungary, 1890; d. 1959). Composer. Studied Prague Conservatory. To U.S. 1941. Vis. prof. composition Princeton 1941–53. Living in France from 1953.

MAUROIS, André (b. Elbeuf, Normandy, 1885; d. 1967). Writer. To U.S. 1940. In U.S. during World War II except for period of service as officer in North Africa 1943. Returned to France 1946. *History of the United States* (1944). Académie française 1938.

MAYER, Maria Goeppert (b. Kattowitz, Germany, 1906). Physicist. Ph.D. Göttingen 1930. To U.S. 1930; nat. 1933. Volunteer asso. Johns Hopkins 1933–39. Lect. Columbia 1939–46. Senior physicist Argonne Natl. Lab. 1946–60. Volunteer prof. U. Chicago 1946–59; prof. 1959–60. Prof. U. Calif. La Jolla from 1960. Natl. Acad. Sci. Nobel Prize in physics 1963 with Eugene Wigner and J. H. D. Jensen for her and Jensen's "discoveries concerning the shell structure of atomic nuclei."

MENDELSOHN, Erich (b. Allenstein, East Prussia, 1887; d. 1953). Architect. Studied Charlottenburg and Munich with Theodor Fischer 1907–11. Practicing architect Munich 1911–14. Served in German Army in World War I. Major commissions in Germany 1921–33. To England 1933; partner of Serge Chermayeff. British subject 1938. To U.S. 1941. In practice in Calif. till his death.

MENGER, Karl (b. Vienna 1902). Mathematician. Ph.D. Vienna 1924. Prof. Vienna 1927–37. To U.S. 1937; nat. 1942. Prof. Notre Dame 1937–46. Prof. Illinois Inst. of Technology from 1946.

MEYERHOF, Otto (b. Hannover, Germany, 1884; d. 1951). Biochemist. M.D. Heidelberg 1909. Director Kaiser Wilhelm Inst. Physiology Heidelberg 1929–38. Directeur de recherche Paris 1938–40. To U.S. 1940; nat. 1946. Research prof. U. Pennsylvania from 1940. Natl. Acad. Sci. Nobel Prize in physiology or medicine 1922 with A. V. Hill "for his discovery of the fixed relationship between the consumption of oxygen and the metabolism of lactic acid in the muscle."

MICHAEL, Franz (b. Freiburg 1907). Sinologist, political scientist. Dr. Juris. Freiburg 1933. Attaché German For. Service 1933–34. Prof. Natl. Chekiang U. China 1934–38. To U.S. 1939; naturalized. Fac. Johns Hopkins 1939–42. Prof. hist. modern China U. Washington from 1942.

MIDDELDORF, Ulrich (b. Stassfurt, Germany, 1901). Art historian. Ph.D. Berlin 1924. Curator Kunsthistorisches Institut Florence 1928–35. To U.S. 1935. Asst. prof. art U. Chicago 1935, prof. 1941–53. Director Kunsthistorisches Institut Florence from 1953. Pres. Coll. Art Asso. Am. 1939–40. *Raphael's Drawings* (1945).

MIES VAN DER ROHE, Ludwig (b. Aachen, Germany, 1886). Architect. Director Bauhaus 1930–33. To U.S. 1938; nat. 1944. Director Schl. Architecture Illinois Inst. Tech. 1938–58; designer IIT campus Chicago. One-man show Museum Modern Art (N.Y.) 1947. Feltrinelli International prize for architecture.

MILHAUD, Darius (b. Aix-en-Provence 1892). Composer. Studied Conservatoire de Musique Paris. Composer since 1912. Member Conseil supérieur Conservatoire de Musique 1937–40. To U.S. 1940. Prof. composition Mills Coll. 1940–47. Returned to France 1947. Prof. Conservatoire from 1947.

MINKOWSKI, Rudolph (b. Strassburg 1895). Astronomer. Ph.D. Breslau 1921. Ausserord. prof. Hamburg 1931–35. To U.S. 1935; nat. 1940. Staff Mt. Wilson Observatory 1935–48; Mt. Wilson and Palomar Observatories 1948–60. Prof. Berkeley from 1961. Natl. Acad. Sci.

MODIGLIANI, Franco (b. Rome 1918). Economist. Dr. Juris. Rome 1939. To U.S. 1939; nat. 1946. Instructor N.J. Coll. for Women 1942; assoc. in econ. and statistics Bard Coll. 1942–44; lect. New Schl. for Soc. Res. 1943–44; chief statistician Inst. World Affairs N.Y.C. 1945–48; asst. prof. New Schl. for Soc. Res. 1946–48; Research in econ. U. Chicago 1949–54. Asso. prof. later prof. U. Illinois 1949–52. Prof. Carnegie Inst. Tech. 1952–60. Prof. Northwestern 1960–62. Prof. industrial management MIT from 1961; also prof. econ. from 1964.

MOHOLY-NAGY, László (b. Borsod, Hungary, 1895; d. 1946). Designer. Grad. in law Budapest 1915. Prof. basic elements of art Bauhaus (Weimar, Dessau) 1923–28. Left Bauhaus with Gropius 1928. Married Sibyl Peech 1933. Worked in Amsterdam 1934; in London 1935–37. To U.S. 1937; nat. 1946. Director New Bauhaus Chicago 1937–38. Pres. Institute of Design Chicago 1939–46. *The New Vision* (1930; 2d ed. 1938; 3d ed. 1946).

MOHOLY-NAGY, Sibyl née Peech (b. Dresden). Historian of architecture. Married László Moholy-Nagy 1933. To U.S. 1937. Head division humanities Inst. of Design Chicago 1941–47; asso. prof. art Bradley U. 1947–49; lect. Berkeley 1949–51. Prof. hist. architecture Pratt Inst. from 1951. *Moholy-Nagy* (1950).

MOLNÁR, Ferenc (b. Budapest 1878; d. 1952). Playwright. To U.S. 1940.

MORGENSTERN, Oskar (b. Görlitz, Germany, 1902). Economist. Dr. rer. pol. Vienna 1925. Privatdozent econ. Vienna 1928–35; prof. 1935–38. To U.S. 1938; nat. 1944. Lect. econ. Princeton 1938; asso. prof. 1941; prof. from 1944. Co-author with John von Neumann, *Theory of Games and Economic Behavior* (1944). Rockefeller Fellow, Harvard, London, Paris, Rome 1925–28.

MORGENTHAU, Hans J. (b. Coburg, Germany, 1904). Political scientist. Practiced law 1927–30. Asst. to law fac. U. Frankfurt 1931; acting pres. Labor Law Court Frankfurt 1931–33. Instructor pol. sci. U. Geneva 1932–35. Prof. internatl. law U. Madrid 1935–36. To U.S. 1937, aided by Emergency Committee; nat. 1943. Instructor gov. Brooklyn Coll. 1937–39; asst. prof. law U. Kansas (Kansas City) 1939–43. Vis. asso. prof. pol. sci. U. Chicago 1943–45, asso. prof. 1945–49, prof. from 1949, Albert A. Michelson prof. from 1963. Director Center for Study of Am. For. Policy U. Chicago from 1950. *Scientific Man vs. Power Politics* (1946).

NACHMANSOHN, David (b. Russia 1899). Biochemist. M.D. Berlin 1926. Fellow Kaiser Wilhelm Inst. for Biology Berlin 1926–30; with Rudolf Virchow Hosp. Berlin 1932–33. Independent investigator at Sorbonne 1933–39. To U.S. 1939; nat. 1945. Instructor Yale Med. Schl. 1939–42. Fac. Coll. of Physicians and Surgeons Columbia from 1942; prof. biochem. from 1954. Natl. Acad. Sci.

NATHAN, Otto (b. Bingen, Germany, 1893). Economist. Ph.D. Würzburg 1920. Fac. Hochschule Polit. Berlin 1928–33; econ. adviser Ministry Economics 1930–33. To U.S. 1933. Vis. lect. Princeton 1933–35. Fac. NYU 1935–58. Literary executor of Albert Einstein. *The Nazi Economic System* (1944). Co-editor *Einstein on Peace* (1960).

NEUGEBAUER, Otto (b. Innsbruck 1899). Historian of mathematics and astronomy. Ph.D. Göttingen 1926. Fac. Göttingen 1927–33. Research in Copenhagen 1934–39. To U.S. 1939, aided by Emergency Committee; naturalized. Prof. hist. of mathematics Brown U. from 1939. At Inst. for Advanced Study Princeton 1945–46, 1950–54, etc. *The Exact Sciences in Antiquity* (1952).

NEUMANN, Franz (b. Kattowitz, Poland, 1900; d. 1954). Political scientist. Dr. Juris. Frankfurt 1923. Labor lawyer, legal adviser to Social Democratic party, lect. Hochschule für Politik Frankfurt 1926–33. In England 1933–36, studied with Harold Laski, London Schl. Econ. To U.S. 1936, aided by Emergency Committee. With Inst. für Sozialforschung Columbia from

1936 till wartime service with OSS. Prof. pol. sci. Columbia. *Behemoth: The Structure and Practice of National Socialism* (1942).

NEUMANN, Sigmund (b. Leipzig 1904; d. 1962). Political scientist. Ph.D. Leipzig 1927. Lect. Hochschule Polit. Berlin 1928–30, prof. 1930–33. Research Fellow Roy. Inst. Internatl. Affairs London 1933–34. To U.S. 1934; nat. 1940. Asso. prof. social sci. Wesleyan U. 1934–44, prof. from 1944, now director Center for Advanced Studies. Also prof. diplomacy Fletcher Schl. Law and Diplom. Tufts from 1949. Consultant OSS 1943–45.

NEURATH, Hans (b. Vienna 1909). Biochemist. Ph.D. Vienna 1933. Instructor Vienna 1932–34. Research Fellow U. London 1934–35. To U.S. 1935; nat. 1941. At U. Minn. 1935–36; fellow Cornell 1936–38. Assoc. biochem. Duke 1938–39, thence to prof. physical chemistry 1946–50. Prof. biochemistry U. Washington from 1950. Natl. Acad. Sci. Ed. *The Proteins* (1953; 2d ed. 1963). Guggenheim Fellow 1954.

NEYMAN, Jerzy (b. Benderey, Bessarabia, 1894). Statistician. Ph.D. Warsaw 1923. Lect. U. Warsaw 1928–34. Special lect. U. Coll. London 1934–35, reader in statistics 1935–38. To U.S. 1938; naturalized. Prof. math. Berkeley from 1938; director Statistical Lab. from 1941. Natl. Acad. Sci.

NOETHER, Emmy (b. Germany 1882; d. 1935). Mathematician. Prof. Göttingen 1922–23. To U.S. 1933, aided by Emergency Committee. Vis. prof. Bryn Mawr 1933–35. With Inst. for Advanced Study Princeton 1934–35.

OCHOA, Severo (b. Luarca, Spain, 1905). Biochemist. M.D. Madrid 1929. Lect. in physiology U. Madrid Med. Schl. 1931–35, head physiol. div. Inst. for Med. Research 1935–36. Guest research asst. in physiology Kaiser Wilhelm Inst. for Med. Heidelberg. Investigator Marine Biological Lab. Plymouth (England) 1937; demonstrator and research asst. biochemistry U. Oxford 1938–40. To U.S. 1940; nat. 1956. Instructor and research asst. pharmacology Washington U. Med. Schl. (St. Louis) 1941–42. Research asso. medicine NYU Med. Schl. 1942–45, prof. pharmacology 1946–54, prof. biochemistry from 1954. Natl. Acad. Sci. For. mem. Roy. Soc. London; USSR Acad. Sci. Hon. doctorates Oxford, Salamanca, Glasgow. Nobel Prize in physiology or medicine 1959 with Arthur Kornberg "for their discovery of the mechanisms in the biological synthesis of ribonucleic and deoxyribonucleic acids."

OPPENHEIM, A. Leo (b. Vienna 1904). Assyriologist. Ph.D. Vienna 1933. Librarian and asst. Orient. Inst. Vienna 1935–38. To U.S. 1941; naturalized. Cataloguer cuneiform tablets N.Y. Public Library 1941–42. Fac. Iranian Inst. N.Y.C. Faculty Oriental Inst. U. Chicago from 1947, prof. from 1955.

PANOFSKY, Erwin (b. Hannover, Germany, 1892; d. 1968). Art historian. Ph.D. Freiburg 1914. Prof. Hamburg 1921–33. Vis. prof. fine arts NYU 1931–35; vis. lect. Princeton 1934–35. Decision to settle in U.S. 1934. Prof. Inst. for Advanced Study Princeton 1935–68. Charles Eliot Norton prof. Harvard 1947–48. Hon. doc. Utrecht, Uppsala, Berlin, Princeton, Harvard, Rome, Columbia. *Studies in Iconology* (1939); *Albrecht Dürer* (1943); *Early Netherlandish Painting* (1953); *Meaning in the Visual Arts* (1955).

ST.-JOHN PERSE, pseud. Alexis Léger (b. Guadeloupe 1887). Poet, diplomat. Licencé in law Ecole des Hautes Etudes Paris. Ambassadeur de France and Sec.-Gén. Ministère des Affaires Etrangères 1933–40. To U.S. 1940. Consultant on French lit. Libr. Cong. 1941–45. Alternating between France and U.S. since 1945. *Exil* (1944); *Vents* (1946); *Amers* (1957); *Oiseaux* (1962). Nobel Prize for literature 1960.

PISCATOR, Erwin (b. Ulm, Germany, 1893; d. 1966). Theatrical producer. Director People's Theater and State Theater Berlin. Head Piscator Dramatic Academy and lect. U. Paris 1936–38. To U.S. 1939. Directed *Saint Joan* 1940. Director Dramatic Workshop New Schl. for Soc. Res. 1940–66.

POGGIOLI, Renato (b. Florence 1907; d. 1963). Literary historian and critic. Litt. D. Rome 1938. To U.S. 1938; nat. 1950. Vis. prof. Smith Coll. 1938–39. Fac. Brown U. 1940–47. Fac. Harvard from 1947, prof. Slavic and Comparative Lit. from 1950, Curt Hugo Reisinger prof. from 1960.

POLANYI, Karl (b. Vienna 1886; d. 1964). Social scientist. Dr. Juris. Budapest 1909. For. ed. *Österreichische Volkswirt* Vienna 1924–33. Lect. extramural delegacy Oxford from 1937. Resident scholar Bennington Coll. 1940–43; vis. prof. Columbia 1947–53, also 1955–56. *The Great Transformation* (1944). Resident in Canada at death.

PRAEGER, Frederick (b. Vienna 1915). Book publisher. Studied Vienna 1933–38; Sorbonne 1934. Asso. ed. publ. hse. Vienna 1935–38. To U.S. 1938. Jewelry salesman, asst. merchandising manager jewelry store chain 1938–41. Served in U.S. Army from private to 1st Lt. 1942–46. Civilian head publ. Mil. Govt. U.S. (Hesse, Germany) 1946–48. Pres. Frederick A. Praeger Inc. N.Y. from 1948. Also chairman Phaidon Press Ltd. Carey-Thomas Award for creative publishing 1957.

PRAGER, William (b. Karlsruhe, Germany, 1903). Applied mathematician. Dr. Engr. Darmstadt 1926. Structural inspector German Airport League Berlin 1929–33. Prof. mechanics Karlsruhe 1933. Prof. mechanics U. Istanbul 1934–41. To U.S. 1941; naturalized. Prof. applied math. Brown U. from 1941, Ballou University prof. 1959–65. Prof. applied math.

U. Calif. San Diego 1965–68. University prof. Brown U. from 1968. Theodore von Kármán Award, Am. Soc. Civil Engrs. 1960.

RABINOWITCH, Eugene (b. St. Petersburg 1901). Physical chemist, editor. Ph.D. Berlin 1926. Research asso. Göttingen 1929–33. Research asso. U. Coll. London 1934–38. To U.S. 1939. Research asso. MIT 1939–44. With Manhattan District 1944–46. Research prof. U. Illinois from 1947. Ed. *Bulletin of Atomic Scientists. Photosynthesis* (1945–56). Kalinga Prize UNESCO 1965.

RASETTI, Franco (b. Castiglione del Lago, Italy, 1901). Ph.D. Pisa 1923. Asst. prof. Rome 1927–30, prof. 1931–38. Fac. Laval U. (Québec) 1939–47. To U.S. 1947; nat. 1952. Prof. physics Johns Hopkins from 1947. Guggenheim Fellow 1959.

REDL, Fritz (b. Klaus, Austria, 1902). Psychoanalyst. Ph.D. Vienna 1925. In training Psychoanalytic Inst. Vienna 1925–36; teacher Vienna public schls. 1925–36. To U.S. 1936; nat. 1943. Research asso. General Educ. Bd. Rockefeller Fdn. 1936–38. Lect. mental hygiene U. Michigan 1938–41. Prof. social work Wayne State U. 1941–53. Chief Child Research Bureau Nat. Insts. Health Bethesda 1953–59. Prof. behavioral sciences Wayne from 1953. *When We Deal with Children* (1966).

REDLICH, Fredrick (b. Vienna 1910). Psychiatrist. M.D. Vienna 1935. Resident Neurol.-Psychiatr. Klinik U. Vienna 1936–38. To U.S. 1938; nat. 1943. Asst. physician Iowa State Hosp. 1938–40. Resident neurol. unit Boston City Hosp. 1940–42; teaching fellow neurol. Harvard Med. Schl. 1941–42. Instructor psychiatry Yale 1942, thence to prof. 1950. Psychiatrist New Haven Hosp. from 1942, psychiatrist-in-chief from 1948. Co-author *Social Class and Mental Illness* (1958).

REICH, Wilhelm (b. Austria 1897; d. 1957). Psychoanalyst. M.D. Vienna 1922. Freud's 1st clinical asst. Psychoanalytic Polyclinic Vienna 1922–28. Director Seminar for Psychoanalytic Therapy Vienna 1924–30. Broke with Freud 1930. In Denmark and Norway 1933–39. To U.S. 1939. Lect. New Schl. for Soc. Res. 1940–42. Established Orgone Energy Lab. Prosecuted by Food and Drug Admin. for "cosmic radiation" treatment of patients; died in prison.

REICHENBACH, Hans (b. Hamburg 1891; d. 1953). Philosopher. Prof. Berlin from 1926. To Istanbul. Left for U.S. 1938. Prof. UCLA from 1938. *Philosophic Foundations of Quantum Mechanics* (1944); *The Rise of Scientific Philosophy* (1951).

REIK, Theodor (b. Vienna 1888). Psychoanalyst. Ph.D. Vienna 1912. Asso. of Sigmund Freud Vienna 1910–38. To U.S. 1938; nat. 1944. Director

Soc. for Psychoanalytic Psychology N.Y.C. from 1941. Also prof. Adelphi U. *Listening with the Third Ear* (1948); *The Need to be Loved* (1963).

REINHARDT, Max (b. Baden bei Wien, Vienna, 1873; d. 1943). Theatrical producer. Actor, later producer, Deutsche Theater Berlin 1895–1932. Left Germany 1933; became citizen of Czechoslovakia. Producer *The Miracle*. To U.S. 1938. Produced motion picture version of *A Midsummer Night's Dream*. Founder of the Salzburg Festival.

ROMAINS, Jules (b. Le Velay, France, 1885). Writer. In U.S. during World War II. Académie française 1946.

ROSENBERG, Hans (b. Hannover, Germany, 1904). Historian. Ph.D. Berlin 1927. Research asso. Fedl. Hist. Commission, Germany, 1928–34; lect. hist. Cologne 1932–33. Research Fellow Inst. Hist. Research U. London 1934–35. To U.S. 1935, aided by Emergency Committee; nat. 1944. Instructor hist. and pol. sci. Ill. Coll. 1936–37. Asst. prof. Brooklyn Coll. 1937, thence to prof. 1952–59. Shepard prof. hist. Berkeley from 1959. *Bureaucracy, Aristocracy and Autocracy: The Prussian Experience 1660–1815* (1958). Guggenheim Fellow 1945–57.

ROSENBERG, Jakob (b. Berlin 1893). Art historian, museum curator. Ph.D. Munich 1922. Keeper of prints State Museum Berlin 1930–35. Lect. Harvard 1937, curator of prints 1939, asso. prof. fine arts 1940, prof. 1948–64. *Rembrandt* (1948); *On Quality in Art* (1964).

ROSENBLITH, Walter (b. Vienna 1913). Biophysicist. Engr. degree U. Bordeaux 1936. Research engineer France 1937–39. To U.S. 1939; nat. 1946. Research asst. NYU 1939–40. Teaching fellow physics UCLA 1939–43. From asst. prof. to asso. prof. South Dakota Schl. Mines 1943–47. Research fellow Psycho-Acoustic Lab. Harvard 1947–51. Asso. prof. communications and biophysics MIT 1951, prof. from 1957. Research asso. otology Harvard Med. Schl. from 1957.

ROSENSTOCK-HUESSY, Eugen (b. Berlin 1888). Educator, social philosopher. Ph.D. Heidelberg 1923. Prof. hist. law and sociology Breslau 1923–33. To U.S. 1933. Lect. Harvard 1933–36. Prof. social philosophy Dartmouth 1935–57. Eugen Rosenstock-Huessy Soc. founded Bielefeld, Germany, 1963. D. Laws (hon.) U. Calif. 1967.

ROSENTHAL, Franz (b. Berlin 1914). Arabist. Ph.D. Berlin 1935. To U.S. 1940; nat. 1943. Asst. prof. semitic langs. Hebrew Union Coll. Cincinnati 1940–48. With OSS 1943–45. Prof. Arabic U. Pennsylvania 1948–56. Leon M. Rabinowitz prof. Arabic Yale from 1956. *History of Muslim Historiography* (1952); ed. Ibn Khaldun, *The Muqaddimah* (1958).

ROSSI, Bruno (b. Venice 1905). Physicist. Studied Padua, Bologna. Prof. physics Padua 1932–38. Research asst. U. Manchester, England, 1939. Asso. in cosmic rays U. Chicago 1939–40. Asso. prof. physics Cornell 1940–45. Prof. physics MIT from 1945, Institute prof. from 1966. *Cosmic Rays* (1964). Natl. Acad. Sci. Accademia dei Lincei (Rome).

ROTHFELS, Hans (b. Kassel 1891). Historian. Ph.D. Heidelberg. Prof. Königsberg 1926–36. Research Fellow St. John's Coll. Oxford 1939–40. To U.S. 1940. Vis. prof. Brown U. 1940–46. Prof. modern hist. U. Chicago 1946–56. Also Prof. modern hist. Tübingen from 1951. *The German Opposition to Hitler* (1948). Pres. Deutsche Historikerverband 1958–62.

SACHS, Curt (b. Berlin 1881; d. 1959). Musicologist. Ph.D. Berlin 1904. Prof. Berlin 1919–33. Chargé de mission Musée de l'Homme Paris 1933–37. To U.S. 1937. Consultant to N.Y. Public Libr. 1937–52. Vis. prof. NYU 1937–57; adjunct prof. Columbia from 1953. *The History of Musical Instruments* (1940).

SACHS, Hanns (b. Vienna 1881; d. 1947). Psychoanalyst. Admitted to the bar 1904. Member of Freud's "Committee." Training analyst Psychoanalytic Inst. Berlin 1920–32. To U.S. 1932. With Boston Psychoanalytic Inst. 1932–43.

SALINAS, Pedro (b. Madrid 1891; d. 1951). Poet, scholar. Prof. Spanish U. Seville. Prof. Madrid from 1930. To U.S. 1936. Vis. prof. Wellesley Coll. 1936–39, prof. 1939. Prof. Johns Hopkins from 1939. *Literatura española siglo XX* (1941). Selected poems trans. Eleanor L. Turnbull: *Lost Angel and Other Poems* (1938); *Truth of Two and Other Poems* (1940).

SALVEMINI, Gaetano (b. Molfetta, Italy, 1873; d. 1957). Historian. Ph.D. Florence 1894. Prof. mediaeval and modern hist. Florence 1916–25. Member Italian Parliament 1919–21. To U.S. 1932; nat. 1940. Lauro de Bosis lect. in hist. Italian civilization Harvard 1933–48. Returned to Italy. *Under the Ax of Fascism* (1936).

SCHEIN, Marcel (b. Trstena, Austria-Hungary, 1902; d. 1960). Physicist. Ph.D. Zürich 1927. Rockefeller Fdn. Fellow U. Chicago 1929–30. Privatdozent Zürich 1931–35. Prof. experimental physics Odessa 1935–37. To U.S. 1938; nat. 1943. Research in cosmic rays U. Chicago 1938–42; asst. prof. physics 1942–45, prof. from 1946. Consultant to Manhattan District 1945–46.

SCHNABEL, Artur (b. Lipnik, Austria, 1882; d. 1951). Pianist. Studied piano Vienna 1891–97. Concert tours from 1896. American debut 1921. Taught piano Hochschule für Musik Berlin 1925–30. Left Germany for Switzerland. To U.S. 1939.

SCHOCKEN, Theodore (b. Germany 1914). Book publisher. Taken by his father to Palestine. To U.S. 1938. Pres. Schocken Books Inc. from 1946.

SCHOENBERG, Arnold (b. Vienna 1874; d. 1951). Composer. Studied Realschule Vienna 1885–91. Taught composition Akademie der Künste Berlin. To U.S. 1936. Prof. music UCLA 1936–44.

SCHWARZSCHILD, Martin (b. Potsdam 1912). Astronomer. Ph.D. Göttingen 1935. Research fellow Inst. Astrophysics Oslo 1936–37. To U.S. 1937; Rutherfurd Observatory Columbia 1940–47. 1st Lt. U.S. Army 1942–45. Prof. astronomy Princeton from 1947, Higgins prof. from 1950. Natl. Acad. Sci. (Henry Draper medal 1961). Eddington medal, Roy. Astron. Soc. London 1963. *Structure and Evolution of the Stars* (1958).

SEGRÈ, Emilio (b. Rome 1905). Physicist. Ph.D. Rome 1928. Director physics lab. Palermo 1936–38. To U.S. 1938; nat. 1944. Research asst. Berkeley 1938–43. Group leader Los Alamos Lab. 1943–46. Prof. physics Berkeley from 1945. Natl. Acad. Sci. Accademia dei Lincei (Rome). Nobel Prize in physics 1959 with Owen Chamberlain "for their discovery of the antiproton."

SERKIN, Rudolf (b. Eger, Austria-Hungary, 1903). Pianist. Child prodigy. Studied piano (and composition with Schoenberg). Concert debut with Vienna Symphony 1915; refused offers to tour till 1920. Married Irene Busch, d. Adolf Busch. Debut in America 1933. Head piano dept. Curtis Inst. Music (Phila.). Artistic director Marlboro Music Schl. and Festival. Presidential Medal of Freedom 1964.

SERT, José Luis (b. Barcelona 1902). Architect. M. Arch. Barcelona 1929. Worked with Le Corbusier Paris 1929–30. In private practice arch. Barcelona 1930–38. To U.S. 1939; nat. 1951. Co-founder, partner, Town Planing Assoc. N.Y. 1941–59. Partner Sert, Jackson, Gourley 1958. Designer prefabricated, other structures for War Production Board 1942–46. Prof. city planning Yale 1944–45. Prof. arch., dean Schl. Design Harvard from 1953.

SFORZA, Carlo, Count (b. Italy 1873; d. 1952). Statesman. Foreign Minister Italy 1920–21. Ambassador to Paris 1921–22. Left office when Mussolini seized power 1922. To Belgium 1926, later to England. To U.S. 1940. Returned to Italy 1943. Pres. Consultative Assembly, then deputy National Assembly 1946. Foreign Minister 1947–51.

SIGERIST, Henry (b. Paris 1891; d. 1957). Historian of medicine. M.D. Zürich 1917. Prof. hist. med. Leipzig 1925–32. Lect. Johns Hopkins 1931; offered William H. Welch professorship and directorship Inst. Hist. Med.

Johns Hopkins 1931. Decision to accept determined by course of events in Germany. At Johns Hopkins 1932–47. Research assoc. Yale from 1947. Returned to Switzerland 1947. *A History of Medicine*, vol. I (1951). Karl Sudhoff medal 1933; William H. Welch medal 1951.

SIMONS, Hans (b. Velbert, Germany, 1893). Dr. Juris. et rer. pol. Königsberg 1921. Director Inst. Pol. Sci. Berlin 1925–29. District governor Upper Silesia 1930–32. To U.S. 1933; naturalized. Prof. internatl. relations New Schl. for Soc. Res. 1935–60, dean Schl. Pol. 1943–50, Pres. New Schl. 1950–60. Consultant OSS 1944. Consultant on gen. educ. to Ford Fdn., India, from 1960.

SOHN, Louis (b. Lwów, Poland, 1914). Legal scholar. Legal degrees Lwów 1935. To U.S. 1939; nat. 1943. Asst. to Judge Manley O. Hudson 1941–48. Research Fellow Harvard Law Schl. 1946–47, lect. law 1947–51, asst. prof. 1951–53, prof. from 1953, Bemis prof. internatl. law from 1961. *World Peace through World Law* (1958).

SOLMSEN, Friedrich (b. Bonn 1904). Classical philologist. Ph.D. Berlin 1928. Asst. prof. classics Berlin 1929–33. Research student Cambridge U. 1933–37. Prof. classics Olivet Coll. (Mich.) 1937–40. Asst. prof. classics Cornell 1940, asso. prof. 1944, prof. 1947–62. Prof. Inst. for Research in Humanities U. Wisconsin 1962–64, Moses Slaughter prof. classical studies from 1964. *Aristotle's System of the Physical World* (1960). Guggenheim Fellow 1947–48.

SPEIER, Hans (b. Berlin 1905). Sociologist. Ph.D. Heidelberg 1928. To U.S. 1933; naturalized. Prof. New Schl. for Soc. Res. 1933–42. Analyst FCC 1942–44; with Office of War Information 1944–45. Asso. chief occupied areas div. U.S. State Dept. 1946–47. Prof. New Schl. 1947–48. Chief social science div. Rand Corp. 1948–60.

SPITZER, Leo (b. Vienna 1887; d. 1960). Comparative philologist. Ph.D. Vienna 1913. Prof. romance langs. Cologne 1930–33. Prof. Istanbul 1933–36. To U.S. 1936. Prof. Johns Hopkins from 1936. *Linguistics and Literary History* (1948); *Essays on English and American Literature* (1962).

STEINBERG, Saul (b. Ramnic-Sarat, Rumania, 1914). Cartoonist. Dr. arch. Milan 1933–40. Cartoonist for magazine *Bertoldo* Milan 1936–39; practicing architect 1939–41. To Dominican Republic 1941. To U.S. 1942; nat. 1943. Lt. U.S. Navy 1943–45. Free-lance cartoonist, largely for *The New Yorker*, from 1941.

STEINBERG, William (b. Cologne 1899). Conductor. General music director Frankfurt Opera Hse. To U.S. 1938. Conductor San Francisco Opera from 1944. Music director Pittsburgh Symphony from 1952. Music director Boston Symphony from 1969.

STERN, Curt (b. Hamburg 1902). Geneticist. Ph.D. Berlin 1923. Investigator Kaiser Wilhelm Inst. Biol. 1923–33; privatdozent Berlin 1928–33. Internatl. Educ. Bd. fellow 1924–26; Rockefeller Fdn. fellow 1932–33. Research asso. zoology U. Rochester 1933–35, asst. prof. 1935, assoc. prof. 1937, prof. 1941–47. Prof. zoology Berkeley from 1947, prof. genetics from 1958. Natl. Acad. Sci. (Kimber Genetics medal 1963). Pres. Am. Genetic Soc. 1950. Pres. Am. Soc. Zoologists 1962. *Principles of Human Genetics* (1949; 2d ed. 1960).

STERN, Otto (b. Sorau, Germany, 1888). Physicist. Ph.D. Breslau 1912. Prof. physical chemistry Hamburg 1923–33. To U.S. 1933. Research prof. physics Carnegie Inst. Tech. 1933–45. Natl. Acad. Sci. Nobel Prize in physics 1943 "for his contribution to the development of the molecular ray method and his discovery of the magnetic moment of the proton."

STERN, William (b. Berlin 1871; d. 1938). Psychologist. Ph.D. Berlin 1893. Prof. Hamburg 1916–33. Lect. then prof. Duke 1934–38.

STOLPER, Gustav (b. Vienna 1888; d. 1947). Economist. Dr. Law and Econ. Vienna 1911. Ed. and pub. *Deutscher Volkswirt* (Berlin) 1926–33. Member German Reichstag 1929–32. To U.S. 1933; naturalized. Consulting economist in N.Y.C.

STRAUSS, Leo (b. Kirchhain, Hesse, Germany 1899). Political philosopher. Ph.D. Hamburg 1921. Research asst. Acad. Jewish Research Berlin 1925–32. Rockefeller Fdn. Fellow France and England 1932–34. To U.S. 1938; nat. 1944. From lect. to prof. pol. sci. and philosophy, New Schl. for Soc. Res. 1938–48. Prof. political philosophy U. Chicago from 1949, later Robert Maynard Hutchins prof. *The Political Philosophy of Hobbes* (1936); *On Tyranny* (1950).

STRAVINSKY, Igor (b. nr. St. Petersburg 1882). Composer. Studied law St. Petersburg. Studied composition with Rimski-Korsakov. To Paris. To U.S. 1939; nat. 1946. Charles Eliot Norton prof. poetry Harvard 1939. Sibelius Prize 1963.

SZELL, George (b. Budapest 1897). Conductor. Child prodigy. Grad. Acad. Music Vienna. Music director German Opera Hse. and Philharmonic Concerts and prof. Acad. Music and Dramatic Arts Prague 1929–37. Guest conductor Europe, outside Germany. Toured Australia 1938–39. To U.S. 1939; nat. 1946. Guest conductor U.S. orchestras 1939–45. Musical director Cleveland Orchestra from 1946.

SZILARD, Leo (b. Budapest 1898; d. 1964). Physicist, biologist. Ph.D. Berlin 1922. Taught U. Berlin 1925–32. Research in nuclear physics St. Bartholomew's Hosp. London and Clarendon Lab. U. Oxford 1934–38. To U.S. 1937; nat. 1943. Research on atomic energy Columbia 1939–42. Chief Physicist Metallurgical Lab. U. Chicago 1942–46, then prof. U. Chicago. Resident fellow Salk Inst. Biol. studies La Jolla 1964. Founded Pugwash Conferences. Atoms for Peace award 1960.

TANGUY, Yves (b. Paris 1900; d. 1955). Artist. To U.S. 1939; nat. 1948. Leading Surrealist. Paintings exhibited regularly from 1927.

TARSKI, Alfred (b. Warsaw 1902). Mathematician, logician. Ph.D. Warsaw 1924. Prof. lycée Warsaw 1925–39. Dozent, adjoint prof. U. Warsaw 1925–39. To U.S. 1939, aided by Emergency Committee; nat. 1945. Research asso. math. Harvard 1939–41. Vis. prof. CCNY 1940. Member Inst. for Advanced Study Princeton 1941–42. Lect. math. Berkeley 1942, asso. prof. 1945, prof. 1946, research prof. 1958–60. Natl. Acad. Sci.

TELLER, Edward (b. Budapest 1908). Physicist. Ph.D. Leipzig 1930. Research asso. Göttingen 1931–33. Rockefeller Fdn. Fellow Copenhagen 1934. Lect. U. London 1935. To U.S. 1935; nat. 1941. Prof. physics George Washington U. 1935–41. With Inst. Nuclear Studies U. Chicago 1945; prof. physics U. Chicago 1946–49, 1951–52. Prof. physics Berkeley 1953–60. Prof.-at-large U. Calif. from 1960. Director Los Alamos Sci. Lab. 1949–51; director Livermore Lab. 1958–60. Natl. Acad. Sci.

TEMKIN, Owsei (b. Minsk 1902). Historian of medicine. M.D. Leipzig 1927. Asst. Inst. Hist. Med. Leipzig 1928–32, privatdozent 1931–33. To U.S. 1932; nat. 1938. Fac. Johns Hopkins Inst. Hist. Med. 1932–58; William H. Welch prof. hist. med. and director Inst. Hist. Med. Johns Hopkins 1958–68. *The Falling Sickness* (1945). Ed. *Bull. Hist. Med.* 1948–68. William H. Welch medal, Am. Asso. Hist. Med. 1952; Sarton medal, Hist. Sci. Soc. 1960; prize for distinguished scholarship in humanities, Am. Council Learned Societies 1962.

TERZAGHI, Karl (b. Prague, Austria-Hungary, 1883; d. 1963). Engineer, expert in soil mechanics. Prof. foundation eng. Constantinople 1918–25. Prof. Robert Coll. Constantinople 1918–25. Prof. soil mechanics and foundation eng. MIT 1925–29. Prof. Technische Hochschule Vienna 1929–38. To U.S. 1939; nat. 1943. Prof. practice of civil eng. Harvard 1946–56. Hon. doctorates Istanbul, Eidgenössische Tech. Hoch. Zürich, Trinity Coll. Dublin. Pres. internatl. conferences soil mechanics and foundation eng. Rotterdam 1948, Zürich 1953.

TILLICH, Paul (b. Starzeddel, Prussia 1886; d. 1965). Theologian. Ph.D. Breslau 1911. Prof. philosophy Frankfurt 1929–33. To U.S. 1933; nat. 1940. Prof. Union Theological Seminary N.Y. 1933–35. University prof. Harvard 1955–62. John Nuveen prof. U. Chicago 1962–65. *The Shaking of the Foundations* (1948); *Systematic Theology* (1951, 1957); *The Courage to Be* (1952). Hon. doctorate Yale, Glasgow, Harvard, Princeton, Chicago, Free U. Berlin. Goethe Prize, Hamburg, 1958.

TOCH, Ernst (b. Vienna 1887; d. 1964). Composer. Ph.D. Heidelberg 1921. To U.S. 1934; nat. 1940. Mozart Prize, Frankfurt 1909; Pulitzer Prize for Third Symphony 1956.

TOLLER, Ernst (b. Samotschin, Posen, 1893; d. 1939). Writer. Pres. Bavarian Socialist Republic 1919. Sentenced to 5 yrs. imprisonment for revolutionary activities 1919. Left Germany 1932. To U.S. Committed suicide N.Y.C. 1939. *Pastor Hall* (i.e., Niemöller; 1939).

TOLNAY, Charles de (b. Budapest 1899). Art historian. Ph.D. Vienna 1925. Lect. hist. art Hamburg 1929–33. Lect. Sorbonne 1934–39. To U.S. 1939; nat. 1945. Inst. for Adv. Study Princeton 1939–48. *Michelangelo* (1943).

TOSCANINI, Arturo (b. Parma 1867; d. 1957). Conductor. Studied Conservatory Parma. Began career as cellist. Conductor La Scala Milan 1898. Conductor Metropolitan Opera N.Y. 1908–15. Guest conductor N.Y. Philharmonic 1926–28; regular conductor 1928–36, musical director 1933–36. To U.S. as refugee 1937. Organizer and conductor NBC Symphony Orchestra 1937–44. Returned to Italy.

ULAM, S(tanislaw). (b. Lwów, Poland, 1909). Mathematician. Dr. Sci. Lwów 1933. To U.S. 1936; nat. 1943. Vis. member Inst. for Advanced Study Princeton 1936. Member Society of Fellows Harvard 1936–39. Lect. math. Harvard 1939–40. Asst. prof. math. U. Wisconsin 1941–43. Staff Los Alamos Sci. Lab. from 1943. Prof. U. Colorado from 1965. Natl. Acad. Sci.

ULICH, Robert (b. Riedermuchl bei Lam, Germany, 1890). Educationist. Ph.D. Leipzig 1914. Counselor in charge Saxon universities 1923–33. Hon. prof. philosophy Dresden Inst. Tech. 1928–33. To U.S. 1934. Lect. comparative educ. Harvard 1934, prof. educ. 1936, James Bryant Conant prof. educ. 1960.

UNDSET, Sigrid (b. Kallundborg, Denmark, 1882; d. 1949). Writer. To Christiania as child. Escaped from Norway via Russia and Japan to U.S. 1940. Wrote children's books in U.S. and recollections of her flight from Norway, *The Return to the Future* (1942). Returned to Norway 1945. Nobel Prize in literature 1928.

VALENTIN, Veit (b. Germany 1885; d. 1947). Historian. Studied Heidelberg, Berlin, Munich. Lect. then asso. prof. Berlin Schl. Econ. 1919–33. Lect. U. London 1933–40. To U.S. Lect. U. Pennsylvania 1940–41. Research grant from Queens Coll. N.Y. 1941–42. Research asso. Fletcher Schl. Diplomacy Tufts U. 1934–44. *1848: Chapters of German History* (1940).

VOEGELIN, Eric (b. Cologne 1901). Political scientist. Dr. rer. pol. Vienna 1922. Privatdozent Vienna 1929, asso. prof. 1936. Dismissed by Nazis. To U.S. 1938; nat. 1944. Instructor Harvard 1938–39; instructor Bennington Coll. 1939. Asst. prof. U. Alabama 1939–42. Asso. prof. Louisiana State U. 1942–46, prof. from 1946, Boyd prof. 1952–58. Prof. pol. sci. Munich from 1958. *The New Science of Politics* (1952).

VON BÉKÉSY, Georg (b. Budapest 1899). Biophysicist. Ph.D. physics Budapest 1923. With research lab. Hungarian Telephone System 1923–46. Prof. experimental physics Budapest 1939–46. Guest investigator Karolinska Inst. Stockholm 1946–47. To U.S. 1947. Research assoc. and lect. Psycho-Acoustic Lab. Harvard 1947–66. Prof. sensory sciences U. Hawaii from 1966. Natl. Acad. Sci. Guyot Prize, Groningen U.; Leibnitz Medal, Acad. Sci. Berlin; gold medals Am. Otological Soc., Acoustical Soc. Am. Nobel Prize in physiology or medicine 1961 "for his discoveries concerning the physical mechanism of stimulation within the cochlea."

VON GRUNEBAUM, Gustave (b. Vienna 1909). Islamist. Ph.D. Vienna 1931. Leader extension inst. Oriental Inst. Vienna 1936–38. To U.S. 1938, aided by Emergency Committee; nat. 1944. Asst. Prof. Arabic and Islamic studies Asia Inst. N.Y. 1938–43. Asst. prof. Arabic and Islamic studies U. Chicago 1943, asso. prof. 1946, prof. 1949. Now prof. hist., director Near Eastern Center UCLA. *Medieval Islam* (1946); *Muhammadan Festivals* (1951).

VON MISES, Ludwig (b. Lemberg, Austria, 1881). Economist. Dr. Law and Soc. Sci. Vienna 1906. Prof. economics Vienna 1913–38. Prof. internatl. econ. relations Geneva 1934–40. To U.S. 1940; nat. 1946. Vis. prof. Natl. U. Mexico 1942. Prof. NYU from 1946. *Human Action, A Treatise on Economics* (1949); *The Anticapitalistic Mentality* (1956).

VON MISES, Richard (b. Austria 1883; d. 1953). Mathematician. Dr. Tech. Vienna 1907. Prof., director Inst. Applied Mathematics Berlin 1920–33. Prof. math. Istanbul 1933–39. To U.S. 1939. Prof. applied math. Harvard 1939. Gordon McKay prof. aerodynamics and applied math. 1944–53.

VON NEUMANN, John (b. Budapest 1903; d. 1957). Mathematician. Ph.D. Budapest 1926. Privatdozent Hamburg 1929. Vis. prof. mathematical physics Princeton 1930, prof. 1931–33. Prof. Inst. for Advanced Study Princeton 1933–57. Member AEC from 1954. Co-author with Oskar Morgenstern *Theory of Games and Economic Behavior* (1944). Natl. Acad. Sci. U.S. Medal for Merit 1947; Medal of Freedom 1956; Enrico Fermi award 1956. Pres. Am. Math. Soc. 1951–53.

VON UNRUH, Fritz (b. Coblenz 1885). Writer. Experience of World War I made him a pacifist. To France 1933. To U.S. 1940. First return to Germany 1948; later settled there.

WACH, Joachim (b. Chemnitz, Germany, 1898; d. 1955). Historian of religion. Ph.D. Leipzig 1922. Prof. hist. religions Leipzig 1924–35. To U.S. 1935; nat. 1946. Vis. prof. Brown U. 1935–37, asso. prof. 1937–46. Prof. hist. religions U. Chicago from 1946. *Sociology of Religion* (1944); *Types of Religious Experience* (1951). Settled in Switzerland.

WACHSMANN, Konrad (b. Frankfurt 1901). Architect. Studied Berlin Acad. 1922–25. In private practice Berlin 1929–32. *Prix de Rome* German Acad. in Rome 1932. In private practice Rome 1932–38. To France 1938, U.S. 1941; nat. 1944. In practice with W. Gropius 1941–48. Prof. Illinois Inst. Tech. from 1950. *The Turning Point of Building* (1960).

WALTER, Bruno (b. Berlin 1876; d. 1962). Conductor. Studied Stern's Conserv. Berlin. Conductor Gewandthaus Orch. Leipzig 1929–33. To U.S. 1933. Asso. conductor with Toscanini, N.Y. Philharmonic 1933–36. Musical director Vienna Opera 1936–38. Returned to U.S. Conductor Metropolitan Opera N.Y. 1941. Conductor and musical adviser N.Y. Philharmonic 1947–49.

WECHSBERG, Joseph (b. Ostrava, Austria-Hungary, 1907). Writer. Graduated U. Prague Law Schl. 1930. To U.S. 1938; nat. 1944. Supported himself as free-lance writer. With *The New Yorker* magazine from 1943. *Looking for a Bluebird* (1945); *Blue Trout and Black Truffles* (1957).

WEILL, Kurt (b. Dessau, Germany, 1900; d. 1950). Composer. Studied Berlin Acad. Music (and with Busoni). Married Lotte Lenya 1926. Left Berlin for Paris 1933. To U.S. 1935. Music for *Knickerbocker Holiday* (1938); *Lady in the Dark* (1941); *One Touch of Venus* (1943); *Street Scene* (opera 1947); *Down in the Valley* (folk opera 1948).

WEINTRAUB, Wiktor (b. Zawiercie, Poland, 1908). Slavic scholar. Ph.D. Cracow 1930. Literary critic Warsaw 1934–37. French govt. scholar Paris 1937–39. Press officer Polish embassy, Moscow and Kuibyshev, 1941–42. Ed. magazine in Jerusalem 1943–45. Staff Polish Min. Information London 1945–50. To U.S. 1950. Vis. lect. Harvard 1950–54, asso. prof. Slavic langs. and lit. 1954–59, prof. from 1959.

WEISKOPF, F(ranz). C. (b. Prague 1900; d. 1955). Writer. Lived in Berlin till 1933. Emigrated via Prague and Paris to U.S. 1938. Returned to Germany 1953. *Vor einem neuen Tag* (1944).

WEISSKOPF, Victor (b. Vienna 1908). Physicist. Ph.D. Göttingen 1931. Research asso. Copenhagen 1932–34. Research asso. Eidgenössische Tech. Hoch. Zürich 1934–37. To U.S. 1937; nat. 1942. Asst. prof. physics U. Rochester 1937–43. With Manhattan Project Los Alamos 1943–46. Prof. physics MIT 1946–60. Director-general CERN Geneva 1961–65. Institute prof. MIT from 1965. Natl. Acad. Sci.

WELLEK, René (b. Vienna 1903). Historian of literature. Ph.D. Charles U. Prague 1926. Fellow and instructor Princeton 1927–30. Instructor Smith Coll. 1928–39. Privatdozent Prague 1930–35. Lect. Schl. Slavonic Studies U. London 1935–39. To U.S. 1939; nat. 1946. Fac. U. Iowa from 1939, prof. English 1944–46. Prof. Slavic and comparative lit. Yale from 1946, Sterling prof. from 1952. Guggenheim Fellow 1951–52, 1956–57, 1966–67. Prize for distinguished service to humanities, Am. Council Learned Societies 1959. Hon. doctorates Oxford, Harvard, Rome. *A History of Modern Criticism* (in progress from 1955).

WERFEL, Franz (b. Prague 1890; d. 1945). Writer. Married Alma Mahler, widow Gustav M. With Kurt Wolff Verlag 1912–14. In Vienna 1917–38. To France 1938. To U.S. 1940; settled in Calif. *Embezzled Heaven* (1940); *Lied der Bernadette* (1941); *Jacobowski und der Oberst* (Stockholm première 1944); *Stern der Ungeborenen* (1946).

WERNER, Heinz (b. Vienna 1890). Psychologist. Ph.D. Vienna 1915. Prof. psychology Hamburg 1926–33. To U.S. 1933; naturalized. Lect. U. Michigan 1933–36. Research asso. Harvard 1936–37. At Wayne County (Mich.) Training Schl. 1937–44. Fac. Brooklyn Coll. 1945–57. Prof. psychology Clark U. from 1947.

WERTHEIMER, Max (b. Prague 1880; d. 1943). Psychologist. Ph.D. Würzburg 1904. Founder of Gestalt psychology. Prof. Frankfurt 1929–33. To U.S. 1934. Prof. New Schl. for Soc. Res. 1934–43. *Productive Thinking* (1945).

WEYL, Hermann (b. Elmshorn, Germany, 1885; d. 1955). Mathematician. Ph.D. Göttingen 1908. Prof. Göttingen 1930–33. Prof. Inst. for Advanced Study Princeton 1933–53. Natl. Acad. Sci. For. mem. Roy. Soc. London. Hon. doctorates Columbia, Eidgenössische Tech. Hoch. Zürich, Paris. *Philosophy of Mathematics and Natural Science* (1949).

WIGNER, Eugene (b. Budapest 1902). Physicist. Dr. Ing. Berlin 1925. Fac. Tech. Hochschule Berlin 1926–33, prof. from 1930. Vis. lect. Princeton

1930. Half-time prof. mathematical physics Princeton 1931–37. Settled in U.S. 1930; nat. 1937. Jones prof. theoretical physics Princeton from 1938. With Metallurgical Lab. Manhattan District U. Chicago 1942–45; director research and development Clinton Labs. 1946–47. Natl. Acad. Sci. Pres. Am. Physical Soc. 1956. U.S. Medal for Merit 1946; Franklin medal 1950; Enrico Fermi award 1958; Atoms for Peace award 1960; Max Planck medal 1961. Nobel Prize in physics 1963 with Maria Goeppert-Mayer and J. H. D. Jensen "for his contributions to the theory of atomic nuclei and elementary particles, especially through the discovery and application of fundamental principles of symmetry."

WIND, Edgar (b. Berlin 1900). Art historian, Ph.D. Hamburg 1922. Privatdozent and research fellow Warburg Inst. Hamburg 1927–33. Deputy director Warburg Inst. London 1934–42; hon. lect. U. Coll. London 1934–42. To U.S. 1942; nat. 1948. Prof. art U. Chicago 1942–44. William Allan Neilson research prof. Smith Coll. 1944–48, prof. philosophy and art 1948–55. Prof. hist. art and fellow Trinity Coll. Oxford 1955–67. Chichele lect. Oxford 1954; Rede lect. Cambridge 1960; Reith lect. BBC 1960. *Bellini's Feast of the Gods* (1948).

WITTFOGEL, Karl (b. Woltersdorf, Germany, 1896). Sinologist. Ph.D. Frankfurt 1928. Res. asso. Inst. für Sozialforschung Frankfurt 1925–33. To U.S. 1934, aided by Emergency Committee; nat. 1941. Research asso. Columbia 1934–39, director Chinese hist. project from 1939. Prof. Chinese hist. U. Washington 1947–66. *Oriental Despotism* (1957).

WOLFF, Kurt (b. Bonn 1887; d. 1963). Publisher. Studied Leipzig. In partnership with Ernst Rowohlt Leipzig 1908–13. Founded Kurt Wolff Verlag 1913. Publ. Werfel, Kafka, Karl Kraus, Heinrich Mann. Left Germany 1929; publ. art books Florence. In Nice in 1930's. To U.S. 1941. Founded Pantheon Books Inc. N.Y. 1942. Publ. English eds. Musil, Hermann Broch (*Death of Virgil*), Pasternak (*Doctor Zhivago*), Lampedusa (*The Leopard*). Left Pantheon and settled in Switzerland 1960. "Helen and Kurt Wolff Books" publ. through Harcourt Brace 1960–63.

WOLFF, Kurt H. (b. Darmstadt 1912). Sociologist. Ph.D. Florence 1935. Taught in Italy 1936–38. To U.S. 1939; naturalized. Asst. in sociology Southern Methodist U. 1939–43. Research Fellow SSRC U. Chicago. Fac. Earlham Coll. 1944–45. Fac. Ohio State U. 1945–59. Prof. sociology Brandeis from 1959.

ZEISEL, Hans (b. Austria-Hungary 1905). Sociologist. Dr. Jur. Vienna 1927. With Wirtschaftspsychologische Forschungsstelle U. Vienna. To U.S.; naturalized. Director research and development McCann-Erickson advertising agency 1943–50; research for Tea Council 1950–53. Prof. law and sociology U. Chicago from 1953. *The American Jury* (1960).

ZIMMER, Heinrich (b. Germany 1890; d. 1943). Indologist. Ph.D. Berlin 1915. Married d. of Hugo von Hofmannsthal. Prof. Heidelberg 1922–38. Lect. Balliol Coll. Oxford 1938–40. To U.S. 1940, aided by Emergency Committee. At Columbia 1941–43. His aid achnowledged by Thomas Mann in *The Transposed Heads*. *Myths and Symbols of Indian Art and Civilization* (1946).

ZUCKMAYER, Carl (b. Nackenheim, Germany, 1896). Writer. Settled in Austria in 1920's. Escaped to Switzerland 1938. To U.S. in 1939. Supported himself and his family as farmer in Vermont. Returned to Europe in 1946; settled in Switzerland. Autobiographical *Second Wind* (1940). *Des Teufels General* (1946).

NOTES ON CONTRIBUTORS

T. W. ADORNO (born Frankfurt-am-Main, 1903), in England 1934–1938; to U.S. 1938; returned to Germany 1953; professor of philosophy and sociology and head of Institut für Sozialforschung, University of Frankfurt.

COLIN EISLER (born Hamburg, 1931), to U.S. 1941; professor of fine arts, Institute of Fine Arts, New York University.

HERBERT FEIGL (born Austria, 1902), to U.S. 1930; professor of philosophy and director, Minnesota Center for Philosophy of Science, University of Minnesota.

DONALD FLEMING (born Maryland, 1923), professor of history, Harvard University.

PETER GAY (born Berlin, 1923), to U.S. 1941; William R. Shepherd professor of history, Columbia University.

H. STUART HUGHES (born New York City, 1916), professor of history, Harvard University.

MARIE JAHODA (born Vienna, 1907), in England 1937–1945; in U.S. 1945–1958, professor of psychology and director, Research Center for Human Relations, New York University; now professor of social psychology, University of Sussex, England.

WILLIAM H. JORDY (born New York, 1917), professor of art, Brown University.

H. W. KUHN (born California, 1925), professor of mathematics, Princeton University.

PAUL F. LAZARSFELD (born Vienna, 1901), to U.S. 1933; Quetelet professor of social sciences and chairman, Bureau of Applied Social Research, Columbia University.

HARRY LEVIN (born Minnesota, 1912), Irving Babbitt professor of comparative literature, Harvard University.

GEORGE MANDLER (born Vienna, 1924), to U.S. 1940; professor of psychology and chairman of the department of psychology, University of California at San Diego.

JEAN MATTER MANDLER (born Illinois, 1929), associate research psychologist and lecturer, University of California at San Diego.

CLAUDE E. SHANNON (born Michigan, 1916), Donner professor of science, Massachusetts Institute of Technology.

LEO SZILARD (born Budapest, 1898; died California, 1964), to U.S. 1937; professor, University of Chicago.

A. W. TUCKER (born Ontario, Canada, 1905), Albert Baldwin Dod professor of mathematics, Princeton University.

S(TANISLAW). ULAM (born Lwów, Poland, 1909), to U.S. 1935; professor of mathematics, University of Colorado.

CHARLES WEINER (born Brooklyn, N.Y., 1931), director of the Center for History and Philosophy of Physics, American Institute of Physics.

INDEX

Italicized page numbers at the end of index entries refer to the list of biographies.